The History of The Manx Grand Prix
1923 - 1998

by

Peter Kneale

&

Bill Snelling

Amulree Publications

Acknowledgments

We should like to give grateful thanks to our many friends and colleagues who have helped to make this book possible.

These include many riders who have contributed stories and articles about their rides, and to the various organisations that contribute so much to the running of the Manx; to the many photographers and organisations who have allowed us to delve into their collections to bring together some rare and unseen pictures for this book; these include; Beryl Corkill, Doug Davidson, John Watterson, Monica Clark of Island Photographics, Steve Colvin, and special thanks to Roger Sims, Head Librarian of the Manx Museum.

Last but not least the photographic laboratory staff at Island Photographics who gave every assistance to ensure the quality of the pictures, despite some less than perfect negatives; Michael Fitzpatrick, Bill Milligan, and Geoff Ralston.

Peter Kneale & Bill Snelling, 1998

A lineup of Manx Grand Prix competitors who were staying at the Cunningham Holiday Camp, c.1930.

Produced with financial assistance from the Manx Heritage Foundation

© Peter Kneale and Bill Snelling
First published 1998

All rights reserved. Except for the purpose of review, criticism or private study no part of this publication may be reproduced, stored in a retrieval system, or transmitted, in any form or by any means, electronic, electrical, chemical, mechanical, optical, photocopying, recording or otherwise without the prior permission of Peter Kneale & Amulree Publications.

Amulree Publications
Lossan y Twoaie , Glen Road, Laxey, Isle of Man, IM4 7AN
Tel: (01624) 862238 • Fax: (01624) 862298 • Email: amulree@mcb.net

ISBN 1 901508 04 8
The History of the Manx Grand Prix 1923 - 1998 (softback)

Contents

Foreword, by G. R. Martin Moore, President, Manx Motor Cycle Club	5
About the authors	6
The Manx Amateur Road Races - the start of it all	7
The Manx Amateur Road Race Championships 1923 - 1929	9
The Manx Grand Prix 1930 - 1938	14
My Winning ride - J. Kelly Swanston, 1935 Senior Manx Grand Prix	19
Index of riders performances 1923 - 1938	25
The Manx Grand Prix 1946 - 1961	30
My Winning ride - Geoff Duke, 1949 Senior Manx Grand Prix	35
My Winning ride - Frank Fox, 1953 Junior Manx Grand Prix	40
The Lost Lap - Drew Herdman, 1955 Senior Manx Grand Prix	43
My Winning rides - Alan Holmes, 1957 Junior and Senior Manx Grand Prix	47
The Manx Grand Prix 1962 - 1982	54
Well, what would you have done? - Doug Rose	57
One man's view of the Manx - George Ridgeon	74
A Newcomer's view - Bill Snelling, 1978 Newcomers	80
Isle of Man TT (and MGP) Marshals Association - Mary Crellin	91
Index of riders performances 1946 - 1982	92
The Manx Grand Prix Supporters Club Helicopter Fund	120
The Manx Grand Prix 1983 - 1997	122
My Winning ride - Mike Casey, 1996 Senior Manx Grand Prix	160
Current race and lap records	167
The Travelling Marshals	168
Index of riders performances 1983 - 1997	169
The Manx Grand Prix Riders Association	190
Manx Facts	191

Foreword by
G. R. Martin Moore, President of the Manx Motorcycle Club

1998 marks the 75th Anniversary of the first Manx Amateur Motorcycle Road Races which ran until 1929 and which then became the Manx Grand Prix.

I am very pleased indeed to have the opportunity to write a foreword for this history of the last 75 years motorcycle racing in the Manx Grand Prix here on the Isle of Man.

Peter Kneale has unrivalled knowledge of the history of the Manx Grand Prix having had a long connection with the organisation of the Races and in particular with Manx Radio's broadcasts of the events.

Bill Snelling, a former Manx Grand Prix competitor, has searched through many photographic collections to add over a hundred images which complement Peter's writing.

The Manx Motorcycle Club had been established in 1912 and provided the enthusiasts with a range of motorcycle sports. In 1923 the Committee, headed by Canon E. H. Stenning decided to promote amateur races for riders to compete over the TT course. Canon Stenning was still President of the Club in the late 1950s when I had the honour to join the organisation initially the Control and then joining the Committee.

Throughout the 75 years of the Manx Grand Prix races as can be seen from this fascinating history which Peter Kneale and Bill Snelling have produced, the M.M.C.C. Committee, with the support of the Government and the people of the Isle of Man has endeavoured to promote attractive road racing which has developed over the years a unique appeal to motorcycle competitors who at considerable cost in time, effort and expense have provided a unique camaraderie in motorcycle sport here on the Island.

The Manx Grand Prix has evolved over the years but its unique character continues. This comprehensive history will provide a fascinating insight to the races year by year and the Manx Motorcycle Club looks forward to many years of continuing motorcycle sport on the Island.

G. R. Martin Moore

Committee members of the Manx Motorcycle Club, 1998. Back row - left to right: Barry Skillicorn, David Stevens, Mike Dean, Harvey Garton, Des Evans, Stephen Harding, Les Quayle, Alan Hampton, Bill Bennett. Front row - left to right: Chris Rowe, Carol Etherington, Neil Hanson, Martin Moore, Les Doherty, David Mylchreest and John Stott. Other committee members who were not present at this time were: Fred Adlem, Jeff North and Gavin Corkill.

About the Authors

Peter Kneale

Peter has been involved with racing on the Isle of Man for the past 52 years. He has seen every race on the T.T. Course, both T.T. and Manx Grand Prix since 1946 when the Manx became the first race on the Mountain Course after World War II. At the age of 16, he became a marshal for the Races in 1950, and even during National Service in the R.A.F. managed to take leave to watch the Races. In 1963 he was invited to join the Timekeepers Box team as a Time Auditor and he carried out these duties again in 1964.

Then in May 1965, he was offered the job of Sports Editor/Announcer with the newly formed Manx Radio, and a month later began commentating on the T.T. For the past 34 years he has been the Grandstand commentator for the T.T. and Manx. For seven years he was the motorcycle commentator for I.T.V.'s World of Sport - from such circuits as Brands Hatch, Donington Park, Mallory Park and even one foreign excursion to the Belgian Grand Prix at Spa Francorchamps. He has been Chief Press Officer for the Island Races since 1986, and has written six books about the events.

Peter Kneale (marshalling alongside flag marshal) watches Bob McIntyre on his winning way in the 1951 Junior Manx. 'Mac' also finished second in the Senior on the same machine.

Bill Snelling

Bill first came to the Island to watch his first TT in 1960 at the age of thirteen. His first job was as mechanic at Arthur Lavington's Velocette emporium in Tooting. From his sixteenth year, he was a regular visitor here until the 1975 TT, when he became an 'MGP stopover' and never went home after the races! Whilst living on the 'adjacent Island', he rode the MCC long-distance trials for many years, winning the overall motorcycle championship two years in succession.

Bill had raced at many UK short-circuit races in the 70s, mainly on Velocette machinery and rode in the first Newcomers Manx on a Velocette Metisse, as well as the 1978 and 1980 Senior Manx Grand Prix, finishing every MGP race he started.

In 1993 he formed Amulree Publications and wrote his first book 'Aurora to Ariel' the story of J. Graham Oates, a Manx motorcycling pioneer. Since that book, Bill has written and/or published twelve books on motorcycling and Manx subjects, in addition to writing two books for a major UK publisher.

In 1997 Bill started FoTTofinders Bikesport Archives, which is actively cataloguing over half a million images of the Manx Grand Prix and the TT.

Currently residing in Laxey with partner Pat and Jeeyl, a big, friendly, soft Rottweiler.

Bill Snelling at Braddan Bridge in the 1978 Senior Newcomers on a Seymour Velocette Metisse.

The Manx Amateur Motor Cycle Road Races
The start of it all

The idea of a race for young motorcycling amateurs and private entrants, on the world famous TT course, was first mooted in the early twenties, indeed a request was made by the Manx Motor Cycle Club to hold a one-lap race for amateurs in the 1921 T.T. meeting, but this was dismissed out of hand by the A.C.U. It would appear that the Motor Cycle Trade Society was a strong voice in arguing against an amateur race.

Another reason was that in 1921, the Auto Cycle Union - organisers of the T.T. Races in the Island since 1907, announced the possibility of the 1922 T.T. races being held in Belgium. This bombshell was met by the Manx Motor Cycle Club, who realised the importance of motorcycle road racing to the Island. The course was ready to use and all the facilities provided but it was still a mammoth task to be faced. As it happened, the TT did not move to Belgium, but the 'Amateur' race went ahead.

One problem faced the organisers - how to define an amateur. Long and complicated rules were drawn up including - 'A person who is not at the time of making entry, or has not been since the first day of January 1923, engaged in the manufacture for sale, or sale or repair, or the exhibition of motor cars or motorcycles, their parts or accessories. Has not since the 1st January 1921, accepted and undertakes not to accept, any monetary benefit or consideration, or the equivalent thereof, from any person or firm engaged or directly interested in the manufacture for sale, or the sale of motor cars or motorcycles, their parts or accessories.'

These were just two of the lengthy paragraphs in the rules to try to define an amateur. Not ideal perhaps, but at least a basis to go ahead with the races. And so the first Manx Amateur Road Race Championship was set to be held on the 20th September 1923. In that first year, and indeed until 1929, there was just one class - 500 cc - with a special award for the best performance by a 350 cc machine. Councillor A. B. Crookall, then Mayor of Douglas, presented the Club with the principal trophy, and *The Motor Cycle* donated the trophy for the best 350. Five laps of the course, one less than the TT, had to be covered - 188.65 miles.

The Manx Amateur Motor Cycle Road Race Championships
1923 - 1929

1923

There were 35 entries, including six 350s for the first 'Amateur', and on September 20th, 31 riders faced the starter. The honour of being first rider to start fell to Ken Twemlow on his 350cc New Imperial. At the end of the first lap, one of the firm favourites Bob Lowe (Norton) led at a speed of 56.44 mph matching exactly the fastest lap in the 1921 Senior TT. But it was two 350cc machines in second and third place! D. Wright (A.J.S.), was two and a half minutes down on the leader, and Ken Twemlow (New Imperial), third. Len Randles (Sunbeam) held fourth place. Lowe increased his lead over Wright on the second lap, and Randles took over third place from Twemlow. On the third lap Lowe continued to forge ahead, and Wright and Randles were overtaken by G. Bower (Norton) and Arthur Marsden (Douglas). Wright retired on the fourth lap, Lowe was seven minutes ahead of Bower with Randles in hot pursuit. The first 'Amateur' was no exception to drama on the last lap. Lowe crashed due to a burst front tyre, Bower took over the lead only to retire with engine trouble at the Bungalow.

Twemlow was the first to finish, but Randles had enough in hand to win by one minute and 17 seconds.

After Twemlow came local rider Arthur Marsden (Douglas), W. H. Houghton (Sunbeam), C. Waterhouse (Sunbeam) and J. W Bezzant (Sunbeam). There were 18 finishers, and 11 medals, the equivalent of today's replicas, were won.

1923 M.A.R.R.C. (5 laps / 188.6 miles) 35 entries

1. Len Randles	Sunbeam	3h. 34m. 32s	52.77 mph
2. Ken Twemlow	New Imperial	3h. 35m. 49s	52.46 mph
3. Arthur Marsden	Douglas	3h. 38m. 18s	51.74 mph
Fastest lap:			
Bob Lowe	Norton	40m. 35s	55.79 mph
350cc class winner:			
Ken Twemlow	New Imperial	3h 35m 49s	52.46 mph

Although Bob Lowe had lapped in 40m. 08s. on his first lap, it was incomplete, as the starting line was some 70 yards before the finishing line. So his second lap was officially the fastest of the race.

The field assemble on the Glencrutchery Road for the first Manx Motorcycle Club's Amateur Road Race Championship. First man away was Ken Twemlow, who took his 350cc New Imperial to runner-up spot.

1924

After such a promising start, it was predicted that the 1923 entry of 35 would easily be beaten for the second Amateur, but it was disappointing that the entry only reached 29, and that more than half the entry - 15 - were on 350s. By virtue of his 1923 win, Len Randles was first away and he led the race from start to finish, increasing his lead on every lap. At the end of the first he was over one minute ahead of Bob Lowe (Norton) with A. Archibald (Norton) third and Manxman Quinton Smith (Triumph) fourth. On lap two Archibald retired, letting Quinton Smith, who had overtaken Lowe, up into second place. Randles lead was up to over four minutes. On lap three Smith held on to second place, now over five minutes down on Randles, and Lowe had been overtaken by two 350s, R. C. Brown (Sunbeam) and Archie Birkin (Cotton). W. L. Birch (Sunbeam) who had been fastest in practice and who had had a slow first lap, got moving well and set the first over 60 mph lap by an Amateur, to move on to the leaderboard. Birkin retired on the fourth lap and Smith slowed, so with one lap to go, Randles was over eight minutes ahead of Brown with Lowe third, and another 350 rider M. R. Edmondes (Chater-Lea) had moved into fourth place. So Len Randles won his second Manx in succession by nine minutes 15 seconds from Brown, Edmondes took third place from Lowe who was fourth, with the top six being completed by Birch and Quinton Smith. There were 17 finishers and seven replicas were won.

1924 M.A.R.R.C. (5 laps / 188.6 miles) 29 entries

1. Len Randles	Sunbeam	3h. 19m. 36s	56.71 mph (record)
2. R. C. Brown	Sunbeam	3h. 28m. 52s	54.20 mph
3. M. R. Edmondes	Chater-Lea	3h. 30m. 00s	53.91 mph
Fastest lap: (record)			
W. L. Birch	Sunbeam	36m. 54s	61.36 mph
350cc class winner:			
R. C. Brown	Sunbeam	3h 28m 52s	54.20 mph

Two out of two for Les Randles and Sunbeam as he accepts the congratulations after his 1924 victory.

1925

H. G. Dobbs poses with his Norton on the Ramsey Promenade.

The races were now taking off, and for 1925, the entry was up to 48, with 16 riders on 350cc machines. Len Randles was obviously the hot favourite for a hat-trick of wins and, starting again at No. 1, he completed his first lap in 36m. 38s. - 16 seconds inside the lap record. But later starters were going even quicker and the leaderboard read, first, Archibald (Norton), second, C. W. Provis (Norton) and then came Randles on his Sunbeam. On lap two Les lapped in 35m. 24s., quicker than Archibald and Provis and so took his by now accustomed first place by 29 seconds. But the hat-trick wasn't to be, for on lap three at Kirk Michael, clutch trouble forced him out. So Archibald was in the lead, but only for a short while; he crashed at Hillberry and managed to push to the pits where he retired. The new leader of the race was now Provis, but he only got as far as Crosby on the fourth lap before retiring also. Sub-Lieut. H. G. Dobbs, who had been having a steady, ride suddenly found himself in the lead at the end of the fourth lap and he made no mistakes, taking the chequered flag on his Norton six minutes and 13 seconds ahead of J. C. Vaughan (Norton) and K. S. Duncan (Norton). The first 350 to finish was J. Morton (New Gerrard) in fourth place. There were 17 finishers, and only the first six received replicas.

1925 M.A.R.R.C. (5 laps / 188.6 miles) 46 entries

1. H. G. Dobbs	Norton	3h. 8m. 46s	59.97 mph (record)
2. J. C. Vaughan	Norton	3h. 14m. 59s	58.06 mph
3. K. S. Duncan	Norton	3h. 15m. 31s	57.90 mph
Fastest lap (record)			
Les Randles	Sunbeam	35m. 24s	63.96 mph
350cc class winner:			
J. Morton	New Gerrard	3h 16m 00s	57.75 mph

1926

For 1926, the number of laps was increased to six, the same as the TT races of the time, a mileage of 226.38 miles. The entry was again up on the previous year - 54, including 12 350s. Riders were still referred to in the programme as 'Mr' - but a number of riders chose to ride under a nom de plume! There were three in total 'A. Menace', 'A. Shortus' and 'A. Reserve'!

The weather was not so good, heavy rain before the event, clearing as the race started, but the mist came down on the Mountain for the latter half of the race. This race proved to be the biggest runaway in the history of the series - and it was 'A. Reserve' (A.J.S.), who led from start to finish. At the end of the first lap he led W. S. Braidwood (A.J.S.), by 38 seconds. By the end of the second lap, he had increased his lead to over three minutes from D. Oldroyd (Sunbeam) with E Archibald (Triumph) third. The first three maintained station on lap three but Braidwood retired and F. A. Brown (Norton) came up to fourth place. The lead for 'A. Reserve' at the end of the third lap was up to five minutes 12 seconds. The fourth lap saw the end of Archibald's race, Brown overtook Oldroyd, and the leader was now eight minutes 19 seconds in front. Brown went out on the fifth lap, and M. I. Dawson (H.R.D.) moved from fifth to second with a quick lap, Oldroyd retained his third place and the leader was 12 minutes 45 seconds ahead. There were no more changes to the leaderboard, so 'A. Reserve', who disclosed his identity as Rex Adams, won by the biggest margin ever - twelve minutes eight seconds - from Dawson with Oldroyd third, followed on the leaderboard by C. W. Provis (Norton), J. O. Cunliffe (Sunbeam) and P. Stables (Scott). There were 20 finishers and 11 replicas were won.

1926 M.A.R.R.C. (6 laps / 226.38 miles) 54 entries

1. Rex Adams	A.J.S.	3h. 52m. 23s	58.46 mph
2. M. I. Dawson	H.R.D.	4h. 4m. 31s	55.56 mph
3. D. Oldroyd	Sunbeam	4h. 9m. 00s	54.56 mph
Fastest lap			
Rex Adams	A.J.S.	36m. 43s	61.67 mph
350cc class winner:			
W. A. Empsall	Velocette	4h 22m 18s	52.00 mph

'A Reserve' - Rex Adams with his A.J.S. Adams was a bank manager, and, fearful of the effect of publicity, rode under the non-de-plume 'A Reserve'. When the story of his win was made public, he was sacked from his job! Touching the front mudguard is Jimmy Simpson, who finished second in the 1926 Junior TT.

The 1926 TT was Len Randle's last race on the TT course, a year later a road accident left him with a stiff knee, and out of racing. There was, at this time, nothing to stop riders entering both the TT and the Manx. Len had a pair of rides in the 1925 TT, finishing sixth in the Senior TT. He also rode in the 1926 Senior TT, but retired.

1927

Entries for the races continued to increase, and in 1927 there was a total of 75, and 23 of the riders had entered 350cc machines. Practice times had been slow, despite conditions for the period being generally good, the fastest lap being by J. C. Vaughan (Norton) in 36m. 22s., some 58 seconds outside Len Randle's 1925 record. But if the practice period conditions had been good, the race days certainly were not - torrential rain, roads very wet and the visibility on the Mountain down to a few yards in places. This race saw the debut of Percy (Tim) Hunt, who was destined to go on to TT victories, including a Junior/Senior double in 1931. However, at the end of the first lap it was W. S. Braidwood (P. & M.) who led, H. Matthews (Norton) was second, G. W. Limmer (Scott) third and Hunt (Norton) fourth. On lap two Matthews took over the lead from Braidwood by 11 seconds, with Limmer and Hunt still third and fourth. Braidwood was back in front at half distance by 39 seconds, followed by Matthews, Limmer and Hunt. The fourth lap saw some dramatic changes - firstly Braidwood retired at Kirk Michael and then Matthews retired after a spill in the Greeba area. Limmer took over the lead at the end of this lap from Hunt, with C. W. Provis (Norton) moving up to fourth place. By the end of the next lap Tim Hunt had closed to within 22 seconds of Limmer - and with a last lap some two minutes quicker than any of his previous ones and the fastest of the day, he won from Limmer by one minute and 41 seconds. Third place went to Dennis de Ferranti (Scott), and the top six were completed by C. W. Provis (Norton), A. Cownley (Norton) and S. Gates (Velocette). There were 25 finishers and five riders won replicas. S. Gates became the last rider to win the 350cc. class, as from 1928, due to the popularity of the 350cc machines, a separate Junior race was held.

1927 M.A.R.R.C. (6 laps / 226.38 miles) 75 entries

1. Tim Hunt	Norton	3h. 53m. 55s	57.66 mph
2. G. Limmer	Scott	3h. 57m. 36s	57.17 mph
3. Dennis de Ferranti	Scott	4h. 3m. 11s	55.86 mph
Fastest lap:			
Tim Hunt	Norton	37m. 27s	60.46 mph
350cc class winner:			
S. Gates	Velocette	4h 21m 55s	51.87 mph

Dennis de Ferranti takes Schoolhouse Corner, Ramsey on his Scott. The corner was known as Crossags Corner in the days before the Ramsey Grammar School was built.

1928

For the first time in the Manx, there was a Junior race in its own right. It was held on the Tuesday with the Senior on the Thursday. Entries were slightly up on the previous year - 28 in the new Junior race and 49 in the Senior - a total of 77 as against the 1927 total of 75.

1928 Junior M.A.R.R.C.

Tim Hunt, winner of the 1927 Senior, was down to ride one of the new 350cc Levis four stroke machines, but despite his ability, he was not considered as one of the favourites for the Junior. But he proved them wrong, however, with an opening lap of 37m. 02s. - some one minute 15 seconds ahead of J. Hanson (Velocette). Third on the first lap was Gilbert Emery (Sunbeam), 23 seconds down on Hanson with 19 year old Harry Meageen (Rex-Acme), fourth. Hunt increased his lead by a further minute at the end of lap two with the top four in the same order. Meageen lapped quicker than the leader on the third lap and drew into second place, but was still two minutes 29 seconds down on Hunt, and a lap later Tim increased his lead by a further seven seconds. There was a sensation on lap five when Meageen's lap time was announced; he had lapped in 35 minutes 20 seconds, breaking the Senior record by four seconds, bringing him to just one minute behind Hunt, and as he had pulled back one minute 56 seconds on the leader on the fifth lap, there was every possibility of a very tight finish to the first ever Junior. Hunt appeared to be holding his lead as he circulated on the sixth lap, but after he was signalled through Creg-ny-Baa he stopped with engine trouble and retired, so Meageen, who had finished the race, was declared the winner by three minutes 45 seconds from J. Hanson (Velocette) with D. M. Chrystal (Velocette) third. The top six leaderboard was completed by W. L. Birch (Sunbeam), D. Jackson (Dot) and F. T. Kilburn (Rex-Acme).

1928 Junior M.A.R.R.C. (6 laps / 226.38 miles) 28 entries

1. Harry Meageen	Rex-Acme	3h. 40m. 36s	61.58 mph
2. J. Hanson	Velocette	3h. 44m. 19s	60.56 mph
3. D. M. Chrystal	Velocette	3h. 54m. 27s	57.95 mph
Fastest lap:			
Harry Meageen	Rex-Acme	35m. 20s	64.08 mph

Harry Meageen takes Ramsey Hairpin in style on his way to victory in the 1928 Junior.

1928 Senior M.A.R.R.C.

The Senior exploded into action with a dead-heat for first place between W. L. Birch (Sunbeam) and Gilbert Emery (Sunbeam) - both had lapped in 33m. 55s. - one minute 29 seconds inside the lap record! Tim Hunt (Norton) was third - one minute down. At the end of lap two, Birch led from Emery by 13 seconds, with Hunt a further one minute 20 seconds down. Lap three saw the start of Hunt's charge; he lapped in 35m. 15s. which lifted him to second place, 34 seconds down on Birch and 15 seconds ahead of Emery. Lap four saw another record from Hunt - 33m. 01s. - and this gave him the lead by just two seconds. Lap five, and another record from Hunt - this time in 32m. 42s. - and he left Birch trailing by almost a minute and a half, with Emery now two minutes down in third place. But Hunt's final lap was a real scorcher - 31m. 52s. - two seconds faster than the TT Senior lap record! This gave him a winning margin of some three minutes 10 seconds over Birch, with Emery, Norman Gledhill (Norton), J. Robinson (Norton) and Eric Lea (Norton) completing the top six. There were just eleven finishers, and, because of the winner's speed, just four replicas were won.

1928 Senior M.A.R.R.C. (6 laps / 226.38 miles) 49 entries

1. Tim Hunt	Norton	3h. 19m. 58s	67.94 mph
			(record)
2. W. L. Birch	Sunbeam	3h. 23m. 08s	66.88 mph
3. Gilbert Emery	Sunbeam	3h. 26m. 29s	65.79 mph
Fastest lap (record)			
Tim Hunt	Norton	31m. 52s	71.05 mph

1929

There was a total entry of 76 for the 1929 races, 34 in the Junior and 42 in the Senior, the same total as the previous year.

1929 Junior M.A.R.R.C.

The weather conditions for the Junior were good - and favourites for the honours were W. H. T. Meageen (Rex-Acme) and J. Hanson (Velocette), first and second in the 1928 Junior. It was Hanson who led at the end of the first lap in 33m. 49s. well inside the 1928 record, but Meageen could only manage sixth place. Second was Eric Lea (Velocette), third was R. S. Sikes (Velocette), with Harold Levings (Velocette) and Doug Pirie (Velocette) also ahead of Meageen. Lap two saw a new lap record again, this time to Meageen - 33m. 24s. - he moved up to be equal second with Sikes, just over one minute behind Hanson. Sikes dropped down the leaderboard on lap three, leaving Meageen in second place, and Lea came up to third, and this top three order remained on lap four. Lap five saw the end of Hanson's race when an engine seizure on the Mountain brought about his retirement Meageen led Lea by over three minutes and looked all set to repeat his 1928 victory, but on the last lap the throttle cable broke near Hillberry - with just a couple of miles to go. By holding the cable with his hand he got going again, but stalled his engine at Governor's Bridge. He then pushed the last half mile to the finish and held his lead by just 12 seconds. But then drama - following a protest, the race

Stewards met and found that Meageen had received 'outside assistance' at Hillberry, by being pushed off by spectators after his throttle cable had snapped and they had no alternative but to disqualify him and award the race to Eric Lea who had finished second on time. The rest of the top six leaderboard then read: D. de Ferranti (New Henley), L. A. Hutchings (Velocette), Harold Hartley (Velocette), E. Forman (Velocette) and R. S. Sikes (Velocette). Fourteen riders finished and four won replicas.

1929 Junior M.A.R.R.C. (6 laps / 226.38 miles) 34 entries

1. Eric Lea	Velocette	3h. 28m. 15s	65.24 mph
2. Dennis Z. de Ferranti	New Henley	3h. 35m. 18s	63.10 mph
3. L. A. Hutchings	Velocette	3h. 43m. 59s	60.65 mph
Fastest lap			
W. H. T. Meageen	Rex-Acme	33m. 24s	67.80 mph

The following is taken from the Isle of Man Weekly Times:
'Mr Sikes is camping with some friends outside Crosby, and during one morning's practice he did two marvellously quick consecutive laps, despite a low-lying mist, took a toss at Signpost Corner, picked himself up, went on, killed a hen, braked too hard at the finish, came off, turned two somersaults, picked himself up again, and went home to cook the breakfast!'

1929 Senior M.A.R.R.C.

The 1929 Senior was to turn out to be even more dramatic than the Junior! There was no hint of this, however at the start when conditions were described as wet roads and poor visibility. At the end of the first lap, the leader was Dennis de Ferranti (New Hudson) from W. H. T. Meageen (Rex-Acme) by just one second at 67.16 mph, with H. J. Bacon (Sunbeam) in third place less than a minute down. By lap two Meageen was in the lead by 10 seconds from de Ferranti, with Bacon closing to just 22 seconds down. J. D. Potts (Grindlay-Peerless) was in fourth place. Meageen held his lead at the end of lap three, but with the fastest lap of the race at 69.99 mph Bacon moved up into second place ahead of de Ferranti, with Potts still fourth but now three minutes down. The fourth lap saw two of the top three out of the race - the leader Meageen retired with engine trouble on the Mountain and third place de Ferranti crashed at Quarter Bridge, and although he continued from there he too shortly retired. So at the end of the fourth lap Bacon had a lead over Potts of almost five minutes with G. W. Wood (Rudge) closing on Potts. Bacon slowed on the fifth lap and Potts was able to close the gap, and Eric Lea (Norton) the Junior winner took third place from Wood. On the last lap Bacon crashed at Ballig and Wood also retired, so Potts now had a lead of over seven minutes from Lea and Levings brought his 350 Velocette into third place, almost fifteen minutes down on Potts. The top six were completed by J. M. Sugg (Norton), C. P. Tutt (Rudge-Whitworth) and Doug Pirie (Velocette). There were 14 finishers and four replicas were won.

1929 Senior M.A.R.R.C. (6 laps / 226.38 miles) 42 entries
(amended after protests)

1. Eric Lea	Norton	3h. 32m. 13s	64.02 mph
2. Harold Levings	Velocette	3h. 40m. 01s	61.74 mph
3. J. M. Sugg	Norton	3h. 44m. 42s	60.46 mph
Fastest lap			
H. J. Bacon	Sunbeam	32m. 21s	69.99 mph

Later that year, rumours began about 'Amateurs' accepting retainers and bonuses, which were against the regulations for the Amateur races. The Auto-Cycle Union held an official enquiry and *The Motor Cycling* of December 1929 - over three months after the race - reported that a special committee had been appointed to probe each individual case. The report read: "That so many entrants could sign affidavits to the effect that they were not in receipt of assistance from the trade, when some of them were being paid as much, or more, than works entered riders in the TT, was a state of affairs liable to bring the whole sport into disrepute and one which could not be allowed to continue. It must be mentioned that it was the riders themselves and not the regulations that were at fault. The trouble was that only with the honest cooperation of competitors could these rules be enforced. This cooperation was not forthcoming and, we believe, never has been forthcoming with regard to the amateur races".

It would appear that the Motor Cycle Manufacturers Union may have been a driving force in agitating against the rules as they stood.

Following the inquiry, the A.C.U. suspended, or recommended the suspension of twenty one riders, and excluded them from such awards as they might have won in the 1929 Amateur. Five of the race Stewards were also suspended.

The results of the Junior race were not affected, but one of the twenty one was J. D. Potts, the Senior winner. Eric Lea, who had finished second to Potts was declared the winner, and, after finishing second in both races, became the first rider in the September races to do the 'double'!

So that was the last of the 'Amateur' races; new rules were about to be drawn up for the Manx Grand Prix for 1930, which would avoid the problems of the 1929 meeting.

A double-winner, by default. Eric Lea at Parliament Square, Ramsey. The caption gives him as finishing second; it was much later in the season that he was awarded the race.

The Manx Grand Prix
1930 - 1939

1930

The year of the birth of The Manx Grand Prix. New regulations for the Manx had been drawn up and it was no longer a race for amateurs, but a race with experts barred. The rules included: "All entrants, who shall be the drivers, must be British or Irish subjects resident in the British Isles or the Irish Free State, and must hold open competition licenses. They must not, since 1920, have been entered as a competitor in any international road race or have held any world motorcycling record. The race to be for machines of up to 350cc and 500cc, and to be over six laps of the TT course, the meeting to be known as the Manx Grand Prix."

Making their Island debut in 1930 were two future stars and TT winners, Freddie Frith on a 350cc Velocette in the Junior and Senior, and Harold Daniell on a Norton in the Senior.

1930 Junior MGP

Torrential rain greeted the riders for the Junior, which turned out to be a Velocette benefit. Frith led at the end of the first lap on his first appearance from J. M. Muir by five seconds, with the local hope Wilf Harding third. Frith dropped to third on lap two, with Muir taking over and leading Harding by one minute 44 seconds. On lap three, Muir set the fastest lap of the race - 34m. 46s. - 65.15 mph and led the race by over four minutes. Lap four however saw the end of Muir when he retired at the 13th Milestone. So was a Manx victory on in the first Manx? Harding led the race by almost one minute from Doug Pirie, who had overtaken Frith. On lap five Pirie pulled back Harding's lead by 50 seconds, with Frith still third, and on the final lap Pirie took over the lead to win by 28 seconds. Harding finished runner-up with Frith third. The top six were completed by Harold Levings, Jock Forbes and T. L. Brookes, and all the top six were on KTT Velocettes. There were 18 finishers, and six replicas were won.

1930 Junior MGP (6 laps / 226.38) 47 entries

1. Doug Pirie	Velocette	3h. 40m. 26s	61.63 mph
2. Wilf Harding	Velocette	3h. 40m. 54s	61.50 mph
3. Freddie Frith	Velocette	3h. 45m. 10s	60.34 mph
Fastest lap:			
J. M. Muir	Velocette	34m. 46s	65.13 mph

Jack McL. Leslie had some good unofficial practice for the 1930 Junior, he was a riding member of the Levis team that completed 50 laps of the course in their attempt to gain the Maudes Trophy.

1930 Senior MGP

The weather conditions for the Senior were in complete contrast to that for the Junior - bright sunshine and perfect visibility. The machine that dominated the Senior was Rudge, the make that had taken the first three places in the 1930 Senior TT. In this first Senior Manx, Ralph Merrill led on his Rudge from start to finish, with Rudge mounted G. W. Wood second throughout. They were chased in the early stages by Norman Gledhill (Norton) and four riders on 350 Velocettes - Frith, Harding, Pirie and Muir. In fact on the fourth lap Frith took third place behind the Rudges, just over two minutes behind the leader, but a lap later his engine expired and he was out of the race. Gledhill (Norton) took over third place, followed by Pirie (Velocette), Muir (Velocette) and S. (Ginger) Woods (Rudge). Merrill won the race by 19 seconds from Wood (G. W.) with Gledhill 2 minutes 11 seconds down in third place, the remaining leaderboard unchanged. There were 24 finishers and 15 replicas were won.

1930 Senior MGP (6 laps / 226.38 miles) 53 entries

1. Ralph Merrill	Rudge	3h. 15m. 30s	69.49 mph
			(record)
2. Ginger Wood	Rudge	3h. 15m. 49s	69.38 mph
3. Norman Gledhill	Norton	3h. 18m. 00s	68.61 mph
Fastest lap (record)			
Ralph Merrill	Rudge	31m. 50s	71.13 mph

The Merrill camp in full celebration of Ralph's record-breaking Senior victory

1931

1931 Junior MGP

In the early stages of the Junior it looked as it Velocette would repeat their previous years success. At the end of lap one, Velocette riders held the first four places - Eric Lea., A. L. Hodgson, Harold Newman and Doug Pirie, and from a standing start, Lea had lapped at over 70 mph - the first time ever in the Junior. He slowed on lap two however and Hodgson took the lead, only to retire on the third lap. This let the 1930 Junior win-

ner, Doug Pirie into the lead, and he never looked back. He won by four minutes 44 seconds from John Carr (New Imperial), with Harold Hartley (Rudge) third almost two minutes down. The top six were completed by H. Widdall (Rudge), J. A. McLean Leslie (Rudge) and Ron Harris (Norton). There were 14 finishers and 10 replicas were won, Lea just missing out on one by finishing 11th.

A. S. Moorhouse (Norton), 8th finisher in the Junior, at Parliament Square.

1931 Junior MGP (6 laps / 226.38 miles) 53 entries

1. Doug Pirie	Velocette	3h. 15m. 13s	69.59 mph
			(record)
2. John Carr	New Imperial	3h. 19m. 57s	67.95 mph
3. Harold Hartley	Rudge	3h. 21m. 51s	67.31 mph
Fastest lap (record)			
Doug Pirie	Velocette	31m. 48s	71.20 mph

Doug Pirie was lucky to race, let alone win. He was thrown from his Velocette on the mountain late in practice, sustaining facial and other injuries. His friends repaired the damaged machine, and he was able to put in a couple of quiet laps on his Senior Excelsior to prove his fitness. His face was swathed in bandages during the race and he all but collapsed at the end of the race.

1931 Senior MGP

Norton riders dominated the opening laps of the Senior, with local rider Wilf Harding leading at the end of the first lap from Norman Gledhill, Kelly Swanston and J. M. Muir, all on Nortons. Harding's race ended however on lap two when he retired and Gledhill took over the lead at the end of lap two. His lead didn't last long however, going out at Union Mills on the third lap. Muir, who had set the fastest lap in the 1930 Junior, went into the lead at the end of the fourth lap, and held on to his lead to clinch his victory. He won by almost 10 minutes from L. R. Courtney (Rudge) who had ridden consistently throughout the race, with John Carr (Norton) third, over three minutes behind Courtney, the top six were completed by Harold Hartley (Rudge), W. L. Stranger (A.J.S.) and Robert Williamson (Rudge). There were 20 finishers, and 17 replicas were won.

1931 Senior MGP (6 laps / 226.38 miles) 55 entries

1. J. M. Muir	Norton	3h. 09m. 15s	71.79 mph
			(record)
2. L. R. Courtney	Rudge	3h. 19m. 14s	68.19 mph
3. John Carr	Norton	3h. 22m. 29s	67.09 mph
Fastest lap (record)			
Norman Gledhill	Norton	30m. 49s	73.47 mph

C. D. Reich had a pair of experts in his pit, Charlie Dodson and Syd Crabtree.

Muir over-braked at the finish of the race, and fell off just after the flag.

Although Dope fuel had been banned for use at the TT, it was still allowed at the Manx. Some riders found their machines had been prepared with its use in mind. One competitor brought over thirty, five-gallon cans of 'bang-water' with him.

1932

1932 Junior MGP

Weather conditions for the 1932 Junior were reasonable, although there was mist on the Mountain, and water on various parts of the course. At the end of the first lap, J. M. Muir (Velocette), winner of the 1931 Senior led from John Carr (New Imperial) and Harold Newman (Velocette), who were jointly 11 seconds down on the leader. Newman took over the lead on lap two, due to a slow lap by Muir, and led Carr by eight seconds, with Doug Pirie (Excelsior) just one second down on Carr. With a new record lap on the third circuit - 31m. 44s. - Pirie took over the lead from Newman by 30 seconds, with Carr third and John 'Crasher' White (Velocette) fourth. The fourth lap saw the end of the race for Pirie who came off at Glen Helen, so Newman was the new leader, and White had moved ahead of Carr. The order remained the same on the fifth lap, with Muir trying hard to make up for his slow second lap. But things really happened on the last lap - Newman hit machine problems and slowed dramatically, and White took over the lead from Carr. But then at Signpost, White's machine broke down and he coasted to Governor's Bridge and pushed in to finish fifth. So Carr won a dramatic race by 52 seconds from Muir, with Austin Munks (Velocette) third. The top six were completed by J. A. McL. Leslie (Rudge), John 'Crasher' White (Velocette) and J. F. Clay (Velocette). Newman finished in eighth place. There were 29 finishers, and 17 replicas were won.

1932 Junior MGP (6 laps / 226.38 miles) 56 entries

1. John Carr	New Imperial	3h. 16m. 08s	69.27 mph
2. J. M. Muir	Velocette	3h. 17m. 00s	68.96 mph
3. Austin Munks	Velocette	3h. 18m. 00s	68.59 mph
Fastest lap (record)			
Doug Pirie	Excelsior	31m. 44s	71.35 mph

1932 Senior MGP

The 1932 Senior has been described as the wettest ever. The forty-four starters who lined up faced torrential rain and driving mist on the Mountain. Despite the conditions, Harold Levings (Norton) led at the end of the first lap with a time of 33m. 31s. and was four seconds ahead of Norman Gledhill (Norton) with Steve Darbishire (Levis) third. Levings retired on the second lap and Darbishire slowed down, eventually to retire, so Gledhill took the lead by over three minutes from J. Fletcher (Sunbeam), with Harold Daniell (Norton) third. Daniell took

over second place on the third lap and "Q. Ack" took his 350 Velocette into third place, but his efforts ended with a retirement on lap four and B. W. Swabey (Rudge) took over the third place. Despite the efforts of Daniell and Swabey, who closed on the leader on the fifth and sixth laps, Norman was in command and won by just over one minute. J. Fletcher (Sunbeam) was fourth, Freddie Frith (Norton) fifth and Ron Harris (Norton) sixth. There were 20 finishers and 11 replicas were won.

1932 Senior MGP (6 laps / 226.38 miles)   48 entries

1. Norman Gledhill	Norton	3h. 21m. 49s	67.32 mph
2. Harold Daniell	Norton	3h. 22m. 51s	66.97 mph
3. B. W. Swabey	Rudge	3h. 25m. 59s	65.96 mph
Fastest lap			
B. W. Swabey	Rudge	32m. 50s	68.97 mph

1933

1933 Junior MGP

For the first time in the Manx, a special Lightweight Trophy for 250cc machines was awarded, the race to be run concurrently with the Junior. The weather was perfect for the Junior and records were well and truly smashed. On lap one 'Crasher' White (Velocette) knocked one minute 38 seconds off the Junior record to lead Austin Munks (Velocette) by 53 seconds, with the Norton challenge headed by third place man Harold Daniell. White made history on the second lap when he became the first rider in the Manx to lap in under 30 minutes - 29m. 56s. - 75.64 mph - 31 seconds inside the Senior record! This gave him a 52 seconds lead over Munks with Daniell still third. By half distance White had increased his lead to 66 seconds over Munks with Daniell 64 seconds down on the second place man. 'Crasher' lived up to his nick-name on the fourth lap when he came off on the Mountain section, and although unhurt, he only managed to get his damaged machine to the pits where he retired. Daniell also went out on this lap, so Austin had an enormous lead of three minutes 20 seconds over Norton rider Freddie Frith, with Doug Pirie and Harold Levings in third and fourth places. There were no more changes on the leaderboard to the end of the race. There was a total of 24 finishers and 11 replicas were won.

In the Lightweight class there had been just four entries, and the new Trophy was won by Ron Harris.

The Manningham Hotel hangs out the flags for their successful riders. Senior winner Norman Gledhill is behind the main trophy; on his left is Junior winner J. H. Carr. On the left (with glasses) is Ron Harris

Austin Munks takes Governors Bridge on his way to the first of his Velocette-mounted victories in the Junior Manx.

1933 Junior MGP (6 laps / 226.38 miles) 56 entries

1. Austin Munks	Velocette	3h. 03m. 15s	74.14 mph (record)
2. Freddie Frith	Velocette	3h. 08m. 21s	72.13 mph
3. Doug Pirie	Norton	3h. 08m. 36s	72.03 mph
250cc class winner:			
Ron Harris	New Imperial	?h ?m ?s	66.47 mph
Fastest lap (record)			
J. H. 'Crasher' White	Velocette	29m. 56s	75.64 mph

1933 Senior MGP

With weather conditions again perfect for the Senior, all records again were broken. At the end of lap one Harold Daniell (Norton), runner-up in 1932, lapped in 29m. 32s., one minute 17 seconds inside the Senior record. Seven seconds down on Harold was Steve Darbishire (Norton) with the top six completed by Harold Levings (Norton), Jock Forbes (Norton), 'Crasher' White (350 Velocette) and J. M. Muir (Norton). At the end of lap too, Daniell had increased his lead over Darbishire to 25 seconds, and Doug Pirie, Junior winner in 1930 and 1931, had moved up from seventh to joint third with Forbes, White and Muir remained fifth and sixth. The third lap saw the end of the race for Darbishire, off at Glen Helen, Pirie retired after Ballacraine and Forbes also retired. This left Harold with a lead over Kelly Swanston (Norton) of two minutes 31 seconds, followed by Muir (Norton), Norman Gledhill (Norton), Ron Harris (Norton) and Austin Munks (Velocette). There were no further changes on the leaderboard to the end of the race. Harold went on to win by two and a half minutes, despite a record lap on the sixth circuit by Swanston at 77.86 mph. There were 24 finishers, and nine replicas were won.

1933 Senior MGP (6 laps / 226.38 miles) 62 entries

1. Harold Daniell	Norton	2h. 56m. 29s	76.98 mph (record)
2. J. Kelly Swanston	Norton	2h. 59m. 00s	75.90 mph
3. J. M. Muir	Norton	3h. 00m. 52s	75.11 mph
Fastest lap (record)			
J. Kelly Swanston	Norton	29m. 05s	77.86 mph

1934

1934 Lightweight MGP

For 1934, there was a separate race for 250cc machines, which was run concurrently with the Junior. It was a brave step, as in 1933 there had been just four 250cc machines entered. For 1934 this number rose to 15. At the end of the first lap, Bob Foster (New Imperial) led C. V. Moore (New Imperial) and T. Cogan-Verney (New Imperial). The order remained the same at the end of lap two, with Foster 42 seconds ahead of Moore, and Cogan-Verney 17 seconds down on Moore. Lap three saw no change in the leading three, but on the fourth lap Donald Mitchell (Cotton) came up to third place, only four seconds behind Moore, who was two minutes 41 seconds down on the leader Foster. Mitchell continued his charge on lap five, and took second place from Moore, and with the fastest lap of the race on the final circuit, 34m. 18s. snatched victory from Foster by 34 seconds. Cogan-Verney finished third ahead of Moore, Ken Bills (Rudge) finished fifth and R.H. Robinson (Dunelt) was sixth. There were eight finishers, and they all won replicas.

1934 Lightweight MGP (6 laps / 226.38 miles) 15 entries

1. W. Donald Mitchell	Cotton	3h. 33m. 58s	63.49 mph
2. Bob Foster	New Imperial	3h. 34m. 32s	63.33 mph
3. T. Cogan-Verney	New Imperial	3h. 36m. 08s	62.86 mph
Fastest lap			
W. Donald Mitchell	Cotton	34m. 18s	66.02 mph

1934 Junior MGP

J. H. 'Crasher' White led the Junior from start to finish. Riding a Norton he led Doug Pirie (Norton), Austin Munks (Norton) and Freddie Frith (Norton) at the end of he first lap. By the a end of the second lap White was 53 seconds ahead of Pirie, who in turn had an advantage of 26 seconds over Munks. Frith was still fourth, Bertie Rowell (Velocette) was fifth and Steve Darbishire (Norton) sixth. Pirie reduced White's lead by 12 seconds an lap three to 41 seconds, and the remaining leaderboard places were unchanged. By the end of the fourth lap, White was really in charge, his lead over Pirie was one minute 58 seconds with Munks still third, followed by Frith, Rowell and Darbishire. White continued to pull away from the rest of the field on the fifth lap, with the placings unchanged. So 'Crasher' White went on to win the Junior by three minutes nine seconds from Doug Pirie who finished just four seconds ahead of Munks. Frith slowed on the final lap to finish in sixth place behind Rowell and Darbishire. There were 25 finishers and nine replicas were won.

1934 Junior MGP (6 laps / 226.38 miles) 52 entries

1. J. H. 'Crasher' White	Norton	2h. 59m. 44s	75.59 mph (record)
2. Doug Pirie	Norton	3h. 02m. 53s	74.29 mph
3. Austin Munks	Norton	3h. 02m. 57s	74.26 mph
Fastest lap (record)			
J. H. 'Crasher' White	Norton	29m. 25s	76.97 mph

1934 Senior MGP

Crasher White makes for a front wheel landing on Union Mills Bridge, prior to his retirement from the lead of the race at almost the same spot.

White was the favourite for the Senior, but at the end of the first lap he was only in fourth place behind Freddie Frith, Doug Pirie and Steve Darbishire, all Norton mounted. At the end of the second lap Frith was 30 seconds ahead of Pirie who was 17 seconds ahead of Darbishire, White was still fourth, Kelly Swanston (Norton) fifth and Ron Harris (Norton) sixth. On the third lap White broke the lap record at 81.74 mph, the first 80 mph lap in the history of the Manx, and led Frith by over four seconds. By the end of the fourth lap White increased his lead over Frith to 52 seconds, and the double looked on. Pirie was third, Swanston fourth, Harris fifth and Bertie Rowell (Velocette) sixth. But there was still drama to come in this race. 'Crasher' again lived up to his nick-name on the fifth lap when he came off at Union Mills after his footrest caught the pavement. Frith took over the the lead by 12 seconds from Pirie with Swanston third. But on the final lap, Freddie Frith ran out of petrol above Ramsey, so Doug Pirie went on to win his third Manx by four minutes 21 seconds seconds from Swanston, who finished six minutes five seconds in front of Harris. Rowell and L. R. Courtney (Velocette) tied for fourth place, and Bob Foster brought his Sunbeam into sixth place. There were 25 finishers and six replicas were won.

1934 Senior MGP (6 laps / 226.38 miles) 62 entries

1. Doug Pirie	Norton	2h. 51m. 34s	79.19 mph
			(record)
2. J. Kelly Swanston	Norton	2h. 55m. 55s	77.27 mph
3. Ron Harris	Norton	3h. 02m. 00s	74.64 mph
Fastest lap (record)			
J. H. 'Crasher' White	Norton	27m. 42s	81.74 mph

1935

1935 Lightweight MGP

The entry for the Lightweight increased from 15 in 1934 to 25. It was a race that Ron Harris (New Imperial) led from start to finish. By the end of the first lap he was one minute ahead of Harold Rowell (Rudge) who led P. R. Warren (New Imperial) by 13 seconds. By the end of the second lap, a new record at 69.11 mph, Harris led Rowell by two minutes 17 seconds, with Rowell 12 seconds in front of C.A.W. Durno (Cotton), Warren having stopped at the pits at the end of the first lap. By half distance, Harris was three minutes eight seconds in front of Rowell, who was still 12 seconds in front of Durno. Harris added almost two more minutes to his lead by the end of the fourth lap, and Durno had taken second place from Rowell by six seconds. Durno's brave effort ended on the fifth lap when he retired with a seized engine, Harris led Rowell by five minutes 24 seconds, with Frank Cadman (New Imperial) four minutes down in third place. So Ron Harris went on to win by a massive 11 minutes 14 seconds from Harold Rowell, Cadman was third, Denis Parkinson (Excelsior) fourth, K. B. Leach (Excelsior) fifth and J. Longstaff (C.T.S.) sixth. There were nine finishers and six replicas were won.

1935 Lightweight MGP (6 laps / 226.38 miles) 25 entries

1. Ron Harris	New Imperial	3h. 18m. 06s	68.56 mph
			(record)
2. Harold Rowell	Rudge	3h. 29m. 20s	64.90 mph
3. Frank Cadman	New Imperial	3h. 32m. 32s	63.92 mph
Fastest lap (record)			
Ron Harris	New Imperial	32m. 23s	69.93 mph

Freddie Frith (left) and Ron Harris in the winners enclosure after their record-breaking runs.

1935 Junior MGP

Freddie Frith made no mistake in the Junior, leading from start to finish, and winning in record breaking style. At the end of the first lap his Norton was 32 seconds in front of Kelly Swanston (Norton) who led Jack Blyth (Norton) by just one second. Steve Darbishire (Norton), Bertie Rowell (Velocette) and Tommy McEwan (Norton) completed the top six. Frith increased his lead to 54 seconds over Darbishire at the end of the second lap, and Blyth was still third, three seconds down on Darbishire. Swanston had dropped to fourth, followed by McEwan and Rowell. Strangely enough, there were no changes to the top six positions on the next three laps, with Frith increasing his lead lap by lap, at the end of the third it was one minute 13 seconds, by the end of the fourth, one minute 29 seconds, and at the end of the fifth he was one

My Winning Ride - by J. Kelly Swanston, 1935 Senior Manx

After a second place in both the 1933 and 1934 Senior Manx, I approached Norton in 1935 to see if they would lend me a 350 to go with my Senior machine, which they did.

I took things a bit too easy in the Junior race, and was given the 'hurry-up' at the mid-race pit-stop by my crew! I upped the pace and finished third (behind Freddie Frith and Steve Darbishire).

As I weighed in for the Senior, a drip was noticed under my machine - the petrol tank had sprung a leak! Norton were unable to provide a replacement tank and suggested that I used the tank of the Junior machine. But, I said, this is a 3fi gallon tank, I needed a 3fl gallon for the Senior. "That'll be alright", they said! so I had apply for an extension to take the bike out of weigh-in and change it.

Race day dawned, and I was the last to leave the hall where the bikes had been stored overnight. As I was riding up to the start, a black cat crossed my path. "That's a very good sign", I thought, and made my way to the start. The machine was nicely warmed up by now, so I changed the plug for a racing one. Just then, Dennis Mansell, son of the Managing Director of Norton, came up to me and said,

"We would like you to use this plug for the race".

"But that's a KLG and I am using Lodge" I said.

"Never mind, we would like you to use this plug". I was a bit puzzled by this, but did as they asked.

When I started the race, it was immediately obvious to me that there was something wrong with the plug. Instead of having a nice deep sound coming from the engine, it had a higher pitch than normal. As I accelerated out of Quarter Bridge, it misfired once, the next slow corner, approaching Glen Helen, and it misfired twice. At Ramsey, I didn't think it would start again, and finally, on the exit to Governors Bridge, it completely died. I almost felt like retiring, after all these years, I had a defunct machine.

As I went to lean it against the wall, a chap leaned over and said, "What's wrong chum".

"I've burnt out a plug" was my reply.

"Aren't you going to change it?"

Well, I thought I better had, so I re-fitted the plug I had intended to use, it must have taken me about a minute and a half. Just then I heard a sound of another machine coming round Governors and the marshal said, "You will have to wait until he has gone past". Lo and behold, it was my old sparring partner Steve Darbishire (who started number 30 to my number 28), so I thought, well, I will have a good run with him. As we passed the pits I could see him in the distance and I very quickly caught him up at Braddan Bridge. I was unable to get past until Greeba Castle, where Steve went to pass Tommy McEwan and ran slightly wide, I was able to nip past the pair of them and made my escape. Steve was tailing me at this point, listening to where I shut off, then leaving it a second or so later. Unfortunately, he left it a little to late at Ballacraine, and had to take the slip road!

I carried on until the end of the third lap, pit stop time, where I was informed that I was lying second to Freddie Frith, who was leading by a minute and a half, but I was gaining about half a minute a lap on him.

I motored on in style for the next three laps and finished. Freddie had started number 38, so I had to wait until he crossed the finishing line, when the Tannoy gave the news that I had won by over 40 seconds, setting new race and lap records on the way, and gaining my third club team prize for the Kircaldy M.C.C., with Tommy McEwan and Jack Blyth (6th and 16th).

I never mentioned the plug episode to Nortons; they had been very good to me over the years, I would send my engine down for reconditioning and they would send it back, sometimes they would fit a bronze head, other times it would be an all-alloy motor, and all they charged me was £10!

I had five glorious years at the Manx and would liked to have gone on but my father told the Mansell's; "My son is a doctor, he must get these motorcycles out of his system, let him carry on with the medicine", so I retired from racing to pursue my chosen career.

I did ride once more, the Yorkshire Sand Racing Championship at Redcar in 1936, I won both 500 and Unlimited events.

J.K.Swanston. 1st in Senior M.G.P. 1935

minute 32 seconds in front. There was to be no drama in this race, and Freddie won from Steve Darbishire by one minute 32 seconds with Swanston third, 22 seconds down on Darbishire. Blyth maintained his fourth place, and the only change on the leaderboard was Rowell snatched fifth place from McEwan. There were 22 finishers and 13 replicas were won.

1935 Junior MGP (6 laps / 226.38 miles) 54 entries

1. Freddie Frith	Norton	2h. 58m. 43s	76.02 mph (record)
2. Steve Darbishire	Norton	3h. 01m. 14s	74.96 mph
3. Kelly Swanston	Norton	3h. 01m. 36s	74.81 mph
Fastest lap (record)			
Freddie Frith	Norton	29m. 11s	77.59 mph

1935 Senior MGP

Freddie Frith was again the favourite for the Senior, and at the end of the first lap he led Steve Darbishire by 51 seconds with Austin Munks third, a further 29 seconds down. Ron Harris was fourth, Jack Blyth fifth and Kelly Swanston sixth. All six were Norton mounted. Frith was one minute 27 seconds ahead at the end of the second lap, and it was Swanston who was second, with Darbishire third, Munks fourth, Harris fifth and Blyth sixth. There were no changes to the top six to the end of the race, but the battle between Frith and Swanston kept the crowd on their toes. At the end of the third lap, Swanston had pulled back 21 seconds to trail Frith by one minute six seconds. He continued his charge and was only 31 seconds down at the end of the fourth, and just three seconds behind Frith as they started their last lap. There was nothing Frith could do about it and Swanston took the chequered flag 43 seconds ahead of Frith, and for good measure broke the lap record on the last lap at 81.84 mph Darbishire finished third, two minutes eight seconds down on Freddie, with Austin Munks, Ron Harris and Jack Blyth completing the top six. There were 20 finishers and nine replicas were won.

1935 Senior MGP (6 laps / 226.38 miles) 42 entries

1. J. Kelly Swanston	Norton	2h. 50m. 38s	79.62 mph (record)
2. Freddie Frith	Norton	2h. 51m. 21s	79.29 mph
3. Steve Darbishire	Norton	2h. 53m. 29s	78.31 mph
Fastest lap (record)			
J. Kelly Swanston	Norton	27m. 40s	81.84 mph

A number of Manx Grand Prix riders were employed as extras on George Formby's TT film 'No Limit', including Harold and Bertie Rowell, Jack Cannell, Jock Fairweather and TT star Paddy Johnston. Harold Rowell recalled many incidents during the filming. The regular stunt riders were very quickly rendered 'hors de combat', so the locals were pressed into service. Jack Cannell 'volunteered' to crash at Creg Willies Hill for the film, he executed the stunt perfectly. The next MGP, Harold had retired in the Glen Helen area and was supping tea in Kitty Brew's Cafe when word came through that Jack Cannell had crashed at the exact spot used in the film. "Is Jack still practising for a film role?" was Harold's comment.

1936

1936 Lightweight MGP

The Lightweight entries again increased, the total being 37. Denis Parkinson (Excelsior) led at the end of lap one by nine seconds from P. R. Warren (New Imperial) who was 57 seconds ahead of Laurence Longstaff (C.T.S.). Frank Cadman (New Imperial), Charlie Brett (Excelsior) and R. Hooper (New Imperial) completed the top six. Parkinson increased his lead over Warren to 52 seconds at the end of the second lap with Longstaff a further 53 seconds down. By half distance Parkinson was 55 seconds up on Warren, but Longstaff was closing on Warren, being just 22 seconds behind. But Warren's race ended on the fourth lap when he came off at Windy Corner, and Parkinson led Longstaff by four minutes 53 seconds, with F. J. Hudson (O.K. Supreme) up into third place, one minute 16 seconds down on Longstaff. By the end of lap five Parkinson had increased his lead to six minutes 52 second, from Longstaff, who in turn was over one minute up on Hudson. So Denis Parkinson went on to win his first Manx by seven minutes 58 seconds. Longstaff retired on the final lap, and second place went to F. R. W. England (Python) who finished 48 seconds ahead of the third place man F. J. Hudson. The top six were completed by R. Hooper (New Imperial), Charlie Brett (Excelsior) and H. W. Boswell (Cotton). There were eight finishers and the first six won replicas.

1936 Lightweight MGP (6 laps / 226.38 miles) 37 entries

1. Denis Parkinson	Excelsior	3h. 26m. 51s	65.68 mph
2. F. R. W. England	Python	3h. 34m. 49s	63.25 mph
3. F. J. Hudson	OK Supreme	2h. 53m. 27s	63.06 mph
Fastest lap			
Denis Parkinson	Excelsior	33m. 51s	69.90 mph

Second placeman 'Lofty' England went on to manage the Jaguar racing team that took great success at Le Mans in the 1950s.

R. J. Edwards practiced on an Excelsior 'Mechanical Marvel' which had been ridden to victory in the 1933 Lightweight TT by Sid Gleave.

1936 Junior MGP

The Junior race of 1936 attracted an entry of 44, and quite a race it turned out to be. Maurice Cann (Norton) led at the end of the first lap by seven seconds from Jack Blyth (Norton) who was 29 seconds ahead of the third place man Austin Munks (Velocette). Three Norton riders completed the first lap leaderboard - Bertie Rowell, Tommy McEwan and W. L. Dawson. At the end of the second lap, Cann and Blyth were exactly level on time and 50 seconds ahead of Munks in third place. Rowell and McEwan held their places and Jack Cannell (Velocette) came into sixth place. But what a change around by the end of lap three, Maurice Cann came off at Sulby Bridge, Munks, put on a spurt and moved from third to first, 11 seconds in front of Blyth, with Rowell one minute down in third place, Cannell was fourth, Harry Ogden (Norton) fifth and Johnnie Lockett (Norton) sixth. The lead changed yet again at the end of the fourth lap - Blyth led by 43 seconds from Munks who in turn was one minute 15 seconds in front of Rowell. Ogden, Lockett,

and J. F. R. Martin (Norton) completed the top six. On lap five, Munks began his fight back and closed the gap between himself and Blyth to 17 seconds, with Rowell two minutes down, with the rest of the leaderboard unchanged. It was a two-man race to the flag, and Austin Munks took victory from Jack Blyth with Bertie Rowell in third place two and a half minutes down. Harry Ogden finished fourth, Johnnie Lockett fifth and J. F .R. Martin sixth. There were 21 finishers and seven replicas were won.

1936 Junior MGP (6 laps / 226.38 miles) 44 entries

1. Austin Munks	Velocette	3h. 03m. 47s	73.93 mph
2. Jack Blyth	Norton	3h. 03m. 54s	73.88 mph
3. Bertie Rowell	Norton	3h. 06m. 25s	72.88 mph
Fastest lap			
Austin Munks	Velocette	29m. 36s	76.50 mph

1936 Senior MGP

Phil Heath with his first Manx machine. Phil finished second in the 1948 Junior before joining the Continental Circus.

With 47 entries for the Senior, the total for the 1936 Manx was 127. Ken Bills (Norton) led at the end of the first lap by two seconds from Jack Blyth (Norton) who was just four seconds ahead of the Junior winner Austin Munks (Norton). The first lap leaderboard was completed by Maurice Cann (Norton), Harold Rowell (Norton) and Albert Moule (Rudge). Munks took over the lead at the end of the second lap by seven seconds, Blyth remained second, six seconds ahead of Bills. Cann, Tommy McEwan (Norton) and Moule completed the top six. Munks increased his lead to 21 seconds at half distance over Blyth who was 19 seconds up on Bills, followed by McEwan, Moule and Rowell. Maurice Cann retired on the third lap. By the end of the fourth lap Munks had added a further five seconds to his lead over Blyth who was now 41 seconds ahead of Bills. McEwan and Moule remained fourth and fifth, but with Harold Rowell's retirement, H. Trevor-Battye (Norton) came on to the leaderboard in sixth place. The tank on Munk's Norton developed a leak on the fifth lap and he led Blyth by 20 seconds, and pulled in to top up with petrol, could he complete the double? McEwan had moved up to third ahead of Bills, Moule and Trevor-Battye. Austin Munks' caution in topping up the tank at the end of the fifth lap paid off, and he completed his double, the first genuine 'winning' double, following Lea's efforts in 1929 when he finished second in both races, but the winner in both cases was disqualified. Munks finished 10 seconds in front of Blyth who had an advantage of one minute 15 seconds over Ken Bills. McEwan finished fourth, Trevor-Battye fifth and Harry Ogden sixth, with Albert Moule (Rudge) the first non Norton rider in seventh place. There were 21 finishers and nine replicas were won.

1936 Senior MGP (6 laps / 226.38 miles) 47 entries

1. Austin Munks	Norton	2h. 52m. 14s	78.88 mph
2. Jack Blyth	Norton	2h. 52m. 24s	78.80 mph
3. Ken Bills	Norton	2h. 53m. 39s	78.24 mph
Fastest lap			
Tommy McEwan	Norton	27m. 57s	81.01 mph

1937

1937 Lightweight MGP

Denis Parkinson after his second Manx win.

The total entry for the 1937 meeting was an all time record, 139, and 31 of these were in the Lightweight. It was an unusual race, in that the first three remained unchanged throughout the six laps. The 1936 winner Denis Parkinson (Excelsior) led Harold Rowell (Rudge) by 54 seconds at the end of the first lap with Laurence Longstaff (C.T.S.) third. Rowell pulled back on the second lap to trail Parkinson by just five seconds, and led Longstaff by 29 seconds. But from there on, Parkinson increased his advantage lap by lap, 35 seconds on lap three, one minute 20 seconds on lap four and over two minutes on lap five, and eventually won his second Manx in succession from Rowell by three minutes 31 seconds with Longstaff third, three minutes 26 seconds down in third place. S. M. Miller (O.K. Supreme) finished fourth, J. A. Worswick (Excelsior) fifth and Reg Board (Excelsior) sixth. There were 16 finishers and the first seven won replicas.

1937 Lightweight MGP (6 laps / 226.38 miles) 35 entries

1. Denis Parkinson	Excelsior	3h. 14m. 59s	69.68 mph
			(record)
2. Harold Rowell	Rudge	3h. 18m. 30s	68.45 mph
3. Laurence Longstaff	C.T.S.	3h. 21m. 56s	67.28 mph
Fastest lap (record)			
Denis Parkinson	Excelsior	31m. 45s	71.32 mph

1937 Junior MGP

The entry for the Junior totalled 46, and it gave Maurice Cann (Norton) a start to finish victory, and strangely enough, as in the Lightweight race, the first three remained unchanged, Ken Bills (Norton) in second place and Johnnie Lockett (Norton) third. By the time lap two had been completed Cann was 20 seconds up on Bills who led Lockett by 17 seconds. Tommy McEwan (Norton) was fourth, Albert Moule (Norton) fifth and H. Taylor (Norton) sixth. At half distance Cann was 24 seconds up on Bills who led Lockett by 33 seconds. Moule had taken fourth place from McEwan and Bertie Rowell (Norton) came on to the leaderboard in sixth place. Bills put in a spurt on the fourth lap and closed to within three seconds of Cann, and Bills was 51 seconds down on Bills. Moule and McEwan were still fourth and fifth, with sixth place being taken by T. W. Holmes (A.J.S.). At the end of lap five, the difference between Cann and Bills was seven seconds, and Lockett in third place was followed by Moule, McEwan and Rowell. But Maurice Cann got the message and made no mistakes, winning from Ken Bills by 45 seconds, with Johnnie Lockett one minute 29 seconds behind Bills in third place. The top six were completed by McEwan, Moule and C. Bayley (Norton) with Bertie Rowell in seventh place. There were 25 finishers and 14 replicas were won.

1937 Junior MGP (6 laps / 226.38 miles) 46 entries

1. Maurice Cann	Norton	2h. 58m. 13s	76.23 mph
			(record)
2. Ken Bills	Norton	2h. 58m. 58s	75.91 mph
3. Johnny Lockett	Norton	3h. 00m. 27s	75.29 mph
Fastest lap			
Maurice Cann	Norton	29m. 18s	77.28 mph

Double-winner Maurice Cann and Johnny Lockett, first and third in the Junior Manx. Both riders were to feature in post-war GPs, Maurice with his home-brewed double-knocker Guzzi and Johnny with the works Norton team.

1937 Senior MGP

The Senior attracted an entry of 62 riders, and unlike the Junior and Lightweight races, the leaderboard was constantly changing. Tommy McEwan (Norton) led Maurice Cann (Norton) by 44 seconds at the end of the first lap with Ken Bills (Norton) a further four seconds down in third place. Bertie Rowell (Norton), Albert Moule (Norton) and Harold Rowell (Norton) completed the top six. McEwan increased his lead over Cann at the end of lap two to 31 seconds, and Bills closed to within one second of Cann. The brothers Bertie and Harold Rowell were fourth and fifth with Moule sixth. Tommy McEwan's race ended on the third lap following a spill at Laurel Bank, and at the end of the lap Cann and Bills dead-heated for

1937 Lightweight: Stan Miller (OK) gets the show on the road. Others shown include C. J. Tompsett (Sunbeam, 7), R. S. Simpson (Excelsior, 8) and R. J. Weston (Rudge, 9). All featured were destined to finish the race; Miller was fourth, Simpson 7th, Tompsett 12th, and Weston 13th

first place, 27 seconds ahead of Bertie Rowell, who was followed Moule, Harold Rowell and Ron Harris (Norton). Junior winner Cann took a clear lead over Bills by 11 seconds at the end of lap four, with Bertie Rowell 19 seconds behind Bills. Moule, Harris and Harold Rowell completed the leaderboard. Cann increased his lead to 27 seconds at the end of the fifth lap, but it was Bertie Rowell in second place, five seconds ahead of Bills, who was followed by Moule, Harris and C. D. Foord (Norton). Maurice Cann went on to complete the double by one minute and seven seconds from Ken Bills who finished 17 seconds ahead of Bertie Rowell, with C. D. Foord fourth, Ron Harris fifth and Albert Moule sixth. Harold Rowell took seventh place. There were 31 finishers and 15 replicas were won. Maurice Cann made Manx Grand Prix history with the first ever 80 mph plus average speed for a race.

1937 Senior MGP (6 laps / 226.38 miles) 62 entries

1. Maurice Cann	Norton	2h. 46m. 24s	81.65 mph	(record)
2. Ken Bills	Norton	2h. 47m. 31s	81.10 mph	
3. Bertie Rowell	Norton	2h. 47m. 48s	80.97 mph	
Fastest lap (record)				
Tommy McEwan	Norton	26m. 58s	83.93 mph	

1938

And so to the last Manx Grand Prix for eight years. The total entry was down on the previous years record, being just 104, and of these, 35 were in the Lightweight race.

1938 Lightweight MGP

Strangely enough, Denis Parkinson (Excelsior) was not leading at the end of the first lap, he was just one second down on J. A. Worswick (Excelsior)! Peter Aitchison (C.T.S.) was in third place, 22 seconds down on Parkinson. But by the end of the second lap Parkinson was in his accustomed first place, by 54 seconds from Worswick who was one minute and seven seconds ahead of Aitchison. The order remained the same on laps three and four, by which time Parkinson was just over two minutes in front. Lap five saw the first change in the top three, Parkinson still led the race, by two minutes 14 seconds from Worswick, but Laurence Longstaff (C.T.S.) took third place from Aitchison, and was four minutes 16 seconds down on the second place man. Aitchison retired on the last lap, and Denis Parkinson completed the first ever hat-trick of wins by two minutes 22 seconds from J. A. Worswick with Laurence Longstaff five minutes 21 seconds behind in third place. Roland Pike (Rudge) was fourth, Reg Board (Excelsior) fifth and Ben Drinkwater (Excelsior) sixth. There were 14 finishers and eight replicas were won.

1938 Lightweight MGP (6 laps / 226.38 miles) 33 entries

1. Denis Parkinson	Excelsior	3h. 11m. 14s	71.05 mph	(record)
2. J. A. Worswick	Excelsior	3h. 13m. 36s	70.08 mph	
3. Laurence Longstaff	C.T.S.	3h. 18m. 57s	68.29 mph	
Fastest lap (record)				
Denis Parkinson	Excelsior	31m. 01s	73.00 mph	

1938 Junior MGP

There were 32 entries for the Junior, a race that gave Ken Bills, runner-up in both the Junior and Senior in 1937, a record breaking win. At the end of the first lap, Ken Bills (Norton) led Johnnie Lockett (Norton) by 54 seconds, with Tommy McEwan (Norton) in third place a further 16 seconds down. Fourth was J. F. R. Martin (Norton) fifth C. D. Foord (Norton) and sixth Albert Moule (Norton). Johnnie Lockett retired at Kirk Michael on the second lap, at the end of which Bills led McEwan by one minute 58 seconds with Martin 15 seconds down on McEwan. Foord, Moule and Eric Briggs (Norton) completed the leaderboard. By half distance, Bills was two minutes and four seconds in front of Martin, who had taken second place from McEwan by four seconds. Moule, Briggs and W. Dawson (Velocette) completed the top six. At the end of the fourth lap, Bills was one minute 13 seconds in front of McEwan, who had opened up a gap of one minute 57 seconds between himself and Martin, with the rest of the leaderboard unchanged. Bills was one minute and 20 seconds in the lead at the end of lap five, and the only change to the top six was that R. Lee (Norton) replaced Dawson in sixth place. So, after finishing second twice, Ken Bills won his first Manx Grand Prix, and also set the first 80 mph lap in the Junior. He beat Tommy McEwan by one minute 42 seconds, with J. F. R. Martin in third place over three minutes behind McEwan. Moule finished fourth, Briggs fifth and Lee sixth. There were 21 finishers, and the first seven won replicas.

1938 Junior MGP (6 laps / 226.38 miles) 62 entries

1. Ken Bills	Norton	2h. 52m. 30s	78.76 mph	(record)
2. Tommy McEwan	Norton	2h. 54m. 12s	77.99 mph	
3. J. F. R. Martin	Norton	2h. 57m. 27s	76.56 mph	
Fastest lap (record)				
Ken Bills	Norton	28m. 09s	80.44 mph	

Ernie Lyons with his first Island mount, a very standard looking Triumph twin, bearing a prophetic number. This bike failed to finish the course, but he was to be victorious on a derivative of this machine in the next Senior Manx Grand Prix, which was run eight years later.

1938 Senior MGP

There was an entry of 39 for the Senior, which again saw lap and race records broken. Johnnie Lockett (Norton) led at the end of lap one by 11 seconds from Ken Bills (Norton) who was in turn 36 seconds ahead of Tommy McEwan (Norton). Peter Aitchison, Eric Briggs and Albert Moule, all on Nortons completed the first lap leaderboard. Lockett increased his lead over Bills to 16 seconds at the end of the second lap with McEwan one minute 20 seconds down in third place, Aitchison remained fourth, but Moule moved ahead of Briggs. The difference between Lockett and Bills at half distance was 12 seconds, and McEwan was almost two minutes behind Bills, Aitchison was fourth, and there was a tie for fifth place between Moule and Denis Parkinson (Norton). But then Bills got into his record breaking stride and at the end of the fourth lap he led Lockett by 56 seconds, with McEwan now over two minutes down on the second place man. The top six were completed by Aitchison, Moule and Briggs. Parkinson's race ended at the end of this fourth lap, his exhaust came off at Governors Bridge, he arrived at the pits with it under his arm, but repairs could not be effected and he retired.

Lap five saw quite a few changes, third place man McEwan retired with engine trouble at Ramsey, and sixth place Briggs hit trouble and slowed to eventually finish 20th. But Bills just got on with the job and at at the end of the lap had an advantage of one minute seven seconds over Lockett, who was six minutes 31 seconds ahead of the new third place man Aitchison. Moule was fourth and J. F. R. Martin and R. Lee, both on 350 Nortons were fifth and sixth. Moule discovered that his petrol tank was leaking on the fifth lap, but despite taking on petrol at the end of the lap, he retired on the final circuit, out of petrol. So Ken Bills completed the third Junior/Senior double in successive years by one minute and 25 seconds from Lockett, with Aitchison third, Lee finished fourth, J. A. Worswick (B.M.W.) fifth and Guy Newman (Velocette) sixth. There were 13 finishers and, such was the pace, just the first three won replicas.

1938 Senior MGP (6 laps / 226.38 miles) 39 entries

1. Ken Bills	Norton	2h. 40m. 11s	84.81 mph
(record)			
2. Johnny Lockett	Norton	2h. 41m. 36s	84.07 mph
3. Peter Aitchison	Norton	2h. 51m. 40s	79.14 mph
Fastest lap (record)			
Ken Bills	Norton	26m. 14s	86.31 mph

Despite the threat of war, plans went ahead for the 1939 event, some competitors were in fact on the landing stage at Liverpool, waiting for the Isle of Man Steam Packet Company to ferry them and their machines to the island when the event was deferred. And so that was it for eight long years, and Ken Bills had to wait that amount of time for an unusual hat-trick!

Ken Bills at the completion of the last pre-war Manx double. Standing behind Ken is Wilf Harding, himself a Manx leaderboard man. After losing his arm in a car accident, Wilf gave much advice to later Manx GP riders.

INDEX OF RIDERS 1923 - 1938
Key to Abbreviations

S. Senior Manx Grand Prix; J. Junior Manx Grand Prix; L. Lightweight

R. Retired; D. Disqualified; Ex. Excluded; N.F. Non-finisher; F. Finisher *The figures equal the position at end of race.*

Prior to 1928 there was one class only in the Manx Amateur TT Road Race Championship.

Example:

Ashley, A.
1928 J.R.	Excelsior	
1929 J.D.	Excelsior	
1929 S.D.	Excelsior	
1930 S.12	Rudge	
1931 S.13	Rudge	
1932 S.R.	Rudge	

A. Ashley, riding an Excelsior, retired from the 1928 Junior. He was disqualified from the results of the 1929 races. In 1930, riding a Rudge, he finished 12th in the Senior MGP. The following year he finished 13th in the Senior, again riding a Rudge. In 1932, he retired from the Senior MGP, again Rudge mounted.

Adams, Rex D.
1926 1 — A.J.S.

Adamson, J. W., Jun.
1937 J.19 — Norton
1937 S.R. — Norton

Adcock, H.
1931 J.R. — Raleigh

Agar, E.
1926 R. — Royal Enfield

Aitchison, Peter M.
1937 S.R. — Vincent/H.R.D.
1933 L.R. — C.T.S.
1938 S.3 — Norton

Alexander, J.
1934 J.8 — Velocette
1934 S.10 — Velocette
1935 J.11 — Velocette

Allen, R.
1929 J.6 — Sunbeam
1930 S.22 — Sunbeam
1932 J.14 — Velocette
1933 J.11 — Norton
1933 S.13 — Norton
1934 J.11 — Norton
1934 S.14 — Norton

Anderton, Sylvester
1937 S.24 — Norton

Andrews, Stanley T.
1936 S.21 — Norton

Archibald, A.
1924 R. — Norton

Archibald, E.
1925 R. — Norton
1926 R. — Triumph
1927 R. — Triumph

Armytage, R. D.
1930 J.8 — Velocette

Arter, Tom E.
1938 J.14 — A.J.S.

Ashley, A.
1928 J.R. — Excelsior
1929 J.D. — Excelsior
1929 S.D. — Excelsior
1930 S.12 — Rudge
1931 S.13 — Rudge
1932 S.R. — Rudge

Ashton, G. D. W.
1925 R. — A.J.S.

Bacon, Harry J.
1928 J.D. — Chater Lea
1928 S.R. — Norton
1929 S.R. — Sunbeam

Ballard, E.
1934 S.R. — Norton

Bamford, C.
1936 L.8 — Dunelt Python

Barawitzke, R. G.
1934 S.R. — Norton

Barnett, Jim W.
1934 S.R. — Excelsior
1935 J.12 — Velocette

Batchelor, J. L.
1937 J.R. — Norton
1938 L.R. — Excelsior

Bayly, C.
1936 S.R. — Norton

Beamish, W. R.
1931 S.R. — Rudge
1936 L.R. — New Imperial

Beevers, J. Bill
1934 S.R. — Norton

Bennett, C. V.
1924 R. — Triumph
1925 R — O.E.C. Atlanta

Bentley, R. G.
1928 J.R. — B.S.A.

Berry, N.
1938 L.R. — O.K. Supreme

Bevan, W. G.
1929 J.8 — A.J.S.

Bezzant, J. W.
1923 6 — Norton
1925 5 — P. & M. Panther

Bickell, C. Ben
1930 J.R. — Chater Lea

Bills, Ken
1934 L.5 — Rudge
1934 S.7 — Vincent-H.R.D.
1935 J.9 — Velocette
1935 S.R. — Vincent-H.R.D.
1936 J.R. — Norton
1936 S.3 — Norton
1937 J.2 — Norton
1937 S.2 — Norton
1938 J.1 — Norton
1938 S.1 — Norton

Birch, Walter
1923 R. — Sunbeam
1924 5 — Sunbeam
1926 R. — P. & M. Panther
1927 8 — Sunbeam
1928 J.4 — Sunbeam
1928 S.2 — Sunbeam
1929 J.R. — A.J.S.
1929 S.R. — Sunbeam

Bird, D. G.
1927 R. — Scott

Birkin, Archie
1924 R. — Cotton
1925 R. — Cotton

Blair, George D.
1938 L.R. — Rudge

Blyth, Jack H.
1932 J.12 — Norton
1932 S.R. — Velocette
1933 J.9 — Norton
1933 S.9 — Norton
1934 J.R. — Norton
1935 J.4 — Norton
1935 S.6 — Norton
1936 J.2 — Norton
1936 S.2 — Norton

Board, Reg M.
1936 L.R. — Excelsior
1937 L.6 — Excelsior
1938 L.5 — Excelsior

Boardman, J. K.
1935 J.R. — Norton
1935 S.17 — Norton
1936 J.R. — Norton
1937 S.8 — Norton

Bolshaw. T. H.
1925 R. — New Imperial

Bookless, T. L.
1930 J.6 — Velocette
1930 S.R. — Velocette
1932 S.12 — Norton

Booth, C. V. M.
1934 L.6 — Cotton

Boswell, H. W.
1936 L.6 — Cotton

Bower, G.
1923 11 — Norton
1924 8 — Norton

Bowman, E. J.
1937 L.R. — O.K. Supreme

Braidwood, W. S.
1925 R. — A.J.S.
1926 R. — A.J.S.
1927 R. — P. & M. Panther

Bramwell, J. C.
1926 R. — Ariel
1927 22 — H.R.D.

Brand, F. C.
1931 S.R. — Sunbeam

Brassington, Arthur R.
1938 L.9 — Excelsior

Bretherton, H.
1937 J.R. — A.J.S.
1938 J.R. — A.J.S.
1938 S.R. — A.J.S.

Brett, Charlie F.
1935 L.R. — Excelsior
1936 L.5 — Excelsior

Brewin, A.
1927 13 — Sunbeam
1928 S.R. — Sunbeam
1929 J.D. — Raleigh
1929 S.D. — Raleigh

Bridgham, H.
1926 R. — A.J.S.

Briggs, Eric E.
1938 J.5 — Norton
1938 S.R. — Norton

Brocklington, P. A. C.
1927 12 — A.J.S.

Brookes, J.
1926 R. — Norton
1927 R. — H.R.D.

Brooks, L. T.
1929 J.R. — Excelsior

Brown, F. A.
1926 R. — Norton

Brown, R. C.
1924 2 — Sunbeam
1925 R. — Sunbeam

Buchan, Jimmy Sen.
1933 J.7 — Velocette
1934 J.9 — Velocette

Buckley, Jack
1932 S.R — Sunbeam
1933 S.R. — Buckley D.O.T.

Bucknall, A. G.
1931 J.R. — A.J.S.

Burgess, F.
1930 J.R. — S.G.S.

Byrne, J. E.
1928 J.R. — A.J.S.

Cadman. Frank S.
1934 L.R. — New Imperial
1935 L.3 — New Imperial
1936 L.R. — New Imperial
1937 L8 — New Imperial

Calverley, R. D.
1931 S.R. — Rudge
1933 S.R. — Rudge

Campbell, R. M.
1931 S.16 — Norton

Cann, Maurice
1931 J.R. — Velocette
1931 S.9 — Velocette
1935 J.7 — Norton
1935 S.10 — Norton
1936 J.R. — Norton
1936 S.R. — Norton
1937 J.1 — Norton
1937 S.1 — Norton

Cannell, Jack
1934 J.19 — Velocette
1934 S.22 — Norton
1935 J.10 — Velocette
1935 S.8 — Velocette
1936 J.R. — Velocette
1936 S.12 — Velocette
1937 J.11 — Norton
1937 S.10 — Norton
1938 S.R. — B.M.W.

"Carlisle, W. T."
1928 S.11 — Scott

Carr, John H.
1929 J.D. — Norton
1929 S.D. — Norton
1930 J.13 — Velocette
1930 S.11 — Velocette
1931 J.2 — New Imperial
1931 S.3 — Norton
1932 J.1 — New Imperial
1932 S.9 — Norton
1933 J.R. — New Imperial
1933 S.R. — New Imperial

Carter, Harry
1936 J.10 — Norton
1937 J.R. — Norton
1937 S.25 — Vincent-H.R.D.

Carter, T. H.
1935 S.R. — Norton
1936 S.17 — Norton
1937 S.30 — Vincent-H.R.D.
1938 J.R. — Norton

Catt, A. E. Jun.
1923 13 — Scott

Chamberlin, G. A.
1934 J.25 — Norton
1935 S.17 — Norton
1936 J.9 — Norton
1936 S.10 — Norton

Chatwin, H. A.
1932 J.R. — Velocette

Cherriman, L. B.
1937 S.R. — Norton
1938 J.10 — Norton

Cheston, P. B.
1923 18 — Scott

Christmas, Noel
1933 S.R. — Scott
1934 J.7 — Velocette
1934 S.R. — Scott

Chrystal, D. M.
1928 J.3 — Velocette

Clarke, C. P.
1936 S.20 — Rudge

Clarke, Harry
1937 J.20 — Norton

Clarke, R. E. H.
1937 S.R. — Norton

Clay, J. F.
1930 J.R. — Velocette
1931 J.R. — Velocette
1932 J.6 — Velocette
1933 J.R. — Velocette

Clayton, H.
1924 R. — Chater Lea

Clayton, H.
1933 J.16 — Velocette

Cogan-Verney, T.
1934 L.3 — New Imperial
1935 L.4 — New Imperial
1936 J.11 — Norton
1936 S.R. — Norton
1937 J.R. — Norton

Cole, G. A.
1934 S.R. — Vincent H R.D.

Collison, Arthur H.
1935 J.R — A.J.S.

Cook, E. J.
1925 16 — Norton
1926 R. — Douglas

Cook, Harry
1931 J.R. — Velocette
1931 S.R. — Velocette
1932 J.R. — Velocette
1932 S.19 — Velocette

Cooke, J. F.
1932 J.25 — Velocette
1933 J.10 — Velocette

Coombs, F. B.
1932 J.24 — Velocette

Cooper, E.
1936 S.13 — Sunbeam

Cooper, S. W.
1933 S.21 — Sunbeam
1934 S.R. — Sunbeam
1935 S.R. — Sunbeam
1937 S.R. — Norton

Cooper, W. C.
1929 S.8 — Triumph
1930 S.24 — Triumph

Corfield, Edward A.
1933 J.R. — Velocette
1934 J.R. — Velocette
1934 S.23 — Velocette

Corfield, Walter
1933 J.R. — A.J.S.
1933 S.R. — A.J.S.
1934 J.R. — A.J.S.

Corkill, J. R.
1933 J.R. — Norton
1934 S.R. — Norton

The History of the Manx Grand Prix 1923-1998 25

1936 J.12	Norton	1936 J.R.	Norton	1936 L.R.	Excelsior	1933 J.R.	Rudge	**Harris, C. L. R.**	
Cornes, W.		1937 J.8	Norton	1937 L.R.	Excelsior	1934 J.R.	Rudge	1931 J.R.	Velocette
1929 J.D.	Rex Acme	1938 J.7	Velocette	**Eisner, C. A.**		1935 J.20	Rudge	**Harris, Ron**	
1930 J.11	Rex Acme	**Dear, Les A.**		1923 R.	Cotton	1937 L.15	Excelsior	1930 J.R.	A.J.S.
Corney, G.		1936 L.7	New Imperial	**Emery, Gilbert L.**		**Frith, Freddie L.**		1930 S.R.	Norton
1930 J.R.	Raleigh	1937 L.R.	New Imperial	1928 J.R.	Sunbeam	1930 J.3	Velocette	1931 J.6	Norton
Corteen, Gilbert		**Dearden, Reg W.**		1928 S.3	Sunbeam	1930 S.R.	Velocette	1931 S.10	Norton
1933 J.21	Velocette	1929 S.R.	Norton	**Emery, S. J.**		1932 J.R.	Norton	1932 J.R.	New Imperial
1933 S.R.	Velocette	1933 S.R.	Norton	1931 J.9	Velocette	1932 S.5	Norton	1932 S.6	Norton
1934 J.15	Velocette	1937 S.R.	Norton	1933 J.15	Norton	1933 J.2	Norton	1933 L.1	New Imperial
1935 J.18	Velocette	1938 J.16	Norton	1933 S.20	Norton	1933 S.R.	Norton	1933 S.5	Norton
Courtney, L. R.		1938 S.R.	Norton	**Empsall, W. A.**		1934 J.6	Norton	1934 J.R.	Norton
1931 S.2	Rudge	**de Ferranti, Dennis Z.**		1926 8	Velocette	1934 S.R.	Norton	1934 S.3	Norton
1934 J.R.	Velocette	1927 3	Scott	1927 19	Rudge	1935 J.1	Norton	1935 L.1	New Imperial
1934 S.5	Velocette	1929 J.2	New Henley	**England, F. R. W.**		1935 S.2	Norton	1935 S.5	Norton
Coward, F.		1929 S.R.	New Hudson	1935 L.R.	Cotton	**Fry, Frank**		1936 L.R.	New Imperial
1923 15	Scott	**Derrick, M. W.**		1936 L.2	Cotton-Python	1938 J.12	Velocette	1936 S.R.	Norton
1925 15	Scott	1926 21	H.R.D.	**Essex, G.**				1937 J.14	Norton
Cownley, A.		**Deschamps, Harvey P.**		1926 R.	Norton	**Gardner, M. G.**		1937 S.5	Norton
1927 5	Norton	1938 J.R.	Norton	**Etherington, W. B.**		1932 J.R.	Norton	1938 J.R.	Velocette
Craine, W. Harry		1938 S.8	Norton	1937 J.R.	Velocette	**Gates, S.**		1938 S.R.	Norton
1935 S.12	Norton	**Dinsmore, J. R.**		**Evetts, P. S.**		1927 6	Velocette	**Harrison, A. C.**	
Croft, Norman		1932 J.R.	Chater Lea	1934 L.R.	O.K. Supreme	**Gauterin, Charles**		1933 J.R.	Norton
1929 J.R.	Norton	**Dixon, K.**		**Farquharson, R.**		1936 J.13	Norton	**Harrison, H.**	
1930 J.R.	Norton	1927 R.	O.K. Supreme	1926 14	Royal Enfield	**Geeson, Bob E.**		1927 R.	H.R.D.
1930 S.R.	Norton	**Dobbs, H. G.**		1927 17	Royal Enfield	1938 L.R.	Excelsior	**Hartley, Harold**	
1932 J.11	Rudge	1925 1	Norton	**Fassett, T. W.**		**Gilchrist, A. J. G.**		1929 J.4	Velocette
1932 S.7	Rudge	1926 R.	Norton	1931 S.R.	Ariel	1925 R.	A.J.S.	1929 S.N.F.	Rudge
1934 J.R.	Rudge	**Dodds, S. H.**		**Fell, J. H.**		**Gledhill, Norman M. N.**		1931 J.3	Rudge
1934 S.R.	Rudge	1932 J.30	Norton	1927 23				1931 S.4	Rudge
Crone, W. M.		1933 S.R.	Ariel	1933 S.R.	Sunbeam	1928 S.4	Norton	1932 J.18	Norton
1927 R.	Chater Lea	**Dodson, Charlie J. P.**		1934 J.10	Sunbeam	1929 S.R.	Norton	1932 S.R.	Norton
1928 R.	Chater Lea	1924 9	Sunbeam	1934 S.9	Sunbeam	1930 S.3	Norton	1933 J.14	Rudge
Crossland, M. E.		1925 R.	Sunbeam	**Fellowes, H. F.**		1931 S.R.	Norton	1933 S.17	Rudge
1930 J.R.	Velocette	**D'Olier, E. W.**		1925 R.	Norton	1932 J.10	Norton	1934 L.8	O.K. Supreme
1932 J.28	Norton	1926 R.	Norton	1926 R.	Norton	1932 S.1	Norton	1934 S.16	O.K. Supreme
Crossley, Don G.		**Doswell, A. R.**		**Fernihough, Eric G.**		1933 J.5	Norton	1935 L.R.	Rudge
1938 L.R.	O.K. Supreme	1935 S.R.	Rudge	1925 R.	New Imperial	1933 S.4	Norton	1935 S.18	Velocette
Crosthwaite, V. F.		**Drabble, A. L**		**Fidgeon, R.**		**Goddard, S. H.**		**Hartley, Herbert**	
1923 10	Beardmore Precision	1924 12	Cotton	1932 J.7	Norton	1931 J.R.	Goddard-Levis	1930 S.14	Rudge
1924 15	Beardmore Precision	**Dresser, H. C. W.**		**Fleet, J. A.**		1932 S.R.	Excelsior	1931 S.12	Norton
1926 20	Norton	1931 J.13	Levis	1928 S.R.	A.J.S.	1934 L.7	Calthorpe	**Harvey, F.**	
Crowey, A. C.		1932 J.19	Levis	1929 S.R.	Scott	1935 S.R.	O.K. Supreme	1932 S.R.	Norton
1928 S.R.	Triumph	1933 S.15	Norton	1930 J.17	A.J.S.	**Gorst, J. T.**		1933 J.R.	H.R.D.
Cullis, T. C.		**Drew, Frank**		**Fletcher, J.**		1934 J.R.	Velocette	**Havercroft, H.**	
1927 16	Sunbeam	1934 L.R.	Levis	1930 S.R.	Sunbeam	**Grace, G. H.**		1934 S.R.	Rudge
1928 J.R.	Sunbeam	1935 L.R.	O.K. Supreme	1931 J.R.	Sunbeam	1929 S.R.	Rudge	1935 S.R.	Rudge
1928 S.R.	Sunbeam	1937 J.23	Norton	1931 S.7	Sunbeam	**Greenwood, J. H. W.**		1936 S.R.	Rudge
Culpan, Norman R.		**Drinkwater, R. T. 'Ben'**		1932 S.4	Sunbeam	1933 S.R.	Rudge	1937 S.R.	Rudge
1928 S.10	Rudge	1937 L.R.	Excelsior	1933 J.24	Sunbeam	**Gregory, L.**		**Haverfield, J. D.**	
1929 S.R.	Rudge	1938 L.6	Excelsior	1933 S.8	Sunbeam	1932 J.R.	Rudge	1933 J.R.	Norton
Cunliffe, J. O.		**Drysdale, I. D.**		**Fletcher, R.**		**Grundman, B.**		**Hay, G. B. M.**	
1924 11	Norton	1938 L.8	Excelsior	1934 J.R.	Norton	1933 S.R.	Norton	1926 R.	Temple
1926 5	Sunbeam	**Dudding, J.**		**Fletcher, R. S.**		**Haines, G. L.**		1927 R.	New Hudson
1927 R.	H.R.D.	1929 J.D.	Rex Acme	1927 R.	Cotton	1936 J.20	Norton	**Hayden, G. H.**	
Cupples, F. J.		**Duff, W. A.**		**Floyd, A. St. J.**				1936 J.R.	Velocette
1926 R.	A.J.S.	1937 S.R.	Norton	1931 S.R.	Norton	**Hall, J. G.**		1936 S.11	Velocette
		Dulson, J. R.		**Foord, C. D.**		1928 S.R.	Scott	**Hayes, J. E.**	
Daniell, Harold L.		1936 J.21	Norton	1936 J.R.	Norton	1929 S.R.	Scott	1938 J.17	Velocette
1930 S.R.	Norton	1936 S.R.	Norton	1936 S.8	Norton	**Hampton, T. A.**		1938 S.11	Velocette
1931 S.R.	Norton	**Duncan, K. S.**		1937 J.12	Norton	1932 J.R.	New Imperial	**Heath, Phil**	
1932 J.9	Excelsior	1925 3	Norton	1937 S.4	Norton	**Hancocks, H.**		1936 S18	Vincent-H.R.D.
1932 S.2	Norton	**Durno Charles A. W.**		1938 J.R.	Norton	1926 13	Sunbeam	1937 S.R.	Vincent-H.R.D.
1933 J.R.	Norton	1935 L.R.	Cotton	**Forbes, Jock W.**		1927 R.	Sunbeam	1938 L.7	New Imperial
Darbishire, Steve B.		**Earle, H. A. R.**		1930 J.5	Velocette	1928 S.R.	Sunbeam	**Heaton, J.**	
1931 S.R.	Norton	1938 J.8	Velocette	1932 S.R.	Velocette	**Hands, C. J.**		1925 R.	Norton
1932 S.R.	Levis	**Eastwood, V. E.**		1933 S.R.	Norton	1932 J.R.	Velocette	1926 R.	Ariel
1933 S.R.	Norton	1933 S.24	Rudge	**Forman, E.**		**Hanson, J.**		**Hewison, E. F.**	
1934 J.5	Norton	**Edmonds, M. R.**		1929 J.D.	Velocette	1927 R.	Velocette	1926 R.	A.J.S.
1934 S.R.	Norton	1924 3	Chater Lea	1930 J.7	Velocette	1928 J.2	Velocette	**Hewstone, W. J.**	
1935 J.2	Norton	1925 6	Chater Lea	1930 S.25	Velocette	1929 J.R.	Velocette	1930 J.R.	Velocette
1935 S.3	Norton	**Edmondson, A. L.**		1931 J.7	Velocette	1929 S.R.	Velocette	**Hickey, J. R.**	
Davenport, A.		1932 J.R.	Velocette	**Forsyth, C. V.**		**Harding, C. J.**		1930 J.20	Norton
1927 14	H.R.D.	**Edwards, Eric S.**		1925 17	Norton	1931 S.14	Sunbeam	**Higginbottom, Ben**	
"David, Bill"		1931 S.R.	Sunbeam	**Fortune, Tom B.**		1932 S.21	Sunbeam	1935 L.R.	New Imperial
1933 S.R.	Rudge	**Edwards, J.**		1938 S.9	Rudge	**Harding, Wilf A.**		1936 L.R.	New Imperial
Davis, C. H.		1928 S.R.	Norton	**Foster, A. Bob**		1930 J.2	Velocette	1937 L.11	New Imperial
1938 S.R.	Vincent H.R.D.	**Edwards, R. A.**		1933 J.R.	New Imperial	1930 S.19	Velocette	1938 L.13	Excelsior
Dawson, M. J.		1934 J.24	Norton	1933 S.R.	New Imperial	1931 J.R.	Velocette	**Higginson, R.**	
1926 2	H.R.D.	1934 S.R.	Norton	1934 L.2	New Imperial	1931 S.R.	Velocette	1927 R.	H.R.D.
1927 R.	X-J.A.P.	**Edwards, Robert J.**		1934 S.6	Sunbeam	**Harrington, R. V.**		**Higson, L.**	
1930 8	Norton	1934 L.R.	Cotton	**Foster, W. E.**		1927 R.	Norton	1926 18	New Imperial
Dawson, W. L.		1935 L.8	Cotton	1934 S.R.	O.K. Supreme	**Harrington, W. T.**		**Hilbert, E. A.**	
1935 J.15	Norton			**Fox, Alfred**		1929 J.D.	Velocette	1928 S.R.	Norton

26 The History of the Manx Grand Prix 1923-1998

Year	Race	Machine
1929	S.R.	Norton
1930	S.R.	Norton

Hill, G.
| 1933 | S.R. | O.K. Supreme |

Hill, W.
| 1930 | J.R. | Levis |
| 1931 | J.R. | Levis |

Hislop, J. D.
| 1928 | S.R. | Rudge |

Hodges, G. H.
| 1933 | J.R. | Zenith-J.A.P. |

Hodgson, A. L.
| 1930 | J.R. | A.J.S. |
| 1931 | J.R. | Velocette |

Hodgson, C. R.
1933	S.R.	Norton
1934	J.R.	Norton
1934	S.24	Norton

Hogg, Arnold S.
1923	16	Cotton
1924	R.	Cotton
1925	R.	O.K. Blackburne
1926	R.	O.K. Supreme
1927	R.	O.K. Supreme
1928	J.R.	O.K. Supreme
1929	J.10	O.K. Supreme
1930	J.R.	O.K. Supreme

Hoggarth, P.
| 1924 | 17 | Scott |

Holland, W.
| 1935 | S.R. | Norton |

Holme, R. A. E.
| 1929 | S.R. | Rudge |

Holmes, T. W.
1936	J.8	Velocette
1936	S.9	Velocette
1937	J.9	A.J.S.
1937	S.R.	A.J.S.

Hooper, Ronald
1934	S.18	Sunbeam
1935	S.14	Sunbeam
1936	L.4	New Imperial

Hornby, C.
| 1928 | S.R. | A.J.S. |

Hornby, W. G.
1934	S.R.	Norton
1936	J.R.	Velocette
1936	S.16	Velocette

Horne, A. G.
| 1938 | L.R. | O.K. Supreme |

Hough, F.
| 1926 | R. | H.R.D. |

Houghton, W. H.
1923	4	Sunbeam
1924	R.	Sunbeam
1925	R.	Sunbeam
1926	12	Sunbeam

Hoult, John H.
| 1934 | S.R. | Norton |

Hovenden, D. A.
| 1937 | J.R. | Norton |
| 1937 | S.22 | Norton |

Howard, A.
| 1923 | 14 | Scott |
| 1924 | 7 | Sunbeam |

Howe, A. M.
| 1927 | R. | Sunbeam |

Howitt, A. L.
| 1934 | S.R. | Scott |
| 1935 | S.R. | Scott |

Hudson, F. J.
| 1936 | L.3 | O.K. Supreme |
| 1936 | S.R. | O.K. Supreme |

Hughes, A.
| 1932 | S.17 | Sunbeam |

Hunt, F.
| 1928 | S.R. | A.J.S. |

Hunt, Tim P.
1927	1	Norton
1928	J.R.	Levis
1928	S.1	Norton

Hunter, A.
| 1934 | S.R. | Norton |

Hutchings, L. A.

1926	R	Sunbeam
1927	25	Velocette
1928	J.R.	Velocette
1929	J.3	Velocette

Illingworth, P. H. C.
| 1936 | L.R. | Royal Enfield |

Ivin, L. F.
| 1934 | S.R. | Scott |

Jackson, D.
1927	R.	Norton
1928	J.7	Velocette
1928	S.R.	Norton

Jackson, V.
| 1928 | S.9 | Rudge |
| 1930 | S.R. | Cotton |

Jefferies, Alan
| 1933 | S.R | Scott |

Jenness, W. J.
| 1932 | J.R. | Norton |

Jennings, Reg
1937	J.R.	Norton
1938	J.19	Norton
1938	S.R.	Norton

Jervis, H.
| 1928 | S.R. | Ariel |
| 1929 | S.D. | Ariel |

Job, William G.
| 1935 | J.21 | Velocette |
| 1936 | J.19 | Velocette |

Johnson, J. W.
| 1927 | R. | New Hudson |

Jones, A. W.
| 1925 | 11 | Royal Enfield |

Jones, E. T.
| 1927 | 24 | A.J.S. |

Jones, J. H.
| 1931 | S.R. | Sunbeam |

Jones, K. P.
| 1935 | S.9 | Norton |

'Jones, Mr.'
| 1931 | S.R. | Rudge |

Jones, R. A.
1927	15	H.R.D.
1928	S.R.	Velocette
1928	J.7	Velocette

Jones, T. F.
| 1933 | J.R. | O.K. Supreme |

Jones, W.
| 1938 | L.R. | Excelsior |

Jones, W. L.
| 1928 | J.11 | Velocette |

Jordan, W. Noel
1929	J.R.	Sunbeam
1930	J.10	A.J.S.
1930	S.R.	New Hudson
1931	S.R.	Sunbeam
1932	J.R.	Rudge
1932	S.R.	Excelsior

Keay, J. T.
| 1927 | R. | Rudge |

Kellas, A. C.
| 1934 | S.R. | Norton |

Kemble, H. R.
| 1930 | S.18 | Rudge |

Kemp, H. J.
| 1938 | S.R. | New Imperial |

Kenyon, D.
| 1930 | S.13 | Sunbeam |
| 1931 | S.R. | Sunbeam |

Kenyon, J.
| 1930 | S.R. | Sunbeam |

Kermode, J.K.
| 1937 | S.R. | Scott |
| 1938 | S.7 | Norton |

Kidd, H. A.
| 1937 | S.27 | Velocette |

Kilburn, F. T.
| 1928 | J.6 | Rex Acme |

Kilburn, G. A.
| 1930 | S.R. | Rex Acme |

Kirby, H.

| 1931 | J.R. | Montgomery |
| 1932 | J.17 | Norton |

Kirkpatrick, W. J.
| 1937 | S.R. | Norton |

Kitchen, Les W.
1934	J.17	Norton
1935	J.8	Norton
1938	J.R.	Norton

Kneenshaw, R.
| 1928 | S.R. | Rudge |

Kniveton, A. A.
| 1927 | R. | Sunbeam |

Knowles, H. D.
1936	J.R.	Velocette
1937	L.R.	Rudge
1938	L.R.	Rudge

Knox, E. J.
| 1934 | J.R. | Norton |
| 1935 | J.19 | Norton |

Ladyman, J. E.
| 1934 | J.R. | Levis |

Lafone, J. H.
| 1932 | S.R. | Norton |
| 1933 | J.R. | Rudge |

Lamacraft, Harry C.
1931	J.R.	Velocette
1932	J.13	Velocette
1933	J.R.	Velocette
1933	S.16	Velocette

Lambert, J.
| 1928 | S.R. | Scott |

Lansdale, P.
| 1935 | L.R. | C.T.S. |
| 1938 | J.9 | Norton |

Lea, Eric N.
1928	S.6	Norton
1929	J.1	Velocette
1929	S.1	Norton
1931	J.11	Velocette
1931	S.R.	Norton

Leach, K. B.
1933	J.R.	Norton
1934	J.R.	Norton
1935	L.6	Excelsior

Lee, N. R.
| 1930 | J.R. | B.S.A. |

Lee, Reg
1937	J.R.	Norton
1937	S.28	Norton
1938	J.6	Norton
1938	S.4	Norton

Lees, S.
1928	J.9	Sunbeam
1929	S.6	Sunbeam
1930	S.R.	Sunbeam

Leitch, A. M.
| 1932 | S.R. | Rudge |
| 1933 | S.R. | Rudge |

Lennie, G. H.
1929	J.9	A.J.S.
1930	J.R.	Velocette
1931	J.R.	Velocette

Leonard, P. J.
| 1927 | R. | Royal Enfield |

Leslie, Jack A. McL.
1930	J.R.	Levis
1931	J.5	Rudge
1932	J.4	Rudge
1932	S.R.	Rudge
1933	J.6	Velocette
1933	S.11	Velocette

Levings, Harold
1929	J.R.	Velocette
1929	S.2	Velocette
1930	J.4	Velocette
1930	S.R.	Sunbeam
1932	J.R.	Norton
1932	S.R.	Norton
1933	J.4	Norton
1933	S.R.	Norton

Lewis, O.
| 1933 | J.12 | Norton |

Limmer, G. W.
| 1927 | R. | Scott |

| | | Lind, R. |
| 1934 | S.R. | Rudge |

Lindsay, D. B.
1934	J.R.	Velocette
1936	J.R.	Norton
1937	J.15	Norton
1937	S.20	Norton

Lockett, Johnny
1936	J.5	Norton
1937	J.3	Norton
1937	S.9	Norton
1938	J.R.	Norton
1938	S.2	Norton

Lodge, G. F.
| 1938 | S.R. | Norton |

Logan, S. G.
| 1933 | J.R. | Velocette |

Lomas, J. E.
| 1927 | R. | Scott |

Lomonosoff, G.
| 1927 | R. | McEvoy |

Long, K. E.
| 1924 | R. | Cotton |

Longstaff, J.
1935	L.7	C.T.S.
1936	L.R.	C.T.S.
1937	L.9	C.T.S.
1938	L.R.	C.T.S.

Longstaff, Lawrence
1931	S.R.	Rudge
1933	S.18	Norton
1934	S.R.	Norton
1935	L.R.	C.T.S.
1935	S.11	Norton
1936	L.R.	C.T.S.
1937	L.3	C.T.S.
1938	L.3	C.T.S.

Louks, A. E
| 1924 | 10 | Sunbeam |

Lowe, J. R.
1927	R.	Norton
1928	J.8	Cotton
1929	J.R.	Cotton

Lowe, Bob O.
| 1923 | R. | Norton |
| 1924 | 4 | Norton |

Lyons, Ernie
| 1938 | S.R. | Triumph |

McClafferty, J.A.
1936	J.18	Norton
1937	J.18	Norton
1937	S.31	Norton

McDermid, R.A.
1928	S.R.	Norton
1929	J.D.	Calthorpe
1929	S.D.	Sunbeam
1930	J.9	Cotton-Blackburne
1930	S.R.	Cotton-Blackburne

MacDonald, J. A.
| 1934 | S.13 | Rudge |

McEwan, Tommy
1933	S.R.	Norton
1934	J.12	Velocette
1934	S.8	Velocette
1935	J.6	Norton
1935	S.16	Norton
1936	J.R.	Norton
1936	S.4	Norton
1937	J.4	Norton
1938	J.2	Norton
1938	S.R.	Norton

'Macintosh, A.'
| 1930 | J.16 | Velocette |
| 1930 | S.R. | Rudge |

Maclennan, D.
| 1925 | 9 | H.R.D. |

Major, Frank
| 1926 | 11 | Sunbeam |
| 1927 | R. | Sunbeam |

Manders, Charlie H. W.
| 1929 | J.D. | Sunbeam |
| 1929 | S.D. | Sunbeam |

Marsden, Arthur J.

1923	3	Douglas
1924	R.	Douglas
1925	R.	H.R.D.

Martin, J. F. R.
1936	J.6	Norton
1936	S.R.	Norton
1937	J.10	Norton
1937	S.12	Norton
1938	J.3	Norton
1938	S.R.	Norton

Martin, W. B.
| 1938 | J.R. | Norton |

Matthews, H.
| 1926 | R. | Norton |
| 1927 | R. | Norton |

Mavrogordato, Noel
1926	7	Scott
1928	S.R.	Scott
1929	S.R.	Scott
1930	S.R.	Scott
1931	S.R.	Scott
1932	S.14	Scott

Meageen, W. Harry T.
1927	7	H.R.D.
1928	J.1	Rex Acme
1928	S.R.	Rex Acme
1929	J.D.	Rex Acme
1929	S.D.	Rex Acme

Meikle, John
| 1935 | L.9 | Excelsior |

Mellors, Ted A.
| 1927 | 10 | P & M Panther |

Merrill, C. W. H.
| 1925 | R. | Rex Acme |

Merrill, E. Ralph
| 1928 | S.R. | Rudge |
| 1930 | S.1 | Rudge |

Metters, H.
| 1934 | L.R. | New Imperial |

Middleton, T. E.
| 1928 | J.R. | Rex Acme |

Miller, Sam M.
| 1937 | L.4 | O.K. Supreme |

Millington, A. K.
1934	J.14	Velocette
1935	J.R.	Velocette
1937	J.16	Norton

Mills, H. L.
| 1931 | J.R. | O.K. Supreme |
| 1932 | J.R. | Velocette |

Milner, W.
| 1928 | S.R. | Norton |

Mitchell, D. K.
| 1923 | R. | Scott |

Mitchell, W. Donald
| 1934 | L.1 | Cotton |

Monk, E. W.
| 1930 | J.R. | New Hudson |

Moore, C. V.
| 1934 | L.4 | New Imperial |
| 1935 | L.5 | New Imperial |

Moore, J. S.
| 1923 | R. | Triumph |

Moore, T. G. M.
| 1928 | S.R | Rudge |

Moorhouse, R. S.
1927	R.	Norton
1930	J.12	Norton
1930	S.17	Norton
1931	J.8	Norton
1931	S.R	Norton
1932	J.16	Norton

Morison, F. M.
| 1934 | S.R. | Excelsior |

Morton, J. H. M.
1925	4	New Gerrard
1926	9	H.R.D.
1927	11	H.R.D.

Moule, Albert E.
1936	S.7	Rudge
1937	J.5	Norton
1937	S.6	Norton
1938	J.4	Norton
1938	S.R.	Norton

The History of the Manx Grand Prix 1923-1998

Muir, Jock M.
1930 J.R. Velocette
1930 S.5 Velocette
1931 J.R. Velocette
1931 S.1 Norton
1932 J.2 Velocette
1932 S.R. Norton
1933 J.13 Norton
1933 S.3 Norton
Munks, Austin
1931 J.R. Velocette
1932 J.3 Velocette
1933 J.1 Velocette
1933 S.6 Velocette
1934 J.3 Velocette
1935 J.R. Velocette
1935 S.4 Norton
1936 J.1 Velocette
1936 S.1 Velocette
Murray, S. H.
1929 S.R. Sunbeam
Myers, Harry B.
1936 J.R. Norton
1936 S.R. Norton
Nash, F. J. A.
1936 J.R. Velocette
Nash, J.
1927 R. Scott
Needham, C. F.
1928 J.R. New Hudson
Nelson, R.
1928 S.R. New Hudson
Ness, M.
1937 J.25 Norton
Newman, C.
1928 S.R. New Hudson
Newman, Guy
1937 J.R. Velocette
1937 S.R. Norton
1938 J.11 Velocette
1938 S.6 Velocette
Newman, Harold E.
1930 S.10 Sunbeam
1931 J.R. Velocette
1932 J.8 Velocette
Newman, L. C.
1934 S.12 Sunbeam
1935 S.R. Sunbeam
1936 S.R Sunbeam
1937 S.26 Sunbeam
Nichols, Frank
1930 J.R A.J.S.
Nicholson, H. E.
1929 S.R. H.R.D.
1930 S.23 Rudge
Norris, J. H.
1936 J.R. Velocette
1936 S.19 Velocette
Norris, W. C.
1936 S.R. Grindley Peerless
Noterman, A.
1927 N.F. Montgomery
Ogden, Harry
1935 J.R Norton
1936 J.4 Norton
1936 S.6 Norton
Oldroyd, D.
1926 3 Sunbeam
1927 9 Sunbeam
1928 S.R. Sunbeam
Ovens, Edgar
1934 S.R. Norton
Owen, N.
1923 9 Norton

Packham, J. V.
1933 S.R. Excelsior
Parker, Len
1923 R. Douglas
Parker, R.
1930 J.R. Velocette
Parkinson, Dennis

1932 J.29 Norton
1933 J.23 O.K Supreme
1933 S.22 Norton
1934 J.R. Norton
1934 S.19 Norton
1935 L.R. Excelsior
1935 S.20 Norton
1936 L.1 Excelsior
1936 S.R. Norton
1937 L.1 Excelsior
1937 S.13 Excelsior
1938 L.1 Excelsior
1938 S.R. Norton
Parkinson, Ronnie F.
1925 R. A.J.S.
1926 R. A.J.S.
Parrish, B.
1930 J.R. Velocette
1932 J.21 Velocette
Parsons, Len W.
1931 J.R. Sunbeam
Paterson, George L.
1934 S.R. Excelsior
Pattison, J.
1932 S.R. Norton
1934 S.R. Norton
Pearson, Austin
1935 L.R. Excelsior
1936 L.R. O.K. Supreme
Perrin, H. K.
1938 L.14 New Imperial
Perryman, Bert C.
1937 L.R. Excelsior
Phillips, J. S.
1938 J.R. Norton
Pike, L.
1935 J.R. A.J.S.
1936 J.16 Norton
1937 J.22 A.J.S.
1937 S.19 Norton
Pike, Roland H.
1937 L.R. Rudge
1938 L.4 Rudge
Pike, W. H. Stan
1937 S.23 Rudge
1938 L.R. Excelsior
Pink, Ted T.
1938 L.12 Excelsior
Pirie, Doug J.
1929 J.7 Velocette
1929 S.5 Scott
1930 J.1 Velocette
1930 S.4 Velocette
1931 J.1 Velocette
1931 S.R. Excelsior
1932 S.R. Excelsior
1933 J.3 Norton
1933 S.R. Norton
1934 J.2 Norton
1934 S.1 Norton
Plevin, Syd
1931 J.R. Sunbeam
1932 J.R. Excelsior
1935 J.R. Norton
1937 L.R. O.K. Supreme
1937 S.17 Norton
Pope, Noel B.
1933 J.R. Velocette
Potts, H. Y.
1924 14 A.J.S.
1925 8 Sunbeam
1927 20 Sunbeam
Potts, J. D.
1927 R. H.R.D.
1928 S.R. Zenith-J.A.P.
1929 J.D. Grindlay-Peerless
1929 S.D. Grindlay-Peerless
Potts, J. W.
1929 S.R. A.J.S.
1930 J.R. A.J.S.
Poyser, D. R.
1930 J.R. Sunbeam
Prescott, H. V.

1923 8 Scott
1924 13 Scott
1925 R. P. & M. Panther
1926 15 Scott
1927 R. Scott
1928 S.R. Scott
1929 S.R. Scott
Provis, C. W.
1925 R. Norton
1926 4 Norton
1927 4 Norton
Pugh, K.
1935 S.19 Ariel
Purslow, C. C.
1927 R. A.J.S.
"Q. Ack"
1932 S.R. Velocette
Quinn, W. E.
1932 J.20 Norton

Radley, W.
1932 S.R. Excelsior
Rae, G.
1929 S.7 Sunbeam
Randles, Les
1923 1 Sunbeam
1924 1 Sunbeam
1925 R. Sunbeam
Redfearn, C.
1932 S.13 Norton
Redfern, G. A.
1929 J.11 Rex-Acme
Reed, W. C.
1938 L.R. New Imperial
Reich, C. D.
1930 S.R. Sunbeam
1931 S.11 Excelsior
1932 S.R. Excelsior
1934 J.R. Excelsior
1934 S.R. Excelsior
Reid, D.
1937 L.14 Excelsior
1938 L.10 Excelsior
Reid, J. S.
1937 J.R. A.J.S.
Reid, L. A.
1927 R. Norton
Renwick, J. L.
1934 S.R. Norton
Reynolds, J. C.
1927 R. A.J.S.
Reynolds, L. R.
1930 J.R. O.K. Supreme
Riding, J.
1924 R. Norton
Riefstahl, A.
1936 J.17 Norton
1936 S.R. Norton
Rigg, W. H.
1930 S.20 Rudge
1931 S.R. Rudge
Riley, J.
1928 S.R. P. & M. Panther
Riley, W.
1930 J.14 Sunbeam
1931 J R. Sunbeam
1932 J.R. Sunbeam
Roberts, E. Lionel
1930 J.R. Grindlay-Peerless
Roberts, Wilfred
1931 S.R. Rudge
1932 J.26 Velocette
1933 J.R. Velocette
Robinson, F.
1934 S.21 Rudge
Robinson, J.
1925 13 Norton
1926 R. OK. Supreme
1927 R. Chater Lea
1928 S5 Norton
Robinson, R. H.
1934 L.6 Dunelt Python
Robson, Norman

1930 J.18 New Hudson
Rogerson, R.
1930 S.R. Rudge
1932 J.R. Norton
1932 S.18 Norton
Ronan, D. W.
1934 S.17 Rudge
Rose, W. H.
1931 J.R. Norton
Rowbotham, T. J.
1932 J.R. Velocette
1933 J.R. Velocette
Rowell, Harold M.
1935 L.2 Rudge
1936 L.R Rudge
1936 S R. Norton
1937 L.2 Rudge
1937 S.7 Norton
Rowell, W. Bertie
1932 J.R. Velocette
1932 S.15 Velocette
1933 J.12 Velocette
1933 S.10 Velocette
1934 J.4 Velocette
1935 J.5 Velocette
1935 S.7 Velocette
1936 J.3 Norton
1936 S.R. Norton
1937 J.7 Norton
1937 S.3 Norton
Rudge, E. A.
1937 L.16 Excelsior
1938 L.18 Velocette
1938 S.13 Velocette

Salkfield, W. E.
1928 S.R. Norton
Salter, F. L. D.
1925 14 Norton
1926 R. Sunbeam
Sanders, A. A.
1923 17 Triumph
1924 16 Montgomery-J.A.P.
1931 S.R. Montgomery-J.A.P.
1934 S.R. Triumph
Sandison, James
1936 L.R. Rudge
1936 S.15 Norton
1937 J.17 Norton
1937 S.R. Norton
Schofield, J.
1931 S.R. Rudge
Scott, S.
1934 J.23 Rudge
1936 R. O.K. Supreme
Seiffert, M.
1927 R. B.S.A.
Sharrock, W. L.
1926 R Norton
Shaw, Albert E.
1936 L.R. Excelsior
1937 L.10 Excelsior
1938 L.R. Excelsior
Sheirs, R.
1931 J.14 Sunbeam
1932 J.22 Norton
Shelbourne, A.
1926 6 Scott
1927 R. Scott
Shenstone, J. R.
1937 L.R. New Imperial
Shillings, F. Pat
1936 J.R. Norton
1937 J.R. Norton
1937 S.14 Norton
1938 J.R. Norton
1938 S.R. Norton
Shorrock, F.
1923 D. Sunbeam
Short, J. C.
1929 S.D. Scott
Sikes, Somerville

1932 J.15 Velocette
Sikes, R. S.
1929 J.5 Velocette
Simpson, R. S.
1937 L.7 Excelsior
Singleton, W. H.
1929 S.R. Sunbeam
1931 S.13 Sunbeam
1932 J.23 Velocette
1933 J.R. Velocette
1934 J.R. Velocette
Skelly. A.
1927 R. Norton
Smith, A.
1938 S.10 Norton
Smith, A. P.
1938 J.15 Velocette
Smith, E. G.
1937 S.21 Norton
Smith, George
1930 J.R. Montgomery
1932 J.27 Norton
1933 J.R. Norton
Smith, H.
1938 S.12 Scott
Smith, N.
1924 R. New Scale
Smith, Quentin
1923 R. Triumph
1924 6 Triumph-Ricardo
1925 R. Triumph
Spavin, R. W.
1937 J.R. O.K. Supreme
Spikins, F. R. G.
1923 R. Hawker
Staples, R. P. H.
1926 6 Scott
1927 R. Scott
Stephens, Edward
1931 S.R. Sunbeam
Stewart, A. D.
1931 J.R. Rudge
Stobart, R.
1930 J.R. Cotton-Blackburne
1930 S.15 Scott
1931 S.R. Scott
1932 S.R. Excelsior
Stranger, W. L.
1931 J.R. A.J.S.
1931 S.5 A.J.S.
Sugg, J. M.
1928 S.7 Norton
1929 S.3 Norton
1931 S.8 Norton
1932 S.16 Norton
1933 S.19 Norton
1934 J.21 Norton
1934 S.20 Norton
1935 L.R. Sunbeam
Sunderland, Milton
1937 J.24 Norton
1937 S.R. Norton
1938 J.21 Norton
Sutherland, C. B.
1937 J.R. Norton
1937 S.R. Norton
Swabey, B. W.
1930 S.R. Rudge
1931 S.R. Rudge
1932 S.3 Rudge
Swan, J.
1930 S.R. Norton
Swanston, James K.
1931 S.R. Norton
1932 S.10 Norton
1933 J.17 Velocette
1933 S.R. Norton
1934 J.18 New Imperial
1934 S.2 Norton
1935 J.3 Norton
1935 S.1 Norton
Symons, G. R.
1923 R. Sunbeam

Taylor, H.		1929 S.R.	New Hudson	1936 J.15	Velocette	1931 J.R.	Velocette	1933 S.12	Rudge
1933 J.R.	Velocette	**Tutt, C. P.**		1936 S.R.	Velocette	1931 S.R.	Velocette	**Williamson, John R.**	
1934 J.13	Velocette	1929 S.4	Rudge	**Warburton, T. S.**		1932 J.5	Velocette	1934 J.22	New Imperial
1935 J.13	Velocette	1930 S.R.	Rudge	1931 J.10	New Imperial	1933 J.R.	Velocette	**Williamson, Robert G.**	
1936 J.R.	Norton	**Twemlow, Edwin**		1932 S.R.	Royal Enfield	1933 S.7	Velocette	1931 S.6	Rudge
1937 J.R.	Norton	1923 7	Sunbeam	**Ward, J. S.**		1934 J.1	Norton	**Williman, K. H.**	
Tedham. Percy		**Twemlow, Kenneth**		1932 S.R.	Sunbeam	1934 S.R.	Norton	1930 S.21	Norton
1938 J.13	A.J.S.	1923 2	New Imperial	1933 S.14	Sunbeam	**Whitehead, W. E.**		**Willows, J. H.**	
Thomas, Ernie M.				**Wareing, V. M.**		1930 J.5	Sunbeam	1935 L.R.	S.O.S.-J.A.P.
1927 R.	Rex Acme	**Valente, J.**		1937 S.R.	Calthorpe	1933 J.19	Velocette	**Wills, S. A. P.**	
Thompson, R. W.		1937 S.16	Norton	**Warren, P. R.**		1933 S.23	Velocette	1931 S.R.	Rudge
1936 L.R.	O.K. Supreme	**Varey, Frank**		1934 L.D.	New Imperial	1934 J R.	Velocette	**Wilson, Arthur D.**	
1937 L.R.	O.K. Supreme	1938 L.R.	D.K.W.	1935 L.R.	New Imperial	1934 S.11	Velocette	1929 S.D.	Sunbeam
1937 S.R.	O.K. Supreme	1938 S.R.	Norton	1936 L.R.	New Imperial	1935 J.14	Velocette	**Wilson, G. W.**	
1938 L.R.	O.K. Supreme	**Vaughan, J. C.**		**Warwick, C. A.**		1935 S.15	Velocette	1928 J.R.	Sunbeam
1938 S.R.	O.K. Supreme	1925 2	Norton	1927 18	Rudge	**Whitehouse, F. A.**		**Wilson, T. G.**	
Thomson, Allan S.		1926 R.	Norton	**Waterhouse, C.**		1937 S.R.	Rudge	1935 J.R.	Velocette
1937 J.R.	Norton	1927 R.	Norton	1923 5	Sunbeam	**Whittingham, D. J. P.**		**Wilson, W. L.**	
1938 L.R.	Rudge	1928 S.R.	Norton	**Webster, F. E.**		1931 J.12	A.J.S.	1925 R.	New Imperial
Thomson, J. S.		**Verity, P. S.**		1926 10	Sunbeam	**Whittingham, S. R.**		1926 R.	New imperial
1936 L.R.	New Imperial	1931 S.15	Norton	**Webster, G. W.**		1938 L.R.	New Imperial	1927 R.	Cotton
1937 L.R.	New Imperial	**Verner-Jeffrys, R. D.**		1934 S.R.	Sunbeam	**Whittle, W. L.**		1928 J.R.	Cotton
1937 S.29	Norton	1934 S.25	Rudge	1935 L.R.	Sunbeam	1928 S.8	Grindlay-Peerless	**Wing, Billy A.**	
Thorn, J. A.		**Vigers, E. J.**		1935 S.13	Sunbeam	1928 J.R.	Grindlay-Peerless	1935 J.R.	Velocette
1925 R.	Sunbeam	1936 L.R.	New Imperial	**Weddell, Jock A.**		1929 J.D.	Grindlay-Peerless	**Wood, G. W.**	
Tindle, Tommy F.		**Vince, S. C.**		1937 J.13	Norton	1929 S.D.	Grindlay-Peerless	1929 S.R.	Rudge
1933 J.R.	Velocette	1930 S.16	Norton	**West, J. M. 'Jock'**		**Whitworth, M. David**		1930 S.2	Rudge
Tinning, W.		1932 S.11	Norton	1931 S.R.	Ariel	1935 S.R.	Vincent-H.R.D.	**Wood, Tommy L.**	
1925 12	Norton			1932 S.20	Ariel	1936 L.R.	Cotton	1937 J.R.	Velocette
Tompsett, C. J.		**Waddington, H. B.**		**Weston, G. C.**		**Whyte, J. W.**		**Woods, S.**	
1936 J.R.	Norton	1937 J.R.	Norton	1928 S.R.	Triumph	1925 7	Norton	1930 S.6	Rudge
1937 L.12	Sunbeam	1937 S.18	Norton	**Weston, R. J.**		1926 R.	Sunbeam	**Worsick, C. A.**	
1938 L.11	Excelsior	**Wainwright, N.**		1935 L.R.	Rudge	1927 R.	Sunbeam	1926 16	Toreador
Tong, R. D.		1933 S.R.	Norton	1936 L.R.	Rudge	**Widdall, H.**		**Worsick, J. A.**	
1929 S.R.	Scott	1934 J.16	Velocette	1937 L.13	Rudge	1931 J.4	Rudge	1937 L.5	Excelsior
Trevor-Battye, Hugh		1935 J.16	Velocette	1938 S.R.	Norton	**Wilkinson, J. C.**		1937 S.15	B.M.W.
1931 S.R.	Scott	1936 J.14	Norton	**Weston, R. M.**		1931 J.R.	Rudge	1938 L.2	Excelsior
1932 S.R.	Scott	1936 S.14	Norton	1927 R.	Cotton	1932 J.R.	Rudge	1938 S.5	B.M.W.
1933 J.22	Velocette	**Waite, W. J.**		1928 J.10	H.R.D.	**Wilkinson, S.**		**Wright, D.**	
1934 J.R.	Velocette	1931 S.R.	Rudge	**Wheeler, Arthur F.**		1926 R.	Cotton	1923 R.	A.J.S.
1935 J.R.	Velocette	**Wakefield, J. P.**		1937 J.R.	Velocette	**Williams, Frank**		**Young, H. L.**	
1936 S.5	Norton	1933 J.18	Velocette	**Wheller, H. J.**		1932 S.8	Sunbeam	1923 R.	A.J.S.
1937 S.R.	Norton	1933 S.R.	Velocette	1931 J.R.	D.O.T.	1933 S.R.	Sunbeam		
Tromans, D. V.		**Walker, W.**		**Whistance, Ken**		**Williams, Jack**			
1937 J.R.	Norton	1934 J.R.	New Imperial	1932 J.R.	New Imperial	1930 S.7	Rudge		
Turner, R. F.		1934 S.R.	New Imperial	**White, J. H. 'Crasher'**		**Williamson, J. P.**			

1935. The entry, having collected their machines from Faragher and Ashton's (later Mylchreest Motors) ride through the streets of Douglas on their way to the start.

The Manx Grand Prix
1946 - 1961

1946

The 1946 Manx Grand Prix races were the first to be held on the TT course after the end of World War II. A record entry of 191 was received, 86 in the Senior, 64 in the Junior and 41 in the Lightweight, so the three race pattern of pre-war years was to continue. After the eight year gap there was only a sprinkling of experienced riders - including the 1938 double winner Ken Bills, three times Lightweight winner Denis Parkinson, Eric Briggs, Albert Moule and locals Jack Cannell and Harold Rowell. The Junior and Lightweight races were run concurrently on the Tuesday with the Senior on its own on the Thursday, all races over six laps of the course, a distance of 226.38 miles.

1946 Lightweight MGP

The first rider away in a post-war race was P. H. Weston (Rudge) who had drawn No. 1 in the Lightweight. At the end of the first lap Ben Drinkwater (Excelsior) and Don Crossley (Excelsior) tied for the lead in 34m. 14s. Third was R. J. Edwards (C.T.S.), fourth A. G. Horne (Rudge), fifth L. W. Parsons (Rudge) and there was also a tie for sixth place between B. Holden (C.T.S.) and W. Reeve (Excelsior). Crossley came off in Ramsey on the second lap, and although unhurt and able to continue, he dropped off the leaderboard and finished eighth. Drinkwater, with the fastest lap of the race at 66.76 mph, increased him lead to one minute over Edwards, Parsons moved up to third, Reeve and Holden fourth and fifth with New Imperial mounted Ray Petty coming into sixth place. The leaderboard remained the same at the end of the third lap, and Drinkwater had increased his lead by another 35 seconds. Lap four saw Parsons move up to second place and close the gap on the leader to just 44 seconds. Edwards was third. Reeve went out at Ballaugh, and Holden at the Bungalow so Petty moved up to fourth, and R. S. Simpson and Jack Brett come into the top six. On the fifth lap Parsons lapped in 34m. 12s. against Drinkwater's 34m. 26s. and led by 30 seconds. Drinkwater pulled back two seconds on the final lap, but Parsons had a winning margin of 28 seconds at the flag. Simpson took third spot, with Edwards, Petty and Brett completing the top six. There were 17 finishers and six won replicas.

1946 Lightweight MGP (6 laps / 226.38 miles) 41 entries

1. L. W. Parsons	Rudge	3h. 28m. 39s	65.11 mph
2. Ben Drinkwater	Excelsior	3h. 29m. 07s	64.96 mph
3. R. S. Simpson	Excelsior	3h. 36m. 16s	62.82 mph
Fastest lap			
Ben Drinkwater	Excelsior	33m. 55s	66.76 mph

1946 Junior MGP

The Junior gave Ken Bills an unusual hat-trick, separated by eight years, he had won the 1938 Junior and Senior and took the 1946 Junior with a start to finish victory. On five of the six laps the same four Norton mounted riders featured in the top four places. At the end of the first lap Bills led Tommy McEwan by 18 seconds followed by Peter Aitchison and Denis Parkinson. On lap two Ken increased his lead to 36 seconds over Tommy, but on the third circuit Aitchison and Parkinson got in front of McEwan, but Ken Bills lead had increased to 52 seconds. McEwan was back up to second place at the end of the fourth lap, 48 seconds down, but a lap later Ken led by one minute eight seconds, and McEwan was only 15 seconds ahead of Aitchison. But on the sixth lap McEwan ran out of petrol at Creg-y-Baa so Aitchison and Parkinson completed the top three. Harold Rowell (Norton) was fourth, Jack Cannell (Velocette) fifth and Charlie Salt (Norton) sixth. There were 40 finishers and 14 replicas were won.

Ken Bills at Quarter Bridge.

1946 Junior MGP (6 laps / 226.38 miles) 64 entries

1. Ken Bills	Norton	3h. 03m. 08s	74.18 mph
2. Peter Aitchison	Norton	3h. 03m. 53s	73.89 mph
3. Denis Parkinson	Norton	3h. 06m. 27s	72.87 mph
Fastest lap			
Ken Bills	Norton	30m. 09s	75.10 mph

1946 Senior MGP

Ernie Lyons and crew in the winning enclosure with the prototype GP Triumph.

The 1946 Senior has been described as the "wettest" race ever, but turned out to be a tremendous race. At 10.30 a.m. on Senior day there was no actual rain falling, but as soon as the race got under way, down came the rain and mist. Nortons, with five riders in the top seven on the practice leaderboard, were favourites to win and Ken Bills was all out for his second successive double. But Ernie Lyons, from Co. Kildare, on the sole Triumph in the race had other ideas. At the end of the first lap he led Bills by 43 seconds, followed by Peter Aitchison, Denis Parkinson, Eric Briggs and Harold Rowell, all on Nortons. By the end of lap two Ernie had increased his lead to one minute eleven seconds with a lap in 29m. 11s., and as the weather got worse, the Irishman got quicker. His third lap was completed in 28m. 44s. and he led the field by two minutes six seconds. Tragically on this lap Peter Aitchison came off at the 33rd and sustained fatal injuries. Rowell, Briggs, Parkinson and Barnett completed the top six. The fourth lap, which included pit stops was slow, but Ernie increased his lead over Ken by a further 10 seconds. On lap five Ernie set the second fastest lap of the day in 29m. 09s. and gained another five seconds. On the final lap Bills pulled back eight seconds but the 'Tiger' had Triumphed! Harold Rowell took third place, Denis Parkinson fourth, Albert Moule fifth, and Velocette mounted Peter Goodman was sixth. Eric Briggs slowed towards the end of the race and finished 20th. There were 31 finishers and seven replicas were won.

1946 Senior MGP (6 laps / 226.38 miles) 86 entries

1. Ernie Lyons	Triumph	2h. 57m. 03s	76.73 mph
2. Ken Bills	Norton	2h. 59m. 16s	75.78 mph
3. Harold Rowell	Norton	3h. 06m. 18s	72.93 mph
Fastest lap			
Ernie Lyons	Triumph	28m. 44s	78.80 mph

1947

Entries for 1947 were again an all time record - 284, forty-six in the Lightweight, 111 in the Junior and 127 in the Senior. The sensation of the practices was a young Irishman, Benjy Russell, who, despite using 'Pool' petrol lapped on his Guzzi in 30m 58s., beating the official Lightweight lap record, set in 1938 by Denis Parkinson, by three seconds. Eric Briggs (Norton) topped both the Junior and Senior leaderboards.

1947 Junior MGP

The Junior and Lightweight races as usual were run concurrently on the Tuesday, but for the first time ever, the Juniors started first. From a total entry for both races of 157, 140 came to the line, 100 in the Junior and 40 in the Lightweight. The riders were started from the timing box, not the centre of the grandstand as in the past, so the first lap could qualify as a lap record. With so many riders on the course, the timekeepers issued lap times without deducting the starting times, so all the lap times on the first circuit appeared very slow. Denis Parkinson was said to be leading with a lap in 42m. 22s., with Eric Briggs, who had appeared to have gained on Parkinson, credited with a lap some 55 seconds slower! However, the error was spotted and the first lap leaders were confirmed as Eric Briggs leading Albert Moule by 15 seconds with Denis Parkinson 12 seconds down in third place, and R. P. Sifflett, H. Carter and W McVeigh completed the top six, and all were on Nortons. On lap two. J. E. C. Purnell (Velocette) seventh on lap one moved into fourth place with Sifflett dropping out of the top six. By half distance Briggs led Moule by one minute 25 seconds, and Moule in turn was 15 seconds ahead of Parkinson, and McVeigh had taken fourth place from Purnell.

Parkinson set the fastest fourth lap of the top three, and moved into second place, one minute three seconds down on Briggs, and as they had started one minute apart at the start of the race, Briggs was just three seconds ahead of Parkinson on the road. They circulated together on laps five and six, and were indicated at Governors Bridge together, but whilst Eric flashed across the line to win, there was no sign of Denis. Moule and Purnell passed him to complete the top three. Denis had problems at Governors and faced the long heart-breaking push to the finish, he took fourth place with Sid Barnett (Norton) and Arthur Wheeler (Velocette) completing the leaderboard. There were 65 finishers and 33 replicas were won

1947 Junior MGP (6 laps / 226.38 miles) 111 entries

1. Eric Briggs	Norton	3h. 02m. 01.2s	74.64 mph
2. Albert Moule	Norton	3h. 04m. 49.8s	73.50 mph
3. J. E. C. Purnell	Velocette	3h. 07m. 13.0s	72.57 mph
Fastest lap			
Eric Briggs	Norton	29m. 45s	76.11 mph

1947 Lightweight MGP

Firm favourite for the Lightweight was Benjy Russell (Guzzi) who had broken the lap record in practice, with the main opposition likely from three times winner Austin Munks on another Guzzi. But surprisingly, at the end of the first lap, the leader was Freddie Hawken (Excelsior), five seconds ahead of

Austin Munks hits the bottom of Bray Hill, flattening the rear tyre. This was the first Manx win on a foreign machine.

Russell, who in turn was 10 seconds ahead of Munks.

The leaderboard was completed by Ray Petty (E.M.C.), Reg Armstrong (Excelsior) and R. S. Simpson (Excelsior). Russell turned on the power on lap two with a lap of 31m. 47s to lead Hawken by 40 seconds, with Munks 27 seconds down on the Excelsior rider. By the end of the third lap, Russell had increased his lead over Hawken to over one minute, and Munks had closed to within 16 seconds in third place. On lap four, Austin Munks lapped 69 seconds faster than Benjy Russell, and brought him to within 17 seconds of the leader. and Hawken's brave effort on the Excelsior was slowing and he was some one minute 22 seconds behind Munks. Sadly on the fifth lap, Benjy Russell sustained fatal injuries in a crash at Schoolhouse Corner, near Ramsey. Austin Munks went on to win his fourth Manx Grand Prix by four minutes 48 seconds from Freddie Hawken (Excelsior) with R. S. Simpson (Excelsior) third. The top six were completed by Ray Petty (E.M.C.), Reg Armstrong (Excelsior) and R. J. Edwards (C.T.S.). There were 18 finishers and eight replicas were won.

1947 Lightweight MGP (6 laps / 226.38 miles) 46 entries

1. Austin Munks	Guzzi	3h. 12m. 21.0s	70.63 mph
2. Freddie Hawken	Excelsior	3h. 17m. 09.4s	68.91 mph
3. R. S. Simpson	Excelsior	3h. 23m. 00.2s	66.92 mph
Fastest lap			
Austin Munks	Guzzi	31m. 13s	72.95 mph

1947 Senior MGP

There were 106 starters for the Senior. Nortons were again favourites to win, with five of the top six in practice riding these machines, Briggs, Barnett, Scott, Cannell and Parkinson, with Arthur Wheeler (Velocette) in sixth place. Denis Parkinson was all out to make up for his bad luck in the Junior, and at the end of the first lap led Eric Briggs by four seconds, with Albert Moule third a further eight seconds down. Completing the leaderboard were Don Crossley, Charlie Salt and Jim Crow, all the top six were on Nortons. Parkinson and Briggs completed the second lap in exactly the same time - 28m. 43s. - so were still separated by four seconds, Albert Moule was still third and Don Crossley fourth, but Salt and Crow had dropped off the leaderboard to be replaced by Cromie McCandless and Sid Barnett, again all Nortons. Conditions deteriorated on lap three, yet McCandless turned in what was to be the fastest lap of the race - 28m. 22s. and moved up to fourth place. Parkinson lapped three seconds faster than Briggs, and increased his lead to seven seconds, Moule was still third, and behind McCandless were Crossley and Salt. Pit stops were taken at the end of this

The winners and their attendant sponsors after the 1946 Senior Manx. Left to right: Steve Lancefield and Eric Briggs, winner Denis Parkinson and Francis Beart, and Albert Moule.

third lap, and Denis had a slower stop than Eric, and at the end of the fourth lap, Briggs was in fact 22 seconds ahead of Parkinson, with Moule still third, 36 seconds down. McCandless retired at Creg-ny-Baa on this lap, so Salt, Crossley and Barnett made up the rest of the leaderboard. Briggs doubled his lead on lap five, and, with a lightly slipping clutch, Denis finished some 50 seconds behind Eric, and the top six at the end of the race were completed by Albert Moule, Charlie Salt, Don Crossley and Bill McVeigh, all on Nortons. There were 60 finishers and 15 replicas were won.

1947 Senior MGP (6 laps / 226.38 miles) 127 entries

1. Eric Briggs	Norton	2h. 53m. 25.4s	78.33 mph
2. Denis Parkinson	Norton	2h. 54m. 15.2s	77.96 mph
3. Albert Moule	Norton	2h. 54m. 26.0s	77.88 mph
Fastest lap (record)			
Cromie McCandless	Norton	28m. 22s	79.92 mph

1948

Twenty-five years after the first 'Amateur', and in Silver Jubilee Year of the Manx, there were a number of alterations. Following the record entry of 1947, when 284 riders applied, the problem the club found themselves with was how to keep entries at a reasonable level. It was decided that 350cc machines would be barred from the Senior - in 1947 60 of the entry of 127 were on 350's - run the Lightweight as a separate race, with a trophy of its own, on the same day as the Senior, and the Junior would open the proceedings. Starters for each of the two race days would be limited to 100. The entries received in 1948 were: Senior 64, Lightweight 39, Junior 107, just 10 over the 200, so just about everyone who arrived on the Island got a race.

1948 Junior MGP

The weather for Junior day, heavy rain and thick mist caused a postponement until the Wednesday. Three Nortons, two A.J.S. and one Velocette topped the Junior practice leaderboard, with Bill McVeigh fastest. He was not to feature on the leaderboard however due to a very slow start, and finished eighth, whilst another favourite Cromie McCandless came off at Quarter bridge on the first lap and retired. At the end of the first circuit Denis Parkinson (Norton) led Geoff Duke (Norton) and Phil Heath (A.J.S.) by 17 seconds, followed by Don Crossley, Reg Armstrong and R. Allen. The top six were all inside the post war lap record, and only 37 seconds separated them. At the end of lap two, Denis drew in for a pit stop, Geoff went straight through and was only two seconds down. Phil Heath was third, four seconds behind Duke and Reg Armstrong in fifth place was just five seconds down on Heath. As always on the TT course, pit stops alter leaderboards, and at the end of the third lap Geoff led the race from Phil by three seconds, with Denis a further two seconds down, fourth was Don Crossley, fifth Charlie Salt and equal sixth Reg Armstrong and Chris Horn. The fourth lap saw the end of Duke's race, when he retired with a split oil tank on the Mountain, Denis led Phil by some 52 seconds and Reg Armstrong had moved up to third. Armstrong set the fastest lap of the race on his fifth lap in 28m. 28s. to stay third, and Heath closed to within 46 seconds of the leader. Armstrong retired on the final lap at the Guthrie Memorial, bringing Don Crossley into third place behind Phil Heath. Denis Parkinson added the Junior title to his three Lightweight victories by 50.6 seconds. There were 62 finishers and 31 replicas were won.

1948 Junior MGP (6 laps / 226.38 miles) 107 entries

1. Denis Parkinson	Norton	2h. 53m. 44.4s	78.19 mph
2. Phil Heath	Norton	2h. 54m. 35.0s	77.81 mph
3. Don Crossley	Velocette	2h. 55m. 40.2s	77.35 mph
Fastest lap			
Reg Armstrong	A.J.S.	28m. 28s	79.54 mph

1948 Lightweight MGP

The hot favourite for honours in the Lightweight was Dickie Dale (Guzzi) who topped the practice leaderboard by exactly one minute from Ernie Barrett (Guzzi), with Gill's Excelsior in third place, 50 seconds down on Barrett. True to form at the end of the first lap, Dale led Barrett by 71 seconds and was only 26 seconds outside the record. Gill held third place, 44 seconds down on Barrett, followed by R. J. Edwards (C.T.S.), H. R. Penton (Endura) and R. J. Wilkinson (Rudge). At the end of lap two, Dale came into the pits for fuel, and even with the slowing down he had knocked nine seconds off the Lightweight record in 30m. 52s., and increased his lead over Barrett to over two minutes. Edwards had pulled equal to Gill and they shared third place, and with the retirement of both Penton and Wilkinson, W. Clark (Excelsior) and T. Clegg (C.T.S.) came into the top six. At half distance Dale was leading Barrett by two minutes 43 seconds, and Barrett in turn was now over four minutes ahead of Gill. Clegg was just one second ahead of Clark, and Frank Fletcher (Excelsior) came into sixth place. Dale smashed the record again on his fourth lap, and the only change to the fourth lap leaderboard was that Clark and Fletcher overtook Clegg, as did D. Whelan (Rudge) who was sixth. At the end of the fifth lap the order was the same, but on lap six Fletcher retired. Dickie Dale won at a record speed of 75.56 m.p.h by nine minutes 32.4 seconds from Ernie Barrett with Gill almost six minutes down it third place. The top six were completed by W. Clark (Excelsior), R. W. Marsh (Rudge) and P. H. Weston (Rudge). There were 12 finishers and three replicas were won.

H. R. Penton with his home-brewed Endura

1948 Lightweight MGP (6 laps / 226.38 miles)   39 entries

1. Dickie Dale	Guzzi	3h. 05m. 10.4s	73.36 mph (record)
2. Ernie Barrett	Guzzi	3h. 14m. 42.8s	69.77 mph
3. P. D. Gill	Excelsior	3h. 20m. 13.4s	67.86 mph
Fastest lap (record)			
Dickie Dale	Guzzi	30m. 27s	74.36 mph

1948 Senior MGP

Don Crossley (Triumph) topped the Senior leaderboard by nine seconds from Charlie Salt (Norton) who was just one second faster than Denis Parkinson (Norton). First of the favourites to go out was Parkinson who retired at the Highlander on the first lap. It was Crossley who led at the end of the first lap by 27 seconds from Bill McVeigh (Triumph) with Charlie Salt third. The leaderboard was completed by Phil Heath (Norton), Reg Armstrong (Triumph) and Cromie McCandless (Norton), exactly one minute covered the first six.

McVeigh retired on the Mountain on the second lap, and with a lap in 28m. 03s. Armstrong moved from fifth to second, 45 seconds down on Crossley, and just one second ahead of Salt. Heath remained fourth, McCandless moved up to fifth and R. Lee (Norton) took sixth spot. At half distance Crossley's lead over Armstrong was cut to 35 seconds, Salt was still third with McCandless, Lee and Heath making up the top six. Armstrong continued his charge on the fourth lap, closing to within 13 seconds of Crossley. McCandless went out on this lap at Ramsey so 'Anno Domini' came into the top six. Reg Armstrong's challenge faded on lap five when he lost all gears except top, but Crossley could not relax as Salt set the fastest lap of the race in 27m. 29s. and had closed to within nine seconds of the leader. Lee was third, 'Domini' fourth, Armstrong fifth and Heath sixth. So just nine seconds between Crossley and Salt with one lap to go. At Kirk Michael the gap was down to five seconds, at the Mountain Box it was three seconds and at Creg-ny-Baa just one second. Crossley, who was No. 84 finished, and waited to see if Salt, No. 103 could take the race. Charlie's engine however stopped at Governors Bridge and he had that long push to the flag. 'Anno Domini' (Norton) took second place, over three minutes down, with Salt taking third place. Reg Armstrong, Arthur Wheeler (Triumph) and Phil Heath completed the leaderboard. There were 31 finishers, and 18 replicas were won.

1948 Senior MGP (6 laps / 226.38 miles)   64 entries

1. Don Crossley	Triumph	2h. 48m. 30.0s	80.62 mph
2. 'Anno Domini'	Norton	2h. 51m. 36.2s	79.17 mph
3. Charlie Salt	Norton	2h. 52m. 48.2s	78.62 mph
Fastest lap			
Charlie Salt	Norton	27m. 29s	82.38 mph

1949

For 1949 the Lightweight race was dropped from the programme. In 1948 there were just 12 finishers, and some 15 minutes separated the first three, with the 12th finisher taking 10 minutes per lap longer than the winner. The reason, of course, was the age of the 250s, with the exception of the couple of Guzzi's which had dominated this class from 1946 to 1948. So it was just Junior and Senior for the 1949 meeting.

1949 Junior MGP

The Junior, held in good conditions, attracted an entry of 108,

Cromie McCandless in the winners enclosure, with wife Phoebe and Francis Beart.

of which 98 faced the starter. Cromie McCandless had topped the practice leaderboard some 44 seconds faster than the second place man Don Crossley, who in turn was just two seconds ahead of Bill Lomas. Geoff Duke did not figure on the Junior leaderboard, but would obviously be well up during the race. Cromie was the first of the favourites to complete the first lap, his time was 28m. 22s. but Geoff lapped in 27m. 52s. - 81.25 mph - 17 seconds inside the Junior record set in 1938 by Ken Bills! So Geoff led Cromie by 30 seconds with Don Crossley (A.J.S.) third. Velocette riders Jim Crow, Bill Lomas and Cecil Sandford completed the top six. On lap two Cromie set a new lap record in 27.m 41s. but Geoff went even quicker - 27m. 33s. - to increase his lead to 38 seconds. Crossley was still third, 34

'Anno Domini' in the winners enclosure. In 1997 his identity was revealed to be Norman Culpan, who had ridden to 10th place in his maiden Manx on a Rudge in 1928. Norman chose a nom-de-plume when he returned to race after the war for business reasons.

seconds down and just 16 seconds ahead of Crow, with Peter Romaine coming into fifth place ahead of Bill Lomas, Sandford had dropped just off the leaderboard. At half distance, Cromie - with another record - 27m. 23s. - had reduced Geoff's lead to 28 seconds, Crow had taken third place from Crossley who was equal fourth with Romaine, and despite a spill at the Waterworks, Lomas was still sixth. On lap four Cromie pulled back a further 11 seconds on Geoff, and Crow was one and a half minutes down in third place. Cromie lapped in 27m. 12s. on lap five, yet another record, but Geoff slid off at Ramsey Hairpin, and although he quickly remounted, Cromie had a lead of 35 seconds. Crow was also off on the fifth lap, at Quarter Bridge, he also remounted quickly but dropped to fifth, with Crossley third and Romaine fourth. Not content with his new record, Cromie broke it again on the final lap to win by one minute 15.2 seconds from Geoff with Don Crossley third. The top six were completed by Peter Romaine (A.J.S.), Cecil Sandford (Velocette) and Bill Lomas (Velocette). There were 69 finishers and 21 replicas were won.

1949 Junior MGP (6 laps / 226.38 miles) 108 entries

1. Cromie McCandless	Norton		2h. 46m. 02.4s	81.82 mph
				(record)
2. Geoff Duke	Norton		2h. 47m. 18.0s	81.20 mph
3. Don Crossley	A.J.S.		2h. 50m. 57.2s	79.47 mph
Fastest lap (record)				
Cromie McCandless	Norton		27m. 07.4s	83.50 mph

1949 Senior MGP

There were 84 entries for the 1949 Senior, but all eyes would be on just two riders - Cromie McCandless who topped the practice leaderboard in 27m. 09s. and Geoff Duke, second fastest in 27m. 23s. These two riders who had had such a battle in the Junior were clear favourites for victory. The weather was perfect and the race and lap records, which had stood since 1938, looked certain to be bettered. At the end of the first lap Geoff was within two seconds of the lap record in 26m 16s., 23 seconds ahead ahead of Cromie, both of course were riding Nortons. Denis Parkinson (Norton) was third, already 47 seconds down on McCandless. The top six were completed by Chris Horn (Norton), Don Crossley (Triumph) and D. Marshal (Triumph). Cromie broke the record on lap two in 26 minutes - 14 seconds inside the 1938 figure, but Geoff was even quicker in 25m. 53s. and increased his lead over Cromie to 30 seconds. Horn had overtaken Parkinson, Crossley remained fifth and Harold Clark (Norton) came up into sixth place. McCandless had re-fuelled at the end of lap two, whereas Duke had gone straight through, so at the end of lap three, half distance, Geoff led Cromie by one minute nine seconds, with the rest of the leaderboard unchanged. Geoff had a longer pit stop than Cromie, and as the two of them were timed at various places around the course it was seen that Cromie was really biting into Geoff's lead, and with a lap in exactly 26 minutes, against Geoff's 27m. 5s. - the difference was down to just four seconds. Horn was now over four minutes down in third place and Parkinson, Crossley and Clark retained their positions on the leaderboard. Cromie pressed on and lapped in 26m. 13s. on lap five, 14 seconds faster than Geoff, so the Irishman led by 10 seconds with one lap to go. Geoff pulled out the stops on lap six, and by Ramsey had turned a 10 second deficit into a 10 second advantage. He maintained his 10 seconds advantage at Creg-ny-Baa and all looked set for a close finish. But Cromie, who was trying for four laps on a tankful, having stopped at the end of lap two, had to stop at Cronk-ny-Mona to hoist his bike up a bank to coax some petrol into the carburettor. Geoff went on to win by 42.8 seconds. Chris Horn (Norton) was third, Denis Parkinson (Norton) fourth, and with Don Crossley's retirement on the last lap, Harold Clark (Norton) took fifth place ahead of Peter Romaine (348 A.J.S.). This was the same machine that Peter had ridden into fourth place in the Junior, and his race

My Winning Ride - by Geoff Duke, 1949 Senior Manx

Following a win in the Senior Clubman's TT, I was looking forward to the Manx Grand Prix.

Senior race day was fine with less wind than earlier. McCandless was number 2, Denis Parkinson (Norton) was number 12, and I was 23. At the end of the first lap, I led the race from Cromie by 23 seconds, having gone round in 26 min 16 sec (86.2 mph). This was just two seconds outside the all-time Senior MGP record.

On lap two, Cromie made his stop to refuel, taking 24 seconds, having completed the lap in 26 minutes exactly (87.09 mph) to establish a new lap record. However, I did not slow down to stop and refuel, so my second lap was seven seconds faster at 87.48 mph-which remained unbeaten to the end of the race.

My third lap also took precisely 26 minutes when I stopped for fuel, but the delay of 35 seconds cost me 11 seconds, while Cromie, with time to get back into his stride after the earlier pit stop, was now really flying. The end of lap four saw my lead cut to just four seconds.

The end of the fifth lap saw Cromie in the lead by ten seconds, but at the Bungalow on the last time around, I was apparently back in the lead by four seconds, though unaware of the situation as my signalling arrangements had gone awry. Fate had taken a hand in the proceedings, yet again. On the downhill approach to Hillberry, the small amount of fuel remaining in Cromie's tank had swilled forward and left the feed to the carburettor dry. Realising what had happened, Cromie had to stop and run his machine's front wheel up the bank to refill the float chamber.

The result of the race was now no longer in doubt. At the finish I was 43 seconds ahead at an average speed of 86.063 mph - only 0.865 outside the 1949 Senior TT average of 86.928 mph.

times were almost identical - he was 2.6 seconds faster in the Senior! There were 55 finishers and just eight riders won replicas.

1949 Senior MGP (6 laps / 226.38 miles) 84 entries

1. Geoff Duke	Norton	2h. 37m. 50.8s	86.06 mph
			(record)
2. Cromie McCandless	Norton	2h. 38m. 33.6s	85.68 mph
3. Chris Horn	Norton	2h. 44m. 00.6s	82.83 mph
Fastest lap (record)			
Geoff Duke	Norton	25m. 53s	87.48 mph

1950

1950 Junior MGP

The pattern of two races continued for 1950, and entries were slightly up on 1949 - 109 in the Junior and 102 in the Senior, of which 45 were riding 350cc machines. The weather conditions were good - bright and clear - and there were 97 starters. The two favourites, Don Crossley (A.J.S.) and Peter Romaine (Norton), were amongst the high numbers, 82 and 68 respectively, and they had been separated on the practice leaderboard by just four seconds. At the end of lap one, Romaine led the race by some 27 seconds from Crossley. With a second lap just one second outside the record, Romaine increased his lead to 47 seconds, with the rest of the leaderboard falling behind the two front runners. At half distance Crossley had pulled back seven seconds and trailed Romaine by 41 seconds, with the top six being completed by Hedley Cox (Velocette) almost three minutes down on Crossley, Robin Sherry (A.J.S.) Jim Crow (Velocette) and W. J. Netherwood (A.J.S.). Romaine took his pit stop at the end of the third lap, but with a large tank, Crossley was planning a non-stop race, and on lap four, with the weight of the fuel lightening, his laps became quicker, and at the end of the lap he was in the lead by nine seconds. At the end of the fifth lap he had increased this to 20 seconds and Sherry, who had moved up to third place was now over seven minutes behind the two leaders. Don won the race by 24.4 seconds from Romaine, but third place man Sherry retired with gearbox trouble, just ten miles from the finish, allowing Cyril Julian (Velocette) into third place, followed by D. Bogie, (Velocette), A. K. Howth (A.J.S.) and J. F. Jackson (Velocette). There were 58 finishers and 14 riders won replicas.

1950 Junior MGP (6 laps / 226.38 miles) 109 entries

1. Don Crossley	A.J.S.	2h. 44m. 30.0s	82.58 mph
			(record)
2. Peter Romaine	Norton	2h. 44m. 55s	82.38 mph
3. Cyril Julian	Velocette	2h. 55m. 10s	77.56 mph
Fastest lap			
Peter Romaine	Norton	27m. 08s	83.45 mph

1950 Senior MGP

The weather for the Senior was not as good as it had been for the Junior, although dry, strong to gale force winds were forecast, and these would be against the riders on the Mountain climb. There were 84 starters, and unlike the Junior, most of the favourites were early starters - Peter Romaine No.1, Denis Parkinson No.5, Don Crossley No. 15 and Mick Featherstone No.49. Lap one saw Romaine (Norton) three seconds ahead of Featherstone (Norton) with Parkinson (Norton) third, but Crossley, the Junior winner, retired in his home town of Ramsey on the first lap. Romaine increased his lead at the end of the second lap to 33 seconds, and Parkinson was still third, but over one minute down on time. By the end of the third lap, Romaine increased his lead over Featherstone to exactly one minute, with Parkinson one minute and 42 seconds down in third place. The leaderboard was completed by Jim Crow (Norton), Harold Clark (Norton) and Dave Bennett (Norton). Lap four saw Featherstone slowing and he was one minute 31 seconds down on Romaine. Parkinson remained third and Clark had taken fourth place from Crow. Romaine sailed on to a comfortable victory from Featherstone by two minutes 35 seconds, but Parkinson retired at Sulby with engine trouble, bringing Harold Clark (Norton) up to third. The rest of the top six were - Dave Bennett, Jim Crow and E. Andrew, all on Nortons. There were 63 finishers and 17 replicas were won.

1950 Senior MGP (6 laps / 226.38 miles) 102 entries

Peter Romaine, first lap and already flat out on Bray Hill. The 'winged' fork shrouds were a Francis Beart speciality.

1. Peter Romaine	Norton	2h. 41m. 30s	84.12 mph
2. Mick Featherstone	Norton	2h. 44m. 05s	82.79 mph
3. Harold Clark	Norton	2h. 47m. 31.6s	81.09 mph
Fastest lap			
Peter Romaine	Norton	26m. 29s	85.55 mph

R. M. Lucas broke his Mk. VIII KTT Velocette in practice, and turned out for the race on this 1928 model. It didn't go too bad, it lasted him five laps and he lapped in under 36 minutes!

1951

1951 Junior MGP

The start of the Junior, which had attracted 106 entries, had to be delayed for one hour due to poor visibility on the Mountain sections of the course. The practice leaderboard had been shared equally by three makes of machine - Norton - Velocette - A.J.S. The order was Harold Clark (A.J.S.), Robin Sherry (A.J.S.), Dave Bennett (Norton), Keith Campbell (Velocette), Don Crossley (Norton) and Cyril Julian (Velocette). Three of the favourites were in the first dozen starters - Sherry No. 1, Bennett No. 11 and and Clark No. 12.

There was a tie for first place at the end of the first lap between Sherry and Crossley who both lapped in 27m. 53s., Bennett was third, 26 seconds down and Campbell was fourth. Campbell came off at Quarter Bridge on lap two, he remounted but then came off at the Stonebreakers Hut where he retired.

Sherry took a clear lead from Crossley at the end of the second lap by three seconds, with Bennett still third. At half distance Sherry increased his lead over Crossley to 12 seconds, Bennett was still third, 43 seconds down, followed by Clark (A.J.S.), Brian Jackson (A.J.S.) and Cyril Julian (Velocette). Bennett began his charge on lap four and took second place from Crossley by six seconds, but Sherry was still in command with a new lap record at 83.91 mph But Bennett's race ended on lap five, when he coasted down to the Creg with a broken primary chain, putting Crossley back into second spot and Clark third. Sherry rode on to a record breaking win, almost two minutes ahead of Crossley, with the leaderboard completed by Harold Clark (A.J.S.). Cyril Julian (Velocette), Dennis Morgan (A.J.S.) and W. J. Netherwood (Velocette). There were 70 finishers and 11 replicas were won.

Robin Sherry at Cronk ny Mona. Robin was a member of the Manufacturers award-winning team in the 1953 Senior TT, and was also a member of the travelling marshal team in the 1980s.

1951 Junior MGP (6 laps / 226.38 miles) 106 entries

1. Robin Sherry	A.J.S.		2h. 44m. 28.8s	82.61 mph (record)
2. Don Crossley	Norton		2h. 46m. 25.0s	81.63 mph
3. Harold Clark	A.J.S.		2h. 50m. 51.8s	79.50 mph
Fastest lap (record)				
Robin Sherry	A.J.S.		26m. 59s	83.91 mph

The 1951 Junior saw the first Manx ride for 'Alexander John', a nom de plume for Alexander Jones, who was Chairman of Llandudno Watch Committee.

1951 Senior MGP

Heavy rain and low cloud caused the postponement of the Senior from the Thursday to the Friday The only problem with the weather was strong winds against the riders on the Mountain climb. From the 110 entries, 93 riders faced the starter. Top six in practice had been Dave Bennett (Norton), Don Crossley (Norton) Denis Parkinson (Norton), Brian Jackson (Norton), Robin Sherry (Matchless) and Ivor Arber (Norton), and five of these riders were on the leaderboard at the end of lap one. Bennett led from Crossley, Sherry, Parkinson and Arber, with Harold Clark (Norton) sixth. Despite the strong winds Bennett broke Geoff Duke's 1949 lap record on the second circuit at 89.75 mph and he led Crossley by 58 seconds, with the same four riders completing the top six. Pit stops were taken at the end of the third lap, when the positions were - Bennett by one minute 25 seconds from Crossley, who in turn was exactly one minute ahead of Sherry, Parkinson was just seven seconds down on Sherry and only one second ahead of Arber with Clark over one minute down in sixth place. Ivor Arber took over third place at the end of lap four, Sherry being relegated to fourth. But his challenge faded on lap five when he retired at Quarry Bends. Sherry should have then taken back his third spot, but Parkinson had lapped quicker and slotted in ahead of Sherry with just one lap to go. Bennett's lead was unassailable, and he crossed the line one minute 43.4 seconds ahead of Crossley with Parkinson almost four minutes down. The top six were completed by Robin Sherry, Harold Clark and Peter Davey (Norton). There were 64 finishers and 16 replicas were won.

Kermeen's dairy farm at Ballacraine provides the backdrop for Dave Bennett as he speeds to victory.

1951 Senior MGP (6 laps / 226.38 miles) 110 entries

1. Dave Bennett	Norton		2h. 36m. 03.2s	87.05 mph
2. Don Crossley	Norton		2h. 37m. 46.6s	86.09 mph
3. Denis Parkinson	Norton		2h. 41m. 37.6s	84.05 mph

The History of the Manx Grand Prix 1923-1998

Fastest lap (record)			
Dave Bennett	Norton	25m. 45s	87.95 mph

The left (plunger) rear suspension unit on D. J. P. Wilkins Norton disintegrated as he approached Creg ny Baa "and bits fell all over the road. The wheel was wobbling badly as he departed for Hillberry."

1952

1952 Junior MGP

Bob McIntyre leads Harold Clark into Ginger Hall. Clark was ahead by 20 seconds, but Bob gradually pulled away to win.

The 1952 Junior attracted the same entry as the previous year, 106, but due to various problems, 93 riders faced the starter, with Harold Clark, third in the 1951 Junior, a hot favourite on his A.J.S. He had bettered the lap record in practice by some 32 seconds. But at the end of lap one, it was the determined Scot Bob McIntyre (A.J.S.) who led Clark by eight seconds, with Derek Farrant (A.J.S.) third some 21 seconds down on Clark. McIntyre and Clark both broke the lap record on lap two, Bob in 26m. 44s., and Clark went even better in 26m. 25s. to lead the race by 11 seconds. Farrant still held third place and Manxman Derek Ennett, also A.J.S. mounted had moved up to fourth place. McIntyre equalled the new record on the third lap, but Clark went even faster, 25m. 59s., to lead at half distance by 37 seconds from McIntyre, with Farrant and Ennett still third and fourth, followed by A. C. Taylor (Norton) and Keith Campbell (Velocette). Neither Clark or McIntyre stopped for fuel, so they were both going for a non-stop race. On lap four Clark reduced the lap record by another four seconds, over a minute quicker than the 1951 record, and increased his lead by a further 10 seconds with Farrant and Ennett still holding their places. But on the fifth lap things began to change, Sulby reported that Bob was a mere six yards behind Clark, he was No. 17 and Clark was 21, so they had started 40 seconds apart, and the gap was closing. By Creg-ny Baa, McIntyre was 14 seconds ahead of Clark. Clark's machine was suffering clutch slip, and he could do nothing about the flying Scot, as he disappeared into the distance to win the race, on his Manx debut, by 39.6 seconds. Clark managed to hold on to second place, one minute 10 seconds ahead of Farrant. The top six were completed by Derek Ennett (A.J.S.)

Harry Pearce (Velocette) and Keith Campbell (Velocette). Taylor, who had been on the leaderboard finished seventh. There were 66 finishers and 25 replicas were won.

1952 Junior MGP (6 laps / 226.38 miles) 106 entries

1. Bob McIntyre	A.J.S.	2h. 38m. 27s	85.73 mph (record)
2. Harold Clark	A.J.S.	2h. 39m. 06s	85.37 mph
3. Derek Farrant	A.J.S.	2h. 40m. 16s	84.76 mph
Fastest lap (record)			
Harold Clark	A.J.S.	25m. 55s	87.37 mph

1952 Senior MGP

The Senior, which attracted an entry of 107, promised to be a real thriller, as the top six in practice, McIntyre, Farrant, Parkinson, Clark, Storr and Christian were separated by just 19 seconds. Bob McIntyre and Derek Ennett both changed from 500 Nortons to 350 A.J.S.'s for the race. Derek Farrant (Matchless) led at the end of the first lap from Bob McIntyre (A.J.S.) with a lap in 25m. 56s., just 11 seconds outside the record, and Clark, Storr and Ennett were tightly bunched on the leaderboard. Lap two saw Peter Davey (Norton) come within five seconds of the record, Clark equalled it, but Farrant had broken it by 14 seconds in 25m. 31s. Farrant led at half distance by 25 seconds from McIntyre on his little A.J.S., Peter Davey (Norton) was third, just two seconds down on McIntyre, and four seconds ahead of Harold Clark (Norton). John Storr (Norton) was a further six seconds down, and the top six were completed by Derek Ennett (A.J.S.). Lap four saw Farrant break the record again, 25m. 17 seconds, 89.57 mph to increase his lead. Storr, who had moved up to fourth, retired at Ballaugh with a broken chain.

There was no stopping Farrant, his fifth lap was another record, 25m. 15.8s. and went on to win the race by one minute 43.4 seconds from McIntyre, whose time for the Senior was some three and a half minutes faster than in the Junior on the same machine. Peter Davey (Norton) took third place with Harold Clark (Norton) fourth Derek Ennett (A.J.S.) fifth and Dennis Christian (Norton) sixth. One of the favourites Denis Parkinson (Norton), finished eighth, but his year was soon to come. There were 66 finishers and 26 replicas were won.

Derek Farrant at Governors Bridge. His machine formed the basis of the Matchless G45.

1952 Senior MGP (6 laps / 226.38 miles) 102 entries

1. Derek Farrant	Matchless		2h. 33m. 13.8s	88.65 mph (record)
2. Bob McIntyre	A.J.S.		2h. 34m. 57.2s	87.67 mph
3. Peter Davey	Norton		2h. 35m. 49.8s	87.17 mph
Fastest lap (record)				
Derek Farrant	Matchless		25m. 15.8s	89.64 mph

1952 was a tragic year for Francis Beart. Both his riders, Ivor Arber and Ken James, were killed in practice accidents.

Arber won the Distinguished Flying Cross in WWII flying Spitfires and he took up racing the replicate the thrill of flying.

1953

1953 Junior MGP

Alistair King's 7R blazes away at Quarter Bridge as Ray Fay (Norton) slips past.

The weather conditions for the Junior could not have been better, they were officially described as "ideal for racing, with perfect weather all round the course". The entries were a little disappointing, 77 compared to the 100 odd the previous years, but the standard of entry promised a good race. Two Manxmen, Dennis Christian (Norton) and Derek Ennett (A.J.S.) had topped the practice leaderboard, and by coincidence, they started together. But this close race wasn't to be, as Derek stopped at Quarter Bridge on the first lap to change a plug, he re-started but with an engine misfire, just got round to the pits where he retired. Another possible, Alistair King (A.J.S.) got no further than Quarter Bridge where he slid off, causing a spectacular sight as his machine burst into flames.

At the end of lap one, Frank Fox (Norton) led from Dennis Christian, with Norton mounted Bob Keeler in third place. Keeler overtook Christian for second place on lap two, and in fact came within striking distance of the leader. At half distance he had taken the lead by 18 seconds from Fox with Derek Powell (Norton) up into third place ahead of Christian. Bob Ritchie (A.J.S.) was fifth, and there was a tie for sixth place between Terry Shepherd (Norton) and Brian Freestone (Norton). But Keeler's lead didn't last long as he retired with engine trouble at Union Mills on lap four. At the end of this lap Fox was back in the lead and Christian had reclaimed second place from Powell. Fox seemed to have the race safe now with a lead of 51 seconds, which he increased to 71 seconds at the end of the fifth lap. Christian had slight problems on the last lap, when his engine seized briefly at the 33rd, but he held on to second place by 26 seconds from Powell. The top six were completed by Bob Ritchie (A.J.S.), Brian Freestone (Norton) and Terry Shepherd (Norton). There were 44 finishers and 25 riders won replicas.

1953 Junior MGP (6 laps / 226.38 miles) 77 entries

1. Frank Fox	Norton	2h. 40m. 18.8s	84.73 mph
2. Dennis Christian	Norton	2h. 42m. 05.0s	83.81 mph
3. Derek Powell	Norton	2h. 42m. 31.0s	83.59 mph
Fastest lap			
Frank Fox)	Norton	26m. 31s	85.41 mph
Bob Keeler)	Norton		

1953 Senior MGP

The Senior made history in more ways than one, Denis Parkinson won his fifth race, more than any other rider, and set the first 90 mph lap in the history of the Manx. There were 69 entries for the Senior and 58 of them came to the start line. Eleven riders had lapped in practice in under 27 minutes, the fastest being Denis Parkinson, Derek Ennett, Jack Wood, Harry Plews, Roy Jervis and Dennis Christian. At the end of lap one Parkinson had a six second advantage over Keeler, and three Manxmen, Ennett, Christian and Wood were in the top six. Denis led by five seconds at the end of the second lap and pulled in to re-fuel, whilst Bob went straight through. Ennett and Christian were tying for third place, Wood was fifth and Brian Freestone (Norton) had come into sixth place. At half distance the top six were Bob Keeler (Norton) by 15 seconds from Denis Parkinson, who was one minute 40 seconds ahead of Derek Ennett (Matchless). Jack Wood (Norton) was fourth just 25 down on Ennett, Roy Jervis (Matchless) was fifth, just five seconds down on Wood, and Dennis Christian (Norton) was sixth, 12 seconds down on Jervis. Lap four saw the end of Christian's race when he retired at the Guthrie Memorial. Parkinson, however, was really flying on this fourth lap and set the first ever 90 mph lap in the Manx - 24m. 58s. 90.69 mph, with Keeler and Ennett still second and third. Denis went even faster on lap five with another record, this time at 90.75 mph and his lead over Keeler was up to 57 seconds, whilst Ennett was three minutes 46 seconds down on Keeler in third place. On the final lap Denis recorded another 90 lap to set a new race record of 89.68 mph

Denis Parkinson on has way to Manx win number five, a Cronk ny Mona shot

The Lost Lap - by Drew Herdman, 1955 Senior Manx

1953 proved to be a good year. I first came to the Manx in 1951, finishing 27th at my first attempt; in 1952 I rode in the Clubman's and then the Senior Manx, coming thirteenth.

In 1953 I was working for T. Garner Motorcycles, Barnsley and had many successes in Ireland and on the mainland. Entries were sent for the 1953 Manx and Tom Garner said to me "take a hack bike and get yourself off to the Island", this was a week before practice began, staying as usual with George and Margaret Woolams as I had done before. I rode five laps a day, no matter what the weather was, to get my geography right.

At the start of practice I had got the course off pat, knowing exactly where to go, as I had walked the most difficult parts of the course during the week.

Practice went off well. Following strict instructions from my mechanic and friend John Mason, I was instructed to go slow to Ramsey, then fast over the Mountain. Next lap, fast to Ramsey and then slow over the Mountain.

I attracted the attention of the management of Norton Motors, Alan Wilson and Joe Craig, and after the Thursday afternoon practice, I was asked to bring my 500 to Norton's at Large's Garage in Princes Road, off Victoria Road and have a works engine fitted (the latest short-stroke version). Arriving at their garage, we put the bike up on the bench, took out the engine and then proceeded to open the packing case, only to discover that it contained a 350 - not a 500 unit! After re-assembling our Senior mount, it was back to the garage to bring the 350, into which the engine was installed. Then came a further snag; the exhaust pipe was there, but no megaphone, our one was of the wrong dimensions!

By this time it was 4.00 pm on Friday, with only Saturday morning in which to try the engine. I went down to the Castle Mona and explained the problem to Joe Craig; luckily, he had drawings for a megaphone in his briefcase; but where were to get one made?

Knowing Joe Kelly had a garage just off Derby Square, I dashed there to find him just closing up at 5.00 pm. Telling him of my predicament, he viewed the drawings and said, "yes, I can make it, but it would take me four hours". He duly set to, and by 9.30 pm we had our megaphone, complete with the reverse cone. We rushed it back to our garage in Sydney Street and it fitted like a glove. We fired the bike for the first time at 11.00 pm, but only for a few minutes.

Next morning, 5.00 am, I wheeled it out of the garage, bumped it down the road and up to the start. This was the first time a private entrant had ridden a short-stroke 350 in the Island. Going round that morning, with instructions to do only one lap, I was amazed at the tractability of this engine, it was like an electric motor.

Back to the garage after practice, it was time to discuss race tactics. I was number 61, so way back down the start order. I begged Joe Craig to let us go up a tooth but he was adamant and said "No, it would be ok". Whilst all this was going on, I had got friendly with a (nameless) local girl, we had been out to the pictures etc.

Frank with John Mason, his long-time mechanic.

I must confess I had a wife in Barnsley and I had a feeling that I could win the Manx. My friend John said "Look, if you win and this girl is at the finish; with the pictures all over the papers, it could be embarrassing for you". So we duly asked another friend to take her on his pillion to a place where she could not get out until the race was over. We settled on the 11th Milestone.

Race day; the bike was warmed up and then covered with blankets to keep the heat in prior to the start. Moving down to face the starter, I was approached by Joe Craig, who spoke in my ear. He said "We shall be signalling for you at Ramsey Hairpin, if you are pushed, take the revs up to 8,600 rpm". I was amazed as most 350's only revved to 7,000. I ran the bike at 8,200 all the race and led from the start (see report). Coming down the Mountain on the last lap, with a minute in hand, I revved it to 8,600 rpm, it would have done more.

I cannot describe the feeling of seeing that chequered flag and the honour that goes with winning the Manx.

When we looked closely at the engine, we discovered the engine was stamped G.E.D. 1952; this was the motor that Geoff Duke had used to win the 1952 Junior TT.

P. S. The decision to move the girl to the Eleventh Milestone proved to be correct; Movitone News took a film at the finish which was shown at most local cinemas in Yorkshire!

Bob Keeler was 63.4 seconds down in second place, four minutes 53 seconds ahead of Derek Ennett. The top six were completed by Jack Wood (Norton), Brian Freestone (Norton) and Derek Powell (Norton). Roy Jervis (Matchless), who had been on the leaderboard for most of the race, finished eighth of the 37 finishers, and 16 riders won replicas.

1953 Senior MGP (6 laps / 226.38 miles) 69 entries

1. Denis Parkinson	Norton	2h. 31m. 28.2s	89.68 mph (record)
2. Bob Keeler	Norton	2h. 32m. 31.4s	89.07 mph
3. Derek Ennett	Matchless	2h. 37m. 00.4s	86.52 mph
Fastest lap (record)			
Denis Parkinson	Norton	24m. 57s	90.75 mph

1954

1954 Junior MGP

Jack Wood very nearly picked up a leaderboard place on his Gold Star.

Entries for the Junior were down on the previous year, 86, and non starters reduced this number to 75. The weather was good, apart from some low cloud on the Mountain sections. Manx rider Derek Ennett (A.J.S.) had topped the practice leaderboard followed by John Hartle (A.J.S.), Alistair King (A.J.S.), Jack Wood (B.S.A.), Percy Tait (Norton) and Dave Chadwick (Norton). It was Ennett who led at the end of lap one by six seconds from King, who in turn led Hartle by 17 seconds. Chadwick was fourth, Derek Powell (Norton) fifth and Wood sixth. With a new lap record on lap two in 25m. 48s. - 87.77 mph, King took over the lead by 12 seconds from Ennett, Chadwick had passed Hartle whilst Powell and Wood held their places. At half distance, the end of lap three, Ennett was back in front by nine seconds from King and Powell dropped to ninth place, bringing Geoff Tanner (Norton) into fifth place ahead of Wood. King pulled back three seconds on the fourth lap to trail Ennett by six seconds, with Chadwick, Hartle, Tanner and Wood completing the leaderboard. Ennett increased his lead at the end of lap five to 34 seconds, but fellow Manxman Wood retired at Ballaugh, bringing Powell back onto the leaderboard in sixth place. Alistair King's bad luck in the Manx struck again when he retired on the last lap at Kirk Michael, but he had the consolation of a new Junior lap record. So Derek Ennett became the first Manx born rider to win a Manx Grand Prix. His winning margin over Dave Chadwick was one minute six seconds, with John Hartle third. Geoff Tanner (Norton) remained fourth and Derek Powell (Norton) fifth with A. M. Phillip (Norton) coming into the top six. There were 54 finishers and 32 riders won replicas.

1954 Junior MGP (6 laps / 226.38 miles) 86 entries

1. Derek Ennett	A.J.S.	2h. 37m. 21.4s	86.33 mph (record)
2. Dave Chadwick	Norton	2h. 39m. 27.0s	85.19 mph
3. John Hartle	Norton	2h. 40m. 03.2s	84.87 mph
Fastest lap (record)			
Alistair King	A.J.S.	25m. 48s	87.77 mph

1954 Senior MGP

Entries for the Senior were also down on the previous year, 75, and with 14 non starters there were 61 riders on the line to face the starter. Low cloud on the mountain giving reduced visibility caused a postponement of 30 minutes. Junior winner Derek Ennett (Matchless) had been fastest in practice followed by Geoff Tanner (Norton), John Hartle (Norton), George Costain (Norton), with Dave Chadwick (Norton) and Derek Powell (Norton) tying in sixth place. Practice form was confirmed at the end of the first lap when Ennett led the race by 29 seconds from Hartle with Percy Tait (Norton) third, Chadwick fourth, Costain fifth and James Davie (B.S.A.) sixth. Visibility was deteriorating however and warning flags were shown at Ramsey, and to add to this it was also raining heavily. Chadwick's challenge ended on lap two when he slid off at Quarter Bridge, he remounted but eventually retired at Ballacraine. With the fastest lap of the race, Ennett increased his lead over Hartle to 68 seconds at the end of the second lap, Tait remained third, Costain moved up to fourth and Powell and Dennis Christian (Norton) came on to the leaderboard. Lap three saw Hartle take the lead from Ennett, he lapped in 27m.

Colin Watson, seen here at Union Mills, finished 11th in the '54 Senior on his debut Manx on this International Norton. With a large family and limited funds, his racing was restricted to just a few meetings per year.
Colin was working in the steel mills in Scunthorpe, where you could only take your annual holidays in August, or face the sack. There were three mills in Scunthorpe; Colin was sacked three times after riding in '54, '55 and '56!

33s. to the Manxman's 29m. 06s. to lead by 25 seconds, the only other leaderboard change was that Christian moved ahead of Powell. Another of the leaderboard men, Tait, retired on the fourth lap, his race ended at the Ballahutchin. Ennett appeared to be in trouble as Hartle increased his lead to 70 seconds. Costain moved up to third, Powell was fourth, Gavin Dunlop (Matchless) came into fifth place ahead of Christian. Ennett's problems were confirmed on lap five, when he was reported to be touring at Windy Corner, and he retired at the pits with plug trouble. This gave Hartle a lead of 4 minutes 53 seconds, a lead that appeared unassailable, but this was the TT course and there was still one lap to go. Costain was now second, Powell third, Dunlop fourth, Christian fifth and A. M. Phillip (Norton) coming into the top six. But drama on the last lap, Hartle retired at the Mountain Box, out of petrol! So Manxman George Costain completed a Castletown double by some 13 seconds from Derek Powell, Gavin Dunlop, Dennis Christian, A. M. Phillip and Bob Dowty (Norton). A remarkable race, with only the winner Costain being in the top six at the end of the first lap! There were just 31 finishers, and 15 riders won replicas.

1954 Senior MGP (6 laps / 226.38 miles) 75 entries

1. George Costain	Norton	2h. 47m. 49.0s	80.95 mph
2. Derek Powell	Norton	2h. 48m. 02.6s	80.83 mph
3. Gavin Dunlop	Matchless	2h. 49m. 18.4s	80.23 mph
Fastest lap			
Derek Ennett	Matchless	25m. 49s	87.72 mph

1955

1955 Junior MGP

Entries for the Junior were well up on the previous year, and more in line with the entries received in the early fifties. A total of 116 were received, and of these, 103 came to the starting line. The practice leaderboard had shown James Davie (B.S.A.) to be fastest, followed by R. E. Drysdale (A.J.S.), Jack Wood (B.S.A.), Gavin Dunlop (A.J.S.) with Jimmy Drysdale (A.J.S.) and Jimmy Buchan tying for sixth place. A close race was in prospect as just 14 seconds covered the first six. There was drama at the start, when local hope Alan Holmes (Norton) had machine problems. He was allowed to start at the rear of the field, without any penalty, but the extra traffic he would have to pass would add to his problems. At the end of the first lap the leader was Geoff Tanner (Norton) in 25m. 55s - just seven seconds outside the lap record. He led Alistair King (A.J.S.) by 22 seconds who was in turn just three seconds ahead of Dunlop. Davie held fourth place and R. F. Jerrard (A.J.S.) and Jimmy Buchan (Norton) shared fifth place. Tanner broke the lap record on his second lap in 25m. 21s. - 27 seconds inside the previous best, and he increased his lead over King to 65 seconds. King was just two seconds ahead of Dunlop, Buchan was fourth, Jerrard fifth and Wood brought his B.S.A. into sixth place. Tragically on this second lap, James Davie, who had been fourth on lap one, came off at the Gooseneck, he was taken to Ramsey Cottage Hospital, but his injuries proved fatal. Tanner continued to turn the pressure on and again broke the record on his third lap at 89.51 mph and led new second place man Dunlop by 2 minutes 23 seconds, with King two seconds down in third place. Buchan was fourth, and Alan Holmes (Norton), who had been fighting his way through the field, came up to fifth place ahead of fellow Manxman Wood. Buchan took second place on the fourth lap, two minutes 26 seconds down on Tanner and one second ahead of Dunlop with King now in fourth place, followed by Holmes and Wood. Dunlop's race ended on lap five just past Kirk Michael, Tanner led by over three minutes from

Geoff Tanner (1) eases past P. J. Walsh (B.S.A.) en route to yet another Manx double.

The Lost Lap - by Drew Herdman, 1955 Senior Manx

I think I can say without much fear of contradiction, that I could well have been one of the first people to go on a 'Trip' through sniffing petrol, though in my case it was not in the least intentional.

To explain how this came about, read on. Practice for the 1955 M.G.P. had gone well. My times were competitive, and I had even set the fastest lap, albeit in the wet, which must say something about recklessness. I was really looking forward to the races. The flag dropped for the Junior start, and off I went. Three laps, and a fill up took me on to the last lap. Struggling, as usual, up the Mountain, I felt the clutch slipping; hasty adjustment did not help, and as I passed the Bungalow, it decided that it had done enough, and ceased to work. Speed took me on to Hillberry, and from there on it was push up hill and free wheel down to Governors Bridge, where a final push took me to the finish. At that time the film No Limit was still very popular, and I received a standing ovation to the cheers of "Come on George, " etc. I had not sweated a drop, until I drank two glasses of liquid refreshment, whereupon, I leaked into my leathers from every pore.

Suffice it to say that the offending clutch was replaced and the bike delivered to Faragher and Ashton's garage in time for scrutineering for the Senior. On Thursday morning, bikes were collected, and tanks filled to the brim. As I closed the cap and rocked the bike back on to compression, I smelled petrol. Was it me, or just the general atmosphere? Ignoring it, I started the bike, and amidst the roar of a hundred bikes, joined the parade, and down to the Promenade. Brakes on at the bottom, and again the smell of petrol. A swift visual showed no drip or obvious leak, so on I went. Waiting at the start gave me more time to look, but still nothing. With a mental shrug, and a determination to avenge my disaster of two days earlier, I joined the line of those with numbers on their backs, and grim expressions on their fronts. I came up to the starter. Four steps and drop the clutch, engine fires, catch it as the rev counter passes 2,000, on the megaphone and away.

Up through the gears, St Ninians, and the drop down Bray Hill. Down again, and brakes on for Quarter Bridge. It was at this point that I found the reason for the previous smell of petrol. A full tank had found a small crack in the weld around the very top of the neck of the tank where it nestled round the frame at the fork tube. Petrol splashed out and back into my face. No full face helmets in those days. All I had was a chamois face guard, to take the sting of any insect that happened to stray into my path. There was no avoiding it. Either I retired then and there, a course not to be contemplated, after the previous race, or I went on and took my chance. No contest really, as I screwed the throttle open on my way to Braddan Bridge. The next three laps were exhilarating, and as the fuel level sank in the tank, the splashing did get less. By now, my leathers were soaked in petrol, which even as it dried, had I come off and sparked, would have burned like a torch, with me inside. Not a pleasant prospect. However. youthful folly made me go on into the pits, a change of goggles, fill up. and away again. Tank full, first brake, and soaked again. By Glen Helen, on lap four I had decided that as a tank full had taken me three laps, then I should have enough fuel to finish the race. Strange that it had taken so long to work that out. By now I was flying. and as I went by the Start for the fifth, having swallowed, sniffed, and been soaked by pints of petrol, I seemed to go onto auto pilot, because I cannot really remember anything clearly about that lap. I was well away, and it must have been the level dropping in the tank, and consequently less coming out that brought me back to reality. By Ramsey on the sixth, I was once again more or less back in my tree, and with only half a lap to go, tackled the Mountain once more, with my faculties restored, and a song in my heart, as the old song tells us, only to reach the Bungalow for the last time, where with a splutter and a cough the engine died. OUT OF FUEL. Once more I coasted to Hillberry, but as I came to a stop, I just hadn't the heart to push in again. The bike went into the hedge, and me with it, to await the van which collected the retirees after the race. Ah well, C'est la Vie. but it was fun for all that, and there are years out there still untouched.

Drew Herdman on his 'lost' lap, going well at Cronk ny Mona.

King, Buchan, Holmes, Wood and another local rider Eddie Crooks (Norton). King's dreadful luck struck again when he retired early on the last lap, and Tanner went on to win by three minutes 57 seconds, both Holmes and Wood overtook Buchan, Crooks finished fifth, and Ellis Boyce moved up to sixth place. There were 73 finishers, and 27 replicas were won.

1955 Junior MGP (6 laps / 226.38 miles)   116 entries

1. Geoff Tanner	Norton	2h. 33m. 33.8s	88.46 mph (record)
2. Alan Holmes	Norton	2h. 37m. 31.0s	86.24 mph
3. Jack Wood	B.S.A.	2h. 38m. 15.0s	85.84 mph

Fastest lap (record)
Geoff Tanner	Norton	25m. 18s	89.51 mph

1955 Senior MGP

The entry for the Senior was also well up on 1954, a total of 113, of whom 93 came to the start tine, after a thirty minute delay because of mist on the Mountain. Alistair King (Norton) topped the Senior practice leaderboard just one second faster than Alan Trow (Norton), who was followed by Geoff Tanner (Norton), Ewan Haldane and Jimmy Buchan (Norton) were equal fifth and Ellis Boyce (Norton) was sixth. Tanner took over where he left off in the Junior and at the end of the first lap was 10 seconds ahead of King, who was six seconds up on Boyce. In fourth place was Buchan, six seconds down, fifth was Alan Holmes (Norton), eight seconds down on Buchan and the leaderboard was completed by Jack Wood (B.S.A.). With a new lap record on the second lap in 24m. 36s., King snatched the lead from Tanner by just two seconds, with Boyce still third. Buchan held on to fourth place, but Holmes was reported to be touring on the Mountain with clutch problems, so Wood moved up to fifth and Dennis Christian (Matchless) took over sixth spot. Tanner was back in the lead at half distance by 17 seconds from King with the rest of the leaderboard unchanged. At this stage of a race, pit stops alter the order quite dramatically, and at the end of the fourth lap Buchan had moved from fourth to first and was six seconds up on Tanner. Alistair King was again forced to retire on this lap, just before Ramsey, Boyce was third, Wood fourth, Christian fifth and Alan Trow (Norton) sixth. Tanner got to work on lap five with a new record at 92.38 mph and led Buchan by 53 seconds. Two leaderboard men retired on this lap, Jack Wood with mechanical problems at Sulby, and Ellis Boyce after a Spill at Dorans Bend. Christian took over third place from Trow with B. J. Thompson (Matchless) and Eddie Crooks (Norton) coming on to the leaderboard. Tanner didn't rest on his laurels and broke the record again on the final lap at 93.14 mph to win by one minute 32 seconds, and so become the first rider to complete a double since Eric Briggs in 1947. Buchan and Christian completed the top three, with Alan Trow, B. J. Thompson and Eddie Crooks making up the leaderboard. There were 62 finishers and 16 replicas were won.

1955 Senior MGP (6 laps / 226.38 miles)   113 entries

1. Geoff Tanner	Norton	2h. 28m. 39.0s	91.38 mph (record)
2. Jimmy Buchan	Norton	2h. 30m. 11.0s	90.45 mph
3. Dennis Christian	Norton	2h. 33m. 43.6s	88.36 mph

Fastest lap (record)
Geoff Tanner	Norton	24m. 19s	93.14 mph

1956

1956 Junior MGP

Jimmy Buchan at Cronk ny Mona

The 1956 Junior attracted 115 entries, for various reasons there were 13 non-starters, so 102 lined up for the start of the race. Manxman Alan Holmes had been fastest in practice on his Norton, 12 seconds faster than Alistair King (Norton), with the top six being completed by Bernard Codd (Norton), Eddie Crooks (Norton), Ernie Washer (A.J.S.) and Jimmy Buchan (Norton). Alistair King who has had so much bad luck in the Manx, set off at a cracking pace, breaking the lap record from a standing start at 90.15 mph, the first 90 plus lap in the history of the Junior Manx. He led by 9.8 seconds from Bob Anderson (Norton), who was 18 seconds ahead of Alan Holmes (Norton), who was followed by Jimmy Buchan, Bernard Codd and Eddie Crooks. King went faster on lap two, 91.07 mph, and increased his lead over Anderson to 34 seconds, Holmes was 30 seconds down in third place and the rest of the leaderboard was unchanged. By half distance King was 75 seconds ahead of Holmes, who had overtaken Anderson, Buchan was still fourth, Crooks fifth and Bob Dowty (Norton), who had come on the leaderboard in sixth place, with Codd dropping to seventh. Holmes struck trouble on the fourth lap and pushed in from Governors Bridge, King still led with Anderson 67 seconds down, Buchan took third place. Crooks was fourth, Codd came back into fifth place ahead of Dowty. Lap five saw dramatic changes, King again was forced to retire with engine trouble at Kirk Michael, and Anderson went out at Glentrammon with a broken chain. So Buchan was the new leader, two minutes and 10 seconds ahead of Crooks, Dowty came up to third ahead of Codd and Frank Rutherford (B.S.A.) and Ellis Boyce (Norton) came on to the leaderboard in fifth and six places. There was no more drama on the final lap and no change to the leading six places. Jimmy Buchan (Norton) won by 2 minutes 34 seconds from Eddie Crooks, with Bob Dowty third. Bernard Codd (Norton), Frank Rutherford (B.S.A.) and Ellis Boyce completed the top six. There were 67 finishers, and 28 riders won replicas.

1956 Junior MGP (6 laps / 226.38 miles)   115 entries

1. Jimmy Buchan	Norton	2h. 33m. 25.0s	88.54 mph

2. Eddie Crooks	Norton	2h. 35m. 39.0s	87.09 mph (record)
3. Bob Dowty	Norton	2h. 37m. 14.6s	86.39 mph
Fastest lap (record)			
Alistair King	Norton	24m. 51.8s	91.07 mph

1956 Senior MGP

The Senior also had an entry of 115, but there were more non-starters than in the Junior, 18, so 97 riders set off in the six lap race. The practice leaderboard had shown Bob Anderson (Norton), fastest, 22 seconds ahead of Alistair King (Norton), with Jimmy Buchan, Bernard Codd, Ewan Haldane and Ernie Washer, all on Nortons, completing the fastest six. There was a one hour delay to the start due to the weather, but when it got underway, Alistair King was in his usual first place, 17 seconds ahead of Bob Anderson, who was just 0.8 seconds up on Buchan, local riders Alan Holmes and Bob Dowty on Nortons were fourth and fifth, with Codd in sixth place. Anderson pulled back time on King on lap two and was just 6.8 seconds down, was Kings bad luck about to strike again? Buchan was still in touch in third place just 2.6 seconds down on Anderson. Holmes remained fourth, Codd moved up to fifth and Ewan Haldane (Norton) came into sixth place, with Dowty dropping to eighth. King was in trouble, he came off at Ramsey Hairpin, due to no back brake, he remounted and toured to the pits to retire. It was Buchan who led at half distance, he had lapped at 91.91 mph to snatch the lead from Anderson by four seconds. King was still credited as third at the end of the lap, with Holmes, Codd and Haldane still in the top six. Buchan, with his eyes now set on a Manx double, increased his lead over Anderson at the end of lap four to 5.8 seconds, Holmes moved up to third, and Haldane and Ellis Boyce (Norton) were tying for fifth place ahead of Crooks. Buchan increased his lead by a further six seconds at the end of lap five, and the only change to the leaderboard was Boyce took a clear fourth place with Haldane fifth. Anderson spurted on the final lap and came within just 3.2 seconds of Buchan, the closest ever finish to a Manx at that time. Alan Holmes was also flying on the final lap and set a new record at 93.59 mph to take a secure third place. Boyce finished fourth, Crooks fifth and Dowty sixth, with Haldane just off the leaderboard in seventh place. There were 57 finishers, and 17 replicas were won.

1956 Senior MGP (6 laps / 226.38 miles) 115 entries

1. Jimmy Buchan	Norton	2h. 29m. 32.2s	90.83 mph
2. Bob Anderson	Norton	2h. 29m. 35.4s	90.80 mph
3. Alan Holmes	Norton	2h. 30m. 49.2s	90.06 mph
Fastest lap (record)			
Alan Holmes	Norton	24m. 08.0s	93.59 mph

1957

With even more applications to ride in the Manx in 1957, rather than turn riders away, the Manx Club decided to hold a race for Newcomers. The race, for 500cc and 350cc machines, was to be over four laps of the course, prior to the Manx proper, with the most successful riders in each of the classes competing in the Junior and Senior races.

1957 Junior Newcomers

The Junior class attracted an entry of 78, there were eight non-starters, so 70 riders lined up in perfect weather conditions. Mike Brookes (Norton), was the hot favourite, having topped the practice leaderboard, and having been fastest in every session. At the end of the first lap Brookes led P. Hodgson (A.J.S.) by 35 seconds with Roger Sutcliffe (Norton) third, 32 seconds down. Dennis Pratt (A.J.S.), Jack Nutter (Norton) and John Righton (Velocette), completed the top six. Brookes increased his lead at the end of lap two to 67 seconds, and the only other leaderboard change was that Derek Williams (B.S.A.) came into fifth place, with Righton dropping out. There was drama at the end of lap three, when the race leader, Brookes pushed in from Governors Bridge to retire with a seized engine. Dennis Pratt jumped from fourth place to first, with a lead of 23 seconds over Williams. Sutcliffe remained third, Hodgson was fourth and two new names appeared on the leaderboard in fifth and sixth places - R. Brinnard (Norton) and G. R. Sharp (B.S.A.). Pratt increased his lead at the end of the race to 36.2 seconds. with Williams second, but surprisingly four new names completed the top six - R. Preece (Norton), Cyril Huxley (B.S.A.), E. Whiteside (A.J.S.) and H. Nichol (B.S.A.). Sutcliffe finished eighth and Hodgson was 10th. There were 51 finishers.

Dennis Pratt speeds past the scouts at work on the Scoreboard.

1957 Junior Newcomers (4 laps / 150.92 miles) 78 entries

1. Dennis Pratt	A.J.S.	1h. 49m. 11.2s	82.94 mph
2. Derek Williams	B.S.A.	1h. 49m 47.5	82.49 mph
3. R. Preece	Norton	1h. 51m 04.6s	81.53 mph
Fastest lap			
Mike Brookes	Norton	25m. 57.4s	87.21 mph

1957 Senior Newcomers

Run concurrently with the 350's, the 500 class attracted 40 entries, but non-starters reduced this to 31. Peter Middleton had been fastest in practice in 25m. 56s. - 87.31 mph, followed by Ned Minihan and Roy Mayhew, all on Nortons. At the end of the first lap it was Minihan in the lead followed by Middleton, 22 seconds down with Joe Dunphy (Norton) in third place. M. R. Hancock (Norton) was fourth, Mayhew fifth and M. W. Munday (Norton) sixth. Middleton closed the gap on lap two to 2.2 seconds, but Dunphy retired at the pits with a partially seized engine, allowing G. H. Turner (B.S.A.) into sixth place. Minihan increased his lead over Middleton to 28 seconds at the

end of lap three, followed by Hancock, Mayhew, Turner and Munday. On the final lap Minihan appeared to have lost time, and when he finished his total race time slotted him into fourth place. But fifteen minutes after he had finished, it was announced that he had been stopped in Ramsey on the last lap by order of the Clerk of the course for his machine to be examined. The machine was O.K., and he was given a time allowance of three minutes 16 seconds, two minutes 46 seconds for the time he was stopped and 15 seconds for slowing. This time allowance gave Minihan victory by 17 seconds from Middleton with Hancock third. Mayhew (Norton), Turner (B.S.A.) and Munday (Norton) completed the leaderboard. There were 20 finishers.

1957 Senior Newcomers (4 laps / 150.92 miles) 40 entries

1. Ned Minihan	Norton	1h. 41m. 51.4s	88.90 mph
2. Peter Middleton	Norton	1h. 42m. 08.4s	88.66 mph
3. M. R. Hancock	Norton	1h. 44m. 56.2s	86.30 mph
Fastest lap			
Ned Minihan	Norton	24m. 58.6s	90.63 mph

1957 Junior MGP

The Junior attracted 87 entries, there were 10 non-starters, so the top 23 finishers in the Junior Newcomers class were included to bring the field up to 100. Alan Holmes (Norton) had been fastest in practice, followed by Alan Shepherd (Norton), Alan Craven (B.S.A.), Ken Patrick (Norton), Ellis Boyce (Norton) and Eddie Crooks (Norton). The weather for the Junior was described as perfect. At the end of the first lap Holmes held a narrow three second lead over Crooks with Shepherd some 10 seconds down in third place. Colin Broughton (Norton) was fourth, Craven fifth and Boyce sixth, and just 30 seconds covered the first six. Holmes increased his lead on lap two to 10.8 seconds from Crooks, and Broughton moved into third place, 33 seconds behind Crooks followed by Shepherd, Boyce and Craven. By half distance Holmes was 18 seconds in front and Crooks was 76 seconds up on Broughton, but Shepherd was only 10 seconds behind Broughton. Tom Thorp (Norton) came into fifth place with Boyce sixth. Holmes was now pulling steadily away from Crooks, his advantage at the end of lap four was 46 seconds, Shepherd had taken third place, Boyce was fourth, Broughton fifth and Thorp sixth. The difference between Holmes and Crooks was 68 seconds at the end of the fifth lap, and the only change in the top six was Bob Dowty (Norton) replaced Thorp in sixth place. As they started their last lap Holmes and Crooks seemed to have their places secure, but Crooks retired with engine trouble at Ballaugh. Holmes was now well clear of the field and won by two minutes 34 seconds from Boyce who was 12 seconds ahead of Shepherd. Dowty, Broughton and Thorp completed the top six. There were 63 finishers and 25 riders won replicas, among them Junior Snaefell Newcomers winner Denis Pratt who finished 14th.

1957 Junior MGP (6 laps / 226.38 miles) 100 entries

1. Alan Holmes	Norton	2h. 32m. 24.4s	89.13 mph
2. Ellis Boyce	Norton	2h. 34m. 58.4s	87.66 mph
3. Alan Shepherd	Norton	2h. 35m. 10.2s	87.55 mph
Fastest lap			
Alan Holmes	Norton	25m. 08.6s	90.04 mph

1957 Senior MGP

The Senior had attracted 91 entries, there were 11 non-starters, so the first 20 in the Senior Newcomers were accepted, to bring the starting total up 100. Alan Shepherd (Norton) had topped the practice leaderboard, followed by Ken Patrick (Norton), Ellis Boyce (Norton), Ewan Haldane (Norton), Jim Drysdale (Norton) and Ernie Washer (Norton). Alan Holmes, the Junior winner was not featured, so was the third successive double unlikely? The weather conditions were poor at the start of the race, and at the end of lap one Shepherd was in the lead, but only by 10 seconds from Holmes, who in turn was eight seconds up on Boyce, with Haldane, Washer and Drysdale completing the top six. Shepherd's race ended early on lap two, and Holmes took over the lead by 11 seconds from Boyce, Haldane and Washer maintained their leaderboard places, and were joined by Ned Minihan (Norton) the Senior Snaefell winner, and Bob Dowty (Norton). Boyce really motored on lap three and broke the lap record at 94.06 mph to snatch the lead from Holmes by just under three seconds, Haldane held on to third place, Dowty moved up to fourth, and with Minihan's retirement, Frank Rutherford (Norton) came into fifth place ahead of Washer. Boyce increased his lead over Holmes to 19 seconds at the end of lap four, Haldane retired and Dowty took over third spot, followed by Washer, Rutherford and Eddie Crooks (Norton). Disaster struck Ellis Boyce on the fifth lap when he came off at Glen Helen, he was not injured but machine damage forced his retirement. This mishap let Holmes into the lead at the end of the lap by one minute and 51 seconds from Washer with Dowty third, Rutherford fourth, John Lewis (Norton) and John Hurlstone (Norton) coming into the top six. So Alan Holmes went on to complete his Manx double by over two minutes from Ernie Washer with Bob Dowty third. Frank Rutherford held on to his fourth place, and Hurlstone pipped

Graham T. Downes (A.J.S.) broke a footrest off on the descent of Bray Hill at the start of his second lap, but he still finished the race. "There was no question of retiring, but it was a most uncomfortable ride, the large tank I had borrowed from Jack Williams (head of the AMC race department), meant that I could not rest my foot on the chaincase so it had to dangle for the next four laps." Graham returned as travelling marshal for 1961, and raced in the Sidecar TT in 1963, under the pseudonym 'V.E.R. Boten', as he was signed off from work on the sick at the time!

My Winning Rides - by Alan Holmes, 1957 Senior and Junior Manx

For those who believe in fate there are a number of interesting examples leading up to my 1957 'Manx Double.'

With a second and a third and a record lap already behind me I had taken a comfortable lead in the 1956 Junior, only to have the magneto fail on me at Governors Bridge on the fifth lap. This was of course very disappointing at the time but had I gone on to win there could have been no 'Double' for me the following year. Jimmy Buchan would not have had his '56 'Double', Ernie Washer would have won the '57 Senior instead of in '58 which in turn would have had Eddie Crooks win the '58 Senior instead of in '59 which would have had Tom Thorp win the '59 Senior. Ellis Boyce would have won the '57 Junior instead of in '60 which in turn would have made Roy Mayhew that year's winner

Lady fate is a fickle lady to be sure.

Another example came in the lead up to the first leg of my 'Double'. The 350 Norton had gone well in practice but we were not too happy about the carburation so, along with my sponsor Reg Dearden and best chum the now late Ken Crellin, we repaired to the Ballamodha Straight to see if we could improve it. We got the settings where we wanted them and were ready to leave to go back to the weigh in in Douglas when I persuaded Reg to let me have just one more run up and down the Straight On the way back down the engine started to misfire badly and when we checked the carb it was found that a tiny sliver of a fibre washer had broken off and lodged in the main jet. Had I not made that extra run up and down the Straight it is more than likely that I would have had to retire on the first lap, or at best finished well down the field.

And so to the race itself. I had made the fastest lap in practice and with the Norton now running like a dream I was looking forward to having a good ride

It was a beautiful day with no wind and sunshine all the way. The race itself was totally uneventful and at the end of the first lap I led from my team-mate Eddie Crooks by some 6 seconds This was increased on the second lap and again on the third when the first three places were held by three of Reg Dearden's runners i.e., myself, Eddie, and Colin Broughton,

Alan peels into Governors Bridge on the 350 Manx.

all local riders, with another local, another of Reg's runners, Bob Dowty, just a few places further back. I know that Reg was very proud of this at the time.

My lead increased with each lap and at the end of the fifth I was just over a minute ahead of Eddie who very sadly had to retire at Sulby on the last lap. I well remember going over the mountain on that last lap, knowing from my signal at Ramsey that I had a comfortable lead, humming "Oh Island in the Sun" a hit record at the time, at the same time praying that the Norton would keep going for those last few miles. It did, and I finished at record speed 2fi minutes ahead of Ellis Boyce with Alan Shepherd third and my two stablemates Bob Dowty and Colin Broughton filling fourth and fifth places just 1.8 seconds apart.

The Senior was a different story altogether and was anything but uneventful. Practice leader Alan Shepherd started favourite on no. 80 with Ellis Boyce no. 82 and myself at no. 83. Just 30 seconds separating the three favourites at the start so it looked like being a very interesting race as indeed it was.

Unlike Junior day, the weather was not so good, with high winds and the prospect of rain later in the race.

Sure enough, Alan Shepherd led at the end of the first lap with me 9.8 seconds back in second spot and Ellis third, just 8.6 seconds behind me on corrected time. So after the first 37fl miles just 18.2 seconds separated the first three, and here I would like to mention a very interesting point regarding gearing.

Reg Dearden had always opted for a higher gear in the interests of reliability so I was carrying at least half a tooth higher than most and on the flat section from Douglas to Ramsey on the first lap, I was, on unofficial timing, ten seconds up on Shepherd. On the steep climb up the mountain however, then down into Douglas again, Alan took no less than something like 20 seconds out of me but it wasn't his day and he went out at the Nook on the second lap.

Just ten seconds behind Boyce off the grid, I had all but pulled that back on the first lap and with Ellis in my sights going past the grandstand I was just under ten seconds ahead on corrected time. I got past him going through Crosby and at the end of the second lap was leading the race by some eleven seconds. This really was some race.

All went well on the third lap, with Ellis in my slipstream, until we arrived at the Bungalow which was still standing at the time.

Laying it into the left hander the Norton went into a two wheel drift and my right foot actually clipped the upright of the Bungalow leaving some tell-tale

Alan takes what must be the largest chequered flag in racing - and the double.

yellow paint on my boot. That was a really close shave and whilst all that was going on, Ellis slipped by on the inside and I tucked in behind him going up the straight now known as Hailwood Rise towards Brandywell, the highest point on the course.

Half way up the straight disaster almost struck for a second time in the space of about ten seconds, when a granite chip was thrown up from Ellis' back wheel and smacked me right on the forehead between helmet and goggles, just above my left eye. With the combined speed of the stone and me riding into it I remember very little of the last few miles back to the grandstand where I was due for my refuelling pit stop and lost 13 seconds to Ellis who led at the end of the lap, the half way stage in the race, by just over two seconds..

During my pit stop, some time was lost inspecting the rear of my machine to see if oil had caused my slide at the Bungalow but all was well. Whilst in the pits, Norman Brown, the Clerk of The Course, came to make a routine check and noticed blood running down my face from the wound on my forehead. (I had taken off my goggles to change them). Norman told me later that it was touch and go as to whether he would allow me to continue in the race but fortunately, he called a first aid man to apply a plaster and allowed me to continue.

Unfortunately, all of this time, which counted in the fourth lap, left me some 18 seconds down on Boyce going into lap five.

By now, light rain had started to fall on parts of the course making the going very tricky and one of those to fall foul of the slippery roads was the unfortunate Ellis Boyce who I saw picking himself up off the road as I went round the left hander at Glen Helen. A most unfortunate end to a fine ride but Ellis' day was to come when he justly registered his Junior win three years later

At the end of lap five I led Ernie Washer by almost two minutes and am happy that Ernie too was to register a Senior win the following year.

My signals told me that I now had a comfortable lead going into the last lap but unfortunately the weather had deteriorated further and the roads were now wet over most of the course with high winds, particularly over the mountain section, making the going decidedly dicey.

That last lap was very much like walking on a knife edge but apart from a nasty slide on the right hander after passing Bishop's Court, there was no serious incident and I managed to increase my lead still further to finish at record speed.

Altogether a very satisfying fortnight with two record breaking wins, both by a margin of more than two minutes, the Lady Hill Rose Bowl and the Senior Team prize with Eddie Crooks and Bob Dowty, all of which led to my getting a Norton works ride in the 1958 T.T.

But that's another story!

To the victors - the spoils! A laden table is proof of Reg Dearden's ability to pick Manx winners. From left: Bob Dowty, Ken Crellin, Johnnie Quirk (reporter), Alan Holmes, Reg Dearden, and Eddie Crooks

48 The History of the Manx Grand Prix 1923-1998

Lewis for fifth place at the flag. Peter Middleton, runner up in the Senior Newcomers class finished ninth. There were 60 finishers and 15 replicas were won.

1957 Senior MGP (6 laps / 226.38 miles) 100 entries

1. Alan Holmes	Norton	2h. 28m. 33.6s	91.43 mph (record)
2. Ernie Washer	Norton	2h. 30m. 48.0s	90.08 mph
3. Bob Dowty	Norton	2h. 31m. 18.8s	89.77 mph
Fastest lap (record)			
Ellis Boyce	Norton	24m. 04s	94.06 mph

1958

Swamped with entries again in 1958, the Club organised an additional race, named the Snaefell Race, for 500cc and 350cc machines over four laps, and again both classes would race concurrently, with the fastest in each class gaining entries into the Manx proper. The race was due to be held on the Saturday, but bad weather caused a postponement to Monday. This was O.K. for the Senior riders, but the top 350cc riders would have to be ready to race in the Junior Manx the next day.

1958 Junior Snaefell Newcomers

The 350cc class had an original entry of 95, reduced by non-starters to 76. Gordon Bell had been fastest in practice at 84.31 mph, compared with the fastest lap in the 1957 Newcomers 350 of 87.21 mph set by Mike Brookes. It was Bell who led at the end of lap one by 48 seconds from K. Bannister (Norton), N. Bramhall (A.J.S.), Ginger Payne (Norton), Phil Read (Norton), making his TT course debut, and Jack Adam (Norton). Bell was an incredible two minutes and three seconds in front at the end of the second lap, and the new second place man was Payne, with Read third followed by Adam. On to the leaderboard came Ian Wallace (Norton) and N. Bramhall (A.J.S.). Bell increased his advantage by a further 27 seconds on the third lap, and the only change in the top six was that Bramhall moved up to fourth place. So Gordon Bell went on to win by two minutes and 54 seconds from Payne, Read was third. Adam regained his fourth place ahead of Bramhall and Wallace. There were 62 finishers, a very high percentage.

J. L. 'Ginger' Payne at Signpost Corner.

1958 Junior Snaefell (4 laps / 150.92 miles) 95 entries

1. Gordon Bell	Norton	1h. 47m. 41.6s	84.15 mph
2. Ginger Payne	Norton	1h. 50m. 35.4s	81.89 mph
3. Phil Read	Norton	1h. 51m. 09.8s	81.47 mph
Fastest lap			
Gordon Bell	Norton	26m. 43.8s	84.69 mph

1958 Senior Snaefell Newcomers

The Senior Snaefell race had 30 entries, but there were four non-starters, reducing the field to 26. David Williams (B.S.A.) led at the end of the first lap by just 3.6 seconds from P. Overton (B.S.A.) with John Griffiths (Norton) in third place, followed by Peter Richardson (Norton), John Holder (Norton) and G. C. Young (Norton). Overton took over first place at the end of the second lap by two point six seconds from Williams, Richardson moved up to third ahead of Griffiths, with Holder and Young still fifth and sixth. Williams was back in front on lap three by 27 seconds from Richardson, Griffiths was third, Overton had dropped to fourth, Young was fifth and B. Betts (Norton) came on to the leaderboard in sixth place. Richardson, who had moved up one place on each of the first three laps, did it again on the last lap to snatch victory from Williams by eight point two seconds, whilst Griffiths, Overton, Betts and Young completed the top six. There were 19 finishers.

1958 Senior Snaefell (4 laps / 150.92 miles) 30 entries

1. Peter Richardson	Norton	1h. 46m. 28s	85.06 mph
2. David Williams	B.S.A.	1h. 46m. 36.2s	84.95 mph
3. John Griffiths	Norton	1h. 47m. 37.4s	84.21 mph
Fastest lap			
D. Williams	B.S.A.	25m. 56.6s	87.26 mph

1958 Junior MGP

There were 94 entries for the Junior, but with 13 non-starters, the first 19 in the 350 Snaefell race were accepted to bring the starting line up to 100. The race turned into a start to finish victory for a rider who had come so close in previous years, Alan Shepherd (A.J.S.), and there were remarkably few retirements to leaderboard men throughout the race. At the end of lap one, Shepherd led Ernie Washer (Norton) by 10 seconds, Eddie Crooks (Norton) was a further 14 seconds down in third place, followed by John Lewis (Norton), Ned Minihan (Norton) and T. R. Graham (Norton). Lap two saw Shepherd increase his lead to 43 seconds, with Washer now second, Lewis third, Crooks fourth, Minihan fifth and Tom Thorp (Norton) sixth. At half distance the lead was 30 seconds, with Crooks back up to second, Minihan third, Washer fourth, followed by Lewis and Thorp. By the end of lap four Shepherd's advantage was 60 seconds from Crooks with Washer third ahead of Lewis, Minihan and Thorp. A further eight seconds were added to Shepherd's lead on lap five, with Crooks, Washer and Lewis retaining their places, and they were joined in the top six by John Righton (Norton) and Bob Dowty (Norton). Shepherd slowed on the last lap but still won the race by 48 seconds from Crooks, with Washer third. John Lewis held his fourth place, Bob Dowty took fifth and Jack Adam (Norton) came into sixth place. Gordon Bell, the 350 Snaefell winner finished in 11th place. There were 57 finishers and 30 riders won replicas.

1958 Junior MGP (6 laps / 226.38 miles) 100 entries

1. Alan Shepherd	A.J.S.	2h. 32m. 30.4s	89.08 mph
2. Eddie Crooks	Norton	2h. 33m. 18.2s	88.61 mph
3. Ernie Washer	Norton	2h. 33m. 37.8s	88.42 mph

Fastest lap

Alan Shepherd	A.J.S.	24m. 59.4s	90.58 mph

1958 Senior MGP

Of the 95 entries for the Senior, 14 were non-starters, allowing the top 19 finishers in the 500 Snaefell to compete, bringing the field up to the maximum 100. Junior third place man Ernie Washer (Norton) had topped the practice leaderboard followed by Bob Dowty (Norton), John Lewis (Norton), Eddie Crooks (Norton), Alan Shepherd (Norton) and Tony Godfrey (Norton). The weather conditions were perfect. At the end of lap one, Junior winner Alan Shepherd (Norton) led Bob Dowty (Norton) by three point four seconds, with Tony Godfrey (Norton) a further nine seconds down. The top six were completed by Ernie Washer (Norton), Ned Minihan (Norton) and Eddie Crooks (Norton). Shepherd was nine seconds in front at the end of lap two, and Godfrey and Washer were tying for second place, Dowty had dropped to fourth, only two point six seconds down, Crooks was fifth and Mike Brookes (Norton) came into sixth place. It was still tight at half distance, Shepherd was just 11.2 seconds in front of Dowty, who was nine seconds up on Washer, Godfrey had dropped to fourth, with Crooks and Brookes still in the top six. Shepherd had opened up a 30 second gap by the end of lap four, Washer was up to second place, Crooks third, Dowty fourth, Minihan fifth and John Hurlstone had come into sixth spot. Washer really motored on lap five and halved Shepherd's lead to 15 seconds with just one lap to go. Crooks was still third, but Hurlstone had passed both Minihan and Dowty. But just when it looked as if Alan Shepherd was going to be the fourth rider in succession to complete a Manx double, came the news that he had retired with engine trouble at Laurel Bank. With a lap record on his final lap at 94.40 mph, Washer left us with the question, would he have won even if Shepherd had finished? Washer's winning margin over Crooks was one minute 48 seconds, with Minihan third, Hurlstone fourth, Dowty fifth and Mike Kelly (Norton) sixth. David Williams (B.S.A.), runner up in the Senior Snaefell race finished 11th. There were 55 finishers and 22 replicas were won.

Ernie Washer at speed on Glencrutchery Road.

1958 Senior MGP (6 laps / 226.38 miles) 100 entries

1. Ernie Washer	Norton	2h. 26m. 09.8s	92.94 mph (record)
2. Eddie Crooks	Norton	2h. 27m. 27.0s	91.81 mph
3. Ned Minihan	Norton	2h. 29m. 15.0s	91.02 mph

Fastest lap (record)

Ernie Washer	Norton	23m. 58.8s	94.40 mph

1959

1959 Junior MGP

So nearly a winner - Tom Thorp at Cronk ny Mona.

The race programme for the 1959 Manx reverted to a two-race meeting, the Junior and Senior. The entry for the Junior was fantastic, 132, and with just 10 non-starters, there would be 122 starters. The Junior record had not been beaten in practice, John Lewis had been fastest on his Norton. He was followed by David Williams (Norton), Mike Brookes (Norton), Phil Read (Norton), Jack Adam (Norton) and Derek Williams (A.J.S.). Weather conditions were reasonable, but sea fog on the lower stretches of the course slowed the pace somewhat. Local rider Eddie Crooks, (Norton) set the early pace and at the end of lap one led Tom Thorp (Norton) by 10 seconds, with Peter Middleton (Norton) a further 20 seconds down in third place. John Lewis (Norton) was fourth, Mike Brookes (Norton) fifth and Ron Langston (Norton) sixth. Lap two saw Crooks increase his lead over Thorp to 13 seconds, with Middleton still third, but now 55 seconds adrift of the second place man. Lewis was still fourth, but Brookes had retired at Union Mills, so Langston moved up to fifth and Tony Godfrey (A.J.S.) came up to sixth. But the race was over for Eddie Crooks on lap three when he retired with mechanical problems, so Thorp took over the lead from Lewis by one minute 17 seconds, with Middleton third, Langston fourth. Derek Williams (A.J.S.) fifth and Mike Kelly (Norton) sixth. John Lewis's second place didn't last long, he retired at the Bungalow with engine problems on the fourth lap. Thorp now led the race from Middleton by one minute 32 seconds, with Langston, Bob Ritchie (A.J.S.), Godfrey and Ellis Boyce (Norton) completing the leaderboard. Thorp added a further two seconds to his lead at the end of the fifth lap, Langston was still third, but Godfrey and Boyce had both passed Ritchie.

Then, as often happens on the last lap of a race on the TT course, drama struck. With a comfortable lead, Thorp struck trouble at the Bungalow, he managed to free wheel and push his way to the finish and took equal 44th place, what really bad luck. So Peter Middleton went on to win from Ron Langston by 54 seconds, and Ritchie took third place. Ellis Boyce (Norton), Tony Godfrey (A.J.S.) and Cyril Huxley (A.J.S.) completed the top six. There were 78 finishers and 40 riders won replicas.

1959 Junior MGP (6 laps / 226.38 miles) 132 entries

1. Peter Middleton	Norton	2h. 33m. 06s	88.73 mph
2. Ron Langston	Norton	2h. 34m. 00s	88.20 mph
3. Bob Ritchie	A.J.S.	2h. 34m. 05s	87.66 mph
Fastest lap			
Eddie Crooks	Norton	24m. 54.6s	90.89 mph

1959 Senior MGP

Eddie Crooks speeds through Union Mills.

The Senior had also attracted an entry of 132, but there were 26 non-starters, leaving 106 riders to face the starter in perfect conditions. Mike Brookes (Norton) had topped the practice leaderboard followed by John Lewis (Norton) and Eddie Crooks (Norton) and all three were faster than the lap record. The top six in practice were completed by Phil Read (Norton), Roy Mayhew (Matchless) and Peter Middleton (Norton). Junior winner Peter Middleton led at the end of the first lap from Tom Thorp by six seconds, with Eddie Crooks third, eight seconds down. John Lewis, Tony Godfrey (Norton) and Ellis Boyce (Norton) completed the top six. The records began to go on lap two, firstly Thorp in 23m. 41s., Crooks in 23m. 40.8s. Thorp therefore took the lead from Crooks by seven seconds, and Middleton had dropped to fourth, 16 seconds down on Crooks, with the other places unchanged. Crooks turned on the power on the third lap with another record - 23m. 31.2s. 96.30 mph - the fastest lap of the race, and snatched the lead from Thorp by just 3.8 seconds. With Middleton now over one minute down in third place. Ned Minihan (Matchless) is now fourth, Lewis fifth and Alan Rutherford (Norton) is sixth. Crooks increased his lead on lap four to 24 seconds from Thorp, Middleton was still third with Minihan, Rutherford and Boyce making up the top six. At the end of the fifth lap, Crooks added four seconds to his lead over Thorp, but Middleton, who had had a long pit stop at the end of the fourth lap adjusting his rear wheel, had dropped to sixth, with Minihan third, Rutherford fourth and Boyce fifth. So Eddie Crooks, who had had a consistent Manx career, finally achieved his ambition and won from Tom Thorp by 30.6 seconds with Minihan third. The top six were completed by Rutherford, Boyce and Middleton. There were 62 finishers and 25 replicas were won.

1959 Senior MGP (6 laps / 226.38 miles) 132 entries

1. Eddie Crooks	Norton	2h. 23m. 11.4s	94.87 mph
			(record)
2. Tom Thorp	Norton	2h. 23m. 42.0s	94.53 mph
3. Ned Minihan	Norton	2h. 27m. 27.6s	92.12 mph
Fastest lap (record)			
Eddie Crooks	Norton	23m. 31.2s	96.30 mph

1960

1960 Junior MGP

Entries for the Junior numbered 110, but 13 non-starters reduced the field to 97. Weather conditions on the Tuesday were described as dreadful, and an early decision to postpone the race until Wednesday was made, and it proved to be absolutely right as Wednesday gave perfect conditions.

No one had come near the record in practice, Colin Huxley (A.J.S.) had been fastest, followed by Bob Ritchie (A.J.S.), Derek Williams (A.J.S.), Ned Minihan A.J.S.), Jack Adam (Norton) and Phil Read (Norton). Two of the possibles went out on the first lap, Phil Read at Ramsey with engine trouble - a dropped valve - and Ned Minihan at Crosby with a seized engine. Ron Langston (Norton) led at the end of lap one with a lap in 25 minutes, some 26 seconds ahead of Ellis Boyce (Norton), who in turn was 19 seconds ahead of David Williams (Norton). They were followed by Robin Dawson (A.J.S.), Ian Wallace (Norton) and Roy Mayhew (A.J.S.). Langston broke the lap record which had stood since 1956 on his second lap, 24m. 42s. - 91.69 mph and increased his lead over Boyce to over 40 seconds, Mayhew moved up to third place, almost one minute down on Boyce, Wallace remained fourth; with Williams and Dawson dropping to fifth and sixth. At half distance Langston increased his lead over Boyce to 90 seconds and Mayhew was just 30 seconds down in third place. Wallace was

Ellis Boyce at Quarter Bridge.

still fourth, one minute down, Ginger Payne (A.J.S.) and Bob Ritchie (A.J.S.) came on to the leaderboard with Dawson dropping to eighth. Williams had problems and never regained a leaderboard place, finishing eventually 21st. Then sensation on lap four, Langston was out - he retired at Barregarrow with engine trouble. This gave Boyce a comfortable lead over Mayhew of one minute 18 seconds, with Wallace third, 38 seconds down. Colin Huxley (A.J.S.) came up to fourth place, Dawson came back on the leaderboard in fifth place, and sixth place was taken by Frank Reynolds (A.J.S.). The order remained exactly the same on lap five, and the only change on the last lap was that Reynolds retired at Guthries with a seized engine. So Ellis Boyce won by 72 seconds from Mayhew, Wallace was third, Huxley fourth, Dawson fifth and Ritchie sixth. There were 62 finishers and 32 replicas were won.

1960 Junior MGP (6 laps / 226.38 miles)   110 entries

1. Ellis Boyce	Norton	2h. 30m. 52.0s	90.04 mph (record)
2. Roy Mayhew	A.J.S.	2h. 32m. 04.8s	89.32 mph
3. Ian Wallace	Norton	2h. 33m. 08.0s	88.71 mph
Fastest lap (record)			
Ron Langston	A.J.S.	24m. 42s	91.69 mph

1960 Senior MGP

The Senior attracted 120 entries, the maximum permitted, and with 14 non-starters, 106 riders faced the starter in good weather conditions. Jack Adam (Norton) topped the practice leaderboard, just 17 seconds outside the record and six seconds faster than Phil Read (Norton), third was Ron Langston (Matchless) followed by Mike Brookes (Norton), Peter Darvill (Norton) and the Junior winner Ellis Boyce (Norton). Phil Read, No. 34, appeared to be going really well on the first lap, and at the end of it he was leading with a lap in 23m. 40.2s. - just nine seconds outside the record from a standing start. He was leading Jack Adam (Norton) by 25 seconds with David Williams (Norton) third, just 4.6 seconds down. Fourth was Ned Minihan (Norton), fifth Ellis Boyce (Norton) and sixth Ginger Payne (Matchless). Read set a new record on lap two, 23m. 19s. - 97.09 mph and increased his lead over Adam to 43 seconds, Williams, Minihan and Boyce retained their places, but Roy Mayhew (Matchless) replaced Payne in sixth place. At half distance, Read was almost a minute up on Adam, who in turn was over a minute ahead of Boyce. Minihan, Mayhew and Mike Brookes (Norton) completed the top six. But Boyce had a very long pit stop, changed plugs, and had a long push to get away, this dropped him right down the field and he finished in 28th position. Williams and Brookes both retired, at Barregarrow and the pits respectively, so the lap four leaderboard read, Read, 59 seconds in front of Adam, Minihan, one minute 34 seconds down in third place, Roy Mayhew, Ian Wallace (Norton), and Mike Kelly (Norton). Read extended his lead by a further 12 seconds on the fifth lap, Mayhew moved ahead of Minihan, and Kelly overtook Wallace. No drama on the final lap, Read beat Adam by one minute 26.2 seconds, Roy Mayhew followed his second place in the Junior with a fine third place, with Ned Minihan, Mike Kelly and Ian Wallace completing the top six leaderboard. There were 62 finishers, and 20 riders won replicas.

1960 Senior MGP (6 laps / 226.38 miles)   120 entries

1. Phil Read	Norton	2h. 22m. 25.0s	95.38 mph (record)
2. Jack Adam	Norton	2h. 23m. 51.2s	94.43 mph
3. Roy Mayhew	Matchless	2h. 25m. 26.4s	93.40 mph
Fastest lap			
Phil Read	Norton	23m. 19s	97.09 mph

1961

The scoreboard clocks had a new look this year, being reduced to four places on the course, the Start, Glen Helen, Ramsey and the Bungalow, with the scoreboard light still coming on when the rider has passed Signpost Corner.

1961 Junior MGP

There were 110 entries for the Junior, the maximum permitted now by the Manx Club. and non-starters reduced this number to 102, as compared to 97 last year. The forecast was not too promising, cloudy with hill fog patches, with rain and drizzle at times. However there was no delay to the start, and the race got under way promptly at 10.45 a.m., with Vern Wallis (Velocette) starting the proceedings. The likely winners appeared to be Fred Neville (A.J.S.), Roy Mayhew (A.J.S.), Derek Woodman (A.J.S.), Frank Reynolds (Norton) and Denis Pratt (Norton) who were all on the practice leaderboard, with Neville's best lap at 92.38 mph The rains came however and conditions were far from good as could be judged by the first lap speeds. Fred Neville led with a lap in 27m. 23s. - 82.70 mph - 27 seconds ahead of Frank Reynolds with Roy Mayhew third. The top six were completed by Robin Dawson (A.J.S.), Bob Ritchie (Norton) and D. E. Watson (Norton). The gap between the two leaders narrowed on lap two to 12 seconds, and the average speed of Neville dropped to 81.57 mph - Dawson passed Mayhew and Watson moved ahead of Ritchie. By the end of lap three there was a new leader, Neville took over from Reynolds by 31 seconds, Mayhew re-took third place from Dawson, Watson held on to fifth place and Alan Newstead (A.J.S.) came up to six place, improving on his 13th place at the end of the first lap. At the end of lap four, Neville was back in front of Reynolds with a lead of 22 seconds, Dawson was third ahead of Mayhew, Newstead was fifth and Watson sixth. Neville was turning on the power and by the time lap five was completed he had opened up a gap of just over two minutes on Reynolds, and increased the average speed to 82.29 mph, Dawson was now third. Newstead came up to fourth ahead of Mayhew with Watson sixth. But tragedy struck on the final lap when Fred Neville came off at Greeba Bridge, and received injuries which proved to be fatal. So Reynolds had a comfortable lead, and went on to win from Robin Dawson by over three minutes, with Alan Newstead taking third place. Denis Pratt was fourth followed by D. E. Watson and Gordon Bell (A.J.S.). There were 50 finishers, and 21 replicas were won.

1961 Junior MGP (6 laps / 226.38 miles)   110 entries

1. Frank Reynolds	A.J.S.	2h. 47m. 08.6s	81.28 mph
2. Robin Dawson	A.J.S.	2h. 50m. 11.2s	79.82 mph

3. Alan Newstead	A.J.S.	2h. 52m. 30.2s	78.75 mph
Fastest lap			
Fred Neville	A.J.S.	26m. 34.6s	85.22 mph

1961 Senior MGP

The maximum entry of 110 was again received for the Senior, but non-starters reduced the field to 92. The winner is likely to come from the top four in practice - Roy Mayhew (Matchless), David Williams (Norton), Ned Minihan (Norton) and Mike Kelly (Norton). The weather conditions were much improved, given as almost perfect, good visibility but a little on the cool side. At the end of lap one, Ned Minihan, winner of the 1957 Senior Newcomers race, led by 20 seconds from Roy Mayhew, with Junior winner Frank Reynolds (Norton) third. Mike Kelly was holding fourth ahead of David Williams and Joe Dunphy (Norton). A really close race was developing with just 40 seconds covering the first four at the end of the second lap. Minihan was just 4.2 seconds ahead of Mayhew, Williams was 30 seconds down on Mayhew, but just on fifth of a second ahead of Kelly, and Reynolds and Dunphy completed the top six. Mayhew took the lead from Minihan at the end of the third lap by 16 seconds, Williams was still third, just three seconds up on Kelly, with Reynolds and Dunphy still on the leaderboard. But it was not to be Mayhew's race, he retired on lap four at Ballaugh with engine trouble. So Minihan was back in front at the end of the lap by 73 seconds from Williams with Kelly 13 seconds down in third place. Robin Dawson (Norton) came on to the leaderboard in fourth place ahead of Dunphy, whilst Norman Price (Norton) took over sixth place. Minihan was 76 seconds ahead of Williams at the end of lap five, Kelly was 22 seconds down on Williams. Dawson maintained his fourth place but Price took fifth place from Dunphy. No drama on the final lap, Ned Minihan won by one minute 15 seconds from Dave Williams, Mike Kelly took third place, just 15 seconds down, and Dawson, Price and Dunphy completed the top six leaderboard. There were 64 finishers and 34 riders won replicas.

1961 Senior MGP (6 laps / 226.38 miles) 110 entries

1. Ned Minihan	Norton	2h. 24m. 59s	93.69 mph
2. Dave Williams	Norton	2h. 26m. 14s	92.89 mph
3. Mike Kelly	Norton	2h. 26m. 29s	92.73 mph
Fastest lap			
Roy Mayhew	Matchless	23m. 39.6s	95.66 mph

The end of an era - the last unfaired winner of the Manx. Ned Minihan heels into Signpost Corner.

The Manx Grand Prix
1962 - 1982

1962

There were a number of rule changes after the 1961 race meeting, the main alteration was that streamlining was allowed in Manx Grand Prix races for the first time.

1962 Junior MGP

Again the maximum number of entries were received for the Junior, but 13 non-starters reduced the field to 97. Dave Downer (Norton) was fastest in practice, followed by Peter Darvill (A.J.S.) and Joe Dunphy (A.J.S.). The weather early on Tuesday morning was atrocious, with torrential rain and mist. Conditions did slowly improve, and after an hours postponement the race got under way. Robin Dawson (A.J.S.) led at the end of the first lap by five seconds from David Williams (Norton) with Peter Darvill (A.J.S.) third, 11 seconds down. Fourth place was taken by Fred Fisher (Norton), with Joe Dunphy (A.J.S.) and Neil Kelly (A.J.S.) completing the leaderboard. Another Kelly, Mike, came off at Creg-ny-Baa, but remounted and continued. Fisher put in a quick lap second time round and moved into second place, just three seconds down on Dawson, Darvill remained third, but another local rider Dennis Craine (Norton) came into fourth place followed by Selwyn Griffiths (A.J.S.) and Dave Downer (Norton). Joe Dunphy had dropped to seventh place, and a spill at Sulby Bridge had dropped Neil Kelly back to 12th place. Fisher took the lead at half distance, by 11.4 seconds from Darvill, with Dawson third, Craine fourth, Griffiths fifth and Alan Hunter (Norton) sixth. Dunphy had retired with mechanical problems. By the time the fourth lap had been completed, pit stops had levelled out, and Dawson was back in front of Darvill by 11.2 seconds, and Dawson in turn was 30.6 seconds ahead of Fisher. Griffiths had moved ahead of Craine, and Mike Kelly came on to the leaderboard in place of Hunter who was seventh. Dawson increased his lead to 30 seconds on the fifth lap and the only change to the top six was that Kelly took fifth place from Craine in the battle of the locals. The top six retained their positions on the final lap, Robin Dawson won by 42.4 seconds from Peter Darvill, Fred Fisher finished third ahead of Selwyn Griffiths, Mike Kelly and Dennis Craine. There were 62 finishers and 26 replicas were won.

Leaderboard men for the 1962 Junior Manx. Winner Robin Dawson (A.J.S., 106) is flanked by Peter Darvill (A.J.S., 100) and Fred Fisher (Norton, 7) right. Reg Dearden, for many years a sponsor and supporter of the Manx, is to Fisher's right.

1962 Junior MGP (6 laps / 226.38 miles) 110 entries

1. Robin Dawson	A.J.S.	2h. 32m. 36.0s	89.02 mph
2. Peter Darvill	A.J.S.	2h. 33m. 18.4s	88.61 mph
3. Fred Fisher	Norton	2h. 34m. 16.0s	88.06 mph

Fastest lap (record)

Robin Dawson	A.J.S.	24m. 38.6s	91.87 mph

1962 Senior MGP

Joe Dunphy at Signpost Corner.

Entries for the Senior did not quite reach the maximum of 110, 106 was the number, and of these 94 faced the starter.

Peter Darvill (Norton) had been fastest in practice, 10 seconds faster than David Williams (Norton), followed by Fred Fisher (Norton), Joe Dunphy (Norton), Robin Dawson (Matchless) and Gordon Bell (Matchless). Weather conditions were reasonable, but it started to rain midway through the race. David Williams set the early pace with a lap in 23m. 47.4s. (95.16 mph) to lead Joe Dunphy by 13 seconds with Fred Fisher a further eight seconds down in third place. Robin Dawson was fourth, Peter Darvill fifth and B. Lindley (Matchless) sixth. On lap two, with the fastest lap of the race at 96.79 mph Dunphy took the lead from Williams by four seconds, Fisher, Dawson and Darvill were next, and Norman Price (Norton) came into sixth spot in place of Lindley. There was no change in the top three at the end of the third lap, Dunphy had increased his lead to 14 seconds, but Darvill had got in front of Dawson. On lap four, Dunphy was increasing his lead, but over a new second place man, Fisher having overtaken Williams by 6.2 seconds, Darvill, Dawson and Price completed the top six. On lap five Dunphy had a comfortable lead over Fisher of 68 seconds and Darvill had overtaken Williams, Dawson was still fifth and Mike Kelly (Norton) came into sixth place. Fred Fisher's race ended at Rhencullen on the last lap when he retired with gearbox trouble, so Joe Dunphy (Norton) won at 91.83 mph from Peter Darvill (Norton), with David Williams (Norton) third. Robin Dawson (Matchless) took fourth place with Mike Kelly (Norton) repeating his fifth place in the Junior, and Norman Price (Norton) held on to sixth place. There were 57 finishers and 20 riders won replicas.

1962 Senior MGP (6 laps / 226.38 miles) 106 entries

1. Joe Dunphy	Norton	2h. 27m. 54.8s	91.83 mph
2. Peter Darvill	Norton	2h. 29m. 30.4s	90.86 mph
3. David Williams	Norton	2h. 30m. 27.6s	90.29 mph

Fastest lap

Joe Dunphy	Norton	23m. 38s	96.79 mph

1963

1963 Junior MGP

Finally a winner, Peter Darvill takes his 7R out of Parliament Square, Ramsey.

Entries for the Junior totalled 107, but non-starters reduced the field to 97. Peter Darvill (A.J.S.), runner-up in both races last year headed the practice leaderboard from Alan Hunter (A.J.S.) David Williams (A.J.S.), Selwyn Griffiths (A.J.S.), Mike Kelly (Norton) and Jimmy Guthrie (Norton). Williams, however had changed to a Norton for the race. Riders were warned that the roads were wet all around the course, especially the Ballacraine to Glen Helen section, but that the strong winds should have dried out the mountain section before the first man reached there. Despite these conditions, Peter Darvill set a fast pace and lapped at 91.48 mph to lead Alan Hunter by 25 seconds, with David Williams third, eight seconds down on Hunter. Gordon Bell (A.J.S.) was fourth, Selwyn Griffiths fifth and Griff Jenkins (A.J.S.) sixth. Darvill broke the lap record on lap two to increase his lead over Hunter to almost one minute, Williams, Bell and Griffiths held their places, but Bill Fulton (Norton) displaced Jenkins in sixth place. By half distance, Darvill was leading Hunter by one minute 19 seconds, Griffiths moved up to third and Fulton took fourth place. John Evans (Norton) came up into fifth place and Brian Warburton (Norton) to sixth, with Williams down to seventh and Jenkins to 11th. The first three remained the same on lap four, with Darvill stretching his lead, Williams came up to fourth place, Warburton was fifth and Jenkins came back into the top six. Strangely enough, for Manx races, the order remained unchanged on laps five and six, so Peter Darvill won from Alan Hunter by one minute and 13 seconds, with Selwyn Griffiths third, David Williams fourth, Brian Warburton fifth and Griff Jenkins sixth. There were 66 finishers and 35 of them won replicas.

1963 Junior MGP (6 laps / 226.38 miles) 107 entries

1. Peter Darvill	A.J.S.	2h. 26m. 53.8s	92.48 mph

The History of the Manx Grand Prix 1923-1998

				(record)
2. Alan Hunter	A.J.S.	2h. 28m. 06.6s	91.72 mph	
3. Selwyn Griffiths	A.J.S.	2h. 28m. 39.2s	91.38 mph	
Fastest lap (record)				
Peter Darvill	A.J.S.	24m. 07s	93.87 mph	

1963 Senior MGP

Griff Jenkins at Bedstead Corner.

Entries for the Senior were slightly down on previous years, 99, and non-starters reduced the field to 84. Weather conditions were described as 'not to bad' for the race, and with it proving to be a record breaker, this was perhaps an understatement! Roger Hunter (Matchless) had been fastest in practice, 11 seconds faster than David Williams (Norton). Junior winner Peter Darvill (Norton) was third, followed by Ron Chandler (Matchless), Selwyn Griffiths (Matchless) and Griff Jenkins (Norton). It was Williams who led at the end of lap one, just 3.4 seconds faster than Hunter with Jenkins third, 13 seconds slower. Griffiths, Darvill and Mike Kelly (Norton) completed the leaderboard. Williams broke the lap record on lap two by 11 seconds - 23m. 08.2s. - and increased his lead over Hunter to seven seconds and the rest of the leaderboard was unchanged. Lap three saw another record from Williams - 23m. 3.4s. - 98.18 mph and his lead over Hunter increased to 16 seconds, Jenkins was still third, but Selwyn Griffiths retired at the Bungalow, Darvill took over fourth place, Kelly moved up to fifth and Ron Chandler (Matchless) came into sixth place. Hunter took over the lead from Williams at the end of lap four - by just eight-tenths of a second! Williams however pulled into his pit suffering from cramp - he recovered and got away in just over two minutes. Meanwhile Jenkins and Darvill remained third and fourth, but Mike Kelly had retired after a spill at Waterworks, so Chandler was now fifth and Denis Craine (Norton) came up to sixth. Due to Williams stop, Hunter had a comfortable lead at the end of the fifth lap of 79 seconds over Jenkins, Darvill was still third, just 11 seconds down on Jenkins, Chandler, Craine and Chris Williams (Norton) made up the top six. Williams race ended on this fifth lap when he walked to Glentrammon and reported that his engine had seized. But there was more drama to come - Hunter was reported to be late at Sulby Bridge, and eventually went out at the Gooseneck - out of petrol. So Griff Jenkins, who had been third for the first four laps won at a record breaking speed of 96.10 mph from Peter Darvill by just 26 seconds, Jimmy Guthrie (Norton) the son of the late great Jimmy Guthrie brought his Norton into third place. He was followed by Bob McGregor (Norton) in fourth place. Dennis Craine (Norton) came off at the Gooseneck on the last lap but quickly remounted and held on to his fifth place with D. Phillips (Norton) coming into sixth place. It had been quite a race. There were 45 finishers and 18 replicas were won.

1963 Senior MGP (6 laps / 226.38 miles) 99 entries

1. Griff Jenkins	Norton	2h. 21m. 21.2s	96.10 mph
			(record)
2. Peter Darvill	Norton	2h. 21m. 47.2s	95.81 mph
3. Jimmy Guthrie	Norton	2h. 27m. 35.2s	92.04 mph
Fastest lap (record)			
David Williams	Norton	23m. 03.4s	98.18 mph

1964

1964 Lightweight MGP

Terry Grotefeld, Gordon Keith and Rex Butcher.

The 1964 Manx returned to being a three race meeting, with the re-introduction of the Lightweight, last held in 1948. And the return of the 250 class proved very popular, with an entry of 86, which was reduced by non-starters to 66. The fastest lap in practice had been set by Terry Grotefeld (Aermacchi) in 27m. 8.4s. - 83.43 mph compared to the record held by Dickie Dale (Guzzi) of 30m. 27s. - 74.36 mph set in 1948. Weather conditions were perfect for the four lap Lightweight race held on the Tuesday morning, and for the first time in the Manx, riders were were started in pairs at 10 second intervals, as opposed to singularly in the past. It was Southern Rhodesian Gordon Keith (Greeves) who led at the end of the first lap from George Collis (Yamaha) by 10 seconds. Rex Butcher (Aermacchi) was third just five seconds down on Collis, with Chris Fenton (Aermacchi), Terry Grotefeld (Aermacchi) and Gerry Borland (Aermacchi) completing the leaderboard. By the end of lap two Keith had increased his lead to 29 seconds and Butcher had moved up to second place, ahead of Collis, Grotefeld, Fenton and Borland. Lap three saw the first leaderboard retirement when Fenton retired, the first four remained the same with Keith's lead up to 53 seconds, and John Blanchard (Aermacchi) came into fifth place with Borland still sixth. The fastest lap of the race, and obviously a new record

Well, what would you have done? - by Doug Rose

Well, what would you have done?

I suppose it was because I was just as interested in developing a racing machine as I was in riding the thing, and as I was hardly likely to be able to improve on Joe Craig's work, thoughts fell to different capacity machines.

As my build and weight suited the smaller, lighter class, an MOV 248cc Velocette was acquired and much development poured into it. The little machine acquired Teledraulic forks and a swinging arm frame. The enhanced mechanicals included special cams, hairpin valvesprings, high-compression piston, close-ratio gears, etc., etc. After full development this little machine was capable of nearly 100 mph using alcohol fuel and brought me good results at Cadwell, Mallory, Osmaston, Silverstone etc.

By this time a Mk VIII KTT Velocette had been acquired, but in the late 50s this proved to be uncompetitive, so a decision was made to build a lightweight frame to house the MK VIII gearbox and engine which was converted to 248cc capacity. After some initial snags this machine proved very reliable and was good enough to give me third place in the 1960 Southern 100.

In 1961 Honda brought to the UK a limited number of their 250cc twin cylinder CB72s. Now with development, what could we do with one of these? Even special race parts were promised, so in anticipation, one of these models was acquired. Unfortunately the race kit turned out to be a pair of megaphones, various sprockets and that's about all, but by the time we had fitted a pair of Mk II Amals, modified camshafts and raised compression ratio, we had a really competitive little bike.

Acquaintance with the Isle of Man Mountain circuit had been made in 1952 with an attempt at the Clubman's TT and the MGP, the machine being a 'specially built for the Clubman's' 350cc BSA Gold Star. This plunger-framed beast gave me a lowly 33rd place in the Clubman's, due partly to a badly slipping clutch and a N.F. in the Manx due to failure of the clutch sprocket at Glen Helen on the last lap. And what a headache I had on the following day due to 'hospitality' in the Glen Helen!

The magic of the mountain had been injected. What would it be like to ride the little Honda round the TT course? But there wasn't a 250 Manx and hadn't been for years. Well let's try to change this.

During the 1963 Manx week a meeting was held of all the known and interested 250 riders, and a letter was composed and sent to the Manx Club requesting the reinstatement of the 250 class. Early in 1964 it was announced that the Lightweight class would be in the programme for that year.

But it was also announced that the cut-off age for competitors would be 40 - and I already exceeded that age.

What would you have done?

Confession time. Instead of being D. R. Rose, Electrician, born 13.8.22, I suddenly became D. Rose, Steel tube maker, born 1.6.25 - and got away with it, but only for one year!

Yes, the little Honda finished the course. One megaphone broke off on the second lap at Quarter Bridge (see below) which dropped the revs from 10,000 to 8,500, but I received a solid silver (yes, they were solid silver in those days) finishers award for finishing in 27th place.

And that is why my name appears twice in the 'History of the Manx Grand Prix' - and I think I must be one of the very few people with *two* M.G.P. Competitors Badges, one with a date bar 1952 and the other with a date bar 1964.

Top: D. R. Rose, 1952 Junior, Governors Bridge. Right: D. Rose 1964 Lightweight, Quarter Bridge. Spot the difference! Most of the nearside megaphone on the Honda is just about to depart!

was set by Keith on his final lap in 25m. 50.4s. - 87.61 mph, and he won by one minute 16 seconds from Rex Butcher, Terry Grotefeld moved up to third ahead of John Blanchard, George Collis and Gerry Borland. There were 56 finishers and 16 riders won replicas.

1964 Lightweight MGP (4 laps / 150.92 miles) 86 entries

1. Gordon Keith	Greeves	1h. 45m. 04.8s	86.19 mph
			(record)
2. Rex Butcher	Aermacchi	1h. 46m. 21.0s	85.15 mph
3. Terry Grotefeld	Aermacchi	1h. 49m. 00.6s	83.08 mph
Fastest lap (record)			
Gordon Keith	Greeves	25m. 50.4s	87.61 mph

1964 Junior MGP

Conditions remained perfect for the Junior, held on the Tuesday afternoon, the race had attracted 110 entries, and with 10 non-starters, exactly 100 riders faced the starter. David Williams (MW Special), runner up in last years Senior, set the pace from the beginning and at the end of the first lap had an advantage of six seconds from George Buchan (Norton), who in turn was just one second ahead of Malcolm Uphill (A.J.S.), Selwyn Griffiths (A.J.S.) was fourth just three seconds down on Uphill and Jimmy Guthrie (Norton) and Tom Holdsworth (A.J.S.) completed the leaderboard - there were just 38 seconds separating the first six. By the end of lap two, Williams was 27 seconds ahead of Buchan who was just one second up on Uphill, Griffiths remained fourth, Guthrie was fifth and Mike Kelly (A.J.S.) came into sixth place with Holdsworth dropping to eighth. At half distance Williams was 33 seconds ahead, but Uphill was now second, with Buchan third, Kelly up to fourth, Dave Degens (A.J.S.) fifth and Bill Milne (A.J.S.) sixth. The gap between Williams and Uphill at the end of the fourth lap was 50 seconds, with Buchan still third, Kelly fourth, Neil Pendreigh (Norton) fifth and Degens sixth. Milne had dropped to seventh and retired on lap five. The first four remained unchanged at the end of the fifth lap, Bill Fulton (A.J.S.) came up to fifth with Pendreigh in sixth place. So Williams, after seven appearances, went on to win at a record speed of 92.54 mph, but his fastest lap was just 1.2 seconds outside the record. Malcolm Uphill took second place with George Buchan third. Fourth place went Mike Kelly, Bill Fulton was fifth and Neil Pendreigh was sixth. There were 52 finishers and 19 replicas were won.

1964 Junior MGP (6 laps / 226.38 miles) 110 entries

1. David Williams	MW Special	2h. 26m. 47.0s	92.54 mph
			(record)
2. Malcolm Uphill	A.J.S.	2h. 27m. 25.2s	92.15 mph
3. George Buchan	Norton	2h. 28m. 07.8s	91.71 mph
Fastest lap			
David Williams	MW Special	24m. 08.2s	93.79 mph

Buchan missed seeing the chequered flag and set off on a seventh lap, he was eventually stopped at Ramsey, and he toured back to the finish.

1964 Senior MGP

The Senior attracted an entry of 100, but non-starters reduced this number to 84. Selwyn Griffiths (Matchless) had been fastest in practice in 23m. 40.6s., 57 seconds faster than Malcolm Uphill (Norton). The top six were completed by Mike Kelly (Norton), Rex Butcher (Norton), John Sear (Matchless) and D. Reid (Norton). Race day, and the conditions were fine, warmer than on Tuesday. Lap one saw Selwyn Griffiths take the lead by 15 seconds from George Buchan (Norton), Rex Butcher, Bill Fulton (Matchless) and Mike Kelly. Griffiths increased his lead over Buchan to 23 seconds on lap two, Fulton took third place from Buchan, and Uphill and Kelly remained fifth and sixth. At the end of lap three, half distance, Griffiths led Buchan by 23 seconds with Fulton third. Kelly had moved up to fourth, with Uphill fifth and Reid sixth, with Butcher just off the leaderboard. The only change on lap four was Butcher retaking fourth place from Kelly, and Reid dropped to seventh. But Bill Fulton's fine race ended at Union Mills on lap five when he was forced out with engine trouble. Griffiths still led Buchan, and these two were pulling ahead of the field. Kelly was up to third, just 5.2 seconds ahead of Butcher with Uphill and Reid completing the leaderboard. So Selwyn Griffiths won his Manx by 30.4 seconds from George Buchan, local rider Mike Kelly finished a fine third. Butcher was fourth, but Uphill and Reid both went out on the last lap, bringing Randall Cowell (Norton) and Robin Good (Matchless) into the top six. There 34 finishers and 11 replicas were won.

Selwyn Griffiths at Governors, just ahead of George Buchan

1964 Senior MGP (6 laps / 226.38 miles) 100 entries

1. Selwyn Griffiths	Matchless	2h. 21m. 06.0s	96.27 mph
2. George Buchan	Norton	2h. 21m. 36.4s	95.93 mph
3. Mike Kelly	Norton	2h. 24m. 27.2s	94.04 mph
Fastest lap			
Selwyn Griffiths	Matchless	23m. 14.4s	97.41 mph

1965

1965 Lightweight MGP

The 1965 Lightweight attracted the maximum 110 entries, but non-starters reduced the field to 96. Hopes were high for a local win as two Manx riders featured on the practice leaderboard - Dennis Craine (Greeves) was fastest with Peter Williams (Greeves) second and another Manx rider Neil Kelly

(Royal Enfield) third. In good conditions, the lap record was broken on the opening lap, Brian Warburton (Yamaha) lapped at 88.66 mph to lead Dennis Craine by 6.8 seconds. Peter Williams was third, 22 seconds down on Craine, Kelly was in fourth place with Colin Fenton (Aermacchi) and John Wetherall (Cotton) completing the leaderboard. Craine broke the record again on lap two at 89.48 mph and led Warburton by nine seconds, Williams was some 43 seconds down in third place, followed by Fenton, Kelly and Ron Pladdys (Honda), Wetherall having retired. Lap three saw Craine increase his lead over Warburton to 24 seconds, and Kelly with a quick lap, moved up to third place, just five seconds down on Warburton, Williams, Fenton and Pladdys completed the top six. But Kelly's charge ended on the final lap when he retired at the Guthrie Memorial. Dennis Craine went on to score the first local victory since 1959 by 17.8 seconds from Brian Warburton, with Peter Williams third. The leaderboard was completed by Colin Fenton, Ray Ashcroft (Yamaha) and Ron Pladdys. There were 53 finishers and 20 riders won replicas

Victor and vanquished! Dennis Craine (left) and Brian Warburton in the winners enclosure.

1965 Lightweight MGP (4 laps / 150.92 miles) 110 entries

1. Dennis Craine	Greeves	1h. 42m. 29.0s	88.37 mph (record)
2. Brian Warburton	Yamaha	1h. 42m. 46.8s	88.12 mph
3. Peter Williams	Greeves	1h. 44m. 02.2s	87.05 mph
Fastest lap (record)			
Dennis Craine	Greeves	25m. 18.0s	89.48 mph

1965 Junior MGP

The Junior also attracted the maximum 110 entries, but by a strange coincidence, there were again 14 non-starters like the Lightweight, so 96 riders faced the starter. The practice leaderboard had been led by George Buchan (Norton), followed by Malcolm Uphill (A.J.S.) and John Lishman (A.J.S.) At the end of lap one Buchan led Uphill by 18 seconds with Joe Thornton (Norton) third a further 10 seconds down. Bill Milne (A.J.S.) was fourth, Colin Davey (Norton) fifth and Nigel Warren (Norton) sixth. With a record lap at 93.96 mph second time round, Buchan increased his lead to 45 seconds from Uphill with Thornton 32 seconds down. Warren moved up to third place, Davey remained fifth and Milne dropped to sixth. Buchan led at half distance by 25 seconds from Uphill who was 40 seconds ahead of the new third place man Warren, Thornton dropped to fourth, Milne was fifth and John Lishman (A.J.S.) came up to sixth. Buchan's race ended at Bishopscourt on lap four when he was forced out with engine trouble, so Uphill took the lead by 15 seconds from Warren, Thornton was third, 19 seconds down, followed by Milne, Lishman and George Logan (A.J.S.). A close finish looked in prospect at the end of lap five, Warren led Uphill by just three fifths of a second, Thornton was still third, but now 42 seconds down, Milne still held fourth place, and Logan moved ahead of Lishman. It looked as if another local victory was on the cards as Warren completed his final lap, but he was pipped at the line by Uphill who won by six seconds. Thornton held his third place, with Milne, Lishman and Jimmy Guthrie (Norton) completing the top six. There were 58 finishers and 25 replicas were won.

What would this lineup be worth today. The 1965 Junior entry after scrutineering in Mylchreest's Garage, Douglas.

1965 Junior MGP (6 laps / 226.38 miles) 110 entries			
1. Malcolm Uphill	A.J.S.	2h. 28m. 55.0s	91.22 mph
2. Nigel Warren	Norton	2h. 29m. 01.0s	91.16 mph
3. Joe Thornton	Norton	2h. 30m. 10.0s	90.46 mph
Fastest lap (record)			
George Buchan	Norton	24m. 05.6s	93.96 mph

1965 Senior MGP

The maximum entry of 110 was also received for the Senior, which was delayed due to heavy rain. There were 18 non-starters, reducing the field to 92. Keith Heckles (Norton) topped the practice leaderboard, followed by George Buchan (Norton) and Malcolm Uphill (Norton). Heckles led at the end of the first lap by 3.4 seconds from Uphill, who was 52 seconds in front of Buchan. Brian Warburton (Norton) was fourth, Jimmy Guthrie (Norton) fifth and Steve Spencer (Norton) sixth. Uphill took the lead on lap two by 33 seconds from Heckles with Buchan 11 seconds behind Heckles. Guthrie moved up to fourth place ahead of Warburton and Cyril Davey (Norton) came up into sixth place. Uphill increased his lead by half distance to 71 seconds, and Heckles was 39 seconds in front of Buchan, with the rest of the leaderboard unchanged. Heckles bad luck continued, and on lap four he retired at the Guthrie Memorial, giving Uphill a lead of two minutes 41 seconds over Buchan, who in turn was one minute 36 seconds up on Guthrie. Warburton and Spencer were fourth and fifth and Nigel Warren (Matchless) came into sixth place. Uphill was three minutes 12 seconds ahead of Buchan at the end of the fifth lap, and Buchan in turn had a comfortable lead of two minutes three seconds over Warburton, Guthrie had dropped to fourth, followed by Spencer and Warren. Both the leaders lapped in almost identical time on the final lap giving Malcolm Uphill a Manx double by three minutes 11.2 seconds from George Buchan. Brian Warburton finished third, two minutes and 45 seconds down, Jimmy Guthrie took fourth place, Steve Spencer fifth and Nigel Warren sixth. Cyril Davey, who had been on the leaderboard early in the race, finished 12th. There were 64 finishers, and 17 riders won replicas.

Malcolm Uphill splashes his way round Quarter Bridge on the first lap.

1965 Senior MGP (6 laps / 226.38 miles) 99 entries			
1. Malcolm Uphill	Norton	2h. 31m. 27.0s	89.69 mph
2. George Buchan	Norton	2h. 34m. 38.2s	87.85 mph
3. Brian Warburton	Norton	2h. 37m. 21.4s	86.33 mph
Fastest lap			
Malcolm Uphill	Norton	24m. 45.2s	91.46 mph

1966

The three race pattern continued in 1966, and the first race of the week as usual was the four-lap Lightweight, which attracted 107 entries.

1966 Lightweight MGP

Bob Farmer at speed on Glencrutchery Road.

John Wetherall (Cotton) had topped the practice leaderboard, followed by Neil Kelly (Royal Enfield) and Bob Farmer (Aermacchi). Wetherall confirmed his practice form by leading at the end of lap one by 16 seconds from Paul Smart (Greeves), who in turn led Alan Dickinson (D.M.W.) by 28 seconds. Don Padgett (Yamaha), Jimmy Guthrie (Greeves) and Bob Farmer completed the top six. Lap two saw Wetherall almost double his lead, he was 30 seconds ahead of Dickinson with Farmer up to third place. Smart had stopped at Glen Helen for 15 minutes making adjustments, he got going again but retired at Ramsey, Padgett was fourth, Martin Watson came on to the leaderboard in fifth place and Guthrie was sixth. Wetherall's lead was cut at the end of the third lap to fourteen seconds, and it was Farmer who was second, Dickinson third, Guthrie fourth. Ken Watson (Ducati) fifth and Brian Ball (B.A. Special) sixth. Padgett's race had ended with a retirement at Kerrowmooar. There was again drama on the last lap when the leader Wetherall retired at Kirk Michael, so Bob Farmer, who had been sixth on the first lap, won by one minute 15 seconds from Watson with Ball third, the top six were completed by Jimmy Guthrie, Martin Watson and Ernie Johnson (Aermacchi). There were 51 finishers and 21 replicas were won.

1966 Lightweight MGP (4 laps / 150.92 miles) 110 entries			
1. Bob Farmer	Aermacchi	1h. 45m. 03.6s	86.20 mph
2. Ken Watson	Ducati	1h. 46m. 18.0s	85.19 mph
3. Brian Ball	B.A. Special	1h. 46m. 55.0s	84.70 mph

Fastest lap				
John Wetherall	Cotton	25m. 25.6s	89.02 mph	

Amongst the finishers, in 19th place, on a Greeves, was a rider who went on to win eight TT Races, Chas. Mortimer.

1966 Junior MGP

The Junior entry of 110 had been reduced to 97 by non-starters. Alan Barnett (A.J.S.) had been fastest in practice, with Keith Heckles (Norton) next followed by Mick Bennett (Norton). George Buchan (Norton), who had been second in the 1964 and 1965 Senior races, made no mistake this time, leading the race from start to finish. At the end of lap one he led Heckles by 10 seconds, with Tom Dickie (A.J.S.) a further 25 seconds down. Bennett held fourth place, Cyril Davey (Norton) was fifth and Nigel Warren (A.J.S.) was sixth. The top three remained the same on lap two, Buchan had increased his lead by a further two seconds, and Heckles was pulling away from Dickie. Alan Barnett had jumped into fourth place with Davey and Warren still fifth and sixth. Buchan led Heckles by 28 seconds at half distance, and the only change to the top six was that Steve Spencer (Norton) took sixth place from Warren who had retired at the pits. On lap four the top six remained unchanged, and Buchan had doubled his advantage over Heckles to 56 seconds. By the end of lap five, he led by over one minute with Heckles, Dickie, Barnett maintaining their places, but Davey retired with clutch trouble, bringing Spencer up to fifth and Joe Thornton on to the leaderboard in sixth place. So, after missing out on the honours twice, George Buchan rode to a record breaking win with a new lap record for good measure. Keith Heckles finished second, one minute and 19 seconds down with Tom Dickie third, Alan Barnett, Steve Spencer and Joe Thornton completed the top six leaderboard. There were 55 finishers and 23 replicas were won.

1966 Junior MGP (6 laps / 226.38 miles) 110 entries

1. George Buchan	Norton	2h. 26m. 17.8s	92.86 mph (record)
2. Keith Heckles	Norton	2h. 27m. 36.4s	92.03 mph
3. Tom Dickie	A.J.S.	2h. 27m. 57.6s	91.81 mph
Fastest lap (record)			
George Buchan	Norton	24m. 03.8s	94.07 mph

1966 Senior MGP

The maximum entry of 110 was again received for the Senior, and with just 23 seconds covering the top three in practice, a close race was certainly in prospect. Keith Heckles (Norton) had topped the practice leaderboard followed by Alan Barnett (Matchless) and Junior winner George Buchan (Norton). Heckles led at the end of lap one by 12 seconds from Buchan with local rider Nigel Warren (Matchless) third, 24 seconds down. Brian Warburton (Norton) was fourth, Jimmy Guthrie (Norton) fifth and Alan Barnett (Matchless) sixth. But Heckles bad luck in the Manx struck again on lap two when he stopped at Barregaroo to make adjustments. He eventually restarted and rode on gamely to finish 25th. So George Buchan took the lead by 19 seconds from Warren who was 29 seconds ahead of Guthrie with Barnett, Warburton and Steve Spencer (Norton) completing the leaderboard. At half distance Buchan's lead over Warren had been cut to 16 seconds and Spencer moved up to third. Tom Dickie (Matchless), who had had a slow start due to plug trouble was now firing on all cylinders and came into fourth place ahead of Guthrie and Warburton, Barnett having retired just past Signpost Corner. Buchan's nearest challenger, Warren, retired on lap four at Union Mills, so he now had a lead of 52 seconds over Dickie who was 57 seconds up on Guthrie, with Spencer, Warburton and Roy Good (Matchless) filling the leaderboard. On lap five Dickie, who had started at No. 108, really started to fly and cut Buchan's lead back to just 21 seconds, Spencer had taken third place from Guthrie. Warburton remained fifth and Bill Milne (Matchless) came into sixth place. Buchan finished the race, and waited for Dickie to come in, and when he crossed the line, it was announced that he had snatched a dramatic last lap win by 11.2 seconds, robbing Buchan of a coveted Manx double. Steve Spencer finished third, Jimmy Guthrie fourth, Brian Davis (Matchless) fifth place ahead of Roy Good. Milne retired at Quarter Bridge on the last lap and Warburton just missed a top six place, finishing seventh. There were 48 finishers and 14 riders won replicas.

1966 Senior MGP (6 laps / 226.38 miles) 110 entries

1. Tom Dickie	Matchless	2h. 24m. 03.2s	94.30 mph
2. George Buchan	Norton	2h. 24m. 14.6s	94.18 mph
3. Steve Spencer	Norton	2h. 26m. 58.0s	92.43 mph
Fastest lap			

Showing a similar style at Ramsey Hairpin: George Buchan (left) and Keith Heckles (right), 1966 Senior.

| Tom Dickie | Matchless | 23m. 19.2s | 97.08 mph |

1967

1967 Lightweight MGP

From the maximum entry of 110 for the Lightweight, some 96 riders made it to the starting line. Frank Whiteway (Suzuki) was fastest in practice with an unofficial lap record in 24m. 54.2s. Neil Kelly (Kawasaki) was second fastest with Alan Dickinson (Kawasaki) third. But any thoughts of new records on race day were literally washed away. On the morning of the race there was torrential rain and gale force winds, and the start was delayed for one hour, and the distance reduced from four laps to three. Brian Ball (B.A. Special) led at the end of the first lap by 5.8 seconds from Whiteway who in turn was eight seconds ahead of Don Padgett (Yamaha). Cyril Davey (Aermacchi) was fourth, George Green (Yamaha) fifth and Bill Day (Greeves) sixth. Ball extended his lead at the end of the second lap to 25.8 seconds, and with the race length reduced was not going to have a pit stop, Whiteway, on the other hand had fitted a small tank, which meant even though the race was three laps, he would still have to stop, and it cost him 36 seconds. Padgett was still in third place, 10.8 seconds down on Whiteway, with Davey fourth, and Day up to fifth ahead of Green. Brian Ball went on to win by one minute 00.2 seconds from Frank Whiteway, with Don Padgett one minute 08.6 seconds down in third place. Don had also been going for a non-stop ride, but had to stop twice on the course to clear water from the magneto! The top six were completed by Bill Day, Cyril Davey and Mike Scruby (Yamaha) with George Green finishing seventh. There were 57 finishers and 16 riders won replicas.

1967 Lightweight MGP (3 laps / 113.98 miles) 110 entries

1. Brian Ball	B.A. Special	1h. 21m. 07.0s	83.73 mph
2. Frank Whiteway	Suzuki	1h. 22m. 07.2s	82.71 mph
3. Don Padgett	Yamaha	1h. 23m. 15.8s	81.58 mph
Fastest lap			
Brian Ball	B.A. Special	26m. 37.6s	85.02 mph

1967 Junior MGP

The weather conditions were still poor for the Junior, which had also attracted the maximum entry of 110, but with 11 non-starters, there were 99 riders on the grid. Keith Heckles (Norton) topped the practice leader board followed by Mike Hatherill (Aermacchi) and Mike Bennett (Norton). At the end of lap one, Joe Thornton (Norton), with a lap at 84.49 mph, led Heckles by 30.8 seconds with Nigel Warren (A.J.S.), a further 4.4. seconds down in third place. Gordon Daniels (A.J.S.), John Wetherall (Norton) and Clive Brown (Norton) completed the top six. At the end of the second lap, Joe Thornton pushed into the pits from Governors Bridge and retired. Heckles led Warren by 3.8 seconds with Daniels in third place, 15.8 seconds down on Warren. Wetherall was fourth, Brown fifth and John Findlay (Norton) came onto the leaderboard in sixth place. Warren took over the lead at half distance, and led Wetherall by 14 seconds, with Heckles now third a further 8.2 seconds down and Daniels, Brown and Findlay completed the leaderboard. By the end of the fourth lap, Heckles was up to second place, six seconds down on Warren, with Wetherall 2.8 seconds behind Heckles. Daniels and Brown remained fourth and fifth, and with John Findlay's retirement, John Duffy (Norton) took over sixth place. Warren lost fifth gear on the fifth lap and slowed, Heckles took over the lead from Wetherall by 12.2 seconds, with Warren 32.6 adrift of the second place man, Duffy moved up to fourth, Mike Bennett (Norton) fifth and Peter Elmore (Norton) sixth. But there were dramatic changes to come, Keith Heckles luck again ran out, and he retired at the Mountain Box. John Wetherall took the chequered flag ahead of the slowing Nigel Warren by 57.6 seconds, Warren in turn was five minutes 38.2 seconds ahead of the third man John Duffy. Mike Bennett was fourth, Charles Wild (Aermacchi) fifth and Colin Dixon (Triumph) sixth. Peter Elmore, sixth on the fifth lap, slid off at Quarter Bridge on the final lap. There were 52 finishers and 21 riders won replicas.

1967 Junior MGP (6 laps / 226.38 miles) 110 entries

1. John Wetherall	Norton	2h. 43m. 14.2s	83.22 mph
2. Nigel Warren	A.J.S.	2h. 44m. 11.8s	82.74 mph
3. John Duffy	Norton	2h. 49m. 50.0s	79.98 mph
Fastest lap			
John Wetherall	Norton	26m. 42.2s	84.77 mph

1967 Senior MGP

Once again the Senior attracted the maximum entry of 110, and of these, 88 made it to the starting line. In contrast to the Tuesday, conditions were perfect for the Senior. Keith Heckles (Norton) was fastest in practice followed by Jimmy Guthrie (Norton) and Nigel Warren (Matchless). Heckles went straight into the lead, and at the end of the first lap he was 21.2 seconds ahead of Guthrie, who in turn was 28.4 seconds in front of Brian Warburton (Norton). Mike Bennett (Norton) was fourth, Warren fifth and Ray Pickrell (Triumph) sixth. The gaps between the first three increased on lap two. Heckles, plus 50.8 seconds on Guthrie, who was one minute 2.6 seconds up on Warren. Two of the first lap top six retired on lap two, Brian Warburton at the pits, and Ray Pickrell on the Mountain. Heckles led Guthrie at half distance by one minute 18.2 seconds. Warren stopped to make adjustments at Glen Helen, got away and round to the pits and proceeded from there but lost his leaderboard place. Bennett took over third place, one minute 50.2 seconds down on Guthrie, Wetherall and Dixon remained

Jimmy Guthrie at Sulby Bridge.

fourth and fifth, and Gordon Pantall (Matchless), came on to the leaderboard in sixth place. But Heckles dreadful luck at the Manx struck again on the fourth lap. He was reported to be misfiring at the Bungalow, and had to push in to the pits to retire. Bennett also retired on this lap at Sulby with a seized engine. So Guthrie led Wetherall by three minutes 30 seconds and Pantall jumped up to third place, 21.2 seconds down on Wetherall. Brian Ball (Norton) was fourth, Peter Elmore (Matchless) fifth and Bill Fulton (Norton) sixth. Dixon stopped in the pits for adjustments. Guthrie extended his lead on the fifth lap to three minutes 50.6 seconds over Pantall, who had snatched second place from Wetherall by just 0.4 seconds. Ball was fourth, Elmore fifth and Warren came back onto the leaderboard in sixth place. Bill Fulton's race ended with a spill at Quarter Bridge on his fifth lap. So, thirty years after his famous father lost his life in the German Grand Prix, Jimmy Guthrie followed in his father's footsteps with a win on the TT course. He won by three minutes 50.6 seconds from Gordon Pantall, who was 15 seconds in front of John Wetherall, and Brian Ball, Peter Elmore and Nigel Warren completed the top six. There were 39 finishers and 16 replicas were won.

1967 Senior MGP (6 laps / 226.38 miles) 110 entries

1. Jimmy Guthrie	Norton	2h. 23m. 01.2s	94.98 mph
2. Gordon Pantall	Norton	2h. 26m. 13.4s	92.90 mph
3. John Wetherall	Norton	2h. 26m. 28.4s	92.74 mph
Fastest lap (record)			
Keith Heckles	Norton	22m. 53.8s	98.87 mph

1968

1968 Lightweight MGP

The Crooks Suzuki was a better (and safer) ride! Frank Whiteway gets a bumpy ride in the 'winners chair' to the stage, ably assisted by sponsor Eddie Crooks (front left).

The entries for the Lightweight reached the maximum of 110, and with 15 non-starters, 95 riders faced the starter. In practice, Ian Richards (Yamaha) had topped the leaderboard, Stan Woods (Yamaha) was next fastest followed by Frank Whiteway (Suzuki). Woods broke the lap record on the opening lap in 25m. 01.8s. to lead Whiteway by 14.2 seconds, third was Bill Milne (Bultaco), 7.4 seconds down, with Richards fourth, M. G. Scruby (Yamaha) fifth and Peter Grove (Yamaha) sixth. Woods had refuelled at the end of the first lap, so Whiteway took the lead from him at half distance by 6.2 seconds, and Richards moved up to third, just over a second down on Woods. Scruby, Ray Ashcroft (Yamaha) and Peter Berwick (Villiers) completed the top six. Milne had retired at Ballaugh Bridge. By the end of the third lap Woods was back in front by 8.8 seconds from Whiteway, and with Richards retiring at Sulby with a seized engine, Mick Bancroft (Bancroft Special) came straight into third place. Berwick, Chas Mortimer and D. J. Page (Bultaco) completed the top six. But Stan Woods hit trouble on the last lap and slowed to finish in ninth place.

Frank Whiteway went on to win by two minutes 21.4 seconds from Mick Bancroft, Peter Berwick took third place followed by Page, Mortimer and Barry Davis (Ducati/Yamaha). There were 47 finishers and 11 riders won replicas.

1968 Lightweight MGP (4 laps / 150.92 miles) 110 entries

1. Frank Whiteway	Suzuki	1h. 42m. 18.6s	88.52 mph
			(record)
2. Mick Bancroft	Bancroft Special	1h. 44m. 40.0s	86.52 mph
3. Peter Berwick	Villiers	1h. 45m. 19.2s	85.99 mph
Fastest lap (record)			
Stan Woods	Yamaha	25m. 01.8s	90.45 mph

1968 Junior MGP

The Junior also attracted the maximum 110 entries, and with just nine non-starters, 101 riders came to the line. Robin Duffty (Norton) had topped the practice leaderboard, followed by Nigel Warren (A.J.S.) and Dave Thomas (Kawasaki). At the end of lap one it was Thomas in the lead by 0.8 of a second from John Findlay (Norton), with Clive Brown (Norton) 3.8 seconds down. Tony Monk (B.S.A. Special) was fourth, with Gordon Pantall (A.J.S.) and John Griffith (Greeves) completing the top six. Thomas increased his lead over Findlay to nine seconds at the end of the second lap with Brown still third, but now 14.8 seconds down. Monk and Pantall held their places but Warren came up to sixth place. Thomas retired at Quarter Bridge on the third lap with the seat on his Kawasaki broken, one of the more unusual reasons for retiring, so Findlay took the lead at the end of the lap by 10.8 seconds from Brown, with Pantall 22 seconds down in third place. Monk and Warren were fourth and fifth with Robin Duffty taking sixth place. A close race looked on when the fourth lap times were announced as Findlay led Brown by just 0.2 seconds! Warren had taken over third place from Pantall with Monk and Duffty fifth and sixth. Findlay increased his lead over Brown at the end of lap five to 22.6 seconds and Warren was just 10 seconds behind Brown with the rest of the leaderboard unchanged. On the final dramatic lap, the second and third place riders went out, Clive Brown was black-flagged at Ballacraine as he had lost one footrest, and Warren came off at Dorans Bend, suffering a broken leg. So John Findlay went on to win by a comfortable one minute 19.8 seconds from Pantall, with Monk third. Duffty took fourth place with Gerry Borland (Aermacchi) coming into fifth place, and Peter Elmore (A.J.S.) finished sixth.

1968 Junior MGP (6 laps / 226.38 miles) 110 entries

1. John Findlay	Norton	2h. 31m. 10.8s	89.85 mph
2. Gordon Pantall	A.J.S.	2h. 32m. 30.4s	89.08 mph
3. Tony Monk	B.S.A. Special	2h. 34m. 28.4s	87.94 mph
Fastest lap			
Dave Thomas	Kawasaki	24m. 31.4s	92.31 mph

1968 Senior MGP

Again the maximum 110 entries were received for the Senior, and with just 10 non-starters, exactly 100 riders faced the starter. Junior winner John Findlay (Norton) had been fastest in practice, followed by Gordon Pantall, the Junior runner-up and third was Nigel Warren (Matchless), but Nigel was one of the non-starters due to his spill in the Junior. At the end of the first lap, Joe Thornton (Mularney Special) led by 22.8 seconds from Clive Brown (Mularney Special) who in turn led the third place man Gordon Daniels (Matchless) by 14 seconds. The top six were completed by Findlay, Tony Dunnell (Norton) and Pantall. Thornton increased his lead over Brown on lap two to 40 seconds and Findlay took third place, just seven seconds down. Daniels was fourth and Pantall took fifth place from Dunnell. Thornton's race ended on the third lap when he came off at Creg-ny-Baa. Pantall, fifth on lap two, shot into the lead by just 9.4 seconds from Findlay, who in turn was 11.4 seconds ahead of Daniels. Dunnell was fourth and Peter Elmore (Matchless) and Malcolm Moffatt (Matchless) came into the top six. Pantall held his lead at the end of lap four, but only just, he was 2.2 seconds up on Findlay who was now over two minutes ahead of the third place man Dunnell. Elmore was fourth, Bill Milne (Matchless) came into fifth spot ahead of Moffatt. But the leader Pantall came off at Braddan Bridge on lap five, so Findlay had a comfortable lead of two minutes 18.2 seconds over Dunnell, Elmore was now third, 57 seconds down, followed by Milne, Colin Dixon (Norton) and John Duffy (Norton). With a Manx double in sight, John Findlay slowed on the last lap to win from Tony Dunnell by one minute 47.6 seconds, Bill Milne took third place, and with the retirements of Elmore at Bishopscourt, and John Duffy out of petrol at the Gooseneck, Nigel Rollason (Metisse) came up to fourth place with C. D. Wild (Norton) and Malcolm Moffatt completing the top six. But there was more drama to come, Bill Milne was excluded from the results for using an engine in the Senior race that was under 350cc. So Rollason took third place, Wild fourth, Moffatt fifth and Chris Owen (Norton) came into sixth. There were 51 finishers and 23 replicas were won.

1968 Senior MGP (6 laps / 226.38 miles) 110 entries

1. John Findlay	Norton	2h. 30m. 41.8s	90.14 mph
2. Tony Dunnell	Norton	2h. 32m. 29.4s	89.09 mph
3. Nigel Rollason	Seeley Metisse	2h. 38m. 31.0s	85.70 mph
Fastest lap			
Joe Thornton	Mularney Special	23m. 44.0s	95.39 mph

1969

1969 Lightweight MGP

The entry for the Lightweight was 110, but non-starters reduced this number to 91. Peter Berwick (Suzuki) was fastest in practice with Mick Bancroft (Suzuki) second fastest. At the end of the first lap, Ernie Johnson (Yamaha), with a lap record at 90.38 mph, led Alex George (Yamaha) by 11.8 seconds, with John Griffiths (Yamaha) third a further 26.2 seconds down. Bancroft was fourth, Ronnie Mann (Bultaco) fifth and Ron Bryant (Yamaha) sixth. But George, with another record lap at 92.40 mph took the lead at the end of the second lap by 52.8 seconds from Griffiths, Ernie Johnson having retired at Sulby with engine trouble. Bancroft was in third place, 13.2 seconds down on Griffiths, and the top six were completed by Mann, Don Padgett (Yamaha) and Noel Clegg (Yamaha). George increased his lead over Griffiths to one minute 39.2 seconds at the end of lap three, and Padgett took third place from Bancroft, over one minute down on Griffiths, Clegg was fifth and P. J. Leahy (Yamaha) sixth. Alex George went on to win from John Griffiths by one minute 57.8 seconds, with Padgett third, 47.4 seconds down. Noel Clegg finished fourth, A. M. Lea (Yamaha) fifth and Mick Bancroft sixth. There were 57 finishers and 15 replicas were won

1969 Lightweight MGP (4 laps / 150.92 miles) 110 entries

1. Alex George	Yamaha	1h. 39m. 55.6s	90.63 mph (record)
2. John Griffiths	Yamaha	1h. 41m. 53.4s	88.89 mph
3. Don Padgett	Yamaha	1h. 42m. 40.8s	88.21 mph
Fastest lap (record)			
Alex George	Yamaha	24m. 30.0s	92.40 mph

1969 Junior MGP

The Junior also attracted an entry of 110, and non-starters were slightly less than in the Lightweight, so 94 riders faced the starter. Clive Brown (Norton) was fastest in practice followed by Roger Sutcliffe (A.J.S.), and Robin Duffty (Aermacchi). At the end of the first lap Bill Milne (Aermacchi) led Duffty by 0.6 seconds, with Brian Warburton (Yamaha) in third place, a further 6.6 seconds down. The top six were completed by Gordon Pantall (Yamaha), Gerry Mateer (Aermacchi) and R. Bilsborrow (Aermacchi). It was still close at the end of the second lap, with Milne 4.4 seconds ahead of Duffty who was 0.4 seconds in front of Warburton. Pantall remained fourth, Danny Shimmin (Aermacchi) was fifth and Mateer sixth. The lead changed at the end of the third lap, Duffty having an advantage of 1.2 seconds over Milne. Shimmin, with the fastest lap of the race - 93.21 mph, took third place, 28.4 seconds down on Milne, Brian Warburton having retired at the pits. Pantall, Andy

John Findlay takes Signpost in fine style.

Chapman (Yamaha) and A. M. Warner (Aermacchi) completed the leaderboard. Duffty was one minute 0.2 seconds ahead at the end of the fourth lap, and the only change to the leaderboard was that Peter Elmore (A.J.S.) came into sixth place. Bill Milne retired with engine trouble on the fifth lap, so Duffty led Chapman by one minute 57.4 seconds. Shimmin came off at Brandywell but was able to continue, and held third place, 20.6 seconds down on Chapman. Clive Brown came on to the leaderboard in fourth place, followed by Roger Sutcliffe (A.J.S.) and Warner. Robin Duffty won the race by two minutes 30.4 seconds from Andy Chapman, who finished 5.2 seconds in front of Clive Brown. Shimmin finished fourth, Peter Elmore fifth and M. Collins (Seeley) sixth. There were 57 finishers and 29 replicas were won.

Robin Duffty at Quarter Bridge.

1969 Junior MGP (6 laps / 226.38 miles)   110 entries

1. Robin Duffty	Aermacchi	2h. 27m. 09.6s	92.31 mph
2. Andy Chapman	Yamaha	2h. 29m. 40.0s	90.76 mph
3. Clive Brown	Norton	2h. 29m. 45.2s	90.71 mph
Fastest lap			
Danny Shimmin	Aermacchi	24m. 17.2s	93.21 mph

1969 Senior MGP

The Senior also attracted the maximum entry of 110, but unfortunately there were 22 non-starters, so 88 riders lined up for the start. Clive Brown (Norton) had also topped the Senior practice leaderboard with Gerry Mateer (Norton) second. It was Gordon Daniels (Matchless) who led at the end of lap one by 27.8 seconds from Gordon Pantall (Seeley), who in turn was 11.2 seconds front of Brian Warburton (Norton). Gerry Mateer (Norton), Tony Dunnell (B.S.A.) and Peter Elmore (Matchless) completed the top six. Daniels increased his lead at the end of the second lap to 52.6 seconds. Mateer was in second place, and Pantall, who had slid off at Governors Bridge and quickly remounted, was third, just 0.2 seconds down on Mateer. Warburton was fourth, Dunnell fifth and Elmore sixth. The next of the leaderboard men to retire was Mateer, who stopped between Braddan Bridge and Union Mills, so at the end of the third lap, Daniels led Pantall by one minute 03.8 seconds, Warburton third, Nigel Rollason (Seeley) fourth, Dunnell fifth and Roger Sutcliffe (Matchless) sixth. Lap four saw the end of Tony Dunnell's race, he retired after a spill at the Waterworks, but Pantall began a charge and was just 24.2 seconds down on Daniels, with Warburton over 2 minutes down in third place, Sutcliffe moved up to fourth, Rollason was fifth and Elmore sixth. Pantall made his move on the fifth lap and snatched the lead from Daniels by 22.2 seconds and the rest of the leaderboard was unchanged. Daniels fought back on the last lap, and with the fastest lap of the race at 96.66 mph, won by just seven seconds from Pantall who was one minute 46.6 seconds ahead of third place Warburton. Nigel Rollason retired after coming off at Milntown, and the top six were completed by Roger Sutcliffe, Peter Elmore and R. C. Davies. There were 48 finishers and 25 replicas were won.

Gordon Daniels seems to be dwarfed by the Cowles Matchless as he exits Governors Bridge.

1969 Senior MGP (6 laps / 226.38 miles)   110 entries

1. Gordon Daniels	Cowles Matchless	2h. 25m. 23.8s	93.43 mph
2. Gordon Pantall	Seeley	2h. 25m. 30.8s	93.36 mph
3. Brian Warburton	Norton	2h. 27m. 17.4s	92.23 mph
Fastest lap			
Gordon Daniels	Cowles Matchless	23m. 25.2s	96.66 mph

The 48th finisher (on a Velocette) was none other than Mick Grant, who was to go on to win seven TT races!

1970

1970 Lightweight MGP

Entries for the Lightweight were slightly down on 1969, 103 riders entered, and of these, 84 made it to the starting line. Allan Steele (Yamaha) was fastest in practice followed by Ivan Hodgkinson (Yamaha) and Ernie Johnson (Yamaha). At the end of the first lap, George Collis (Yamaha) led the race by 30 seconds from Steele with John Griffiths (Yamaha) in third place, 10.6 seconds down on Steele. Noel Clegg (Yamaha) was fourth, Charlie Williams (Yamaha) fifth and Les Trotter (Suzuki) sixth. Steele took over the lead from Collis at the end of lap two by 11.2 seconds, and Griffiths was 22 seconds down on Collis. Williams took fourth place, Trotter fifth and Clegg sixth. Collis retired on the third lap when he came off at Handleys Corner, and at the end of the lap Steele led Griffiths by one minute 21.8 seconds with Trotter in third place, 35.8 seconds down. Williams, Clegg and Mick Bancroft (Suzuki) completed the third lap leaderboard. Allan Steele won the race from John Griffiths by two minutes 02.6 seconds with Les Trotter a further 29.8 seconds down. Noel Clegg finished fourth, Charlie

Williams fifth and Mick Bancroft sixth. There were 48 finishers and 13 replicas were won.

1970 Lightweight MGP (4 laps / 150.92 miles) 110 entries

1. Allan Steele	Yamaha	1h. 40m. 08.6s	90.44 mph
2. John Griffiths	Yamaha	1h. 42m. 11.2s	88.63 mph
3. Les Trotter	Suzuki	1h. 42m. 41.0s	88.20 mph
Fastest lap			
Allan Steele	Yamaha	24m. 32.6s	92.24 mph

1970 Junior MGP

The maximum entry of 110 was received for the Junior, but 20 non-starters reduced the field to 90. Clive Brown (Aermacchi) again topped the practice leaderboard with Gordon Pantall (Yamaha) second fastest and Nigel Rollason (Yamaha) third. Pantall led Brown at the end of the first lap by 22 seconds with Roger Sutcliffe (Aermacchi) in third place, 31.6 seconds down on Brown. Danny Shimmin (Aermacchi) was fourth, Joe Thornton (Mularney Special) fifth and Dave Thomas (Kawasaki) sixth. The first four remained the same on lap two, Pantall increasing his lead to 35.6 seconds. Thomas moved up to fifth place and Rollason with a new lap record after a slow start at 95.32 mph took sixth place. The record didn't stand for long as Pantall set a new one at 96.21 mph and at the end of the third lap led Brown by 34.8 seconds who in turn led Sutcliffe by one minute 43 seconds. Rollason, Shimmin and Thornton completed the top six. But Pantall was in trouble, he had a long pit stop, eventually got away, but only as far as Ballacraine where he retired with a seized engine. Brown took the lead at the end of the fourth lap by 42.2 seconds from Sutcliffe who in turn led the third placeman Rollason by 29.2 seconds, Thornton was fourth, Steve Moynihan (Norton) fifth and Thomas sixth. Brown really flew on the fifth lap and increased his lead to over one minute from Sutcliffe, and Rollason closed on the second place man, being just 4.6 seconds down with the rest of the leaderboard unchanged. Clive Brown went on to win by one minute 07.6 seconds from Rollason, who snatched second place from Sutcliffe by just 6.2 seconds. Thornton finished fourth,

Roger Sutcliffe (left) and Nigel Rollason (right) congratulate Clive Brown. Sid Lawton, who knew a thing or two about making the Aermacchi motor, is between the two riders.

Moynihan fifth and Dave Thomas sixth. There were 49 finishers and 24 replicas were won.

1970 Junior MGP (6 laps / 226.38 miles) 110 entries

1. Clive Brown	Beart Aermacchi	2h. 24m. 56.2s	93.74 mph
			(record)
2. Nigel Rollason	Yamaha	2h. 26m. 02.8s	93.02 mph
3. Roger Sutcliffe	Lawton Aermacchi	2h. 26m. 09.0s	92.95 mph
Fastest lap (record)			
Gordon Pantall	Yamaha	23m. 31.8s	96.21 mph

1970 Senior MGP

The Senior attracted an entry of 110, of which 17 were non-starters, so 93 riders lined up on the grid. Gordon Pantall (Seeley) topped the practice leaderboard followed by Roger Sutcliffe (Matchless) and Ken Huggett (Norton). Pantall led at the end of the first lap by 12.8 seconds from Sutcliffe, with Clive Brown (Norton Special) a further 12.6 seconds down in third place. Peter Elmore (Seeley) was fourth, Chris Griffith, (Matchless) fifth and Brian Warburton (Norton) sixth. Pantall increased his lead over Sutcliffe to 15.8 seconds at the end of lap two, and Brown was 45.4 seconds behind Sutcliffe. Elmore remained fourth, Huggett came onto the leaderboard in fifth place, with Griffiths sixth. Pantall's race ended at Sulby Bridge on lap three when he retired with engine trouble, so Sutcliffe grabbed the lead at the end of the lap by one minute 21.6 seconds from Huggett who had moved up to second place 3.8 seconds in front of Brown. Elmore, Griffiths and David Pearce (Petty Manx) completed the top six at half distance. Huggett reduced Sutcliffe's lead at the end of the fourth lap to one minute 09.2 seconds, and Brown trailed Huggett by 35.6 seconds, followed by Griffiths, Elmore and Nigel Rollason (Seeley). By the end of the fifth lap the difference between Sutcliffe and Huggett was down to 48.4 seconds, and Brown was one and a half minutes down in third place. Griffiths and Elmore maintained their places, but Rollason retired at Glentrammon with engine trouble, and Pearce came back on to the leaderboard in sixth place. By Ballacraine on the last lap Sutcliffe's lead was 34 seconds, at Ballaugh it was 30 seconds, and by Ramsey it was down to 26 seconds. At the Bungalow it was 25 seconds. Huggett finished first and the clocks ticked away, Sutcliffe seemed to be late, but he crossed the line to win by just 4.8 seconds, and Huggett had set the fastest lap of the race on the sixth lap at 97.27 mph. Two of the leaderboard men hit trouble on the final lap, Clive Brown's chain broke at Governors Bridge and he pushed in to finish 11th, and Peter Elmore came off at the Nook, remounted and finished 15th. So the leaderboard was completed by Chris Griffiths, David Pearce, Alan Rogers (Matchless) and George Short (Matchless). There were 44 finishers and 24 replicas were won.

1970 Senior MGP (6 laps / 226.38 miles) 110 entries

1. Roger Sutcliffe	Cowles Matchless	2h. 23m. 53.0s	94.41 mph
2. Ken Huggett	Norton	2h. 23m. 57.8s	94.37 mph
3. Chris Griffiths	Cowles Matchless	2h. 26m. 33.6s	92.69 mph
Fastest lap			
Ken Huggett	Norton	23m. 16.4s	97.27 mph

1971

1971 Lightweight MGP

There was an entry of 99 for the Lightweight, but a high percentage of non-starters - 21 - reduced the field to 78. Charlie Williams (Yamaha) topped the practice leaderboard, followed by John Weeden (Yamaha) and Don Padgett (Yamaha). It was no surprise when Williams led at the end of the first lap, and he had broken the record from a standing start in 23m. 41.6s. to lead Phil Carpenter (Yamaha) by 20.6 seconds with Ernie Johnson (Yamaha) in third place 12.6 seconds down. The top six were completed by Danny Shimmin (Suzuki), George Green (Yamaha) and Alf Mayrs (Yamaco). Charlie really flew on lap two and smashed the record again in 23m. 19s. - 97.09, faster than the Junior lap record. He increased his lead over Carpenter to two minutes 56 seconds, whilst Carpenter in turn had improved his advantage over Johnson to 50 seconds. The remaining leaderboard men remained unchanged. Williams added almost a minute to his lead at the end of the third lap, Carpenter remained second but Johnson had had a long pit stop of some two and a half minutes, and eventually finished 12th. This brought Shimmin up to third, Roger Cope, (Yamaha) came on to the leaderboard in fourth place, ahead of Green and Mayrs. So Charlie Williams won his first race on the TT course, in record breaking style from Phil Carpenter by three minutes 04.2 seconds, Danny Shimmin took third place, Roger Cope was fourth, Don Padgett came up to fifth place and Green was sixth. Alf Mayrs dropped to 10th place at the finish. There were 47 finishers and 12 riders won replicas.

Charlie Williams at Creg ny Baa

1971 Lightweight MGP (4 laps / 150.92 miles) 110 entries

1. Charlie Williams	Yamaha	1h. 36m. 21.2s	93.99 mph
			(record)
2. Phil Carpenter	Yamaha	1h. 39m. 25.6s	91.09 mph
3. Danny Shimmin	Crooks Suzuki	1h. 42m. 05.2s	88.71 mph
Fastest lap (record)			
Charlie Williams	Yamaha	23m. 19.0s	97.09 mph

1971 Junior MGP

The Junior entry was 108 and 19 non-starters reduced the field to 89. Nigel Rollason (Yamaha) was fastest in practice followed by Peter Elmore (Norton) and Ken Huggett (Norton). Steve Moynihan (Aermacchi) led at the end of the first lap by 0.6 seconds from Murray Warner (Yamaha) who was 16.2 seconds ahead of Harvey Porter (Kawasaki). Alan Rogers (Seeley), Dave Hughes (A.J.S.) and Joe Thornton (Mularney Special) completed the top six. Moynihan increased his lead on lap two to 35 seconds, and second place was taken by Hughes, Porter was third, 3.6 seconds down on Hughes, Rogers remained fourth, Thornton moved up to fifth and Roger Haddock (A.J.S.) came into sixth place. Warner retired on this second lap. The leaderboard changed dramatically on lap three, Hughes retired at Ramsey, Haddock at the pits and Porter was black flagged at Ramsey because of a loose exhaust, he repaired it and continued to finish 12th. Moynihan still led by one minute 27 seconds from Thornton, Rogers was third just two seconds down and the three new men on the leaderboard were Chris Griffiths (A.J.S.), Dave Williams (A.J.S.) and Peter Elmore (Norton). After the shake up on lap three, there were no changes to placings on the fourth lap, and Moynihan increased his lead to one minute 49.2. seconds. By the time the fifth lap had been completed, Moynihan was over two minutes ahead of Thornton, Griffiths had moved up to third ahead of Rogers, and Williams and Elmore remained fifth and six. Thornton's race ended on the final lap, when he retired at Crosby. Moynihan won by two minutes 45 seconds from Griffiths and third place went to Alan Rogers. Peter Elmore, Dave Williams and Henry McEwan (Aermacchi) completed the top six. There were in 55 finishers and 26 replicas were won

Steve Moynihan at Quarter Bridge.

1971 Junior MGP (6 laps / 226.38 miles) 108 entries

1. Steve Moynihan	Lawton Aermacchi	2h. 29m. 00.2s	91.17 mph
2. Chris Griffiths	Cowles A.J.S.	2h. 31m. 45.2s	89.52 mph
3. Alan Rogers	Seeley	2h. 32m. 27.0s	89.11 mph
Fastest lap			
Steve Moynihan	Lawton Aermacchi	24m. 28.4s	92.50 mph

1971 Senior MGP

Once again the maximum number of entries were received for the Senior, 110, but non-starters reduced the field to 98. Joe Thornton (Mularney Special) topped the practice leaderboard, Bill Milne (Matchless) was next fastest, followed by George Short (Seeley). Ken Huggett (Norton) led at the end of the first lap by 11 seconds from Nigel Rollason (Yamaha), with John Dawson (Matchless) third, 2.4 seconds down. He was followed by Peter Elmore (Norton), Alan Ryall (Seeley) and Don

Padgett (Yamaha). Huggett increased his lead at the end of the second lap to 29 seconds from Elmore, Dawson moved up to third and Rollason dropped to fourth, place, Ryall was still fifth and Joe Thornton came on to the leaderboard in sixth place. By half distance, the end of lap three, Huggett led Elmore by 47.2 seconds, Rollason came up to third with Ryall, Dawson and Thornton completing the top six. Lap four saw Huggett again extend his lead over Elmore to 56 seconds, and Elmore in turn had a comfortable one minute lead over Rollason. Thornton had moved up to fourth ahead of Dawson and Ryall. At the start the final lap Huggett had what appeared to be an unbeatable lead over Elmore of one minute 34 seconds, but Rollason was closing on Elmore, being only 23 seconds down. Thornton retired on the fifth lap at Ballaugh and Dawson came off at the Gooseneck, he remounted and carried on only to retire at the pits. So the remainder of the leaderboard was Neil Kelly (Matchless), Ryall and Roger Bowler (Mularney Special). But there was more drama to come, Ken Huggett's machine, as he said, "just stopped at Governors Bridge", robbing him him of certain victory. Elmore, second at the end of lap five seemed to be the winner, but Rollason, with the fastest lap of the race at 97.36 mph, took first place by just 6.2 seconds from Huggett who had pushed in from Governors, Elmore took third place, Kelly fourth, Ryall fifth and Bowler sixth. There were 53 finishers and 21 riders won replicas.

Nigel Rollason, first Senior Manx GP winner on a two-stroke.

1971 Senior MGP (6 laps / 226.38 miles)   110 entries

1. Nigel Rollason	Yamaha	2h. 23m. 52.8s	94.42 mph
2. Ken Huggett	Kettle Norton	2h. 23m. 58.6s	94.35 mph
3. Peter Elmore	Norton	2h. 24m. 21.8s	94.10 mph
Fastest lap			
Nigel Rollason	Yamaha	23m. 15.2s	97.36 mph

1972

1972 Lightweight MGP

The entries for the Lightweight totalled 97, but non-starters reduced the field to 85. Phil Carpenter (Yamaha) topped the practice leaderboard followed by Danny Shimmin (Yamaha) and Vic Wright (Yamaha). These three featured on the leaderboard at the end of the first lap, Carpenter led by 43 seconds from Don Padgett (Yamaha), who in turn led Wright by just 2.1 seconds. Shimmin was fourth, Dave Arnold (Yamaha) fifth and Eddie Roberts (Yamaha) sixth. At the end of the second lap, Carpenter had increased his lead to 2 minutes 14 seconds from the new second place man Roberts, who held a five second advantage over Shimmin, Padgett had dropped to fourth, Ernie Johnson (Yamaha) came on to the leaderboard in fifth place and Wright was sixth. With pit stops playing an important part as always, Carpenter's lead at the end of the third lap was 18 seconds, Roberts was still second, but now 61 seconds up on Shimmin, Johnson was fourth, Dave Arnold fifth and Padgett sixth. Roberts race ended on the last lap at the Guthrie Memorial when he ran out of petrol, so Phil Carpenter won by one minute 45 seconds from Ernie Johnson who took second place from Shimmin by just 0.6 seconds! Arnold, Padgett and Wright completed the top six leaderboard. There were 52 finishers and 14 replicas were won.

Phil Carpenter leaves Governors Bridge.

1972 Lightweight MGP (4 laps / 150.92 miles)   110 entries

1. Phil Carpenter	Yamaha	1h. 35m. 15.0s	95.07 mph
			(record)
2. Ernie Johnson	Dugdale Yamaha	1h. 37m. 00.6s	93.94 mph
3. Danny Shimmin	Dugdale Yamaha	1h. 37m. 01.2s	93.33 mph
Fastest lap			
Phil Carpenter	Yamaha	23m. 24.6s	96.70 mph

1972 Junior MGP

The Junior attracted the maximum entry of 110, but 15 non-starters reduced the field to 95. Ken Huggett (Aermacchi) topped the practice leaderboard with Phil Haslam (Yamaha) and Dave Williams (Cowles Yamaha). Huggett led at the end of the first lap by 8.2 seconds from Williams with Alan Ryall a further 9.2 seconds down, the top six was completed by Haslam, Chris Curtis (Aermacchi) and Rex Wainwright (Yamaha). Ryall's race ended on lap two when he came off at the Black Dub, sustaining a broken leg and arm. Huggett led at the end of the second lap by 14.8 seconds from Williams, who was two minutes ahead of third place John Foy (Yamaha). Haslam was fourth, followed by Roger Haddock (A.J.S.) and Wainwright. Huggett's lead was exactly halved at the end of the third lap, 7.4 seconds over, Williams and Foy was now three minutes six seconds down on Williams, followed by Wainwright, Alan Rogers (Seeley) and Haslam. Williams, however, had a long pit stop, and Huggett increased his advantage at the end of the fourth lap to one

minute nine seconds, but second place Williams had an advantage of three minutes over Haslam in third place, Foy had dropped to fourth, Rogers was fifth and Trevor Parker (Aermacchi) came on to the leaderboard in sixth place. The difference between Huggett and Williams at the end of the fifth lap was one minute 30 seconds, Haslam came off at the Waterworks and retired, bringing Foy up to third place, Parker was fourth followed by Dave Hughes (A.J.S.) and Bill Milne (Aermacchi). Dave Williams hit trouble on the last lap, retiring at Appledene with clutch trouble, so Ken Huggett went on to a deserved win by a margin of seven minutes 10 seconds from John Foy, Trevor Parker took third place, Dave Hughes was fourth, Bill Milne fifth and Chris Curtis sixth. There were 42 finishers and 14 riders won replicas.

Ken Huggett at Quarter Bridge. In later years, Ken was mine host at the Hawthorn public house.

1972 Junior MGP (6 laps / 226.38 miles) 108 entries

1. Ken Huggett	Lawton Aermacchi	2h. 22m. 08.0s	95.56 mph (record)
2. John Foy	Yamaha	2h. 29m. 18.2s	90.97 mph
3. Trevor Parker	Aermacchi	2h. 30m. 14.8s	90.40 mph
Fastest lap (record)			
Ken Huggett	Lawton Aermacchi	23m. 15.2s	97.35 mph

1972 Senior MGP

The Senior entry of 110 was reduced to exactly 100 by non-starters. Local rider Danny Shimmin (Suzuki) topped the practice leaderboard, Ken Huggett (Seeley), the Junior winner was next and Brian Hussey (Norton) was third. Huggett's race ended very quickly when he slid off at Braddan Bridge on the opening lap, ending his dreams of a double. Shimmin led by 15.4 seconds at the end of the first lap from Tom Newell (Norton), who was in turn 19.2 seconds ahead of Alan Rogers (Seeley). They were followed by Joe Thornton (Mularney Special), Dave Hughes (Matchless) and Ralph Grew (Suzuki). Shimmin increased his lead over Newell at the end of lap two to 30.4 seconds, but Hughes closed right up on Newell, just 0.4 seconds down. Grew moved up to fourth place as both Rogers and Thornton retired at Barregarrow, and Ken Inwood (Norton) and Keith Martin (Suzuki) came into the top six. Danny continued to pull away from the rest of the field on lap three, his lead over Hughes was 56 seconds, and Hughes had taken second spot from Newell by 33.8 seconds. Dave Williams (Matchless) came on to the leaderboard in fourth place followed by Grew and Martin. At the end of the fourth lap, Shimmin was one minute 7.8 seconds ahead of Hughes, who in turn had increased his advantage over Newell to one minute 40 seconds and the remaining leaderboard places were unchanged. At the start of the last lap Shimmin was almost a minute and a half ahead of Hughes, who was two and a half minutes up on Williams, with Newell now in fourth place ahead of Grew and Martin. But as so often happens on the TT course, drama struck on the final lap. Danny Shimmin, with a commanding lead, was forced to retire at Glen Trammon with engine trouble, so Dave Hughes, with a comfortable margin in hand, went on to win by two minutes 54.4 seconds from Dave Williams with Keith Martin third, 32.6 seconds down on Williams. Tom Newell took fourth place, Ken Inwood finished fifth and, with the retirement of Ralph Grew due to a spill at Glen Helen, Ernie Pitts took sixth place. There were 65 finishers and 19 replicas were won.

1972 Senior MGP (6 laps / 226.38 miles) 110 entries

Dave Hughes (Arter Matchless) leaving Ballaugh Bridge.

1. Dave Hughes	Arter Matchless	2h. 25m. 01.2s	93.66 mph
2. Dave Williams	Cowles Matchless	2h. 27m. 55.4s	91.82 mph
3. Keith Martin	Crooks Suzuki	2h. 28m. 27.6s	91.49 mph
Fastest lap			
Danny Shimmin	Suzuki	23m. 04.6s	98.09 mph

1973

1973 Lightweight MGP

Adverse weather conditions caused the postponement of Tuesday's racing to the Wednesday. The Lightweight attracted an entry of 102 riders, non-starters reduced this to 88. Fastest in practice was Vic Wright (Yamaha) who finished sixth in the race last year, Bob McComb (Yamaha) was next best and third fastest was Don Padgett (Yamaha), fifth last year. It was Dave Arnold (Yamaha), however, who led at the end of the first lap by 16.8 seconds from Wright, with Paddy Reid (Yamaha) a further 15.2 seconds down. McComb was fourth with Chris Revett (Yamaha) and Alf Mayrs (Yamaha) completing the leaderboard. Arnold broke the lap record on his second circuit in 23m. 04.0s. and led Wright by 20.2 seconds, Reid was still third, but now 45 seconds down on Wright. McComb came off at Ramsey Hairpin, he remounted and continued to finish in

tenth place. His spill brought Revett up to fourth place, followed by Mayrs and Padgett came into the top six. Arnold was going the race distance non-stop, and at the end of lap three he had increased his lead to one minute 10 seconds from Wright, who was only 2.6 seconds ahead of Reid. Mayrs moved ahead of Revett and Padgett remained sixth. Dave Arnold broke the lap again on the final lap in 23m. 00.0s. a speed of 98.42 mph to win by one minute 48.8s. from Reid, who took second place from Wright by 6.6 seconds. Mayrs and Revett retained their places, but Padgett retired on the last lap, bringing Peter McKinley (Yamaha) into sixth place. There were 55 finishers and 18 riders won replicas.

1973 Lightweight MGP (4 laps / 150.92 miles) 110 entries

1. Dave Arnold	Walker Yamaha	1h. 33m. 07.8s	97.23 mph
			(record)
2. Paddy Reid	Yamaha	1h. 33m. 56.6s	96.39 mph
3. Vic Wright	Yamaha	1h. 34m. 03.2s	96.28 mph
Fastest lap			
Paddy Reid	Yamaha	23m. 00.0s	98.43 mph

Andy Abram (seen here in practice) gave this reason for his lowly 53rd position in the 1973 Lightweight. "It wasn't an outstanding result but my Yamaha went onto one cylinder shortly after the start. I retired at Ballacraine, had a drink in the pub, and autographed a girl's arm! When I came out of the pub, I bump started the bike to ride back to the pits on the back roads and it burst into life on two cylinders. I rejoined the race twenty minutes behind and still avoided being last!"

1973 Junior MGP

The maximum entry of 100 was received for the Junior, and the sensation of practice was Phil Haslam (Yamaha) who became the first rider in the lap to lap at over 100 mph His best lap was at 102.17 mph, and the top three in practice were completed by Alan Rogers (Yamaha) and Danny Shimmin (Yamaha). True to practice form Phil Haslam entered his name in the history books when he officially became the first 100 mph plus man in the history of the Manx. His opening lap was completed in 22m. 09.2s., 102.18 mph and he led Doug Lunn (Yamaha) by 56 seconds. Third, 27.8 seconds down, was Dave Williams (Yamaha), followed by Danny Shimmin, Joe Thornton (Harley Davidson) and Roger Cope (Yamaha). Haslam went even quicker on lap two - 21m. 56.8s, 103.15 mph, and increased his lead over Lunn to one minute 42.6 seconds. Shimmin had taken third place from Williams, and was 41 seconds behind Lunn. Eddie Roberts (Yamaha) and Steve Tonkin (Yamaha) came on to the leaderboard in fifth and sixth places. At the end of the third lap, Haslam's lead was one minute 21.8s. from Lunn, who was still 41 seconds ahead of Shimmin. Williams was still fourth, Roberts was fifth and sixth place was shared by Cope and Tony Randle (Yamaha). On the fourth lap, Haslam slid off at Signpost, he quickly remounted and proceeded, completing the lap at an average speed of over 99 mph! His lead was now two minutes 22 seconds over Lunn, who had an advantage of 22.8 seconds over Roberts. Williams was still in fourth place, followed by Tonkin and Cope, but Shimmin came off at Quarter Bridge and retired. At the end of the fifth lap, Haslam led Lunn by one minute 37.8 seconds, and Lunn had increased his lead over Roberts to over one minute, and the only other change to the top six saw Randle taking sixth place. So Phil Haslam went on to a record breaking victory at an average speed of 99. 42 mph. Doug Lunn finished second, one minute 30.6 seconds down, but 51.2 seconds ahead of third place man Roberts. Dave Williams, Steve Tonkin and Tony Randle completed the top six. There were 56 finishers and 15 replicas were won.

1973 Junior MGP (6 laps / 226.38 miles) 108 entries

1. Phil Haslam	Pharaoh Yamaha	2h. 16m. 37.2s	99.42 mph
			(record)
2. Doug Lunn	Bryans Yamaha	2h. 18m. 07.8s	98.33 mph
3. Eddie Roberts	Dugdale Yamaha	2h. 18m. 59.0s	97.73 mph
Fastest lap (record)			
Phil Haslam	Pharaoh Yamaha	21m. 56.8s	103.15 mph

Phil Haslam at Quarter Bridge.

1973 Senior MGP

Entries for the Senior were 115, and with just eight non-starters, 107 riders faced the starter. In practice, George Short (Suzuki) was fastest, Tony Rogers (Suzuki) was second and Dave Williams (Matchless) third fastest. At the end of the first lap only one of these featured in the top six. Don Padgett. (Yamaha) led by 2.6 seconds from Paddy Reid (Yamaha), with Williams 11 seconds behind Reid in third place. Les Trotter (Suzuki), Brian Hussey (Norton) and John Goodall (Seeley) completed the top six. On lap two, with the fastest lap of the race and a new record, 22m. 44.0s. - 99.58 mph, Williams took the lead from Padgett by 22.8 seconds and Reid was third, 13.8 seconds behind Padgett Trotter was still fourth, Goodall moved up to fifth and Tony Rogers came up into sixth place. Williams increased his lead to 53 seconds at half distance, and Reid was in second place, 37.8 seconds behind Padgett with the rest of the leaderboard unchanged. Dave Williams retired on lap four at Ballaugh Bridge with big end problems, so Reid took the lead by 12.2 seconds from Padgett, Goodall took third place, almost two minutes down on Padgett, Joe Thornton (Aermacchi) came into fourth place, Mick Poxon (Suzuki) fifth and Alf Mayrs (Yamaha) sixth. Reid increased his lead at the end of lap five to 51 seconds from Padgett who had a two minute advantage over Goodall, Thornton was still fourth and Ernie Pitt (Norton) and Brian Peters (Suzuki) came into the top six. But Padgett again suffered bad luck when he retired at Ginger Hall, and Paddy Reid went on to win by three minutes six seconds from Joe Thornton who pipped John Goodall for second place by 13.2 seconds, Ernie Pitt took fourth place, Les Trotter was fifth and Mick Poxon finished sixth. There were 54 finishers and 23 replicas were won.

John Goodall (2), Joe Thornton (101) and Paddy Reid in the winners enclosure. John Goodall still rides the same machine in the Classic races today.

1973 Senior MGP (6 laps / 226.38 miles) 115 entries

1. Paddy Reid	Yamaha	2h. 20m. 11.4s	96.89 mph (record)
2. Joe Thornton	Aermacchi	2h. 23m. 17.4s	94.79 mph
3. John Goodall	Seeley	2h. 23m. 30.6s	94.64 mph
Fastest lap (record)			
Dave Williams	Matchless	22m. 44.0s	99.58 mph

1974

1974 Lightweight MGP

The Lightweight attracted an entry of 102. Weather conditions caused a postponement of one hour, and the length of the race was reduced from four laps to three. Danny Shimmin topped the practice leaderboard with the first 100 plus lap in the Lightweight. Second fastest was Eddie Roberts (Yamaha) and third fastest was Roger Nott (Yamaha). Weather conditions however, were against records. At the end of the first lap, Roberts led Steve Ward (Yamaha) by 22.8 seconds with Don Padgett (Yamaha) third, 15.6 seconds down. Steve Parrish (Yamaha), Roger Cope (Yamaha) and Donal Cormican (Yamaha) made up the top six. Roberts increased his lead over Ward dramatically on lap two, extending it to 54.6 seconds, with Padgett just nine seconds down on Ward. Russ Webb (Yamsel) came on to the leaderboard in fourth place, followed by Cormican and Parrish. At the end of the race, Eddie Roberts had a margin of 58.8 seconds over Don Padgett who had passed Steve Ward. Danny Shimmin, with the fastest lap of the race, took fourth place, Russ Webb was fifth and Cormican sixth. Steve Parrish finished in seventh place. There were 65 finishers and 21 riders won replicas.

1974 Lightweight MGP (3 laps / 113.98 miles) 102 entries

Steve Ward, Don Padgett and Eddie Roberts

1. Eddie Roberts	Maxton Yamaha	1h. 15m. 10.0s	90.35 mph
2. Don Padgett	Padgett Yamaha	1h. 16m. 08.8s	89.18 mph
3. Steve Ward	Yamaha	1h. 16m. 30.0s	88.77 mph
Fastest lap			
Danny Shimmin	Yamaha	24m. 33.6s	92.17 mph

1974 Junior MGP

The entry of 110 for the Junior was reduced by non-starters to 94. Dave Williams (Yamaha) was the fastest in practice, followed by Neil Kelly (Yamaha) and Jack Higham (Yamaha). Despite the earlier delay, the Junior race was not reduced from the original six laps. Alan Jackson (Yamaha) led at the end of the first lap by 2.6 seconds from Joe Lindsay (Yamaha), with Joe Thornton (Yamaha) a further 4.8 seconds down. Bernard Murray (Yamaha), Wayne Dinham (Yamaha) and S. Jones (Yamaha) completed the top six. On lap two, Jackson retired with a broken gear lever, and Dinham shot into the lead from

fifth place! He led Thornton by 2.6 seconds with Murray in third place, Brian Hussey (Harley Davidson) was fourth, Lindsay was fifth and Tom Newell (Norton) came on to the leaderboard in sixth place. At half distance Dinham was 10.2 seconds ahead of Murray, who in turn had an advantage of 4.8 seconds over Hussey. Ian Tompkinson (Yamaha) came into the top six in fourth place, John Goodall (Aermacchi) was fifth and Lindsay had dropped to sixth. Tom Newell retired on this third lap at Ginger Hall. Murray took over the lead from Dinham on lap four by 28 seconds, with Hussey still third, but now 50.2 seconds adrift of Dinham. Lindsay moved up to fourth, Goodall was fifth with Tompkinson sixth. Murray almost doubled his lead at the end of lap five, he was 54 seconds ahead of Dinham and Hussey had closed to within 17 seconds of Dinham. Goodall, Tompkinson and Sammy McClements (Yamaha) completed the top six, with Lindsay dropping to seventh. Bernard Murray went on to win by over one minute from Dinham, with Hussey third, and the rest of the leaderboard unchanged. There were 51 finishers and 19 replicas were won.

Bernard Murray, 1974 double-winner.

1974 Junior MGP (6 laps / 226.38 miles) 108 entries

1. Bernard Murray	Maxton Yamaha	2h. 21m. 20.0s	96.10 mph
2. Wayne Dinham	Yamaha	2h. 22m. 26.2s	95.36 mph
3. John Goodall	Lawton Aermacchi	2h. 23m. 52.0s	94.41 mph
Fastest lap			
Brian Hussey	Harley Davidson	22m. 49.2s	99.20 mph

1974 Senior MGP

Bernard Murray completed a Junior/Senior double when he won the Senior, despite not appearing on the leaderboard until the fifth lap! Eddie Roberts (Yamaha) was fastest in practice, followed by Roger Nott (Yamaha) and Joe Thornton (Aermacchi H.D.). It was Roberts, the Lightweight winner, leading at the end of the first lap by 18.6 seconds from Thornton, who was 6.6 seconds ahead of Sammy McClements (Yamaha). Fourth was Les Trotter (Suzuki), fifth D. Hunt (Yamaha) and sixth Dave Williams (Matchless). With the first ever 100 mph lap in the Senior Manx - 22m. 36.6s. 100.12 mph - Roberts increased his lead over Thornton to 44.2 seconds with McClements still third, 20 seconds behind Thornton. Trotter and Hunt retained their places and Roger Nott (Yamaha) came up into sixth place. Roberts broke the record again on his third lap - 22m. 19.2s. 101.42 - to increase his lead over Thornton to one minute 18.4 seconds, with McClements a further 41 seconds down in third place. Hunt took fourth place from Trotter and Joe Lindsay (Yamaha) was sixth. Lap four was quite dramatic, Thornton retired on Bray Hill, Trotter was reported as touring at Handleys Corner and eventually retired, and even Roberts had a problem, he was black flagged at Ballacraine because the rear filler cap was open, he was stopped for four seconds and then continued. At the end of the lap his lead was two minutes 43.2 seconds from the new second place man McClements, who in turn led Trotter in third place by just 12.8 seconds. Nott was fourth, Lindsay moved up to fifth and Brian Peters (Suzuki) took over sixth place. The next of the leaderboard men to retire was McClements who went out at Ballagarey with a seized engine, so at the end of the fifth lap Roberts led the race by a staggering five minutes 11 seconds from Nott, and seemed certain of a Lightweight/Senior double. Murray was third, 58 seconds down on Nott, Peters, Tom Newell (Norton) and John Goodall (Vendetta) completed the top six. But if the fourth lap had been dramatic, the final one was even more so. Eddie Roberts, with that lead of over five minutes retired at the Bungalow, robbed of certain victory. So Nott looked the likely winner, but he had a spill at Glentrammon which put him out! So Bernard Murray went on to complete the double by just 3.4 seconds from Norman Tricogulus (Yamaha), who was 44.2 seconds ahead of Tom Newell, Peters took fourth place, Don Padgett (Yamaha) was fifth and John Carpenter (Yamaha) was sixth. There were 53 finishers in this dramatic Senior, and 21 won replicas.

1974 Senior MGP (6 laps / 226.38 miles) 115 entries

1. Bernard Murray	Maxton Yamaha	2h. 25m. 36.4s	93.28 mph
2. Norman Tricogulus	Walker Yamaha	2h. 25m. 40.0s	93.24 mph
3. Tom Newell	Kettle Norton	2h. 26m. 24.2s	92.77 mph
Fastest lap (record)			
Eddie Roberts	Yamaha	22m. 19.2s	101.42 mph

1975

1975 Lightweight MGP

Entries for the Lightweight were slightly down on previous years, 89, and 15 non-starters reduced the field to 74. Lee Heeson (Yamaha) topped the practice leaderboard followed by Don Padgett (Yamaha) and Alan Jackson (Yamaha). Heeson's promising practice times however came to no avail as he retired at Ballig on the first lap. Jackson led at the end of lap one by 27.6 seconds from Rick Burrows (Yamaha) with Steve Ward (Yamaha) in third place, just 4.4. seconds down on Ward. Roger Cope (Yamaha), Richard Watkins (Yamaha) and Nick Jefferies (Yamaha) completed the top six first time round. Jackson increased his lead to just over one minute at the end of the second lap. Ward had moved up to second place, eight seconds ahead of Cope who had taken third place from Burrows. Watkins and Jefferies remained fifth and sixth. Ward retired on lap three with electrical problems and Jackson led Cope by 46.4

seconds with Burrows 17.4 seconds down on Cope. Roger Nott (Yamaha) came on to the leaderboard in fourth place, John Baker (Yamaha) was fifth and Jefferies sixth. Alan Jackson made no mistake this time and won by 25 seconds from Roger Cope who set the fastest time of the day on his final lap - 23m. 04.0s. - to finish 36.2 seconds ahead of Burrows and Nott, Baker and Jefferies completed the first six leaderboard. There were 51 finishers and 19 riders won replicas.

1975 Lightweight MGP (4 laps / 150.92 miles) 89 entries

1. Alan Jackson	Lambert Yamaha	1h. 33m. 44.8s	96.59 mph
2. Roger Cope	Yamaha	1h. 34m. 09.8s	96.16 mph
3. Rick Burrows	Yamaha	1h. 34m. 47.0s	95.53 mph
Fastest lap			
Roger Cope	Yamaha	23m. 04.0s	98.14 mph

1975 Junior MGP

Entries for the Junior totalled 114, but non-starters reduced this figure to 96. Wayne Dinham (Yamaha), runner up in last years Junior, was fastest in practice. exactly 10 seconds faster than Dave Williams (Yamaha) with Les Trotter (Yamaha) third fastest. Dinham made no mistake this year, leading the race from start to finish. At the end of the first lap he led Trotter by 17.6 seconds, having lapped from a standing start at 102.28 mph Trotter in turn led Sammy McClements (Yamaha) by 11.6 seconds and Danny Shimmin (Yamaha) was just one second down on McClements. Richard Swallow (Yamaha) was fifth and Dave Williams (Yamaha) sixth. Dinham increased his lead over Trotter to 56.6 seconds on lap two and McClements was a further 21.4 seconds down in third place. Shimmin remained fourth and Williams took fifth place from Swallow. With the fastest lap of the day on lap three - 102.71 mph - Dinham was one minute 44.6 seconds in front of McClements. Trotter had been slowed by plug trouble. Williams was now third, 6.4 seconds down on McClements, Shimmin still held fourth place, Ian Tompkinson (Yamaha) was fifth and Geoff Kelly (Yamaha) sixth. At the end of the fourth lap Dinham led by two minutes from Williams who had overtaken McClements and had a 6.4 seconds advantage. Shimmin was fourth, Alan Duffus (Yamaha) fifth and Tony Randle (Yamaha) sixth. The positions at the end of lap five were Dinham, two minutes 25 seconds ahead of Williams who in turn was eight seconds in front of McClements, Shimmin, Randle and Ken Inwood (Yamaha). There were no changes to the top six at the finish so Dinham won at only his second attempt by two minutes 24 seconds and at a record race speed. There were 60 finishers and 18 replicas were won.

1975 Junior MGP (6 laps / 226.38 miles) 114 entries

1. Wayne Dinham	Yamaha	2h. 14m. 10.2s	101.23 mph
			(record)
2. Dave Williams	Yamaha	2h. 16m. 35.0s	99.44 mph
3. Sam McClements	Yamaha	2h. 17m. 00.8s	99.13 mph
Fastest lap			
Wayne Dinham	Yamaha	22m. 02.4s	102.71 mph

1975 Senior MGP

There were 113 starters for the Senior, the original entry of 126 having been reduced by 13 due to non-starters. Wayne Dinham (Yamaha) the Junior winner set the fastest practice lap with Danny Shimmin (Yamaha) next, followed by Tony Randle (Yamaha). At the end of the first lap, Keith Trubshaw (Yamaha) led by eight seconds from Sammy McClements (Yamaha) who was just 2.8 seconds up on Steve Ward (Yamaha) in third place. Jack Higham (Yamaha), Les Trotter (Suzuki) and Danny Shimmin (Yamaha) completed the top six. With a record lap second time round, McClements snatched the lead from Trubshaw by just 1.2 seconds, Higham took over third spot from Steve Ward who retired an this lap, Trotter and Shimmin moved up to fourth and fifth, and Dave Williams (Matchless) came on to the

Line astern at Keppel Gate, 1975 Senior. Neil Kelly (RaceWaye, 71) leads Ron Mellor (Seeley, 72) and Rick Burrows (Yamaha). Burrows finished 5th, Mellors 17th but Neil Kelly retired the innovative Clive Waye built machine.

One man's view of the Manx - by George Ridgeon

One man's view of the Manx.

To the racing motorcyclist, to ride in the 'Manx' is a dream, a hope, a vision. Having started racing in March 1964 on a humble BSA Bantam, it would have been a miracle! In 1965 I owned a quick Greeves Silverstone and, although the seed was sown, it faded as I did not have the mechanical ability to keep the machine going. It was not until 1970, when I owned another Greeves, that it started to blossom again. I entered the 1971 MGP. I had a chance meeting with an old friend, Ray Wakefield-

"Fancy mechanicking for me?"

"Yes."

So the team was set. Friends and other riders passed on tips, handed down over the years:- a plug bag; get up and watch any practice you are not riding in; go out in the rain! As any newcomer will know, I got no sleep the night before first practice. I had only had the trip round on the Crossley Tours, so that first lap was very steady. Would you believe that I went down to third gear for the second rise before Glen Vine! I did two laps; I kept saying to my friends in the digs (Doris Jackson's 'Boheme'), "Tell me I've done two laps."

I qualified to start. The bike developed a clutch problem halfway through the race, but I did manage to finish; what a warm feeling as you come out of Governor's dip for the last time.

1972. I again entered the Greeves; it was a 1967 RES. I now knew a lot of the tricks to keep it going. We rekindled friendships made in 1971 along with those riders we already knew, like the late Richard Swallow; although they were opponents, everyone helped each other. In the evenings we all would descend on a pub somewhere.

I remember a night in The George in Castletown, renowned for good nights at the Southern 100. About twenty riders were singing, with actions, 'Old Macdonald's Farm!'.

I feel this was my best year, finishing 24th. There were 22 Yamahas and Les Trotter on the Crook's Suzuki in front, out of 86 entrants.

1973 was my first heartbreak. Although moving up to a G50 with limited sponsorship (the owner put the engine together and owned half the bike), it blew up in practice. Help was at hand; John Goodall and Roger Haddock put it back together with some new bits. I was the 'gofer'! That old Manx atmosphere. I finished practice, but five laps into the race, the big end went. I remember my mother saying, "it doesn't go very well without a big end!" I did however enjoy the first riders' party, as it was the Golden Jubilee meeting.

The next years were mixed in fortune;

1974; I brought Les Hart to his first Manx. I pushed in to finish, yet a mile from home I was in replica time!

1975. It was Mike Dunn's first Manx; although Mike had trouble all week, I was flying, but you know the saying 'Piston broke'. I only made Ballalough, Mike had a good finish.

1976. I was 23rd at 88 mph, my best lap on the island was 91.5, but no replica. The riders' parties were still good.

1977. This was the Queen's Jubilee Year; I held a party and got a finish. (46th)

1978. Mike Dunn offered me his 250 Greeves (he was now living in the Island), as the classes had changed, allowing me to ride in the Junior on the

George celebrates Dave Pither's 1984 Senior Manx win.

G50. Two finishes. (Lightweight 54th, Junior 30th)

1979. I retired on the Greeves, but I limped home on the G50. In fact it was a five-lap finish; the race was shortened as the weather worsened whilst I was in the pits making adjustments at the end of that fifth and final lap. I remember this year well; Princess Michael was giving out the awards. Not only did I wear my Union Jack waistcoat, I kissed her hand on the stage, to the roar of the crowd!

1980. I entered a Trident I bought in a box of bits, and a 7R I had hoped to borrow. In the end I had to take the G50 and a plea brought Richard Swallow to my aid with a 350 Greeves Oulton. It was a long story, but I upset the chief scrutineer, Ken Harding. Sometimes we still laugh about it when we see each other! I managed two finishes. (57th Junior, 56th Senior).

Little did I know that 1981 would be my last Manx. The Trident had already had a finish at the Southern 100. This year's ride at the Manx was the best I had had, since 1972, with a trouble-free ride and my highest average speed, 89 mph for six laps, but only a 90 mph fastest lap.

I rode a few short-circuits at home. One memory is riding at Brands Hatch on the shortest day, 23rd October. I finished third, although it was going dark and the crowd were leaving with their lights on! This turned out to be my last ride on a motorcycle.

On November 16th, I attended a fire at 12.30 am, being a fireman, which was a little like riding in the Manx perhaps? Exciting, enjoyable, as you are helping people; a little of the unknown. Sadly, I woke up in hospital the next day with a broken neck. I was transferred to Stoke Mandeville some days later.

A great number of riders from all over Great Britain dropped in to see me; these included Eric McFarlane and Howard Selby from Scotland. They called in when racing at Brands. In 1981 they camped next to us. Rupert and Ann Murden were weekly visitors from Kent; the list was endless. One local friend offered to fly me to the Island. By June time I was in a wheelchair regularly exercising. The Southern 100 was coming up and they said I could go to that, so, with two good Fire Service friends, Frank and Pete to look after me, I had a very enjoyable, if not emotional, three days, seeing all my Southern 100 and MGP friends and officials. I think missing the 1982 Manx, being then in a nursing home, was the worst time of my life. I did keep getting TT Special reports of the Manx, which did make me feel I was there in Spirit, as I sent messages as well.

Time progressed, I was slowly getting used to my disability. Getting a car with hand controls and a wheelchair lift transformed my life. I drove to the 1983 Southern 100 and found out there was to be a parade of old riders at the Diamond Jubilee Manx; I wanted to do this. There were a few problems, but at last there was something I wanted to do. We overcame every problem, and I did the lap on the back of Mick Grant on an 850 Commando, raising money for charity from it!

I also had three bikes racing in the Manx; Rob Price on my Greeves; he finished sixth; Les Trotter was a retirement on my G50, but Gordon Morss got a finish on my Trident in the Senior. It was the year I also ended up on the Manx Grand Prix Riders' Association committee.

With the TT running an Historic race in '84, I asked Eric McFarlane to ride my Seeley; sadly, it broke in practice. I ended up helping a Canadian, Gary McCaw with his 500 Velo. He let me team manage him and I was pleased he had a good finish, only saddened to find that his 11-year old son John had Cystic Fibrosis. They had cheered me up so much, that I raised £2,600 for Cystic Fibrosis, Cancer, Spinal Injuries and the Manx Helicopter Fund in just six weeks. The draw took place at the 1984 MGP presentations, with Senior winner and fellow Gloucester rider Dave Pither and others attending. Sadly, John McCaw died in 1987, aged 15.

I kept the G50 running for some years. It has achieved a third and fourth with Tony Russell on board. With no 250 race for some years, I had a friend get a special 350 Greeves Oulton together. Now with the problems of disability, I just campaign the 350 Greeves.

Becoming chairman of the MGPRA in 1986, I instituted, and am still running the annual get-together. During the Manx, there are always social get-togethers, the 38th Milestone during race days, plus the AGM to attend.

I can say, having raced for seventeen years, eleven at the Manx, and being disabled for sixteen, I still have not lost my passion for racing, although it is getting harder; but the friendships I have made over the years, this is something that a truly amateur event like the Manx can do. So a big thank-you to all at the MGP for all the pleasure over the years; it has been a privilege to have been associated with it.

Sam McClements at Creg ny Baa.

leaderboard in sixth place. At half distance, McClements was 15 seconds ahead of Trubshaw with Higham over one minute down in third place. Trotter was fourth, Williams fifth and John Goodall (Matchless) came in to sixth place, Danny Shimmin having retired at the pits. By the time lap four was completed, McClements had built up a lead of one minute 35 seconds over Trubshaw with Higham still third, 6.4 seconds down, Williams had taken fourth place from Trotter, and Ian Tompkinson (Yamaha) came on to the leaderboard in sixth place. Trubshaw pulled back 17 seconds on McClements on lap five and improved his lead on Higham to 46 seconds. with the rest of the leaderboard unchanged. Williams came off at Ballaugh on the last lap. Sammy McClements won by 59 seconds from Trubshaw who finished one minute 13 seconds ahead of Higham. Les Trotter was fourth, Rick Burrows (Yamaha) fifth and Roger Nott (Yamaha) sixth, with Ian Tompkinson taking seventh place. There were 60 finishers and 16 riders won replicas.

1975 Senior MGP (6 laps / 226.38 miles) 116 entries

1. Sam McClements	Crawford Yamaha	2h. 14m. 25.6s	101.04 mph (record)
2. Keith Trubshaw	Maxton Yamaha	2h. 15m. 24.2s	100.31 mph
3. Jack Higham	Yamaha	2h. 16m. 07.6s	99.41 mph
Fastest lap (record)			
Sam McClements	Crawford Yamaha	21m. 57.4s	103.10 mph

The Manx Club lifted their ban on women pit attendants this year, and Bob Simmons wife, Freddie, was the first to take advantage of this rule change.

1976

1976 Lightweight MGP

Entries for the Lightweight were well up on the previous year totalling 105, and 12 non-starters reduced the field to 93. Danny Shimmin (Yamaha) set the fastest practice lap, followed by Bryan Robson (Yamaha) and John Stone (Yamaha). Local rider Shimmin set the pace on the opening lap and led Ivor Greenwood (Yamaha) by 5.4 seconds, just 0.8 seconds down in third place was Robson. Stone was fourth followed by Mick Grice (Yamaha) and Don Padgett (Yamaha). Shimmin increased his lead at the end of lap two to 12.8 seconds, and Robson moved into second place, 20 seconds ahead of Greenwood. Stone remained fourth, Padgett moved up to fifth and Stephen Davies (Yamaha) came into sixth place. By the time the fourth lap was completed, Shimmin led Robson by 30.4 seconds. Stone moved up to third ahead of Grice, Greenwood and Davies. So Danny Shimmin became the first Manx rider to win a Manx since 1965 when Dennis Craine won the Lightweight Race. He won by 29.2 seconds from Bryan Robson, and Mick Grice with a new record on his final lap took third place. John Stone, Ivor Greenwood and Norman Tricogulus (Yamaha) completed the top six, with Stephen Davies taking seventh place. Don Padgett, who had been on the leaderboard for the first two laps eventually finished 17th after having problems with a broken gear lever. There were 71 finishers and 35 replicas were won.

1976 Lightweight MGP (4 laps / 150.92 miles) 105 entries

1. Danny Shimmin	Harrison Yamaha	1h. 31m. 23.8s	99.07 mph (record)
2. Bryan Robson	Yamaha	1h. 31m. 53.0s	98.55 mph
3. Mick Grice	Maxton Yamaha	1h. 31m. 58.4s	98.45 mph
Fastest lap (record)			
Mick Grice	Maxton Yamaha	22m. 26.0s	100.91 mph

1976 Junior MGP

Danny Shimmin aviates the front wheel at Kerrowmoar.

From 110 entries for the Junior, non-starters reduced the field to exactly 100. Kevin Riley (Yamaha) topped the practice leaderboard, followed by Keith Trubshaw (Yamaha) and Ronnie Russell (Yamaha). It was Dave Williams (Yamaha) however, who led at the end or the first lap by 0.2 seconds from Trubshaw who was just 0.8 seconds ahead of Riley - one second covering the first three! Jim Heath (Yamaha) was fourth, only two seconds down on Riley and Joe Lindsay (Yamaha) was fifth ahead of Russell. Williams was 1.8 seconds up on Riley at the end of the second lap, Heath was third - 18.2 seconds down - Lindsay was fourth, Trubshaw dropped to fifth and Russell remained sixth. The first of the leaderboard men to retire was Jim Heath, who went out on lap three at the Gooseneck with gearbox trouble. Williams led Riley by 14.6 seconds at half distance, with Lindsay third, 48 seconds behind Riley. Russell moved up to fourth place, Trubshaw was fifth and Jack Higham (Yamaha) came on to the leaderboard in sixth place. Riley had a long pit stop at the end of the third lap due to brake problems, so dropped

of the fourth lap leaderboard. Williams led Lindsay by over one minute, Russell moved up to third, 38 seconds down on Lindsay. Trubshaw was fourth, John Knowles (Yamaha) fifth and John Golding (Yamaha) sixth. Williams luck again ran out on lap five when he came off at the 11th Milestone. Lindsay took over the lead from Trubshaw by 35.8 seconds with Russell in third place. Jim Balmer (Yamaha) came into the top six in fourth place, followed by Golding and Higham. Russell was the next to taste misfortune when he came off at Schoolhouse Corner in Ramsey on the final lap. So Joe Lindsay took the chequered flag by a minute and a half from Trubshaw. Kevin Riley made up for his long pit stop with a couple of quick laps to take third place from Jim Balmer, with Ron Jones (Yamaha) fifth and John Knowles sixth. There were 57 finishers and 30 riders won replicas.

1976 Junior MGP (6 laps / 226.38 miles) 110 entries

1. Joe Lindsay	Maxton Yamaha	2h. 14m. 04.6s	101.30 mph (record)
2. Keith Trubshaw	Yamaha	2h. 14m. 34.0s	100.19 mph
3. Kevin Riley	Fowler Yamaha	2h. 16m. 49.0s	99.27 mph
Fastest lap			
Dave Williams	Yamaha	21m. 25.8s	105.63 mph

1976 Senior MGP

Les Trotter gets lined up for the jump at Rhencullen.

The Senior Manx Grand Prix was postponed from the Thursday to the Friday because of poor weather conditions. The entry was 114, and with just seven non-starters a large field of 107 faced the starter. Jim Heath (Yamaha) was fastest in practice followed by Kevin Riley (Yamaha) and Les Bibby (Yamaha). At the end of lap one, Keith Trubshaw led by 11.6 seconds from Danny Shimmin who was 10.4 seconds in front of Don Padgett (Yamaha), with Ken Inwood (Yamaha), Bryan Robson (Yamaha) and Les Trotter (Suzuki) completing the top six. Keith Trubshaw's luck ran out on the second lap when he retired at Ballaugh with plug trouble. Shimmin took over the lead by 11.4 seconds from Padgett, and Inwood took third place, 20 seconds behind Padgett. Chris Revett (Suzuki) came on to the leaderboard in fourth place ahead of Trotter and Roger J. Wilson (Yamaha) came up to sixth place. With Shimmin taking a pit stop at the end of the second lap, Padgett took over the lead at the end of the third by 52.8 seconds, and Shimmin was 35.2 seconds ahead of Trotter, Wilson, Revett and Nick Jefferies (Yamaha) completed the top six. Padgett went out on lap four and Shimmin had a comfortable lead of two minutes over Trotter who in turn was 34 seconds ahead of Wilson. Robin Buxton (Yamaha) and Les Bibby (Yamaha) came on to the leaderboard in fourth and fifth places ahead of Ronnie Russell. But once again drama struck on the final lap of a Manx, Les Trotter was No. 1, and started the final lap 55 seconds down on Danny Shimmin who was No. 71, their starting difference was five minutes 50 seconds. Les finished the race and then the rains came, Danny was losing ground mile by mile in the wet conditions and eventually finished second to Les by just 1.4 seconds after 226 miles of racing. It was the closest ever finish to a Manx at that time. Robinson finished third, Les Bibby fourth, Robin Buxton fifth and Roger J. Wilson sixth. Despite the fact that there were 107 starters, only 37 finished the race, and of these, 14 won replicas.

1976 Senior MGP (6 laps / 226.38 miles) 114 entries

1. Les Trotter	Crooks Suzuki	2h. 17m. 55.8s	98.47 mph
2. Danny Shimmin	SS	2h. 17m. 57.2s	98.45 mph
3. Brian Robinson	Yamaha	2h. 21m. 20.8s	96.09 mph
Fastest lap			
Chris Revett	Suzuki	22m. 08.4s	102.24 mph

1977

1977 Lightweight MGP

Entries for the Lightweight were again up, totalling 112, but 16 non-starters reduced the line up to 96. Dave Hickman (Yamaha) was fastest in practice, followed by Norman Tricogulus (Yamaha) and Bryan Robson (Yamaha). On the opening lap, Hickman lapped at 100.09 mph to lead Richard Swallow (Yamaha) by 1.8 seconds, third place was held by Clive Watts (Yamaha), 17.4 seconds down on Swallow and the top six were completed by Mick Grice (Yamaha), Dick Cassidy (Yamaha) and Bob Jackson (Yamaha). Hickman broke the lap record on lap two at 101.28 mph and led Clive Watts by 36.2 seconds, with Swallow now third, 19.4 seconds down. Grice came off at Ballacraine on this lap and Jackson took over fourth place, Mick Shirlaw (Yamaha) came on to the leaderboard in fifth place and Cassidy was sixth. Hickman forged ahead on lap

Dave Hickman in fine style at Union Mills.

three and led Swallow by 55.4 seconds with Watts down to third place. Jackson remained fourth, Don Padgett (Yamaha) was fifth and Drew Alexander (Yamaha) sixth. Cassidy had dropped to ninth. It was Swallow who motored on the final lap, breaking the record at 101.30 mph to close to within 3.8 seconds of Hickman. Watts finished third, Jackson fourth, Shirlaw fifth and Padgett sixth. Drew Alexander finished ninth. There were 69 Finishers and 22 replicas were won.

1977 Lightweight MGP (4 laps / 150.92 miles) 89 entries

1. Dave Hickman	Maxton Yamaha	1h. 30m. 35.8s	99.95 mph (record)
2. Richard Swallow	Yamaha	1h. 30m. 39.6s	99.88 mph
3. Clive Watts	Fowler Yamaha	1h. 31m. 17.0s	99.19 mph
Fastest lap (record)			
Richard Swallow	Yamaha	22m. 20.8s	101.30 mph

1977 Junior MGP

Because of worsening weather conditions the Junior was postponed until the Wednesday. The entry was 109, and 10 non-starters reduced this figure to 99. Fred Broadbent (Yamaha) set the fastest lap in practice followed by Jack Higham (Yamaha) and Ron Jones (Yamaha). At the end of the first lap Kevin Riley (Yamaha), who had finished third in the 1976 Junior led from Jim Heath (Yamaha) by 30 seconds, with Mick Capper (Yamaha) in third place, 1.4 seconds down on Heath. Ron Jones was fourth, John Knowles (Yamaha) fifth and John Golding (Yamaha) sixth. The first four remained unchanged on lap two, and Riley added another 7.8 seconds to his lead. Geoff Johnson (Yamaha) and Ronnie Russell (Yamaha) came on to the leaderboard in fifth and sixth places, Golding and Knowles dropping to seventh and eighth. At half distance, Riley led the new second place man Capper by one minute 5.6 seconds, Jones also moved up one place to third with Heath relegated to fourth place, Russell moved up to fifth and Golding came back into the top six. Riley's lead at the end of the fourth lap was 46 seconds and Heath had retaken second place from Capper by 17 seconds. Jones was fourth followed by Russell and Golding. Heath had a slow fifth lap and dropped out of the top six. Riley led from Capper by one minute 27 seconds with Jones third, Russell fourth, Golding fifth and Knowles sixth. Two of the leaderboard men went out on the last lap, Capper came off at Laurel Bank and Knowles retired with engine trouble. So Riley won at a record breaking pace by one and a half minutes from Jones who finished 32.4 seconds ahead of Russell. Heath took fourth place and John Robinson (Yamaha) and Alan Lee (Yamaha) came into the top six. There were 49 finishers and 19 replicas were won.

1977 Junior MGP (6 laps / 226.38 miles) 109 entries

1. Kevin Riley	Beresford Yamaha	2h. 12m. 20.6s	102.63 mph (record)
2. Ron Jones	Yamaha	2h. 13m. 50.6s	101.48 mph
3. Ronnie Russell	Yamaha	2h. 14m. 23.0s	101.07 mph
Fastest lap			
Kevin Riley	Beresford Yamaha	21m. 33.6s	105.00 mph

1977 Senior MGP

"Snuffy" Davis at Governors Bridge.

The entry for the Senior totalled 115, and exactly 100 riders lined up at the start. Ron Jones (Yamaha) had set the fastest practice time, followed by the Junior winner Kevin Riley and Mick Grice (Yamaha). Jones completed the first lap at 100.86 mph to lead John Golding (Yamaha) by two seconds with Jim Heath in third place, 0.6 seconds down. Snuffy Davis (Yamaha) was fourth and Jack Higham (Yamaha) and Ronnie Russell (Yamaha) completed the top six. On lap two Davis snatched the lead from Jones, but only by 0.2 seconds, and the same margin separated Heath in third place from Jones. Golding was fourth, Bob Jackson (Yamaha) fifth and Jack Higham sixth. Only 11 seconds separated the first six, and Russell had dropped to seventh. More changes on lap three - Jones was back in front by 0.4 seconds from Russell who was 11 seconds up on Davis. Jackson took fourth place from Golding who retired at Ballaugh with a broken chain. George Linder brought his Suzuki into fifth place and Heath was sixth. Yet another change of leader on lap four - this time Heath was in front by 22.8 seconds from Russell who was 41 seconds up on Jones. Davis was fourth and the top six was completed by Linder and Mick Capper (Yamaha). Davis regained the lead on lap five by 3.8 seconds, Russell retired at Ginger Hall, so Linder was up to second place with Jones third, a further 10 seconds down, Heath, Capper and Nick Jefferies (Yamaha) were next. And so to the final lap, and two more of the top men were in trouble, Jones came off at Douglas Corner, Kirk Michael and Heath had a long pit stop at the end of the fifth lap and retired on the sixth. Davis went on

Kev Riley lets the Beresford Yamaha fly on Quarter Bridge Road.

to win by 17.2 seconds from Linder and Nick Jefferies came up to third place. Steve Bradley, (Suzuki) finished fourth ahead of Capper, and Kevin Jackson (Yamaha) took sixth place. There were 47 finishers and 16 replicas were won.

1977 Senior MGP (6 laps / 226.38 miles) 115 entries

1. Snuffy Davis	TZ Yamaha	2h. 15m. 10.2s	100.48 mph
2. George Linder	RG Suzuki	2h. 15m. 27.4s	100.27 mph
3. Nick Jefferies	Yamaha	2h. 19m. 36.0s	97.29 mph
Fastest lap			
George Linder	RG Suzuki	22m. 02.0s	102.88 mph

1978

Newcomers races were re-introduced to the programme in 1978, there were three classes - 500cc, 350cc and 250cc They were to be held on the Tuesday morning over four laps, followed by the Junior over six laps, with the Lightweight race over four laps being transferred to the Thursday morning followed by the Senior over six laps.

1978 Senior Newcomers

Dave Ashton on Bray Hill, a practice shot.

Weather conditions caused the postponement of the Newcomers races to the Wednesday. All classes were to be run concurrently. Even on Wednesday the weather was poor, causing a two hour delay, and the reduction of the races to three laps. The Senior class had attracted 29 entries, and with just three non-starters, 26 riders faced the starter. Dave Ashton (Suzuki) set the fastest practice lap, followed by John Davies (Yamaha) and Davy Gordon (Sparton). At the end of the first lap Ashton led by 22.6 seconds from Davies with Mark Middleton (Suzuki) third a further 17.4 seconds down. Then the rains came and slowed the pace right down. Ashton increased his lead to 2 minutes 1.6 seconds at the end of the second lap from Davies with Middleton still third, 14 seconds down. Ashton won by one minute 53 seconds from Davies, but Middleton came off in Parliament Square on the last lap and retired bringing Gordon into third place. Mal Marsden (Honda); Phillip Odlin (Honda) and Kenny Harmer (Yamaha) completed the top six. There were 20 finishers.

1978 Senior Newcomers (3 laps / 113.19 miles) 29 entries

1. Dave Ashton	Suzuki	1h. 23m. 35.0s	81.25 mph
2. John Davies	Maxton Yamaha	1h. 25m. 28.0s	79.46 mph
3. Davy Gordon	Sparton	1h. 26m. 56.6s	78.11 mph
Fastest lap			
Dave Ashton	Suzuki	26m. 50.4s	84.34 mph

1978 Junior Newcomers

There were 33 entries for the Junior Newcomers, and non-starters reduced this total to 29. Conor McGinn (Yamaha,) topped the practice leaderboard followed by Jackie Hughes (Yamaha) and Tony Rennie (Yamaha). But at the end of the first lap, Island International footballer Rob Brew (Yamaha) led the race, by one minute 1.6 seconds from McGinn, with Rennie nine seconds down on McGinn. Brew more than doubled his lead over McGinn on lap two to two minutes 28 seconds and Hughes (Yamaha) took third place from Rennie, but was one minute three seconds down on McGinn. Brew motored on to win from McGinn by just over three minutes, with Hughes over two minutes down on McGinn. Fourth place was taken by Rob Britton (Yamaha), fifth was Tony Rennie (Yamaha) and sixth was John Crellin (Yamaha). There were 26 finishers.

1978 Junior Newcomers (3 laps / 113.19 miles) 33 entries

1. Rob Brew	CBG Yamaha	1h. 17m. 04.6s	88.11 mph
2. Conor McGinn	MB Yamaha	1h. 20m. 05.6s	84.79 mph
3. Jackie Hughes	Shepherd Yamaha	1h. 22m. 06.0s	82.72 mph
Fastest lap			
Rob Brew	CBG Yamaha	24m. 56.6s	90.75 mph

1978 Lightweight Newcomers

The entry of 23 for the Lightweight Newcomers was reduced by non-starters to 19. Phil Mellor (Yamaha) topped the practice leaderboard followed by Brian Reid (Yamaha) and Dave Broadhead (Yamaha). Mellor shot straight into the lead at the end of the first lap by one minute 5.4 seconds from Broadhead with Reid a further 14 seconds down. It was quite a dramatic second lap, Broadhead retired at Governors Bridge and Reid came off at Cruickshanks Corner, Ramsey. This left Mellor with a lead of five minutes 24.4 seconds over Allan Brew (Yamaha) with Mick Noblett (Suzuki) in third place. Mellor added over two minutes to his advantage on the last lap to win from Brew, with Noblett holding on to third place. The top six leaderboard was completed by Gareth Lawrence (Yamaha), Robert Maltby (Harley Davidson) and Rex Edwards (Yamaha). There were 13 finishers.

1978 Lightweight Newcomers (3 laps / 113.19 miles) 23 entries

1. Phil Mellor	Maxton Yamaha	1h. 19m. 38.4s	85.27 mph
2. Allan Brew	Yamaha	1h. 27m. 06.6s	77.96 mph
3. Mick Noblett	Yamaha	1h. 30m. 55.8s	74.68 mph
Fastest lap			
Phil Mellor	Maxton Yamaha	25m. 48.2s	87.73 mph

1978 Lightweight MGP

At the conclusion of the Newcomers, weather conditions had worsened, and the Junior race was postponed until the Friday. The weather was not too good on the Thursday either,

A first-timers view - by Bill Snelling

Having spectated and mechanicked at the Manx for many years, 1978 saw the opportunity to get a ride. I had recently bought a Velocette Metisse that had originally been built by the Velo specialist Ralph Seymour at Thame. It had been ridden by Anthony Woollon, who finished 36th in the 1971 Senior Manx.

I had moved to the Island during 1977, so a lot of spare time was used in getting the sequence of bends memorised, more important than trying to get a real racing line sorted, especially for a newcomer. Living in Castletown and working in Ramsey meant a half-lap session getting to work; the other half was completed going home.

First practice session, all went well to start with, but going down the Cronk y Voddy straight, something whacked me on the bum - I thought I must have picked up a stone or something. Later that lap I was aware that the rear suspension had stiffened up, so took it easy back to the paddock, where we found the top lug had snapped off a rear suspension! What had smacked my backside was a top collet! I had ridden most of a lap with the suspension fully compressed. (those aware of my physical proportions - my tailor calls my size 'short portly' - think it happens all the time!).

The machine ran real well through practice, but my excess of 'avoirdupois' (flab) meant that it was a struggle to get the bike to pull up the mountain. The close-ratio Velo box is a bit like a five-speeder with the middle gear missing - rev the nuts off it in second, hit third and it bogs down. Even sticking a boot in the mega didn't help so I was resigned to pootling up to Guthrie's in second, watching the rev counter creep up, then rolling it back to save revving out. Later, on the last day of practice, rounding the Creg I gave it some stick, round to 6,000, a bit more - 6,200 then 6,400 when all of a sudden it took off and whanged round to 7,000! A boot into second, and it went there again! Same again in third, and by the time Brandish was getting very adjacent, it was showing 6,400 in top, which equated to over 130! [Note: a standard Velo would have grenaded itself at those revs; this one had parallel rollers, coil valve springs, rocker return springs and a flanged drive side shaft - don't try it unless you have a spare engine with you].

I mentioned my exciting discovery to Vern Wallis, then chief mechanic at Seymour's and got bawled out for doing it! (I resisted using those sort of revs in the race - wish I had done so).

We had a wet Thursday afternoon practice, but that was nothing compared to the weather experienced in the race. I had been allocated No. 1, so when the flag dropped, I ran like crazy down towards Bray Hill for what seemed like ages before hitting the saddle and it fired. A split-second later I heard Stephen Winn's Seeley Matchless burst into life and I thought "If they stop the race now, I've won!" We 'led' round to Ballacraine before being passed by a pair of Yamahas. Got back past them through Laurel Bank (all those hours memorising the course paid off), past again at Cronk y Voddy, and we played tag all the way round to the Sulby Straight, where they buggered off for good.

Schoolhouse Corner was one I did not like, a bump on the way in unsettled both of us - bike and me, so I took it steady through there - so steady that I went in laying about fourth on the road, and exited it somewhere like twenty fourth! It was snowing riders; they must have been queueing up for miles back.

The mountain this day was very, very misty and I was groping my way along the white line towards Windy when I was aware of a rider in front. I could not see or hear him, but the distinctive smell of unburnt two-stroke oil was wafting in through my (open) visor. I came upon the back of a rider and slipped past. I glanced at his number - 25 - and thought, "He must be going well" After Windy, the mist lifted and a millisecond later, No. 25 Dave Ashton (Suzuki) flew past at a rate of knots that made me look like a pedestrian. (Can I stake my claim now to being the only rider in this race to have passed the eventual winner?).

We bimbled our way on, passing a few on the lower stretches, then watching them go past up the mountain, cursing the lack of a middle gear and/or the excess of pud that the 'little' 500 was assigned to be pulling. Even at 'supposed' racing speeds, it was easy to spot some clubmates around the circuit, but I am sure the race was longer than the two laps they appeared to be indicating as I went past!

We eventually finished twelfth out of 20 finishers, and went on to have a further two finishes. The finishers medal may be small, but it means the most to me!

Irrefutable proof that the 'short-portly' publisher of this august publication led the 1978 Newcomers (on the road at least). Bill Snelling leads Steve Winn (Matchless) on the first lap, but the roles were reversed by the end of the race!

and the Lightweight race was postponed for two hours and reduced to three laps. The entry was 95, and with 12 non-starters, 83 riders lined up for the start. Bryan Robson (Yamaha) was fastest in practice followed by Bob Jackson (Yamaha) and Cliff Paterson (Yamaha). At the end of the first lap, Lee Heeson (Yamaha) led from Richard Swallow by 3.8 seconds with Jackson third, 1.6 seconds down. Paterson was fourth, Rob Brew (Yamaha) fifth and Robson sixth. Heeson retired at Union Mills on lap two, and Robson at Sulby Bridge. Jackson went into the lead by 12 seconds from Swallow with Paterson third, just one second down on Swallow. Phil Mellor (Yamaha), Ron Jones (Yamaha) and Jackie Hughes (Yamaha) came on to the leaderboard. Jackson had a slow last lap, whilst Paterson set the fastest lap of the race, so Paterson won by 35.6 seconds from Swallow who beat Jackson by 11.2 seconds. Mellor finished fourth, Jones fifth and Hughes sixth. There were 65 finishers and 22 replicas were won.

Cliff Paterson (Yamaha), Bray Hill.

1978 Lightweight (4 laps / 150.92 miles) 95 entries

1. Cliff Paterson	Yamaha	1h. 10m. 33.6s	96.25 mph
2. Richard Swallow	Maxton Yamaha	1h. 11m. 09.2s	95.44 mph
3. Bob Jackson	Lambert Yamaha	1h. 11m. 40.4s	94.75 mph
Fastest lap			
Cliff Paterson	Yamaha	22m. 33.8s	100.33 mph

1978 Senior MGP

The Senior entry totalled 114, and with just 11 non-starters, 103 riders came to the starting line. Local rider Mike Kneen (Suzuki) topped the practice leaderboard, Steve Ward (Yamaha) was next with Conor McGinn (Yamaha) third. Ward grabbed the early advantage and led George Linder (Suzuki) at the end of the first lap by 6.6 seconds with Jim Heath (Yamaha) 3.8 seconds down in third place. Dave Pither (Yamaha), McGinn and Marty Ames (Lockyam) completed the first lap leaderboard. Ward increased his lead over Linder to 8.4 seconds at the end of lap two. Pither moved up to third, Ronnie Russell (Suzuki) came on to the leaderboard in fourth place Ames moved up to fifth and Heath dropped to sixth. By half distance, Ward was 16.8 seconds up on Linder, and Russell took third place from Pither and was 28.6 seconds behind Linder. McGinn was fourth, John Robinson (Yamaha) fifth and Pither sixth. At the end of the fourth lap Ward had added three seconds to his lead over Linder, and Russell, with a new lap record at 105.09 mph closed to within 25.6 seconds of Linder. Pither came back up to fourth place, McGinn was fifth and Robinson sixth. Linder fell a further three seconds behind Ward on lap five, the difference being 24.6 seconds. Russell retired at Ballaugh and McGinn took over third place, one minute 23.6 seconds down. Robinson, Pither and Jim Dunlop (Yamsel) completed the top six. Linder appeared to be closing the gap on Ward on the last lap, and when the final times were announced, he took victory by 8.8 seconds. McGinn had problems at Ballacraine when he stopped to replace the chain and eventually finished 22nd. Pither finished third, Phil Nichols (Yamaha) took fourth place, Clive Watts (Yamaha) fifth and Steve Bradley (Yamaha) sixth. There were 64 finishers and 22 replicas were won.

1978 Senior (6 laps / 226.38 miles) 114 entries

1. George Linder	Suzuki	2h. 12m. 48.0s	102.28 mph
			(record)
2. Steve Ward	Padgett Yamaha	2h. 12m. 56.8s	102.16 mph
3. Dave Pither	Yamaha	2h. 16m. 05.6s	99.80 mph
Fastest lap (record)			
Ronnie Russell	Suzuki	21m. 32.4s	105.09 mph

1978 Junior MGP

The Junior, postponed to the Friday, had an entry of 115, and despite the delay, there were just 12 non-starters, giving a field of 103. John McEntee (Yamaha) was fastest in practice followed by Steve Ward (Yamaha). the Senior runner-up and Bob Jackson (Yamaha). Local rider Mike Kneen (Yamaha) led at the end of the first lap by three seconds from Ward who in turn was 9.8 seconds ahead of Nick Jefferies (Yamaha). John Webb (Yamaha) was fourth, Jackson fifth and Richard Swallow (Yamaha) sixth. Kneen increased his lead over Ward to 27.2 seconds at the end of the second lap, with Webb up into third place, 26 seconds down on Ward. Jackson was fourth, Jefferies fifth and Swallow sixth. Ward closed to just two seconds of Kneen at the end of the third lap, with Webb trailing Kneen by 28.2 seconds. Swallow moved in to fourth place, Clive Watts (Yamaha) came on to the leaderboard in fifth place and Jim Dunlop (Yamsel) come up to sixth. Jackson was seventh and Jefferies eighth. Ward snatched the lead from Kneen at the end of the fourth lap by just 0.2 seconds, with Webb still third, but now 39.2 seconds down on Kneen. Jackson took fourth place ahead of Swallow and Watts. Nick Jefferies retired at Ballacraine. A close race was still in prospect at the end of the fifth lap, with Ward just 0.4 seconds up on Kneen, Webb was still third, Watts was up to fourth, Jackson dropped to fifth and Swallow was sixth. But the close last lap lasted only as far as Ballaugh Bridge, where Kneen retired with a broken gear lever. So Ward made up for his narrow defeat in the Senior, winning by three minutes 22.6 seconds from Jackson with Watts third, nine seconds down. Swallow, Webb and John Knowles (Yamaha) completed the top six. There were 53 finishers and 14 replicas were won.

1978 Junior (6 laps / 226.38 miles) 115 entries

1. Steve Ward	Padgett Yamaha	2h. 15m. 22.4s	100.33 mph
2. Bob Jackson	Lambert Yamaha	2h. 18m. 45.0s	97.89 mph
3. Clive Watts	Cowles Yamaha	2h. 18m. 54.0s	97.78 mph
Fastest lap (record)			
Mike Kneen	Yamaha	21m. 52.6s	103.48 mph

1979

1979 was Millennium Year in the Isle of Man. The race programme for the Manx remained the same but the capacity for the Junior was increased to 500cc and for the Senior to 750cc

1979 Senior Newcomers

The Senior Newcomers attracted an entry of 23, of which non-starters reduced the field to 20. Dave Raybon (Yamaha) was fastest in practice followed by Gordon Brown (Suzuki) and Fred O'Callaghan (Norton). Raybon took command of the race from the start and at the end of the first lap led Bob Eyre (Yamaha) by 56.2 seconds with Brown third, 7.6 seconds down. By the time the second lap was completed Raybon was in a commanding lead of three minutes 6.2 seconds from Alan Couldwell (Honda) with Allan Evans (Yamaha) third, Brown having dropped to sixth.place. At the end of the third lap Raybon led Couldwell by three minutes 27 seconds and the new third place man was John Loder (Fahron) with Evans down to fifth. Raybon won comfortably by five minutes 23.8 seconds from Couldwell with Loder third. Fourth place was taken by Evans, fifth by John Trickett (Suzuki) and sixth by Rob Claude (Honda). There were 14 finishers.

1979 Senior Newcomers (4 laps / 150.92 miles) 23 entries

1. Dave Raybon	Yamaha	1h. 35m. 28.6s	94.84 mph (record)
2. Alan Couldwell	Honda	1h. 40m. 52.4s	89.76 mph
3. John Loder	Fahron	1h. 41m. 36.6s	89.11 mph
Fastest lap (record)			
Dave Raybon	Yamaha	23m. 24.4s	96.17 mph

1979 Junior Newcomers

An entry of 29 was received for the Junior Newcomers, and 27 riders came to the line. Rob McElnea (Yamaha) set the fastest practice lap, second was Steve Bamford (Yamaha) with Stewart Cole (Yamaha) third. McElnea led at the end of the first lap by 24.6 seconds from Roger Luckman (Yamaha) who in turn led Bamford by seven seconds. Luckman closed the gap on McElnea by three seconds at the end of lap two, and Cole was 28 seconds down on Luckman with Bamford in fourth place. Cole took the lead by one second from McElnea on lap three, with Luckman 11.4 seconds down in third place.

The final lap saw drama once again, Cole retired, McElnea came off above May Hill, Ramsey, hurt his elbow and damaged the fairing, but remounted and proceeded. Whilst all this was going on, Luckman broke the lap record at 100.68 mph and won the race by just 2.8 seconds from McElnea! Bamford finished third, Gary Radcliffe (Yamaha) fourth, Andy Bassett (Yamaha) fifth and Peter Wild (Yamaha) sixth. There were 18 finishers.

1979 Junior Newcomers (4 laps / 150.92 miles) 29 entries

1. Roger Luckman	T. Tim Yamaha	1h. 33m. 11.0s	97.17 mph (record)
2. Rob McElnea	Yamaha	1h. 33m. 13.8s	97.12 mph
3. Steve Bamford	Yamaha	1h. 35m. 08.8s	95.17 mph
Fastest lap (record)			
Roger Luckman	T. Tim Yamaha	22m. 29.0s	100.68 mph

1979 Lightweight Newcomers

There were 30 entries for the Lightweight Newcomers, and five non-starters reduced the field to 25. Mike Booys (Yamaha) set the fastest practice lap and Roger Hurst (Yamaha) was second. But it was Andy McGladdery (Yamaha) who took command of the race from the start. He led Mark Johns at the end of the first lap by 2.6 seconds with Booys third, a further 8.8 seconds down. Johns retired on the second lap and McGladdery led Booys by 27.8 seconds and the new third place man was Steve Williams (Yamaha). At the end of lap three McGladdery still led the race, but from Williams by 25 seconds, with Booys relegated to third place, 30.2 seconds down on Williams. So McGladdery won from Williams by 32.8 seconds with Booys 56 seconds down in third place. The top six were completed by Derek Best (Yamaha) Trevor Wise (Yamaha) and Bob Eva (Yamaha). There were 17 finishers.

1979 Lightweight Newcomers (4 laps / 150.92 miles) 30 entries

1. Andy McGladdery	Yamaha	1h. 35m. 49.6s	94.49 mph (record)
2. Steve Williams	Fowler Yamaha	1h. 36m. 21.8s	93.96 mph
3. Mike Booys	Yamaha	1h. 37m. 17.4s	93.07 mph
Fastest lap (record)			
Andy McGladdery	Yamaha	23m. 06.0s	98.00 mph

1979 Junior MGP

The Junior, which had the capacity increased this year to 500cc, attracted the maximum 114 entries. and 11 non-starters reduced the field to 103. It was not surprising that the fastest practice lap was set by Clive Watts (500 Suzuki) but Donnie Robinson (Yamaha) was second, with Phil Mellor (Yamaha) third. Watts led at the end of the first lap, but only by one second from Conor McGinn (Yamaha) with Con Law Yamaha) third, seven seconds down. Fourth was Bob Jackson (Yamaha). fifth Mellor and sixth Dave East (Yamaha). Watts broke the lap record second time round at 108.10 mph and increased his lead over McGinn to 16.4 seconds with Law still third, 11.2 seconds behind McGinn. Jackson remained fourth, Mellor fifth and Mike Kneen (Yamaha) replaced East in sixth place, East dropping to 10th. Watts gradually increased his lead each lap, at the end of the third it was 20.6 seconds from

Roger Luckman takes the Tiger Tim Yamaha through Whitegates.

McGinn with the remainder of the leaderboard unchanged. At the end of the fourth lap Watts was 29 seconds up on McGinn, but with Con Law retiring, Jackson took third place 46.4 seconds down. Mellor moved up to fourth, John Robinson (Yamaha) was fifth and Rob Britton (Yamaha) sixth, Kneen having retired on Bray Hill. Watts broke the lap record again on the fifth lap at 108.61 mph and led McGinn by 34.2 seconds, and the only change to the leaderboard was that Mellor took third place from Jackson. There were no changes to the leaderboard on the final lap, so Watts won by 56.8 seconds from McGinn with Mellor in third place 39 seconds down on McGinn. Jackson took fourth place followed by Robinson and Britton. There were 60 finishers and 20 replicas were won.

1979 Junior (6 laps / 226.38 miles) 114 entries

1. Clive Watts	Cowles Suzuki	2h. 07m. 26.0s	106.58 mph
			(record)
2. Conor McGinn	MB Yamaha	2h. 08m. 22.8s	105.80 mph
3. Phil Mellor	Maxton Yamaha	2h. 09m. 02.2s	105.26 mph
Fastest lap (record)			
Clive Watts	Cowles Suzuki	20m. 50.6s	108.61 mph

1979 Lightweight MGP

The entry for the Lightweight totalled 96, but 11 non-starters reduced this number to 85 starters. Con Law was fastest in practice, Dave Broadhead (Yamaha) second and Tony Rennie (Yamaha) third. The race was postponed for an hour and a half due to bad weather, and reduced in distance from four laps to three. Con Law led at the end of the first lap by 23.6 seconds from Conor McGinn (Yamaha) with Bob Jackson (Yamaha) third just 4.2 seconds down on McGinn. Brian Reid (Yamaha) was fourth, Richard Swallow (Yamaha) fifth and Rennie sixth. Law increased his advantage over McGinn to 44.4 seconds at the end of the second lap and and Jackson was a further 17.8 seconds down in third place. Brian Reid retired at Ballaugh on this second lap and Swallow moved up to fourth followed by Ronnie Mann (Yamaha) and Rennie. Con Law's winning margin at the end of the race was 50.6 seconds over McGinn, with Jackson taking another top three place in third spot. Swallow held on to fourth place, Mann moved up to fifth and Rob Britton (Yamaha) took sixth place. There were 63 finishers and 24 riders won replicas.

1979 Lightweight (3 laps / 150.92 miles) 96 entries

1. Con Law	Yamaha	1h. 06m. 43.4s	101.78 mph
2. Conor McGinn	MB Yamaha	1h. 07m. 38.0s	100.41 mph
3. Bob Jackson	Yamaha	1h. 08m. 18.2s	99.43 mph
Fastest lap (record)			
Con Law	Yamaha	20m. 05.0s	102.51 mph

1979 Senior MGP

Once again the Senior attracted the maximum entry of 115, but 17 non-starters reduced this to 98. Mike Kneen (Suzuki) was fastest in practice with Rob Brew (747 Yamaha) next and Junior winner Clive Watts (Suzuki) third. As in the Junior, Clive Watts took command right from the flag, and led the race from start to finish. At the end of the first lap his advantage was 40.4 seconds over Brew, with Geoff Johnson (Yamaha) third, just 2.6 seconds down on Brew. Marty Ames (Yamaha) was fourth, Dave East (Yamaha) fifth and John Robinson (Yamaha) sixth. Watts led at the end of the second lap by one minute 29.4 seconds from Johnson and Ames was third, East fourth, Brew fifth and Robinson sixth. At half distance Watts led Johnson by just over two minutes who in turn was 44.6 seconds in front of the new third place man Keith Trubshaw (Yamaha), Ames was now fourth, Robinson fifth and Jim Heath sixth, with East seventh. The difference between Watts and the second place man at the end of lap four was exactly the same two minutes two seconds, but Ames was now second, 23.6 seconds ahead of Johnson. East was back up to fourth, Robinson fifth and Brew came back on to the leaderboard in sixth place. Watts increased his advantage at the end of lap five by another 53 seconds, but it was over Johnson, who retook second place from Ames by 35.6 seconds. Robinson, East and Brew completed the top six. So Clive Watts went on to complete a unique Junior/Senior double, riding the same machine in both races! He won from Johnson by three minutes 24.6 seconds with Ames in third place. Robinson finished fourth, Brew fifth and East sixth. There 59 finishers and 19 riders won replicas.

1979 Senior (6 laps / 226.38 miles) 115 entries

1. Clive Watts	Cowles Suzuki	2h. 09m. 01.0s	105.27 mph
			(record)
2. Geoff Johnson	Lambert Yamaha	2h. 12m. 25.6s	102.56 mph
3. Marty Ames	Yamaha	2h. 13m. 25.4s	101.80 mph
Fastest lap (record)			
Clive Watts	Cowles Suzuki	20m. 57.4s	108.02 mph

1980

1980 Senior Newcomers

There were just 13 entries for the Senior Newcomers and with two non-starters, only 11 riders were on the line for the start of the race. Steve Richardson (Yamaha) was fastest in practice followed by John Leech (Yamaha) and Steve Renton (Honda). Richardson led at the end of the first lap by an amazing three minutes 27.4 seconds from John Limerick (Yamaha) with John Nightingale (Honda) third a further 21.8 seconds

Con Law - classic style at Ballaugh Bridge.

down. The difference between Richardson and Limerick at the end of lap two was three minutes 55 seconds, and Fred Curry (Yamaha) was in third place, 34 seconds behind Limerick. The order at the end of lap three was Richardson, Nightingale and Limerick, and there was no changes on the final lap, so Steve Richardson won by seven minutes 31.2 seconds from Nightingale with Limerick third, one minute nine seconds down. Steve Renton (Honda), Colin Pearson (Yamaha) and Martin Lee (Honda) completed the top six, and Curry, third on lap two, finished ninth of the nine finishers.

1980 Senior Newcomers (4 laps / 150.92 miles) 13 entries

1. Steve Richardson	Yamaha	1h. 40m. 23.4s	90.92 mph
2. John Nightingale	Kerby Honda	1h. 47m. 54.2s	83.92 mph
3. John Limerick	Yamaha	1h. 49m. 03.8s	83.02 mph
Fastest lap			
Steve Richardson	Yamaha	24m. 28.4s	92.50 mph

1980 Junior Newcomers

There were 32 entries for the Junior Newcomers, and seven non-starters reduced the field to 25. Kenny Shepherd (Yamaha) was fastest in practice, Kevin Wilson (Yamaha) was second fastest followed by Chris Grose (Yamaha). Shepherd led at the end of the first lap by 19.8 seconds, having broken the lap record at 100.89 mph. Wilson was second, 37.4 seconds ahead of Paul Cranston (Yamaha). Wilson set a new record of 102.38 mph on lap two, to lead Shepherd by six seconds with Cranston 35 seconds behind Shepherd. Wilson increased his advantage on the third lap over Shepherd to 21 seconds, and Cranston was two minutes 21 seconds down in third place. But things happened on the final lap, Wilson retired at Cruickshanks Corner with exhaust problems. Shepherd stopped at Bishopscourt to make adjustments, proceeded and took the chequered flag one minute one second in front of Cranston, Allan Hannay (Yamaha) took third place, Alan Coulter (Yamaha) fourth, Dave Thurlow (Yamaha) fifth and Graham King (Yamaha) sixth. There were 13 finishers.

1980 Junior Newcomers (4 laps / 150.92 miles) 32 entries

1. Kenny Shepherd	Yamaha	1h. 32m. 16.2s	98.13 mph
			(record)
2. Paul Cranston	Yamaha	1h. 33m. 17.2s	97.06 mph
3. Allan Hannay	Yamaha	1h. 37m. 04.4s	93.28 mph
Fastest lap (record)			
Kevin Wilson	Yamaha	22m. 06.6s	102.38 mph

1980 Lightweight Newcomers

The Lightweight Newcomers attracted an entry of 24, but non-starters reduced this number to 20. Gary Padgett (Yamaha) was fastest in practice followed by Stephen Boyes (Yamaha) and Steve Hodgson (Yamaha). Padgett led Boyes at the end of the first lap by one minute 10.2 seconds, having set a new lap record at 99.36 mph. Chris Faulkner (Yamaha) was third, 40 seconds down on Boyes. Surprisingly these three riders maintained their positions to the end of the race, and on lap two Padgett set another new record at 99.39 mph, and increased his lead each lap. At the end of lap three it was two minutes 31 seconds. and Gary went on to win from Boyes by four minutes eight seconds with Faulkner in third place. the top six were completed by Hodgson, Simon Anderson (Yamaha) and Sean Collister (Yamaha). There were 17 finishers.

1979 Senior: Clive Watts heels the Cowles Suzuki into Parliament Square.

1980 Lightweight Newcomers (4 laps / 150.92 miles) 24 entries

1. Gary Padgett	Padgett Yamaha	1h. 32m. 49.2s	97.55 mph (record)
2. Steve Boyes	Maxton Yamaha	1h. 36m. 57.2s	93.39 mph
3. Chris Faulkner	Maxton Yamaha	1h. 37m. 55.8s	92.46 mph

Fastest lap (record)

Gary Padgett	Padgett Yamaha	22m. 46.6s	99.39 mph

1980 Junior MGP

Manxman Mike Kneen at Sulby Bridge.

The maximum entry for the Junior, which was back to 350cc machines, was reduced by non-starters to 104. Brian Reid (Yamaha) was fastest in practice followed by Rob Britton (Yamaha) and Andy McGladdery (Yamaha). Brian Reid led at the end of the first lap from Mike Kneen (Yamaha) by 13.6 seconds with Keith Trubshaw just 0.2 seconds down on Kneen in third place. Nick Jefferies (Yamaha), McGladdery and Gordon Brown (Yamaha) completed the first six. Reid led by 29.4 seconds at the end of lap two from Trubshaw, who had taken second place from Kneen by 1.4 seconds. Jefferies was still fourth, Dave East (Yamaha) fifth and Brown sixth. On lap three Reid came off at Ramsey Hairpin and retired, so at half distance Trubshaw was the new leader by 3.6 seconds from Kneen, who in turn was just two seconds up on Jefferies - 5.6 seconds covering the first three. Brown moved up to fourth, East was fifth and Geoff Johnson (Yamaha) came into sixth place. At the end of lap four Kneen was in the lead, but only by 0.8 seconds from Trubshaw who in turn had a 16.2 second advantage over Jefferies, Johnson was fourth, Brown fifth and Mick Capper (Yamaha) sixth. East retired on this fourth lap after a spill in Kirk Michael. Kneen increased his lead over Trubshaw to 21.6 seconds at the end of lap five, with the remainder of the top six unchanged. And so Mike Kneen became the first Manx rider to win the Junior since 1957, with a margin of 25 seconds over Trubshaw, with Jefferies third. Johnson took fourth place, Brown fifth and Mick Capper sixth. There were 57 finishers and 26 replicas were won.

1980 Junior (6 laps / 226.38 miles) 115 entries

1. Mike Kneen	Yamaha	2h. 10m. 40.2s	103.94 mph
2. Keith Trubshaw	Maxton	2h. 11m. 03.2s	103.64 mph
3. Nick Jefferies	Yamaha	2h. 11m. 07.2s	103.59 mph

Fastest lap

Mike Kneen	Yamaha	21m. 17.6s	106.31 mph

1980 Lightweight MGP

The entry for the Lightweight was down on last year, 85, and with an unusually high number of non-starters, the field was reduced to 71. Bob Jackson (Gregg Yamaha) led at the end of the first lap by 2.6 seconds from Williams (Fowler Yamaha) with Andy McGladdery (Yamaha), a further 7.4 seconds down in third place. Alan Atkins (Yamaha), Geoff Tunstall (Yamaha) and Stephen Boyes (Yamaha) completed the top six. At the end of the second lap, Williams led from Jackson by 5.4 seconds with McGladdery losing ground, 56 seconds behind Jackson. Tunstall and Boyes moved up to fourth and fifth, Ray Campbell (Yamaha) was sixth, and Atkins dropped to ninth. Jackson was back in the lead at the end of lap three by 31.4 seconds from Williams, but Andy McGladdery's race ended when he retired with mechanical problems. This brought Boyes in to third place, Atkins came back up to fourth place, Chris Faulkner (Yamaha) came on to the leader-board in fifth place and Campbell was sixth. So after one second place and two thirds, was this to be Jackson's year. As their progress was followed on the last lap, Williams was gaining, he was just 3.6 seconds behind at Ballaugh, by Ramsey he was leading by just one second, and at the Bungalow he was 6.4 seconds in front. Jackson fought back on the descent and split seconds would decide the winner. Williams took the race by 2.8 seconds from Jackson, with Boyes third. Atkins was fourth and the leaderboard was completed by Faulkner and Campbell. There were 56 finishers and 21 replicas were won.

1980 Lightweight (4 laps / 150.92 miles) 85 entries

1. Steve Williams	Fowler Yamaha	1h. 31m. 10.8s	99.31 mph
2. Bob Jackson	Gregg Yamaha	1h. 31m. 13.6s	99.26 mph
3. Stephen Boyes	Maxton Yamaha	1h. 33m. 55.4s	96.41 mph

Fastest lap

Gary Padgett	Yamaha	22m. 07.8s	102.29 mph

1980 Senior MGP

The entry for the Senior was 115, and with 11 non-starters, 104 riders faced the starter. Rob Britton (Yamaha) was fastest in practice followed by Geoff Johnson (Yamaha) and Keith Trubshaw (Yamaha). At the end of the first lap, the leader was Brian Reid (Suzuki) by 5.2 seconds from Johnson, who in turn led Mike Kneen (Suzuki) the Junior winner, 11.6 seconds down on Johnson. Britton was fourth, Phil Daniels (Yamaha) fifth and Rob Vine Yamaha) sixth. Johnson took over the lead from Reid by 20.4 seconds at the end of lap two and Kneen was 11.6 seconds down in third place. Nick Jefferies (Yamaha) came on to the leaderboard in fourth place followed by John Crellin (Yamaha) and Daniels, Vine was seventh and Britton 10th. Reid was back in front by 7.4 seconds at the end of the third lap and Johnson held second place by 26.4 seconds from Kneen. Jefferies remained fourth, Mick Capper (Yamaha) was fifth and Daniels sixth, Vine was eighth, Crellin ninth and Britton 12th. At the end of the fourth lap, Johnson was back in front by 39.4 seconds from Kneen, who in turn led Reid by 36.4 seconds. Jefferies, Daniels and Mick Noblett (Yamaha) completed the top

six. Johnson maintained the lead at the end of the fifth lap by 37.2 seconds, and Reid was back up to second, 25.4 seconds in front of Kneen, Jefferies, Daniels and Capper completed the top six with Noblett seventh. So Johnson won the Senior by 58 seconds from Reid, and Kneen completed a good meeting for him with third place, just two seconds down on Reid. Jefferies finished fourth, Daniels fifth and Noblett sixth, with Capper seventh. There were 66 finishers and 22 replicas were won.

Geoff Johnson at Greeba; the first of many wins on the TT course.

1980 Senior (6 laps / 226.38 miles) 115 entries

1. Geoff Johnson	Yamaha	2h. 11m. 19.2s	103.69 mph
2. Brian Reid	Cowles Suzuki	2h. 12m. 17.2s	102.67 mph
3. Mike Kneen	Suzuki	2h. 12m. 19.2s	102.65 mph
Fastest lap			
Geoff Johnson	Yamaha	21m. 08.4s	107.08 mph

1981

1981 Senior Newcomers

The Senior Newcomers attracted an entry of 29, and 25 of these came to the line. Adrian Jardine (Suzuki) was fastest in practice with Mike Pellow (Yamaha) next and Keith Storey (Yamaha) third. Pellow was never headed in the race, at the end of the first lap he was 45.2 seconds in front of Roger White (Yamaha) with Pete Beale (Yamaha) third. At the end of the second lap, his lead was two minutes 27 seconds from Beale, and with White's retirement, Steve Linsdell (Royal Enfield) took third place. On lap three, Beale retired at the Hawthorn, and Pellow led Linsdell by two minutes 28.6 seconds with Adrian Jardine up in to third place. Pellow took the chequered flag three minutes 24.2 seconds from Linsdell with John Raybould (Yamaha) third, Jardine took fourth place ahead of Colin Stockdale (Honda) and Colin Parker (Honda). There were 14 finishers.

1981 Senior Newcomers (4 laps / 150.92 miles) 29 entries

1. Mike Pellow	Yamaha	1h. 32m. 14.6s	98.16 mph
			(record)
2. Steve Linsdell	Royal Enfield	1h. 35m. 38.4s	94.67 mph
3. John Raybould	Yamaha	1h. 36m. 34.6s	93.76 mph
Fastest lap (record)			
Mike Pellow	Yamaha	22m. 26.2s	100.89 mph

1981 Junior Newcomers

Twenty-two riders entered for the Junior Newcomers and of these 19 faced the starter. Norman Brown (Yamaha) was fastest in practice, Graham Cannell (Yamaha) was second fastest with Simon Beaumont (Yamaha) third. Cannell broke the lap record from a standing start at 106.36 mph and led Brown by 7.2 seconds with Beaumont third 27.8 seconds down. Cannell retired at Sulby Bridge on the second lap, and Brown smashed the record, lapping at 108.07 mph to lead Beaumont by one minute 22.2 seconds, with Martin Nelson (Yamaha) taking third place. Beaumont was the next of the leaderboard men to retire, going out at the Hawthorn. This gave Brown a lead of over three minutes from Nelson and Craig Ryding (Yamaha) took over third place. Brown won at a record speed of 103.76 mph, by four minutes 18.4 seconds from Ryding with Nelson third. Nick Smith (Yamaha) finished fourth, Mark Dilnot (Yamaha) fifth and Dave Brown (Yamaha) sixth. There were 12 finishers.

1981 Junior Newcomers (4 laps / 150.92 miles) 22 entries

1. Norman Brown	Yamaha	1h. 27m. 16.2s	103.76 mph
			(record)
2. Craig Ryding	Yamaha	1h. 31m. 34.6s	98.88 mph
3. Martin Nelson	Yamaha	1h. 31m. 44.0s	98.71 mph
Fastest lap (record)			
Norman Brown	Yamaha	20m. 56.8s	108.07 mph

1981 Lightweight Newcomers

There were just 16 entries for the Lightweight Newcomers and three non-starters reduced the field to 13. Buddy Yeardsley (Yamaha) was fastest in practice with Gary Clark (Yamaha) and Alan Douglas (Yamaha) next best. Clark led at the end of the first lap by 20.8 seconds from Douglas, with Yeardsley third, 14.2 seconds down. Clark increased his lead at the end of the second lap to 32.4 seconds, but from Yeardsley who had taken second place from Douglas by 25 seconds. At the end of lap three Yeardsley was in front of Clark by 9.8 seconds with Douglas still third, 49.2 seconds behind Clark. On the fourth lap, Clark was reported to be touring at Ramsey, where he retired. Yeardsley won by two minutes 20 seconds from Douglas, who in turn was four minutes eight seconds ahead of the third place man Paul Davies (Yamaha). The top six were completed by Geoff Gates (Suzuki), Pete Bateson (Yamaha) and Richard Freak (Yamaha). There were 10 finishers.

1981 Lightweight Newcomers (4 laps / 150.92 miles) 16 entries

1. Buddy Yeardsley	Yamaha	1h. 33m. 31.8s	96.81 mph
2. Alan Douglas	Yamaha	1h. 35m. 52.0s	94.45 mph
3. Paul Davies	Yamaha	1h. 40m. 00.6s	90.54 mph
Fastest lap			
Buddy Yeardsley	Yamaha	22m. 55.8s	99.45 mph

1981 Junior MGP

The Junior once again attracted an entry of 115, and with just nine non-starters, the starting grid totalled 106 riders. Rob Vine (Yamaha) was fastest in practice, followed by Rob Britton (Yamaha) and Kenny Shepherd Yamaha). At the end of the first lap Dave Broadhead (Yamaha) led Shepherd by just two seconds, with Vine a further 3.8 seconds down. Kevin Wilson (Yamaha), Keith Trubshaw (Yamaha) and Dave Ashton

(Yamaha) completed the top six, and with just 17.4 seconds covering the first six, a close race was in prospect. Broadhead led by seven seconds at the end of the second lap from Vine, with Shepherd third, five seconds down on Vine. Wilson and Ashton remained fourth and fifth with Dave East (Yamaha) coming into sixth place and Trubshaw dropping to seventh. Vine completed lap three 14 seconds faster than Broadhead and took the lead by seven seconds and Shepherd was the same margin down in third place. Ashton took fourth place from Wilson and Andy Cooper (Yamaha) replaced East in sixth place. Vine stretched his lead on lap tour to 40.4 seconds, and Broadhead and Shepherd tied for second place. Ashton and Wilson remained fourth and fifth and East regained sixth place from Cooper. At the end of lap five Broadhead had closed to within 18 seconds of Vine, Ashton took third place from Shepherd, Wilson remained fifth and East sixth. But Vine had a long pit stop at the end of the fifth lap with gear lever problems and lost his chance. Broadhead won by 19 seconds from Ashton with Shepherd 3.6 seconds down in third place. Wilson was fourth, Vine fifth and Chris Grose (Yamaha) sixth. Vine's pit stop took one minute 38 seconds, and he finished one minute 36.2 seconds down on Broadhead - it could well have been a nail biting finish! There were 60 finishers and 30 replicas were won.

Dave Broadhead skirts the railings at Ginger Hall.

1981 Junior (6 laps / 226.38 miles) 115 entries

1. Dave Broadhead	Yamaha	2h. 08m. 14.8s	105.91 mph
			(record for 350cc)
2. Dave Ashton	Yamaha	2h. 08m. 33.8s	105.65 mph
3. Kenny Shepherd	Yamaha	2h. 08m. 37.4s	105.60 mph
Fastest lap (record for 350cc)			
Rob Vine	Yamaha)		
Dave Broadhead	Yamaha)	20m. 58.2s	107.95 mph

1981 Lightweight MGP

For the Lightweight, 91 entries were received, and of these, 80 lined up for the start of the race. Graham Cannell (Rotax) was fastest in practice, followed by Chris Grose (Yamaha) and John McEntee (Yamaha). Cannell opened up with a lap at 103.22 mph and led Norman Brown (Yamaha) by 29 seconds, with Chris Fargher (Yamaha) third, 13 seconds down on Brown. Grose was fourth, Keith Trubshaw (Yamaha) fifth and Cliff Gobell (Yamaha) sixth. Three Manx riders in the first six, Cannell, Fargher and Grose. At the end of lap two Cannell was 23 seconds ahead of Brown and Fargher 26 seconds down in third place. Grose remained fourth, Gobell moved up to fifth and sixth place was taken by Chris Faulkner (Yamaha). Brown closed the gap between himself and Cannell to 13.4 seconds at the end of lap three, and Grose look third place from Fargher with Gobell and Faulkner remaining fifth and sixth. Cannell got the message that Brown was closing on him. and set a new lap record on lap four at 105.60 mph to win by 16.8 seconds, with Grose third, 35 seconds behind Brown. Fargher, Gobell and Faulkner completed the top six. There were 52 finishers and 19 replicas were won.

1981 Lightweight (4 laps / 150.92 miles) 91 entries

1. Graham Cannell	Cotton Rotax	1h. 27m. 45.0s	103.19 mph
			(record)
2. Norman Brown	Yamaha	1h. 28m. 01.8s	102.86 mph
3. Chris Grose	Yamaha	1h. 28m. 36.8s	102.18 mph
Fastest lap (record)			
Graham Cannell	Cotton Rotax	21m. 26.2s	105.60 mph

1981 Senior MGP

The maximum entry of 115 was received for the Senior, and with just eight non-starters, 107 riders lined up for the start of the race. Mark Johns (Yamaha) was fastest in practice followed by Nick Jefferies (Suzuki) and Dave Broadhead (Suzuki). But it was Rob McElnea who led at the end of the first lap. He set a new lap record from a standing start at 108.48 mph and led Allan Brew (Suzuki) by 8.8 seconds with Johns third, a further 6.8 seconds down. Dave East (Suzuki), Dave Ashton (Yamaha) and Kenny Shepherd (Yamaha) completed the top six. McElnea increased his lead at the end of the second lap to 15.8 seconds from Johns who had an advantage of 18.8 seconds over third place man Brew. Rob Vine (Suzuki) took fourth place, Shepherd was fifth and Ashton sixth, East was seventh. At half distance, McElnea led by 19.8 seconds from Johns with Ashton taking over third place, East was fourth, Shepherd fifth and Steve Boyes (Yamaha) came on to the leaderboard in sixth place. Rob Vine retired at Ballacraine, with a broken gear lever, the same problem that he had in the Junior. There were dramatic changes to the top six on lap four. McElnea retired at the 26th Milestone with a flat rear tyre, Johns retired at Hillberry and Ashton also went out, both with engine trouble. The new leader at the end of lap four was East who had an advantage of 7.4 seconds over Brew, who in turn led Shepherd by 44.4 seconds. Boyes was fourth, Kieron Hunt (Suzuki) fifth and Brian Robinson (Yamaha) sixth. East set a new record lap on the fifth circuit, 108.64 mph and with Brew's retirement, East led the race by a massive five minutes six seconds from Robinson, who was just 2.2 seconds in front of Neil Fowler (Yamaha). Shepherd was fourth, Dick Coates (Yamaha) fifth and Norman Kneen (Suzuki) sixth. East won the race by six minutes 11.4 seconds and Robinson finished second, 13.4 seconds in front of Fowler, Dick Coates finished fourth, Gordon Farmer (Yamaha) fifth and Steve Richardson (Suzuki) sixth. Shepherd had gear lever problems, his pit crew swopped it over to the right side of the machine, and he managed to finish in 14th place, and Norman Kneen finished seventh. There were 56 finishers and 21 replicas were won.

Dave East at Union Mills.

1981 Senior (6 laps / 226.38 miles)   115 entries

1. Dave East	RG Suzuki	2h. 07m. 49.4s	106.26 mph (record)
2. Brian Robinson	Yamaha	2h. 14m. 00.8s	101.35 mph
3. Neil Fowler	NEBCO Yamaha	2h. 14m. 13.4s	101.19 mph
Fastest lap (record)			
Dave East	RG Suzuki	20m. 50.2s	108.64 mph

1982

1982 Senior Newcomers

The entry for the Senior Newcomers totalled 34, and five non-starters reduced the line up to 29. Ian Ogden (Suzuki) was fastest in practice, followed by Stephen Mainwaring (Suzuki) and Rick White (Suzuki). Practice form was confirmed when these three riders filled the first three places at the end of the first lap. Ogden led Mainwaring by 0.8 seconds and White was 5.4 seconds down in third place. Ogden increased his advantage at the end of lap two to three minutes 17.8 seconds. The reason - Mainwaring came off at Cruickshanks Corner and White retired at Ballacraine. Brian Appleton (Suzuki) was second and Richard Kneen (Yamaha) third, 13 seconds down on Appleton. The first three remained the same at the end of lap three, and Ogden increased his lead to four minutes 15.8 seconds with Kneen half a minute down on Appleton. On the last lap Appleton came off at Greeba Bridge, so Ogden had a comfortable victory by five minutes 43.8 seconds from Kneen who in turn was one minute 25 seconds in front of the third place man David Davies. Fourth was Patrick Martin (Yamaha) fifth was John Smith (Honda) and sixth Ned Bowers (Ducati). There were 22 finishers.

1982 Senior Newcomers (4 laps / 150.92 miles)   34 entries

1. Ian Ogden	Suzuki	1h. 34m. 02.6s	96.28 mph
2. Richard Kneen	Yamaha	1h. 39m. 44.0s	90.79 mph
3. David Davies	Maxton Yamaha	1h. 41m. 09.0s	89.52 mph
Fastest lap			
Ian Ogden	Suzuki	22m. 48.4s	99.25 mph

1982 Junior Newcomers

Twenty seven riders entered for the Junior Newcomers, and 24 of them made it to the starting line. Gary Hislop (Yamaha) was fastest in practice, Gerry Brennan (Yamaha) was second fastest and Phillip Kneen (Yamaha) third. Strangely enough, as in the Senior class, the first three in practice were the first three at the end of the first lap. Hislop led Brennan by 20.6 seconds who in turn was 10 seconds in front of Kneen. Hislop increased his lead to one minute over Brennan at the end of the second lap, but Kneen retired at Ballaugh, and Grant Goodings (Yamaha) took third place. Hislop forged ahead and led Brennan by two minutes 17 seconds at the end of the third lap, and Ralph Sutcliffe (Yamaha), son of the 1970 Senior winner Roger, took third place from Goodings who dropped to fourth. Hislop went on to win by three minutes 37 seconds from Sutcliffe with Goodings third. The top six were completed by Terry Nichol (Yamaha), Robert Howe (Yamaha) and Damion Fairhurst (Maxton). Gerry Brennan retired at the Wild Life Park, Ballaugh, on the final lap. There were 18 finishers.

1982 Junior Newcomers (4 laps / 150.92 miles)   27 entries

1. Gary Hislop	Yamaha	1h. 30m. 35.0s	99.96 mph

Newcomers victors: left to right. Brian Lund (Lightweight), Gary Hislop (Junior) and Ian Ogden (Senior).

2. Ralph Sutcliffe	Yamaha	1h. 34m. 12.2s	96.12 mph
3. Grant Goodings	Yamaha	1h. 34m. 50.0s	95.48 mph
Fastest lap			
Gary Hislop	Yamaha	22m. 04.6s	102.57 mph

1982 Lightweight Newcomers

Twenty four of the original entry of 25 made it to the starting grid for the Lightweight Newcomers. Brian Lund (Yamaha) was fastest in practice followed by Graham Taylor (Yamaha) and Robert Haynes (Yamaha). At the end of the lap Lund led Alistair Rae (Yamaha) by 53 seconds with Peter Cook (Yamaha) third, a further 10.2 seconds down. The order of the first three remained unchanged on laps two and three, with Lund increasing his lead each lap. But on the final lap, Rae retired at the 32nd Milestone, so Lund won by three minutes 12.2 seconds from Peter Cook with Dave Auckland (Yamaha) third. Dave Leach (Yamaha) finished fourth, Haynes fifth and Ian Tunstall (Yamaha) sixth. There were 17 finishers.

1982 Lightweight Newcomers (4 laps / 150.92 miles) 25 entries

1. Brian Lund	Yamaha	1h. 33m. 16.0s	97.08 mph
2. Peter Cook	Yamaha	1h. 36m. 28.2s	93.86 mph
3. Dave Auckland	Yamaha	1h. 37m. 04.2s	93.28 mph
Fastest lap			
Brian Lund	Yamaha	22m. 51.2s	99.05 mph

1982 Junior MGP

The entry for the Junior was 113, and five non-starters reduced the field to 108. Dick Coates (Waddon) was fastest in practice with Chris Fargher (Yamaha) second and Gary Padgett (Yamaha) third. Chris Faulkner (Yamaha) led at the end of the first lap by 16.4 seconds from Coates, who was just three seconds in front of Andy Cooper (Yamaha). Fourth was Kevin Wilson (Yamaha), fifth Gary Radcliffe (Yamaha) and sixth Dave Pither (Yamaha). At the end of the second lap Faulkner led Cooper by 52.4 seconds, with Coates third by 8.8 seconds. Wilson and Radcliffe remained fourth and fifth, but Dave Pither retired, and Nick Jefferies (Yamaha) came up to sixth. Faulkner marched on on lap three and led by 45.6 seconds from Cooper, Wilson was third, 11.4 seconds down, followed by Radcliffe, Jefferies and Mick Noblett (Yamaha). Dick Coates had stopped in Ramsey to make adjustments, he got going again and finished 17th. Lap four saw dramatic changes to the top six - both Chris Faulkner and Kevin Wilson, first and third at the end of lap three, retired at Ballaugh. Cooper took the lead from Radcliffe by 39.6 seconds and Jefferies was third, a further 54.6 seconds down on Radcliffe. Noblett moved up to fourth, Gordon Farmer (Yamaha) was fifth and Cliff Mylchreest (Yamaha) sixth. There were no changes on lap five, and Cooper increased his advantage over Radcliffe to 55.6 seconds. So Cooper took the chequered flag by one minute from Radcliffe with Jefferies third. Gordon Farmer took fourth place from Noblett and Mylchreest finished sixth. There were 54 finishers and 21 replicas were won.

1982 Junior (6 laps / 226.38 miles) 113 entries

1. Andy Cooper	Yamaha	2h. 12m. 03.4s	102.85 mph
2. Gary Radcliffe	Fowler Yamaha	2h. 13m. 03.4s	102.08 mph
3. Nick Jefferies	Yamaha	2h. 14m. 11.0s	101.22 mph
Fastest lap			
Chris Faulkner	Yamaha	21m. 28.0s	105.45 mph

1982 Lightweight MGP

There were 92 entries for the Lightweight, and with six non-starters, 86 riders lined up for the start of the race. Chris Fargher (Cotton) was fastest in practice followed by Mike Booys (Rotax) and Sean Collister (Yamaha). But it was Lightweight Newcomers class winner Brian Lund (Yamaha) who led at the of the first lap by 9.2 seconds from Collister with Booys a further 42.8 seconds down in third place. Robert Haynes (Yamaha), Phil Kneen (Yamaha), and Dave Leach (Yamaha) completed the top six. Collister took the lead from Lund on the second lap by 10.8 seconds, and Booys was 15.6 seconds down on Lund. Haynes and Kneen remained fourth and fifth, and Dave Auckland (Yamaha) was sixth, with Leach dropping to 10th. Lund's race ended on the third lap when he retired at the 9th Milestone. Collister led Haynes by 53.8 seconds at the start of the last lap, Booys was third, 8.8 seconds down on Haynes, Paul Todd (Yamaha) was fourth, Alan Jackson (Yamaha) fifth and Auckland sixth. Kneen had dropped to ninth. Collister got a signal that he was 50 seconds in front at the Gooseneck on the last lap, and with visibility on the mountain poor, he eased off, but too much. He lost the race by 17.2 seconds to Haynes, and finished just four seconds ahead of the third place man Booys. Todd, Leach and Alan 'Bud' Jackson completed the top six and Auckland finished seventh. There were 58 finishers and 21 replicas were won.

1982 Lightweight (4 laps / 150.92 miles) 92 entries

1. Robert Haynes	Yamaha	1h. 42m. 51.4s	88.03 mph
2. Sean Collister	Yamaha	1h. 43m. 08.6s	87.79 mph
3. Mike Booys	Pinford Rotax	1h. 43m. 12.6s	87.73 mph
Fastest lap			
Brian Lund	Yamaha	24m. 19.2s	93.08 mph

1982 Senior MGP

The entry for the Senior was 113, and non-starters reduced the field to exactly 100. Buddy Yeardsley (Suzuki) was fastest in practice, second fastest was Nick Jefferies (Suzuki) and third was Kevin Wilson (Suzuki). Gary Radcliffe (Yamaha) led at the end of the first lap by 8.8 seconds from Wilson, who in turn led Andy Cooper (Yamaha) by 6.4 seconds. Jefferies was fourth, Ray Campbell (Yamaha) fifth and Dave Pither (Suzuki) sixth. Wilson led at the end of the second lap by 8.2 seconds from Cooper, Jefferies was third. 6.2 seconds down, and Radcliffe dropped to fourth. Campbell was fifth and Steve Richardson (Suzuki) came up to sixth, with the retirement of Dave Pither. Wilson increased his lead on lap three to 51 seconds from Jefferies with Radcliffe third. Campbell, Mick Noblett (Suzuki) and Gordon Farmer (Yamaha) completed the top six. Cooper retired and Richardson was seventh. Jefferies took over the lead at the end of lap four by 38 seconds from Wilson, who retired at the pits. Third was Radcliffe, followed by Steve Boyes (Yamaha), Farmer and Richardson, with Noblett in 12th place. Jefferies increased his lead to one minute 7.4 seconds at the end of the fifth lap from Farmer and Radcliffe, with

Richardson, Simon Beaumont and Buddy Yeardsley (Suzuki) filling the remaining leaderboard places, Steve Boyes having retired. Jefferies had an eventful last lap. The engine seized at Milntown, he free-wheeled to Ramsey where it fired up again. Then it seized again on the Mountain Mile, and after free wheeling again, it fired up and he managed to complete the race, but lost so much time Farmer and Gary Radcliffe both passed him. Farmer won by 15.8 seconds with Radcliffe 21.6 seconds in front of Jefferies. Yeardsley was fourth, Richardson fifth and Phil Daniels (Yamaha) sixth. There were 60 finishers and 37 replicas were won.

1982 Senior (6 laps / 226.38 miles) 113 entries

1. Gordon Farmer	Yamaha	2h. 15m. 10.6s	100.48 mph
2. Gary Radcliffe	Suzuki	2h. 15m. 26.4s	100.28 mph
3. Nick Jefferies	Suzuki	2h. 15m. 48.0s	100.02 mph
Fastest lap			
Kevin Wilson	Suzuki	21m. 27.6s	105.48 mph

Gordon Farmer at Braddan Bridge.

ISLE of MAN T.T. MARSHALS ASSOCIATION

The Isle of Man TT Marshals Association (which includes the Manx Grand Prix) was formed in 1962 by amongst others Alan (Kipper) Killip, who is Chief Travelling Marshal, Selwyn Taggart and John Preston who regularly marshals at Brandish. The first Chairman was the Deputy Chief Constable at the time, Bob Kermeen and the first Secretary was the late Sergeant Underhill. In fact the positions of Secretary and Chairman were filled by serving police officers, until 1988 when Mary Crellin became the first civilian as well as first female Secretary. In 1995 Mr Roger Hurst became the first civilian Chairman of the Association, a position he still holds.

The aim of the Association was to maintain and improve the standard of marshalling, to foster an esperit de corp amongst the marshals, to establish liaison between marshals and race organisers, to encourage the training of marshals in incident management, basic first aid, handling of crashed motorcycles, crowd control, race procedure, communications, correct use of flags, prohibited areas and, most importantly, powers of a Special Constable, as under the Road Racing Act, all marshals while on duty have the same powers as a Special Constable.

Each winter the Association run Incident Management Courses, which are held on one night a week, over four weeks and cover all the points that the Association was formed for, Further details of these courses, for anyone interested in doing one can be obtained from the Chairman, Mr Roger Hurst on 851881.

Also during the winter months the Association tries to organise one or two social functions. Sometimes trips may be organised to such as the Lloyds Bowmaker Scottish Motorcycle Show which is held in March just outside Edinburgh.

Having taken the time to read this we very much hope that you will consider becoming a Marshal - remember we can never have too many marshals as the Mountain Course is nearly 38 miles long.

Q. Who can marshal on the famous TT Course?
A. Anyone, male or female, providing you are physically fit, have good hearing and are over 16. (Between 16 and 18 the consent of a parent or guardian is required.)

Q. Do I need marshalling experience?
A. No, but if you do so much the better. Basically just good common sense as your own safety is paramount.

Q. Do I need to be an Island resident?
A. Definitely Not, your assistance will be welcome.

Q. Can I marshal at the TT and the Manx Grand Prix?
A. Yes, one or the other, but both is even better.

Q. Can I move to different locations for different sessions?
A. Yes, but if you do move please let the Sector Chief Marshal or a deputy know so that marshalling distribution is known, but to get to know a particular area is extremely useful.

Q. Do I have to marshal all practice and race sessions?
A. No, If you can and want to, fine, but any assistance for any session is greatly appreciated.

Q. Can I carry a camera or, tape recorder while I marshal?
A. No.

Q. Can I drink alcohol while I marshal?
A. No, as during all practice and race sessions you are a Special Constable.

Q. How can I sign on?
A. Call at the Race Office at the rear of the Grandstand any morning during practice week, or contact a Sector Chief Marshal at various points on the course at road closing.

The course is divided into twelve sections with a Sector Chief Marshal in charge of each Sector; he in turn has Deputy Sector Marshals in charge of the various corners/bends in his sector.

Once you have signed on as a marshal, you may apply to become a member of the Isle of Man TT Marshals Association. At present this will cost you £20 plus a passport type photograph. Your membership will entitle you to certain discounts at various retail outlets plus the Steam Packet Co. (but not during the TT period).

Mary Crellin

INDEX OF RIDERS 1946 - 1982
Key to Abbreviations

S. Senior Manx Grand Prix; S(N). Senior Newcomers; S(Sn.). Senior Snaefell; J. Junior Manx Grand Prix; J(N). Junior Newcomers; J(Sn.). Junior Snaefell; L. Lightweight; Cl. Classic

R. Retired; D. Disqualified; Ex. Excluded; N.F. Non-finisher; F. Finisher *The figures equal the position at end of race.*

Example:
Alexander, P. A.
1955	J.R.	A.J.S.
1958	J.50	B.S.A.
1959	S.R.	Matchless

P.A. Alexander, riding an A.J.S., retired in the 1955 Junior Race. In 1958 he finished 50th on a B.S.A. In 1959 he rode a Matchless in the Senior, but retired.

Abbey, B.
1962 J.R. — A.J.S.
Ablett, Ian
1961 J.R. — A.J.S.
1962 J.R. — A.J.S.
1963 J.30 — A.J.S.
Abbott, Roger
1977 L.26 — Brown Yamaha
1978 L.26 — Brown Yamaha
1979 L.R. — Brown Yamaha
1979 J.24 — Brown Yamaha
1981 J.38 — Axtell-Pool Yamaha
Abrahams, Dave J.
1973 S.R. — Vincent
1974 S.35 — Hillgate Vincent
1975 S.39 — B.S.A.
1976 S.R. — Vincent
1977 S.R. — Vincent
Abram, Andy
1973 L.53 — Yamaha
1974 L.R. — Yamaha
Ackroyd, Stephen E.
1965 L.R. — Fosstar
1966 L.27 — Fosstar
Adam, John McC.
1958 J(Sn) 4 — Norton
1958 J.8 — Norton
1959 J.R. — Norton
1959 S.11 — Norton
1960 J.11 — Norton
1960 S.2 — Norton
Adams, Brian G.
1966 J.41 — Norton
Adams, George
1980 L/N.R. — Yamaha
1980 L.41 — Yamaha
1981 L.18 — Yamaha
1981 J.32 — Yamaha
1982 L.12 — Yamaha
1982 J.14 — Yamaha
Adams, Michael C.
1955 J.73 — B.S.A.
1955 S.60 — B.S.A.
Addie, H. J.
1947 J. R. — Velocette
1947 S.R. — Rudge
Adger, Ken
1961 S.53 — Matchless
1963 S.R. — Matchless
1965 J.37 — Norton
Aiken, Alex G.
1982 S/N.R. — Yamaha
Ainge, Alan J.
1962 S.57 — Norton
1963 S.28 — Norton
1964 S.R. — Norton
1965 S.R. — Norton
1966 S.13 — Norton
1967 J.R. — Norton
1967 S.38 — Norton
1968 S.R. — Norton
1969 S.R. — Norton
1970 S.32 — Norton
1971 S.R. — Norton
1972 S.R. — Norton
1973 S.R. — Norton
1974 S.41 — Norton
1975 L.R. — Vernon Yamaha
1976 S.R. — Norton
Ainscough, Kevin
1976 J.R. — Yamaha
Ainslie, Anthony
1981 L/N.9 — Ducati
Aitchison, Peter M.
1946 J.2 — Norton
1946 S.R. — Norton
Aitken, Alex
1957 S(N).R. — Norton Triumph
Aitken, M.
1960 S.52 — Matchless/Norton
Ajax, Dave R.
1960 S.R. — Norton
1961 J.32 — Norton
Akerman, Derek
1970 L.R. — Alpha
1972 L.37 — Yamaha
1973 L.R. — Yamaha
1974 L.32 — Yamaha
1976 L.R. — Yamaha
1977 S.R. — Yamaha
Alcock, Dave C.
1960 S.23 — Matchless
1961 S.R. — Matchless
Alcock, Geoff D.
1950 S.49 — Norton
1956 J.32 — B.S.A.
1956 S.32 — B.S.A.
1957 J.29 — A.J.S.
1957 S.41 — A.J.S.
1960 S.49 — B.S.A.
Aldridge, Colin
1976 L.45 — Yamaha
1977 L.R. — Grinstead Yamaha
Aldridge, James W.
1971 L.R. — Yamacette
1972 J.R. — DMW/Yamaha
1973 J.R. — DMW/Yamaha
Aldworth, J. R.
1967 L.39 — Aermacchi
Alexander, Andy J. P.
1972 S.R. — Tri-Metisse
1974 S.44 — Metisse
Alexander, Drew
1974 L.R. — Yamaha
1975 L.10 — Yamaha
1976 L.11 — Yamsel
1976 S.18 — Yamsel
1977 L.9 — Yamaha
1977 S.R. — Yamaha
Alexander, J.
1945 S.R. — Velocette
'Alexander, John'
1951 J.11 — A.J.S.
1952 J.R. — A.J.S.
1953 J.26 — A.J.S.
1953 S.25 — Matchless
Alexander, P. A.
1955 J.R. — A.J.S.
1958 J.50 — B.S.A.
1959 S.R. — Matchless
Allan, Derek J.
1976 L.R. — Yamsel
1977 L.R. — Yamsel
1978 L.22 — Yamsel
1979 S.R. — Yamaha
1980 L.13 — Yamaha
1980 L.R. — Yamaha
1981 L.31 — Yamaha
1981 J.R. — Yamaha
1982 L.R. — Cotton
1982 J.40 — Yamaha
Allan, Roddy
1979 L/N.9 — Yamaha
1979 L.61 — Yamaha
1980 S.44 — Yamaha
1980 J.R. — Yamaha
Allcott, M. L.
1968 J.32 — A.J.S.
Allen, B. P.
1957 J(N).45 — Norton
1958 J(Sn).51 — Norton
Allen, David
1973 L.R. — Greeves
Allen, L.
1961 J.48 — B.S.A.
Allen, R.
1947 J.14 — Norton
1947 S.R. — Norton
1948 J.R. — Norton
1948 S.14 — Norton
Allman, Dave
1976 S.43 — Norton
1977 S.R. — Norton
1979 J.58 — Honda
1980 S.R. — Honda
Allum, Ken W.
1960 S.58 — Norton
Almond, W. J.
1957 J(N).R. — B.S.A.
1958 J(Sn).63 — B.S.A.
Ames, Marty
1977 S.R. — Lockyam
1978 S.13 — Lockyam
1979 S.3 — Yamaha
Anchell, David
1976 L.R. — Yamaha
Anderson, A.
1962 J.49 — Norton
Anderson, Anthony T.
1967 S.R. — Matchless
1968 S.R. — Matchless
1969 S.34 — Matchless
Anderson, Bill R.
1954 J.39 — Norton
1955 J.R. — Norton
1955 S.13 — Norton
1957 J.24 — Norton
1957 S.24 — Norton
1959 J.R. — Norton
1959 S.41 — Norton
Anderson, Brian L.
1969 J.R. — Norton
Anderson, G. J.
1946 S.30 — Norton
1947 S.R. — Norton
Anderson, James
1979 J/N.R. — Yamaha
1980 S.21 — Ducati
1981 S.10 — Ducati
Anderson, Bob H. F.
1955 S.8 — Matchless
1956 J.R. — Norton
1956 S.2 — Norton
Anderson, Simon
1980 L/N.5 — Yamaha
1980 L.R. — Yamaha
1981 J.R. — Yamaha
1981 S.19 — Yamaha
Anderton, Syd
1947 S.26 — Triumph
1948 J.11 — A.J.S.
1948 S.I 7 — Triumph
Andrews, D. R.
1954 S.23 — B.S.A.
1955 J.30 — B.S.A.
1955 S.R. — B.S.A.
Andrews, E.
1947 J.40 — Norton
1948 J.22 — Norton
1948 S.13 — Norton
1949 J.19 — Norton
1949 S.7 — Norton
1950 S.6 — Norton
1951 J.17 — A.J.S.
1951 S.13 — Norton
Andrews, Jack A.
1963 J.63 — Norton
1964 J.R. — Norton
1965 J.R. — Norton
Andrews, Richard J.
1979 J/N.14 — Yamaha
1980 J.R. — Yamaha
1980 S.R. — Yamaha
1981 J.R. — Yamaha
1981 S.15 — Yamaha
1982 J.R. — Yamaha
1982 S.R. — Yamaha
Antill, D. P. L.
1951 J.R. — Norton
1952 J.54 — Velocette
1953 J.28 — Earles Velocette
1954 J.R. — A.J.S.
1954 S.14 — A.J.S.
Appleby, Roger
1976 L.48 — Yamsel
1977 L.22 — Yamaha
1978 L.33 — Yamaha
1979 L.21 — Yamaha
1980 L.R. — Yamaha
1981 L.R. — Yamaha
1981 J.12 — Yamaha
Appleton, Brian
1982 S/N.R. — Suzuki
Appleyard, Colin B.
1956 S.R. — Triumph
1958 J.R. — A.J.S.
1958 S.51 — A.J.S.
1959 J.64 — A.J.S.
Arber, Ivor K.
1951 S.R. — Norton
Archard, Norman G.
1962 J.31 — A.J.S.
1963 J.42 — A.J.S.
1965 S.26 — Matchless
1966 S.R. — Matchless
1967 J.11 — A.J.S.
1967 S.R. — Matchless
Archer, Les R.
1947 L.R. — New Imperial
1947 S.R. — New Imperial
Armson, Paul
1976 S.R. — Yamaha
Armstrong, George B.
1964 S.R. — Triton
Armstrong, George
1980 J/N.R. — Armstrong Ducati
1981 J.R. — Armstrong Ducati
1981 S.45 — Suzuki
Armstrong, Graham J.
1982 L/N.R. — Yamaha
1982 L.52 — Yamaha
Armstrong, H. Reg
1947 L.5 — Excelsior
1948 J.R. — A.J.S.
1948 S.4 — Triumph
Armstrong, John
1964 J.R. — A.J.S.
Armstrong, Jack
1972 L.R. — Yamaha
Armstrong, James
1982 L/N.R. — Yamaha
1982 L.52 — Yamaha
Armstrong, Raymond
1964 J.R. — B.S.A.
Armstrong, Wilfred T.
1964 J.R. — Norton
1965 J.R. — Norton
1967 J.R. — Norton
1967 S.R. — Triumph
Arnell-Smith, John J.
1965 S.48 — Triumph/Norton
1966 S.41 — Triumph/Norton
Arnold, Dave
1971 L.16 — Aermacchi
1972 L.4 — Yamaha
1973 L.1 — Yamaha
1973 S.17 — Harley Davidson
Arnold, G.
1954 J.R. — B. S. A.
Arnold, M. D.
1953 J.42 — B. S. A.
1954 J.35 — A.J.S.
1954 S.R. — A.J.S.
1955 J.29 — A.J.S.
1955 S.R. — A.J.S.
1956 J.41 — B.S.A.
1956 S.26 — B.S.A.
1957 J.51 — A.J.S.
1957 S.15 — Norton
Arnott, P.
1961 S.57 — Norton
Ascott, L. D.
1960 S.62 — B.S.A.
Ascott, R. M.
1957 J(N).R. — Douglas
1958 J(Sn).59 — Douglas
Ashcroft, Raymond
1959 S.50 — Norton
1964 L.8 — Yamaha
1965 L.5 — Yamaha
1966 L.12 — Yamaha
1967 L.R. — Yamaha
1968 L.R. — Yamaha
Ashton, David
1978 S/N.1 — Suzuki
1978 S.R. — Triumph
1979 J.16 — Yamaha
1979 S.17 — Triumph
1980 J.R. — Yamaha
1980 S.19 — Triumph
1981 J.2 — Yamaha
1981 S.R. — Yamaha
1982 J.2 — Yamaha
1982 S.R. — Yamaha
Ashton, Gordon
1975 L.41 — Ducati
1976 L.18 — Ducati
Ashton, James
1964 J.36 — A.J.S.
1965 J.31 — A.J.S.

Ashton, J.M.
1968 J.R. Norton
Ashton, Martyn
1982 S/N.12 Yamaha
Askey, J.
1956 J.67 Norton
1957 J.R. B.S.A.
Aspell, J. D.
1960 S.48 B.S.A.
1961 J.R. B.S.A.
Atkin, M. A.
1958 J(Sn).33 B.S.A.
1959 S.R. B.S.A.
1962 J.33 Norton
Atkins, Alan
1975 L.34 Yamaha
1976 L.30 Yamaha
1977 L.20 Yamaha
1978 L.13 Yamaha
1979 L.11 Yamaha
1979 J.25 Yamaha
1980 L.4 Yamaha
1980 J.12 Yamaha
1981 L.R. Yamaha
1981 J.14 Yamaha
1982 J.R. Yamaha
1982 S.7 Yamaha
Atkins, Paul J.
1966 L.33 Greeves
Atkinson, Chris
1982 J/N.12 Yamaha
Attenborough, Michael
1974 S.50 Norton
Attenborough, Richard
1974 J.41 Bultaco
Auckland, David
1982 L/N.3 Yamaha
1982 L.7 Yamaha
Austin, R. F.
1950 S.57 B.S.A.
Avis, A. S.
1957 J(N).19 A.J.S.
1957 J 46 A.J.S.
1958 J.R. Velocette
Ayers, Alex
1968 S.42 Velocette
1970 S.R. Matchless
1971 S.19 Matchless
1972 S.13 Matchless
1973 J.27 Aermacchi
1973 S.10 Matchless
1974 S.13 Matchless
1975 J.R. Aermacchi
1975 S.R. Seeley Matchless
1976 J.33 Aermacchi
1976 S.R. Seeley Matchless
1977 S.17 Honda

Babb, Gerry
1966 L.35 Honda
1967 L.35 Honda
1969 J.R. Honda
1970 L.R. Suzuki
1971 L.R. Crooks Suzuki
1973 L.49 Suzuki
1974 L.19 Crooks Suzuki
1975 J.R. Yamaha
Bacon, Chris J.
1982 L/N.12 Fahron
1982 L.51 Fahron
Bagshaw, P.
1951 S.45 B.S.A.
1952 J.43 A.J.S.
1952 S.44 A.J.S.
Bailey, Graham L.
1967 S.R. Triumph
1971 L.R. Crooks Suzuki
Bailey, M. J.
1967 J.R. Norton
1968 J.R. A.J.S.
Bain, Geoff S.
1966 L.R. Aermacchi
1967 L.R. Suzuki
Baker, Clifford E.
1969 L.42 Yamaha
1970 L.11 Yamaha
Baker, F. R.
1967 L.R. Royal Enfield
Baker, John
1974 J.20 Aermacchi
1975 L.5 Yamaha
Baker, John R.
1979 L/N.13 Wilkinson Yamaha
1982 L.47 Wilkinson Yamaha
Baker, Norman
1965 L.R. Greeves
1972 L.R. Royal Enfield
Baker, T. A. H.
1972 L.27 Honda
1974 J.R. Bartel
Baldock, Robert T.
1965 L.49 Ducati
1966 L.46 Ducati
1968 L.42 Ducati
1969 L.53 Ducati
Baldwin, Stewart
1970 S.39 Petty Manx
1971 S.R. Seeley
1973 S.R. Norton
Ball, B.
1962 S.50 B.S.A.
Ball, Brian A.
1963 J.R. Norton
1963 S.19 Norton
1964 L.9 Mondial
1964 S.R. Norton
1965 L.7 Mondial
1965 S.R. Norton
1966 L.3 B.A. Spl.
1966 S.R. Norton
1967 L.1 B.A. Spl.
1967 S.4 Norton
Ball, D.
1957 J(N).R. B.S.A.
Ballinger, John
1966 J.R. Norton/B.S.A.
Balmer, Jim
1974 L.20 Yamaha
1975 L.14 Yamaha
1976 J.4 Yamaha
1976 S.10 Yamaha
Balmer, Mike
1971 J.R. A.J.S.
1973 L.42 Greeves
1974 L.R. Yamaha
1975 L.R. Yamaha
1976 J.55 Bultaco
1977 L.60 Suzuki
Bamford, Jack
1963 S.43 Norton
1964 J.31 Norton
1965 J.23 Norton
Bamford, Steve
1979 J/N.3 Yamaha
1979 S.R. Yamaha
Bancroft, David A.
1973 L.R. Suzuki
Bancroft, Mick
1960 J.R. A.J.S.
1961 J.36 A.J.S.
1962 J.16 A.J.S.
1963 J.19 A.J.S.
1963 S.R. Matchless
1967 L.R. Suzuki
1968 L.2 Bancroft Spl.
1969 L.6 Suzuki
1970 L.6 Suzuki
1972 L.10 Yamaha
1972 S.R. Matchless
1973 L.R. Norton
1974 L.R. Norton
Bandeen, Chad
1975 L.50 Suzuki
1978 L.R. Suzuki
1980 L.51 Suzuki
1981 L.48 Yamaha
1982 S.53 Yamaha
Banglestein, Brian T. M.

1973 S.41 Norton
1974 S.33 Norton
1975 S.45 Manx Norton
1976 J.48 Manx Norton
Banks, John R.
1955 J.67 Velocette
Bannister, K. W.
1958 J(Sn).R. Norton
1959 J.R. Norton
Barber, Roy
1975 S.52 Triton
1976 L.R. Suzuki
1977 L.35 Yamaha
1982 J.42 Yamaha
Barfoot, Ken
1958 J(Sn).10 Norton
1958 J.41 Norton
1959 S.23 Norton
Barham, A. J.
1950 S.48 Norton
1951 J.13 Norton
1951 S.23 Norton
Barker, Anthony H.
1971 S.44 Tri-Manx
Barlow, J. D.
1968 L.R. DMW
Barnacle, George
1961 J.33 A.J.S.
1962 J.21 A.J.S.
Barnard, John
1976 J.52 A.J.S. 7R
Barnato, Peter M.
1971 S.R. Petty Norton
Barnes, E. W.
1958 J(Sn).35 A.J.S.
Barnes, Ray
1959 S.R. Norton
1960 S.55 Norton
1962 S.45 Norton
1963 S.R. Norton
Barnett, Alan J.
1964 J.R. A.J.S.
1965 J.10 A.J.S
1965 S.10 Matchless
1966 J.4 A.J.S.
1966 S.R. Matchless
Barnett, Syd
1946 J.R. Norton
1946 S.8 Norton
1947 J.5 Norton
1947 S.R. Norton
Barnwell, A. T.
1954 J.54 Norton
Baron, James D.
1970 S.R. Matchless
Barr, Andy
1972 J.32 Yamaha
Barr, Martin
1977 L.30 Esler Yamaha
1977 L.9 Yamaha
Barrett, Ernie A.
1947 J.R. Norton
1947 S.R. Norton
1948 L.2 Moto Guzzi
Barrett, John
1966 L.51 Aermacchi
1967 L.R. Aermacchi
Barrett, Paul
1978 J/N.10 Aermacchi
Barrow, J.D.
1968 L.R. D.M.W.
Barry, Neil
1971 S.28 Norton
Barstard, Geoff
1975 S.38 Crescent
1976 S.R. Ryan Crescent
1978 S.15 Yamaha
1979 J.R. Yamaha
1979 S.55 Yamaha
1980 J.18 Yamaha
1980 S.15 Yamaha
Barton, J. D.
1969 J.R. Triumph
Bass, M. T.

1968 L.22 Bultaco
Bass, R.
1967 S.R. Triumph
1968 S.R. Triumph
Bassett, Andy
1979 J/N.5 Yamaha
1982 J.22 Maxton Yamaha
Bassett, A. D.
1951 J.29 A.J.S.
1951 S.R. A.J.S.
Bates, P. E.
1970 S.R. Triumph
Bateson, N.
1951 S.R. Norton
Bateson, Peter
1981 L/N.5 Yamaha
1981 L.53 Yamaha
1982 L.R. Maxton Rotax
Batty, Lew
1976 L.R. Yamaha
1977 L.25 Yamaha
1978 L.9 Yamaha
Battey, Thomas F.
1965 J.55 B.S.A.
Baxter, Barrie
1978 S/N.14 Honda
1979 J.57 Yamaha
1979 S.R. Yamaha
1980 J.41 Yamaha
1980 S.R. Yamaha
Baxter, Michael W.
1982 S/N.17 Honda
Baxter, Walter J.
1965 L.R. Greeves
Baybutt, Mick
1975 L.R. Ducati
Bayle, David J.
1965 S.55 Norton
1966 S.27 Norton
1967 J.R. B.S.A.
1967 S.18 Norton
1969 J.39 B.S.A.
Bayley, J. A.
1970 J.R. A.J.S.
Baylie, Ron W.
1963 J.R. Norton
1964 J.39 Norton
1965 J.57 A.J.S.
1966 J.36 A.J.S.
Bayly, Keith
1976 J.22 Yamaha
1977 S.R. Norton
Beale, Peter
1981 S/N.R. Yamaha
1982 S.R. Suzuki
Beames, Martin D.
1965 L.44 Greeves
Beasley, Doug St. J.
1946 L.15 Excelsior
1947 L.15 Excelsior
Beaumont, Simon
1981 J/N.R. Yamaha
1981 S.12 Yamaha
1982 J.R. Yamaha
1982 S.R. Yamaha
Bebbington, R.
1970 L.R. Yamaha
Beck, Stan
1978 S/N.20 Bill Head Honda
1978 S.60 Bill Head Honda
1979 J.R. Honda
1979 S.R. Honda
Beckett, D. J.
1958 J(Sn).39 B.S.A.
Bedford, Brian
1975 L.40 Hi-Tac Yamaha
1976 S.44 Suzuki
Bedlington, J. David
1965 L.48 Greeves
1966 L.30 Greeves
Bedward, Chris
1971 L.31 Ducati
1972 L.R. Ducati
1973 L.44 Yamaha
1975 L.17 Yamaha

1977 S.25 Cowles Metisse
1978 S.48 Triumph
1980 J.R. Yamaha
1980 S.54 Yamaha
Begg, George N.
1955 J.28 A.J.S.
1955 S.25 A.J.S.
Beharrell, Trevor
1966 J.R. A.J.S.
Beighton, A. M.
1972 J.36 Yamsel
Bell, Dennis M.
1965 L.45 N.S.U.
1966 L.43 N.S.U.
1967 L.R. Yamaha
Bell, Derek
1982 L/N.10 Yamaha
1982 L.42 Yamaha
Bell, Dermot
1979 L/N.16 Yamaha
Bell, Dudley
1979 S/N.12 Honda
Bell, Gordon
1958 J(Sn).I Norton
1958 J.11 Norton
1959 J.18 A.J.S.
1959 S.15 Matchless
1961 J.6 A.J.S.
1961 S.16 Matchless
1962 J.R. A.J.S.
1963 J.R. A.J.S.
Bell, G. D.
1958 J(Sn).R. Norton
1959 J.R. Norton
Bell, Michael J.
1966 L.37 Bultaco
1967 L.32 Kawasaki
1968 L.R. Kawasaki
Benfield, Alan A.
1966 J.R. Aermacchi
1967 J.R. Aermacchi
1968 J.41 Aermacchi
1969 J.R. Aermacchi
Bennett, Brian A.
1961 J.35 A.J.S.
1962 J.R. A.J.S.
1963 S.31 Triumph
1964 S.33 Triumph
Bennett Dave E.
1950 J.8 Norton
1950 S.4 Norton
1951 J.R. Norton
1951 S.1 Norton
Bennett, Michael L.
1963 S.24 Norton
1964 J.11 Norton
1964 S.R. Norton
1965 S.R. Norton
1966 J.8 Norton
1966 S.R. Norton
1967 J.4 Norton
1967 S.R. Norton
Bennett, R.
1951 S.37 Norton
1952 S.52 Norton
1953 S.32 Norton
1954 S.28 Norton
Bennison, W.
1948 J.50 A.J.S.
1949 J.50 A.J.S.
1950 J.R. B.S.A.
Benskin, Robert W.
1969 J.35 Norton
Benson, William G.
1964 L.32 Honda
Bent, Harold
1951 S.55 Norton
1952 S.56 Triumph
1953 S.R. Triumph
1954 S.29 Triumph
1955 S.59 Triumph
1956 J.R. A.J.S.
1957 J.60 A.J.S.
1959 S.R. Triumph

The History of the Manx Grand Prix 1923-1998 93

1960 J.57	B.S.A.
Bentley, Robert L.	
1970 J.15	Aermacchi
1971 J.R.	Aermacchi
1972 J.20	Aermacchi
Bentley, R. W.	
1969 J.35	Norton
Bentman, Graham F.	
1970 S.22	Norton
1971 J.R.	Norton
1971 S.20	Norton
Bernier, Robert L.	
1982 J/N.17	Yamaha
Berrill, Mick	
1962 S.48	G.B.S.
Berwick, Peter	
1964 L.35	J.D. DOT
1966 L.31	DOT
1967 L.9	DOT
1968 L.3	P.B. Villiers
1968 S.R.	Norton
Best, Derek	
1979 L/N.4	Yamaha
Bethell, Roy	
1964 J.R.	A.J.S.
Bethell, Roy G.	
1947 J.8	Norton
Bettison, Peter	
1960 J.24	Norton
1961 J.20	Norton
1961 S.14	Norton
1962 J.17	Norton
1962 S.10	Norton
Betts, B.	
1958 S(Sn).5	Norton
1958 S.R.	Norton
1960 S.R.	Norton
Bevan, Colin	
1977 J.R.	Yamaha
1978 J.18	Pantall Yamaha
1978 S.11	Pantall Yamaha
1979 L.R.	Yamaha
1979 J.22	Yamaha
Bevan, Dave	
1970 S.38	Norton
1971 S.24	Petty Norton
1972 S.23	Norton
1973 S.23	Matchless
1974 S.42	Matchless
Bexon, Dave	
1977 J.R.	Yamaha
Bezer, Ian H.	
1969 L.50	Greeves
1970 L.R.	Greeves
Bibby, Les	
1972 S.R.	Seeley
1973 S.R.	Seeley
1974 L.46	Yamaha
1975 L.8	Yamaha
1976 J.R.	Yamaha
1976 S.R.	Yamaha
Biggs, Geoff	
1971 J.49	B.S.A.
1972 J.R.	Norton
1973 J.R.	Aermacchi
1974 S.R.	Lawton H.D.
Bills, Ken	
1946 J.1	Norton
1946 S.2	Norton
Bilsborrow, Edward	
1966 S.R.	Matchless
1967 S.R.	Matchless
1968 S.41	Matchless
1970 S.R.	Seeley
1972 J.R.	Yamaha
Bilsborrow, Richard	
1966 J.R.	A.J.S.
1967 J.21	A.J.S.
1968 J.23	A.J.S.
1969 J.R.	Aermacchi
1969 S.R.	Matchless
1970 J.R.	Aermacchi
1971 J.R.	Aermacchi
Binnie, Jim S. G.	
1972 L.R.	Yamaha
1973 L.55	Yamaha
1974 L.R.	Maxton Yamaha
1975 L.27	Maxton Yamaha
1976 J.R.	Maxton Yamaha
1977 J.R.	Maxton Yamaha
1978 J.R.	Maxton Yamaha
1979 S.R.	Maxton Yamaha
1980 L.29	Maxton Yamaha
1981 S.R.	Norton
Birch, Kenneth E.	
1971 S.R.	Norton
Bird, Mick R.	
1967 J.47	A.J.S.
1968 J.R.	A.J.S.
1969 J.R.	A.J.S.
1970 J.R.	A.J.S.
1971 S.12	Seeley
1972 J.8	Aermacchi
1972 S.R.	Seeley
1973 J.R.	Yamaha
1973 S.13	Yamaha
1974 J.8	Broad Yamaha
1974 S.R.	Broad Yamaha
1980 L.33	Yamaha
Birkenhead, Robert C.	
1968 L.R.	Yamaha
1969 J.53	A.J.S
Birrell, D. C.	
1951 S.R.	Norton
1952 J.23	Norton
1952 S.28	Norton
Bisbey, Roy	
1959 J.R.	A.J.S.
1960 J.R.	A.J.S.
1961 J.R.	Norton
Biscardine, Bob	
1965 J.32	Norton
1968 L.R.	Yamaha
Bishop, Julian	
1977 J.34	Maxton Yamaha
Bissett, Alan	
1978 L/N.9	Yamaha
1978 L.51	Yamaha
1979 L.48	Yamaha
Black, Paul	
1982 L/N.R.	Yamaha
1982 L.R.	Yamaha
Blackburn, Neil	
1982 S/N.R.	Seeley Triumph
Bladon, Chris	
1974 S.52	Seeley Matchless
1975 S.R.	Matchless
1976 S.39	Seeley
1977 J.R.	Aermacchi
Blair, J. S.	
1951 S.59	A.J.S.
1952 J.13	A.J.S.
1952 S.21	A.J.S.
Blanch, Christopher H.	
1971 J.31	A.J.S.
Blanchard, John E.	
1964 L.4	Aermacchi
1965 L.24	Greeves
1966 L.22	Greeves
1967 L.R.	Greeves
1968 L.32	Greeves
Bland, Martyn J.	
1968 J.38	Norton
1969 J.R.	Norton
Blanning, R.	
1957 J(N).20	B.S.A.
1957 J.R.	B.S.A.
1958 J.40	B.S.A.
1958 S.45	B.S.A.
Bloomfield, Fred A.	
1963 J.R.	A.J.S.
Bloyce, Christopher F.	
1969 J.R.	Norton
1970 J.7	Norton
Blueman, Andy	
1969 L.29	Yamaha
Blum, Jack	
1951 J.65	Norton

Blunt, Dave G.	
1973 L.39	Greeves
1974 L.54	Greeves
Blyth, Jim H.	
1948 J.19	Norton
1948 S.R.	Norton
1949 J.30	Norton
1949 S.16	Norton
Boarer, E. T.	
1958 S(Sn).9	Norton
1958 S.38	Norton
Boast, Peter	
1982 J/N.18	Ducati
Bogie, D.	
1949 J.54	Velocette
1950 J.4	Velocette
1950 S.D.	Velocette
1951 J.30	Velocette
1951 S.R.	Norton
Bolland, Kevin	
1980 L/N.R.	Yamaha
1980 L.43	Yamaha
Bolton, Clifford J.	
1966 S.38	Norton
1967 S.30	Norton
Bond, Chris	
1968 S.35	Tri-Metisse
1969 S.40	Norton
1970 S.R.	Norton
1971 S.26	Norton
1972 S.R.	Norton
1974 J.26	Yamaha
1975 J.14	Yamaha
1976 J.21	Yamaha
1976 S.22	Yamaha
1977 J.23	Yamaha
1977 S.R.	Yamaha
1978 L.41	Yamaha
1978 J.35	Yamaha
Boniface, Jeffrey C.	
1969 S.R.	Norton
1970 S.R.	Norton
Bonney, George A.	
1963 J.R.	Norton
1964 J.R.	Norton
1965 J.R.	Norton
Bool, Rich	
1975 L.51	Ducati
1976 L.66	Ducati
1977 L.63	Ducati
1978 J.R.	Honda
1979 L.56	Honda
1980 S.61	Norton
1982 L.R.	Yamaha
Booys, Mike	
1979 L/N.3	Yamaha
1979 L.23	Yamaha
1982 L.3	Pinfold Rotax
Borland, Gerald A.	
1963 J.57	B.S.A.
1963 S.22	Matchless
1964 L.6	Aermacchi
1965 L.R.	J.D. Spl.
1967 L.37	J.D. Spl.
1967 S.13	J.D. Spl.
1968 J.5	Aermacchi
1968 S.R.	J.D. Spl.
Borman, David	
1975 S.61	Matchless Metisse
1976 S.R.	Velocette
Borthwick, William McF.	
1969 L.R.	Greeves
Boughey, Roy	
1955 J.45	Velocette
1955 S.34	Velocette
1957 J.R.	Norton
1957 S.29	Norton
Boult, L. D.	
1948 J.58	Velocette
1952 J.55	A.J.S.
1952 S.59	A.J.S.
Bowen, J. M.	
1952 J.17	B.S.A.
1952 S.34	B.S.A.

1953 J.8	B.S.A.
1953 S.11	B.S.A.
Bowers, Ned	
1982 S/N.6	Ducati
Bowers, Peter	
1978 L/N.R.	Suzuki
1978 L.64	Cathcart Suzuki
Bowers, Steve	
1974 J.51	Ducati
1975 S.48	H1R Kawasaki
Bowie, A. S.	
1954 J.21	B.S.A.
1954 S.15	B.S.A.
Bowler, Roger D.	
1967 J.18	Husqvarna
1968 J.R.	Norton
1968 S.32	Triumph
1969 S.9	A.J.S.
1969 S.9	Triumph
1970 J.11	Norton
1970 S.R.	Norton
1971 J.R.	Mularney Spl.
1971 S.6	Mularney Spl.
Bowring, Roger, V.	
1962 S.R.	Triumph/Norton
1963 S.R.	R.V.B.-Triumph
1964 S.R.	R.V.B.-Triumph
1965 S.R.	R.V.B.-Triumph
1966 J.R.	Triumph
1966 S.37	Triumph
1967 S.R.	Triumph
1968 S.R.	Triumph
1969 S.R.	Triumph
1970 S.R.	R.V.B. Spl.
1971 S.54	R.V.B. Spl.
Boxall, Roger	
1980 J/N.10	Yamaha
1981 J.45	Yamaha
Boyce, Ellis F.H.	
1953 J.15	A.J.S.
1953 S.R.	A.J.S.
1954 J.19	Norton
1954 S.R.	Norton
1955 J.6	Norton
1955 S.R.	Norton
1956 J.6	Norton
1956 S.4	Norton
1957 J.2	Norton
1957 S.R.	Norton
1959 J.4	Norton
1959 S.5	Norton
1960 J.1	Norton
1960 S.28	Norton
Boyes, Tony M.	
1968 J.25	Aermacchi
1969 J.R.	Aermacchi
Boyes, Stephen	
1980 L/N.2	Maxton Yamaha
1980 L.3	Maxton yamaha
1981 J.R.	Padgett Yamaha
1981 L.R.	Padgett Yamaha
1982 J.R.	Yamaha
1982 S.R.	Padgett Yamaha
Boyton, H. J. D.	
1946 S.R.	B.S.A.
1949 J.32	Norton
1949 S.9	Norton
1950 J.33	B.S.A.
1950 S.16	B.S.A.
Bradburn, Geoff M.	
1962 S.R.	Norton
Bradbury, A. E.	
1970 S.41	B.S.A./Metisse
Bradley, Steve	
1974 J.22	Yamaha
1976 J.16	Yamaha
1977 J.R.	Yamaha
1977 S.4	Yamaha
1978 J.R.	Yamaha
1978 S.6	Yamaha
1979 J.29	Yamaha
1979 S.R.	Yamaha
1980 J.R.	Yamaha
1980 S.R.	Yamaha

Bradshaw, D. N.	
1950 J.R.	Norton
Braine, E.	
1946 J.R.	Norton
1946 S.29	Norton
1947 J.53	Norton
1947 S.R.	Norton
Bramhall, N.	
1958 S(Sn).5	A.J.S.
1958 J.R	A.J.S.
Brassington, Arthur R.	
1946 L.13	Excelsior
1947 L.R.	Excelsior
1948 J.R.	A.J.S.
1949 J.18	A.J.S.
1950 J.12	A.J.S.
1951 J.32	A.J.S.
1952 J.34	A.J.S.
Bratt, C. L	
1947 J.33	Norton
1947 S.35	Norton
Brayne, Peter G.	
1967 J.46	Norton
1968 J.R.	Norton
1969 L.45	Honda
1970 L.40	Ducati
1971 L.R.	Honda
1972 L.41	Honda
1973 L.32	Honda
Brazier, V. R.	
1957 J(N).41	A.J.S.
1959 S.47	Matchless
Brennan, Gerard	
1982 J/N.R.	Yamaha
Bretherton, H.	
1947 S.R.	Rudge
Brett, Jack	
1946 L.6	Excelsior
1946 J.6	Velocette
1946 S.7	Velocette
Brew, Allan	
1978 L/N.2	Yamaha
1978 S.21	Yamaha
1979 J.15	Yamaha
1979 S.21	Yamaha
1980 J.R.	Z Parts Yamaha
1980 S.R.	Z Parts Yamaha
1981 J.R.	Brew Suzuki
1981 S.R.	RG Suzuki
Brew, J.	
1949 J.R.	Velocette
Brew, Rob	
1978 J/N.1	CBG Yamaha
1978 L.8	Yamaha
1979 J.12	Yamaha
1979 S.5	Yamaha
Bridger, Michael J.	
1967 J.R.	Norton
1968 J.33	Norton
1969 J.47	Norton
Briggs, A. G.	
1951 J.R.	Norton
1952 S.47	Norton
Briggs, Eric E.	
1946 J.R.	Norton
1946 S.20	Norton
1947 J.1	Norton
1947 S.1	Norton
Briggs, Gordon E.	
1958 J(Sn).11	B.S.A.
1958 J.48	B.S.A.
1959 J.R.	B.S.A.
1960 S.44	A.J.S.
Briggs, H. D.	
1955 J.63	B.S.A.
1955 S.3	B.S.A.
Brillard, Jock N.	
1965 S.R.	Norton
Brindley, J. Derek	
1955 J.25	Norton
1955 S.18	Norton
Brinnand, R. J.	
1957 J(N).R.	Norton
1958 J.30	Norton

94 The History of the Manx Grand Prix 1923-1998

1958 S.R.	Norton	1964 S.27	B.S.A.	1968 J.50	Norton	1956 S.R.	Triumph	1970 S.29	Matchless
1960 J.R.	Norton	**Broughton, Colin**		1969 J.37	Aermacchi	1960 J.R.	B.S.A	**Buxton, Arthur W.**	
1960 S.42	Norton	1954 J.28	B.S.A.	1970 J.25	Aermacchi	**Buckwell, R. C.**		1968 L.30	Greeves
Briscoe, R. D.		1956 J.14	B.S.A.	1971 J.R.	Aermacchi	1967 S.R.	Norton	1969 L.R.	Greeves
1951 S.11	Norton	1956 S.R.	B.S.A.	1972 J.18	Yamaha	1968 L.40	Greeves	1970 L.R.	Greeves
Bristow, Fred		1957 J.5	Norton	1973 J.22	Yamaha	**Buffham, J. W.**		1971 L.R.	Greeves
1973 J.51	Aermacchi	1960 S.R.	Norton	1975 L.R.	Yamaha	1958 J(Sn).47	B.S.A.	1972 L.R.	Greeves
1974 J.R.	Aermacchi	1960 J.R.	Norton	1976 J.36	Yamaha	**Bull, Stephen**		1973 L.R.	Greeves
1975 J.40	Seeley	1961 J.R.	Norton	1977 J.25	Yamaha	1980 L/N.10	Yamaha	1974 L.R.	Greeves
1976 J.R.	Yamsel	1962 J.R.	Norton	**Brown, L. L.**		**Bullock, Jack**		1975 L.45	Yamaha
Bristow, John A.		**Broughton, F. P. L.**		1959 J.R.	Norton	1956 S.17	Triumph	1976 J.R.	Yamaha
1969 J.42	Norton	1949 J.55	B.S.A.	**Brown, Malcolm**		1957 S R.	Matchless	**Buxton. N. E.**	
Britton, David F.		1949 S.49	B.S.A.	1980 L/N.15	Yamaha	1958 J.32	Velocette	1951 J.51	A.J.S.
1965 J.44	A.J.S.	1951 J.R.	B.S.A.	1980 L.44	Yamaha	1958 S.R.	Matchless	1952 J.63	A.J.S.
1966 J.16	A.J.S.	**Brown, A.**		**Brown, Norman**		**Bullock, P.**		1952 S.60	A.J.S.
Britton, Rob		1949 J.R.	A.J.S.	1981 J/N.1	Yamaha	1959 J.60	B.S.A.	**Buxton, Robin R.**	
1978 J/N.4	Yamaha	**Brown, Arthur C.**		1981 L.2	Yamaha	1960 S.32	Norton	1971 S.R.	Norton
1978 S.44	Yamaha	1965 S.R.	Norton	**Brown, Ron**		**Burgess, Brian A.**		1972 S.33	Norton
1979 L.6	Yamaha	**Brown, A. D.**		1979 L.R.	Yamaha	1962 S.R.	Norton	1973 J.24	Yamaha
1979 J.6	Yamaha	1950 J.13	A.J.S.	1980 L.53	Yamaha	**Burgess, F.**		1974 J.R.	Yamaha
1980 J.R.	Yamaha	1951 J.31	A.J.S.	1981 L.R.	Maxton Yamaha	1955 J.39	Norton	1975 J.10	Yamaha
1980 S.R.	Yamaha	1951 S.R.	A. J. S.	1982 L.R.	Maxton Yamaha	1955 S.40	Norton	1976 J.9	Yamaha
1981 J.R.	Yamaha	1952 J.40	A.J.S.	**Brown, R. B.**		1956 S.30	Norton	1976 S.5	Yamaha
Broad, M. J.		**Brown, Anthony M. G.**		1968 S.R.	Norton	1956 S.R.	Norton	1977 J.R.	Maxton Yamaha
1967 S.R.	Matchless	1972 J.R.	Aermacchi	**Brown, S.**		1957 S.N.F.	B.S.A.	1977 S.R.	Maxton Yamaha
Broadbent, Fred		1973 J.R.	Yamaha	1970 L.R.	Royal Enfield	1958 J.R.	Norton	1978 L.16	Maxton Yamaha
1976 L.63	Suzuki	**Brown, B. A.**		**Brown, T.**		1958 S.34	Norton	1978 L.R.	Maxton Yamaha
1977 J.10	Yamaha	1967 J.R.	Norton	1958 J(Sn).27	Norton	1959 J.R.	Norton	**Byles, Christopher J.**	
Broadey, A. L.		1968 J.R.	Norton	1958 S.R.	Norton	1959 S.R.	Norton	1966 S.19	Norton
1953 J.40	A.J.S.	**Brown, Chas**		**Brown, T. W.**		**Burgess, John D.**		1967 S.22	Norton
1953 S.35	A.J.S.	1975 J.R.	Velocette	1952 J.47	A.J.S.	1966 J.43	Norton	1968 S.17	Norton
1955 J.66	A.J.S.	1976 J.R.	Aermacchi	1952 S.45	A.J.S.	**Burman, Alan P.**		**Byrne, Roger**	
1955 S.55	A.J.S.	1977 J.40	Aermacchi	**Brown, Wattie**		1982 S/N.7	Yamaha	1962 S.R.	Norton
Broadhead, Dave		1978 J.43	Aermacchi	1981 S/N.R.	Honda	**Burrows, Rick**		1963 S.23	Norton
1978 L/N.R.	Yamaha	1978 S.42	Aermacchi	1982 J.R.	Maxton Yamaha	1973 S.R.	Seeley	**Caffrey, John B.**	
1978 L.12	Yamaha	1979 J.R.	Aermacchi	**Brown, W. D.**		1974 J.10	Yamaha	1971 S.R.	Metisse
1979 L.7	Yamaha	1980 J.34	Yamaha	1961 S.31	Norton	1975 S.5	Yamaha	1972 S.R.	Norton
1979 J.14	Yamaha	1980 S.30	Yamaha	1962 S.R.	Norton	1975 L.3	Yamaha	1973 S.R.	Vendetta Weslake
1980 L.R.	Yamaha	**Brown, Clive**		**Browne, R. B.**		**Burton, Chris J.**		1974 S.40	Vendetta Weslake
1980 J.44	Yamaha	1962 S.17	Matchless	1970 S.33	Norton	1970 J.R.	Greeves	1975 S.56	Vendetta Weslake
1981 J.1	Yamaha	1963 J.25	Norton	**Brownrigg, Brian**		1971 J.34	Yamaha	1976 S.28	Vendetta Weslake
1981 S.R.	Suzuki	1963 S.R.	Matchless/Norton	1982 J/N.16	Yamaha	1972 J.R.	Yamaha	**Cain, Peter**	
Brock, W.		1965 J.R.	M.W. Norton	**Bryant, Ernest R.**		1973 J.R.	Yamaha	1978 S/N.R.	Yamaha
1957 J(N).42	B.S.A.	1965 S.8	M.W. Norton	1968 L.38	Yamaha	1974 J.R.	Yamaha	1979 J.51	Yamaha
1958 J(Sn).61	B.S.A.	1966 J.7	Norton	1969 L.40	Yamaha	1976 J.R.	Yamaha	1979 S.R.	Yamaha
1959 J.71	B.S.A.	1966 J.R.	Norton	**Bryant, Ron W.**		1977 J.R.	Yamaha	1980 J.47	Yamaha
Brodrick, Alan W.		1967 J.R.	Norton	1965 S.28	B.S.A.	**Burton, Colin R.**		1980 S.49	Yamaha
1953 S.R.	Triumph	1967 J.R.	Norton	1966 S.R.	B.S.A.	1964 S.R.	Matchless	1981 S.41	Yamaha
Brookes, J. E.		1968 J.R.	Norton	1967 S.19	B.S.A.	**Burton, M. J.**		1982 J.36	Yamaha
1950 J.14	B.S.A.	1968 S.R.	Matchless	1968 S.11	B.S.A.	1959 S.56	Norton	**Cain, Stanley T. W.**	
1950 S.R.	B.S.A.	1969 J.3	Norton	1969 L.57	Yamaha	**Bury. L. J.**		1962 J.58	Norton
1951 J.R.	Norton	1969 S.30	Norton	1969 L.21	B.S.A.	1959 J.R.	A.J.S.	1963 J.50	Norton
Brookes, Mervyn S.		1970 J.1	Aermacchi	1970 J.33	Velocette	1960 J.R.	A.J.S.	**Cain, W. H.**	
1970 L.R.	Greeves	1970 S.11	Norton	1970 S.19	B.S.A.	**Busswell, Peter J.**		1967 L.44	Bultaco
Brookes, Michael T.		**Brown, David**		1971 S.R.	B.S.A.	1966 L.39	Bultaco	1968 L.45	D.M.W.
1957 J(N).R.	Norton	1964 S.30	Norton	1972 S.R.	B.S.A.	1967 L.R.	Bultaco	**Callow, Stephen**	
1958 J.R.	Norton	1965 S.38	Norton	1973 J.R.	Velocette	**Butcher, A. J.**		1982 S/N.10	Suzuki
1958 S.R.	Norton	**Brown, David**		1973 S.R.	Matchless	1952 J.R.	B.S.A.	**Calvert, Dave**	
1959 J.R.	Norton	1969 S.29	Matchless	1974 J.R.	Seymour Velocette	1953 J.33	A.J.S.	1975 J.42	Yamaha
1959 S.R.	Norton	1970 S.R.	Matchless	1975 J.44	Seymour Velocette	1953 S.30	A.J.S.	1976 L.36	Yamaha
1960 S.R.	Norton	1971 S.18	Seeley	1976 J.50	Yamaha	1954 J.40	A.J.S.	**Cammack, Brian**	
Brooks, A. P.		1972 J.R.	Seeley	1977 J.27	Yamaha	1954 S.31	A.J.S.	1962 S.R.	B.S.A.
1952 J.51	Velocette	1972 S.9	Seeley	**Buchan, George B.**		**Butcher, Rex E.**		1963 J.R.	Norton
1953 S.R.	Velocette	1973 S.27	Seeley	1963 J.13	A.J.S.	1961 J R.	Norton	1964 J.26	Norton
Brooks, Peter J.		**Brown, David E**		1964 J.3	Norton	1962 S.29	Norton	1965 J.36	A.J.S.
1973 L.11	Yamaha	1981 J/N.6	Yamaha	1964 S.2	Norton	1963 J.26	Norton	1966 J.R.	A.J.S.
1974 S.R.	Yamaha	1981 S.34	Yamaha	1965 J.R.	Norton	1963 S.R.	Norton	1967 J.37	A.J.S.
1974 J.R.	Yamaha	1982 L.11	Yamaha	1965 S.2	Norton	1964 L.2	Aermacchi	1968 S.R.	Norton
1976 L.12	Yamaha	1982 J.R.	Yamaha	1966 J.1	Norton	1964 S.4	Norton	1969 J.31	Ducati
Brooks, Richard		**Brown, Gordon**		1966 S.2	Norton	**Butler, G. R.**		1970 J.R.	Ducati
1978 L/N.8	Yamaha	1979 S/N.R.	Suzuki	**Buchan, Jimmy Jun.**		1956 S.33	Norton	1971 J.20	Ducati
1978 L.36	Yamaha	1979 S.7	Suzuki	1955 J.4	Norton	1957 J.36	Norton/B.S.A.	1972 J.R.	Ducati
1979 L.28	Yamaha	1980 L.16	Yamaha	1955 S.2	Norton	1957 S.19	Norton	1972 S.R.	Ducati
1980 L.23	Yamaha	1980 J.5	Yamaha	1956 J.1	Norton	1958 J.R.	Norton/B.S.A.	1973 J.43	Ducati
Broom, Mick J.		1981 J.R.	Spondon Yamaha	1956 S.I	Norton	1958 S.10	Norton	**Butler, R.**	
1970 S.R.	Triumph	1981 S.R.	Spondon Yamaha	**Buchanan, J. H.**		1954 J.R.	A.J.S.	1973 S.45	Matchless
Broome, V. F.		**Brown, Graham**		1960 J.R.	A.J.S.	**Butler, William**		1976 S.45	Honda
1958 S(Sn).7	B.S.A.	1978 J/N.8	Yamaha	1961 J.41	Norton	1977 L.47	Suzuki	**Campbell, J. D.**	
1958 S.48	B.S.A.	1979 J.R.	Yamaha	1962 J.50	A.J.S.	1978 L.30	Suzuki	1952 J.61	Norton
1961 S.56	Norton	1979 S.R.	Yamaha	**Buckley, Keith**		1979 L.R.	Yamaha	**Campbell, J. H.**	
1962 S.R.	Norton	**Brown, H. H.**		1975 J.36	Jerkoff Yamaha	1980 L.30	Yamaha	1957 J(N).R.	B.S.A
Brough, Kenneth G.		1952 J.65	Norton	1976 J.12	Metro Yamaha	1981 L.25	Yamaha	1960 S.37	Norton
1960 S.R.	B.S.A.	**Brown, J. Keith**		**Buckmaster, Ken G.**		**Butterworth, Mark**		1962 S.44	Norton
1962 S.41	B.S.A.	1967 J.45	Norton	1955 S.57	Triumph			**Campbell, Keith E. R.**	

Year	Race	Machine	Year	Race	Machine	Year	Race	Machine	Year	Race	Machine	Year	Race	Machine
1951	J.R.	Velocette	1960	J.10	Norton	1946	S.36	Norton	1953	J.2	Norton	1982	S.41	Suzuki
1952	J.6	Velocette	1960	S.19	Norton	1947	S.40	Norton	1953	S.R.	Norton	**Clegg, Noel**		
1952	S.14	Norton	**Carpenter, John D.**			**Caven, John**			1954	J.13	Norton	1968	L.12	Yamaha
Campbell, Raymond			1968	L.R.	Cotton	1971	L.14	Yamaha	1954	S.4	Norton	1969	L.4	Yamaha
1977	L.33	Yamaha	1969	L.15	Cotton	**Chadwick, Dave V.**			1955	J.R.	A.J.S.	1970	L.4	Yamaha
1978	L.R.	Yamaha	1970	L.16	Cotton	1953	J.R.	Velocette	1955	S.R.	Matchless	**Clegg, T**		
1979	L.12	Yamaha	1970	S.R.	Mistral	1954	J.2	Norton	**Christian, Doug S.**			1947	L.R.	Rudge
1980	L.6	Yamaha	1971	L.18	Cotton	1954	S.R.	Norton	1982	S/N.11	Suzuki	1948	L.10	C.T.S.
1980	J.R.	Yamaha	1972	L.R.	Yamaha	**Challis, M. C.**			**Christian, Tom Q.**			**Clifford, H. S.**		
1981	J.18	Yamaha	1973	L.14	Yamaha	1956	J.R.	A.J.S.	1972	J.16	Aermacchi	1951	S.57	Triumph
1981	S.R.	Anderson Suzuki	1974	S.6	Yamaha	**Chambers, Fred I.**			1973	J.R.	Aermacchi	1952	S.62	Triumph
1982	J.R.	Anderson Suzuki	1974	L.14	Yamaha	1963	J.35	B.S.A.	1974	L.27	Shenco Yamaha	1953	S.R.	Triumph
1982	S.R.	Anderson Suzuki	**Carpenter, W. Phil**			**Chambers, R.**			1975	J.31	Lawton Aermacchi	**Clough, Robert D.**		
Candy, Maurice J			1969	L.9	Yamaha	1957	S(N).R.	B.S.A.	1976	J.35	Yamaha	1970	S.R.	Norton
1956	J.34	Velocette	1970	L.R.	Yamaha	1958	J(Sn).60	A.J.S.	**Christie, D.**			1972	J.R.	Norton
1956	S.R.	Norton	1971	L.2	Yamaha	**Chambers, Tom**			1972	L.R.	Greeves	1973	S.R.	Yamaha
Cannell, Graham			1971	S.R.	Yamaha	1979	J/N.18	Ducati	**Chwistek, Erwin**			1974	J.29	Poco Yamaha
1981	J/N.R.	Yamaha	1972	L.1	Yamaha	1980	J.55	Ducati	1975	J.46	Yamaha	1975	L.24	Maxton Yamaha
1981	L.1	Cotton Rotax	1972	S.R.	Yamaha	1981	S.44	Ducati	**Clague, Cliff S.**			1976	J.R.	Maxton Yamaha
Cannell, Jack			**Carr, Brian B.**			1981	J.R.	Yamaha	1964	L.R.	Greeves	**Coates, James E.**		
1946	J.5	Velocette	1957	J(N).R.	B.S.A.	**Chandler, H.**			**Clark, Derek**			1956	J.R.	Norton
1946	S.10	Norton	1958	J.R.	Norton	1967	S.9	Norton	1971	S.49	Norton	**Coates, Richard**		
1947	J.R.	Norton	1959	J.R.	Norton	**Chandler, Ron S.**			1972	S.R.	Norton	1978	J/N.7	Yamaha
1947	S.13	Norton	1960	J.31	Norton	1961	S.52	Matchless	**Clark, D. G. A.**			1979	J.31	Yamaha
Cannell, John C.			1961	J.R.	Norton	1963	J.15	A.J.S.	1947	S.32	Norton	1979	S.15	Yamaha
1962	S.42	Norton	1961	S.20	Norton	1963	S.R.	Matchless	**Clark, Gary E.**			1980	J.R.	Yamaha
1963	S.26	Norton	1962	J.R.	Norton	1964	J.R.	A.J.S.	1981	L/N.R.	AMR	1980	S.R.	Yamaha
Cannon, Rick			1962	S.R.	Norton	1964	S.R.	Matchless	1981	L.R.	AMR	1981	J.19	Yamaha
1975	L.R.	Aermacchi	**Carr, J. E.**			**Chapman, Andy C.**			**Clark, G. P.**			1981	S.R.	Yamaha
1976	S.33	Suzuki	1956	J.43	Norton	1968	L.R.	Yamaha	1950	S.R.	Norton	1982	L.R.	Cotton
1977	S.R.	Suzuki	**Carr, Louis**			1969	J.2	Yamaha	1951	J.R.	Norton	1982	J.17	Waddon
1978	L.39	Yamaha	1952	S.23	Triumph	**Chapman, Frank**			1952	J.28	A.J.S.	**Cocks, Roger C.**		
1979	L.27	Yamaha	1953	S.18	Triumph	1974	L.R.	Yamaha	1952	S.R.	A.J.S.	1970	J.R.	Ducati
1980	L.17	Yamaha	**Carr, P.**			**Chapman, Joe**			**Clark, Harold**			1972	L.R.	Aermacchi
1980	J.R.	Yamaha	1954	J.32	A.J.S.	1960	S.R.	Norton/B.S.A.	1946	J.18	Norton	1973	J.40	Aermacchi
1981	L.15	Yamaha	1954	S.R.	A.J.S.	1961	S.46	Norton/B.S.A.	1946	S.14	Norton	1974	S.R.	Aermacchi HD
1981	J.26	Yamaha	1955	J.R.	A.J.S.	1962	J.45	A.J.S.	1947	J.20	Norton	1975	S.R.	Aermacchi HD
1982	L.15	Yamaha	1955	S.41	A.J.S.	1963	J.29	A.J.S.	1947	S.R.	Norton	1976	S.26	Norton
1982	J.R.	Yamaha	1958	J.R.	A.J.S.	1964	J.14	A.J.S.	1948	J.12	Velocette	1977	S.40	Suzuki
Cant, George W.			**Carter, B.**			**Chappell, Dennis E.**			1948	S.10	Norton	1978	S.49	Suzuki
1967	J.52	Norton	1950	S.28	Triumph	1970	L.R.	Greeves	1949	J.11	Norton	1980	S.R.	Suzuki
1968	J.35	Norton	**Carter, E.**			1973	L.50	Yamaha	1949	S.5	Norton	**Codd, Bernard D.**		
1969	J.R.	Norton	1958	J.(Sn).50	B.S.A.	**Chappell, J.**			1950	J.R.	Norton	1956	J.4	Norton
1970	J.R.	Norton	**Carter, Harry**			1960	J.N.F.	Norton	1950	S.3	Norton	1956	S.R.	Norton
1971	S.R.	Norton	1946	J.13	Norton	**Chappell, John**			1951	J.3	Norton	**Cole, Stewart**		
1972	S.R.	Norton	1946	S.R.	Vincent-H.R.D.	1976	L.54	Yamaha	1951	S.5	A.J.S.	1979	J/N.R.	Yamaha
1974	S.28	Norton	1947	J.R.	Norton	1977	J.12	Yamaha	1952	J.2	A.J.S.	1979	L.18	Yamaha
Capes, Derek E. E.			1947	S.R.	Norton	**Charles, Tony**			1952	S.4	Norton	1980	L.R.	Yamaha
1964	L.R.	B.S.A	**Carter, Phil H.**			1977	L.45	Yamaha	**Clark, John R.**			1980	J.20	Yamaha
1970	L.R.	Ducati	1949	S.19	Norton	**Charlesworth, Keith R.**			1950	J.43	Douglas	**Coleman, F. C.**		
1972	L.45	Ducati	1950	J.47	Norton	1982	L/N.15	Yamaha	**Clarke, A. E.**			1948	L.R.	Excelsior
1974	L.41	Aermacchi	1950	S.14	Norton	1982	L.48	Yamaha	1957	J(N).36	A.J.S.	**Coleman, John**		
1977	L.52	Aermacchi	**Cash, Douglas**			**Chatterton, Mick**			1958	J(Sn).44	A.J.S.	1978	J/N.22	Yamaha
1978	L.47	Aermacchi	1965	S.R.	Norton	1964	L.17	D.M.W.	**Clarke, Christopher M.**			1978	S.R.	Yamaha
1979	L.49	Aermacchi	**Cassidy, Dick**			1965	L.12	D.M.W.	1969	J.26	A.J.S.	1979	S.56	Yamaha
Capner A. Roy			1976	J.38	Yamaha	1966	J.R.	Norton	1970	J.R.	A.J.S.	1980	J.30	Yamaha
1950	J.R.	Norton	1977	J.8	Yamaha	**Chatterton, V. Derek**			**Clarke, I.**			1980	L.R.	Yamaha
1952	J.R.	B.S.A.	1978	L.42	Yamaha	1967	L.R.	Ducati	1955	J.R.	Norton	1981	J.52	Yamaha
1953	J.25	B.S.A.	1978	J.R.	Inglewood Yamaha	**Cheers, Eric**			1956	S.31	Norton	1982	S.R.	Yamaha
Capper, Mick			**Castle, R.**			1954	J.25	B.S.A.	1957	J.R.	A.J.S.	**Collard, William J.**		
1976	L.31	Yamaha	1955	J.50	B.S.A.	1954	S.17	B.S.A.	1957	S.R.	Norton	1973	S.46	Norton
1977	S.5	Yamaha	1955	S.58	Norton	**Ching, S. H.**			1958	S.16	Norton	1974	S.R.	Petty Manx
1977	J.R.	Yamaha	1956	S.28	B.S.A.	1946	J.27	Norton	1959	J.53	Norton	1978	L.48	Yamaha
1980	J.6	Yamaha	1956	S.24	B.S.A.	1946	S.R.	Norton	1959	S.R.	Norton	1979	L.40	Yamaha
1980	S.7	Yamaha	1957	J.R.	B.S.A.	**Chivers, C. A.**			**Clarke, J. L.**			1980	L.35	Yamaha
1981	S.R.	Sheppard Yamaha	1957	S.11	B.S.A.	1957	J(N).34	A.J.S.	1971	J.41	Norton	1981	L.36	Yamaha
1981	J.R.	Yamaha	1959	J.79	A.J.S.	1960	S.41	A.J.S.	1972	S.42	Norton	1981	J.36	Yamaha
Capper, Roland C.			**Castles, Leo G. C.**			1962	J.R.	A.J.S.	**Clarke, M. A. C.**			**Collett, G. E.**		
1963	J.34	A.J.S.	1972	J.35	Honda	**Chivers, F. G.**			1946	J.33	Norton	1952	S.R.	B.S.A.
Capstick, Alan B.			**Catchpole.P.**			1959	J.77	B.S.A.	**Clarke, W.**			1953	J.R.	A.J.S.
1964	L.R.	Ceer/B.S.A.	1960	S.60	B.S.A.	**Cholerton, D. S.**			1948	L.4	Excelsior	1953	S.R.	A.J.S.
1965	L.R.	Ceer/B.S.A.	**Cathcart, Alan**			1955	S.36	B.S.A.	**Clarkson, Dave**			**Collings, E. F.**		
Carman, R. H.			1976	J.42	Aermacchi	**Chrich, T. M.**			1969	J.R.	A.J.S.	1949	J.R.	Norton
1954	J.33	A.J. S.	1977	J.R.	Aermacchi	1955	J.R.	B.S.A.	1973	J.R.	Yamaha	**Collings, A. C. R.**		
1954	S.R.	A.J.S.	**Catlin, George A.**			1955	S.R.	B.S.A.	1974	J.17	Yamaha	1949	J.57	A.J.S.
1955	J.22	A.J.S.	1954	J.R.	Norton	**Christian, Dennis**			1975	J.R.	Yamaha	1949	S.51	Norton
1955	S.29	A.J.S.	1954	S.25	Norton	1949	J.16	Velocette	**Clarkson, S.**			**Collins, Michael**		
1956	S.18	Norton	**Catterson, David F.**			1949	S.11	Velocette	1970	L.R.	Greeves	1969	J.6	Seeley
1957	J.15	B.S.A.	1970	L.21	Bultaco	1950	J.11	Norton	**Claude, Rob**			**Collis, George R. V.**		
1957	S.27	A.J.S.	1971	L.R.	Bultaco	1950	S.7	Norton	1979	S/N.6	Rickman Honda	1964	L.5	Yamaha
1958	J.14	A.J.S.	1972	L.R.	Bultaco	1951	J.10	Norton	1980	S.R.	Yamaha	1967	L.12	Aermacchi
1958	S.13	A.J.S.	1973	L.R.	Bultaco	1951	S.R.	Norton	**Clay, Barry**			1967	S.R.	Triton
1959	J.R.	A.J.S.	1974	L.51	Fleming Yamaha	1952	J.8	Norton	1982	J/N.15	Spondon Yamaha	1968	L.R.	G.C. Special
1959	S.26	A.J.S.	**Caunce, Wilfred**			1952	S.6	Norton	**Clay, Paul**			1968	S.R.	Norton

1969 L.R.	Yamaha	1952 S.24	Norton	1954 J.10	Norton	1973 J.R.	Aermacchi	1970 L.15	Ducati
1969 S.11	Norton	1959 J.29	Norton	1954 S.1	Norton	1974 J.R.	Aermacchi	1971 L.R.	Ducati
1970 L.R.	Yamaha	1959 S.38	Norton	**Costain, George D. C.**		**Craine, Dennis**		**Crooks, Eddie**	
Collison, Tony		**Cope, E. Frank**		1966 J.R.	Aermacchi	1961 S.R.	Norton	1952 J.R.	A.J.S.
1971 L.38	Suzuki	1948 L.R.	A.J.S.	1967 L.R.	Aermacchi	1962 J.6	Norton	1953 J.13	A.J.S.
Collister, Sean		1949 J.51	A.J.S.	1968 L.R.	Aermacchi	1963 J.12	Norton	1953 S.10	Norton
1980 L/N.6	Yamaha	1949 S.R.	A.J.S.	**Cotgrave, Geoffrey**		1963 S.5	Norton	1954 J.8	A.J.S.
1980 L.R.	Yamaha	**Cope, Roger J. E.**		1982 L/N.11	Rankin Yamaha	1964 L.R.	Royal Enfield	1954 S.12	Matchless
1981 L.8	Prews Yamaha	1969 L.R.	Suzuki	1982 L.44	Rankin Yamaha	1965 L.1	Greeves	1955 J.5	Norton
1982 L.2	Yamaha	1970 L.20	Suzuki	**Cott, Paul J.**		**Crann, R. G.**		1956 S.6	Norton
1982 J.10	Padgett Yamaha	1971 L.4	Yamaha	1968 S.23	Norton	1956 J.65	A.J.S.	1956 J.2	Norton
Conn, Chris R		1972 L.R.	Yamsel	**Cottrell, Peter**		1957 J.61	A.J.S.	1956 S.5	Norton
1961 S.30	Norton	1972 S.R.	Yamsel	1966 S.35	B.S.A.	**Cranston, Paul**		1957 J.R.	Norton
Connell, Don		1973 J.R.	Yamsel	1968 S.44	B.S.A.	1980 J/N.2	Yamaha	1957 S.7	Norton
1980 L/N.R.	Yamaha	1973 S.R.	Yamsel	1969 S.R.	B.S.A.	1980 L.R.	Yamaha	1958 J.2	Norton
1980 L.R.	Yamaha	1974 L.R.	Yamaha	**Couldwell, Alan**		1981 J.R.	Neill Yamaha	1958 S.2	Norton
Connolly, Ed		1975 S.R.	RN Special	1979 S/N.2	Honda	1981 S.R.	Starplan Yamaha	1959 J.R.	Norton
1976 S.R.	Norton	1975 L.2	Yamaha	1980 J.R.	Yamaha	**Craven, Alan**		1959 S.1	Norton
Connor, David		1976 L.R.	Yamaha	1980 S.R.	Luke Honda	1955 J.R.	Norton	**Crosby, Cyril**	
1977 L.36	Yamaha	1976 S.35	Yamaha	**Coulter, Alan**		1955 S.58	Norton	1971 S.37	Seeley
1978 L.R.	Yamaha	**Copeland, Alastair R.**		1980 J/N.4	Yamaha	1956 J.28	B.S.A.	1972 J.R.	Yamaha
1979 L.39	Yamaha	1958 S(Sn).l2	B.S.A.	1981 J.31	Yamaha	1956 S.24	B.S.A.	1973 J.29	Yamaha
1980 L.36	Yamaha	1958 S.42	B.S.A.	1981 L.R.	Yamaha	1957 J.R.	B.S.A.	**Cross, G. A.**	
Conway, Tony		1959 S.31	B.S.A.	**Courtney, Peter**		1957 S.11	B.S.A.	1959 S.58	B.S.A.
1980 J/N.R.	Yamaha	1961 J.26	Norton	1968 L.23	D.M.W.	1958 J.R.	Norton	**Crossland, Philip**	
Cook, Peter		1962 J.15	Norton	1969 L.25	A.J.S.	1958 S.32	Norton	1978 J/N.20	Aermacchi
1982 L/N.2	Rotax	1963 J.10	Norton	**Cousins, John**		1959 J.53	B.S.A.	**Crossley, Don G.**	
1982 L.27	Rotax	1964 J.19	Norton	1975 S.51	Suzuki	1959 S.R.	B.S.A.	1946 L.8	Excelsior
Cook, R. G.		1964 S.10	Norton	1976 S.R.	Seeley Suzuki	1960 J.51	A.J.S.	1946 J.R.	Velocette
1955 J.R.	A.J.S./Norton	1965 J.R.	Norton	**Cowell, G. B.**		**Crebbin, T. Peter**		1946 S.R.	Norton
1955 S.R.	A.J.S.	1965 S.R.	Norton	1960 S.R.	Triumph/Norton	1947 S.R.	Triumph	1947 J.R.	E.M.C.
Cooke, James		1966 J.13	Norton	1961 S.47	Triumph/Norton	1948 S.11	Triumph	1947 S.5	Norton
1973 L.R.	Suzuki	1966 S.R.	Norton	**Cowell, P. T.**		1949 J.29	A.J.S.	1948 J.3	Velocette
1976 L.55	Yamaha	1967 S.R.	Norton	1947 S.54	Triumph	1949 S.22	A.J.S.	1948 S.1	Triumph
Coomber Brian E.		1968 J.R.	Honda	**Cowell, T. Randall**		**Creer, Jimmy**		1949 J.3	A.J.S.
1965 J.R.	Norton	1968 S.R.	Norton	1960 J.33	Norton	1969 L.48	Honda	1949 S.R.	Triumph
Coombes, David		1969 L.27	Ducati	1961 J.13	Norton	1970 L.R.	Aermacchi	1950 J.1	A.J.S.
1972 L.42	Aermacchi	1969 S.R.	Norton	1963 J.R.	Norton	1975 J.32	Yamaha	1950 S.R.	Norton
1974 L.R.	Suzuki	1970 S.R.	Norton	1963 S.7	Norton	1977 J.R.	Yamaha	1951 J.2	Norton
1976 L.33	Suzuki	**Cops, Norman G.**		1964 J.R.	Norton	1978 L.10	Yamaha	1951 S.2	Norton
1977 L.32	Suzuki	1973 L.R.	Yamaha	1964 S.5	Norton	**Crellin, John**		**Crossley, J.**	
1978 L.24	Hejira Suzuki	**Corbett, Ray**		1965 J.R.	Norton	1978 J/N.6	Yamaha	1950 J.44	Norton
Coombes, Mike		1978 S/N.11	Yamaha	1966 J.17	Aermacchi	1979 J.R.	Yamaha	1951 S.32	Vincent-H.R.D.
1976 S.R.	Suzuki	1979 J.52	Yamaha	1966 S.R.	Norton	1980 J.15	Yamaha	**Croucher, V. F. G.**	
1977 S.44	Suzuki	1979 S.R.	Yamaha	1975 L.R.	Glen Cowell Yamaha	1980 S.8	Yamaha	1957 J(N).51	A.J.S.
1978 S.35	Kawasaki	1980 J.42	Yamaha	1976 L.24	Glen Cowell Yamaha	1982 J.50	Yamaha	1958 S(Sn).17	B.S.A.
1979 S.46	Kawasaki	**Corbett, Roger W.**		1978 S.R.	Yamaha	1982 S.10	Yamaha	**Crow, J. M. 'Jim'**	
Coombes, Paul E.		1966 S.R.	Triumph/Manx	**Cowie, John**		**Crellin, Paul**		1946 J.R.	Norton
1969 S.R.	C.R.D.	1967 S.R.	Triton	1971 S.R.	Dresda	1978 J/N.17	Yamaha	1946 S.11	Norton
Coombs, G. C.		**Corlett, G. Ted**		1972 S.15	Seeley	**Crellin, R.**		1947 J.18	Norton
1956 S.R.	B.S.A.	1957 J(N).24	B.S.A.	1973 J.15	Norton	1976 L.R.	Ossa	1947 S.30	Norton
Coope, Brian G.		1958 J.R.	B.S.A.	1973 S.R.	Seeley	**Cresswell, J. V.**		1949 J.7	Velocette
1969 S.R.	Kawasaki	1959 J.45	A.J.S.	**Cowie, Keith**		1946 J.R.	Rudge	1949 S.10	Norton
1971 S.R.	Kawasaki	1960 J.27	A.J.S.	1970 S.28	Norton	**Cretney, David**		1950 J.48	Velocette
1972 S.R.	Kawasaki	**Corley, W. J.**		1971 S.25	Norton	1976 J.R.	Yamsel	1950 S.5	Norton
1975 S.22	Wilson & Collins Special	1949 J.39	A.J.S.	1972 S.21	Norton	1977 S.R.	Yoshimura Honda	1951 J.R.	Velocette
1976 S.32	Yamaha	1949 S.44	A.J.S.	**Cowles, Ray J.**		1978 J.R.	Yamaha	1951 S.R.	Norton
Cooper, Andy		**Cormican, Donald S.**		1961 S.55	Matchless	1978 S.57	Honda	**Crowe, John F. P.**	
1979 J/N.7	Spondon Yamaha	1973 J.25	Aermacchi	1962 S.43	Matchless	1982 S.42	Honda	1963 J.R.	B.S.A.
1979 S.32	Triumph Trident	1974 L.6	Yamaha	1963 J.55	A.J.S.	**Crew, Peter R. G.**		1963 S.R.	Triton
1980 J.11	Spondon Yamaha	**Cornes, Eric**		**Cowley, J. Kevin**		1972 L.29	Yamaha	1964 J.R.	B.S.A.
1980 S.11	Spondon Yamaha	1970 S.34	Norton	1968 J.R.	Norton	1973 L.R.	Yamaha	1964 S.18	Norton
1981 S.52	Spondon Yamaha	1972 S.39	Norton	1969 J.R.	Norton	**Crichton, D. G.**		1965 S.21	Norton
1981 J.7	Spondon Yamaha	1972 S.34	Norton	1970 J.38	Norton	1948 L.R.	New Imperial	1967 S.12	Norton
1982 J.1	Yamaha	1974 S.20	Norton	1971 S.R.	Seeley	**Cripps, J. R.**		**Crowder, Horace**	
1982 S.R.	Spondon Yamaha	1975 S.27	Beale Norton	**Cox, Bruce M.**		1959 J.R.	Norton	1957 J(N).13	B.S.A.
Cooper, David		1975 J.53	Beale A.J.S.	1963 S.R.	Norton/Triumph	1960 J.R.	Norton	1957 J.28	B.S.A.
1979 L/N.10	Yamaha	1976 S.30	Matchless	**Cox, Hedley J.**		1961 J.R.	Norton	1958 J.R.	B.S.A.
1979 L.R.	Yamaha	1977 S.16	Yamaha	1950 J.37	Velocette	**Critten, Adrian**		1958 S.26	B.S.A.
Cooper, Eric R.		1978 J.32	Beale Yamaha	1951 J.R.	Velocette	1980 S/N.8	Kawasaki	1959 J.R.	A.J.S.
1964 J.R.	Norton	1978 S.24	Beale Yamaha	**Cox, Malcolm J.**		1981 S.R.	Kawasaki	**Crowther, R. G.**	
Cooper, Gavin D.		1979 J.55	Yamaha	1969 L.41	Kawasaki	1982 S.R.	Kawasaki	1967 J.R.	A.J.S.
1965 L.R.	Aermacchi	1979 S.31	Yamaha	1970 L.29	Sukiaky	**Croft, David N.**		**Cruse, P. K.**	
Cooper, H.		**Cortvriend, R. Barry**		**Cox, Peter M.**		1971 J.48	A.J.S.	1951 J.50	B.S.A.
1957 J.(N).28	Norton	1954 J.51	A.J.S.	1979 L/N.R.	Yamaha	**Cronan, H. J.**		1955 J.42	A.J.S.
1958 J.50	Norton	1955 J.52	B.S.A.	1979 L.62	Yamaha	1949 J.R.	Norton	1955 S.R.	A.J.S.
1959 J.47	Norton	1955 S.48	B.S.A.	1980 J.R.	Yamaha	1950 J.R.	Norton	**Cubbon, Barry**	
Cooper, John H.		1956 J.50	B.S.A.	1981 S.54	Yamaha	1951 J.69	Velocette	1978 J/N.18	Yamaha
1963 J.R.	Norton	1956 S.R.	Matchless	1981 S.42	Yamaha	**Cronin, Gerald**		**Cudworth, Neil**	
Cooper, Stan		1957 J.45	B.S.A.	1982 J.47	Yamaha	1979 J/N.15	Yamaha	1979 J/N.R.	Yamaha
1950 S.41	A.J.S.	1957 S.30	Matchless	**Cragg, John**		1979 J.R.	Yamaha	1979 S.R.	Yamaha
1951 J.39	Norton	**Costain, George R.**		1982 S/N.R.	Honda	**Cronshaw, John**		1980 J.27	Yamaha
1952 J.36	Norton	1953 J.12	Norton	**Craig, Gordon C.**		1981 S/N.R.	Unity B.S.A.	1980 S.24	Yamaha
		1953 S.R.	Norton	1971 L.R.	Greeves	**Crookes, C. E.**		1981 J.22	Yamaha

Year	Race	Machine
1981	S.R.	Yamaha
1982	J.25	Yamaha
1982	S.32	Yamaha

Cull, Rodney
| 1968 | L.18 | Aermacchi |

Cullen, Paul M.
| 1969 | L.16 | Bultaco |

Culley, J. E.
| 1968 | L.R. | Bultaco |

Culshaw, A.
| 1957 | J(N).30 | A.J.S. |

Culshaw, R.
1958	J(Sn).9	B.S.A.
1958	J.R.	B.S.A.
1959	J.24	Norton
1960	J.R.	Norton
1960	S.R.	B.S.A.
1961	J.30	Norton
1961	S.24	Norton

Cumming, H. M.
| 1967 | L.20 | Ducati |
| 1968 | L.17 | Ducati |

Cunliffe, J. O.
| 1951 | J.64 | A.J.S. |

Currie, L.
1952	S.66	Velocette
1953	J.44	Velocette
1953	S.R.	Velocette

Curry, Fred
1980	S/N.9	Yamaha
1981	J.49	Yamaha
1981	S.36	Yamaha
1982	J.28	Yamaha
1982	S.33	Kawasaki

Curtis, Chris W.
1968	L.44	Ducati
1969	L.17	Aermacchi
1970	J.R.	Aermacchi
1971	J.10	Aermacchi
1972	J.6	Aermacchi
1974	L.35	Yamaha
1975	L.R.	Yamaha
1976	L.35	Yamaha
1977	L.R.	Yamaha

Curzon, H. D. S.
| 1947 | S.57 | Norton |
| 1950 | S.58 | Norton |

Cutts, Richard H.
1977	J.R.	Yamaha
1978	J.36	Yamaha
1979	J.R.	Matchless
1980	S.35	Seeley
1981	J.47	Yamaha
1981	S.R.	Ducati
1982	S.15	Kawasaki

Dakin, Phil L.
1955	J.43	A.J.S.
1955	S.52	A.J.S.
1956	J.R.	A.J.S.
1956	S.30	A.J.S.
1957	J.R.	A.J.S.
1957	S.21	A.J.S.

Dale, Dickie H.
| 1948 | L.1 | Moto Guzzi |
| 1948 | J.13 | Velocette |

Dalgleish, Nisbet C.
| 1965 | J.30 | Norton |
| 1967 | L.51 | Honda |

Dallow, John
1966	J.31	A.J.S.
1967	J.14	Norton
1968	J.R.	A.J.S.
1969	J.43	A.J.S.

Daly, John Jnr
1974	S.R.	Triumph
1976	S.51	Triumph Daytona
1977	S.R.	Triumph Daytona
1978	S.47	Headline Norton
1979	S.45	Triumph
1980	S.R.	Triumph
1981	S.R.	Triumph
1982	S.58	Triumph

Daniels, Gordon J.
1965	L.R.	Cotton
1966	J.20	A.J.S.
1967	J.R.	A.J.S.
1967	S.R.	Matchless
1968	J.13	Cowles Matchless
1968	S.R.	Matchless
1969	S.1	Cowles Matchless

Daniels, John
1964	L.R.	Greeves
1965	L.R.	Ducati
1966	J.R.	N.S.U.

Daniels, J. D.
| 1948 | J.5 | Velocette |
| 1948 | S.R. | Triumph |

Daniels, Ken D.
1966	S.11	Norton
1967	J.R.	Norton
1968	S.R.	Norton

Daniels, Phil
1976	J.27	Yamaha
1977	J.14	Yamaha
1979	J.11	Weston Yamaha
1979	S.13	Weston Yamaha
1980	J.22	Weston Yamaha
1980	S.5	Weston Yamaha
1982	J.R.	Yamaha
1982	S.6	Yamaha

Danks, David
| 1975 | J.16 | Yamaha |

Dann, David
| 1974 | J.37 | Norton |
| 1975 | J.R. | Aermacchi |

Darbishire, J. G.
1949	J.R.	Norton
1950	J.25	Norton
1950	S.59	Norton

Darville, Kenneth A.
1971	J.52	A.J.S.
1972	J.33	A.J.S.
1973	S.R.	Norton

Darvill, Peter J.
1957	S(N).17	P.J.D.-Vincent
1957	S.51	P.J.D.-Vincent
1958	J.55	P.J.D.-Vincent
1958	S.21	P.J.D.-Vincent
1959	J.19	A.J.S.
1959	S.28	Norton
1961	J.R.	A.J.S.
1961	S.19	Norton
1962	J.2	A.J.S.
1962	S.2	Norton
1963	J.1	A.J.S.
1963	S.2	Norton

Davenport, A. F.
1949	J.67	A.J.S.
1950	J.49	A.J.S.
1950	S.62	A.J.S.

Davenport, N. J.
| 1957 | J(N).16 | B.S.A. |

Davey, Cyril
1961	J.24	Norton
1962	J.24	Norton
1963	J.21	Norton
1965	J.R.	Norton
1965	S.12	Norton
1966	J.19	Norton
1966	S.R.	Norton
1967	L.5	Aermacchi
1967	S.28	Norton
1968	L.R.	Aermacchi
1968	S.18	Norton

Davey, D. H.
| 1957 | J(N).16 | B.S.A. |
| 1957 | J.34 | B.S.A. |

Davey, Peter A.
1951	S.6	Norton
1952	J.12	A.J.S.
1952	S.3	Norton

Davie, J. W.
1954	J.12	B.S.A.
1954	S.R.	B.S.A.
1955	S.R.	B.S.A.

Davies, David C. E.
| 1982 | S/N.3 | Maxton Yamaha |

Davies, Eugene P.
1955	J.46	B.S.A.
1956	S.19	Norton
1957	S.9	Norton
1958	J.R.	A.J.S.
1958	S.9	Norton
1959	J.15	Norton
1959	S.R.	Norton
1960	J.22	Norton
1960	S.R.	Norton
1963	J.37	Norton

Davies, John R.
| 1973 | J.R. | Norton |

Davies, John D.
1978	S/N.2	Maxton Yamaha
1978	S.23	Maxton Yamaha
1979	L.29	Maxton Yamaha
1979	J.18	Maxton Yamaha
1980	J.R.	Yamaha
1980	S.R.	Suzuki
1981	L.R.	RDV
1982	J.R.	Yamaha
1982	S.9	Yamaha

Davies, Mike
| 1976 | L.47 | Maxton Yamaha |
| 1978 | L.45 | Maxton Yamaha |

Davies, Paul A.
1981	L/N.3	Yamaha
1981	L.30	Yamaha
1982	L.23	Yamaha
1982	J.23	Daniels Yamaha

Davies, R. B.
| 1967 | S.36 | Norton |

Davies, Roger C.
1966	S.R.	Matchless
1968	S.31	Matchless
1969	S.6	Matchless
1970	S.R.	Matchless
1971	S.R.	Norton
1972	S.7	Norton
1973	S.R.	Norton

Davies, Steven 'Snuffy'
1974	L.R.	Yamaha
1975	L.23	Yamaha
1976	L.7	Yamaha
1977	J.45	Yamaha
1977	S.1	Yamaha

Davies, Steve
| 1977 | L.R. | Yamaha |

Davis, Barry, J.
1964	L.30	Ducati
1965	L.R.	D.M.W.
1967	L.36	Yamaha
1968	L.6	Ducati/Yamaha
1969	L.10	Ducati/Yamaha
1970	L.13	Ducati/Yamaha
1971	L.8	Yamaha

Davis, Brian, J.
1964	J.R.	A.J.S.
1965	J.8	A.J.S.
1965	S.13	Matchless
1966	J.9	A.J.S.
1966	S.5	Matchless

Davis, C. H.
1947	J.54	Velocette
1947	S.R.	Velocette
1948	J.60	Velocette
1949	J.25	Velocette
1949	S.32	Velocette

Davis, J. D. O.
| 1950 | S.55 | A.J.S. |
| 1950 | J.36 | Norton |

Davis, Jeremy R.
1971	L.R.	Yamaha
1972	L.43	Yamaha
1973	L.46	Yamaha
1975	J.50	Yamaha

Davis, P. B.
| 1951 | J.36 | Norton |

Davy, N.
| 1959 | S.44 | Velocette |

Daw, Peter
| 1968 | J.R. | Norton |
| 1969 | S.43 | Matchless |

Dawson, John
1970	S.R.	Matchless
1971	S.R.	Matchless
1968	J.26	A.J.S.
1969	J.11	A.J.S.
1971	S.R.	Matchless

Dawson, M. J.
1960	J.R.	B.S.A.
1961	J.R.	Norton
1956	S.56	Vincent
1957	J.59	B.S.A.
1957	S.57	B.S.A.
1958	J.47	B.S.A.
1958	S.R.	B.S.A.
1959	S.51	Norton

Dawson, Robin P.
1959	J.37	A.J.S.
1960	J.5	A.J.S.
1960	S.11	Matchless
1961	J.2	A.J.S.
1961	S.4	Norton
1962	J.1	A.J.S.
1962	S.4	Matchless

Dawson, Wally
1964	S.R.	Norton
1965	J.7	Norton
1967	J.22	Norton
1967	S.R.	Norton

Day, William H.
1963	S.30	B.S.A.
1964	S.R.	Special
1964	L.R.	Greeves
1966	L.7	Greeves
1967	L.4	Greeves
1968	L.R.	T.S.R.
1968	S.12	Crescent
1970	L.R.	Yamaha
1971	L.R.	Yamaha
1972	L.R.	Yamaha
1973	L.15	Yamaha
1974	L.23	Yamaha Special

Daykin, D. Robin
| 1957 | J(N).40 | A.J.S. |

Deakin, Robert C.
| 1968 | J.20 | A.J.S. |

Dean, Rally
| 1951 | J.58 | Norton |

Dearden, Reg W.
1946	J.26	E.M.C.
1946	S.R.	Norton
1947	J.50	Norton
1947	S.R.	Norton
1948	J.R.	Norton
1948	S.26	Norton
1949	J.45	Norton
1949	S.30	Norton
1950	J.R.	Norton
1950	S.R.	Norton

Deaville, John W.
1957	S(N).R.	Norton
1958	S.R.	Matchless
1973	S.48	Matchless
1974	S.R.	Matchless

Degens, Dave F.
1962	S.R.	Matchless
1963	S.12	Matchless
1964	J.R.	A.J.S.
1964	S.22	Dunstall Dominator

Denehy, Brian L.
1957	S(N).14	Norton
1957	S.R.	Norton
1960	S.R.	Norton

Denny, R. D. L.
| 1966 | L.R. | Yamaha |

Dennis, Joseph T.
1960	J.R.	Norton
1961	J.R.	Norton
1963	S.11	Norton
1963	S.9	Norton

Denniss, Brian A.
| 1956 | S.53 | B.S.A. |
| 1957 | S.45 | Norton |

Dent, Joe D.
1947	S.36	Norton
1948	J.37	A.J.S.
1948	S.32	Norton

Denton, J. B.
| 1954 | J.18 | B.S.A. |
| 1954 | S.R. | B.S.A. |

Denty, John A.
1960	S.56	B.S.A.
1963	J.43	A.J.S.
1964	J.R.	A.J.S.
1964	S.R.	Norton

De Prez, Brian
1964	J.R.	Norton
1967	J.16	Norton
1968	L.11	Yamaha
1969	L.7	Yamaha

Devey, John
1968	S.R.	Norton
1969	S.33	Norton
1970	S.R.	Norton

Devlin, Larry G.
1978	J/N.13	Aermacchi Metisse
1979	J.R.	Aermacchi Metisse
1980	S.46	Bowring Yamaha
1981	S.25	Bowring Yamaha
1981	J.R.	Bowring Aermacchi Metisse
1982	J.32	Aermacchi Metisse

Dewey, J.
| 1973 | J.R. | Aermacchi |

Dibben, Stan J.
| 1952 | J.32 | Norton |

Dickenson, John
1980	L/N.8	Yamaha
1980	L.34	Yamaha
1981	L.29	Yamaha
1981	J.42	Yamaha
1982	L.43	Yamaha
1982	J.R.	Yamaha

Dicker, Dennis J.
1960	J.30	A.J.S.
1961	J.21	A.J.S.
1962	J18	A.J.S.
1962	S.R.	Matchless
1963	J.18	A.J.S.
1963	S.R.	Matchless

Dickie, Tom
1964	S.21	Matchless
1965	J.R.	A.J.S.
1965	S.16	Matchless
1966	J.3	A.J.S.
1966	S.1	Matchless

Dickinson, Alan F.
1964	L.12	D.M.W.
1965	L.8	D.M.W.
1965	S.R.	Norton
1966	L.23	D.M.W.
1967	L.R.	Kawasaki
1968	S.R.	T.S.R.
1968	S.R.	Norton
1969	R.	Norton
1970	S.R.	Norton
1972	S.26	Matchless

Dickinson, Raymond
1964	S.R.	B.S.A.
1965	S.53	B.S.A.
1966	S.R.	Matchless

Dickson, Brian
1971	S.47	N.G.S. Spl.
1973	S.R.	N.G.S.
1974	L.33	Yamaha
1975	L.31	Yamaha

Dickson, G. C.
| 1962 | J.52 | A.J.S. |

Dickson, Peter C.
| 1970 | J.42 | Norton |
| 1972 | J.25 | Norton |

1973 L.17		Yamaha
1974 L.21		Yamaha

Difazio, Jack
1947 J.43 — B.S.A.
1948 J.51 — B.S.A.
1951 J.42 — B.S.A.
1951 S.R. — B.S.A.

Difazio, Richard J.
1961 S.38 — Norton
1962 S.19 — Norton

Dilnot, Mark
1981 J/N.5 — Yamaha
1981 S.24 — Yamaha
1982 J.39 — Yamaha
1982 S.R. — Yamaha

Dinham, Wayne
1974 J.2 — Yamaha
1975 S.R. — Yamaha
1975 J.1 — Yamaha

Dinnie, James McG.
1965 L.17 — Greeves

Ditchborn, Harry W. G.
1947 L.R. — Ariel

Ditchburn, Barry E
1968 S.R. — Triton

Ditchfield, Edward O.
1964 J.R. — Norton
1965 L.13 — D.M.W.
1966 J.35 — B.S.A.
1967 J.33 — B.S.A.

Dixon, C. G.
1967 J.6 — Triumph
1967 S.R. — Norton
1968 J.R. — Triumph
1968 S.R. — Norton

Dixon, Graham D.
1969 L.R. — Yamaha
1970 J.R. — Aermacchi
1971 J.R. — Aermacchi
1972 J.9 — Aermacchi
1973 J.14 — Aermacchi
1974 J.R. — Yamaha

Dixon, Michael G.
1964 J.35 — Norton/B.S.A.
1965 J.47 — Norton/B.S.A.
1966 S.39 — Norton/B.S.A.

Dixon, W. H.
1951 J.56 — Norton
1952 J.57 — Norton
1956 J.62 — Norton
1957 J.25 — B.S.A.
1957 S.R. — B.S.A.
1959 J.R. — B.S.A.
1959 S.61 — B.S.A.

Dobbs, A. W.
1948 J.33 — Velocette
1949 J.R. — Velocette
1949 S.R. — Triumph

Dobson, Charlie E.
1967 J.44 — B.S.A.

Dock, Dave
1977 L.62 — Ducati
1979 L.58 — Ducati
1980 L.54 — Ducati
1980 J.53 — Aermacchi Metisse
1981 L.51 — Desmo Ducati
1982 L.45 — Ducati
1982 S.54 — Aermacchi

Dodd, B.
1970 S.R. — Norton

Doddenhof, Dave
1970 S.R. — Matchless

Dodsworth, John M.
1967 J.R. — A.J.S.

Dolby, J.
1950 J.16 — Velocette
1951 J.26 — Velocette
1951 S.21 — Velocette

Dolman, L. M.
1968 L.31 — Greeves

'Domini, Anno'
1947 J.17 — Norton
1947 S.8 — Norton
1948 J.8. — Velocette

1948 S.2 — Velocette

Donaldson, J. Barry
1957 J(N).43 — Velocette

Donnelly, William B
1964 L.24 — Honda
1965 L.39 — Honda
1966 L.R. — Greeves
1967 L.14 — Greeves

Doran, Bill
1946 J.22 — Norton
1946 S.23 — Norton
1947 J.R. — Norton
1947 S.7 — Norton

Douglas, Alan
1981 L/N.2 — Yamaha
1981 L.R. — Yamaha
1982 J.R. — Yamaha
1982 S.20 — Yamaha

Douglas, Robert W.
1969 J.44 — A.J.S.
1970 S.25 — Matchless
1973 S.29 — Seeley

Douglass, Ken H. J.
1957 S(N).9 — B.S.A.
1957 S.38 — B.S.A
1959 S.R. — Norton

Dow, W. Eddie
1955 J.8 — Norton
1955 S.R. — Norton

Dowey, Steve
1982 J/N.R. — Yamaha

Dowie, Alan F.
1968 J.R. — Honda
1969 J.R. — Honda
1973 S.R. — Suzuki
1974 S.R. — Suzuki

Dowie, George E.
1967 L.R. — Greeves
1968 J.R. — Kawasaki
1969 S.42 — Matchless
1971 S.15 — Matchless
1972 J.R. — Yamaha

Dowland, Richard S.
1971 L.R. — Yamaha
1973 L.18 — Yamaha
1974 L.25 — Norton

Downer, Dave L.
1960 J.R. — Norton
1961 J.R. — Norton
1962 J.R. — Norton

Downes, Graham T.
1955 J.72 — B.S.A.
1955 J.38 — B.S.A.
1956 J.38 — A.J.S.
1956 S.36 — A.J.S.
1957 J.57 — A.J.S.
1957 S.N.F. — A.J.S.
1958 S.35 — A.J.S.
1959 S.42 — Norton

Downing, H. J.
1948 L.R. — Velocette

Dowty, Bob
1951 J.47 — Douglas
1952 S.16 — Douglas
1953 J.R. — Norton
1953 S.R. — A.J.S.
1954 J.R. — Norton
1954 S.6 — Norton
1955 J.10 — Norton
1955 S.12 — Norton
1956 J.3 — Norton
1956 S.6 — Norton
1957 J.4 — Norton
1957 S.3 — Norton
1958 J.5 — Norton
1958 S.5 — Norton

Draper, David
1972 S.30 — Norton
1973 S.19 — Norton

Draper, K. H.
1957 S(N).18 — Norton

Drinkwater, Ben
1946 L.2 — Excelsior
1946 S.16 — Norton

Drinkwater, Frank
1976 L.R. — Ducati
1977 L.54 — Yamaha
1978 L.59 — Ducati
1979 S.57 — Kawasaki

Driver, Robert W.
1969 L.46 — Aermacchi

Drummond, David
1970 S.42 — Norton
1971 S.R. — Norton
1972 S.R. — Norton

Drysdale, I. D.
1947 J.R. — Norton
1947 S.R. — Norton
1948 J.25 — A.J.S.
1948 S.R. — Norton
1949 J.26 — Velocette
1949 S.R. — Triumph

Drysdale, Jimmy
1955 J.R. — A.J.S.
1955 S.11 — Norton
1956 J.8 — A.J.S.
1956 S.9 — Norton
1957 S.R. — Norton

Duckett, Vin F.
1959 J.R. — B.S.A.
1960 S.33 — B.S.A.
1961 S.12 — Matchless
1962 J.R. — A.J.S.
1962 S.8 — Matchless

Duckworth, Dennis R.
1970 J.41 — A.J.S.
1971 S.43 — Matchless

Dudley Ward, Allan J.
1947 S.R. — Norton

Duerden, Tom
1948 S.31 — Norton
1949 S.48 — Norton
1950 S.52 — Norton
1951 J.R. — Norton
1951 S.47 — Norton
1952 J.R. — Norton
1954 J.R. — T.D. Norton
1956 J.R. — Norton
1956 S.R. — Norton

Duffty, Robin G.
1966 J.R. — Norton
1967 J.R. — Norton
1968 J.4 — Petty Norton
1969 J.1 — Aermacchi
1969 S.R. — Norton

Duffus, Alan
1974 J.R. — Oliver Yamaha
1975 J.8 — Yamaha

Duffy, John
1966 J.25 — Norton
1966 S.17 — Norton
1967 J.3 — Norton
1967 S.R. — Norton
1968 J.10 — Norton
1968 S.R. — Norton
1969 J.15 — Norton
1969 S.10 — Norton
1970 J.20 — Norton
1970 S.7 — Norton

Duke, Geoff E.
1948 J.R. — Norton
1949 J.2 — Norton
1948 S.1 — Norton

Dulson, J. R.
1948 L.R. — Velocette

Duncan, D. J.
1958 J(Sn).19 — B.S.A.
1958 J.43 — B.S.A.
1959 J.21 — A.J.S.
1961 J.46 — Norton
1961 S.42 — Norton

Duncan, Ian E.
1964 L.29 — Aermacchi

Duncan, J. C.
1950 S.R. — A.J.S.

1951 J.18 — A.J.S.
1952 J.22 — A.J.S.
1953 J.11 — A.J.S.
1953 S.19 — A.J.S.

Duncan, J. E.
1967 L.56 — Royal Enfield
1968 L.R. — Royal Enfield

Dungworth, Keith
1976 L.39 — Yamaha
1977 J.R. — Yamaha

Dunham, Cyril G. H. F.
1947 J.24 — Velocette
1948 J.18 — Velocette

Dunham, L.
1952 S.57 — B.S.A.

Dunlop, Charles W.
1969 J.51 — Norton

Dunlop, Gavin R.
1953 J.24 — A.J.S.
1953 S.20 — A.J.S.
1954 J.15 — A.J.S.
1954 S.3 — Matchless
1955 J.R. — A.J.S.

Dunlop, Jim
1977 J.R. — Yamsel
1978 J.7 — Yamsel
1978 S.7 — Yamsel
1980 L.10 — Yamaha
1980 J.R. — Yamaha
1981 J.11 — Yamaha
1981 S.22 — Yamaha

Dunlop, Malcolm P.
1981 S/N.10 — Seeley Suzuki
1981 S.49 — Seeley Suzuki
1982 S.55 — Seeley Suzuki

Dunn, Mike
1975 S.43 — Seeley
1976 S.R. — Yamaha
1977 S.R. — Yamaha
1978 J.13 — Yamaha
1979 J.19 — Yamaha
1979 S.10 — Yamaha
1982 J.16 — Yamaha
1982 S.R. — Yamaha

Dunn, Robert
1972 S.R. — Honda

Dunne, John Brian
1958 S(Sn).14 — Norton

Dunnell, Tony D.
1965 S.40 — Triton
1966 S.R. — T.D. Triton
1967 S11 — Triton
1968 S.2 — Norton
1969 S.R. — Norton
1971 S.R. — T.D. Triumph
1972 S.R. — Norton
1973 S.R. — Norton
1974 S.R. — Norton
1976 S.R. — Yamaha
1978 S.R. — Honyam
1979 J.R. — Yamaha
1980 S.53 — Honda
1981 S.50 — Honda

Dunning, Michael K.
1969 L.35 — Greeves

Dunphy, P. Joe
1957 S(N).R — Norton
1958 S.R. — Norton
1959 J.R. — Norton
1960 S.R. — Norton
1961 S.6 — Norton
1962 J.R. — A.J.S.
1962 S.1 — Norton

Dunscombe, Alan
1969 L.31 — Ducati

Dunwell, Peter B.
1965 L.R. — Royal Enfield

Durkin, Philip
1965 S.62 — Norton

Dyde, Albert H.
1964 L.21 — Royal Enfield
1965 L.R. — Royal Enfield

Dyson, Derek S.
1967 J.R. — Aermacchi

1971 J.33 — Aermacchi
1972 S.R. — Aermacchi
1975 S.R. — Yamaha

Dziedzic, George
1976 L.25 — Yamaha

Eadie, Graham
1976 J.37 — Yamaha

East, Chris
1965 J.50 — A.J.S.
1966 J.50 — A.J.S.
1967 S.R. — Matchless
1968 S.16 — Matchless
1969 S.28 — Matchless
1970 S.18 — Matchless
1971 S.14 — Matchless
1972 S.12 — Matchless
1974 S.39 — Matchless

East, Dave
1976 S.R. — Velocette
1977 S.37 — Velocette
1978 J.19 — Yamsel
1978 S.27 — Yamsel
1979 J.R. — Yamaha
1979 S.6 — Yamaha
1980 J.R. — Yamaha
1981 J.8 — Yamaha
1981 S.1 — Yamaha

Easton, D. W.
1958 S(Sn).11 — B.S.A.

Eaton, D.
1967 L.33 — Bultaco

Eatough, Neil R.
1964 L.R. — Aermacchi
1965 L.28 — Aermacchi

Eberhardt, Paul
1966 L.R. — Bultaco
1967 L.34 — Bultaco

Eccles, Geoff L.
1958 J(Sn).15 — B.S.A.
1958 J.31 — B.S.A.
1959 J.34 — B.S.A.

Eckhart, John
1956 J.13 — B.S.A.
1956 S.13 — Norton

Edgar, F. G.
1946 S R. — Vincent H.R.D.

Edge, Dave
1980 L/N.7 — Yamaha
1980 L.26 — Yamaha

Edgson, A. W.
— B.S.A.

Edwards, Anthony
1973 L.R. — Greeves
1974 L.R. — Yamaha
1975 L.R. — Yamaha
1976 S.47 — Crescent
1978 L.34 — Yamaha
1979 L.R. — Yamaha
1980 J.26 — Yamaha
1980 S.R. — Yamaha
1981 J.R. — Yamaha
1981 S.R. — Yamaha
1982 J.24 — Yamaha
1982 S.R. — Yamaha

Edwards, Arthur
1974 J.R. — Aermacchi
1975 J.37 — Aermacchi

Edwards, Brian S.
1966 J.R. — Aermacchi
1967 J.R. — Norton
1968 J.R. — Kettle Norton

Edwards, Colin F.
1963 J.R. — Norton
1964 J.29 — Norton
1965 J.27 — Norton

Edwards, C. R.
1959 J.70 — A.J.S.

Edwards, G.
1948 J.44 — A.J.S.
1949 J.37 — A.J.S.
1949 S.R. — A.J.S.
1951 J.34 — Velocette

Edwards, Keith R.

The History of the Manx Grand Prix 1923-1998 99

1971 S.R.	Seeley
1972 S.27	Seeley
1973 S.R.	Seeley
1974 S.17	Seeley
1975 S.R.	Seymour Velocette
1976 S.25	Seymour Velocette
1977 S.26	Seymour Velocette
1978 J.37	Seymour Velocette
1980 J.39	Yamaha
1981 J.R.	Yamaha
1982 J.29	Yamaha

Edwards, Neil
1975 J.38	Yamaha
1976 J.R.	Gaskell Yamaha
1977 J.R.	Yamaha

Edwards, Rex
| 1978 L/N.6 | Yamaha |

Edwards, Robert
| 1979 J/N.16 | Aermacchi |

Edwards, Roberts J.
1946 L.4	C.T.S.
1946 J.R.	Norton
1947 L.6	C.T.S.
1948 L.R.	C.T.S.

Edwards, Terry R. L.
| 1972 S.44 | Seeley |
| 1975 J.R. | Manx Norton |

Eglinton, R. W.
| 1970 L.28 | Bultaco |

Elder, N. G.
| 1970 S.R. | Norton |

Eldridge, Ronald A.
| 1964 L.23 | Greeves |

Eldridge-Smith, Robert J.
| 1965 L.51 | Ducati |

Elkin, S.
| 1957 S(N).R. | B.S.A. |

Ellerby, Cliff
| 1952 J.R. | A.J.S. |

Elliott, Jasper L.
| 1965 S.R. | NorB.S.A. |

Elliott, Richard
1978 J/N.24	Yamaha
1979 J.R.	Yamaha
1979 S.R.	Yamaha
1980 J.R.	Yamaha
1980 S.64	Yamaha

Elliott, R. C.
| 1958 S(Sn).R. | Triumph |

Ellis, B.
| 1959 S.R. | Norton |
| 1960 S.R. | Norton |

Ellis, Don J.
| 1960 S.53 | Matchless |
| 1961 S.45 | Matchless |

Ellis, Stephen H.
| 1965 S.51 | Matchless |

Elmore, Peter N.
1961 S.R.	B.S.A.
1962 S.32	Matchless
1963 S.14	Matchless
1964 S.R.	Matchless
1965 S.15	Matchless
1966 J.14	A.J.S.
1966 S.9	Matchless
1967 J.R.	A.J.S.
1967 S.5	Matchless
1968 J.6	A.J.S.
1968 S.R.	Matchless
1969 J.5	A.J.S.
1969 S.5	Matchless
1970 J.R.	Seeley
1970 S.15	Seeley
1971 J.4	Norton
1971 S.3	Norton

Elworthy, Stanley J.
| 1969 L.R. | Greeves |
| 1970 L.38 | Greeves |

Emerson, R.
| 1959 J.65 | Norton |

Emuss, Alan E.
| 1966 S.46 | Vincent |

Endean, David C.
| 1972 S.R. | Metisse |

1973 S.26	Metisse
1974 S.R.	Suzuki
1975 S.14	Suzuki

Ennett, Derek
1951 S.R.	B.S.A.
1952 J.4	A.J.S.
1952 S.5	A.J.S.
1953 J.R.	A.J.S.
1953 S.3	Matchless
1954 J.1	A.J.S.
1954 S.R.	Matchless

Eva, Robert
1979 L/N.6	Yamaha
1980 J.R.	Yamaha
1980 S.48	Yamaha
1981 J.R.	Yamaha

Evans, A.
| 1956 S.R. | Norton |
| 1957 S.N.F. | Norton |

Evans, Alan
1979 S/N.4	Yamaha
1981 J.R.	Yamaha
1982 J.37	Yamaha
1982 S.34	Yamaha

Evans, Desmond
| 1964 L.R. | Norvel |
| 1965 L.35 | Yamaha |

Evans, Gwynfryn
1961 J.R.	A.J.S.
1962 J.47	A.J.S.
1963 J.56	A.J.S.
1964 J.25	A.J.S.
1966 J.R.	A.J.S.
1967 J.R.	A.J.S.
1968 J.R.	A.J.S.

Evans, John
1957 S(N).R.	Norton
1958 J(Sn).12	B.S.A.
1959 J.49	B.S.A.
1960 S.27	Norton
1961 S.R.	Norton
1962 J.R.	Norton
1963 J.9	Norton

Evans, John H.
1960 S.34	Norton
1961 S.34	Norton
1962 S.24	Norton
1963 S.18	Norton
1964 J.R.	Norton
1964 S.19	Norton
1965 S.29	Norton
1966 J.26	Norton
1966 S.29	Norton

Evans, John G
| 1982 L/N.13 | Yamaha |
| 1982 L.40 | Yamaha |

Evans, Larry E.
1955 J.69	A..J.S.
1956 J.61	B.S.A.
1957 J.54	B.S.A.
1957 S.55	B.S.A.

Evans, P. R.
| 1960 S.R. | Matchless |

Evans, Ray
1977 J.R.	Yamaha
1980 J.32	Maxton Yamaha
1980 S.R.	Maxton Yamaha
1981 J.44	Maxton
1981 S.26	Maxton
1982 L.R.	Yamaha
1982 J.27	Maxton

Evans, Russell
1972 S.38	Matchless
1973 S.37	Metisse
1974 S.30	Matchless Metisse
1975 S.R.	Matchless Metisse
1976 S.R.	Matchless Metisse
1977 S.R.	Yamaha
1978 S.26	Yamaha
1979 S.22	Yamaha
1980 J.37	Yamaha
1980 S.R.	Yamaha
1981 S.R.	Yamaha
1982 J.38	Yamaha

| 1982 S.29 | Maxton Yamaha |

Evans, W.
| 1961 S.59 | Norton |
| 1962 S.28 | Norton |

Ewer, G. N.
| 1950 J.R. | A.J.S. |
| 1951 J.33 | A.J.S. |

Eyre, Robert
| 1979 S/N.R. | Yamaha |
| 1979 S.37 | Yamaha |

Faben, John P.
1969 J.R.	Norton
1970 J.R.	Aermacchi
1971 S.42	Norton
1972 S.R.	Yamaha

Face, Donald C.
1970 S.R.	B.S.A.
1971 S.41	B.S.A.
1973 L.24	Yamaha

Fairbairn, F.
1947 J.R.	Norton
1948 J.16	A.J.S.
1948 S.R.	Norton

Fairclough, Jeffrie
1959 S.54	Matchless
1960 S.50	Matchless
1961 S.R.	Matchless
1962 S.52	Norton
1963 S.R.	Norton
1964 S.20	Norton

Fairhurst, Damion
| 1982 J/N.6 | Maxton |

Fairhurst, Paul
1974 L.56	Yamaha
1975 L.38	Yamaha
1977 L.48	Yamaha

Fairweather, George
1972 J.40	Aermacchi
1975 J.R.	Norton
1976 J.49	Cowles Aermacchi

Falls, S. Brian
| 1981 L/N.8 | Yamaha |
| 1981 L.R. | Yamaha |

Faragher, Robert W.
| 1982 J/N.9 | Yamaha |
| 1982 L.14 | Yamaha |

Fargher, Chris
1980 L.15	Harris Yamaha
1981 L.4	Yamaha
1981 J.R.	Yamaha
1982 L.R.	Reeves Cotton
1982 J.R.	Reeves Yamaha

Farmer, Robert G.
| 1965 L.R. | Aermacchi |
| 1966 L.1 | Aermacchi |

Farmer, Gordon
1976 L.32	Yamsel
1981 J.R.	Yamaha
1981 S.5	Yamaha
1982 J.4	Yamaha
1982 S.1	Yamaha

Farnhill, Vic
1974 J.R.	Norton
1975 J.R.	Norton
1976 J.51	Manx Norton

Farrant, Derek K.
1951 J.14	Velocette
1952 J.3	A.J.S.
1952 S.1	Matchless/A.J.S.

Farrar, John
1958 J(Sn).R.	Norton/Velocette
1959 S.59	Velocette
1960 J.R.	B.S.A.
1961 J.R.	B.S.A.
1962 J.R.	B.S.A.
1963 J.38	B.S.A.

Faulkner, Chris
1980 L/N.3	Maxton Yamaha
1980 L.5	Maxton Yamaha
1981 L.6	Yamaha
1982 J.R.	Wallace Yamaha
1982 S.18	Yamaha

Fawkes, J. N.
| 1956 J.40 | A.J.S. |

Fawsitt, Kevin
| 1979 J/N.R. | Yamaha |

Fay, Ray
1952 J.60	Norton
1953 J.R.	Norton
1953 S.27	Norton

Fearnhead, J. K.
| 1950 J.38 | Norton |
| 1950 S.53 | Norton |

Featherstone, David
1968 L.R.	Greeves
1969 J.R.	A.J.S.
1973 J.9	Yamaha
1975 S.12	Yamaha
1975 J.12	Yamaha
1976 J.R.	Yamaha

Featherstone, Mick
| 1950 S.2 | Norton |

Fellows, W. D.
1956 J.39	B.S.A.
1957 J.30	B.S.A.
1957 S.R.	B.S.A.
1958 J.R.	B.S.A.
1958 S.39	B.S.A.
1959 J.42	B.S.A.

Fenn, Arthur A.
| 1947 J.30 | Norton |

Fenning, L. M. F.
| 1947 S.52 | Norton |

Fenton, Colin Mc P.
1962 S.19	Matchless
1963 S.17	Norton
1964 L.R.	Aermacchi
1965 L.2	Aermacchi
1966 L.8	Greeves
1967 L.23	Aermacchi

Fiddament, E. G.
| 1957 S(N).8 | Norton |
| 1957 S.36 | Norton |

Fiedler, Colin
1962 J.56	B.S.A.
1963 J.62	A.J.S.
1964 J.R.	A.J.S.
1965 J.33	A.J.S.

Finch, Brian
| 1968 L.10 | Greeves |
| 1969 L.R. | Yamaha |

Findlay, John T.
1965 S.56=	Velocette
1966 S.R.	Norton
1967 J.15	Norton
1967 S.R.	Norton
1968 J.1	Norton
1968 S.1	Norton

Fish, R. W.
| 1946 L.R. | Excelsior |
| 1947 L.R. | Excelsior |

Fisher, A.
1957 J(N).27	B.S.A.
1958 J.R.	Norton
1959 J.36	Norton
1960 S.R.	Norton
1961 S.32	Norton
1962 J.44	Norton
1962 S.R.	Norton

Fisher, C. R.
1949 J.44	A.J.S.
1949 S.43	A.J.S.
1950 J.R.	A.J.S.
1950 S.R.	A.J.S.

Fisher, Fred
1958 J(Sn).26	Norton
1958 S.R.	Norton
1959 S.25	Norton
1960 S.17	Norton
1961 J.17	Norton
1961 S.13	Norton
1962 J.3	Norton
1962 S.R.	Norton

Fisher, J. W. C.
| 1949 J.23 | Velocette |
| 1949 S.R. | Velocette |

Fitzgerald, John T
| 1982 S/N.15 | Moriwaki Kawasaki |

Fitzsimmons, Richard A.
1969 L.51	Suzuki
1970 L.R.	Suzuki
1971 L.R.	Suzuki
1972 L.R.	Suzuki
1973 L.R.	Suzuki
1974 L.R.	RAF Suzuki
1975 L.R.	RAF Suzuki
1976 L.60	Suzuki
1977 L.55	Suzuki
1978 L.49	Suzuki
1979 L.51	Suzuki
1980 L.R.	Suzuki
1981 L.R.	Suzuki
1982 L.57	Suzuki

Fitzsimmons, W. N.
1955 J.68	Norton
1956 S.R.	Norton
1957 J.R.	Norton
1957 S.R.	Norton

Fleming, Peter
1976 J.R.	Aermacchi
1977 J.48	Aermacchi
1978 J.R.	Aermacchi
1979 J.R.	Yamaha

Fletcher, Arnold H.
| 1964 J.R. | A.J.S. |

Fletcher, D. G.
| 1957 S(N).19 | B.S.A. |

Fletcher, Frank
1947 L.10	Excelsior
1948 L.R.	Excelsior
1949 J.R.	A.J.S.

Fletcher, H. J.
| 1958 J.17 | B.S.A. |

Fletcher, Martin
| 1981 J/N.R. | Yamaha |
| 1981 S.38 | Yamaha |

Fletcher, Tony G.
1968 S.46	Matchless
1969 S.R.	Matchless
1970 S.R.	Matchless

Flury, Lawrence
1956 J.54	A.J.S.
1956 S.R.	A.J.S.
1957 J.R.	A.J.S.
1957 S.53	A.J.S.

Foale, Tony E.
1971 J.55	Bultaco
1972 J.R.	Aermacchi
1973 J.52	Aermacchi
1974 J.50	Aermacchi

Fogarty, George L.
1963 J.60	Norton
1964 J.R.	Aermacchi
1964 S.R.	Norton

Forrest, J. A.
1967 J.R.	Norton
1968 J.R.	Norton
1970 J.40	Aermacchi

Forrest, Rob
| 1976 J.R. | Yamaha |

Forrester, David
| 1973 S.40 | Metisse |

Forrester. Robert
| 1964 L.20 | Aermacchi |
| 1965 L.R. | Aermacchi |

Fotherby, D.
| 1952 S.R. | Ariel |

Foulkes, David R.
| 1966 S.R. | Norton |

Fountain, Paul C.
| 1969 L.R. | Yamaha |

Fowler, Neil
1980 J/N.R.	Yamaha
1981 J.15	NEBCO Yamaha
1981 S.3	NEBCO Yamaha

Fowles, Raymond
| 1965 S.61 | Matchless |

Fox, Frank
| 1951 J.27 | Norton |

Year/Race	Rider/Machine	
1952 S.13		Norton
1953 J.1		Norton
1953 S.R.		Norton

Fox, Roy
1963 J.64 — A.J.S.
1964 J.42 — A.J.S.
1965 J.R. — A.J.S.
1966 L.R. — Aermacchi

Fox, R. E.
1958 J(Sn).25 — A.J.S.
1958 S.R. — A.J.S.

Foy, John R.
1967 J.R. — Norton
1968 S.29 — Norton
1969 J.R. — B.S.A.
1971 S.29 — Norton
1972 J.2 — Yamaha
1974 J.23 — Yamaha

Francis, Andy
1974 L.60 — Greeves
1975 L.48 — Greeves
1976 L.R. — Marshalls Greeves
1977 L.43 — Marshalls Cotton
1978 L.37 — Marshalls Cotton
1979 L.60 — Marshalls Cotton
1979 J.49 — Cammack Honda
1980 S.57 — Hildred Honda

Francis, C. H.
1947 J.8 — Norton
1947 S.11 — Norton

Franklin, Paul
1976 L.64 — Ducati
1977 S.45 — Ducati
1978 S.R. — Ducati

'Franklin. Syd'
1948 J.R. — A.J.S.
1949 J.9 — A.J.S.
1949 S.24 — A.J.S.

Freak, Richard J.
1981 L/N.6 — Yamaha
1981 L.44 — Yamaha

Freeman, Andy
1979 J/N.R. — Yamaha
1980 S.12 — Yamaha
1980 J.R. — Yamaha

Freeman, J.
1961 S.R. — B.S.A./Norton

Freeman, Leslie W. N.
1971 L.29 — Bultaco

Freestone, Brian
1951 S.R. — B.S.A.
1953 J.5 — Norton
1953 S.5 — Norton
1955 J.32 — Norton
1955 S.22 — Norton

Friend, W.
1958 S(Sn).19 — D.W. Special

Frost, A. H.
1955 J.47 — A.J.S.
1955 S.49 — A.J.S.
1956 J.64 — A.J.S.
1957 S.R. — Norton

Frost, J. L.
1949 J.R. — Velocette

Frost, Nev
1974 L.36 — JJM Bultaco

Fry, B. J.
1961 S.R. — Norton
1962 J.R. — Norton

Fry, Peter E.
1964 J.R. — B.S.A.
1965 J.21 — Norton

Fry, Stephen L.
1973 J.47 — Ducati

Fryer, Frank
1977 S.41 — Yamaha
1978 J.47 — Yamaha
1978 S.54 — Yamaha
1979 L.36 — Yamaha
1979 J.43 — Yamaha

Fryer, J.
1958 J(Sn).40 — B.S.A.

Fulton, Bill
1956 J.R. — B.S.A.

1956 S.R. — B.S.A.
1957 J.27 — Norton
1957 S.R. — Norton
1958 J.12 — Norton
1958 S.18 — Norton
1959 J.17 — Norton
1959 S.16 — Norton
1960 J.14 — Norton
1960 S.22 — Norton
1961 J.31 — Norton
1961 S.25 — Norton
1962 J.19 — Norton
1962 S.12 — Norton
1963 J.R. — Norton
1963 S.R. — Norton
1964 J.5 — A.J.S.
1964 S.R. — Matchless
1965 J.18 — A.J.S.
1965 S.R. — Norton
1966 J.R. — A.J.S.
1966 S.R. — Norton
1967 J.7 — Norton
1967 S.R. — Norton

Fulton, Gerald
1965 J.R. — A.J.S.
1966 J.21 — A.J.S.
1966 S.18 — Matchless
1967 J.27 — A.J.S.
1967 S.R. — Matchless
1968 J.30 — A.J.S.
1968 S.24 — Matchless
1969 J.16 — A.J.S.
1969 S.R. — Matchless
1970 S.16 — G.F. Spl.
1970 S.R. — G.F. Spl.
1971 J.R. — A.J.S.
1971 S.R. — Matchless

Fyson, Graham
1980 L/N.14 — Yamaha
1981 L.22 — Yamaha
1982 L.30 — Yamaha

Gagen, Allan G.
1966 L.32 — Royal Enfield
1967 L.49 — Yamaha
1968 L.R. — Yamaha
1969 L.R. — Dugdale Spl.

Gain, Victor P.
1971 J.R. — A.J.S.

Gaites, Brett
1977 L.R. — Ducati
1978 S.41 — Rob North Honda
1979 S.44 — Honda

Galbraith, William McC.
1969 L.38 — Ducati
1970 L.25 — Ducati

Gallagher, Derek J.
1947 J.R. — Rudge
1948 J.29 — A.J.S.
1952 S.63 — Triumph

Gandy, David
1978 J/N.26 — Yamaha
1979 J.47 — Yamaha
1979 S.43 — Yamaha
1980 J.R. — Maxton Yamaha
1980 S.R. — Maxton Yamaha
1981 J.R. — Yamaha

Gant, Clive
1974 S.29 — Norton

Gardiner, Alexander
1965 L.43 — Yamaha

Gardiner, John
1970 L.R. — Kawasaki
1971 L.R. — Kawasaki
1972 L.19 — Yamaha
1973 J.21 — Yamaha

Gardner, A. K.
1958 J(Sn).38 — B.S.A.

Garner, Charles P.
1964 L.R. — N.S.U. Special
1965 L.R. — Honda
1966 J.48 — Honda
1967 J.R. — Honda
1968 L.R. — Honda

Garnett, Roy A.
1970 S.R. — Honda
1971 S.R. — Honda
1973 L.35 — Honda
1974 L.26 — Honda
1975 L.32 — Honda
1976 L.67 — Honda
1977 L.R. — Honda

Garratt, Brian D.
1971 S.46 — Velocette
1972 S.R. — Matchless
1973 S.31 — Norton
1974 S.47 — Norton
1975 S.R. — Suzuki Special
1976 S.R. — Suzuki
1977 S.31 — Suzuki
1978 S.46 — Norton Vendetta
1979 S.R. — Suzuki
1980 S.R. — Norton
1981 S.53 — Norton
1982 S.50 — Norton

Garrett, James
1977 J.R. — Yamaha
1982 J.9 — Yamaha
1982 S.19 — Yamaha

Gatenby, Keith
1979 L/N.14 — Yamaha

Gates, Geoffrey
1981 L/N.4 — Suzuki

Gates, Roy W. F.
1962 J.R. — A.J.S.
1963 J.51 — A.J.S.
1964 J.33 — A.J.S.
1965 J.42 — A.J.S.

Gaunt, A. J.
1955 J.56 — Norton
1956 J.49 — Norton
1956 S.R. — Norton

Gaunt, Peter H.
1959 J.68 — B.S.A.
1960 S.40 — B.S.A.
1961 S.R. — B.S.A.

Gavin, Pat
1979 J/N.11 — Yamaha

Gawler, Keith T.
1962 S.R. — Norton

Geeson, Bob E.
1948 L.R. — R.E.G.

George, Alex J. S.
1968 L.R. — Yamaha
1969 L.1 — Yamaha

German, Howard D.
1953 J.R. — Norton
1953 S.31 — J.V. Special

Getley, Malcolm J.
1965 S.R. — Velocette

Gibbons, G. F.
1967 L.R. — D.M.W.

Gibbs, Steven
1979 S/N.10 — Honda
1980 S.52 — Honda

Gibson, G. E.
1950 S.60 — B.S.A.

Gibson, Harry R.
1957 S(N).13 — B.S.A.
1957 S.39 — B.S.A.
1958 S.R. — Matchless

Gibson, James
1982 L/N.17 — Yamaha
1982 L.R. — Yamaha

Gibson, M. J.
1960 S.R. — B.S.A.
1962 S.R. — Norton

Gibson, William T.
1969 J.49 — A.J.S.
1970 L.R. — Aermacchi
1971 J.15 — Aermacchi

Gidlow, Brian D.
1965 J.R. — Norton

Giffin, John
1981 J.R. — Yamaha

Gilbert, H. R.
1946 S.R, — Norton

Gilbert, L. D.

1946 J.23 — Norton
1946 S.35 — Norton
1947 J.61 — Norton
1948 J.24 — Norton

Gilder, Michael D.
1969 S.45 — Norton
1970 S.R. — Norton
1971 L.45 — Suzuki
1972 L.R. — Suzuki
1973 S.28 — Matchless

Giles, A. D.
1968 S.10 — Norton

Giles, R. C.
1970 S.R. — Velocette

Gill, A. B.
1957 J(N).R. — Velocette
1959 S.R. — A.J.S.

Gill, P. D.
1946 J.12 — Velocette
1946 S.12 — Velocette
1948 L.3 — Excelsior
1948 S.38 — Velocette

Gittins, Ian
1974 L.42 — Ducati
1975 L.R. — Walker Ducati
1976 L.51 — Walker Hejira Ducati

Gittins, John B.
1970 L.43 — Ducati
1971 L.37 — Ducati
1973 J.R. — Aermacchi

Gittins, M. J.
1957 S(N).10 — Norton
1957 S.33 — Norton
1958 J.45 — B.S.A.
1958 S.13 — Norton
1959 J.R. — Norton
1959 S.R. — Norton

Gittins, Robert M.
1972 L.51 — Ducati

Gladwin, D. R.
1968 L.36 — Aermacchi

Glasper, Eric P.
1966 S.42 — Norton
1970 J.R. — Ducati
1971 J.R. — Ducati
1972 J.R. — Honda
1973 L.R. — Suzuki
1974 S.38 — Matchless

Glazebrook, A. Joe
1946 J.25 — Norton
1946 S.34 — Norton
1947 S.21 — Norton
1948 J.21 — Norton
1948 S.22 — Norton

Glendenning, Paul
1975 L.R. — Yamaha

Glover, D.
1947 S.R. — Triumph

Glover, D. J. H.
1946 L.R. — Rudge
1947 J.51 — Norton
1952 L.R. — Norton

Gobbett, J.
1956 S.55 — Norton

Gobell, Cliff
1975 L.R. — Yamaha
1976 L.R. — Collier/Day Spl.
1977 L.R. — BDS Special
1978 L.25 — Nice Yamaha
1979 L.R. — Nice Yamaha
1980 L.8 — Nice Yamaha
1981 L.5 — Nice Yamaha
1982 L.R. — Nice Yamaha

Goddard, Ian R.
1961 J.R. — A.J.S.
1962 J.42 — A.J.S.

Godden, Adrian
1974 J.9 — Yamaha

Godfrey, Kevin
1976 J.R. — Yamaha

Godfrey, Tony
1956 J.26 — Velocette

1956 S.R. — Velocette
1957 J.R. — Velocette
1957 S.14 — Norton
1958 J.R. — Velocette
1958 S.R. — Norton
1959 J.5 — A.J.S.
1959 S.R. — Matchless

Godward, Graham
1974 J.R. — Aermacchi
1975 L.35 — Willmott Yamaha
1976 L.41 — Willmott Yamaha

Golding, John
1975 L.R. — Yamaha
1976 L.18 — Yamaha
1977 J.R. — Yamaha
1977 S.R. — Yamaha

Goldsmith, J. C.
1954 J.53 — B.S.A.
1959 J.R. — B.S.A.

Gollins, John
1980 J/N.R. — Yamaha

Good, C. R.
1946 J.R. — Norton
1946 S.27 — Norton

Good, Robin W.
1964 L.R. — Ariel
1964 S.6 — Matchless
1965 L.14 — Ariel
1965 S.11 — Matchless
1966 J.10 — Norton
1966 S.6 — Matchless

Goodall, John H.
1972 S.29 — Seeley
1973 J.R. — Seeley
1974 S.R. — Vendetta
1974 J.3 — Lawton Aermacchi
1975 S.8 — Vendetta Matchless
1975 J.R. — Lawton Aermacchi
1976 J.10 — Vendetta Matchless
1976 S.R. — Vendetta Matchless
1977 J.21 — Lawton Aermacchi
1977 S.12 — Vendetta Matchless
1978 J.R. — Vendetta Matchless
1978 S.R. — Cowles Triumph
1979 J.36 — Vendetta Matchless

Goodfellow, David
1974 S.R. — Crooks Suzuki
1975 S.37 — Crooks Suzuki
1976 S.12 — Crooks Suzuki
1977 J.9 — Yamaha
1977 S.39 — Honda

Goodfellow, Thomas J.
1967 S.R. — H.G.S.
1968 J.R. — Norton
1969 S.R. — Norton
1970 J.12 — Dearden Norton

Goodings, Grant
1982 J/N.3 — Yamaha

Goodman, Peter
1946 J.R. — Velocette
1946 S.6 — Velocette

Goodman, T. H. R.
1947 J.58 — Norton
1947 S.R. — Norton
1948 J.R. — Norton

Goodwin, E.
1947 J.R. — Norton
1947 S.56 — Norton
1949 J.60 — Norton
1949 S.41 — Norton
1950 J.40 — Norton
1950 S.R. — Norton
1951 J.52 — Norton
1951 S.39 — Norton
1953 J.32 — A.J.S.
1953 S.R. — A.J.S.
1954 J.50 — A.J.S.
1956 J.63 — A.J.S.

Gordon, David
1978 S/N.3 — Yamaha

Gourlay, Andrew
1976 L.54 — Aermacchi
1977 J.36 — Aermacchi
1978 J.38 — Aermacchi

The History of the Manx Grand Prix 1923-1998 101

Year	Race	Machine
1979	J.53	Aermacchi
1980	J.52	Yamaha
1980	S.R.	Norton

Graham, E.
1947	J.R.	Norton
1950	J.R.	Norton
1951	J.49	A.J.S.

Graham, Ray
| 1974 | L.37 | Montesa |

Graham, Robert A.
1964	S.R.	Matchless
1966	J.R.	A.J.S. Spl.
1967	J.12	A.J.S.

Graham, Tom R.
1955	J.13	Norton
1955	S.17	Norton
1956	J.10	Norton
1956	S.R.	Norton
1957	J.9	Norton
1957	S.8	Norton
1958	J.R.	Norton
1958	S.8	Norton

Graham, V. R.
| 1957 | J(N).44 | B.S.A. |

Grant, Colin
| 1975 | S.R. | Desmo Ducati |

Grant, Donald McG.
1967	S.20	Norton
1968	S.R.	Norton
1969	S.15	Norton

Grant, Eddie O.
| 1960 | J.61 | Moto Parilla |

Grant, Mick
| 1969 | S.48 | Velocette |

Grant, R. J.
| 1961 | S.R. | Norton |

Graves, Andrew M
| 1982 | J/N.14 | Yamaha |

Graves, W. D.
| 1967 | J.R. | Norton |
| 1968 | J.44 | Norton |

Gray, A.
| 1949 | J.R. | Excelsior |

Gray, Anthony
| 1964 | J.R. | A.J.S. |

Green, George A.
1966	L.29	Yamaha
1967	L.7	Yamaha
1968	L.R.	Yamaha
1969	L.R.	Yamaha
1970	J.R.	Aermacchi
1971	L.6	Yamaha
1972	L.9	Yamaha

Green, J.
| 1948 | J.R. | Triumph |

Green, P. J.
| 1967 | J.41 | Norton |

Greene, Johnne
| 1975 | S.54 | B.S.A. |

Greene, Richard
| 1974 | J.R. | Greeves |
| 1975 | J.R. | Greeves |

Greenham, David
1980	J/N.13	Ducati
1980	L.R.	Aermacchi
1981	J.R.	Maxton Yamaha
1982	J.35	Yamaha

Greenham, Geoffrey J.
1981	J/N.10	Ducati
1981	L.35	Cotton
1982	L.R.	Cotton

Greenwood, David
| 1978 | S/N.8 | Yamaha |

Greenwood, Ivor
| 1976 | L.5 | Yamaha |

Greenwood, Owen E.
1951	S.R.	B.S.A.
1953	J.22	B.S.A.
1953	S.R.	B.S.A.
1954	J.24	B.S.A.
1954	S.10	A.J.S.
1955	J.12	A.J.S.
1955	S.R.	Norton
1956	J.23	B.S.A.

Greenwood, Roger
1967	S.R.	Tri-Manx
1968	S.R.	Tri-Manx
1969	S.32	Norton

Gregson, R. E.
| 1946 | J.R. | Velocette |

Grew, Ralph A.
1969	L.R.	Greeves
1970	J.R.	Bridgestone
1971	J.R.	Bridgestone
1972	S.R.	Suzuki

Gribbin, J. H. Terence
1958	J(Sn).R.	B.S.A.
1959	J.43	B.S.A.
1960	J.34	B.S.A.
1961	J.R.	B.S.A.
1963	J.46	Norton
1964	L.R.	Cotton
1966	L.36	Royal Enfield

Grice, Mick
1975	L.9	Maxton Yamaha
1976	L.3	Maxton Yamaha
1976	S.19	
1977	L.R.	Vladivar Maxton

Griffin, G. J.
| 1960 | S.39 | Norton/B.S.A. |

Griffin, John
| 1977 | L.68 | Yamaha |
| 1978 | L.43 | Yamaha |

Griffin, S.
| 1965 | S.41 | Norton |

Griffiths, Barry A. C.
| 1972 | J.R. | GH |
| 1973 | L.54 | Yamaha |

Griffiths, C. G.
1949	S.40	A.J.S.
1950	J.9	A.J.S.
1950	S.25	Norton
1951	J.20	A.J.S.
1951	S.27	A.J.S.

Griffiths, D. Chris M.
1969	S.8	Matchless
1970	L.10	Cowles A.J.S.
1970	S.3	Cowles Matchless
1971	J.2	Cowles A.J.S.
1971	S.R.	Cowles Seeley
1977	J.17	Beart Aermacchi
1978	S.16	Yamaha
1978	J.R.	Aermacchi
1979	J.R.	Aermacchi
1979	S.35	Cowles Matchless

Griffiths, John E
1958	S(Sn).3	Norton
1958	S.R.	Norton
1959	J.R.	Norton
1959	S.18	Norton

Griffiths, John T.
1959	J.40	Norton
1960	J.39	Norton
1960	S.29	Norton
1961	J.19	A.J.S.
1962	J.32	A.J.S.
1963	J.24	A.J.S.

Griffiths, John V.
1967	L.13	Greeves
1968	L.R.	Greeves
1969	L.2	Yamaha
1970	L.2	Yamaha

Griffiths, Michael
| 1982 | S/N.8 | Laverda |

Griffiths, Paul D.
| 1973 | L.22 | Yamaha |

Griffiths, Selwyn G.
1961	J.22	A.J.S.
1962	J.4	A.J.S.
1963	J.3	A.J.S.
1963	S.R.	Matchless
1964	J.R.	A.J.S.
1964	S.1	Matchless

Griffiths, Terence
| 1975 | L.R. | Honda |
| 1976 | L.71 | Honda |

1977	L.R.	Machin Yamaha
1978	L.53	Maxton Yamaha
1979	S.52	Yamaha
1980	J.R.	Yamaha
1981	L.23	Yamaha
1981	J.60	Yamaha
1982	L.R.	Yamaha
1982	J.R.	Yamaha

Grimson, R. G.
| 1967 | J.17 | Norton |

Grindley, Howard W.
| 1949 | S.19 | Norton |
| 1950 | S.11 | Norton |

Gripton, Peter J.
| 1971 | L.28 | Yamaha |
| 1972 | L.R. | Yamaha |

Grose, Chris
1980	J/N.R.	Yamaha
1980	L.7	Yamaha
1981	L.3	Yamaha
1981	J.6	Reeves Yamaha

Grotefeld, Terry P.
| 1964 | L.3 | Aermacchi |

Grover, Bob
| 1975 | J.60 | Manx Norton |

Grove, Peter H.
| 1968 | L.R. | Yamaha |
| 1973 | J.R. | Yamaha |

Guthrie, Jimmy Jnr.
1962	J.R.	Norton
1963	J.20	Norton
1963	S.3	Norton
1964	J.R.	Norton
1965	J.6	Norton
1965	S.4	Norton
1966	L.4	Greeves
1966	S.4	Norton
1967	L.R.	Greeves
1967	S.1	Norton

Haddock, Roger F.
1968	J.R.	A.J.S.
1969	J.27	A.J.S.
1970	J.26	A.J.S.
1971	J.R.	A.J.S.
1972	J.R.	A.J.S.
1973	J.R.	A.J.S.
1974	S.9	Cowles Matchless

Hadwin, Chris
1979	S/N.R.	Yamaha
1980	S.47	Yamaha
1981	S.40	Yamaha
1982	S.43	Yamaha

Hadwin, Geoff
1979	L/N.17	Yamaha
1980	L.52	Yamaha
1981	L.46	Yamaha
1981	J.59	Yamaha
1982	L.46	Yamaha
1982	S.55	Yamaha

Hagan, Philip E.
1970	L.R.	Greeves
1971	L.R.	Greeves
1972	L.38	Greeves
1973	L.R.	Greeves
1974	L.61	Greeves
1977	L.58	Greeves
1978	L.52	Greeves
1979	L.55	Greeves
1980	L.R.	Greeves
1981	L.R.	Greeves Yamaha

Haldane, Ewan McG.
1953	J.R.	Velocette
1953	S.24	B.S.A.
1954	J.23	Velocette
1954	S.18	Norton
1955	J.19	A.J.S.
1955	S.7	Norton
1956	J.R.	B.S.A.
1956	S.7	Norton
1957	S.R.	Norton

Haley, Wesley
| 1964 | J.34 | P.H. Special |

Hall, Bill

| 1947 | J.R. | Velocette |

Hall, G.
| 1947 | L.R. | Dunelt Python |
| 1948 | J.R. | A.J.S. |

Hall, Graham
| 1970 | L.14 | Yamaha |
| 1973 | L.R. | Yamaha |

Hall, Harold
| 1963 | J.R. | Norton |

Hall, J. Barry
1971	J.18	Seeley
1972	J.R.	Seeley
1973	J.26	Seeley
1973	S.15	Seeley

Hall, P. M.
1951	J.16	A.J.S.
1951	S.R.	A.J.S.
1952	J.25	A.J.S.
1952	S.22	A.J.S.
1954	J.22	A.J.S.
1954	S.16	A.J.S.

Hallett, R. M.
| 1949 | J.28 | B.S.A. |
| 1949 | S.R. | B.S.A. |

Hamilton, J. D.
| 1957 | J(N).R. | A.J.S. |
| 1959 | S.R. | Norton |

Hamilton, Paul
| 1977 | S.32 | Sparton |

Hammond, Colin
1974	L.R.	Bultaco
1975	L.39	TSS Bultaco
1976	L.R.	Bultaco
1977	L.44	Bultaco
1978	L.55	Bultaco
1979	L.44	Honda
1980	L.39	Honda
1981	L.R.	Honda
1982	L.29	Honda

Hammond, George W.
1960	J.R.	B.S.A.
1961	J.43	Norton
1962	J.43	Norton
1963	J.R.	Norton
1963	S.R.	Norton

Hammond, John E.
1970	J.43	Aermacchi
1971	J.54	Aermacchi
1973	J.28	Aermacchi
1974	J.R.	Aermacchi
1975	J.26	Aermacchi
1977	J.29	Aermacchi

Hampton, Kenneth G.
1971	S.31	Norton
1971	J.12	Norton
1973	J.R.	Norton
1973	S.R.	Norton

Hancock, M.R.
1957	S(N).3	Norton
1957	S.18	Norton
1958	J.16	Norton
1958	S.14	Norton

Hancock, William D.
1968	S.38	Triumph
1969	S.37	Tri/B.S.A.
1970	S.R.	Matchless

Hands, Geoffrey
1969	L.R.	Yamaha
1970	L.10	Yamaha
1972	L.15	Yamaha
1973	L.12	Yamaha
1974	S.R.	Yamaha
1974	L.24	Yamaha

Hankin, Jeff G.
| 1965 | S.58 | Norton |

Hanna, Ray S.
1979	L/N.8	Yamaha
1979	L.30	Yamaha
1982	S.23	Yamaha

Hannaford, John
1976	J.R.	Yamaha
1977	J.R.	Yamaha
1978	L.65	Yamaha

Hannan, Ross H.

| 1965 | L.R. | Cotton |

Hannay, Allan
1980	J/N.3	Yamaha
1981	J.R.	R & T Yamaha
1981	S.R.	R & T Yamaha
1982	J.R.	Yamaha
1982	S.27	Yamaha

Hardcastle, Brian
| 1966 | L.R. | Greeves |
| 1967 | L.R. | Greeves |

Harding, Billy
| 1947 | J.57 | A.J.S. |
| 1953 | J.31 | A.J.S. |

Harding, Jack
1947	S.44	Norton
1948	S.39	Norton
1949	J.R.	Norton

Harding, Richard M.
| 1955 | J.26 | A.J.S. |
| 1955 | S.20 | A.J.S. |

Hardman, Andrew
| 1972 | L.R. | Bultaco |
| 1973 | L.40 | Yamaha |

Hardman, Colin
1974	L.52	Ducati
1975	L.37	Yamaha
1979	L.R.	Yamaha
1980	L.R.	Yamaha
1981	J.R.	Yamaha

Hardy, Eric V. C.
| 1947 | S.46 | Norton |

Hardy, R. W.
| 1959 | S.R. | B.S.A. |

Hargreaves, Bernard J.
1949	J.R.	Norton
1951	J.44	Douglas
1951	S.R.	Douglas
1952	J.38	Velocette
1952	S.41	Triumph

Harmer, Kenny
1978	S/N.6	Yamaha
1979	J.R.	Yamaha
1979	S.14	Yamaha
1980	S.50	Yamaha
1982	S.R.	Triumph Bonneville

Harper, A.
| 1959 | S.52 | B.S.A. |
| 1960 | S.R. | B.S.A. |

Harper, M. K.
| 1970 | J.32 | Yamaha |

Harris, Chris A.
1978	S/N.13	Cowles Matchless
1978	S.52	Cowles Matchless
1979	J.40	Cowles Yamaha
1979	S.36	Cowles Yamaha
1980	J.21	Cowles Yamaha
1980	S.R.	Cowles Yamaha
1981	S.9	Yamaha
1981	J.29	Yamaha
1982	J.7	Yamaha
1982	S.R.	Cowles Suzuki

Harris, David
1967	J.R.	D.M.W.
1968	S.R.	Norton
1969	S.R.	Norton

Harris, John L.
| 1969 | S.36 | Triton |

Harris, Peter K.
| 1969 | L.32 | Greeves |
| 1970 | L.23 | Yamaha |

Harris, Paul R.
| 1969 | L.R. | Greeves |
| 1970 | J.39 | Aermacchi |

Harris, Ron
| 1947 | L.7 | Moto Guzzi |

Harrison, Brian
1978	J/N.R.	Craig Yamaha
1979	L.19	Yamaha
1979	J.27	Yamaha

Harrison, David R.
1967	S.35	Norton
1968	J.R.	A.J.S.
1969	J.R.	A.J.S.
1970	J.9	Aermacchi

1971	J.R.	Aermacchi
1971	S.R.	Cowles Matchless
1973	J.R.	Aermacchi
1974	J.R.	A.J.S.
1975	S.R.	Bee Bee Matchless
1976	S.R.	Bee Bee Matchless
1978	J.24	Yamaha

Harrison, J.
| 1947 | S.R. | | Ariel |

Harrison, Jon
| 1982 | L/N.8 | Mainline Yamaha |
| 1982 | L.R. | Mainline Yamaha |

Harrison, Kenny
| 1976 | L.49 | Yamaha |
| 1977 | L.7 | Yamaha |

Harrison, Mike A.
1972	L.39	Ducati
1973	J.48	Aermacchi
1974	J.30	Aermacchi
1975	J.48	Aermacchi
1976	J.47	Aermacchi
1977	J.41	Aermacchi
1979	S.42	Ducati
1980	S.37	Ducati
1981	S.23	Ducati

Harrison, R. E. D.
| 1949 | S.21 | Triumph |

Harrison, R. J.
1950	S.R.	Triumph
1955	S.31	Norton
1957	S.R.	Norton
1958	S.36	Norton

Hart, John P.
1971	L.24	D.M.W./Yamaha
1972	L.R.	D.M.W./Yamaha
1973	L.27	Yamaha

Hart, Johannes R.
1973	J.R.	Ducati
1974	L.48	Maxton Yamaha
1975	L.22	Maxton Yamaha
1976	L.R.	Maxton Yamaha
1977	L.24	Maxton Yamaha
1978	L.27	Maxton Yamaha
1979	L.25	Yamaha
1980	L.R.	Yamaha
1981	L.17	Yamaha

Hart, Leslie R.
| 1973 | L.R. | Yamsel |
| 1974 | L.R. | Yamsel |

Harthern, M. W.
| 1967 | L.40 | Greeves |
| 1968 | J.R. | Greeves |

Hartle, John
1953	J.21	A.J.S.
1953	S.15	Norton
1954	J.3	Norton
1954	J.D.	Norton

Hartley, Clive
| 1978 | S/N.R. | Suzuki |
| 1978 | S.R. | Suzuki |

Hartree, O. P.
1948	J.R.	Velocette
1949	J.R.	Velocette
1949	S.R.	Velocette

Harvey, E. B.
| 1949 | J.R. | B.S.A. |

Harvey, Robert
1978	J/N.23	Aermacchi
1980	L.55	Aermacchi
1981	L.50	Aermacchi
1981	L.57	Aermacchi
1982	L.49	Aermacchi

Haslam, N.
| 1967 | L.47 | Aermacchi |

Haslam, Phil
| 1972 | J.R. | Yamaha |
| 1973 | J.1 | Yamaha |

Hatherhill, Michael F.
| 1966 | L.20 | Cotton |
| 1967 | J.R. | Aermacchi |

Hattersley, John
| 1978 | N.7 | Seeley |
| 1981 | S.R. | Seeley |

Haw, J. R.
| 1968 | L.R. | | Yamaha |

Hawken, Freddie C.
1946	J.9	Norton
1946	S.R.	Norton
1947	L.2	Excelsior

Hawkins, F. J.
1965	L.R.	Greeves
1967	L.52	Cotton
1968	L.R.	Cotton

Hawthorne, Maurice H.
1960	S.R.	B.S.A.
1961	S.R.	Norton
1962	S.R.	Norton
1963	S.R.	Norton

Hawthorne, William H.
| 1962 | S.R. | B.S.A. |

Hay, I. McK.
| 1947 | J.35 | Norton |
| 1947 | S.39 | Norton |

Haydon, Norman
| 1957 | J(N).22 | Norton |
| 1957 | J.R. | Norton |

Haynes, Ray
1978	J/N.14	Yamaha
1979	S.R.	Yamaha
1980	L.32	Yamaha
1980	J.28	Yamaha
1981	L.21	Yamaha
1981	J.24	Yamaha
1982	S.R.	Yamaha

Haynes, Rob
| 1982 | J/N.5 | Yamaha |
| 1982 | L.1 | Yamaha |

Hayward, M.
1959	S.R.	B.S.A.
1960	S.25	B.S.A.
1961	S.51	Velocette
1962	S.20	Matchless

Hazlehurst, Ronnie J.
| 1948 | J.31 | Velocette |

Hazlewood, E.
| 1968 | L.R. | Yamaha |

Head, Terry V.
| 1973 | S.38 | Matchless |
| 1974 | S.49 | Matchless |

Head, Bill
| 1977 | L.41 | Yamaha |
| 1978 | S.51 | Velocette |

Heap, Derek
| 1982 | J/N.10 | Yamaha |

Heard, Michael J.
| 1968 | L.R. | Suzuki |
| 1969 | L.18 | Suzuki |

Heath, Graham
1977	J.22	Yamaha
1978	S.17	Heath Yamaha
1979	J.20	Yamaha
1980	J.35	Yamaha
1980	S.58	Suzuki

Heath, James W.
1969	J.29	Norton
1970	J.R.	Norton
1971	J.R.	Norton
1971	S.R.	Manx T.5
1972	J.R.	Yamaha
1973	J.42	Yamaha
1975	J.17	Yamaha
1976	J.R.	Yamaha
1976	S.R.	Yamaha
1977	J.4	Yamaha
1977	S.R.	Yamaha
1978	S.R.	Yamaha
1979	J.10	Yamaha
1979	S.9	Norton

Heath, F. Phil
1946	J.17	Norton
1946	S.13	Norton
1947	S.37	Norton
1948	J.2	A.J.S.
1948	S.6	Norton

Heaton, T.

Heckles, Keith
1959	J.R.	B.S.A.
1961	J.R.	B.S.A.
1962	J.53	B.S.A.
1963	J.R.	Norton
1964	J.R.	Norton
1965	S.R.	Norton
1966	J.2	Norton
1966	S.25	Norton
1967	J.42	Norton
1967	S.R.	Norton

Hedley, J.
| 1951 | S.48 | Norton |
| 1952 | J.67 | A.J.S. |

Hedley, P. A.
1960	J.58	Norton
1961	J.R.	Norton
1962	J.R.	Norton

Heenan, David
| 1982 | J/N.13 | Yamaha |

Heenan, Peter
1975	L.25	Yamaha
1976	L.R.	Yamaha
1977	L.27	Yamaha
1978	J.R.	Yamaha

Heeson, Lee
1974	J.R.	Yamaha
1975	L.R.	Yamaha
1977	L.69	Stapeley Yamaha
1978	L.R.	Yamaha
1979	L.R.	Stapeley Yamaha

Hegbourne, A. V.
| 1956 | J.15 | Norton |
| 1956 | S.R. | Norton |

Heinze, G.
| 1950 | S.51 | Norton |

Heller, Ian
| 1965 | L.47 | Moto Guzzi |
| 1966 | L.R. | Moto Guzzi |

Helm, Richard
| 1970 | S.R. | Norton |
| 1971 | S.35 | Norton |

Hemming, Malcolm J.
| 1965 | L.R. | Aermacchi |
| 1966 | L.45 | Ducati |

Henderson, Francis W.
| 1969 | J.R. | Aermacchi |
| 1970 | L.R. | Yamaha |

Henderson, George
1946	J.R.	Norton
1946	S.R.	Norton
1947	J.41	Norton
1947	S.R.	Norton
1948	J.34	Norton
1948	S.R.	Norton
1949	J.R.	Norton
1949	S.27	Norton
1950	J.35	A.J.S.
1950	S.42	Norton

Henson, J. T.
| 1964 | J.47 | A.J.S. |
| 1965 | J.13 | A.J.S. |

Hensworth, H. R.
| 1947 | J.65 | Triumph |

Henthorn, A.
1946	L. R.	New Imperial
1947	L.R.	New Imperial
1948	L.12	Velocette
1951	J.70	B.S.A.
1951	S.61	B.S.A.
1952	J.R.	B.S.A.

Herbert, Angus S.
1949	J.31	A.J.S.
1949	S.20	A.J.S.
1950	J.19	A.J.S.
1950	S.R.	Norton

Herbert, Kenneth E.
| 1966 | S.R. | Triumph/Norton |

Herdman, Andy
1953	J.R.	Norton
1955	J.54	B.S.A.
1955	S.R.	B.S.A.

Herley, Tom
| 1973 | L.R. | Ducati |

Herrod, D.
| 1955 | J.R. | A.J.S. |

Heseltine, Donald W.
| 1966 | L.R. | Greeves |

Hesketh, Tom C.
| 1957 | S(N).R. | Norton |

Heward, Harry P.
1964	L.R.	Greeves
1965	L.R.	Greeves
1967	L.R.	Greeves
1969	L.R.	Greeves
1970	L.46	Greeves

Hewitt, Ronnie
1976	L.68	Yamaha
1978	L.46	Yamaha
1979	J.R.	Yamaha
1979	L.53	Yamaha

Hewson, Colin
| 1969 | L.R. | Ducati |

Hicken, Stuart
1971	S.53	Matchless
1972	S.R.	Scott
1973	S.52	Matchless
1974	S.R.	Vendetta G50
1975	S.R.	Vendetta G50
1976	S.42	Vendetta Kawasaki

Hickman, David
1976	L.10	Yamaha
1977	L.1	Maxton Yamaha
1977	S.R.	Crighton Honda

Hickson, J. G.
| 1952 | J.R. | A.J.S. |

Higginbottom, Ben
| 1946 | L.7 | Excelsior |
| 1947 | L.R. | C.T.S. |

Higginson, A.
| 1958 | J(Sn).29 | B.S.A. |
| 1959 | J.67 | B.S.A. |

Higginson, Frank
1968	S.R.	Domistar
1969	S.R.	Norton/B.S.A.
1970	S.R.	Norton
1971	S.R.	Norton
1972	S.R.	Norton
1974	S.22	Norton
1975	S.R.	Suzuki
1976	S.48	Suzuki
1977	J.R.	Yamaha
1978	S.30	Yamaha
1979	S.R.	Yamaha
1980	S.31	Yamaha
1980	J.R.	Yamaha

Higgs, Eric
| 1970 | L.R. | Yamaha |
| 1971 | L.R. | Yamaha |

Higham, Jack
1968	J.R.	Norton
1969	J.R.	Norton
1970	J.R.	Norton
1971	J.R.	Petty Norton
1972	S.10	Petty Norton
1973	J.R.	Yamaha
1974	S.R.	Petty Weslake
1974	J.R.	Yamaha
1975	S.3	Yamaha
1975	J.R.	Yamaha
1976	J.45	Shepherd Suzuki
1976	S.R.	Shepherd Suzuki
1977	J.19	Hall Yamaha
1977	S.R.	Hall Yamaha

Hilditch, F. A.
| 1949 | S.R. | Norton |
| 1950 | J.39 | Norton |

Hill, Billy
| 1975 | S.R. | Vortex |
| 1976 | S.27 | Vortex |

Hill, Jim D.
1974	S.R.	Petty Manx
1976	L.R.	Yamaha
1978	L.R.	Yamaha
1979	L.38	Yamaha
1980	L.27	Yamaha
1981	J.43	Yamaha
1981	S.R.	Yamaha
1982	S.R.	Yamaha

Hill, Ray
| 1978 | S/N.R. | Yamaha |
| 1979 | L.13 | Yamaha |

Hill, Robert C.
1971	J.39	Aermacchi
1972	J.11	Aermacchi
1973	J.R.	Aermacchi
1977	S.R.	Suzuki
1979	J.R.	Honda

Hill, S. R.
| 1956 | J.44 | B.S.A. |
| 1956 | S.R. | B.S.A. |

Hill, W. J.
1957	S(N).7	Matchless
1957	S.34	Matchless
1959	J.55	Norton
1959	S.R.	Triumph

Hilton, Victor E.
1964	J.50	A.J.S.
1964	J.24	Norton
1966	J.R.	Norton
1966	S.22	Norton

Hilton, W.
| 1946 | J.R. | Norton |

Hirst, Bob
1969	S.38	Velocette
1970	S.R.	Velocette
1971	S.R.	Matchless
1972	S.R.	Matchless
1973	S.20	Matchless
1974	S.R.	Matchless
1975	S.R.	Matchless
1976	S.R.	Matchless
1977	S.20	Seeley Matchless
1978	S.28	Seeley Matchless
1979	S.29	Seeley
1980	S.R.	Seeley Matchless
1981	S.R.	Seeley Matchless

Hislop, Alistair
1958	J(Sn).13	B.S.A.
1958	J.R.	B.S.A.
1959	J.31	Norton
1960	J.23	Norton

Hislop, Gary
| 1982 | J/N.1 | Yamaha |
| 1982 | L.61 | Yamaha |

Hitchcock, Simon P.
1965	L.33	Greeves
1966	L.R.	Bultaco
1967	L.R.	Bultaco

Hobbs, Grahame
| 1977 | J.R. | Fowler Yamaha |

Hobson, Mac
| 1958 | S(Sn).8 | B.S.A. |
| 1958 | S.R. | B.S.A. |

Hodge, R. D.
| 1965 | S.64 | B.S.A. |

Hodges, Maurice S.
1965	S.23	Norton
1966	S.16	Norton
1967	J.26	Norton
1967	S.34	Norton
1968	S.9	Norton
1969	J.12	Norton
1970	J.R.	Norton
1971	S.R.	Norton
1972	J.R.	Norton
1973	S.R.	Norton
1975	J.29	Manx Norton
1977	L.38	Yamaha

Hodgkinson, Ivan A.
| 1969 | L.R. | Norton |
| 1970 | L.R. | Ossa |

Hodgkiss, Phil
| 1968 | J.R. | Velocette |
| 1977 | J.R. | Aermacchi HD |

Hodgson, P. R.	1957 J.1 Norton	**Howe, Graham D.**	1971 J.26 A.J.S.	1971 S.R. Kettle Norton
1957 J(N).10 A.J.S.	1957 S.1 Norton	1969 L.30 Greeves	1971 S.9 Seeley	1972 S.41 Norton
1957 J.23 A.J.S.	**Holt, D.**	1970 L.R. Greeves	1972 J.42 Seeley	1973 S.R. Norton
Hodgson, Steve	1946 J.20 Velocette	1971 L.R. Yamaha	1972 S.R. Seeley	1974 J.6 Harley Davidson
1980 L/N.4 Maxton Yamaha	1946 S.R. Velocette	1981 L.16 Yamaha	1973 J.31 A.J.S.	**Hutchinson, Ian R.**
1980 L.14 Maxton Yamaha	**Holt, John A.**	1981 J.35 Yamaha	1973 S.16 Matchless	1966 J.54 B.S.A.
Hodgson, Tony H.	1966 L.R. D.M.W.	1982 L.21 Yamaha	1974 S.R. Beale Yamaha	**Hutchinson, John**
1948 S.28 Triumph	1967 L.22 D.M.W.	1982 J.R. Yamaha	1974 J.39 Beale Yamaha	1958 J(Sn).R B.S.A.
1949 J.53 A.J.S.	**Holywell, R. W.**	**Howe, Robert K.**	1975 J.22 Beale Yamaha	**Hutchinson, Nigel**
1950 J.R. A.J.S.	1948 S.R. Triumph	1982 J/N.5 Yamaha	1975 S.18 Beale Yamaha	1980 J/N.7 Maxton Yamaha
Hodson, James T.	**Hone, John W.**	**Howth, A. K.**	1976 J.44 A.J.S.	1981 S.50 Maxton Yamaha
1981 S/N.R. Honda	1969 S.R. Norton	1949 J.R. Norton	1976 S.21 Matchless	1981 J.R. Maxton Yamaha
1982 J.34 Maxton Yamaha	**Honey, John S. C.**	1950 J.5 A.J.S.	1977 J.R. Norton	1982 S.11 Yamaha
1982 S.R. Honda	1963 J.R. A.J.S.	**Howton, David E.**	**Hunt, E. W. L.**	**Hutton, C. R. B.**
Hodson, Laurie	1964 J.48 A.J.S.	1965 S.R. Norton	1950 S.29 Norton	1967 S.39 Matchless
1974 J.33 Ducati	1967 J.R. A.J.S.	1966 S.R. Norton	1952 S.R. Velocette	1968 S.45 Matchless
Hogg, D. A.	**Hope, Colin J.**	1968 S.R. Norton	**Hunt, Kieron**	**Huxley, Cyril**
1955 J.62 B.S.A.	1971 S.R. Suzuki	**Huby, Peter**	1979 J/N.R. Yamaha	1957 J(N).4 B.S.A.
1955 S.R. B.S.A.	**Hopkins, Alan H.**	1960 J.44 B.S.A.	1980 J.R. Yamaha	1957 J.32 B.S.A.
1956 J.R. B.S.A.	1969 L.R. Suzuki	1961 J.25 A.J.S.	1980 S.R. Yamaha	1958 J.27 B.S.A.
Holcroft, V. J.	1970 L.R. Yamaha	1962 J.13 A.J.S.	1981 J.9 Yamaha	1959 J.6 A.J.S.
1950 S.R. A.J.S.	1972 L.R. Yamaha	**Hudson, E.**	1981 S.R. Suzuki	1959 S R. A.J.S.
Holden, B.	**Hopwood, C. M.**	1972 J.28 Yamaha	1982 J.R. Yamaha	1960 J.4 A.J.S.
1946 L.R. C.T.S.	1949 J.R. A.J.S.	**Hudson, F. J.**	1982 S.13 Yamaha	1961 J.12 A.J.S.
1947 L.9 C.T.S.	1949 S.31 A.J.S.	1946 L.R. O.K. Supreme	**Hunt, Michael**	1961 S.8 Matchless
Holden, C.	**Horan, J.**	**Hudson, H.**	1974 J.40 Desmo Ducati	**Huxley, Derek**
1948 L.9 Excelsior	1956 J.R. A.J.S.	1956 J.R. Norton	1975 J.R. Ducati	1973 L.20 Yamaha
Holder, John R.	**Horn, Chris**	**Hudson, John R.**	1979 L.R. Ducati	**Huxley, Gordon**
1958 S(Sn).R. Norton	1948 J.6 A.J.S.	1957 J(N).46 Velocette	**Hunt, Michael A.**	1980 J/N.R. Yamaha
1959 S.14 Norton	1949 J.35 A.J.S.	1959 J.R. Velocette	1966 L.44 Ducati	**Hyland, V. G.**
1960 J.R. A.J.S.	1949 S.3 Norton	1962 J.60 Honda	1967 S.33 Triumph	1952 J.46 Norton
1960 S.R. Matchless	**Hornby, Brian**	**Huggett, Ken J.**	1968 S.R. Triumph	**Hylton, P. H. 'Pip'**
Holding, H. R.	1960 S.R. B.S.A.	1966 S.34 Norton	1969 S.19 Norton	1946 L.9 Rudge
1946 J.37 Norton	1961 J.R. Norton	1968 S.22 Norton	**Hunt, R. V.**	**Ibberson, Douglas**
1946 L.R. Norton	**Horne, A. G.**	1969 J.54 Norton	1949 J.40 Norton	1981 S/N.8 Suzuki
Holdsworth, Thomas T.	1946 L.R. Rudge	1969 S.R. Norton	1950 J.32 Velocette	**Iffland, Ted N.**
1961 S.40 Matchless	**Horne, Graham A. T.**	1970 J.8 Aermacchi	1950 S.38 Triumph	1946 J.34 A.J.S.
1962 S.27 Matchless	1965 J.R. B.S.A.	1970 S.2 Norton	**Hunter, Anthony R.**	**Ing, M. E.**
1963 S.8 Matchless	1967 L.R. Bultaco	1971 J.R. Norton	1963 J.23 A.J.S.	1967 L.R. D.M.W.
1964 J.R. A.J.S.	1969 S.41 R.E./Triumph	1971 S.2 Kettle Norton	**Hunter, Alan R. C.**	1968 L.15 D.M.W.
Holley, W. F. J.	**Horsfield, Alan**	1972 J.1 Aermacchi	1959 S,R. A.J.S.	**Ingham, William**
1957 J(N).48 A.J.S.	1966 L.38 Aermacchi	1972 S.R. Seeley	1960 S.R. Norton	1970 S.R. Velocette
1958 J(Sn).34 B.S.A.	**Hosie, Duncan T.**	**Hughes, Charles**	1961 S.26 Norton	1971 S.R. Norton
Holliland, Derrick	1967 S.R. Norton	1977 L.R. Yamaha	1962 J.R. Norton	1972 S.R. Norton
1972 S.R. Norton	1968 S.43 Norton	1979 L.16 Yamaha	1962 S.R. Norton	**Ingleson, Richard J.**
1973 S.51 Norton	1969 S.44 Norton	1979 J.9 Yamaha	1963 J.2 A.J.S.	1969 L.22 Royal Enfield
1975 S.R. Manx Norton	**Hosking, B. S.**	**Hughes, David J.**	1963 S.R. Matchless	1970 L.31 Royal Enfield
1976 S.R. Manx Norton	1952 J.19 Norton	1969 J.R. A.J.S.	**Hunter, Bernard**	1971 L.R. Yamaha
1977 S.R. Manx Norton	1952 S.25 Norton	1970 J.R. A.J.S.	1956 J.48 Velocette	**Innocent, Bill W.**
1978 J.51 Norton	**Houseley, Eric**	1971 J.R. A.J.S.	1957 J.R. Velocette	1963 S.42 Triumph/Norton
1980 S.62 Norton	1951 S.R. B.S.A.	1972 J.4 A.J.S.	1958 J.R. F.B.S.	1964 S.R. Triumph/Norton
1981 S.48 Norton	1952 J.R. Norton	1972 S.1 Matchless	1958 S.R. F.B.S.	1965 S.45 Triumph/Norton
1982 S.52 Norton	1952 S.10 Norton	**Hughes, Donal**	1959 S.36 Norton	**Inwood, Ken F. H.**
Hollings, R. S.	**Houston, D. E.**	1978 L/N.12 Yamaha	1961 S.60 Norton	1963 S.R. Norton
1949 S.36 Norton	1960 J.50 B.S.A.	1979 L.50 Yamaha	**Hunter, Brian W.**	1964 S.R. Norton
Hollis, Vic	1961 J.R. Norton	**Hughes, Jackie**	1969 J.19 A.J.S./Coleshill	1965 J.R. Norton
1977 L.66 Yamaha	**Houston, Robert E.**	1978 J/N.3 Shepherd Yamaha	**Hunter, Graham**	1965 S.17 Norton
1980 S.63 Dresda Honda	1970 L.36 Bultaco	1978 L.6 Yamaha	1963 J.44 B.S.A.	1966 J.R. Norton
Holloway, J. C.	**Hovenden, D. A.**	**Hughes, J. A.**	1964 J.R. B.S.A.	1966 S.R. Norton
1956 J.R. A.J.S.	1946 J.15 Norton	1968 S.38 Nortri	1964 S.R. Norstar	1967 J.35 Norton
1957 J.62 A.J.S.	1946 S.R. Norton	1970 S.10 Matchless	1965 J.43 Norstar	1967 S.15 Norton
1957 S.R. A.J.S.	1947 J.52 Norton	**Hughes, Peter**	1965 S.R. Norton	1968 S.14 Norton
1958 J.51 A.J.S.	1947 S.38 Norton	1962 J.35 Norton	**Hunter, J. B. T.**	1969 J.19 Norton
1959 J.72 A.J.S.	**Howard, Cyril W. J.**	1963 J.14 Norton	1950 J.58 Velocette	1969 S.16 Norton
1960 J.53 A.J.S.	1963 J.53 Moto Guzzi	1964 J.R. Norton	**Hurlstone, John R.**	1970 J.45 Norton
1961 J.R. A.J.S.	**Howard, W.**	1964 S.7 Norton	1955 S.26 Triumph	1970 S.21 Norton
Holman, R. P.	1949 J.R. A.J.S.	**Hughes, W. A.**	1956 J.11 Norton	1971 J.R. Norton
1958 S(Sn).16 B.S.A.	1949 S.31 A.J.S.	1959 S.60 B.S.A.	1956 S.R. Norton	1971 S.10 Norton
Holmes, Fred	1950 J.R. A.J.S.	**Hull, Jack H.**	1957 J.33 Norton	1972 J.17 Norton
1971 S.16 Matchless	1950 S.44 B.S.A.	1957 J(N).R. B.S.A.	1957 S.5 Norton	1972 S.5 Norton
Holmes, John	1951 J.R. A.J.S.	1958 J.19 Norton	1958 S.4 Norton	1973 J.23 Norton
1974 L.29 Yamsel	1951 S.24 Norton	1960 S.R. B.S.A.	1959 J.R. Norton	1973 S.8 Norton
Holmes, Steve	**Howarth, Edward**	**Humber, Peter R.**	**Hurst, Graham R.**	1974 S.R. Norton
1978 S/N.R. Yamaha	1978 L/N.R. Yamaha	1965 L.30 Greeves	1971 L.25 Yamaha	1974 J.18 Norton
1978 S.56 Norton Domiracer	1979 L.43 Yamaha	1966 L.15 D.M.W.	**Hurst, Roger**	1975 S.15 Manx Norton
Holmes, Tony	1980 L.42 Yamaha	**Humble, J. R.**	1979 J/N.R. Yamaha	1975 J.6 Yamaha
1982 L/N.16 Yamaha	**Howarth, G.**	1961 S.R. Matchless	1979 S.R. Yamaha	1976 J.7 Yamaha
Holmes, W. Alan	1956 J.R. A.J.S.	**Hunt, David G.**	**Husher, George F. J.**	1976 S.R. Yamaha
1953 J.R Norton	1957 J.63 A.J.S.	1973 J.53 Aermacchi	1968 J.R. Norton	**Ireland, A.**
1953 S.7 Norton	**Howe, D.**	**Hunt, David W.**	1969 J.56 Norton	1964 S.N.F. B.S.A.
1955 J.2 Norton	1955 J.48 Norton-B.S.A.	1966 J.R. Duke Gold Star	**Hussey, Brian**	**Irlam, H.**
1955 S R Norton	1955 S.43 Norton-B.S.A.	1968 S.25 Norton	1968 S.R. Matchless	1958 S(Sn).R. Norton
1956 J.R. Norton	1956 J.24 Norton	1969 S.27 Norton	1969 S.R. Norton	1959 S.49 Norton
1956 S.3 Norton	1957 J.31 Norton	1970 S.9 Norton	1970 S.R. Seeley Matchless	

1960 S.51	Norton	**Jacques, Bernard**		1963 J.6	A.J.S.	1972 J.41	Aermacchi	1978 L.R.	Yamaha
1961 S.R.	Norton	1982 S/N.14	Suzuki	1963 S.1	Norton	1973 J.R.	Yamaha	1979 L.37	Yamaha
Irvine, Thomas A.		**Jacques, John A.**		**Jenkins, H. A.**		**Jones, A. W.**		1980 L.28	Yamaha
1966 L.R.	Aermacchi	1961 S.43	B.S.A.	1956 J.R.	Norton	1947 L.R.	Rudge	1980 J.45	Yamaha
Iszard, Joe A.		1962 S.18	Norton	1956 S.14	Norton	1948 L.R.	Rudge	**Jordan, W. A.**	
1963 J.52	A.J.S.	1963 J.R.	A.J.S.	1958 J.R.	Norton	**Jones, C. L**		1947 J.R.	Norton
1964 J.15	A.J.S.	1963 S.10	Norton	**Jenness, W. J.**		1959 J.R.	Norton	1947 S.4l	Norton
1965 J.12	A.J.S.	**James, A. H. B.**		1946 L.R	O.K. Supreme	**Jones, Clive**		**Jorgensen, Martin I.**	
Ives, Peter F.		1953 J.37	B.S.A.	1948 L.R.	Excelsior	1974 J.R.	Yamaha	1970 L.45	Yamaha
1970 S.12	Matchless	**James, L. A.**		1949 J.66	Norton	**Jones, Derek A.**		**Joseph, Adrian**	
Ivin, L. F.		1957 J(N).29	Norton	1949 S.55	Norton	1963 S.41	B.S.A.	1975 L.R.	Yamsel
1955 J.R.	B.S.A.	1958 J.25	Norton	1950 J.52	Norton	1964 S.N.F.	B.S.A.	**Jowett, N.**	
		1958 S.27	Norton	1950 S.61	Norton	**Jones, D. L.**		1946 J.16	Velocette
Jackson, Alan 'Bud'		1959 J.20	Norton	**Jennings, Roger**		1947 S.47	Norton	1946 S.R.	A.J.S.
1979 J.34	Bill Rae Yamaha	1959 S.22	Norton	1973 S.R.	Seeley	**Jones, David**		1947 J.9	Velocette
1980 L.24	Jackson Yamaha	**James, P. B.**		1974 S.R.	Seeley	1974 L.11	Yamaha	1948 J.R.	A.J.S.
1981 L.12	Yamaha	1961 J.28	Norton	1976 S.50	Seeley	**Jones, Douglas**		1949 J.R.	Velocette
1982 L.6	Yamaha	1962 J.25	Norton	**Jerrard, R. E.**		1975 S.50	Seeley	1950 J.27	Velocette
1982 J.R.	Jackson Yamaha	**James, Patrick J. N.**		1955 J.R.	A.J.S.	1976 J.17	Yamaha	1951 J.R.	Velocette
Jackson, A. J.		1973 J.19	Aermacchi	**Jervis, D.**		1977 L.53	Yamaha	1951 S.36	Velocette
1957 S(N).R.	Triumph	**Jardine, Adrian**		1955 J.34	B S A.	1977 S.R.	Yamaha	**Judkins, Robert K.**	
Jackson, Alan E.		1981 S/N.4	Suzuki	**Jervis, Roy**		1978 J.R.	Yamaha	1960 J.56	A.J.S.
1970 J.35	Aermacchi	**Jarman, D. J.**		1950 S.35	Norton	1978 S.R.	Yamaha	1962 S.R.	Norton
1971 J.30	Yamaha	1955 J.60	A.J S.	1951 S.54	Triumph	**Jones, Eric B.**		1963 S.R.	Norton
1972 J.13	Yamaha	1955 S.37	A.J.S.	1952 S.15	Norton	1952 S.19	Triumph	**Julian, Cyril**	
1973 J.17	Yamaha	1956 J.R.	A.J.S.	1953 S.8	Matchless	**Jones, F. B.**		1948 J.R.	Velocette
1973 S.11	Suzuki	1956 S.R.	A.J.S.	1954 S.R.	Norton	1946 J.R.	Norton	1949 J.27	Velocette
1974 S.18	Brew Suzuki	1957 J.11	Norton	1955 J.11	Norton	1946 S.R.	Norton	1950 J.3	Velocette
1974 J.R.	Yamaha	1957 S.R.	Norton	1955 S.10	Norton	**Jones, Frank**		1950 S.17	Velocette
1975 S.R.	Brew Suzuki	**Jarvis, P. V.**		1956 J.7	Norton	1977 J.R.	Ducati	1951 J.4	Velocette
1975 L.1	Lambert Yamaha	1959 J.R.	B.S.A.	1956 S.R.	Norton	1978 J.52	Honda	1951 S.10	A.J.S.
Jackson, Bob		**Jarvis, Tony**		**Jessop, Stephen L.**		**Jones, Gareth**		**Kalinins, W.**	
1975 L.29	Crooks Suzuki	1975 J.27	Yamsel	1973 L.51	Greeves	1974 J.27	Yamaha	1956 J.R.	A.J.S.
1976 L.16	Lambert Yamaha	1976 J.R.	Yamaha	1974 S. N.F.	Daytona	1975 J.R.	Yamaha	**Kane, William L.**	
1977 S.R.	Lambert Yamaha	1977 J.R.	Yamaha	1975 J.R.	Aermacchi Metisse	**Jones, G. H.**		1966 S.33	Norton
1977 L.4	Yamaha	**Jealous, G. R.**		**Johns, Mark**		1950 J.45	A.J.S.	1967 S.R.	Matchless
1978 L.3	Lambert Yamaha	1954 J.R.	B.S.A.	1979 L/N.R.	Yamaha	1951 J.46	A.J.S.	1968 S.13	Matchless
1978 L.2	Lambert Yamaha	1955 J.18	B.S.A.	1979 L.R.	Yamaha	**Jones, J. Clive**		**Keane, Patrick**	
1979 L.3	Yamaha	1955 S.23	B.S.A.	1980 S.14	Yamaha	1969 L.R.	Bultaco	1978 L/N.10	Yamaha
1979 L.4	Clucas Yamaha	1956 J.29	B.S.A.	1980 J.R.	Yamaha	1970 L.R.	Bultaco	1978 L.R.	Yamaha
1980 L.2	Gregg Yamaha	1956 S.R.	B.S.A.	1981 J.R.	Yamaha	1971 J.19	Aermacchi	1979 L.48	Yamaha
1980 J.8	WLT Yamaha	**Jefferies, Nick**		1981 S.R.	Yamaha	1973 J.17	Aermacchi	**Keating, Robin**	
Jackson, Brian A.		1975 L.6	Yamaha	**Johnson, E. A.**		1974 J.R.	Yamaha	1968 J.31	Aermacchi
1950 J.R.	B.S.A.	1976 L.13	Yamaha	1958 J(Sn).R	B S A.	**Jones, John W.**		**Keeler, Bob D.**	
1951 S.R.	Norton	1976 S.R.	Yamaha	**Johnson, Ernie J.**		1966 J.R.	Norton/B.S.A.	1953 J.R.	Norton
Jackson, J. F.		1977 L.16	Yamaha	1965 L.16	Aermacchi	**Jones, John**		1953 S.2	Norton
1946 J.R.	Norton	1977 S.3	Yamaha	1966 L.6	Aermacchi	1981 J.27	Yamaha	**Keeton, Stuart**	
1946 S.R.	Norton	1978 J.R.	Yamaha	1969 L.R.	Yamaha	**Jones, M. J.**		1976 J.53	Aermacchi
1947 J.19	Norton	1978 S.R.	Yamaha	1970 L.R.	Yamaha	1957 S(N).12	Norton	**Keith, Colin**	
1947 S.R.	Norton	1979 J.8	Yamaha	1971 L.12	Dugdale Yamaha	1957 S.48	Norton	1974 L.47	Yamaha
1948 J.36	Norton	1979 S.R.	Yamaha	1972 L.2	Yamaha	**Jones, Noel**		1976 L.R.	Yamaha
1949 J.R.	Velocette	1980 J.3	Yamaha	1973 L.7	Yamaha	1959 J.R.	Norton	1977 J.R.	Yamaha
1950 J.6	Velocette	1980 S.4	Yamaha	1973 S.R.	Yamaha	1960 J.55	Norton	1978 L.7	Yamaha
1950 S.R	Norton	1981 J.R.	Yamaha	**Johnson, E. L.**		**Jones, N. E.**		1979 L.10	Yamaha
1951 J.19	Velocette	1981 S.R.	Suzuki	1946 J.35	Norton	1947 L.R.	Rudge	1979 J.13	Yamaha
1951 S.29	Velocette	1982 J.3	Yamaha	**Johnson, Geoff**		**Jones, N. R.**		**Keith, Gordon A.**	
1952 J.20	Velocette	1982 S.3	Suzuki	1976 J.11	Yamaha	1962 J.36	Norton	1964 L.1	Greeves
1952 S.R.	Velocette	**Jeffery, Maurice A.**		1977 J.R.	Crooks Suzuki	**Jones, Ron**		**Kelly, D. Raymond**	
1953 J.29	Velocette	1968 J.19	Norton	1977 S.R.	Crooks Yamaha	1972 S.R.	Seeley	1955 S.R.	Triumph
1953 S.29	Velocette	**Jeffrey, Laurence**		1978 J.R.	DRM Yamaha	1973 J.41	A.J.S.	1958 S.24	Matchless
1954 J.R.	A.J.S.	1976 L.R.	Yamaha	1978 S.8	DRM Yamaha	1975 J.R.	Normanque	1959 J.R.	Norton
1954 S.R.	A.J.S.	1977 L.29	Yamaha	1979 J.R.	Lambert Yamaha	1976 J.5	Yamaha	1959 S.33	Norton
1955 J.25	A.J.S.	1978 L.28	Yamaha	1979 S.2	Lambert Yamaha	1977 J.2	Yamaha	**Kelly, David A.**	
1955 S.30	A.J.S.	**Jeffrey, R. R.**		1980 J.4	Yamaha	1977 S.R.	Yamaha	1979 L/N.11	Yamaha
1956 J.R.	Norton	1949 S.50	A.J.S.	1980 S.1	Yamaha	1978 L.5	Maxton Yamaha	1979 L.42	Yamaha
1956 S.R.	Norton	**Jeffreys, Mick**		**Johnson, M.**		1978 J.R.	Yamaha	1980 L.31	Yamaha
1957 J.19	Norton	1977 J.R.	Yamaha	1959 S.R.	B.S.A.	**Jones, R. G.**		1981 L.48	Yamaha
1957 S.N.F	Norton	1978 L.R.	Yamaha	**Johnson, Stephen**		1961 J.27	Norton	1981 S.46	Yamaha
1958 J.35	A.J.S.	**Jeffries, Anthony**		1979 J/N.10	Yamaha	**Jones, Robert S.**		1982 J.41	Spondon Yamaha
1959 J.R.	B.S.A.	1968 S.R.	Triumph	**Johnson, T.**		1967 L.R.	Greeves	1982 S.R.	Yamaha
Jackson, Kevin		**Jeffries, Brian R.**		1947 J.R.	Norton	1968 L.R.	Greeves	**Kelly, Derek A. 'Decca'**	
1976 S.17	Crooks Suzuki	1964 L.33	Ducati	**Johnston, Stan**		**Jones, Stuart J.**		1976 L.40	Yamaha
1977 S.6	Yamaha	1965 L.R.	Ducati	1974 L.R.	Yamaha	1981 J.37	Yamaha	1977 L.23	Yamaha
1978 J.17	Yamaha	**Jeffs, Christopher**		1975 S.58	Honda	**Jones, Stuart R.**		1978 L.35	Yamaha
1978 S.18	Yamaha	1982 S/N.13 Spondon Yamaha		**Johnstone, A.**		1969 L.23	Yamaha	1978 J.R.	Yamaha
1979 S.23	Duckett Yamaha	**Jenkins, D. F.**		1951 S.50	Norton	1973 J.R.	Yamaha	1979 J.41	Yamaha
1980 S.42	Kawasaki	1952 J.53	B.S.A.	**Jolly, Bob**		1974 J.15	Yamaha	1979 S.18	Yamaha
1982 L.R.	Cotton Armstrong	1952 S.54	B.S.A.	1974 J.R.	Yamaha	**Jones, Tony G.**		1980 J.25	Maxton Yamaha
Jackson, Michael J.		**Jenkins, Griff A.**		**Jones, A. C.**		1970 L.42	Ducati	1980 S.23	Maxton Yamaha
1965 J.R.	A.J.S.	1958 S(Sn).13	Norton	1970 L.27	Suzuki	1971 L.35	Ducati	1981 J.R.	Maxton Yamaha
1966 J.R.	A.J.S.	1959 S.46	Norton	1972 S.R.	Suzuki	1972 J.R.	A.J.S.	1981 S.R.	Maxton Yamaha
Jacob, A. C. B.		1960 S.14	Norton	**Jones, A. J.**		1973 J.55	Ducati	1982 J.R.	Maxton Yamaha
1947 S.R.	Norton	1961 S.R.	Norton	1972 L.28	Yamaha	1974 J.46	Aermacchi	1982 S.R.	Maxton Yamaha
		1962 S.11	Norton	**Jones, Anthony T.**		1977 L.56	Yamaha		

The History of the Manx Grand Prix 1923-1998 105

Kelly, Geoff
1975	J.34	Yamaha
1976	S.20	Suzuki
1977	J.R.	Yamaha

Kelly, Peter T.
1968	J.45	A.J.S.
1969	J.36	A.J.S.
1970	J.22	A.J.S.
1971	J.13	A.J.S.
1975	J.52	A.J.S.

Kelly, Mike
1957	J(N).7	B.S.A.
1957	J.37	B.S.A.
1958	J.R.	Norton
1958	S.6	Norton
1959	J.9	Norton
1959	S.7	Norton
1960	J.8	Norton
1960	S.5	Norton
1961	J.R.	Norton
1961	S.3	Norton
1962	J.5	Norton
1962	S.5	Norton
1963	J.R.	Norton
1963	S.R.	Norton
1964	J.4	A.J.S.
1964	S.3	Norton

Kelly, T. Neil
1960	J.37	B.S.A.
1961	J.R.	Norton/B.S.A.
1962	J.R.	A.J.S.
1964	L.R.	Royal Enfield
1965	L.R.	Royal Enfield
1966	L.R.	Royal Enfield
1967	L.R.	Kawasaki
1967	S.25	Velocette
1968	J.R.	Orpin Special
1968	S.R.	Orpin Special
1969	S.R.	Velocette
1970	J.18	Orpin Special
1970	S.24	Velocette
1971	S.4	Cowles Matchless
1973	J.16	Yamaha
1973	S.R.	Suzuki
1974	S.11	Suzuki
1974	J.R.	Yamaha
1975	S.R.	Racewaye
1975	J.R.	Yamaha
1976	S.9	Racewaye

Kemp, H. J.
1946	S.25	Norton
1947	S.22	Norton
1948	S.8	Norton
1949	S.17	Norton
1950	S.9	Norton
1951	S.15	Norton
1953	S.R.	Norton
1954	S.22	Norton

Kemp, R. D.
| 1968 | L.R. | Greeves |

Kemp-Perrin, H.
1947	J.26	Norton
1947	S.R.	Norton
1948	J.28	Norton

Kendrick, Anthony P.
| 1968 | S.49 | Norton |

Kenna, Geoff J.
1971	L.36	Ducati
1972	L.48	Ducati
1973	L.R.	Suzuki

Kent, Mick
| 1977 | S.29 | Yamaha |

Kentish, J. F.
| 1947 | J.31 | Norton |
| 1947 | S.17 | Norton |

Kenyon, G. J.
1959	J.R.	B.S.A.
1960	S.R.	B.S.A.
1961	S.7	Norton
1962	S.R.	Norton

Kenyon, Ivor B.
1961	S.44	B.S.A.
1962	S.R.	B.S.A.
1963	J.39	Norton

| 1963 | S.R. | Norton |

Kermode, Peter
1976	J.R.	Seymour Velocette
1977	J.R.	Seymour Velocette
1978	S.R.	Velocette
1979	S.R.	Suzuki

Kershaw, B.
1954	J.R.	A.J.S.
1954	S.R.	Norton
1955	J.31	A.J.S.
1955	S.16	Norton
1956	J.17	A.J.S.
1956	S.16	Norton
1957	J.R.	A.J.S.
1957	S.R.	Norton

Kershaw, Kevin
1975	J.R.	Yamaha
1976	J.R.	Yamaha
1977	J.R.	Yamaha
1978	J.34	Yamaha
1979	J.R.	Yamaha
1980	J.R.	Yamaha
1981	J.50	Yamaha
1981	S.32	Velocette
1982	S.R.	Yamaha

Kewley, Robert
1964	L.22	Greeves
1965	L.R.	Greeves
1965	S.63	Norton
1966	L.R.	Greeves
1966	S.R.	Norton

Keys, Basil E.
| 1946 | J.31 | Norton |

Kielty, Peter J.
| 1962 | S.37 | B.S.A. |

Kiely, T.
| 1951 | J.67 | A.J.S. |

Kimberley, Peter D.
| 1972 | L.R. | Yamaha |
| 1974 | L.R. | Yamaha |

King, Alastair
1953	J.R.	A.J.S.
1954	J.R.	A.J.S.
1954	S.R.	Matchless
1955	J.R.	Norton
1955	S.R.	Norton
1956	J.R.	Norton
1956	S.R.	Norton

King, Graham W.
1980	J/N.6	Yamaha
1981	S.18	Yamaha
1981	J.R.	Yamaha
1982	J.R.	Yamaha
1982	S.14	Yamaha

King, M.
| 1957 | J(N).31 | B.S.A. |

King, Michael J.
| 1959 | J.80 | B.S.A. |
| 1960 | J.46 | B.S.A. |

King, R. H.
| 1950 | S.19 | Norton |

Kingsnorth, David R.
| 1971 | L.R. | Greeves |
| 1973 | L.R. | Suzuki |

Kirby, David
1967	S.10	Matchless
1970	S.R.	Dresda Triumph
1971	S.48	Triumph
1972	S.22	Triumph
1973	S.R.	Triumph
1974	S.32	Velocette Metisse

Kirby, D.
1965	S.32	Matchless
1967	L.25	Bultaco
1968	L.R.	Yamaha

Kirby, P. A.
| 1951 | J.R. | Velocette |
| 1952 | J.26 | Velocette |

Kirk, Eric J.
1963	J.R.	A.J.S.
1964	J.R.	A.J.S.
1965	J.35	A.J.S.
1966	J.R.	A.J.S.

1963	S.R.	Norton
1968	J.R.	A.J.S.
1969	J.30	A.J.S.
1970	J.R.	A.J.S.
1971	J.R.	A.J.S.
1972	J.R.	A.J.S.
1973	S.R.	Matchless

Kirk, George I.
1965	J.46	A.J.S.
1966	J.37	A.J.S.
1967	J.37	A.J.S.
1968	J.37	A.J.S.
1969	J.45	A.J.S.
1971	J.R.	A.J.S.
1975	J.51	Maxton Yamaha

Kirkcaldy, Alistair
| 1967 | L.R. | Greeves |
| 1968 | L.19 | Greeves |

Kirwan, Dave S.
1965	L.32	Honda
1969	L.R.	Yamaha
1970	L.19	Aermacchi
1971	J.35	Aermacchi
1972	J.R.	Aermacchi
1973	J.R.	Yamaha
1974	J.R.	Wynnstay Yamaha
1975	J.20	Yamaha

Kirwan, Mal L.
1969	L.24	Aermacchi
1970	L.R.	Aermacchi
1972	J.R.	Aermacchi
1973	J.11	Yamaha
1974	S.15	Yamaha
1974	J.13	Yamaha
1975	S.R.	Yamaha
1975	J.9	Yamaha

Kitchen, L. W.
| 1947 | J.15 | Norton |
| 1947 | S.9 | Norton |

Klein, Max O.
1946	J.R.	Norton
1946	S.R.	Ariel
1947	J.45	Norton
1947	S.R.	Norton

Kneen, Chris
1980	S/N.R.	Honda
1981	L.41	Kerby Honda
1981	J.55	Yamaha
1982	L.34	Yamaha
1982	J.45	Yamaha

Kneen, Kenny
1978	J/N.25	Yamaha
1981	L.39	Yamaha
1982	L.28	Yamaha

Kneen, Mike
1977	J.R.	Yamaha
1978	J.R.	Wilson & Collins Yamaha
1978	S.R.	IOMRS Suzuki
1979	J.R.	Yamaha
1979	S.R.	IOMRS Suzuki
1980	J.1	Yamaha
1980	S.3	Suzuki

Kneen, Norman
1978	S/N.10	Yamaha
1979	J.50	Yamaha
1979	S.26	Yamaha
1980	J.17	Yamaha
1980	S.R.	Yamaha
1981	J.13	Yamaha
1981	S.7	Yamaha
1982	J.R.	Yamaha
1982	S.R.	Yamaha

Kneen, Phil
| 1982 | J/N.R. | Yamaha |
| 1982 | L.9 | Yamaha |

Kneen, Richard
| 1982 | S/N.2 | Yamaha |

Knight, Edward G. A.
1967	J.R.	Aermacchi
1968	J.39	Aermacchi
1969	J.34	Aermacchi
1970	J.R.	Aermacchi
1971	J.25	Aermacchi
1972	J.R.	Aermacchi

| 1973 | L.21 | Yamaha |
| 1973 | S.43 | Triumph |

Knight, Ray L.
1962	S.56	Red Plum
1963	J.49	Hughes-Triumph
1963	S.32	Hughes-Triumph
1964	J.R.	Hughes-Triumph
1964	S.R.	Hughes-Triumph
1965	S.R.	Hughes-Triumph
1966	J.24	Hughes-Triumph
1966	S.30	Hughes-Triumph

Knowles, John
1971	J.44	A.J.S.
1972	J.23	Aermacchi
1973	J.22	Seeley
1974	S.10	Seeley
1975	S.20	Chell Honda
1976	J.6	Yamaha
1976	S.7	Yamaha
1977	J.R.	Yamaha
1977	S.R.	Yamaha
1978	J.6	Fiveways Yamaha
1978	S.R.	Fiveways Yamaha
1979	J.R.	Yamaha
1979	S.16	Yamaha
1980	S.R.	Seeley
1981	J.17	Yamaha
1981	S.R.	Yamaha
1982	J.R.	Yamaha

Koring, E. V.
1946	J.32	Norton
1946	SR.	Norton
1947	J.13	Norton
1947	S.R.	Norton

Laing, A. F.
| 1958 | J(Sn).54 | B.S.A. |

Lambert, G. K.
1951	S.R.	Norton
1952	S.R.	A.J.S.
1952	S.R.	A.J.S.
1953	J.R.	A.J.S.
1953	S.R.	A.J.S.

Lamont, Norman
1966	J.51	A.J.S.
1967	J.48	A.J.S.
1968	J.48	A.J.S.
1969	J.41	A.J.S.
1972	J.34	A.J.S.
1973	J.56	A.J.S.

Landeg, Phil
1974	S.R.	Cowles Matchless
1975	J.30	Maxton Yamaha
1979	S.R.	Suzuki
1981	J.27	Cowles Yamaha
1981	S.11	Cowles Suzuki

Lang, David I.
| 1964 | S.26 | Norton/B.S.A. |

Lang, Gordon
| 1966 | S.R. | Norton |

Langlands, I.
| 1957 | S(N).16 | Norton |
| 1957 | S.R. | Norton |

Langston, Ron J.
1959	J.2	Norton
1960	J.R.	A.J.S.
1960	S.R.	Matchless

Langton, D.
1948	J.R.	Norton
1949	S.37	Norton
1950	S.47	Norton
1952	J.42	Norton
1952	S.51	Norton
1953	J.30	Norton
1953	S.17	Norton

Laporte, R. H.
| 1954 | J.R. | B.S.A. |
| 1954 | S.27 | B.S.A. |

Larkin, Stewart M.
| 1969 | L.49 | Suzuki |

Lashmar, Dennis G.
| 1949 | J.13 | A.J.S. |

Lattimer, G.

| 1955 | J.R. | B.S.A. |

Law, Adrian E.
| 1982 | J/N.R. | Yamaha |

Law, Con
1977	L.10	Yamaha
1978	J.8	Glen-Cowell Yamaha
1978	L.R.	Glen-Cowell Yamaha
1979	L.1	Glen-Cowell Yamaha
1979	L.R.	Glen-Cowell Yamaha

Lawrence, Gareth
1978	L/N.4	Yamaha
1978	L.R.	Yamaha
1979	L.45	Yamaha

Lawrence, William
| 1977 | J.R. | Grimstead Yamaha |
| 1978 | S.12 | Grimstead Yamaha |

Lawson, S.
| 1946 | L.R. | Rudge |
| 1947 | L.11 | Rudge |

Lawton, Alan T.
1960	J.42	B.S.A.
1961	J.R.	Norton
1962	J.23	Norton
1963	J.22	Norton
1964	J.R.	Norton
1964	S.15	Norton
1965	J.9	Norton
1965	S.31	Norton
1966	J.R.	Norton
1966	S.10	Norton

Lawton, Barry
| 1964 | L.14 | Aermacchi |
| 1965 | L.I0 | Aermacchi |

Lea, Aubrey
1967	L.R.	Yamaha
1968	L.R.	Yamaha
1969	L.5	Yamaha

Leach, Dave
| 1982 | L/N.4 | Yamaha |
| 1982 | L.5 | Yamaha |

Leah, Chris
| 1979 | L/N.R. | Yamaha |

Leahy, Peter J.
| 1969 | L.R. | Yamaha |

Learmonth, John J.
1966	J.R.	Norton
1967	J.10	Norton
1968	J.16	Norton
1968	S.15	Norton

Leary, P.
| 1962 | S.53 | B.S.A. |

Lee, Alan M.
1973	J.R.	Aermacchi
1974	L.16	Yamaha
1975	L.11	Yamaha
1976	J.R.	Visnews Yamaha
1976	S.11	Visnews Yamaha
1977	J.6	Visnews Yamaha
1977	S.R.	Visnews Yamaha

Lee, Brian I. H.
1968	J.15	Aermacchi
1969	J.R.	Aermacchi
1969	S.17	Aermacchi
1970	L.R.	Aermacchi
1970	S.8	Aermacchi

Lee, D.
| 1960 | S.61 | B.S.A. |

Lee, Edward C.
| 1964 | J.R. | B.N.S. |

Lee, Jim
| 1963 | S38 | Norton |
| 1964 | S.29 | Norton/B.S.A. |

Lee, Martin J.
1980	S/N.6	Honda
1981	S.R.	Honda
1982	J.R.	Yamaha
1982	S.R.	Yamaha

Lee, Reg
1946	J.R.	Velocette
1946	S.R.	Velocette
1947	L.R.	Norton
1948	J.R.	Norton
1948	S.R.	Norton

Leece, Ernest H.
1964 J.43 B.S.A.
Leech, John
1981 S/N.R. Suzuki
Lees, Roger M.
1970 S.R. Rickman Metisse
1971 S.40 Triumph
1972 S.17 Triumph Metisse
1973 S.R. Triumph Metisse
Legg, D. T.
1948 J.57 Norton
1948 S.R. Norton
1949 J.R. Norton
1949 S.47 Norton
Legge, Dave P.
1956 J.R. B.S.A.
1956 S.R. B.S.A.
Leigh, George E.
1946 S.22 Norton
1947 J.16 Norton
1947 S.24 Norton
1948 J.26 Norton
1948 S15 Norton
Leighton, Ron
1976 J.29 Yamaha
1977 J.R. Yamaha
Lennon, Reg
1973 L.37 Aermacchi
1974 L.R. Yamaha
1975 L.28 Yamaha
1976 L.23 Yamaha
1977 L.28 Maxton Yamaha
Lerego, Leon
1974 J.R. Yamaha
Leslie, Graham
1981 J/N.R. Yamaha
1982 J.R. Yamaha
Lewis, Gerald T.
1968 L.R. Greeves
1969 L.R. Yamaha
1970 L.12 Yamaha
Lewis, John H. L.
1955 S.39 B.S.A.
1957 J.R. Norton
1957 S.6 Norton
1958 J.4 Norton
1958 S.R. Norton
1959 J.R. Norton
1959 S.R. Norton
Lewis, J. R.
1948 J.R. A.J.S.
Lewis, S. L.
1957 S(N).11 Matchless
1957 S.37 Matchless
1957 J.R. A.J.S.
1958 S.30 Matchless
Leyshon, W. F.
1948 L.R. Rudge
Lilley, R. H.
1956 J.36 B.S.A.
1956 S.15 Norton
Limerick, John
1980 S/N.3 Yamaha
1980 L.R. Yamaha
1981 J.58 Yamaha
1981 L.R. Yamaha
1982 L.50 Yamaha
1982 J.52 Yamaha
Linder, George
1977 S.2 Suzuki
1978 S.1 Suzuki
Lindley, Barry
1958 S(Sn).R. B.S.A.
1959 S.37 B.S.A.
1960 S.31 B.S.A.
1961 S.27 Matchless
1962 S.22 Matchless
Lindsay, David G.
1964 J.R. A.J.S.
1965 L.23 Aermacchi
1966 L.18 Greeves
Lindsay, Joe
1971 J.R. Aermacchi
1972 J.15 Aermacchi

1973 J.12 Yamaha
1974 S.7 Yamaha
1974 J.7 Yamaha
1975 S.R. Yamaha
1975 J.R. Yamaha
1976 S.R. Yamaha
1976 J.1 Yamaha
Lindsay, Ken A.
1957 J.32 B.S.A.
1958 J.49 B.S.A.
1959 J.48 B.S.A.
1960 J.59 B.S.A.
1961 J.29 B.S.A.
1962 J.22 Norton
Lindup, Ron
1960 J.29 Norton
1961 J.R. Norton
1961 S.23 Norton
Linsdell, Steve
1981 S/N.2 Royal Enfield
1982 S.21 Ducati
Linton, Dick
1973 J.50 Aermacchi
1974 J.R. Aermacchi
1975 J.28 Drixton Aermacchi
1976 J.28 Aermacchi
1977 J.R. Aermacchi
1977 S.21 FCL Aermacchi
Lishman, John B.
1963 J.54 Norton
1964 J.21 Norton
1965 J.5 A.J.S.
1966 J.R. A.J.S.
1966 S.21 Norton
1967 J.9 A.J.S.
1968 J.R. A.J.S.
Lister, Robin G. M.
1961 S.63 Matchless
1962 S.38 Matchless
1963 S.40 Matchless
1964 L.R. Yamaha
1965 L.37 Yamaha
Little, G.
1956 S.R. Moto Guzzi
Little, Keith
1974 S.53 Triumph
1975 S.36 Kawasaki
1976 S.R. Davick Kawasaki
1977 S.30 Kawasaki
Littler, D. L.
1970 J.29 Yamaha
Lloyd, Kevin
1982 L/N.14 Yamaha
1982 L.38 Yamaha
Loan, Derek
1969 S.R. Norton
Loder, John
1979 S/N.3 Fahron
1980 J.R. Fahron Yamaha
1980 S.R. Fahron
1982 S.R. Fahron
Logan, George
1963 J.36 A.J.S.
1965 J.R. A.J.S.
Logan, John David
1970 J.47 JDLS Bridgestone
1971 J.R. Lostone
1973 S.54 Seeley
1974 S.12 Seeley
Logan, John James
1973 L.34 Yamaha
1974 L.39 Yamaha
1975 L.11 Yamaha
1976 L.14 Harrison Yamaha
Lomas, Bill A.
1948 L.7 Royal Enfield
1949 J.6 Velocette
1949 S.R. Velocette
Longman, G. A.
1954 J.41 Velocette
1954 S.R. Velocette
1955 J.R. Velocette
1955 S.51 Velocette
1957 J.R. Velocette

1957 S.N.F. Velocette
Lord, H.
1950 J.R. Norton
Loughridge, Tom
1966 L.42 Aermacchi
1967 L.38 Aermacchi
Lovatt, Peter K.
1967 S.31 Goldton
1968 S.34 Goldton
1969 J.R. A.J.S.
1970 J.R. A.J.S.
1971 J.R. Ducati
1972 J.R. Ducati
1973 J.38 Yamaha
1974 J.19 Maxton Yamaha
1975 J.21 Maxton Yamaha
1976 J.32 Maxton Yamaha
1977 J.47 Maxton Yamaha
1978 J.R. Maxton Yamaha
1979 J.R. Maxton Yamaha
1980 J.38 Maxton Yamaha
1981 J.R. Maxton Yamaha
Lovell, M.
1947 S.R. Norton
Lovell, R. W.
1968 S.30 D. W. Special
Lowdon, Derek R.
1979 S/N.9 Honda
1980 S.38 Seeley Trident
Lowe, Graham
1978 L/N.R. Yamaha
1979 L.46 Yamaha
Lucas, Malcolm S.
1972 S.25 Norton/B.S.A.
Lucas, R. M.
1949 J.R. Velocette
1950 J.R. Velocette
1950 S.R. Velocette
Luckman, Roger
1979 J/N.1 Tiger Tim Yamaha
1979 S.R. Tiger Tim Yamaha
1980 J.16
Wilson & Collins Yamaha
1980 S.16
Wilson & Collins Yamaha
Ludlam, Paul
1965 L.36 Ducati
1966 L.34 Ducati
1966 S.R. Triumph
1967 L.41 Ducati
Lumsdon, D.
1965 L.R. Aermacchi
Lund, Bernie
1955 J.R. Velocette
1956 J.22 B.S.A.
1956 S.22 B.S.A.
1957 J.35 B.S.A.
1957 S.22 B.S.A.
1958 J.R. B.S.A.
1958 S.R. Norton
1960 J.26 Norton
1960 S.N.F Norton
1961 J.R. Norton
1961 S.R. B.S.A.
1962 J.12 A.J.S.
1962 S.9 Matchless
1963 J.11 A.J.S.
1963 S.R. Norton
1964 J.9 A.J.S.
Lund, Brian
1982 L/N.1 Yamaha
1982 L.R. Yamaha
Lund, G.
1955 L.R. B.S.A.
Lunde, Marty C.
1965 J.20 A.J.S.
Lunn, Doug
1971 L.17 Suzuki
1972 S.R. Suzuki
1973 J.2 Yamaha
Lurock, E. R.
1957 J(N).15 B.S.A.
1957 J.R. B.S.A.
Luton, C. K.

1968 L.35 Ducati
Luton, E. G.
1972 L.35 D.M.W.
Lyons, Ernie
1946 J.8 Velocette
1946 S.1 Triumph
Lyons, Roger
1976 L.61 Yamaha
1977 L.18 Yamaha
1978 L.R. Yamaha
1978 J.20 Yamaha

McAllister, J. B.
1948 J.61 Norton
McBain, David
1965 J.39 Norton
1967 J.R. Norton
1968 J.24 Norton
1969 J.25 Norton
1969 S.R. Norton
1971 J.27 Norton
1971 S.27 Norton
McBride, John
1979 J/N.17 Yamaha
1980 J.56 Yamaha
1981 S.37 Spondon Yamaha
1981 J.R. Spondon Yamaha
1982 S.R. Yamaha
McCandless, W. A. Cromie
1947 J.R. Norton
1947 S.R. Norton
1948 J.R. Norton
1948 S.R. Norton
1949 J.1 Norton
1949 S.2 Norton
MacClean, William I.
1964 J.41 Norton
1965 J.38 Norton
1966 S.20 Norton
1967 S.16 Norton
McClements, Sam A.
1972 S.11 Norton
1973 J.R. Aermacchi
1973 S.25 Norton
1974 S.R. Carson Yamaha
1974 J.5 Carson Yamaha
1975 S.1 Crawford Yamaha
1975 J.3 Yamaha
McClements, Stephen
1982 J/N.R. Yamaha
1982 L.22 Yamaha
McComb, Robert B.
1972 L.R. Honda
1973 L.16 Yamaha
1974 L.9 Yamaha
McCormick, John D.
1982 S/N.18 Yamaha
McCready, Errol T. P.
1969 J.39 Bultaco
1970 L.18 Yamaha
1971 L.R. Yamaha
1972 L.20 Yamaha
1973 J.R. Yamaha
1974 S.23 Yamaha
1976 S.R. Yamaha
1979 J.48 Yamaha
1980 J.R. Yamaha
1980 S.R. Yamaha
1981 J.R. Yamaha
MacDonald, Angus
1982 S/N.19 Suzuki
McDonald, Don
1976 L.R. Suzuki
1977 L.R. Suzuki
1978 L.58 Suzuki
McDonald, R.
1949 J.42 Velocette
MacDonnell, M.
1958 J(Sn).22 B.S.A.
McDougall, Peter
1965 L.R. Royal Enfield
1966 L.R. Royal Enfield
McElnea, Rob
1979 J/N.2 Yamaha

1979 S.R. Yamaha
1981 S.R. Yamaha
McEntee, John
1975 L.20 Fowler Yamaha
1976 L.20 Yamaha
1977 J.R. Fowler Yamaha
1977 S.R. Fowler yamaha
1978 J.14 Fowler Yamaha
1978 S.R. Fowler Yamaha
1979 L.R. Fowler Yamaha
1979 S.12 Fowler Yamaha
1980 J.19 Fowler Yamaha
1980 S.17 Fowler Yamaha
1981 J.16 Fowler Yamaha
1981 L.R. Fowler Yamaha
McEwan, Henry
1965 J.R. Norton/B.S.A.
1966 J.R. Norton
1967 J.23 Norton
1968 J.18 Aermacchi
1969 J.14 Aermacchi
1970 J.13 Aermacchi
1971 J.6 Aermacchi
McEwan, Tommy
1946 J.R. Norton
1946 S.R. Norton
McFarlane, Eric
1977 S/N.R. Laverda
1981 S.R. Ducati
McFarlane, V. G.
1950 J.R. Velocette
1951 J.R. Velocette
1952 J.59 Velocette
1952 S.48 Velocette
McFarlane, Vincent
1957 J(Sn).59 Velocette
McGarrity, Malcolm
1963 J.48 Norton
1964 J.18 Norton
1965 J.29 Norton
1965 S.27 Norton
1966 J.18 Norton
McGeagh, Michael R.
1951 J.R. Velocette
McGill, John
1975 S.R. Hi-Tac Suzuki
McGinn, Conor
1978 J/N.2 MB Yamaha
1978 S.22 MB Yamaha
1979 L.2 MB Yamaha
1982 J.22 MB Yamaha
McGladdery, Andy
1979 L/N.1 Yamaha
1979 L.14 Yamaha
1980 L.R. Yamaha
1980 J.24 Yamaha
MacGregor, Bob
1963 J.33 Norton
1963 S.4 Norton
McGuiness, Brian
1954 J.R. B.S.A.
1955 J.R. A.J.S.
1955 S.R. A.J.S.
1957 J.10 Norton
1957 S.60 Norton
McGurk, Anthony
1964 S.R. Matchless
1965 S.7 Matchless
MacIntosh, Ian C.
1971 J.R. A.J.S.
1972 S.R. Seeley
McIntyre, Bob
1952 J.1 A.J.S.
1952 S.2 A.J.S.
McIvor, A.
1956 J.66 Velocette
1956 S.54 Velocette
McIvor, Joe
1977 J.37 Yamaha
McKane, Terry
1972 S.R. Suzuki
1973 S.R. Suzuki
1974 L.17 Yamaha
1975 S.16 Marriott Yamaha

1975 J.49	Yamaha	1948 S.R.	Triumph	1982 S.25	Honda	1969 S.R.	Norton	1982 J.R.	Shepherd Yamaha
Mackay, Andrew		**McVeigh, Jack J.**		**Martin, Eddie**		**Matthews, G. A.**		**Mellor, Ron L.**	
1977 L.40	Yamaha	1947 J.56	Norton	1976 J.25	Yamaha	1948 S.R.	Sunbeam	1973 S.39	Seeley
Mackay, G. T.		1947 S.51	Norton	1977 S.10	Yamaha	1949 S.53	Sunbeam	1974 S.17	Seeley
1955 J.R.	Velocette	1948 J.41	Norton	1977 J.R.	Yamaha	**Matthews, John T.**		1974 S.17	Seeley
McKechnie, Ewen		1948 S.25	Norton	**Martin, Gary P.**		1972 J.R.	Norton	1975 J.15	Yamaha
1973 L.33	Yamaha	**Machan, G. T.**		1978 J.49	Yamaha	1973 L.52	Suzuki	1977 J.11	Yamaha
1974 S.48	Suzuki	1946 L.18	Cotton	1979 J.R.	Yamaha	1974 J.45	Taylor Honda	**Menzies, David R. I.**	
1975 S.44	Yamaha	**Mackay, G. T.**		1980 S.36	Yamaha	1975 J.R.	Honda	1964 S.28	Norton
1976 S.R.	Sparton	1955 J.R.	Velocette	1980 J.R.	Yamaha	**Mavrogordato, Noel M.**		1965 S.52	Norton
McKee, Stanley		**Maddrick, Bill J.**		1982 S.R.	Yamaha	1946 L.R.	D.K.W.	1966 S.31	Norton
1978 J/N.15	Yamaha	1946 J.R.	Norton	**Martin, Geoffrey D.**		**Maw, R. J. G.**		1967 S.7	Norton
1979 J.33	Yamaha	1946 S.R.	Norton	1980 J/N.R.	Yamaha	1956 J.57	B.S.A.	**Mercier, T.**	
1979 S.R.	Yamaha	1947 L.13	Excelsior	1981 J.39	Yamaha	1958 J.44	Norton	1968 J.47	A.J.S.
1982 S.R.	Yamaha	1947 S.20	Norton	1981 S.R.	Yamaha	1959 S.43	Norton	**Middleton, Jeffrey**	
McKenna, Raymond		**Madsen-Mygdal, David**		1982 J.R.	Yamaha	**Mawby, Robert F. J.**		1967 J.43	B.S.A.
1981 S/N.13	Yamaha	1982 L/N.R.	Yamaha	1982 S.54	Yamaha	1960 J.54	Norton	1968 J.29	Norton
1981 S.54	Yamaha	1982 L.35	Yamaha	**Martin, Guy E.**		1961 J.42	Norton	1969 J.32	Norton
McKenzie, Ian		**Maguire, Ian M.**		1969 L.33	Greeves	1962 J.48	Norton	1974 J.43	Suzuki
1982 S/N.R.	Ducati	1960 J.R.	Velocette	1970 S.R.	Rickman Metisse	1963 S.R.	Norton	1975 S.R.	Suzuki
McKillop, Willie J.		1961 J.40	Norton	**Martin, Keith**		**Mawdsley, Joseph**		1976 S.31	Suzuki
1972 L.34	Greeves	1962 J.28	Norton	1969 L.47	Suzuki	1966 L.R.	D.M.W.	1977 J.R.	Suzuki
1973 L.43	Greeves	**Mahon, Rodney M.**		1970 L.22	Suzuki	1967 L.R.	D.M.W.	**Middleton, Mark**	
1974 L.R.	Johnson Yamaha	1963 S.R.	Norton	1971 L.7	Suzuki	1968 L.24	Ducati	1978 S/N.R.	Suzuki
1977 J.13	Yamaha	1964 S.R.	Norton	1972 L.12	Yamaha	**Mawson, Bob A. D.**		1978 S.R.	Suzuki
1978 J.25	Yamsel	1965 S.20	Norton	1972 S.3	Crooks Suzuki	1951 S.52	Norton	1979 L.15	Suzuki
1978 S.19	Yamsel	1966 S.15	Norton	**Martin, Paddy R.**		1952 J.R.	Norton	1980 S.18	Yamaha
McKimm, J.		**Mainwaring, Stephen**		1982 S/N.4	Yamaha	1952 S.42	Norton	1980 J.R.	Yamaha
1949 J.22	A.J.S.	1982 S/N.R.	Suzuki	**Martin, Paul W.**		1953 S.R.	Norton	**Middleton, Peter C.**	
1949 S.R.	A.J.S.	**Malam, A. D.**		1975 J.R.	Shepherd Suzuki	1954 J.42	B.S.A.	1957 S(N).2	Norton
1951 J.25	A.J.S.	1958 J(Sn).41	B.S.A.	1977 S.42	Shepherd	1954 S.R.	Norton	1957 S.9	Norton
McKinley, Peter J.		1959 J.62	B.S.A.	1978 J.27	Shepherd	**Maxwell, Charles**		1958 S.7	Norton
1973 L.6	Yamaha	**Maltby, Robert**		1978 S.50	Shepherd Suzuki	1982 L/N.7	Rotax	1959 J.1	Norton
McKinstry, David		1978 L/N.5	Yamaha	1979 J.R.	Shepherd Suzuki	1982 L.26	Rotax	1959 S.6	Norton
1979 J/N.9	Yamaha	1978 L.40	Yamaha	1979 S.R.	Shepherd	**May, Donald P.**		**Millar, Jimmy**	
1980 J.R.	McFarland Yamaha	**Manley, Mick W.**		1980 L.37	Shepherd Yamaha	1964 S.32	Norton	1977 J.49	Aermacchi
McKitterick, Bryan		1960 J.47	Norton	1980 J.R.	Shepherd Yamaha	1965 J.41	Norton	**Millard, Stephen M.**	
1979 J/N.R.	Yamaha	1961 J.40	Norton	1981 J.46	Suzuki	1965 S.34	Norton	1964 L.R.	Yamaha
McLaughlin, Patrick		**Mann, Michael G.**		1981 S.R.	Suzuki	1966 J.N.F.	Norton	1965 L.R.	Yamaha
1980 J/N.12	Yamaha	1969 S.R.	Triton	1982 J.20	Yamaha	1966 J.R.	Norton	1966 J.34	A.J.S.
1981 L.R.	Yamaha	**Mann, Ronnie**		1982 S.40	Suzuki	1967 J.R.	Norton	**Millea, A. H.**	
1981 J.R.	Yamaha	1969 L.R.	Bultaco	**Martin, Roger K.**		1967 S.R.	Norton	1946 J.R.	Norton
1982 L.18	Yamaha	1973 L.8	Yamaha	1969 L.26	Ducati	**Mayes, Roger A.**		1946 S.17	Norton
MacLean, Brian J.		1979 L.5	Yamaha	1970 L.R.	Ducati	1964 L.R.	Greeves	**Millar, P. P.**	
1963 S.36	Norton	1979 J.R.	Yamaha	**Martin, Tony**		1965 L.29	Aermacchi	1970 L.R.	Yamaha
1964 S.26	Norton	**Manning, G.**		1981 J/N.8	Yamaha	**Mayhew, Roy S.**		1971 L.26	Yamaha
1965 S.36	Norton	1947 J.R.	Norton	1982 J.46	Yamaha	1957 S(N).4	Norton	**Miller, D.**	
1966 S.20	Norton	1947 S.R.	Norton	**Mash, D. A.**		1957 S.R.	Norton	1967 S.21	T.N.S.
1967 S.16	Norton	**Marriott, Glyn**		1965 J.52	Norton	1958 J.10	A.J.S.	1968 S.R.	Norton
McLean, O. T.		1976 L.38	Yamaha	**Maskell, David**		1958 S.R.	Norton	**Miller, Gerald**	
1967 L.16	Bultaco	1977 L.17	Yamaha	1962 J.R	Velocette	1959 J.10	A.J.S.	1978 J/N.16	Yamsel
McLean, William I.		**Marrs, Colin**		1964 L.R.	D.M.W.	1959 S.10	Matchless	1979 S.41	Yamsel
1966 J.44	Norton	1977 L.R.	Aermacchi	1965 L.22	D.M.W.	1960 J.2	A.J.S.	**Miller, John**	
1969 J.24	Norton	**Marsden, Malcolm**		1966 L.R.	D.M.W.	1960 S.3	Matchless	1969 J.52	Norton
McLoughlin, P. S.		1978 S/N.4	Honda	1967 L.R.	D.M.W.	1961 J.7	A.J.S.	1970 J.R.	Aermacchi
1956 J.R.	A.J.S.	1979 J.38	Honda	1968 L.R.	Ducati	1961 S.R.	Matchless	**Miller, Mick J.**	
1957 J.R.	A.J.S.	1979 S.33	Honda	1970 L.R.	Ducati	**Mayne, G. T. W.**		1960 J.49	A.J.S.
McManus, John		1980 S.28	Honda	**Mason, David**		1949 J.69	Velocette	1961 J.23	A.J.S.
1982 S/N.16	Kawasaki	1981 J.R.	Yamaha	1972 L.17	Yamaha	**Mayrs, Alfred**		1962 J.26	A.J.S.
McMeeken, John		1981 S.R.	Ducati	1973 J.7	Yamaha	1968 L.21	Bultaco	**Miller, Robert W.**	
1976 L.44	Yamaha	**Marselle, K. G.**		**Mason, Neil**		1969 L.13	Bultaco	1965 S.R.	M.C.N./S.S.
1977 L.14	Yamaha	1967 J.R.	Norton	1971 J.38	Yamaha	1970 L.9	Yamaha	**Millins, Roger**	
McMillan, David J.		**Marsh, Adrian**		1972 J.R.	Aermacchi	1971 L.10	Yamaha	1959 J.58	A.J.S.
1966 L.40	Ducati	1976 J.8	Yamaha	1973 J.R.	Aermacchi	1972 L.11	Yamaha	1960 J.36	A.J.S.
1967 L.54	Ducati	1977 J.32	Yamaha	1974 L.10	Yamaha	1973 L.4	Yamaha	1961 J.R.	A.J.S.
1968 L.25	Ducati	1977 S.28	Suzuki	**Massam, Dave**		1973 S.47	Yamaha	1962 S.R.	Matchless
1969 L.28	Ducati	**Marsh, R. W.**		1974 J.R.	Yamaha	**Meddings, Malcolm W. J.**		1963 S.R.	Matchless
McMillan, P. C.		1947 L.14	Excelsior	**Masson, R.**		1964 J.26	Yamaha	1964 J.40	A.J.S
1959 S.35	B.S.A.	1948 L.5	Excelsior	1957 J(N).18	Norton	**Meier, R. R.**		1964 S.R.	Matchless
McStay, M. A.		**Marshal, Alan**		1957 J.39	Norton	1946 S.31	Ariel	**Mills, Derek J.**	
1956 S.R.	B.S.A.	1982 J/N.8	Yamaha	1958 J.38	Norton	1947 S.50	Ariel	1967 J.R.	A.J.S./Metisse
1957 S.R.	Norton	1982 L.16	Yamaha	1958 S.R.	Norton	1948 S.R.	Ariel	1968 J.R.	A.J.S.
1958 S.40	Norton	**Marshal, A. H. E.**		1960 S.45	Norton	1949 S.45	Ariel	1969 J.R.	A.J.S.
1959 S.19	Norton	1947 J.R.	Norton	1961 S.48	Norton	1950 J.R.	A.J.S.	**Mills, Graham T.**	
1960 S.R.	Norton	1948 S.R.	Norton	**Matchett, John**		1951 J.48	A.J.S.	1946 L.R.	Excelsior
1961 S.33	Norton	**Marshal, D.**		1979 L/N.R.	Yamaha	**Mellor, Phil**		**Mills, H. L.**	
MacTaggart, James W.		1948 S.20	Triumph	**Mateer, Gerry**		1978 L/N.1	Maxton Yamaha	1949 J.63	Velocette
1966 S.R.	Norton	1949 S.R.	Triumph	1965 J.R.	Norton	1978 L.4	Maxton Yamaha	1949 S.25	Velocette
McVeigh, Bill		**Marston, Philip**		1966 J.12	Norton	1979 L.R.	Maxton Yamaha	1950 J.R.	Velocette
1946 J.R.	Norton	1976 L.65	Ducati	1967 J.13	Norton	1979 J.3	Maxton Yamaha	1950 S.26	Norton
1946 S.15	Norton	1978 J.R.	Suzuki	1967 S.R.	Norton	**Mellor, Philip, G.**		1951 J.40	Velocette
1947 J.R.	Norton	**Martin, Dean C.**		1968 S.7	Norton	1981 L/N.R.	Yamaha	1951 S.26	Norton
1947 S.6	Norton	1978 J/N.11	Yamaha	1969 J.R.	Aermacchi	1981 L.R.	Yamaha	1952 J.41	A.J.S.
1948 J.10	Velocette	1978 S.58	Yamaha			1982 L.36	ISR	1952 S.35	A.J.S.-Triumph

1953 J.36	A.J.S.	1974 J.35	Honda	1964 J.10	A.J.S.	**Moss, Frank**		1978 L.60	Aermacchi
1953 S.R.	A.J.S.	1975 S.23	Yoshimura Honda	1964 S.N.F.	Norton	1972 S.46	Norton	1979 J.R.	Aermacchi
Mills, John		1976 S.14	Honda	1965 J.19	A.J.S.	1973 J.36	A.J.S.	1981 L.R.	Aermacchi
1969 J.R.	Norton	1977 S.13	Honda	1965 S.35	Norton/B.S.A.	1977 S.33	Honda	1982 J.58	Aermacchi
Milne, Bill		1978 J.44	Honda	1966 L.14	Yamaha	1978 S.38	Moss Honda Spl.	**Murphy, George C. A.**	
1958 J(S n).R.	B.S.A.	1978 S.37	Honda	1966 S.R.	Norton	1979 S.30	Moss Honda	1955 J.24	A.J.S.
1959 J.R.	Norton	**Montgomery, David R.**		1967 J.25	Norton	1982 S.36	Honda	1955 S.21	A.J.S.
1960 J.25	Norton	1978 S/N.15	Aermacchi	1967 S.R.	Matchless	**Moss, P.**		1956 J.16	A.J.S.
1961 J.R.	A.J.S.	1978 S.R.	Seeley Commando	1968 S.26	Matchless	1947 J.38	B.S.A.	1956 S.R.	A.J.S.
1962 J.8	A.J.S.	1979 J.54	Meadows Aermacchi	1969 L.11	Yamaha	1949 J.36	A.J.S.	1957 J.7	A.J.S.
1963 J.7	A.J.S.	1979 S.R.	Triumph	1969 S.20	Matchless	1949 S.26	A.J.S.	1957 S.R.	Matchless
1964 J.R.	A.J.S.	1980 J.51	Aermacchi	1970 L.7	Yamaha	1950 J.15	A.J.S.	1958 J.7	Norton
1965 J.4	A.J.S.	1980 S.R.	Meadows B.S.A.	1971 J.24	Yamaha	1950 S.18	A.J.S.	1958 S.R.	Norton
1966 L.R.	N.S.U.	1981 J.R.	Meadows Aermacchi	1971 S.34	Matchless	1951 J.23	A.J.S.	**Murray, Bernard M.**	
1966 S.R.	Matchless	1981 S.R.	Suzuki	1972 L.22	Yamaha	1951 S.R.	A.J.S.	1972 S.20	Seeley
1967 L.R.	Bultaco	1982 J.R.	Yamaha	1973 L.28	Yamaha	1952 J.31	A.J.S.	1973 J.8	Yamaha
1967 S.R.	Matchless	1982 S.12	Suzuki	**Morgan, Peter**		1952 S.35	A.J.S.	1974 S1	
1968 L.R.	Bultaco	**Montgomery-Swan, Jeremy**		1967 J.49	A.J.S.	**Moss, Richard J.**			Dugdale Maxton Yamaha
1968 S.Ex.	Matchless	1976 L.43	Yamaha	1968 J.R.	Greeves	1981 L/N.R.	Shepherd Yamaha	1974 J.1	
1969 J.R.	Aermacchi	1977 L.34	Maxton Yamaha	1969 J.R.	Greeves	1981 L.R.	Shepherd Yamaha		Dugdale Maxton Yamaha
1970 J.R.	Cowles/A.J.S.	**Moore, Eddie P.**		1970 L.34	Suzuki	1982 L.R.	Yamaha	**Murray, William**	
1970 S.49	Cowles Matchless	1971 J.45	Aermacchi	**Morgan, P. E.**		**Moss, Tony J.**		1981 S/N.R.	M.M.C.
1971 S.7	Cowles Matchless	1972 J.29	Aermacchi	1956 S.R.	Norton	1972 J.27	A.J.S.	1981 S.R.	M.M.C.
1972 J.5	Cowles Aermacchi	1973 J.R.	Aermacchi	**Morley, D. K.**		**Mould, John A.**		**Muxlow, Harvey**	
1972 S.R.	Matchless	1974 J.31	Aermacchi	1950 J.20	B.S.A.	1981 J/N.R.	Maxton Yamaha	1970 S.R.	Triumph
1973 J.R.	Yamaha	1975 S.R.	Suzuki	**Morphew, F.**		1981 L.43	Maxton Yamaha	**Mylchreest, Cliff**	
1973 S.24	Harley Davidson	1976 J.40	Suzuki	1961 J.49	A.J.S.	1982 J.12	Maxton Yamaha	1972 J.35	Bultaco
Minchell, John		1978 S.R.	Suzuki	**Morrell, Stuart S.**		**Moule, Albert E.**		1973 J.30	Yamaha
1978 J/N.7	Yamaha	**Moore, J. W.**		1971 J.16	Aermacchi	1946 J.7	Norton	1974 J.24	Yamaha
1980 J.R.	Yamaha	1946 L.7	Excelsior	1972 J.R.	Aermacchi	1946 S.5	Norton	1975 J.25	Yamaha
Minihan, Ned		1947 J.R.	B.S.A.	1973 J.R.	Ducati	1947 J.2	Norton	1976 J.R.	Yamaha
1957 S(N).l	Norton	1947 S.R.	Triumph	1974 J.R.		1947 S.3	Norton	1977 J.R.	Yamaha
1957 S.R.	Norton	1948 J.R.	B.S.A.		Walker Harley Davidson	**Moyce, Asa**		1978 J.11	Yamaha
1958 S.3	Norton	1948 S.30	B.S.A.	1975 J.7	Beart Aermacchi	1975 S.R.	Ducati	1978 S.14	Yamaha
1959 J.13	A.J.S.	1950 J.R.	A.J.S.	1976 J.R.	Beart Aermacchi	1976 S.R.	Yamaha	1979 J.17	Yamaha
1959 S.3	Matchless	1951 J.41	B.S.A.	**Morris, A. R.**		**Moynihan, Steve B.**		1979 S.19	Yamaha
1960 J.R.	A.J.S.	1953 J.23	B.S.A.	1955 J.33	Norton	1969 J.21	Norton	1980 J.10	Yamaha
1960 S.4	Norton	1954 J.R.	B.S.A.	1955 S.28	Norton	1970 J.5	Norton	1980 S.10	Yamaha
1961 J.R.	Norton	**Moore, Michael**		1956 J.R.	Norton	1971 J.1	Aermacchi	1981 L.R.	Yamaha
1961 S.1	Norton	1979 J/N.8	Yamaha	1956 S.28	Norton	1971 S.R.	Norton	1981 J.R.	Yamaha
Minion, F. Peter		1980 S.33	Yamaha	**Morris, F. A. J.**		**Muir, I. R.**		1982 J.6	Yamaha
1955 J.23	B.S.A.	1980 J.R.	Yamaha	1947 J.55	Norton	1950 S.R.	Norton	1982 S.8	Yamaha
1955 S.33	B.S.A.	**Moore, Robert A.**		**Morris, K. C.**		1951 J.R.	Norton		
Minter, Derek		1981 L/N.10	Yamaha	1952 J.30	Norton	1951 S.35	Norton	**Naintre, V. M. L.**	
1955 S.35	B.S.A.	1981 L.47	Yamaha	1952 S.R.	Norton	**Muir, Terry R.**		1956 S.47	B.S.A.
Minto, Roy		1982 J.57	Yamaha	**Morris, T.**		1957 J(N).50	A.J.S.	1957 J.55	B.S.A.
1958 J(Sn).21	Norton	1982 S.57	Yamaha	1954 J .44	B.S.A.	1958 J(Sn).55	A.J.S.	1957 S.R	B.S.A.
1958 J.42	Norton	**Moore, W. R.**		1954 S.8	B.S.A.	1959 J.75	A.J.S.	**Nairn, J. R.**	
1959 J.R.	Norton	1947 S.55	Norton	1955 J.40	B.S.A.	1960 J.45	Norton	1952 J.49	Velocette
1960 J.19	A.J.S.	**Moorhead, M. J.**		1955 S.R.	B.S.A.	1961 J.R.	Norton	**Nanson, Kenneth**	
1961 J.R.	A.J.S.	1972 L.50	Ducati	1956 J.46	B.S.A.	1962 J.R.	Norton	1969 S.36	Velocette
Mitchell, Hugh M.		**Moorhouse, Chris J.**		1956 S.35	B.S.A.	1963 J.47	Norton	1970 S.37	A.J.S.
1971 L.R.	Yamaha	1973 J.39	Aermacchi	**Morrison, Robert**		1964 J.30	Norton	1971 J.R.	A.J.S.
1973 L.26	Yamaha	1974 J.R.	Aermacchi	1982 L/N.R.	Yamaha	**Muirhead, Paul**		1972 S.24	Matchless
Mitchell, Steve		1975 J.R.	Maxton Yamaha	1982 L.R.	Yamaha	1979 J/N.12	Yamaha	1973 S.35	Matchless
1977 J.16	Yamaha	1976 J.14	Duckett Yamaha	**Morss, Gordon**		1980 J.R.	Yamaha	1974 S.31	Matchless
1978 S.R.	Yamaha	1977 L.R.	Yamaha	1978 L.57	Greeves	1980 S.R.	Yamaha	**Naris, H. A.**	
1979 J.R.	Yamaha	**Morecock, P. G. E.**		1980 L.R.	Greeves	1981 S.R.	Yamaha	1952 J.R.	B.S.A.
1979 S.R.	Yamaha	1959 J.57	A.J.S.	1981 L.40	Yamaha	1982 S.R.	Norton	**Nash, David**	
Mizen, W. Sid		1960 J.R.	A.J.S.	1982 L.R.	Yamaha	**Munday, M. W.**		1976 J.R.	Yamaha
1954 J.31	Norton	**Morgan, Alan T.**		1982 J.48	Yamaha	1957 S(N).6	Norton	1977 J.35	Yamaha
1954 S.19	Norton	1966 J.40	A.J.S.	**Mortimer, Charles S.**		1957 S.28	Norton	**Nash, Tony**	
1956 J.12	A.J.S.	1967 J.R.	A.J.S.	1966 L.19	Greeves	1958 S.31	Norton	1974 J.R.	Yamaha
1956 S.21	A.J.S.	1971 S.R.	Matchless	1967 L.57	Greeves	1959 S.45	Norton	**Nayler, B.**	
1957 J.10	A.J.S.	**Morgan, C. L.**		1968 L.5	Aermacchi	1960 S.26	Norton	1959 S.57	Norton
1957 S.13	Norton	1961 S.49	Velocette	1968 S.R.	Greeves	1961 S.29	Norton	**Naylor, Alan**	
Moffatt, Malcolm A. C.		1962 S.R.	Velocette	**Morton, C.**		1962 S.R.	Norton	1982 S/N.R.	Honda
1965 J.R.	B.S.A.	1964 S.11	Norton	1972 S.R.	Seeley	**Mundy, Bill J.**		**Naylor, David A.**	
1966 S.R.	Norton	1965 J.R.	Norton	**Morton, J. D.**		1947 J.36	A.J.S.	1971 J.23	Aermacchi
1968 S.5	Matchless	**Morgan, Dennis E. R.**		1956 J.27	A.J.S.	1947 J.R.	Norton	1972 J.R.	Aermacchi
Moncrieff, D.		1948 J.32	A.J.S.	1957 J.17	B.S.A.	1950 J.R.	Norton	**Neale, J. R.**	
1948 J.54	B.S.A.	1949 J.17	A.J.S.	1957 S.52	B.S.A.	1950 S.32	Norton	1951 S.35	Norton
1949 J.38	A.J.S.	1949 S.8	Norton	1958 J.54	A.J.S.	**Munks, Austin**		**Needle, Barry**	
Monk, Anthony J.		1950 J.18	A.J.S.	1958 S.44	A.J.S.	1947 L.1	Moto Guzzi	1976 J.20	Yamaha
1960 J.40	B.N. Special	1950 S.10	Norton	1959 J.R.	B.S.A.	**Munn, J. C.**		1977 J.7	Yamaha
1961 J.R.	B.N. Special	1951 J.5	A.J.S.	1959 S.R.	B.S.A.	1966 L.R.	Yamaha	**Nelson, A. Martyn**	
1962 J.30	B.N. Special	1951 S.19	Norton	1960 S.35	B.S.A.	1967 L.19	Yamaha	1981 J/N.3	Yamaha
1966 J.R.	B.S.A. Spl.	1952 J.R.	A.J.S.	1961 S.36	Matchless	1968 L.R.	Yamaha	1981 S.20	Yamaha
1966 S.R.	Norton	1952 S.26	A.J.S.	**Morton, R. G.**		**Munro, J. I.**		1982 J.R.	Yamaha
1967 J.R.	B.S.A.	**Morgan, G. H.**		1968 L.46	Ducati	1966 J.32	A.J.S.	1982 S.R.	Yamaha
1968 J.3	B.S.A.	1946 L.11	New Imperial	**Moses, Brian**		1967 J.8	A.J.S.	**Netherwood, W. J.**	
Monnery, Roger		1947 L.R.	New Imperial	1966 S.N.F.	Norton/B.S.A.	**Murden, Rupert C. H.**		1948 J.23	A.J.S.
1973 L.36	Honda	**Morgan, Geoffrey H.**		1967 S.R.	Norton	1973 L.R.	Greeves	1950 J.R.	A.J.S.
		1963 J.40	A.J.S.	1968 J.11	Aermacchi	1976 L.70	Ducati	1951 J.6	Velocette

The History of the Manx Grand Prix 1923-1998 109

Neve, Christopher E.			1973 J.R.	Norton	O'Brien, J. B.		1970 S.3	Norton	Palmer, Peter	
1964 J.45	A.J.S.		1977 L.R.	Yamsel	1961 J.45	Norton	Osborne, N.		1954 J.20	B.S.A.
1965 J.R.	A.J.S.		**Nobbs, David**		**O'Brien, Steve**		1948 S.R.	Triumph	1954 S.R.	B.S.A.
1966 J.47	A.J.S.		1980 L/N.16	Yamaha	1978 S/N.19	Cowles Yamaha	1949 J.58	A.J.S.	**Palmer, S.**	
1966 S.R.	Matchless		1981 J.56	Yamaha	1978 S.61	Cowles Yamaha	**Oscroft, Richard**		1956 J.58	Norton
Neville, Fred A.			1981 L.R.	Yamaha	1979 S.54	Cowles Yamaha	1974 L.28	Yamaha	1956 S.R.	Norton
1960 J.9	Norton		1982 L.37	Yamaha	1980 S.29	Cowles Yamaha	**Oswin, A. J.**		**Pantall, Gordon C.**	
1961 J.R.	A.J.S.		1982 J.51	Yamaha	1980 J.R.	Cowles Yamaha	1967 J.38	A.J.S.	1965 J.11	A.J.S.
Newall, J.			**Noble, Ben**		**O'Callaghan, Fred**		1968 J.43	A.J.S.	1967 J.R.	A.J.S.
1955 S.61	B.S.A.		1964 S.R	B.S.A.	1979 S/N.14	Norton	**Overton, P.**		1967 S.2	Matchless
1956 S.57	B.S.A.		1965 S.42	B.S.A.	1981 S.R.	Triumph	1958 S(Sn).4	B.S.A.	1968 J.2	A.J.S.
1957 S.59	B.S.A.		1966 J.46	Norton	**Odlin, Phillip**		1958 S.R.	B.S.A.	1968 S.R.	Matchless
1958 S.54	B.S.A.		1967 J.32	Norton	1978 S/N.5	Honda	1959 S.R	Norton/B.S.A.	1969 J.R.	A.J.S.
1959 S.R.	B.S.A.		1968 J.46	Norton	**Offer, Clive**		**Owen, B.**		1969 S.2	Matchless
Newcombe, L. C.			1970 J.34	Norton	1965 L.11	Aermacchi	1961 S.64	Norton	1970 J.R.	Padgett Yamaha
1949 J.56	A.J.S.		1971 J.R.	Norton	**Ogden, Ian**		**Owen, C. M.**		1970 S.R.	Cowles Seeley
1949 S.46	A.J.S.		1972 J.26	Norton	1982 S/N.1	Suzuki	1967 S.27	Norton	**Pantlin, Eddie**	
Newell, Tom H.			1973 J.44	Norton	**Older, Derek G.**		1968 S.6	Norton	1951 J.38	A.J.S.
1967 J.R.	A.J.S.		1974 J.44	Norton	1970 J.48	Norton			1952 J.18	A.J.S.
1968 J.R.	Greeves		1975 J.55	Norton	1972 J.R.	Norton	**Packer C. E.**		1952 S.20	Norton
1969 J.10	Aermacchi		1976 J.R.	Norton	1973 S.R.	Norton	1956 S.34	Matchless	**Park, Brian E.**	
1970 S.R.	Monty Triumph		**Mick D.**		1975 J.R.	Maxton Yamaha	1958 J.R.	A.J.S.	1960 S.R.	B.S.A.
1971 S.R.	Norton		1978 L/N.3	Yamaha	1976 S.34	Norton	1958 S.R.	Matchless	1961 S.R.	Norton
1972 J.R.	A.J.S.		1978 S.R.	Suzuki	1977 S.18	Manx Norton	1959 S.21	Matchless	1962 S.R.	Norton
1972 S.4	Norton		1979 L.17	Yamaha	1978 J.R.	Manx Norton	**Padgett, Don**		1963 S.16	Norton
1973 J.R.	Yamaha		1979 J.R.	Yamaha	1979 J.R.	Inwood Yamaha	1964 L.25	Yamaha	1965 S.19	Norton
1973 S.R.	Norton		1980 S.6	Yamaha	1979 S.R.	Inwood Yamaha	1965 L.19	Yamaha	1967 S.8	Norton
1974 S.3	Kettle Norton		1980 J.R.	Yamaha	1980 S.25	Inwood Yamaha	1966 L.R.	Yamaha	**Parker, Colin T.**	
1974 J.R.	Egerton Yamaha		1981 J.R.	Yamaha	1980 J.R.	Inwood Yamaha	1967 L.3	Yamaha	1981 S/N.6	Honda
Newstead, Alan			1981 S.R.	Suzuki	1981 S.35	Manx Norton	1969 L.3	Yamaha	1981 S.R.	Egli Honda
1954 J.34	A.J.S.		1982 J.5	Yamaha	**Oldfield, G. E.**		1969 S.22	Yamaha	1982 J.56	B.S.A.
1955 J.20	A.J.S.		1982 S.31	Suzuki	1958 J(Sn).62	B.S.A.	1970 L.R.	Padgett Yamaha	1982 S.R.	Kawasaki
1956 J.20	A.J.S.		**Nofer, Marek**		1959 S.73	B.S.A.	1970 S.R.	Padgett Yamaha	**Parker, Trevor C.**	
1957 J.18	A.J.S.		1981 J/N.11	Yamaha	1960 S.46	Norton	1971 L.5	Padgett Yamaha	1965 J.11	Norton
1958 J.15	A.J.S.		1982 J.R.	Yamaha	**Oldfield, W. R.**		1971 S.R.	Padgett Yamaha	1966 J.38	Norton
1959 J.R.	Norton		1982 S.39	Yamaha	1954 J.16	A.J.S.	1972 L.5	Yamaha	1967 J.39	Aermacchi
1960 J.I8	A.J.S.		**Normanton, J.**		1954 S.R.	A.J.S.	1972 S.R.	Yamaha	1968 J.36	Aermacchi
1961 J.3	A.J.S.		1957 S(N).20	Norton	1955 J.15	A.J.S.	1973 L.R.	Yamaha	1969 S.23	Aermacchi
Nichol, H.			1957 S.R.	Norton	1955 S.R	A.J.S.	1973 S.R.	Yamaha	1970 J.19	Aermacchi
1957 J(N).6	B.S.A.		**Norris, F.**		**Oldham, Dennis**		1974 L.2	Padgett Yamaha	1970 S.26	Norton
1957 J.R.	B.S.A.		1946 S.R.	Norton	1978 J/N.21	Aermacchi	1974 S.5	Padgett Yamaha	1971 J.8	Aermacchi
Nichol, Ridley			1947 S.R.	Norton	**O'Leary, M.**		1975 L.19	Padgett Yamaha	1971 S.21	Norton
1964 S.R.	B.S.A.		1948 S.24	Norton	1947 L.R.	Endura	1975 S.9	Padgett Yamaha	1972 J.3	Aermacchi
1965 S.60	A.J.S./B.S.A.		1949 J.15	Velocette	**Oliver, David**		1976 L.17	Padgett Yamaha	1972 S.8	Norton
Nichol, Terry			1949 S.18	Norton	1974 J.R.	Yamaha	1976 S.R.	Padgett Yamaha	1973 J.13	Aermacchi
1982 J/N.4	Yamaha		1950 J.R.	Velocette	1975 J.47	Yamaha	1977 L.6	Padgett Yamaha	1973 S.12	Norton
1982 S.28	Yamaha		1950 S.R.	Norton	1976 J.30	Yamaha	1977 S.R.	Padgett Yamaha	1974 J.R.	Mularney Norton
Nicholls, K.			1951 J.R.	Velocette	1977 S.R.	Yamaha	**Padgett, Gary**		1974 S.R.	Mularney Norton
1955 J.R.	B.S.A.		1951 S.12	Norton	1977 J.31	Yamaha	1980 L/N.1	Padgett Yamaha	1976 J.46	
1955 J.52	B.S.A.		**Norris, John F.**		1978 J.R.	Yamaha	1980 L.19	Padgett Yamaha		Dugdale Maxton Yamaha
Nicholls, Phil			1973 S.R.	Matchless	1978 S.R.	Yamaha	**Padgett, Peter**		1976 S.16	
1968 L.43	D.M.W.		1974 L.34	Yamaha	1979 J.R.	Yamaha	1965 L.42	Yamaha		Dugdale Maxton Yamaha
1969 L.14	Greeves		1975 L.R.	Yamaha	1979 S.R.	Yamaha	**Pados, F.**		1977 J.26	Maxton Yamaha
1970 L.8	Ducati/Yamaha		1976 L.R.	Brockliss Yamaha	1980 J.36	Yamaha	1948 J.R.	Norton	1978 S.20	Maxton Yamaha
1971 L.R.	Yamaha		1977 J.R.	Maxton Yamaha	1980 S.32	Yamaha	**Page, D. J.**		1979 J.30	Maxton Yamaha
1972 J.R.	Aermacchi		1978 J.50	Bultaco	**Oliver, G.**		1965 L.40	Bultaco	1979 S.34	Maxton Yamaha
1973 J.R.	Aermacchi		1979 J.R.	Yamaha	1948 J.45	Velocette	1966 L.9	Bultaco	1980 J.48	Maxton Yamaha
1973 S.32	Suzuki		**North, K.**		**Oliver, J. A.**		1967 L.15	Bultaco	1980 S.20	Maxton Yamaha
1974 J.14	McVeigh Yamaha		1959 S.62	Norton	1960 S.47	B.S.A.	1968 L.4	Bultaco	1981 J.30	Maxton Yamaha
1975 S.13	Norton		**Nott, Roger R.**		1961 S.R.	B.S.A.	**Pails, Robert S.**		1981 S.21	Maxton Yamaha
1975 J.R.	Norton		1968 J.40	A.J.S.	1962 S.46	Norton	1968 S.R.	Norton/B.S.A.	1982 J.11	Yamaha
1977 S.R.	Yamaha		1969 J.R.	Bultaco	1965 S.56	H.K.W.	1969 S.R.	Norton/B.S.A.	1982 S.26	Yamaha
1977 L.65	Yamaha		1970 J.27	Bultaco	1966 S.40	H.K.W.	1970 J.46	Aermacchi	**Parkes, Jonathan**	
1978 S.4	Maxton Yamaha		1971 L.15	Yamaha	**Oliver, Roger E.**		1971 J.50	Drixton Aermacchi	1974 S.R.	Matchless
1978 J.R.	Maxton Yamaha		1972 L.16	Yamaha	1977 J.R.	Yamaha	1972 J.39	Aermacchi	1975 S.21	G50Matchless
1979 J.23	Yamaha		1973 L.9	Yamaha	1978 S.33	Yamaha	1973 L.48	Suzuki	1976 S.37	Matchless
1979 S.11	Yamaha		1974 S.R.	Maxton Yamaha	1980 J.46	Yamaha	1974 L.45	Suzuki	**Parkin, O.**	
Nicholls, Roger L.			1974 L.R.	Yamaha	**Ollerenshaw, H. J.**		1975 L.56	Yamaha	1957 J(N).23	B.S.A.
1969 J.22	A.J.S.		1975 S.6	Yamaha	1951 S.46	A.J.S.	1976 J.46	Maxton Yamaha	1957 J.R.	B.S.A.
1970 J.14	A.J.S.		1975 L.4	Yamaha	1952 J.50	A.J.S.	**Pain, Stephen D.**		1958 J.33	Norton
Nicholson, Colin A.			**Nunn, D. G.**		1952 S.R.	Norton	1982 J/N.7	Yamaha	1958 S.55	Norton
1969 J.R.	A.J.S./Norton		1970 L.41	Ducati	**O'Neill, Brian J.**		**Pallister, Terence G.**		**Parkin, Robert K.**	
Nicholson, Robert A.			**Nutter, Jack T.**		1971 S.50	Norton	1964 L16	Cotton	1968 L.R.	Yamaha
1970 L.R.	Greeves		1957 J(N).R.	Norton	1972 S.R.	Norton	1965 L.R.	Cotton	1969 L.R.	Yamaha
1971 L.R.	Greeves		1958 J.21	A.J.S.	**Oram, M. R.**		**Palmer, Alfred J.**		**Parkinson, Dennis**	
1972 L.44	Ducati		1959 J.26	A.J.S.	1957 J(N).17	B.S.A.	1969 S.31	Triumph	1946 J.3	Norton
1973 J.R.	Aermacchi		1959 S.30	A.J.S.	1957 J.58	B.S.A.	1970 S.30	Triumph	1946 S.4	Norton
Nicholson, Bill			1960 J.13	A.J.S.	**Orchard, L. M.**		1971 S.R.	Triumph	1947 J.4	Norton
1947 J.R.	B.S.A.		1960 S.R.	A.J.S.	1965 L.52	Greeves	1972 S.16	Triumph	1947 S.2	Norton
Nightingale, John			1961 J.11	A.J.S.	**de Orfe, G.**		**Palmer, G.**		1948 J.1	Norton
1980 S/N.2	Kerby Honda		1961 S.21	Matchless	1957 J(N).R.	Norton	1957 J(N).39	A.J.S.	1948 S.R.	Norton
1981 S.43	Kerby Honda		1962 J.11	A.J.S.	**Orford, S.**		1960 J.R.	Norton	1949 S.4	Norton
Niven, Ron F.			1962 S.7	Matchless	1947 L.R.	Excelsior	1961 J.16	A.J.S.	1950 S.R.	Norton
1972 J.R.	Yamsel				**Orgee, Martin J.**		1962 J.34	A.J.S.	1951 S.3	Norton

1952 S.8	Norton	**Patrick, D. E.**		1966 J.23	Norton	1961 S.R.	Norton	1973 L.R.	Yamaha
1953 S.1	Norton	1962 S.R.	Matchless	**Peck, R.**		1962 S.47	Norton	**Pink, Anthony P.**	
Parkinson, Ian		**Patrick, John F.**		1965 J.49	A.J.S.	1963 S.R.	Norton	1967 L.R.	Greeves
1975 J.39	Yamaha	1957 J(N).21	Norton-Velocette	**Pellow, Mike C.**		1964 J.28	Norton	1969 L.54	Yamaha
1976 J.R.	Yamaha	1957 J.43	Norton-Velocette	1981 S/N.1	Yamaha	1964 S. R.	Norton	1970 L.R.	Yamaha
1977 J.R.	Yamaha	1958 J.31	Norton-Velocette	**Pemberton, Tom**		1965 J.28	Norton	1971 J.42	Yamaha
1979 J.60	Yamaha	1958 S.41	Norton-Velocette	1977 S.R.	Kawasaki	1965 S.R.	Norton	**Pink, Ted T.**	
1980 J.50	Yamaha	1959 J.50	Velocette	1978 J.33	Kawasaki	1966 J.42	Norton	1946 L.R.	Excelsior
Parkinson, J.		**Patrick, Ken H.**		1978 S.31	Kawasaki	1966 S.R.	Norton	1947 L.12	Excelsior
1957 J(N).R.	A.J.S.	1955 J.21	B.S.A.	**Pemberton, William J.**		**Pettit, J. H.**		1947 S.23	Norton
Parkinson, N. R.		1955 S.14	B.S.A.	1981 S/N.7	Norton	1946 S.24	Norton	1948 S.14	A.J.S.
1960 S.54	B.S.A.	1956 J.R.	B.S.A.	**Pendlebury, Daryl**		1947 J.34	Norton	1948 S.R.	Norton
Parris, Lawrence		1956 S.11	B.S.A.	1967 S.R.	Norton	1947 S.28	Norton	1949 J.10	A.J.S.
1977 J.38	Aermacchi	1957 J.R.	Norton	1968 S.R.	Norton	1948 J.R.	Norton	1949 S.13	Norton
1978 J.R.	Aermacchi	1957 S.R.	Norton	**Pendreigh, Neil L.**		**Petty, Ray J. A.**		**Pinks, Kenny**	
1979 J.R.	Aermacchi	**Patt, Derwent**		1960 J.38	Norton	1946 L.5	New Imperial	1980 J/N.R.	Yamaha
Parrish, Steve		1980 J/N.9	Yamaha	1961 J.15	Norton	1946 S.R.	Norton	1981 S.13	Yamaha
1974 L.7	Revett Yamaha	1981 J.R.	Yamaha	1962 J.R.	Norton	1947 L.4	E.M.C.	1981 S.13	Yamaha
1975 J.R.	Coppock Yamaha	1982 J.43	Maxton Yamaha	1962 S.14	Matchless	**Peverett, L.**		1982 J.19	Yamaha
1975 S.R.	Yamaha	**Paulson, D. E.**		1963 J.45	Norton	1948 J.20	Norton	1982 S.R.	Yamaha
Parrott, Philip J.		1968 S.R.	Seeley G50	1963 S.R.	Matchless	**Phillips, A. M.**		**Pither, Dave**	
1980 L/N.13	Yamaha	**Payne, Ginger J. L.**		1964 J.6	Norton	1952 S.12	Norton	1974 J.R.	Norton
1981 L.34	Muffitt Yamaha	1958 J(Sn).2	Norton	1964 S.R.	Matchless	1953 S.12	Norton	1975 S.29	Kettle Norton
1982 L.31	Yamaha	1958 J.26	Norton	1966 J.R.	Norton	1954 J.6	Norton	1976 S.R.	Yamaha
Parry, A. Len		1959 J.22	Norton	1966 S.12	Norton	1954 S.5	Norton	1977 S.R.	Manx Norton
1948 L.R.	New Imperial	1959 S.R.	Norton	1968 J.21	A.J.S.	**Phillips, Alan J.**		1978 S.3	Yamaha
Parry, David		1960 J.7	A.J.S.	1968 S.R.	Norton	1978 L/N.7	Craig Yamaha	1979 J.R.	Yamaha
1973 S.44	Norton	1960 S.R.	Matchless	**Penfold, Brian E.**		1978 L.31	Craig Yamaha	1979 S.20	Yamaha
1974 J.34	Aermacchi	**Payne, K. A.**		1968 J.28	A.J.S.	1980 J.33	Yamaha	1981 J.R.	Yamaha
1975 S.30	Norton	1958 J(Sn).18	A.J.S.	1969 J.R.	A.J.S.	1980 S.34	Yamaha	1981 S.8	Suzuki
1976 J.34	Yamaha	1958 J.R.	A.J.S.	1970 J.23	A.J.S.	1981 J.R.	Yamaha	1982 J.R.	Yamaha
1977 J.33	Aermacchi	1960 S.R.	A.J.S.	1971 J.R.	Norton	1981 S.27	Yamaha	1982 S.R.	Suzuki
1978 J.R.	Suzuki	1961 J.R.	A.J.S.	1971 S.32	Norton	1982 S.56	Norton	**Pitt, Ernie T. J.**	
1979 L.34	Yamaha	**Payze, Ian M.**		1972 J.R.	Kettle Norton	**Phillips, Derek W.**		1967 S.R.	Triton
1980 L.22	Yamaha	1965 J.58	B.S.A.	1974 S.R.	Norton	1959 S.32	Norton	1970 S.20	Norton
1981 L.19	Yamaha	1969 J.R.	A.J.S.	1975 S.28	Kettle Norton	1961 S.R.	Norton	1971 J.21	Norton
1982 J.R.	Yamaha	**Peacock, E.**		1976 S.R.	Norton	1962 S.R.	Norton	1971 S.R.	Norton
1982 S.R.	Yamaha	1955 J.64	B.S.A.	1977 S.R.	Kettle Norton	1963 J.28	Norton	1972 J.R.	Norton
Parsonage, Colin A.		1956 S.R.	B.S.A.	**Penny, R. J.**		1963 S.R.	Norton	1972 S.6	Norton
1957 J(N).26	B.S.A.	**Peacock, T. G. J.**		1948 L.R.	Excelsior	**Phillips, John D.**		1973 J.R.	Norton
1958 J.37	Norton	1955 J.53	A.J.S.	1951 S.63	Norton	1982 L/N.18	Yamaha	1973 S.4	Norton
1959 S.39	Norton	**Peake, I. N. D.**		**Pennington, J. Grenville**		1982 L.56	Haigh Yamaha	**Pitt, K. E.**	
1962 J.55	Norton	1966 L.16	Royal Enfield	1955 J.58	A.J.S.	**Phillips, Maurice**		1958 J(Sn).7	Norton
Parsons, G. F.		**Pearce, David A.**		1955 S.R.	A.J.S.	1975 L.49	Ducati	1958 J.28	Norton
1947 J.7	Norton	1968 S.3	Petty Norton	1956 J.R.	A.J.S.	**Phillips, P. L.**		**Pladdys, Ron F.**	
1947 S.16	Norton	1969 S.24	Petty Norton	**Pennycook, R.**		1948 J.R.	A.J.S.	1964 L.10	Honda
Parsons, Laurie D. S.		1970 J.24	Petty Norton	1947 J.R.	Norton	**Phillips, R. G.**		1965 L.6	Honda
1970 J.R.	A.J.S.	1970 S.4	Petty Norton	**Penson, G. K.**		1948 S.R.	Scott	1967 L.R.	Yamaha
1973 S.53	Norton	**Pearce, Graham**		1957 J(N).R.	Velocette	**Phillips, Tom R.**		1968 L.R.	Yamaha
Parsons, Len W.		1975 J.R.	Yamaha	1958 J(Sn).8	Velocette	1962 J.R.	Norton	**Plenderleith, Archie**	
1946 L.1	Rudge	1976 J.R.	Maxton	1958 J.R.	Velocette	**Phillipson, T. H.**		1964 L.R.	Honda
1947 L.R.	Rudge	1977 J.30	Maxton	**Penton, H. R.**		1955 J.59	A.J.S.	**Plews, Harry**	
Parton, Ken		**Pearce, Harry A.**		1948 L.R.	Endura	1955 S.56	A.J.S.	1951 J.21	Norton
1977 L.50	Yamaha	1948 L.R.	Excelsior	1949 J.62	Norton	1956 J.R.	A.J.S.	1953 J.18	Norton
1979 L.47	Yamaha	1949 J.48	Norton	1950 J.R.	A.J.S.	1956 S.38	A.J.S.	1953 S.13	Norton
Partridge, Michael A. R.		1951 J.9	Velocette	1950 S.21	A.J.S.	1957 J.16	A.J.S.	**Plummer, David**	
1971 L.46	Greeves	1951 S.9	Velocette	**Pepper, John R.**		1957 S.42	A.J.S.	1982 L/N.17	Yamaha
Passmore, F. J.		1952 J.5	Velocette	1961 J.R.	A.J.S.	**Pickering, David J.**		**Polak, R.**	
1950 S.20	Norton	1952 S.7	Norton	**Pepper, Mick J.**		1970 S.43	Daytona	1958 J(Sn).42	Norton
1951 S.30	Velocette	**Pearson, Alan**		1972 J.R.	Yamaha	1976 S.R.	Yamaha	1959 S.R.	Norton
1952 S.37	Norton	1979 J/N.13	Yamaha	**Perks, L.**		**Pickrell, Ray**		1960 J.52	Norton
Paterson, Clifford		**Pearson, Colin**		1950 J.R.	Velocette	1967 S.R.	Triumph	**Pope, Maurice W.**	
1976 L.28	Yamsel	1980 S/N.5	Yamaha	**Perrier, R.**		**Pidcock, Ian**		1965 J.26	A.J.S.
1978 L.1	Yamaha	1980 S.41	Suzuki	1968 J.R.	Norton	1976 S.49	Seeley Suzuki	1966 J.R.	A.J.S.
Paterson, George		1981 J.R.	Intervend Yamaha	**Perry, D. L. E.**		1977 S.R.	Seeley Suzuki	**Porteous, Gavin C.**	
1972 J.38	Aermacchi	1981 S.28	Suzuki	1953 J.R.	A.J.S.	1978 S.R.	Aermacchi	1960 J.R.	B.S.A.
1973 J.45	Aermacchi	1982 J.30	Yamaha	1954 J.R.	A.J.S.	**Piles, Rex**		**Porter, Alan A.**	
1974 J.42	Yamsel	1982 S.37	Suzuki	1955 J.R.	B.S.A.	1973 L.R.	Greeves	1968 J.R.	A.J.S.
1975 J.57	Yamsel	**Pearson, John P.**		1957 J.R.	A.J.S.	1974 J.R.	Arter A.J.S.	1970 J.R.	A.J.S.
1976 J.39	Yamaha	1982 L/N.9	Yamaha	**Petch, Bill**		1975 J.R.	Aermacchi	1971 J.17	Aermacchi
1977 J.28	Yamaha	1982 L.33	Yamaha	1947 J.32	Velocette	**Pilling, Dave**		1971 S.R.	Norton
1978 J.26	Yamaha	**Pearson, Kevin M.**		**Peters, J. Brian**		1958 J(Sn).46	A.J.S.	1972 J.R.	Norton
1978 S.39	Yamaha	1981 S/N.R.	Suzuki	1969 S.R.	Norton	1959 J.61	A.J.S.	1972 S.R.	Norton
1979 J.R.	Yamaha	1981 L.26	Yamaha	1970 S.31	Norton	1960 S.43	A.J.S.	1973 J.R.	Norton
1979 S.R.	Suzuki	1982 S.60	Suzuki	1971 S.R.	Norton	1961 J.R.	Norton	1976 J.R.	Aermacchi
1980 J.R.	Yamaha	**Pearson, Michael N.**		1972 S.R.	Norton	1962 J.R.	A.J.S.	**Porter, Harvey**	
1980 S.R.	Suzuki	1965 L.R.	Bultaco	1973 S.7	Suzuki	1963 J.58	A.J.S.	1968 S.28	Norton
1981 J.34	Maxton	1966 L.R.	Bultaco	1974 J.12	Vincent Yamaha	**Pinch, George**		1969 S.R.	Norton
1981 S.R.	Suzuki	1967 L.R.	Bultaco	1974 S.4	Vincent Suzuki	1975 L.15	Yamaha	1970 S.13	Norton
1982 S.R.	Suzuki	1968 L.16	Bultaco	1975 J.R.	Yamaha	**Pinckard, A. D.**		1971 J.12	Kawasaki
Paterson, J. L.		1969 L.20	Shepherd	1975 S.R.	McVeigh Yamaha	1950 S.56	A.J.S.	1971 S.R.	Norton
1946 L.12	New Imperial	**Peatman, W. A.**		**Peters, John R.**		1951 J.R.	A.J.S.	**Porter, L. S.**	
Paterson, Kenneth		1958 J(Sn).57	Norton	1966 S.47	Velocette	**Piner, Eric R.**		1968 J.R.	Norton
1976 L.34	Yamaha	**Peck, Alan C.**		**Pettifer, Donald J.**		1972 L.14	Yamaha	**Porter, Ross W.**	

The History of the Manx Grand Prix 1923-1998 111

1951 S.34	A.J.S.	1957 J.R.	Norton	**Radcliffe, Gary**		**Rawlinson, A.**		1978 L/N.R.	Yamaha
1952 J.27	A.J.S.	1958 S.19	Norton	1979 J/N.4	Yamaha	1970 L.44	Ducati	1979 L.R.	Yamaha
1952 S.36	A.J.S.	**Prentice, G. C.**		1979 S.25	Yamaha	**Ray, D.**		1980 J.R.	Yamaha
Potter, Alan		1959 J.51	Norton-B.S.A.	1980 J.9	Yamaha	1958 J(Sn).48	Norton	1980 S.2	Cowles Suzuki
1981 S/N.14	Yamaha	1960 J.48	Norton-B.S.A.	1980 S.13	Yamaha	1959 S.R.	Norton	**Reid, D.**	
1982 L.R.	Yamaha	1962 J.R.	A.J.S.	1981 J.R.	Yamaha	**Ray, P.**		1963 J.41	Norton
1982 J.53	Yamaha	**Prentice, M.**		1981 S.R.	Yamaha	1968 L.R.	Aermacchi	1963 S.13	Norton
Potter, Don		1965 L.38	Cotton	1982 J.2	Fowler Yamaha	**Raybon, David**		1964 J.8	Norton
1978 J/N.R.	Yamaha	**Price, C. A.**		1982 S.2	Fowler Yamaha	1979 S/N.1	Yamaha	1964 S.R.	Norton
1978 S.R.	Yamaha	1960 J.R.	A.J.S.	**Radford, B. S.**		1980 J.29	Grasmere Yamaha	**Reid, Geoff G.**	
1979 S.28	Yamaha	1961 J.R.	A.J.S.	1953 J.43	Velocette	1980 S.R.	Grasmere Yamaha	1965 J.R.	A.J.S.
1980 J.R.	Yamaha	1962 J.R.	Norton	**Rae, Alastair J.**		**Raybould, John B.**		1966 J.28	A.J.S.
1981 S.51	Yamaha	1963 J.49	Norton	1982 L/N.R.	Yamaha	1981 S/N.3	Yamaha	**Reid, Paddy H.**	
Potter, J. C.		**Price, G. G.**		1982 L.10	Yamaha	**Rayner, Harry W.**		1972 L.8	Yamaha
1947 J.60	Norton	1960 J.R.	A.J.S.	**Rae, Bill**		1959 J.54	A.J.S.	1973 L.2	Yamaha
1947 S.R.	Norton	**Price, L.**		1959 J.38	A.J.S.	1960 J.32	A.J.S.	1973 S.1	Yamaha
Potter, William H.		1947 L.R.	Excelsior	**Rae, James S.**		1962 J.29	A.J.S.	**Reilly, Vincent**	
1966 L.R.	Ducati	**Price, Norman J.**		1959 J.25	Norton	**Raynor, A.**		1957 J(N).R.	B.S.A.
Potts, Stephen		1952 S.49	Norton	**Rae, Ronnie C.**		1952 J.R.	Velocette	1958 J(Sn).28	A.J.S.
1978 S/N.17	Yamaha	1953 S.23	Norton	1964 L.R.	Velocette	1953 J.38	Velocette	1958 S.46	A.J.S.
Povey, Laurence G.		1954 J.29	Velocette	1965 J.R.	A.J.S.	1954 J.49	A.J.S.	1959 J.52	A.J.S.
1951 J.66	Norton	1954 S.R.	Norton	1966 J.R.	A.J.S.	1958 J.53	A.J.S.	**Reilly, Wilf**	
1954 J.47	B.S.A.	1955 J.27	Velocette	**Raineri, L. G.**		1958 S.52	A.J.S.	1955 S.62	Norton
1954 S.R.	B.S.A.	1956 J.25	Velocette	1947 L.16	Excelsior	**Raynor, Brian**		**Rennie, Tony**	
1956 J.45	B.S.A.	1957 S.10	Norton	**Ralston, Frank**		1981 J/N.R.	Aermacchi	1978 J/N.5	Foale Yamaha
1956 S.37	B.S.A.	1958 J.9	Norton	1971 S.R.	Norton	1982 J.R.	Aermacchi	1978 S.R.	Foale Yamaha
1957 J.R.	B.S.A.	1958 S.37	Norton	1972 S.R.	Norton	1982 S.R.	Honda	1979 L.R.	Yamaha
1957 S.35	B.S.A.	1959 J.R.	Norton	1974 S.R.	Seeley Metisse	**Raynor, John B.**		1979 J.R.	Yamaha
Powell, Derek T.		1959 S.12	Norton	**Ramsay, Eric**		1971 J.R.	Norton/B.S.A.	**Rensen, Ralph B.**	
1953 J.3	Norton	1960 J.N.F.	A.J.S.	1971 J.22	A.J.S.	1972 J.R.	Norton/B.S.A.	1953 J.R.	Velocette
1953 S.6	Norton	1960 S.7	Norton	1972 J.30	Norton	1973 J.34	Aermacchi	1954 J.14	A.J.S.
1954 J.5	Norton	1961 J.R.	A.J.S.	1973 J.R.	A.J.S.	1974 J.32	Aermacchi	1954 S.R.	A.J.S.
1954 S.2	Norton	1961 S.5	Norton	1974 J.R.	A.J.S.	**Read, G. E.**		**Renton, Stephen**	
Powell, Martin J.		1962 J.R.	Norton	1975 J.41	A.J.S. 7R	1961 S.8	Norton	1980 S/N.4	Honda
1967 L.24	Honda	1962 S.6	Norton	1976 S.24	Seeley	**Read, Martin N.**		**Revett, Chris P.**	
1968 J.27	Norton	**Prince, K. R. E. 'Kel'**		1977 S.24	Seeley	1971 J.14	Aermacchi	1972 L.25	Yamaha
1969 J.40	Norton	1952 J.21	A.J.S.	1978 S.29	Seeley	1972 J.R.	Yamaha	1973 L.5	Yamaha
1973 S.49	Norton	1952 S.30	A.J.S.	1979 S.47	Seeley	**Read, Phil W.**		1974 L.8	Revett Yamaha
1974 S.16	Honda	**Proctor, E.**		**Randle, Tony**		1958 J(Sn).3	Norton	1974 S.8	Revett Yamaha
1975 S.R.	Honda	1947 J.22	Norton	1971 J.36	Norton	1958 J.17	Norton	1975 J.11	Maxton Yamaha
Powell, Robert J.		1950 S.R.	Norton	1972 J.R.	Norton	1959 J.7	Norton	1975 S.11	Maxton Yamaha
1979 S/N.13	Sparton	**Proctor, Geoffrey**		1973 J.6	Yamaha	1959 S.13	Norton	1976 J.31	Revett Yamaha
1981 S.R.	Yamaha	1966 L.25	Cotton	1974 J.R.	Yamaha	1960 J.R.	Norton	1976 S.R.	Revett Yamaha
Powis, Clive H.		**Proctor, John H.**		1974 S.R.	Yamaha	1960 S.1	Norton	**Revett, Jerry**	
1975 L.30	Yamaha	1962 J.R.	Norton	1975 J.5	Yamaha	**Read, Thomas H.**		1976 L.27	Maxton Yamaha
1976 L.R.	Yamaha	1963 S.45	Norton	1975 S.R.	Yamaha	1963 S.27	Norton	**Reynolds, Andy**	
1977 L.39	Yamaha	**Protheroe, Brian**		**Ranson Humphrey B.**		1964 S.R.	Norton	1978 J/N.19	Aermacchi
1979 L.33	Yamaha	1975 L.47	Honda	1947 J.42	Norton	1965 S.R.	Norton	**Reynolds, Frank**	
1982 L.8	Yamaha	1976 J.56	Honda	1947 S.42	Norton	**Redfern, Ken A.**		1958 J.R.	Norton
Poxon, Michael E.		1978 J.R.	Rickman Honda	**Ranson Llewelyn B.**		1968 J.R.	Norton	1959 J.16	Norton
1970 J.R.	Norton	1979 J.R.	Rickman Honda	1946 S.21	Norton	**Redford, M.**		1960 J.R.	A.J.S.
1972 S.32	Suzuki	1980 S.R.	Suzuki	1947 J.23	Norton	1957 S(N).15	Norton	1960 S.15	A.J.S.
1973 S.6	Suzuki	1982 S.R.	Suzuki	1947 S.27	Norton	1957 S.R.	Norton	1961 J.1	A.J.S.
Prange, Alan D.		**Proudman, Dennis**		**Rapley, Dennis W.**		1958 J.52	Norton	1961 S.R.	Norton
1964 S.17	Matchless	1969 S.R.	Norton	1970 L.48	Ducati	1958 S.R.	Norton	**Reynolds, H. R.**	
1965 S.25	Matchless	1971 S.52	Norton	1971 L.39	Ducati	**Redman, F.**		1960 J.62	A.J.S.
Pratt, Bob		1972 S.R.	Norton	1972 L.30	M.W. Ducati	1955 S.45	Norton	1964 J.52	A.J.S.
1947 J.28	Norton	1973 S.50	Norton	1973 L.R.	Ducati	1957 J.R.	A.J.S.	**Rhodes, Ivan**	
1947 S.43	Norton	**Prudence, M. B.**		1974 L.38	Walker Ducati	1957 S.R.	A.J.S.	1955 J.37	A.J.S.
1948 J.27	Norton	1950 S.22	Norton	1975 L.R.	Yamaha	**Reed, W. C.**		1955 S.38	A.J.S.
1948 S.9	Norton	1951 S.18	Norton	1977 L.67	Yamaha	1946 J.21	Norton	**Rice, J. Melvyn**	
1949 J.8	Velocette	**Pullen, George A.**		**Ratcliffe, G. A.**		1946 S.R.	Norton	1963 J.61	A.J.S.
1949 S.R.	Norton	1966 L.R.	D.M.W.	1967 J.R.	Bultaco	1947 J.R.	Norton	1965 J.R.	A.J.S.
1950 J.29	Velocette	**Purnell, J. E. C.**		**Ratcliffe, K.**		1947 S.R.	Norton	**Rice, Bill**	
1950 S.R.	Norton	1946 J.10	Norton	1951 J.54	A.J.S.	**Rees, Dave**		1977 J.44	Yamaha
Pratt, C.		1946 S.26	Norton	1953 J.R.	B.S.A.	1973 L.R.	Ducati	1978 S.34	Yamaha
1954 J.48	A.J.S.	1947 J.3	Velocette	1953 S.36	B.S.A.	1974 S.R.	Drixton Aermacchi	1979 J.37	Inglewood Yamaha
Pratt, Dennis		1947 S.15	Velocette	1954 J.45	Norton	1975 S.R.		1979 S.38	Inglewood Yamaha
1957 J(N).1	A.J.S.	**Purslow, Brian**		1954 S.R.	Norton		Lawton Drixton Aermacchi	1980 S.65	Inglewood Zeger
1957 J.14	A.J.S.	1952 J.37	Earles-B.S.A.	1955 J.38	Norton	1976 J.26	Baco Yamaha	1981 S.R.	Inglewood Zeger
1958 J.R.	Norton	1952 S.18	Earles-B.S.A.	1955 S.27	Matchless	1977 J.15	Baco Yamaha	1982 S.47	Inglewood Zeger
1958 S.22	Norton	**Purslow, Fron**		1956 J.R.	Norton	1977 S.R.	Baco Yamaha	**Richards, Brian**	
1959 J.11	Norton	1948 J.42	B.S.A.	1956 S.R.	Norton	1978 J.R.	Baco Yamaha	1961 S.50	Matchless
1959 S.9	Norton	**Pusey, Fred**		1957 S.58	Norton	1978 S.25	Baco Yamaha	1962 J.20	A.J.S.
1961 J.4	Norton	1951 S.R.	Norton	**Ravenscroft, Neil**		1979 J.26	Yamaha	**Richards, Ian F.**	
1961 S.10	Norton	1952 J.R.	Norton	1969 J.57	A.J.S.	1979 S.24	Yamaha	1967 L.11	Greeves
Pratt, P. L.		1952 S.R.	Norton	1970 J.R.	Aermacchi	**Rees, E**		1968 L.R.	Yamaha
1949 J.R.	Velocette			1971 J.11	Yamsel	1952 J.R.	A.J.S.	**Richards, P.**	
1950 J.29	Velocette	**Quirk, P. Q.**		1976 J.43	Yamaha	1952 S.29	A.J.S.	1967 L.R.	Greeves
1950 S.R.	Velocette	1953 S.R.	B.S.A	1977 J.R.	Yamaha	**Reeve, William**		1968 L.41	Greeves
Pratt, T. W.				1978 J.22	Yamaha	1946 L.R.	Excelsior	**Richardson, Dennis**	
1962 J.R.	Norton	**Racle, C. F.**		1979 J.R.	Yamaha	**Regen, Ken**		1972 S.36	Norton
Preece, R.		1947 S.60	Norton	**Rawlings, A. W.**		1974 L.57	Montesa	1973 S.21	Norton
1957 J(N).3	Norton	1948 L.8	Excelsior	1959 S.54	A.J.S.	**Reid, Brian**		1974 J.11	Yamsel

112 The History of the Manx Grand Prix 1923-1998

1974 S.R.	Seeley	1976 J.3	Fowler Yamaha	1948 J.59	A.J.S.	**Robson, Bryan**		**Rose, Doug R.**	
Richardson, M.		1976 S.R.	Fowler Yamaha	**Robertson, N.**		1974 L.30	Yamaha	1952 J.R.	B.S.A.
1952 J.R.	A.J.S.	1977 J.1	Beresford Yamaha	1958 J(Sn).49	B.S.A.	1975 L.12	Yamaha	1964 L.27	Honda
1952 S.R	A.J.S.	1977 S.R.	Beresford Yamaha	**Robertson, W.**		1976 L.2	Yamaha	**Rose, Richard W.**	
Richardson, Paul F. D.		**Ritchie, Bob C.**		1967 L.26	Greeves	1976 S.R.	Yamaha	1979 L/N.12	Yamsel
1962 S.R.	Norton	1952 J.9	A.J.S.	1968 L.R.	Suzuki	1977 L.R.	Yamaha	1980 S.27	Fahron
1963 J.R.	B.S.A.	1952 S.11	A.J.S.	**Robinson, Brian**		1977 S.R.	Yamaha	1981 S.57	Fahron
1963 S.R.	Norton	1953 J.4	A.J.S.	1971 L.27	Yamaha	1978 L.R.	Harris Yamaha	1982 S.35	Mafahron
Richardson, Peter E.		1953 S.R.	Matchless	1972 L.R.	Yamaha	1978 J.R.	Maxton Yamaha	**Rose, Stephen R.**	
1958 S(Sn).l	Norton	1957 J.8	A.J.S.	1973 L.23	Yamaha	**Rock, Trevor**		1978 L/N.R.	Ducati
1958 S.R.	Norton	1957 S.R.	Matchless	1974 L.12	Yamaha	1974 L.65	Aermacchi	1979 L.63	Ducati
1959 J.R.	A.J.S.	1958 J.6	A.J.S.	1975 L.16	Yamaha	**Rodda, L. G.**		1980 S.60	Suzuki
1959 S.R.	Norton	1958 S.R.	Matchless	1976 L.22	Yamaha	1961 J.37	A.J.S.	1982 L.R.	Goddard Special
Richardson, Stephen		1959 J.3	A.J.S.	1976 S.3	Yamaha	**Roden, John**		**Rowbottom, R. A.**	
1980 S/N.1	Yamaha	1959 S.8	Matchless	1977 L.19	Maxton Yamaha	1975 L.R.	Ducati	1951 S.17	Triumph
1981 S.6	Suzuki	1960 J.6	A.J.S.	1977 S.R.	Yamaha	**Rodger, Anthony B.**		**Rowe, R. E.**	
1982 J.R.	Yamaha	1960 S.8	Norton	1978 J.R.	Yamaha	1970 J.R.	Aermacchi	1960 S.10	Norton
1982 S.5	Suzuki	1961 J.9	Norton	1978 S.R.	Yamaha	1971 S.11	Seeley	**Rowe, Raymond**	
Riches, James J.		1961 S.9	Norton	1979 J.21	Yamaha	**Roebuck, Brian**		1962 S.26	Norton
1963 J.16	Norton	**Roantree, Aiden**		1979 S.R.	Yamaha	1972 S.31	Norton	1963 S.R.	Norton
1964 J.7	Norton	1977 J.R.	Foale Yamaha	1980 J.14	Yamaha	1973 S.R.	Suzuki	**Rowell, Harold M.**	
1964 S.R.	Norton	**Roberton, W.**		1980 S.R.	Yamaha	**Roebury, Ron C.**		1946 J.4	Norton
1965 J.25	Norton	1954 J.20	B.S.A.	1981 J.R.	Yamaha	1978 S/N.R.	Curry Honda	1946 S.3	Norton
1965 S.44	Norton	1954 S.R.	B.S.A.	1982 S.2	Yamaha	1979 J.45	Curry Honda	**Rowlands, Ron**	
1980 J.R.	Yamaha	**Roberts, Barry**		**Robinson, C.E.**		1979 S.R.	Curry Honda	1969 L.56	Yamaha/Ducati
1980 L.25	Yamaha	1974 J.R.	Yamaha	1962 J.R.	Honda	1980 J.R.	Honda	1971 L.R.	Yamaha
Richmond, Adrian N.		1975 J.35	Yamaha	**Robinson, D. P.**		1980 S.R.	Honda	1972 L.R.	Yamaha
1971 S.45	Norton	1976 J.23	Yamaha	1967 L.29	Bultaco	**Rogers, Alan E.**		1973 L.19	Yamaha
1972 S.43	Norton	**Roberts, Brian**		**Robinson, Don**		1966 S.R.	Norton	1974 L.22	Yamaha
1973 S.36	Norton	1981 J/N.12	Yamaha	1977 L.R.	Yamaha	1968 S.R.	Norton	1975 L.13	Artdean Yamaha
1974 S.34	Norton	**Roberts, C. A. H.**		1978 L.R.	Yamaha	1970 S.5	Matchless	1976 L.19	Artdean Yamaha
Rickard, K.		1946 L.R.	New Imperial	**Robinson, G.W.**		1971 J.3	Seeley	1976 S.R.	Artdean Yamaha
1950 J.R.	A.J.S.	1947 L.R.	New Imperial	1947 J.39	Velocette	1971 S.8	Manx Norton	1977 L.21	Yamaha
Ridge, Maxwell D.		1948 J.62	A.J.S.	1947 S.R.	Velocette	1972 J.R.	Seeley	1977 S.R.	Yamaha
1973 L.38	Ducati	1949 J.R.	New Imperial	1948 J.R.	A.J.S.	1972 S.R.	Seeley	1978 L.14	Yamaha
1974 L.49	Ducati	1952 J.64	B.S.A.	1949 J.20	A.J.S.	1973 J.R.	Yamaha	1978 J.R.	Yamaha
Ridgeon, George F.		**Roberts, David**		1949 S.R.	Norton	1973 S.R.	Suzuki	**Rowles, R. J. E.**	
1971 L.41	Greeves	1974 J.R.	Yamaha	1950 J.10	Velocette	**Rogers, Brian E.**		1958 J(Sn).53	Velocette
1972 L.24	Greeves	1975 S.55	Yamaha	1950 S.23	Triumph	1964 J.R.	Norton	**Roxburgh, Ken**	
1973 S.R.	Matchless	1976 S.R.	Hartley Suzuki	1951 J.R	Norton	1965 J.R.	Norton	1978 S.R.	Yamaha
1974 S.36	Matchless	1977 S.R.	Yamaha	1951 S.16	Norton	1966 J.53	A.J.S.	**Royle, William D.**	
1975 S.R.	Matchless	**Roberts, David, J.**		**Robinson, J. B.**		1966 S.R.	Norton	1967 L.53	D.M.W.
1976 S.23	Seeley	1978 S/N.18	Honda	1961 J.R.	B.S.A.	1967 S.R.	Norton	1968 L.R.	D.M.W.
1977 S.46	Seeley G50	1978 S.59	Honda	1962 J.61	B.S.A.	**Rogers, F.**		1970 L.R.	Suzuki
1978 L.54	Greeves	1979 S.58	Honda	**Robinson, John**		1951 J.R.	B.S.A.	1971 L.R.	Suzuki
1978 J.30	Seeley G50	1980 S.55	Honda	1975 S.31	Honda	**Rogers, H.**		1973 L.47	Suzuki
1979 L.R.	Greeves	1981 L.28	Yamaha	1976 L.9	Yamaha	1948 J.R.	Norton	1974 L.R.	Suzuki
1979 J.59	Seeley	1982 L.R.	Yamaha	1977 J.5	Yamaha	1950 J.50	Norton	1975 L.R.	Yamaha
1980 J.57	Greeves	1982 J.R.	Yamaha	1977 S.7	Yamaha	1951 J.R.	Norton	1976 L.R.	Yamaha
1980 S.56	Seeley	**Roberts, Eddie**		1978 S.R.	Yamaha	**Rogers, Richard O.**		1977 L.64	Yamaha
1981 S.39	Seeley	1971 L.22	Marriott	1979 J.5	Yamaha	1974 S.25	Seeley	1978 L.56	Yamaha
Ridley, J. A.		1972 L.R.	Yamaha	1979 S.4	Yamaha	1976 S.8	Matchless Metisse	1979 L.59	Yamaha
1965 L.27	Greeves	1973 L.3	Yamaha	**Robinson, Mick, S.**		1977 J.R.	Yamaha	1980 L.38	Yamaha
Rigby, Dennis		1974 L.1		1977 L.15	Yamaha	1977 S.R.	Yamaha	1981 L.R.	Spondon Yamaha
1957 J(N).12	B.S.A.		Dugdale Maxton Yamaha	1978 L.20	Yamaha	1978 J.R.	Yamaha	**Rudd, Gerald B.**	
1957 J.R.	B.S.A.	1974 S.R.		1978 J.15	Yamaha	1978 S.R.	Yamaha	1959 J.R.	B.S.A.
1958 J.R.	B.S.A.		Dugdale Maxton Yamaha	1982 S.R.	Honda	1979 J.42	Yamaha	1960 J.R.	Norton/B.S.A.
1958 S.R.	B.S.A.	**Roberts, John**		**Robinson, Michael**		1980 J.43	Yamaha	**Rudge, John G.**	
Rigg, John T.		1977 J.46	Aermacchi	1979 L/N.R.	Yamsel	1980 S.R.	Matchless	1963 S.R.	Norton
1970 J.R.	Norton	1978 J.R.	Aermacchi	**Robinson, M.**		1981 J.R.	Yamaha	**Rudge, Ron H.**	
1971 J.R.	Norton	**Roberts, R. A.**		1972 J.R.	A.J.S.	1981 S.17	Yamaha	1946 L.R.	Cotton
1973 S.R.	Weslake	1961 S.35	B.S.A.	**Robinson, R. A.**		1982 J.13	Yamaha	1947 J.48	Norton
1975 S.49	Weslake Special	1962 S.25	B.S.A.	1960 S.30	Norton	1982 S.24	Yamaha	1947 S.R.	Norton
1976 J.24	Yamaha	**Roberts, Victor G.**		1961 S.22	Norton	**Rollason, Nigel G. A.**		1948 J.30	A.J.S.
1977 J.R.	Yamaha	1966 J.R.	B.S.A.	**Robinson, Roy W.**		1968 S.3	Seeley/Metisse	1949 S.28	Norton
1977 S.R.	Yamaha	1967 J.28	B.S.A.	1968 L.R.	Greeves	1968 J.8	Cowles/Metisse	1950 J.R.	Douglas
1978 J.28	Yamaha	1968 J.R.	B.S.A.	1971 L.32	Ducati	1969 S.R.	Seeley	1950 S.30	Norton
1978 S.R.	Yamaha	1970 J.36	A.J.S.	**Robinson, Spencer**		1970 J.2	Yamaha	1951 J.55	Norton
1979 J.R.	Honda	1973 S.R.	Seeley	1961 J.38	Norton	1970 S.R.	Seeley/Metisse	1951 S.49	Norton
1979 S.40	Honda	1976 S.38	Seeley	1962 J.R.	Norton	1971 J.R.	Yamaha	1952 J.38	Norton
Rigg, Nigel		1977 S.34	Seeley G50	1963 J.27	Norton	1971 S.1	Yamaha	1952 S.50	Norton
1974 J.25	Yamsel	1978 S.R.	Seeley	**Robinson, Steve**		**Romaine, Peter**		**Russell, B. B.**	
1976 J.41	Yamaha	**Roberts, William A.**		1979 S/N.R.	Yamaha	1949 J.4	A.J.S.	1947 L.R.	Moto Guzzi
Righton, John		1963 J.R.	B.S.A.	1979 S.R.	Yamaha	1949 S.6	A.J.S.	**Russell, D. B.**	
1957 J(N).R.	Velocette	1964 J.20	Norton	1981 L.R.	Yamaha	1950 J.2	Norton	1958 J(Sn).R.	Norton
1958 J.R.	Norton	1965 J.15	Norton	1982 L.58	Yamaha	1950 S.1	Norton	1959 J.R.	Norton
Riley, Harry		1965 S.50	Norton	**Robinson, Thomas**		**Rondelli, Gino**		**Russell, Donald 'Ronnie'**	
1955 S.R.	B.S.A.	1966 J.33	Norton	1971 L.40	Yamaha	1982 J/N.R.	Yamaha	1975 J.13	Yamaha
1957 J.41	Norton	1966 S.32	A.J.S.	1972 L.R.	Yamaha	**Rope, David**		1976 J.R.	Yamaha
1958 J.R	Norton	**Robertson, G.**		1973 L.13	Yamaha	1980 L/N.11	Yamaha	1976 S.R.	Yamaha
1958 S.R.	Norton	1961 S.R.	B.S.A.	**Robinson, Thomas D.**		1981 L.R.	Yamaha	1977 J.3	Yamaha
1959 J.35	Norton	**Robertson, J. G.**		1964 L.R	Bultaco	1982 L.20	Yamaha	1977 S.R.	Yamaha
Riley, Kevin		1946 S.R.	Norton	**Robinson, T. N.**		**Rose, Chris**		1978 L.R.	
1975 S.10	McVeigh Yamaha	1947 S.R.	Norton	1951 J.R.	Norton	1979 J/N.R.	Yamaha		Wilson & Collins Yamaha

The History of the Manx Grand Prix 1923-1998 113

1978 S.R.	IOMS Suzuki	1967 L.28	Cotton	1971 L.33	Yamaha	**Shadwell, J. T.**		1949 J.14	A.J.S.
Russell, Gordon		1968 L.27	Cotton	1972 L.18	Yamsel	1947 J.R.	Norton	1949 S.R.	Triumph
1977 S.R.	Honda	**Ryding, Craig**		1973 L.R.	Yamsel	1947 S.R.	Norton	1950 J.R.	A.J.S.
1978 L.19	Lomas Suzuki	1981 J/N.2	Yamaha	1974 L.13	Yamaha	**Shakespeare, John T.**		1950 S.13	Norton
1979 L.24	Yamaha			**Scott, J. R.**		1957 J(N).11	B.S.A.	1951 J.1	A.J.S.
1979 J.32	Yamaha	**Sadler, John H. L.**		1948 L.R.	Rudge	1957 J.R.	B.S.A.	1951 S.4	Matchless
Russell, H. E. M.		1973 L.R.	Greeves	1948 J.R.	Norton	1958 J.18	Norton	**Sherry, Ronan**	
1957 J(N).33	Norton	**Salt, Charlie F.**		**Scott, O. S.**		1958 S.23	Norton	1980 J/N.R.	Yamaha
Russell, R. A.		1946 J.6	Norton	1947 J.10	Norton	**Shannon, Stuart H.**		1981 S.Ex	Yamaha
1953 J.R.	Norton	1946 S.9	Norton	1947 S.R.	Norton	1968 S.R.	Norton	**Shewen, Ronald**	
1953 S.9	Norton	1947 L.R.	Norton	**Scott, R.**		1970 S.40	Norton	1966 L.R.	Greeves
Russell, Tony R.		1947 S.4	Norton	1965 S.R.	Norton	**Sharp, G. R.**		1967 L.R.	Greeves
1969 L.44	Yamaha	1948 J.4	Velocette	**Scott, William**		1957 J(N).9	B.S.A.	1969 J.38	A.J.S.
1970 L.R.	Yamaha	1948 S.3	Norton	1963 S.R.	Matchless	1957 J.40	B.S.A.	1970 J.28	A.J.S.
1972 S.37	Norton	**Salt, George T.**		1964 J.13	A.J.S.	**Sharp, Graham W.**		1971 J.46	A.J.S.
1973 S.R.	Norton	1953 J.14	A.J.S.	1964 S.8	Matchless	1965 S.47	Norton	**Shields, D.**	
1974 J.28	Yamaha	1953 S.23	A.J.S.	1965 S.14	A.J.S.	**Sharp, Peter W.**		1952 S.R.	Norton
1975 J.R.	Yamaha	**Samways, James**		1965 S.14	Matchless	1966 L.R.	Honda	**Shillings, Peter**	
1976 J.R.	Yamaha	1966 J.R.	Norton/B.S.A.	1966 J.15	A.J.S.	**Sharp, Terence R. D.**		1975 J.R.	Yamaha
1977 J.20	Albion Yamaha	**Samways, John**		1966 S.8	Matchless	1961 J.50	A.J.S.	1981 L.24	Yamaha
1978 J.31	Albion Yamaha	1965 S.R.	Triumph	1967 J.R.	A.J.S.	1962 J.54	A.J.S.	1982 L.25	Yamaha
1979 J.R.	Yamaha	1966 J.R.	Norton	1967 S.7	Matchless	1963 J.59	A.J.S.	**Shimmin, Danny**	
1980 L.21	Yamaha	1967 S.26	Norton	**Scott, W. G.**		**Sharpe, Mike**		1965 L.R.	Bultaco
1980 J.49	Yamaha	**Sanby, Charlie**		1951 S.28	B.S.A.	1976 J.R.	Yamaha	1966 L.49	Bultaco
1981 L.13	Yamaha	1964 S.R.	Norton	**Scruby, Mick G.**		**Sharpe, Peter B.**		1967 L.18	Bultaco
1981 J.R.	Yamaha	**Sancto, James W.**		1965 L.26	Greeves	1972 L.52	Yamsel	1968 L.R.	Aermacchi
1982 L.19	Yamaha	1966 L.R.	Bultaco	1967 L.6	Yamaha	1973 L.R.	Yamsel	1969 J.4	Aermacchi
1982 J.R.	Yamaha	1967 L.R.	Bultaco	1968 L.8	Yamaha	**Sharratt, Dave J.**		1970 J.R.	Aermacchi
Russell, S. C.		1968 L.29	Bultaco	**Sculley, Brian**		1973 L.R.	Yamaha	1970 S.16	Seeley
1965 L.53	Royal Enfield	1969 L.R.	Bultaco	1964 L.11	Greeves	1974 S.R.	Suzuki	1971 L.3	Crooks Suzuki
Russell, William T.		**Sanderson, Keith**		1964 S.16	B.G.B.	1975 S.25	Yamaha	1971 S.R.	Yamaha
1960 J.60	Norton	1976 S.R.	Yamaha	1965 J.51	Scott	1976 J.R.	Yamaha	1972 L.3	Yamaha
1962 J.62	Norton	1977 S.15	Yamaha	1965 S.18	Norton	1978 J.R.	Honda	1972 S.R.	Suzuki
1963 J.R.	Norton	1978 J.16	Yamaha	**Sear, John**		1979 J.35	Honda	1973 J.R.	Yamaha
1964 J.51	Norton	1978 S.R.	Yamaha	1962 S.36	O.E.Greenwood	1979 S.27	Honda	1973 S.R.	Suzuki
Rutherford, Frank A.		**Sanderson, Bill**		1963 S.R.	Greenwood Spl	1980 S.26	Honda	1974 L.4	Harrison Yamaha
1952 J.R	Velocette	1962 J.R.	Norton	1964 S.R.	Matchless	1981 S.R.	Honda	1974 S.R.	Brew Suzuki
1953 J.R.	A.J.S.	**Sandford, Cecil C.**		1967 J.R.	Norton	1982 S.30	Honda	1975 J.4	Harrison Yamaha
1953 S.R.	A.J.S.	1949 J.5	Velocette	**Selby, G.**		**Sharrocks, Malcolm**		1975 S.R.	Mylchreest Yamaha
1954 J.26	A.J.S.	1949 S.42	Velocette	1947 J.R.	Norton	1963 J.R.	Norton	1976 L.1	Harrison Yamaha
1955 S.9	Norton	**Sands, Jack**		1947 S.48	Norton	1964 L.R.	Aermacchi	1976 S.2	S.S.
1955 J.R.	A.J.S.	1978 J/N.R.	Yamaha	**Selby, Howard**		1965 L.R.	Aermacchi	**Shirlaw, Roy**	
1955 S.9	Norton	1978 S.55	Yamaha	1981 J/N.7	Yamaha	1965 S.43	Norton	1976 L.26	Yamaha
1956 J.5	B.S.A.	**Sapsford, Brian**		**Sellars, Grant W.**		1967 J.51	Norton	1977 L.5	Yamscot
1956 S.R.	B.S.A.	1965 J.R.	Norton	1969 L.R.	G.W.S.	1968 J.R.	Norton	1977 S.R.	Yamscot
1957 J.12	A.J.S.	**Sapsford, John T.**		1970 S.44	Velocette	**Shaw, Alf E.**		1978 L.18	Yamscot
1957 S.4	Norton	1960 S.R.	B.S.A.	1971 S.39	Velocette	1946 J.R.	Velocette	1978 J.R.	Yamscot
1958 J.R.	Norton	**Savage, L.**		1972 S.R.	Velocette	1947 L.R.	Excelsior	**Shore, Norman**	
1958 S.R.	Norton	1962 S.49	Norton	1974 S.R.	Norton	1948 J.17	Norton	1974 J.49	Ducati
1959 J.12	A.J.S.	**Saville, Dave**		1975 S.R.	Norton	**Shaw, Graham T.**		1975 J.45	Aermacchi
1959 S.4	Norton	1966 S.43	B.S.A.	1976 S.36	Manx Norton	1967 J.R.	Norton	1976 L.21	Yamaha
1960 J.16	Honda	**Saward, G.**		1977 S.R.	Manx Norton	1968 S.R.	Norton/B.S.A.	**Shorey, Dan F.**	
1960 S.R.	Norton	1958 J(Sn).24	Norton	1978 J.42	Manx Norton	1970 S.R.	Norton	1958 J(Sn).31	Norton
Rutherford, Len S.		1958 S.33	Norton	1979 S.R.	Norton	**Sheard, Tim R.**		1958 S.29	Norton
1955 J.49	A.J.S.	1959 J.28	A.J.S.	1980 J.R.	Manx Norton	1946 L.10	Cotton	1959 J.44	Norton
1955 S.R.	A.J.S.	1960 J.28	Norton	1980 S.R.	Norton	1950 S.39	Norton	1959 S.R.	Norton
1956 J.21	A.J.S.	1960 S.R.	Norton	1981 S.31	Norton	**Shearer, Ray**		1960 S.9	Norton
1956 S.R.	A.J.S.	1961 J.R.	Norton	1982 S.R.	Norton	1977 L.49	Yamaha	**Short, George M.**	
Rutter, Frank		**Sawford, Bill J.**		**Senior, G.**		1978 L.29	Yamaha	1964 J.37	Norton
1970 S.35	Norton	1956 J.37	A.J.S.	1960 J.R.	A.J.S.	1979 L.32	Yamaha	1965 J.40	Norton
1971 S.17	Norton	1956 S.12	Matchless	**Seston, Sam T.**		**Sheene, Frank**		1966 J.30	A.J.S.
1972 J.10	Dearden Norton	1958 J.R.	A.J.S.	1950 J.55	Norton	1955 J.44	A.J.S.	1967 J.36	A.J.S.
1972 S.R.	Norton	**Saytch, Malcolm G.**		**Sewart, Geoff E.**		1955 S.44	A.J.S.	1968 J.17	A.J.S.
1973 J.R.	Petty	1973 J.49	Aermacchi	1979 L/N.R.	Cotton	1956 J.51	A.J.S.	1969 J.28	A.J.S.
1973 S.R.	Petty	**Scanes, S. D.**		1979 L.R.	Cotton	1956 S.50	A.J.S.	1969 S.25	Matchless
1974 L.15	Yamaha	1969 L.R.	Honda	1980 L.48	Cotton	**Shekell G. W.**		1970 J.21	A.J.S.
1974 S.R.	Yamaha	1970 J.31	B.S.A./Norton	1981 L.45	Cotton Rotax	1951 S.42	Norton	1970 S.6	Matchless
Rutzen, David W.		**Scarborough, Colin**		1982 L.41	Cotton	**Shepherd, Alan**		1971 J.9	Seeley
1976 L.62	Yamaha	1979 L/N.R.	Yamaha	1982 J.26	Yamaha	1956 S10	Norton	1971 S.R.	Seeley
1977 S.R.	Sparton	1979 L.35	Yamaha	**Sewell, C. A. J.**		1957 J.3	Norton	1972 J.7	Seeley
1978 L.32	Yamaha	**Scholefield, A.**		1967 S.R.	Norton	1957 S.R.	Norton	1972 S.14	Seeley
1979 J.R.	Yamaha	1955 J.R.	B.S.A.	**Seymour, Ralph F.**		1958 J.1	Bancroft-A.J.S.	1973 J.R.	Seeley
1979 S.39	Barton	**Scott, D. John**		1946 J.38	Velocette	1958 S.R.	Norton	1973 S.R.	Suzuki
1980 J.31	Yamaha	1965 L.R.	Ducati	1946 S.R.	Norton	**Shepherd, Kenneth**		**Shortland, Keith A.**	
1980 S.22	Suzuki	**Scott, David J.**		1947 J.21	Velocette	1980 J/N.1	Yamaha	1966 J.R.	A.J.S.
1981 J.21	Yamaha	1962 S.54	Norton	1947 S.R.	Norton	1981 J.3	Yamaha	1967 J.40	A.J.S.
1981 S.R.	Suzuki	1963 S.44	Norton	1948 J.15	Velocette	1981 S.14	Yamaha	1968 J.24	A.J.S.
1982 J.R.	Yamaha	1964 S.31	Triumph/Norton	1948 S.12	Norton	**Shepherd, Terry**		1969 S.R.	A.J.S.
1982 S.16	Suzuki	1965 S.54	Triumph/Special	1949 J.R.	Velocette	1953 J.6	Norton	**Shortt, Thomas F.**	
Ryall, Alan J.		**Scott, G.**		1949 S.12	Norton	**Shepley-Taylor, P.**		1969 J.R.	Bultaco
1971 S.5	Seeley	1957 S(N).R.	Norton	**Shacklady, John**		1952 S.R.	Norton-B.S.A.	1970 J.R.	Drixton
1972 S.R.	Aermacchi	1958 S.15	Norton	1964 L.34	Greeves	**Sheppard, P. M.**		**Shuttleworth, E. S.**	
1975 S.19	Seeley	1959 S.29	Norton	1965 L.R.	Yamaha	1965 S.37	Norton	1965 L.25	Greeves
Ryall, M.		**Scott, James**		1966 L.24	Yamaha	**Sherry, Robin H.**		**Siddles, Bill**	

114 The History of the Manx Grand Prix 1923-1998

1959 J.27	Norton	**Singleton, W. H.**		1958 J.36	A.J.S.	1951 S.62	Norton	**Standivan, R. J.**
1960 J.12	Norton	1946 J.30	Norton	1959 J.32	Norton	1952 J.66	Norton	1952 J.48	A.J.S.
1960 S.R.	Taylor-Dow Sp.	**Skelly, Dave A.**		1960 S.R.	Norton	1952 S.65	Norton	1953 J.35	A.J.S.
1961 J.39	Norton	1971 J.37	A.J.S.	**Smith, David**		1953 J.41	Norton	1954 J.36	A.J.S.
1961 S.37	Norton	1972 L.R.	Suzuki	1976 L.52	Aermacchi	1953 S.37	Norton	1954 S.R.	B.S.A.
Sidey, Iain		1973 J.R.	Yamsel	1977 L.42	Aermacchi	1954 J.R.	Norton	1955 J.41	B.S.A.
1965 S.R.	Triumph-Norton	1974 S.21	Velocette	1978 L.50	Aermacchi	1955 J.57	Norton	1955 S.32	B.S.A.
1966 S.28	Matchless	1976 S.R.	Seymour Velocette	**Smith, David, C. P.**		1955 S.46	Norton	**Stanger, Christopher McK.**
1967 S.24	Matchless	**Skerritt, W.**		1980 J/N.11	Yamaha	1956 J.52	Norton	1966 J.R.	A.J.S.
Sifflett, Richard P.		1951 J.R.	A.J.S.	1981 S.51	Suzuki	1956 S.48	Norton	**Stark, R. L. S.**
1946 J.R.	Norton	**Skinner, Steve**		1982 S.49	Seeley	1957 J.R.	Norton	1952 J.R.	Norton
1946 S.19	Norton	1975 S.46	Arter Matchless	**Smith, G. W.**		**Southcombe, William R.**		**Starkey, Dan E.**
1947 J.R.	Norton	1976 S.R.	Manx Norton	1958 S(Sn).18	B.S.A.	1965 L.R.	Greeves	1971 L.R.	Greeves
1948 J.R.	Norton	1978 S.40	Yamaha	**Smith, Godfery**		1966 L.41	Cotton	1972 L.R.	Greeves
Silversides, J. F.		**Slade, B.**		1977 L.R.	Yamaha	**Sparrow, Jack J. I.**		1974 L.62	Greeves
1968 S.R.	Norton/B.S.A.	1946 J.R.	Norton	1978 L.R.	Yamaha	1948 L.R.	Excelsior	1975 L.R.	Greeves
Simister, John		1946 S.R.	Norton	**Smith, J.**		**Spear, Edward M.**		**Starr, Leo**
1948 J.R.	Norton	**Slade, Paul R.**		1961 J.R.	A.J.S.	1964 J.R.	B.S.A.	1947 S.18	Norton
1948 S.R.	Triumph	1961 J.R	A.J.S.	**Smith, John**		1965 J.56	Norton	1948 J.R.	A.J.S.
1949 J.12	Norton	1962 J.59	A.J.S.	1948 J.53	Norton	1966 J.27	Norton	1948 S.23	Triumph
1949 S.R	Triumph	1963 S.29	Matchless	1948 S.R.	Norton	**Spence, W.**		1949 J.R.	A.J.S.
Simister, Peter		1964 J.N.F.	A.J.S.	1949 J.24	A.J.S.	1952 J.62	Velocette	1949 S 39	A.J.S.
1950 J.24	A.J.S.	1964 S.R.	Matchless	1949 S.15	Triumph	**Spencer, John M.**		1950 J.55	Norton
1950 S.31	A.J.S.	1965 J.R.	A.J.S.	1950 J.R.	A.J.S.	1968 S.46	Norton	**Steele, Allan E.**
1952 J.44	A.J.S.	1965 S.R.	Matchless	1950 S.33	Triumph	**Spencer, Steve**		1965 L.46	Cotton
1952 S.39	Norton	**Slater, J. S.**		1951 J.22	A.J.S.	1964 S.R.	Norton	1966 L.10	Yamaha
Simmons, Roy H.		1946 J.24	Excelsior	1952 J.47	A.J.S.	1965 S.5	Norton	1967 L.R.	Yamaha
1964 S.R.	Norton	1947 J.37	Norton	1952 S.31	Norton	1966 J.5	Norton	1968 L.R.	Yamaha
1965 S.46	Norton	1947 S.25	Norton	1953 J.27	Norton	1966 S.3	Norton	1969 S.R.	Matchless
1966 S.R.	Norton	**Slinger, Peter W.**		1953 S.26	Norton	**Spicer, G. Arthur**		1970 L.1	Dugdale Yamaha
1967 S.23	Norton	1964 S.24	Matchless	1954 J.38	Norton	1947 L.R.	O.K. Supreme	**Steele, Burton**
1968 S.19	Norton	1965 L.R.	Honda	1954 S.R.	Norton	**Spillane, J.**		1966 L.26	Greeves
Simmons, Bob M.		**Smart, Paul A.**		**Smith, Joe A.**		1947 L.18	New imperial	**Steele, David J.**
1967 L.R.	Greeves	1966 S.R.	Greeves	1948 J.R.	Norton	1948 L.R.	New Imperial	1969 L.19	Yamaha
1968 L.20	Greeves	1967 S.R.	Triumph	**Smith, John, N.**		**Spink, Michael J.**		**Steele, Frank J.**
1969 L.R.	Suzuki	**Smith, A.**		1982 S/N.5	Hagon Honda	1971 L.43	Suzuki	1957 J(N).37	B.S.A.
1971 L.19	Suzuki	1946 S.R.	Norton	**Smith, Nicholas**		1972 L.47	Suzuki	1958 J.R.	B.S.A.
1972 J.42	Suzuki	1947 S.R.	Norton	1981 J/N.4	Yamaha	**Spinks, Raymond**		1958 S.R.	B.S.A.
1973 S.R.	Suzuki	1948 S.R.	Norton	1981 S.R.	Yamaha	1964 L.31	Yamaha	1966 S.48	B.S.A.
1974 L.64	Suzuki Special	1949 S.35	Norton	**Smith, Peter J.**		1965 L.R.	Yamaha	1968 L.26	Ducati
1975 S.32	Harrow Suzuki	1950 S.R.	Norton	1971 L.23	Greeves	1966 L.R.	Yamaha	1969 L.36	Ducati
1976 S.R.	Suzuki Special	**Smith, A.**		1972 L.R.	Greeves	**Spivey, L. J.**		1972 L.33	Honda
1977 S.19	Suzuki Special	1952 S.58	Norton	1973 S.R.	Suzuki	1965 J.R.	Aermacchi	1976 J.R.	Beart Norton
1978 L.R.	Fahron Special	**Smith, Anthony J.**		**Smith, R.**		**Spooner, Albert T.**		**Steele, Robert N.**
1978 J.48	Fahron Special	1967 J.R.	B.S.A.	1958 J(Sn).56	B.S.A.	1964 S.R.	Norton	1964 J.27	A.J.S.
1979 J.R.	Fahron	1969 S.R.	B.S.A.	**Smith, Roy E.**		1965 S.R.	Norton	1965 J.R.	A.J.S.
1979 S.59	Fahron	**Smith, Alan L.**		1952 J.R.	Velocette	**Spring, Robin**		1965 S.9	Matchless
1980 J.R.	Fahron	1969 L.R.	Greeves	1952 S.40	Velocette	1978 L/N.13	D.M.W.	1966 J.11	A.J.S.
1980 S.43	Fahron	**Smith, A. M. S.**		1953 J.19	Velocette	1979 L.R.	Cotton	1966 S.R.	Matchless
1981 J.R.	Yamaha	1948 S.18	Norton	1953 S.21	Velocette	**Spruce, David**		**Stenning, Brian A.**
1981 S.56	Suzuki Special	1949 S.21	Norton	**Smith, T. B. N. S.**		1968 J.51	Honda	1966 J.39	A.J.S.
1982 J.R.	Yamaha	1949 S.29	Norton	1946 S.R.	Vincent-H.R.D.	1969 J.R.	Spruce Spl.	1967 J.R.	A.J.S.
1982 S.R.	Suzuki	1950 J.31	Norton	1947 S.R.	Vincent-H.R.D.	1972 J.31	Yamsel	1968 J.R.	A.J.S.
Simpson G.		1950 S.15	Norton	1948 S.R	Vincent-H.R.D.	**Spruce, D. G.**		**Stentiford, Philip D.**
1949 J.64	Rudge	1951 J.20	Norton	1949 S.52	Norton	1968 L.28	Suzuki	1972 S.R.	Seeley
1950 J.R.	Rudge	**Smith, Anthony N.**		1951 S.25	Norton	**Spruce, Kenneth A.**		1973 S.R.	Seeley
Simpson, J.		1973 J.45	Yamaha	1952 S.33	Norton	1962 S.R.	Norton	1974 S.R.	Seeley
1960 J.R.	Norton	**Smith, Alan F.**		**Smits, J. C.**		1963 S.39	Norton	**Stephen, H. L.**
1961 J.R.	Norton	1982 S.N.R.	Honda	1958 J(Sn)32	A.J.S.	**Stacey, Peter**		1950 J.7	A.J.S.
1962 J.10	Norton	**Smith, Brian**		1958 S.R.	A.J.S.	1960 S.38	Norton	**Stephen, Richard**
Simpson, J. R.		1961 S.58	B.S.A.	**Smyth, John**		1961 S.39	Norton	1980 L/N.12	Yamaha
1957 J(N).14	B.S.A.	1962 S.34	B.S.A.	1981 J/N.R.	Yamaha	1962 S.21	Norton	1980 L.40	Yamaha
1957 J.56	B.S.A.	1963 J.35	B.S.A.	1981 S.R.	Yamaha	1963 S.20	Norton	**Stephens, Ralph**
Simpson, R. S.		1964 S.R.	Matchless	**Snape, Tony W.**		1964 L.R.	Cotton	1974 J.47	Norton
1946 L.3	Excelsior	1965 S.33	Matchless	1972 J.R.	Ducati	1965 L.20	Cotton	**Stephens, W. A.**
1947 L.3	Excelsior	1966 S.26	Matchless	1974 L.44	Yamaha	**Staddon, A. E.**		1957 J.48	B.S.A.
Simpson, Bill R.		1967 S.29	Matchless	1975 L.36	Yamaha	1965 L.34	N.S.U.	1957 S.49	B.S.A.
1967 L.21	Greeves	**Smith, B. E.**		1976 L.57	Maxton Yamaha	1967 L.31	Yamaha	**Stephenson, Noel**
1973 L.R.	Yamaha	1965 J.17	Aermacchi	1977 L.R.	Maxton Yamaha	1968 L.14	Yamaha	1961 J.R.	Norton
Sims, Barry G.		**Smith, Bryan J.**		**Snell, R. S.**		**Staley, C. E.**		1962 J.37	Norton
1971 J.32	Norton	1964 J.R.	Norton	1956 S.46	Matchless	1951 J.35	Norton	1963 J.31	Norton
1972 S.40	Suzuki	1965 J.R.	Norton	1957 S.26	Matchless	1952 J.11	A.J.S.	1964 J.12	Norton
1973 S.R.	Suzuki	1967 S.14	Norton	**Snelling, Bill**		1952 S.R.	B.S.A.	**Stephenson, N. R.**
1974 S.26	Difazio Suzuki	1968 L.R.	Ariel	1978 S/N.12		**Staley, V. John**		1947 J.27	Velocette
1975 S.26	Suzuki Special	1968 S.R.	Norton		Seymour Velocette Metisse	1976 S.41	Seeley Suzuki	**Stephenson, S. R.**
Simson, William		**Smith, D. R.**		1978 S.53		1979 S.R.	Seeley Suzuki	1956 S.27	Matchless
1974 L.R.	Bultaco	1959 J.78	A.J.S.		Seymour Velocette Metisse	1980 L.50	Yamaha	1957 S.12	Matchless
1975 L.21	Denholm Yamaha	1960 J.R.	A.J.S.	1980 S.45	Ducati	**Stallard, Eric J.**		**Stevens, C. A.**
1977 L.R.	Denholm Yamaha	1962 J.39	Norton	**Snow, John**		1964 J.38	Norton	1947 J.44	Velocette
1978 S.45	Denholm Yamaha	1963 J.R.	B.S.A.	1968 L.34	Ducati	**Stancer, J. E.**		1947 S.14	Velocette
Sinclair, David		1964 J.R.	B.S.A.	1969 L.R.	Ducati	1961 S.54	Matchless	1948 J.7	A.J.S.
1982 S/N.21	Honda	1965 J.22	B.S.A.	1971 L.44	Ducati	**Standing, Richard S.**		1948 S.7	Triumph
Sinclair, Mark		**Smith, D. W.**		**Southam, R. S.**		1962 J.51	Norton/B.S.A.	**Stevens, David M. F.**
1963 S.R.	B.S.A./Norton	1958 J(Sn).14	A.J.S.	1951 J.R.	Douglas	1963 S.R.	A.J.S.	1972 J.24	Norton

The History of the Manx Grand Prix 1923-1998 115

1973 J.37	Norton	1969 L.R.	Bultaco	1972 L.40	Greeves	1952 S.17	Norton	1949 S.14	Norton
Stevens, J. E.		**Stuart, I.**		1973 L.R.	Greeves	**Taylor, Andy**		1950 J.R.	A.J.S.
1946 J.14	Norton	1955 J.R.	Velocette	1974 L.63	Greeves	1980 J/N.8	Yamaha	1950 S.12	Norton
Stevens, Richard W.		1955 S.R.	Velocette	1975 J.R.	Yamaha	1981 J.20	Yamaha	**Thain, Gerald S.**	
1970 L.26	Suzuki	1956 J.R.	Norton	1976 J.13	Yamaha	1981 S.16	Yamaha	1964 S.R.	Norton
1971 L.R.	Suzuki	1956 S.R.	Norton	1977 L.2	Yamaha	1982 J.15	Yamaha	1967 S.R.	Norton
Stevenson, John R.		**Stuckey, Henry**		1977 S.R.	Yamaha	1982 S.22	Yamaha	1968 L.13	Ducati
1965 J.R.	A.J.S.	1978 J/N.R.	Maxton Yamaha	1978 L.2	Yamaha	**Taylor, Colin J.**		**Thomas, David L**	
Stevenson, W.		1978 S.62	Maxton Yamaha	1978 J.4	Yamaha	1971 S.51	Norton	1965 J.R.	Norton
1965 L.31	Cotton	**Sugden J. A.**		1979 L.4	Yamaha	**Taylor, C. W.**		1966 J.45	Norton
Stewart, Douglas G.		1960 J.17	A.J.S.	**Swannack John**		1968 J.R.	A.J.S.	1967 L.10	Kawasaki
1977 L.R.	Camp Suzuki	**Sugden, T.**		1964 L.R.	Greeves	**Taylor, Derek**		1968 J.R.	Kawasaki
1978 L.61	Suzuki	1958 J(Sn).16	Norton	1964 L.R.	Royal Enfield	1974 J.36	Camp Ducati	1970 J.6	Kawasaki
1980 L.45	Yamaha	**Sullivan, Eric W.**		1965 S.22	B.S.A.	**Taylor, Geoffrey B.**		**Thomas, Gareth N. W.**	
1982 S.51	Honda	1959 S.R.	Norton	**Swarbrick, T. W.**		1971 J.40	A.J.S.	1969 L.55	Ducati
Stewart, Kenneth		**Sunderland, C. M. V.**		1950 S.23	A.J.S.	1972 J.R.	A.J.S.	1970 L.47	Ducati
1972 L.R.	Suzuki	1951 J.57	Norton	1951 J.8	A.J.S.	1973 J.32	Aermacchi	1971 L.28	Aermacchi
1973 L.R.	Aermacchi	**Sunderland, Eric R.**		1951 S.R.	A.J.S.	1974 J.23	Aermacchi	1972 J.21	Aermacchi
Stewart, Mark		1970 J.30	Aermacchi	**Sweetman, N. F.**		1975 J.54	Aermacchi	1973 J.R.	Aermacchi
1977 L.R.	Yamaha	1971 J.47	Aermacchi	1958 J(N).37	B.S.A.	**Taylor, Gordon V.**		1974 J.21	Aermacchi
Stockdale, Colin		1977 L.R.	Pharaoh Yamaha	1959 J.69	B.S.A.	1964 L.R.	Cotton	1975 J.19	Yamaha
1981 S/N.5	Honda	1978 L.11	Pharaoh Yamaha	**Swetman, R. J.**		1965 L.50	Cotton	**Thomas, Geoffrey**	
1981 L.R.	Honda	1979 L.22	Pharaoh Yamaha	1955 J.65	B.S.A.	1966 L.28	Cotton	1975 S.57	Norton
1982 S.46	Honda	1979 J.28	Pharaoh Yamaha	1955 S.54	B.S.A.	1967 L.8	Kawasaki	**Thompson, B. J.**	
Stone, John		1980 L.9	Earnshaw Yamaha	1956 J.53	A.J.S.	1968 L.R.	Kawasaki	1951 J.24	A.J.S.
1975 L.18	Yamaha	1980 J.23	Pharaoh Yamaha	1956 S.R.	A.J.S.	**Taylor, Graham**		1952 J.16	A.J.S.
1976 L.4	Yamaha	1981 L.R.	Earnshaw Yamaha	1957 J.R.	A.J.S.	1982 L/N.R.	Armstrong	1953 J.10	A.J.S.
1977 L.R.	Yamaha	1981 J.25	Pharaoh Yamaha	1957 S.46	A.J.S.	1982 L.R.	Armstrong	1954 J.11	A.J.S.
1977 S.11	Fowler Yamaha	1982 L.R.	Earnshaw Yamaha	1958 J.24	A.J.S.	**Taylor, H.**		1954 S.7	Matchless
1978 L.23	Yamaha	1982 J.18	Pharaoh Yamaha	1958 S.28	A.J.S.	1959 S.R.	Norton	1955 J.R.	A.J.S.
1978 J.40	Yamaha	**Sunderland, Milton**		**Symes, Adrian A.**		1960 S.R	Norton	1955 S.5	Matchless
Stones, Keith E.		1946 J.39	Norton	1976 S.R.	Ducati	1962 S.R.	Norton	1956 J.18	A.J.S.
1966 J.49	Norton	1946 S.32	Norton			**Taylor, Ian**		**Thompson, Leslie**	
Stopford, R. P.		1947 J.46	Norton	**Taft, M. E. J.**		1976 J.R.	Yamaha	1977 J.37	Yamaha
1967 J.34	A.J.S.	1947 S.49	Norton	1951 J.62	B.S.A.	**Taylor, J.**		1979 J.R.	Yamaha
Storer, Norman H.		1948 J.49	Norton	**Tailford, Julian**		1972 S.19	Norton	1979 S.R.	Harris Yamaha
1954 J.R.	A.J.S.	1948 S.27	Norton	1981 S/N.12	Yamaha	**Taylor, John R.**		**Thompson, Paul**	
Storey, Keith		1949 J.61	Norton	1982 S.48	Yamaha	1962 S.R.	Matchless	1977 J.R.	Yamaha
1981 S/N.R.	Yamaha	1949 S.34	Norton	**Tait, Percy**		1963 S.15	Matchless	**Thompson, Peter**	
1982 J.R.	Yamaha	1950 S.56	Norton	1954 J.9	Norton	1964 S.R.	Matchless	1975 L.R.	Yamaha
1982 S.R.	Yamaha	1950 S.40	Norton	1954 S.R.	Norton	1965 J.48	A.J.S.	**Thompson, Peter E.**	
Storr, D. A.		1951 J.61	Norton	**Talbot, Gerry**		1965 S.R.	Matchless	1968 S.48	P.R. Spl.
1947 J.62	Norton	1951 S.38	Norton	1974 L.40	Yamaha	1966 J.R.	A.J.S.	1969 S.R.	P.R. Spl.
1947 S.53	Norton	**Sutcliffe, R. G.**		**Tandy, Geoffrey W.**		1966 S.R.	Matchless	**Thompson, R.**	
1950 J.R.	A.J.S.	1957 J(N).8	Norton	1968 J.R.	Norstar	**Taylor, Martin D. J.**		1957 J.R.	Norton
1951 J.63	A.J.S.	1957 J.53	Norton	1969 J.R.	Norton	1967 J.R.	Triumph	1957 S.16	Norton
1952 J.52	A.J.S.	**Sutcliffe, Ralph**		1971 J.53	A.J.S.	1968 S.50	Triumph	**Thompson, R. W.**	
Storr, John A.		1982 J/N.2	Yamaha	**Tanner, Geoff B.**		**Taylor, M.**		1946 L.R.	O.K. Supreme
1950 J.R.	Velocette	1982 L.13	Yamaha	1954 J.4	Norton	1965 L.R.	Yamaha	1947 J.29	Norton
1951 J.15	Velocette	**Sutcliffe, Roger**		1954 S.R.	Norton	**Taylor, Mick**		1947 S.45	Norton
1951 S.14	Earles Special	1967 J.29	A.J.S.	1955 J.1	Norton	1968 L.R.	Taylor Spl.	1948 J.35	Norton
1952 J.10	Norton	1968 J.9	A.J.S.	1955 S.1	Norton	1972 L.R.	M.N. Ducati	1949 J.R.	Norton
1952 S.R.	Norton	1969 J.50	A.J.S.	**Targett, A. J.**		**Taylor, Peter D.**		**Thompson, Sam D.**	
Storr, William C.		1969 S.4	Matchless	1947 L.R.	Rudge	1981 L.R.	Fahron Yamaha	1972 L.32	Montesa
1948 J.46	Norton	1970 J.3	Aermacchi	1948 L.R.	Rudge	1982 L.54	Jackson	1974 L.R.	D.M.W.
1949 J.65	Norton	1970 S.1	Cowles Matchless	**Taubman, Ken A.**		**Taylor, Robert L.**		1975 L.R.	D.M.W.
Stott, Richard		**Sutcliffe, Stuart K.**		1951 S.58	Triumph	1961 J.R.	A.J.S.	1977 L.57	D.M.W.
1981 S/N.9	Yamaha	1964 L.28	Aermacchi	1952 S.61	Triumph	1962 J.57	A.J.S.	**Thompson, Simon Jr.**	
1982 J.R.	Yamaha	**Sutherland, A. R.**		1953 S.R	Triumph	1963 J.R.	A.J.S.	1981 S/N.11	Yamaha
Stracey, J. F.		1947 J.R.	Norton	1954 S.R.	Matchless	1964 J.R.	A.J.S.	1982 S.R.	Suzuki
1958 S(Sn).R.	Norton	1954 S.21	B.S.A.	1955 S.R.	Matchless	**Taylor, Robert R.**		**Thomson, A. Charles**	
Strachan, J.		1955 J.61	B.S.A.	1956 J.R	B.S.A.	1982 J/N.11	Yamaha	1979 L/N.7	Yamaha
1946 J.33	Norton	1955 S.R.	B.S.A.	1956 S.51	Matchless	**Teare, A. John**		1979 L.26	Yamaha
1947 J.11	Norton	1956 J.42	B.S.A.	1957 J.R.	B.S.A.	1969 L.8	Yamaha	1980 L.11	Yamaha
1948 J.40	Norton	1956 S.R.	B.S.A.	1957 S.50	Matchless	1970 J.R.	Yamaha	1980 J.R.	Yamaha
1948 S.R.	Norton	1957 J.22	Norton	1958 J.R.	B.S.A.	1971 L.9	Yamaha	1981 L.R.	Yamaha
Street, D. J.		1957 S.43	B.S.A	1958 S.R.	B.S.A.	1972 L.R.	Yamaha	1982 J.R.	Yamaha
1970 J.R.	Greeves	**Sutherland, G. A.**		1959 S.R.	Norton/B.S.A.	1972 S.R.	Norton	1982 S.17	Yamaha
Stretch, Ron		1958 J(Sn).52	Norton	1960 S.59	B.S.A.	**Teare, Malcolm**		**Thomson, Christopher**	
1956 J.31	A.J.S.	1959 J.41	Norton	**Taylor, Alan**		1975 L.44	Craig Yamaha	1976 L.56	Yamaha
1956 S.41	A.J.S.	**Sutton, A. M.**		1970 L.R.	Yamaha	1976 L.53	Craig Yamaha	1978 S.R.	Thomson Yamaha
1957 J.13	A.J.S.	1953 J.16	B.S.A.	1971 L.47	Yamaha	1977 L.51	Craig Yamaha	**Thomson, J. A.**	
1957 S.R.	A.J.S.	**Swales, Bill**		1974 L.R.	Yamaha	1978 L.44	Craig Yamaha	1948 J.R.	Norton
Stride, A. A.		1965 J.34	A.J.S.	1975 L.26	Yamaha	1978 J.46	Craig Yamaha	1949 J.R.	Norton
1958 S(Sn).15		1966 J.R.	A.J.S.	1976 L.29	Yamaha	1979 L.41	Craig Yamaha	1950 J.R.	Norton
Strijbis, Jan R.		1968 S.36	Norton	1977 L.R.	Yamaha	1979 L.46	Craig Yamaha	1950 S.45	Norton
1966 L.47	Honda	**Swallow, Alec**		1978 L.21	Yamaha	**Tedder, L. G. 'Les'**		1951 J.28	Norton
1966 S.23	Norton	1975 L.46	Greeves	1979 L.R.	Yamaha	1949 S.R.	Norton	1951 S.40	Vincent
Stringer, G. F.		1976 S.46	Velocette	**Taylor, A. C.**		**Templeton, Malcolm**		1952 J.45	Norton
1967 J.50	A.J.S.	1977 S.47	Velocette	1950 J.30	A.J.S.	1947 J.25	A.J.S.	1952 S.43	Vincent
Strong, P. M.		1978 L.53	Velocette	1950 S.27	A.J.S.	1947 S.19	Norton	**Thomson, John M.**	
1970 L.30	Suzuki	1979 L.R.	Seeley Velocette	1951 J.7	Norton	1948 J.R.	Norton	1967 L.46	Yamaha
Strutt, Jack		1980 S.59	Velocette	1951 S.R.	Norton	1948 S.16	Norton	1969 L.R.	Cotton
1968 L.R.	Suzuki	**Swallow, Richard**		1952 J.7	Norton	1949 J.33	Norton	**Thomson, Tom**	

116 The History of the Manx Grand Prix 1923-1998

1972 S.R. Norton
1973 S.R. Kawasaki
Thomson, William S.
1966 S.44 Tri-Manx
1967 J.R. Norton
1968 S.R. Tri-Manx
Thornton, Joe W.
1961 J.47 Norton
1963 J.R. Norton
1964 J.R. Norton
1965 J.3 Norton
1966 J.6 Norton
1966 S.R. Norton
1967 J.R. Norton
1967 S.R. Norton
1968 J.R. Mularney Spl.
1968 S.R. Mularney Spl.
1970 J.4 Mularney Spl.
1970 S.R. Mularney Spl.
1971 J.R. Mularney Spl.
1971 S.R. Mularney Spl.
1972 J.R. Mularney Spl.
1973 J.R. Harley davidson
1973 S.2 Aermacchi
1974 J.R. Dugdale Yamaha
1974 S.R. Lawton Aermacchi HD
1975 J.R. McVeigh Yamaha
Thorold, John W.
1961 S.61 Norton
1962 S.35 Norton
1964 S.R. Norton
Thorp, Tom
1956 J.19 A.J.S.
1956 S.23 A.J.S.
1957 J.6 Norton
1957 S.R. Norton
1958 J.R. Norton
1958 S.R. Norton
1959 J.45 Norton
1959 S.2 Norton
Thurgood, Alan J.
1960 S.20 Norton
1961 J.18 A.J.S.
1961 S.15 Matchless
Thurlow, Dave
1980 J/N.5 Yamaha
1981 L.33 Yamaha
1981 J.28 Yamaha
1982 L.R. Yamaha
1982 J.R. Yamaha
Thurston, C. A.
1955 S.42 B.S.A.
1956 S.R. B.S.A.
1957 J.50 Special
1957 S.56 Special
Thurston, Jack R.
1953 J.34 B.S.A.
1954 J.R. B.S.A.
1954 S.30 B.S.A.
1955 J.R. B.S.A.
1955 S.53 B.S.A.
1956 J.56 B.S.A.
1956 S.45 B.S.A.
1957 J.38 B.S.A.
1957 S.R. B.S.A.
1958 J.56 B.S.A.
1958 S.R. B.S.A.
1959 J.63 B.S.A.
1960 J.41 Norton
Thurston, Peter
1960 S.57 Norton/Triumph
1961 S.R. Triumph/Norton
1962 S.55 Triumph/Norton
Tibbetts, R. T.
1952 J.R. Norton
Tierney, Derek
1967 J.24 Norton
1968 J.14 Norton
1970 S.R. Norton
1971 S.13 Suzuki
1972 L.23 Yamaha
1972 S.R. Suzuki
Tierney, Norman
1967 S.R. Norton
1968 S.R. Norton
1969 S.47 Norton
Tilley, Kenneth G.
1965 L.15 Aermacchi
1966 L.21 Aermacchi
1967 L.R. Aermacchi
1967 S.R. Norton
1968 J.R. A.J.S.
1968 S.20 Norton
1969 J.17 Norton
1969 S.12 Norton
Tingley, Barry S.
1966 S.45 Norton Spl.
1967 S.37 Tri-Norton
1968 S.40 Tri-Norton
1969 S.39 Tri-Norton
1970 S.36 Tri-Norton
1972 S.45 Norton
1973 S.33 Norton
1974 S.27 Norton
1975 S.34 Norton
Todd, C. S.
1960 J.R. Norton
Todd, Paul A.
1978 J/N.12 Yamaha
1978 S.43 Yamaha
1979 S.50 Triumph
1980 L.20 RDZ Manxman
1981 L.11 RDZ Manxman
1981 J.23 RDZ Manxman
1982 L.4 Yamaha
1982 J.8 Yamaha
Todd, William B.
1964 L.R. Aermacchi
1965 L.21 Aermacchi
Toher, A. A. P.
1950 J.21 A.J.S.
Toleman, Bernie J.
1968 S.33 Triton
1969 S.26 M.B. Triton
1974 S.14 Suzuki
Tomkinson, Ian A.
1972 J.19 Aermacchi
1973 J.10 Yamaha
1974 J.4 Yamaha
1974 S.R. Yamaha
1975 J.R. Fowler Yamaha
1975 S.7 Fowler Yamaha
Tomlinson, Pete
1958 S(Sn).R. Triumph
1960 S.R. Matchless
Tompsett, Clive J.
1946 J.19 Norton
1946 S.R. Norton
Tonge, H. M.
1947 S.34 Norton
1951 S.22 Norton
1955 J.36 B.S.A.
Tonkin, John N.
1962 S.51 Norton
1964 J.32 A.J.S.
Tonkin, Steve
1973 J.5 Yamaha
Toone, Emilio W.
1970 S.R. Triumph
1971 S.R. Triumph
1972 S.48 E.T. Triumph
1974 S.46 E.T. Triumph
1975 S.41 E.T. Triumph
1976 S.R. Triumph
1977 S.43 Triumph
1978 S.32 E.T. Triumph
1979 S.53 E.T. Triumph
Tooze, Michael J.
1964 S.R. Norton
1965 S.24 Norton
1966 S.14 Norton
Tottle, Alan
1970 L.39 Yamaha
1971 L.34 Yamaha
1972 L.R. Yamaha
1974 L.55 Yamaha
Tottle William D.
1971 L.R. Yamaha
Townend, W. B.
1947 S.R. Triumph
Tranter, Robert
1976 J.R. Yamaha
1977 J.R. Yamaha
Tremble, Anthony C.
1968 S.R. Norton
1969 S.R. Norton
1970 S.R. Norton
1973 S.R. Norton
1974 J.16 Yamaha
1975 J.15 Saxon Yamaha
1976 J.R. Saxon Yamaha
1978 L.17 Yamaha
1979 L.R. Yamaha
Trickett, John
1979 S/N.5 Suzuki
Tricogulus, Norman
1973 L.10 Yamaha
1974 L.50 Walker Yamaha
1974 S.2 Walker Yamaha
1976 L.6 Yamaha
Trimby, M. J.
1971 J.R. Aermacchi
1972 J.14 Yamaha
Tromans, D. V.
1947 J.49 Norton
1947 S.33 Norton
Trotter, Les
1963 J.R. B.S.A.
1964 J.R. B.S.A.
1965 J.53 B.S.A.
1966 J.R. B.S.A.
1966 S.R. B.S.A.
1967 J.R. A.J.S.
1968 J.R. Norton
1969 J.18 Suzuki
1970 L.3 Suzuki
1970 S.23 Suzuki
1971 L.11 Crooks Suzuki
1972 L.5 Crooks Suzuki
1973 S.5 Suzuki
1974 S.R. Crooks Suzuki
1975 J.R. Egerton Yamaha
1975 S.4 Crooks Suzuki
1976 L.8 Fowler Yamaha
1976 S.1 Crooks Suzuki
Trow, Alan
1955 J.9 Norton
1955 S.4 Norton
Trubshaw, Keith
1973 L.31 Honda
1974 L.R. Yamaha
1975 L.2 Dugdale Maxton Yamaha
1976 J.2 Yamaha
1976 S.R. Yamaha
1979 J.7 Maxton Yamaha
1979 S.R. Maxton Yamaha
1980 J.2 Maxton
1980 S.R. Maxton
1981 L.14 Maxton Rotax
1981 J.10 Yamaha
1982 J.R. Yamaha
1982 S.R. WLT Suzuki
Trueman, Noel
1974 L.43 Yamaha
Trustham, Jack G.
1953 J.39 A.J.S.
1954 J.R. A.J.S.
1955 J.51 A.J.S.
1955 S.R. A.J.S.
1956 J.R. A.J.S.
1956 S.R. A.J.S.
1957 J.R. A.J.S.
1957 S.31 A.J.S.
1958 S.R. Norton
1959 S.20 Norton
1960 S.16 Norton
1961 J.R. A.J.S.
1961 S.18 Norton
1962 S.23 Norton
1963 S.R. Norton
1964 S.14 Norton
1965 S.30 Triumph
1966 J.29 Norton
1967 J.R. Norton
1967 S.R. Norton
1968 J.22 Norton
1969 J.23 Norton
1969 S.R. Norton
1970 J.R. Norton
1970 S.R. Norton
Tuck. H. G. F.
1950 S.54 A.J.S.
1954 J.R. A.J.S.
Tucker, A. V.
1968 J.49 A.J.S.
Tuke, J. B.
1960 S.43 Norton
Tulley, Peter
1976 J.57 Yamaha
Tunstall, Geoff D.
1968 S.R. Monard
1969 S.R. Monard
1970 S.R. Monard
1971 S.R. Norton
1973 S.R. Norton
1974 S.R. Norton
1975 J.24 Yamaha
1976 S.R. Maxton Yamaha
1977 S.8 Denby Dale Maxton
1978 J.R. Maxton
1978 S.10 Denby Dale Maxton
1979 L.8 Denby Dale Maxton
1979 J.R. Denby Dale Maxton
1980 L.18 Denby Dale Maxton
1980 J.13 Denby Dale Maxton
1981 L.10 Denby Dale Maxton
1981 J.33 Denby Dale Maxton
Turk, A. C. T.
1951 J.12 A.J.S.
Turner, B. L.
1955 J.16 Norton
1955 S.R. Norton
1956 J.R. Norton
Turner, David
1971 J.29 Norton
1972 J.37 Norton
1973 J.46 Norton
1974 J.38 Aermacchi
1975 S.R. Norton
1976 S.R. Manx Norton
Turner, Glyn
1975 L.42 Yamaha
1976 L.50 Yamaha
1977 L.R. Yamaha
1978 L.38 Yamaha
1979 L.R. Yamaha
1980 L.12 Yamaha
1981 L.20 Yamaha
1982 L.R. Yamaha
Turner, G. H.
1957 S(N).5 B.S A.
1957 S.23 B.S.A.
1958 J.23 B.S.A.
1958 S.R. A.J.S.
1959 J.R. A.J.S.
Turner, Kenneth
1964 J.23 Norton
Turner, Michael J.
1966 J.55 Norton
1967 J.R. Norton
1968 J.42 Norton
1969 J.55 Norton
Turner, T. Harry
1947 J.R. Norton
1947 S.10 Norton
Turner, Thomas H. K.
1965 J.R. Norton
1965 S.59 Norton
1966 J.R. Norton
1966 S.R. Norton
1967 J.30 Norton
1968 S.21 Norton
1969 J.20 Aermacchi
1969 S.13 Norton
1970 J.R. Norton
1970 S.17 Norton
1971 L.13 Yamaha
1971 S.22 Norton
Tweddell, J. G.
1957 J(N).38 Norton
1958 J(Sn).43 Norton
Tyack, Pete H.
1958 J(Sn).30 A.J.S.
1958 S.47 A.J.S.
1960 S.36 Norton
1963 S.R. Matchless
1964 J.R. A.J.S.
Tynan, D.
1946 J.29 Norton
1946 S.28 Norton
1947 J.R. Norton
1947 S.29 Norton
1948 J.47 Norton
1949 J.46 Norton
1949 S.33 Norton
1950 J.41 Norton
1951 J.44 A.J.S.
1951 S.43 A.J.S.
Tyson, H. T.
1946 J.36 Velocette
1950 J.R. Velocette

Unwin, E.
1954 J.R. Norton
1956 J.33 B.S.A.
1956 S.20 B.S,A.
1957 J.R. B.S.A.
1958 J.R. B.S.A.
1958 S.R. B.S.A.
Uphill, Malcolm
1962 J.14 Norton
1963 J.8 Norton
1964 J.2 A.J.S.
1964 S.R. Norton
1965 J.1 Norton
1965 S.1 Norton
Urquhart, H. L.
1958 J(Sn).17 A.J.S.
1958 J34 A.J.S.
1959 J.30 A.J.S.

Varlow, J. M.
1948 J.56 A.J.S.
1949 J.34 A.J.S.
1949 S.R. A.J.S.
Vaughan, Bruce
1977 L.59 Yamaha
1978 L.63 Yamaha
Vaughan,Eric E.
1964 J.44 Norton
Vaughan-Jones, Andy R.
1969 L.34 Ducati
1970 L.24 Ducati
1971 L.20 Ducati
1972 S.R. Norton
1973 S.14 Norton
1974 L.R. Ducati
1974 S.R. Norton
1975 S.R. Honda
Vernon, Gary
1980 S/N.7 Milnes Yamaha
1981 L.52 Milnes Yamaha
1982 L.R. Yamaha
Vicaradge, H.
1959 J.R. B.S.A.
Vickery, Graham
1973 L.R. Honda
1974 L.59 Ducati
1975 J.R. Yamaha
1976 J.R. Yamaha
1977 J.39 Yamaha
Vine, Rob
1977 S.R. Yamaha
1978 S.R. Yamaha
1978 S.8 Ely Maxton
1980 J.7 Ely Maxton Yamaha
1980 S.9 Yamaha
1981 J.5 Ely Maxton

1981 S.R.	Yamaha	**Wall, H.**		1966 S.7	Norton	1965 S.6	Matchless	1979 S/N.8	Yamaha
Virco, Alan		1950 S.34	A.J.S.	1967 L.R.	Greeves	1966 J.R.	A.J.S.	**Watt, James G.**	
1956 J.60	B.N. Special	**Wallace, Edward E.**		1967 S.R.	Norton	1966 S.R.	Matchless	1980 S/R.	Laverda
1957 J.49	B.N. Special	1968 S.R.	Triumph	1968 L.7	Yamaha	1967 J.2	A.J.S.	1981 S.55	Laverda
1957 S.47	B.N. Special	1969 L.12	Greeves	1968 S.27	Norton	1967 S.6	Matchless	1982 S.59	Laverda
1958 J.39	B.N. Special	**Wallace, Ian P.**		1969 J.R.	Yamaha	1968 J.R.	A.J.S.	**Watts, Clive**	
1958 S.43	B.N. Special	1958 J(Sn).6	Norton	1969 S.3	Norton	1968 S.R.	Matchless	1976 J.R.	Fowler Yamaha
Vivian, A. H.		1958 J.22	Norton	1970 J.R.	Yamaha	**Warwick, D.**		1977 L.3	Fowler Yamaha
1957 J(N).R.	A.J.S.	1959 J.R.	Norton	1970 S.14	Norton	1951 J.59	Velocette	1978 J.3	Cowles Yamaha
Voice, Harry		1959 S.R.	Norton	**Ward, Anthony M.**		**Washer, Ernie J.**		1978 S.5	Cowles Yamaha
1953 J.7	B.S.A.	1960 J.3	Norton	1964 J.16	Norton	1955 J.17	A.J.S.	1979 J.1	Cowles Suzuki
1953 S.R.	Gilera	1960 S.6	Norton	**Ward, C. E.**		1955 S.24	A.J.S.	1979 S.1	Cowles Suzuki
1954 J.27	B.S.A.	**Waller, J. W.**		1961 J.R.	A.J.S.	1956 J.9	A.J.S.	**Watts, H. B. I.**	
1954 S.13	B.S.A.	1958 J(Sn).58	A.J.S.	1962 J.40	Norton	1956 S.8	Norton	1946 L.R.	O.K. Supreme
1955 J.14	A.J.S.	1959 J.74	A.J.S.	**Ward, Charles H.**		1957 S.2	Norton	1947 L.R.	O.K. Supreme
1955 S.15	A.J.S.	**Walley, Ken**		1964 L.13	L.E./B.S.A.	1958 J.3	Norton	1947 S.R.	Scott
1957 J.R.	A.J.S.	1968 J.R.	Norton	**Ward, E.**		1958 S.1	Norton	**Way, Kenneth G. P.**	
1957 S.54	A.J.S.	**Wallis, C. Vern**		1967 L.55	Yamaha	**Wassell, Maurice**		1964 L.15	Cotton
		1960 S.R.	B.S.A.	1968 L.39	Yamaha	1955 J.70	B.S.A.	**Wayne, D. A.**	
Waddilove, A. William		1961 J.R.	Velocette	**Ward, E. R.**		1957 J.44	A.J.S.	1948 J.48	Norton
1970 S.R.	Velocette	1962 S.31	Norton	1950 J.23	Velocette	1957 S.40	A.J.S.	1949 J.47	Norton
1972 S.47	Velocette	1963 J.R.	Velocette	**Ward, James**		**Wastell, F.**		**Webb, John**	
1973 S.R.	Velocette	1963 S.21	Norton	1963 S.25	Matchless	1946 L.17	Excelsior	1977 L.12	Yamaha
1974 S.R.	Velocette	1964 L.18	Cotton	1964 S.13	Matchless	1947 L.47	Velocette	1978 L.R.	Yamaha
Waddington, Ken D.		1964 S.R.	Norton	1965 L.R.	Royal Enfield	1947 S.58	Moto Guzzi	1978 J.5	Yamaha
1950 J.36	A.J.S.	1965 S.39	Norton	1966 L.17	Royal Enfield	1951 J.68	A.J.S.	**Webb, Keith**	
1950 S.50	A.J.S.	1967 J.R.	Velocette	1967 L.17	Royal Enfield	1951 S.53	A.J.S.	1976 L.37	Yamaha
1952 J.15	A.J.S.	1968 S.R.	Velocette	1968 L.R.	Royal Enfield	1958 J.57	B.S.A.	1977 L.13	Yamaha
1952 S.R.	Triumph	1969 S.R.	Velocette	1969 L.52	Royal Enfield	1958 S.R.	B.S.A.	1978 L.15	Yamaha
Wade, D. J.		1970 S.R.	Velocette	1970 L.R.	Royal Enfield	1959 J.76	B.S.A.	1978 J.45	Yamaha
1970 L.33	Greeves	1971 S.R.	Velocette	1972 L.31	Suzuki	**Wastell, R.**		**Webb, Roger**	
Wade, Harry K.		1972 S.R.	Velocette	**Ward, Keith R.**		1950 J.46	Norton	1974 L.5	Yamsel
1966 L.R.	D.M.W.	1973 S.R.	Velocette	1969 L.R.	Greeves	1950 S.R.	Scott	**Webb, Russ**	
1967 L.43	D.M.W.	**Walmsley, Brian**		1970 L.37	Honda	**Waterer, Richard**		1975 L.R.	Yamaha
Wainwright, R. K.		1961 S.R.	B.S.A.	1971 L.R.	Honda	1964 L.19	Greeves	1976 J.R.	Yamaha
1972 J.R.	Yamaha	1962 J.R.	A.J.S.	**Ward, Mick**		**Watkins, Richard B.**		1977 J.R.	Yamaha
Waite, D. L.		**Walpole, David**		1979 L/N.15	Maxton Yamaha	1964 L.R.	Bultaco	**Webster, Bill N.**	
1958 J(Sn).36	B.S.A.	1969 J.R.	Norton	1979 L.56	Maxton Yamaha	1965 L.R.	Yamaha	1946 L.16	Excelsior
1959 J.66	B.S.A.	**Walsh, P. E.**		1980 L.47	Maxton Yamaha	1967 L.50	Yamaha	**Weedall, N.**	
Waite, J. F.		1950 S.63	Norton	1980 J.54	Maxton Yamaha	1972 L.26	Aermacchi	1968 J.R.	A.J.S.
1951 S.64	Norton	1952 S.64	Triumph	1981 L.38	Spondon Yamaha	1973 L.25	Aermacchi	**Weeden, John**	
Wakefield, G. S.		**Walsh, Pat M.**		1981 J.51	Maxton Yamaha	1974 L.R.	Yamaha	1969 L.21	Yamaha
1946 J.28	Norton	1952 S.32	Vincent	1982 L.55	Maxton Yamaha	1975 L.7	Yamaha	1970 L.35	Yamaha
1946 S.R.	Norton	**Walsh, Peter J.**		1982 J.49	Yamaha	1976 L.R.	Yamaha	1971 L.R.	Yamaha
Walczak, Adolf W. G.		1950 J.54	Norton	**Ward, M. E.**		**Watson, C.**		1972 L.13	Yamaha
1957 J(N).25	B.S.A.	1951 S.56	Triumph	1958 S(Sn).10	Norton	1954 S.11	Norton	**Welfare, Peter D.**	
1958 J.46	B.S.A.	1953 S.R.	Norton	1958 S.53	Norton	1955 S.R.	Norton	1967 J.31	Aermacchi
1959 S.40	Norton	1954 S.24	Norton	**Ward, Peter**		1956 S.25	W.R.S. Special	1968 J.12	Aermacchi
1961 S.62	Norton	1955 J.55	B.S.A.	1966 S.24	B.S.A.	1958 S.R.	Norton	1969 J.33	Honda
1962 S.R.	Norton	1955 S.50	B.S.A.	1967 S.R.	B.S.A.	1959 S.R.	B.S.A.	1970 J.R.	Honda
Wales, Raymond P.		1956 J.35	B.S.A.	1968 S.R.	B.S.A.	**Watson, C. O.**		1970 L.R.	Honda
1966 L.48	N.S.U.	1956 S.R.	B.S.A.	**Ward, Philip**		1959 J.R.	Norton	1971 J.7	Honda
1967 S.R.	Norton	**Walters, E**		1968 L.R.	Ducati	1960 J.35	Norton	1972 J.R.	Honda
Walker, Barrie J.		1950 J.42	A.J.S.	**Ward, Steve**		1961 J.R.	A.J.S.	1973 J.20	Honda
1962 J.9	Norton	**Walters, R. J.**		1974 L.3	Yamaha	1962 S.30	Norton	1973 S.30	Honda
1964 J.R.	Norton	1953 J.R.	A.J.S.	1975 L.R.	Yamaha	**Watson, Colin**		1974 S.24	Suzuki
1964 S.12	Norton	**Walton, Fred**		1975 S.R.	Yamaha	1974 L.58	Yamaha	1975 L.R.	Crooks Suzuki
Walker, E.		1958 J(Sn).R.	B.S.A.	1978 J.1	Padgett Yamaha	1975 L.R.	Yamaha	**Wells, James**	
1948 S.R.	Norton	1959 J.56	B.S.A.	1978 S.2	Padgett Yamaha	**Watson, D. E.**		1974 L.31	Yamaha
1949 S.23	Norton	1960 J.R.	B.S.A.	**Waring, Graham**		1961 J.5	Norton	**West, S. R.**	
Walker, G. W.		1961 J.44	B.S.A.	1974 L.18	Yamaha	1962 J.17	Norton	1947 J.R.	D.K.W.
1956 S.40	Norton	1962 J.46	B.S.A.	**Warner, Alfred M.**		**Watson, Dickie**		**Weston, P. H.**	
1958 S.49	B.S.A.	1963 J.R.	B.S.A.	1965 J.R.	Norton	1976 L.69	Suzuki	1946 L.14	Rudge
1959 S.48	B.S.A.	1964 J.17	B.S.A.	1966 J.22	Norton	**Watson, Kenneth**		1947 L.17	Rudge
1960 S.N.F.	B.S.A.	**Walton, William L.**		1967 J.R.	Norton	1959 S.53	Norton	1948 L.6	Rudge
Walker, Mick J. G.		1963 S.33	Norton	1968 J.8	Aermacchi	1960 S.R.	Norton	1949 J.R.	Norton
1966 L.50	Ducati	**Warburton, Brian J. A.**		1969 J.7	Aermacchi	1961 S.41	Norton	1950 J.R.	Rudge
1967 L.42	Ducati	1957 J(N).R.	Norton	1970 J.44	Aermacchi	1962 S.33	Norton	**Westrum, Rolf**	
1970 L.32	Ducati	1958 J(Sn).20	Velocette	1971 J.R.	Yamaha	1965 L.9	Ducati	1976 J.19	Yamaha
1971 J.30	Ducati	1958 J.R.	Norton	1972 J.R.	Yamaha	1966 L.2	Ducati	1977 J.R.	Yamaha
Walker, R. F.		1959 S.24	Norton	1973 J.R.	Yamaha	1967 L.R.	Suzuki	**Westwood, L.**	
1948 J.R.	Norton	1960 J.R.	Norton	1974 J.48	Yamaha	**Watson, Martin C.**		1950 J.R.	Norton
Walker, T.		1960 S.13	Norton	1975 J.18	Yamaha	1966 L.5	Bultaco	1951 J.R.	Excelsior
1957 J(N).47	B.S.A.	1961 J.14	Norton	1976 J.R.	Yamaha	1966 S.R.	Norton	**Wetherall, John G.**	
1958 J(Sn).R.	B.S.A.	1961 S.17	Norton	1977 J.18	Yamaha	**Watson, T. F.**		1964 L.7	Cotton
1959 J.59	B.S.A.	1962 J.41	Norton	1977 S.R.	Yamaha	1952 S.53	Norton	1965 L.R.	Cotton
1960 S.R.	Norton	1963 J.5	Norton	1978 S.36	Yamaha	1953 S.34	Norton	1966 L.R.	Cotton
1961 S.R.	Norton	1963 S.9	Norton	**Warren, Brian R.**		1954 S.20	Norton	1967 J.1	Norton
1962 S.R.	Norton	1964 J.R.	Norton	1973 J.54	A.J.S.	1955 S.47	Norton	1967 S.3	Norton
Walker, W. B.		1964 S.R.	Norton	**Warren, Nigel R.**		1956 S.43	B.S.A.	**Whalley, David M.**	
1948 J.52	Velocette	1965 L.2	Yamaha	1963 J.17	A.J.S.	1957 J.47	B.S.A.	1966 L.R.	Greeves
Wall, Anthony J.		1965 S.3	Yamaha	1964 J.R.	A.J.S.	1957 S.44	B.S.A.	**Wheeler, Arthur F.**	
1965 L.R.	Greeves	1966 L.13	Yamaha	1964 S.R.	Norton	1958 J.R.	B.S.A.	1946 J.11	Velocette
1966 J.R.	Greeves			1965 J.2	A.J.S.	**Watson, William**		1946 S.10	Velocette

1947 J.6	Velocette	1982 L.24	Yamaha	**Wilkinson, J. F.**		**Williams, John G.**		1980 J/N.R.	Maxton Yamaha
1947 S.12	Velocette	**Whittaker, H.**		1961 S.R.	Norton	1966 L.R.	Greeves	1981 L.7	Yamaha
1948 J.9	Velocette	1948 J.R.	A.J.S.	**Wilkinson, Paul A.**		1967 L.R.	Ducati	1981 J.4	Maxton Yamaha
1948 S.5	Triumph	1949 J.49	Velocette	1969 L.R.	Suzuki	**Williams. John H.**		1982 J.R.	Maxton Yamaha
Wheeler, John		1949 S.R.	Velocette	**Willats, Ron**		1963 S.34	Norton	1982 S.R.	Suzuki
1962 S.N.F.	Velocette	1950 J.R.	A.J.S.	1961 J.R.	A.J.S.	**Williams, Mike F.**		**Wilson, Robert M.**	
Wheeler, Malcolm		**Whittingham, Leonard W.**		1962 J.38	A.J.S.	1982 S/N.9	Ducati	1970 J.49	Norton-B.S.A.
1974 S.R.	Seeley	1946 L.R.	New Imperial	**Willcocks, Richard**		**Williams, Michael P.**		1971 J.51	A.J.S.
1975 S.24	Seeley	1947 L.N.F.	New Imperial	1969 S.R.	B.S.A.	1980 L/N.9	Yamaha	**Wilson, Roger D.**	
1976 S.13	Seeley	**Whittingham, S. R.**		**Willerton, A. E.**		1981 L.32	Yamaha	1970 L.17	Ducati
1977 S.R.	Seeley	1946 J.40	Norton	1956 S.R.	B.S.A.	1982 L.17	Yamaha	1975 J.33	Aermacchi Metisse
1977 J.43	Brightman Aermacchi	1946 S.R.	Norton	1957 J.R.	A.J.S.	1982 J.33	Yamaha	1976 S.R.	Aermacchi Metisse
1978 J.23	Brightman Aermacchi	1947 J.64	Norton	**Williams, Charlie I.**		**Williams, Peter J.**		1977 J.8	Yamaha
Whelan, D.		1947 S.59	Norton	1970 L.5	Yamaha	1964 J.R.	Norton	1978 J.12	Yamaha
1948 L.11	Rudge	1948 J.55	Norton	1971 L.1	Yamaha	1965 L.3	Greeves	1978 S.R.	Yamaha
1950 J.28	A.J.S.	1949 J.68	Norton	**Williams, Chris**		1965 S.R.	Norton	**Wilson, Roger J.**	
1950 S.37	A.J.S.	1949 S.54	Norton	1959 S.R.	Norton	**Williams, Robert**		1975 S.33	Crooks Suzuki
Whillier, P. E.		**Whymark, Barry**		1960 S.R.	Matchless	1964 J.46	Norton	1976 S.6	Yamaha
1954 J.37	B.S.A.	1975 S.40	CR Suzuki	1961 S.R.	Norton	**Williams, Ross**		1977 L.11	Clucas Yamaha
1955 J.R	B.S.A.	1976 S.40	Honda	1962 S.R.	Norton	1980 J/N.R.	Yamaha	1977 S.9	Clucas yamaha
1955 S.19	B.S.A.	1977 S.35	Suzuki	1963 S.R.	Norton	1981 J.R.	Yamaha	1978 J.R.	Clucas Yamaha
White, C. B.		1978 J.41	Suzuki	1967 S.R.	B.S.A.	1981 S.R.	Yamaha	1978 S.9	Clucas Yamaha
1967 L.45	Ducati	**Wicksted, Chris J.**		1968 S.8	B.S.A.	1982 L.R.	Cotton	**Wilson, T. G.**	
1968 L.33	Bultaco	1974 L.R.	Yamaha	1971 S.23	Suzuki	1982 J.31	Yamaha	1947 J.63	Norton
White, John G.		**Widdup, F.**		1972 S.34	Suzuki	**Williams, Stephen**		1947 S.R.	Norton
1969 L.R.	Yamaha	1951 S.51	Norton	1973 S.9	Suzuki	1979 L/N.2	Fowler Yamaha	1948 J.R.	Velocette
White, J. W.		**Wield, Chas**		1974 S.R.	TWS Suzuki	1979 L.20	Fowler Yamaha	1948 S.29	Norton
1948 S.21	Triumph	1971 S.33	Norton	1976 S.R.	Cowles Matchless	1980 L.1	Fowler Yamaha	1949 J. 52	Velocette
White, M. R.		1972 S.18	Norton	**Williams, David**		1980 L.R.	Fowler Yamaha	1949 S.R.	Norton
1965 J.R.	B.S.A.	1974 S.R.	Suzuki	1958 S(Sn).2	Norton	**Williams, Steve**		**Winchester, Brian A.**	
White, N. W.		**Wigan, Mark R.**		1958 S.11	Norton	1974 J.R.	Yamaha	1961 J.R.	A.J.S.
1949 J.43	Velocette	1972 L.R.	Yamaha	1959 J.23	Norton	1975 L.43	Kawasaki	1962 J.R.	A.J.S.
1949 S.38	Velocette	1973 J.35	Yamaha	1959 S.R.	Norton	1976 S.R.	Kawasaki	1963 J.65	A.J.S.
1950 J.34	Velocette	1974 L.53	Honda	1960 J.21	Norton	**Williams, T.**		1964 J.R.	A.J.S.
1950 S.36	Velocette	1975 S.60	Walker Aermacchi	1960 S.R.	Norton	1951 S.R.	Norton	1965 J.54	A.J.S.
1951 J.R.	Velocette	**Wilcox, John**		1961 J.8	Norton	**Williams, V. T.**		1966 J.R.	A.J.S.
1951 S.R.	Velocette	1971 S.R.	Triton	1961 S.2	Norton	1951 S.R.	Triumph	**Winn, Stephen R.**	
White, Robert H.		1972 L.36	Bultaco/Yamaha	1962 J.7	Norton	1952 J.35	A.J.S.	1978 S/N.9	Seeley Matchless
1969 L.R.	Yamaha	1973 L.R.	Yamaha/Bultaco	1962 S.3	Norton	1952 S.R.	A.J.S.	1979 S.51	Seeley
White, Richard		1974 L.R.	Bultaco	1963 J.4	Norton	1953 J.17	Norton	1981 J.41	Maxton Yamaha
1982 S/N.R.	Suzuki	1980 S.R.	Honda	1963 S.R.	M.W. Norton	1953 S.22	Norton	1981 S.R.	Vendetta Matchless
White, Roger E. V.		1981 S.R.	Honda	1964 J.1	M.W. Special	1954 J.7	Norton	1982 J.R.	Maxton Yamaha
1981 S/N.R.	Yamaha	**Wilcox, M.**		1964 S.R.	M.W. Special	1954 S.R.	Norton	**Winter, H. B.**	
1981 S.R.	Yamaha	1951 J.37	A.J.S.	**Williams, David A.**		1955 J.7	A.J.S.	1951 S.60	Norton
1982 J.21	Yamaha	1952 J.R.	A.J.S.	1977 L.70	Honda	1955 S.R.	Norton	1952 J.R.	Norton
1982 S.45	Yamaha	**Wild, Charles D.**		1980 S.66	Suzuki	**Williamson, A. H.**		1952 S.55	Norton
Whitehouse, Ralph		1964 L.R.	Aermacchi	**Williams, David H.**		1957 S(N).F.	B.S.A.	1953 J.R.	Norton
1955 S.R.	Norton	1965 L.R.	Aermacchi	1969 L.37	Aermacchi	1959 S.34	B.S.A.	1954 J.52	Norton
1956 S.29	Norton	1966 J.R.	Aermacchi	1970 J.R.	Cowles Aermacchi	**Williamson, Norman**		**Winter, Nick**	
1957 S.20	Norton	1967 J.5	Aermacchi	1971 J.5	Cowles A.J.S.	1976 J.R.	Aermacchi HD	1965 J.R.	A.J.S.
1958 S.R.	B.S.A.	1968 J.7	Aermacchi	1972 J.R.	Cowles Yamaha	1977 J.R.	Aermacchi HD	1966 J.52	A.J.S.
Whiteside, Alan		1968 S.4	Norton	1972 S.2	Matchless	1978 J.39	Aermacchi HD	1967 J.20	A.J.S.
1961 J.34	A.J.S.	1969 J.13	Norton	1973 J.4	Cowles Yamaha	1979 J.44	Yamaha	1968 J.R.	A.J.S.
1962 S.16	Matchless	1969 S.7	Norton	1973 S.R.	Cowles Matchless	1980 J.40	Yamaha	1969 J.48	Aermacchi
Whiteside, Ted		1973 J.33	Norton	1974 J.R.	Cowles Yamaha	1981 J.40	Yamaha	1970 J.R.	Aermacchi Metisse
1957 J(N).5	A.J.S.	1973 S.R.	Norton	1974 S.R.	Cowles Matchless	1982 J.R.	Yamaha	1972 J.R.	A.J.S.
1957 J.R.	A.J.S.	**Wild, Pete**		1975 J.2	Cowles Yamaha	**Willis, K.**		**Winter, Phillip**	
1958 J.R.	A.J.S.	1979 J/N.6	Yamaha	1975 S.R.	Matchless	1950 J.R.	Norton	1975 J.R.	Roberts Aermacchi
1959 J.R.	Norton	1979 L.R.	Yamaha	1976 J.R.	Cowles Yamaha	1951 J.R.	B.S.A.	1977 S.36	Crooks Suzuki
Whiteway, Frank		**Wilde, L. J.**		**Williams, Derek**		1952 J.29	A.J.S.	**Wise, Trevor**	
1964 L.R.	Triumph	1950 J.57	B.S.A.	1957 J(N).2	B.S.A.	1952 S.27	A.J.S.	1979 L/N.5	Graphic Yamaha
1965 L.R.	Greeves	1951 J.R.	B.S.A.	1957 J.20	B.S.A.	**Willoughby, Peter**		1979 L.31	Graphic Yamaha
1966 L.11	Suzuki	1952 J.56	A.J.S.	1958 J.20	B.S.A.	1967 L.48	Greeves	**Withers, Mick R.**	
1967 L.2	Suzuki	1953 J.R.	A.J.S.	1958 S.20	B.S.A.	1968 L.R.	Yamaha	1974 S.51	Velocette
1968 L.1	Suzuki	1954 J.46	A.J.S.	1959 J.8	A.J.S.	**Wills, A. R.**		1975 S.R.	Velocette
Whitnear, Mike		**Wilkerson, R. J.**		1959 S.17	A.J.S.	1965 S.49	B.S.A.	1976 L.58	Yamaha
1975 S.42	G50 Metisse	1948 L.R.	Rudge	1960 J.20	A.J.S.	**Wills, Dennis A.**		1977 L.31	Yamaha
Whittaker, David M.		**Wilkins, D. J. P.**		1960 S.12	Matchless	1964 J.24	Norton	**Wolton, R.**	
1971 L.42	Aermacchi	1950 S.46	A.J.S.	1962 S.40	Norton	**Wilson, Colin**		1947 J.R.	Excelsior
1972 S.R.	Aermacchi	1951 J.R.	Norton	1963 J.R.	A.J.S.	1975 J.43	Yamaha	**Wood, Davy G.**	
1973 S.42	Norton	1952 J.R.	Norton	1963 S.R.	Norton	**Wilson, G.**		1972 L.46	Honda
1974 S.37	Aermacchi	1953 J.R.	Norton	**Williams, Derek L.**		1956 S.52	Norton	**Wood, Derek R.**	
1975 J.R.	Aermacchi	1953 S.33	Norton	1975 J.59	Yamaha	1957 S.32	Norton	1972 L.R.	Suzuki
1976 L.42	Yamaha	**Wilkinson, Colin**		1976 S.R.	Sparton	1958 S.R.	Norton	1973 L.41	Suzuki
1977 J.42	Harley Davidson	1968 S.47	Norton	1977 S.R.	Sparton	1959 S.R.	Norton	**Wood, J.**	
1978 S.R.	Yamaha	1969 L.R.	Norton	1980 S.R.	Spondon	**Wilson, J.**		1958 J(Sn).23	B.S.A.
Whittaker, Graham J.		1970 S.27	Norton	1982 J.44	Spondon	1958 J(Sn).45	A.J.S.	**Wood, Jackie J.**	
1970 L.R.	Yamaha	1971 S.30	Norton	**Williams, Howard E**		**Wilson, J. S.**		1950 J.26	Norton
1971 L.R.	Yamaha	1972 S.R.	Norton	1963 J.32	A.J.S.	1950 J.51	Velocette	1951 S.7	Norton
1972 L.21	Yamaha	1973 J.R.	Yamsel	1964 J.22	A.J.S.	1951 J.R.	Velocette	1952 J.14	Norton
1973 S.29	Yamaha	1974 J.R.	Yamsel	**Williams, H. L**		1951 S.31	Velocette	1952 S.9	Norton
1979 L.57	Yamaha	1975 S.47	Honda	1950 S.8	Norton	1952 J.R.	Velocette	1953 J.9	Norton
1980 L.46	Yamaha	1976 L.59	Honda	**Williams, Ian**		1952 S.46	Velocette	1953 S.4	Norton
1981 L.37	Yamaha	1977 S.38	Honda	1976 L.R.	Ducati	**Wilson, Kevin**		1954 J.R.	B.S.A.

1954 S.R.	Norton	1961 S.11	Matchless	1981 L.49	Yamaha	**Wroe, Ramon D.**		1982 S.4	Suzuki
1955 J.3	B.S.A.	**Woods. A. W. B.**		1982 J.R.	Yamaha	1954 J.43	Velocette	**Yeatman, John**	
1955 S.R.	B.S.A.	1950 J.R.	Velocette	**Wrettom, Kevin**		1954 S.R.	Velocette	1979 S/N.11	Honda
Wood, Jeff		1951 J.43	Velocette	1976 L.15	Yamaha	1956 J.R.	Velocette	1979 L.52	Yamaha
1975 L.33	Yamaha	1951 S.41	Velocette	**Wright, Alexander**		1957 J.42	Velocette	**York, Jack**	
1976 L.R.	Yamaha	1952 J.24	Velocette	1968 L.R.	Yamaha	1957 S.R.	Velocette	1962 S.R.	G.B.S.
1977 J.R.	Yamaha	1952 S.R.	Velocette	**Wright, Bernie**		1958 J.R.	Norton	1963 S.N.F.	G.B.S.1
1978 J.21	Yamaha	**Woods, Harry S.**		1978 L/N.11	Yamaha	1958 S.23	Norton	1964 S.34	S.B.S.
Wood, Ron		1962 J.R.	Velocette	1980 L.49	Lockyam	1959 J.39	Norton	**Young, G. C.**	
1976 L.R.	Yamaha	1964 L.36	Bultaco	1981 L.27	Lockyam	1960 S.18	Matchless	1957 S(N).R	Norton
Wood, Tony		1965 L.18	Bultaco	1981 J.53	Lockyam	1962 S.R.	B.S.A.	1958 S(Sn).6	Norton
1962 S.R.	B.S.A.	1967 L.27	Bultaco	1982 L.32	Yamaha	1962 S.13	Matchless	1958 S.R.	Norton
1963 J.66	A.J.S.	**Woods, J.**		1982 J.R.	Yamaha	1963 J.R.	B.S.A.	**Young, Lewis P.**	
1964 S.25	Star/7R Special	1966 J.R.	B.S.A.	**Wright, D. A.**		1963 S.R.	Matchless	1955 J.71	A.J.S.
1965 J.16	A.J.S.	**Woods, S.**		1954 J.17	B.S.A.	1964 L.R.	B.S.A.	1956 J.55	A.J.S.
Woodcock, Derek		1966 S.R.	Triumph	1954 S.R.	B.S.A.	1964 S.R.	Matchless	1956 S.49	A.J.S.
1964 J.R.	B.S.A.	1967 J.R.	B.S.A.	**Wright, J.**		**Wyatt, Roger F.**		1957 J.21	A.J.S.
Wooder, Ernie F.		1968 L.9	Yamaha	1951 S.R.	B.S.A.	1971 S.38	Norton	1957 S.R.	J.V. Special
1960 S.24	Matchless	**Woods, Stan V.**		**Wright, Jim**		1972 S.28	Norton	**Young, N. V.**	
1961 S.28	Matchless	1967 L.30	Ducati	1972 S.51	Norton	**Wylie, Graham**		1950 S.R.	Triumph
1962 J.R.	A.J.S.	1968 L.47	S.V. Spl.	1973 S.R.	Manx-Triumph	1975 J.58	Ducati	1951 S.44	A.J.S.
Wooderson, J. N.		**Woodward, John G.**		1974 S.19	Matchless	1976 J.R.	Ducati	**Young, Peter A.**	
1953 J.20	B.S.A.	1981 J/N.9	Yamaha	1975 S.R.	Manx Daytona	1977 S.27	Honda Special	1963 S.37	Norton
1953 S.14	Matchless	1981 S.47	Yamaha	1976 S.29	Lund Matchless	1978 J.29	Aermacchi	1964 J.R.	Norton
Woodhead, John		**Woollon, Anthony M.**		**Wright, J. R.**		1979 J.R.	Aermacchi	1965 J.45	Norton
1974 S.45	Kawasaki	1971 S.36	Seymour Velocette	1958 (J(Sn).R.	Norton	**Wynne, Pat**		**Young, W.**	
1975 S.R.	Kawasaki	**Worgan, H.**		**Wright, Kevin**		1972 L.49	Ducati	1960 J.R.	A.J.S.
1976 S.R.	Kawasaki	1965 L.41	Greeves	1980 L/N.R.	Yamaha	1977 L.61	Yamaha		
1977 S.14	P&S Yamaha	**Worsdall, M. S.**		**Wright, Robert A.**		1978 L.62	Yamaha	**Zealand, A. W.**	
Woodman, Derek		1966 L.R.	Yamaha	1981 S/N.R.	Kawasaki	1979 L.54	Yamaha	1947 J.59	Norton
1956 J.59	B.S.A.	**Worwood, Glyn**		1982 S.38	Kawasaki	1980 L.56	Yamaha	1948 J.R.	Norton
1957 J.26	B.S.A.	1975 S.59	Honda	**Wright, Tony**		1981 L.42	Yamaha	1949 J.R.	Norton
1958 J.29	Norton	**Wotton, B. J.**		1960 S.R.	B.S.A.	1982 L.53	Yamaha	1950 J.R.	Norton
1958 S.25	Norton	1965 L.R.	B.S.A.	**Wright, Victor J.**		**Yeardsley, C. Buddy**		1950 S.43	Norton
1959 J.14	Norton	1966 L.R.	Greeves	1968 J.R.	Greeves	1981 L/N.1	Yamaha	1951 J.60	Norton
1959 S.27	Norton	**Wray, C. H.**		1970 J.R.	Greeves	1981 L.9			
1960 J.15	Norton	1966 S.36	Norton	1971 L.R.	Suzuki		Wilson & Collins Yamaha		
1960 S.21	Norton	**Wren, Edwin**		1972 L.6	Yamaha	1982 J.R.	Yamaha		
1961 J.10	A.J.S.	1981 L/N.7	Yamaha	1973 L.3	Yamaha				

This 'bubble car helicopter was used for many years as a fund-raising vehicle for the Helicopter Fund, seen here in the paddock adjacent to its real live counterpart.

The Manx Grand Prix Supporters' Club Helicopter Fund

An incident which occurred during the 1975 Manx was the catalyst for the formation of the MGP Helicopter Fund, which has to date contributed thousands of pounds to the Manx Motorcycle Club for the provision of the rescue helicopter.

When Mick Bird crashed his Yamaha at Quarry Bends during the Thursday afternoon practice in '75, there was a significant delay waiting for an ambulance to arrive. After the practice, Raymond Caley, the flagman on duty at the scene, was in conversation with Gwen Crellin to see if there was a chance of getting a helicopter for the Manx. From this meeting the MGP Supporters' Club was formed, with the express intent of raising funds for a practice-week 'chopper'.

Thirteen fund-raising events were held during that first year, which paid for the chopper for the 1976 meeting. The cost was £350: in 1997, the club handed over £22,000 towards the cost - some inflation!

The total amount that the Supporters' Club has passed to the M.M.C.C. is over £180,000, all raised from sponsored activities, from dog walks to towing a BMW three-wheeler round the TT course, car boot sales and donations. Pat Wynne has pushed a horse-tram along the length of Douglas Promenade for a great many years, even during 1989, when he was suffering with a broken arm! A recent addition to the fund-raising scene is a Coffee Morning, held at the home of the Membership Secretary Sally Wallis, wife of former MGP rider Vern.

Two of the committee members who have given many years of service to the Club are Gwen Crellin M.B.E., Patron of the Club and John Kermeen, who has been Chairman for the past fifteen years.

Gwen - 'the lady in white' as she is known to the riders is in her prime at 81 years of age, still marshals outside here house, just after leaving Ballaugh village every practice and race day. The dining room table is laden with goodies for riders unfortunate enough to retire during the event. Gwen's house is alive with riders and their wives during race weeks and many drop in out of race times when they visit the Island, she is very proud of the achievements of 'her boys - and girls' as she calls them.

The '98 Manx will be Gwen's 35th year as a marshal for the Manx, and she was awarded the M.B.E. for her services to the community, including her sterling work for the Helicopter Fund.

John Kermeen took over the Chairman's reins fifteen years ago, and has witnessed the growth of the Club and the amount of funds needed to assist the Manx Club's commitment to race safety.

Not dressed as 'the lady in white' this day, Gwen Crellin at Buckingham Palace upon being invested with her M.B.E.

The Supporters' Club is twenty-three years old this year, and is looking forward to celebrating their 25th anniversary at the Millennium.

Membership costs £25 for life membership or £3.00 per year. Please send your membership, and any suggestions for fund-raising activities to Sally Wallis, Riders Retreat, Carrick Park, Sulby, Isle of Man, IM7 2EX.

Pat Wynne and Dave Saville on the 1993 'tram push' along Douglas Promenade, in aid of the Helicopter Fund. Katherine Taylor, daughter of Classic racer Francis, is the passenger.

The Manx Grand Prix
1983 - 1997   The Classics arrive

1983

To celebrate the Diamond Jubilee, the Manx Club decided to introduce a Classic race to the programme, to be held on the Saturday. For the first year there were three classes, 500cc, 350cc and 250cc So popular was this event that it has been included ever since, although the 250cc class was dropped in 1984. Thus the Manx Grand Prix grew into a five race meeting. The three Classic classes were run concurrently over three laps of the course, 113-19 miles.

1983 Senior Classic

The Senior Classic attracted an entry of 56, and non-starters reduced this to 42. American Dave Roper (Matchless) was fastest in practice followed by John Goodall (Matchless) and Bob Hirst (Seeley). Goodall led at the end of the first lap by 19.2 seconds from Hirst, who was 0.4 seconds ahead of Neil Tuxworth (Matchless). Indeed the first three remained unchanged for the three laps, Goodall leading by 17.4 seconds at the end of lap two with Tuxworth 22.4 seconds down on Hirst. At the flag Goodall won by 7.2 seconds from Hirst who finished 42.2 seconds ahead of Tuxworth. Ken Inwood (Norton) was fourth, Richard Cutts (Seeley) fifth and Grant Sellars (Norton) sixth. There were 23 finishers.

1983 Senior Classic (3 laps / 113.19 miles) 56 entries

1. John Goodall	Matchless	1h. 11m. 43.6s	94.68 mph
2. Bob Hirst	Seeley	1h. 11m. 50.8s	94.52 mph
3. Neil Tuxworth	Matchless	1h. 12m. 33.0s	93.61 mph
Fastest lap			
Bob Hirst	Seeley	23m. 39.2s	95.70 mph

1983 Junior Classic

A total of 44 riders entered for the Junior Classic, and five non-starters reduced the field to 39. Chris Griffiths (Aermacchi) was fastest in practice, Paul Barrett (Harley) was second fastest followed by Lawrence Parris (Aermacchi). At the end of the first lap, Barrett led Parris by 46.6 seconds, with Griffiths in third place, a further two seconds down. As in the Junior class, the first three remained unchanged throughout the race. Paul Barrett continued to pull away from his pursuers and won from Parris by one minute 21.8 seconds with Griffiths in third place, 38.6 seconds down on Parris. The top six were completed by Jimmy Millar (Aermacchi), Kobi Haddock (A.J.S.) and Jack Gow (Aermacchi). There were 34 finishers.

John Goodall; victor in 1983, still racing the same machine today.

1983 Junior Classic (3 laps / 113.19 miles) 44 entries

1. Paul Barrett	Harley Davidson	1h. 12m. 48.2s	93.28 mph
2. Lawrence Parris	Aermacchi	1h. 14m. 10.0s	91.56 mph
3. Chris Griffiths	Aermacchi	1h. 14m. 48.6s	90.78 mph
Fastest lap			
Paul Barrett	Harley Davidson	24m. 07.0s	93.80 mph

1983 Lightweight Classic

The Lightweight Classic attracted an entry of 24, which non-starters reduced to 19. Dave Nobbs (Bultaco) was fastest in practice followed by Richard Fitzsimmons (Suzuki) and Dave Smith (Aermacchi). At the end of the first lap Fitzsimmons led Rupert Murden (Aermacchi) by 17.6 seconds, with Tony Ainslie (Ducati) in third place a further 13.6 seconds down. Fitzsimmons increased his lead at the end of the second lap to exactly one minute from Colin Hammond (Bultaco) with Brett Gaites (Greeves) third, 3.2 seconds down. Ainslie had dropped to fourth and Murden had retired. At the finish Fitzsimmons won by one minute 1.2 seconds from Hammond who finished 19.2 seconds in front of Ainslie. Gaites took fourth place, Arthur Wheeler (Guzzi) fifth and Rob Price (Greeves) sixth. There were nine finishers

1983 Lightweight Classic (3 laps / 113.19 miles) 24 entries

1. Richard Fitzsimmons	Suzuki	1h. 21m. 26.8s	83.38 mph
2. Colin Hammond	Bultaco	1h. 22m. 28.0s	82.35 mph
3. Tony Ainslie	Ducati	1h. 22m. 47.8s	82.02 mph
Fastest lap			
Brett Gaites	Greeves	26m. 51.2s	84.30 mph

1983 Senior Newcomers

Capacities for the Senior Newcomers were increased to 600cc and the class attracted an entry of 31, reduced by non-starters to 25. Cliff Tabiner (Suzuki) was fastest in practice followed by Steve Carthy (Suzuki) and Chris Turner (Honda). Tabiner lead Carthy at the end of the first lap by 6.2 seconds, with Brent Gladwin (Yamaha) in third place, 31.6 seconds down. Tabiner increased his lead at the end of the second lap to 17 seconds and Gladwin was one minute 41 seconds down in third place. Carthy took over the lead at the end of lap three, leading Tabiner by 13.2 seconds, Gladwin was still third, but three minutes 5.2 seconds down. Tabiner came off at Bedstead on the last lap, so Steve Carthy won by the comfortable margin of four minutes 17.4 seconds from Gladwin, Bob Price (Yamaha) came up to third, and John Pollack (Yamaha), William McCormack (Kawasaki) and Nat Wood (Honda) completed the top six. There were 14 finishers.

1983 Senior Newcomers (4 laps / 150.92 miles) 31 entries

1. Steve Carthy	Suzuki	1h. 31m. 01.8s	99.47 mph
2. Brent Gladwin	Yamaha	1h. 35m. 19.2s	94.99 mph
3. Bob Price	Yamaha	1h. 35m. 57.8s	94.36 mph
Fastest lap			
Cliff Tabiner	Suzuki	22m. 17.6s	101.54 mph

1983 Junior Newcomers

Forty two entries were received for the Junior Newcomers, and of these, 38 made it to the start line. Ian Newton (Yamaha) was fastest in practice followed by Robert Dunlop (Yamaha) and Lawrence Edwards (Yamaha). Dunlop, younger

Winners all: Steve Carthy (left) and Robert Dunlop wait as Peter Kneale interviews Barrie Middleton.

brother of TT hero Joey, took command of the race from the start, and at the end of the first lap led Steve Hislop (Yamaha) by 18.8 seconds with Keith Nichols (Yamaha) third, just eight seconds down on Hislop. Dunlop stretched his lead to 42 seconds at the end of lap two, and Hislop increased his lead over Nichols to 29.8 seconds. The lead for Dunlop over Hislop at the end of the third lap was a massive two minutes 3.8 seconds, and Ian Lougher (Yamaha) took third place from Nichols. So Dunlop won by one minute 2.6 seconds from Hislop with Lougher third. Nichols took fourth place, Gene McDonnell (Yamaha) fifth and Jerry Crawford (Yamaha) sixth. There were 23 finishers.

1983 Junior Newcomers (4 laps / 150.92 miles) 42 entries

1. Robert Dunlop	Yamaha	1h. 28m. 22.2s	102.46 mph
2. Steve Hislop	Yamaha	1h. 29m. 24.8s	101.27 mph
3. Ian Lougher	Yamaha	1h. 29m. 59.2s	100.62 mph
Fastest lap			
Robert Dunlop	Yamaha	21m. 30.0s	105.29 mph

1983 Lightweight Newcomers

Twenty nine of the 33 entries for the Lightweight Newcomers faced the starter. Gary Beattie (Yamaha) was fastest in practice, Kevin de Cruz (Yamaha) was second fastest with Dennis Quinn (Yamaha) third. At the end of lap one, de Cruz led Dave Dearden (Yamaha) by 20 seconds, with Beattie third. Dearden closed the gap on de Cruz at the end of the second lap to 9.6 seconds, and with Beattie's retirement at the pits, Barrie Middleton (Yamaha) came up to third place just 2.8 seconds down on Dearden. de Cruz dropped right back to sixth place at the end of lap three, and Middleton led from Dearden by 12.2 seconds with Will Williams (Yamaha) up in to third place. Barrie Middleton won by 22 seconds from Williams, who pipped Dave Dearden for second place by 0.8 seconds. de Cruz finished fourth, Quinn fifth and Dave Marsden (Rotax) sixth. There were 19 finishers.

1983 Lightweight Newcomers (4 laps / 150.92 miles) 33 entries

1. Barrie Middleton	Yamaha	1h. 35m. 45.6s	94.56 mph
2. Will Williams	Yamaha	1h. 36m. 08.0s	94.19 mph
3. Dave Dearden	Yamaha	1h. 36m. 08.8s	94.18 mph
Fastest lap			
Kevin de Cruz	Yamaha	23m. 02.2s	98.26 mph

1983 Junior MGP

There were 111 entries for the Junior, and with just six non-starters, 105 riders lined up on the starting grid. Chris Faulkner (Yamaha) was fastest in practice followed by Chris Fargher (Yamaha) and Dick Coates (Yamaha). Faulkner led Coates at the end of the first lap by 10 seconds with Keith Trubshaw (Yamaha) third a further 8.4 seconds down. Fargher was fourth, Gary Radcliffe (Yamaha) fifth and Steve Boyes (Yamaha) sixth. With the fastest lap of the race at 107.54 mph Coates took the lead from Faulkner at the end of lap two by four seconds. Fargher moved up to third, 24 seconds behind Faulkner, Trubshaw was fourth and Boyes was fifth ahead of Radcliffe. Dick Coates race ended at Milntown on lap three when he retired with engine trouble, so Faulkner was back in the lead by 14.4 seconds from Fargher who was 26.6 seconds ahead of Trubshaw. Boyes and Radcliffe were fourth and fifth, with Alan Atkins (Yamaha) coming in to sixth place. Chris Faulkner appeared to be in trouble on lap four, losing ground to his pursuers. Fargher led at the end of the lap by 50.4 seconds from Trubshaw and Radcliffe was third a further 38.4 seconds down. Faulkner came into his pit in fourth place, only to retire with a broken gear lever. Atkins was fifth, and with Boyes retiring with engine trouble, Sean Collister (Yamaha) came on the the leaderboard in sixth place. Fargher's lead was reduced to 28.8 seconds by Trubshaw at the end of the fifth lap and Radcliffe was 19.6 seconds behind Trubshaw in third place. Atkins was fourth, Collister fifth and Paul Todd (Yamaha) sixth. Trubshaw, with two second places to his credit in the Manx already, made a determined effort to go one better, but failed to catch Fargher by 5.6 seconds. Radcliffe, runner up for the 1982 Senior and Junior, took third place, over one minute down. Atkins, Collister and Todd completed the top six. There were 50 finishers and 23 replicas were won.

Chris Fargher leaves Parliament Square.

1983 Junior (6 laps / 226.38 miles) 111 entries

1. Chris Fargher	Yamaha	2h. 09m. 55.4s	104.54 mph
2. Keith Trubshaw	Yamaha	2h. 10m. 01.0s	104.43 mph
3. Gary Radcliffe	Yamaha	2h. 11m. 07.0s	103.59 mph
Fastest lap			
Dick Coates	Yamaha	21m. 03.0s	107.54 mph

1983 Lightweight MGP

The Lightweight, postponed to the Friday, was just about the most dramatic race in the history of the Manx. The entry of 104 was reduced by non-starters to 98. Sean Collister (Yamaha) was fastest in practice followed by Chris Fargher (Rotax) and Craig Ryding (Rotax). Three Manx riders dominated the race. At the end of the first lap Collister led Dick Coates (Cotton) by 10.2 seconds with Fargher third, a further nine seconds down. Steve McClements (Yamaha), Dave Leach (Yamaha) and Pat McLaughlin (Yamaha) completed the top six. At the end of the second lap Collister increased his lead to 18.4 seconds, but it was Fargher second, 24 seconds ahead of Coates. Leach was fourth, McClements fifth and McLaughlin sixth. At the end of the third lap, just nine seconds separated the first three. Coates was in front of Collister by 6.4 seconds, and Fargher was third, 2.6 seconds down on Collister. Leach, Bud Jackson (Yamaha)

and McClements completed the top six, McLaughlin having retired at Ballaugh. So the three Manx lads tore off on the last lap, positions appeared to be changing at each of the commentary points. Coates was the first of the three to finish the race, next was Collister and it appeared that Coates had just beaten him. But Fargher was still on the course, he finished, and everyone waited for the official times. Then came the news - Fargher was the winner, making it a Junior/Lightweight double, by the closest margin ever, 0.6 seconds ahead of Coates who was just 0.8 seconds ahead of Collister. Fourth place went to Leach, Jackson was fifth and McClements sixth. There were 68 finishers and 25 replicas were won.

1983 Lightweight (4 laps / 150.92 miles)   104 entries

1. Chris Fargher	Rotax	1h. 27m. 42.0s	103.25 mph
2. Dick Coates	Cotton	1h. 27m. 42.6s	103.24 mph
3. Sean Collister	Yamaha	1h. 27m. 43.4s	103.22 mph
Fastest lap			
Chris Fargher	Rotax	21m. 33.8s	104.98 mph

The first three finishers comprised the team for the Andreas Racing Association, they finished within 1.4 seconds!

Nick Jefferies at Braddan Bridge. An active trials rider, Nick also won the Manx Two Day. Couple these with his 1993 Formula 1 TT win, and you have a trio of victories that is unlikely to be surpassed.

1983 Senior MGP

The Senior attracted an entry of 111, and 11 non-starters reduced the field to exactly 100. Chris Faulkner (Yamaha) was fastest in practice followed by Mick Noblett (Honda) and Buddy Yeardsley (Suzuki). At the end of the first lap Gary Radcliffe (Yamaha) led Faulkner by 1.2 seconds with Yeardsley third, 3.6 seconds down. The top six was completed by Alan Atkins (Yamaha), Nick Jefferies (Suzuki) and Steve Linsdell (Suzuki). Faulkner took the lead at the end of lap two by two seconds from Yeardsley with Jefferies 0.2 seconds down in third place. Radcliffe was fourth, Keith Trubshaw (Yamaha) fifth and Ian Ogden (Suzuki) sixth. Atkins was ninth and Linsdell seventh. Yet another new leader the end of lap three, Jefferies, 7.2 seconds ahead of Yeardsley, who in turn had a lead of 12.8 seconds over Faulkner, Radcliffe was still fourth, Linsdell was back up to fifth and Steve Richardson (Suzuki) was sixth. Faulkner was back in front at the end of the fourth lap from Jefferies. Steve Dowey (Yamaha) was fourth, Trubshaw fifth and Linsdell sixth, with Radcliffe dropping to seventh place. By the time the riders completed the fifth lap, Jefferies was back in front by nine seconds from Faulkner with Yeardsley still third, 8.6 seconds down. Trubshaw, Dowey and Richardson completed the top six. So Jefferies, so near a victor in previous years, went on to win the Senior by 33.4 seconds from Yeardsley, who pipped Chris Faulkner for second place by just 1.6 seconds. Dowey finished fourth, Trubshaw fifth and Richardson sixth. There were 64 finishers and 26 replicas were won.

1983 Senior (6 laps / 226.38 miles)   111 entries

1. Nick Jefferies	Suzuki	2h. 09m. 09.8s	105.16 mph
2. Buddy Yeardsley	Suzuki	2h. 09m. 43.2s	104.70 mph
3. Chris Faulkner	Yamaha	2h. 09m. 44.8s	104.68 mph
Fastest lap			
Nick Jefferies	Suzuki	21m. 03.2s	107.52 mph

1984

Bad weather caused problems at the start of Manx week in 1984. The Classic races, due to be held on the Saturday, were postponed until the Tuesday, and reduced to two laps. This made the Tuesday the longest race day in the history of the Manx. The Classic race, over two laps, was followed by the Newcomers race over four laps, and the Junior race over six laps. Twelve laps of racing on the one day.

1984 Senior Classic

Dave Pither at Cruickshanks Corner.

The entry for the Senior Classic totalled 49, and non-starters reduced this number to 42. Pete Swallow (Norton) was fastest in practice followed by Bill Swallow (Velocette) and Richard Cutts (Matchless). Dave Pither (Matchless) led at the end of the first lap by 19.2 seconds from Rob Vine (Matchless), who in turn led Alan Lawton (Norton) by 1.4 seconds. John Cronshaw (B.S.A.) was fourth, Bob Hirst (Seeley) fifth and John Goodall (Matchless) sixth. The first five remained unchanged at the end of the race, with Pither winning by 56.2 seconds from Vine who finished one minute 2.2s. ahead of Lawton. Cronshaw and Hirst were joined on the leaderboard by Bill Swallow, with Goodall finishing seventh. There were 32 finishers.

1984 Senior Classic (2 laps / 75.46 miles) 49 entries

1. Dave Pither	Matchless	46m. 39.0s	97.05 mph (record)
2. Rob Vine	Matchless	47m. 15.2s	95.81 mph
3. Alan Lawton	Norton	47m. 17.4s	95.74 mph
Fastest lap (record)			
Dave Pither	Matchless	23m. 00.0s	98.42 mph

1984 Junior Classic

A total of 50 entries were received for the Junior Classic, and 41 riders made it to the starting line. Chris Griffiths (Aermacchi) was fastest in practice followed by Lawrence Parris (Aermacchi) and Jimmy Millar (Aermacchi). At the end of the first lap Parris led Griffiths by 16.2 seconds with John Stephens (Honda) a further 15 seconds down. Dick Irwin (Aermacchi), Chris Bladon (Aermacchi) and Fred O'Callaghan (Aermacchi) completed the top six. Griffiths retired at the 26th Milestone on the last lap and Parris went on to win from Stephens by 35.4 seconds, with Irwin third over one minute down on Stephens. Bladon and O'Callaghan moved up to fourth and fifth, and Eddie Crooks (Suzuki) came up to sixth place. There were 33 finishers.

1984 Junior Classic (2 laps / 75.46 miles) 50 entries

1. Lawrence Parris	Aermacchi	48m. 53.8s	92.69 mph
2. John Stephens	Honda	49m. 29.6s	91.47 mph
3. Dick Irwin	Aermacchi	50m. 45.6s	89.19 mph
Fastest lap			
Lawrence Parris	Aermacchi	24m. 18.4s	93.13 mph

1984 Senior Newcomers

Twenty eight riders entered for the Senior Newcomers, and with just one non-starter, 27 of them lined up on the grid. Colin Wilson (Suzuki) was fastest in practice, John Schoenemann (Suzuki) was next fastest followed by Ted Byers (Suzuki). At the end of the first lap, David Griffin (Suzuki) led Alan Shaw (Yamaha) by 14 seconds, with Stuart Marshal (Honda) third, a further 3.6 seconds down. There were changes on lap two, Griffin retired at Handleys Corner, Byers, fourth on the first lap, took the lead by just 0.4 seconds from Marshal, who in turn led Shaw by 23.4 seconds. Byers increased his lead to one minute 1.2 seconds at the end of lap three over Marshal, who had increased his advantage over Shaw to 57.8 seconds. Marshal pulled back a lot of Byers lead on the final lap, but Byers won the race by 35.4 seconds from Marshal. Shaw retired at Ramsey on the last lap, and Mike Allen (Kawasaki) took third place, over three minutes behind Marshal. Chris Rice (Yamaha), Seamus Rice (Yamaha) and John Samuel (Honda) completed the top six. There were 17 finishers.

1984 Senior Newcomers (4 laps / 150.92 miles) 28 entries

1. Ted Byers	Suzuki	1h. 34m. 35.8s	95.72 mph
2. Stuart Marshal	Honda	1h. 35m. 11.2s	95.13 mph
3. Mike Allen	Kawasaki	1h. 38m. 50.6s	91.61 mph
Fastest lap			
Ted Byers	Suzuki	23m. 13.0s	97.50 mph

1984 Junior Newcomers

From the total entry of 35 for the Junior Newcomers, 32 riders lined up on the grid. Gary Cowan (Yamaha) was fastest in practice followed by Sean McStay (Yamaha) and James Knox (Yamaha). Cowan led the race from start to finish. At the end of the first lap he led McStay by 9.2 seconds with Mike Seward (Yamaha) third, 32.6 seconds down. By the end of the second lap Cowan's advantage over McStay was 20.8 seconds, and with Seward dropping off the leaderboard, Paul Hunt (Yamaha) came up to third place 40.4 seconds down on McStay. The leaderboard changed on lap three, McStay retired and Hunt was touring at the Bungalow. Cowan still led, and he was one minute 55.1 seconds ahead of Steve Hazlett (Yamaha) who in turn led Seward by 22.4 seconds. Cowan won the race by two minutes 27.4 seconds from Seward, who was to go on to make M.G.P. history in 1986. Hazlett finished third, eight seconds down on Seward, and the top six were completed by Stanley Rea (Yamaha), Gordon Rowntree (Yamaha) and Kevin Mawdsley (Yamaha). There were 20 finishers.

1984 Junior Newcomers (4 laps / 150.92 miles) 35 entries

1. Gary Cowan	Yamaha	1h. 29m. 02.8s	101.69 mph
2. Mike Seward	Yamaha	1h. 31m. 30.6s	98.95 mph
3. Steve Hazlett	Yamaha	1h. 31m. 38.6s	98.80 mph
Fastest lap			
Gary Cowan	Yamaha	21m. 55.2s	103.27 mph

1984 Lightweight Newcomers

There were just 19 entries for the Lightweight Newcomers, and five non-starters reduced the field to 14. Declan McCabe (Yamaha) was fastest in practice followed by David Johnston (Yamaha) and Phil Armes (Yamaha). Johnston led McCabe at the end of the first lap by 7.4 seconds, with Armes a further 19.6 seconds down in third place. The first three remained the same at the end of lap two, with Johnston 10.6 seconds in front of McCabe. Armes took the lead at the end of the third lap by one minute 21.6 seconds from Johnston, who had an 11.4 seconds advantage over Dave Grigson (Yamaha). McCabe retired at the pits with a broken frame. Johnston retired on the last lap, so Armes went on to win by 48.8 seconds from Grigson, with Paul English (Yamaha) third. Martin Press (Yamaha), Ian Gray (Yamaha) and Kevin Newberry (Yamaha) completed the leader-board. There were just eight finishers.

1984 250cc Newcomers (4 laps / 150.92 miles) 19 entries

1. Phil Armes	Yamaha	1h. 35m. 04.0s	95.25 mph
2. Dave Grigson	Yamaha	1h. 36m. 52.8s	93.46 mph
3. Paul English	Yamaha	1h. 38m. 23.0s	92.03 mph
Fastest lap			
David Johnston	Yamaha	23m. 08.0s	97.85 mph

1984 Junior MGP

And so to the final race of the day, the Junior. 112 entries were received for the race, and of these, 102 made it to the starting line. Ian Newton (Yamaha) was fastest in practice. Next best was Dave Leach (Yamaha) followed by Alistair Rae (Yamaha). At the end of the first lap Gary Radcliffe (Yamaha) led by 49 seconds from Leach, with Newton a further 5.6 seconds down in third

place. Martyn Nelson (Yamaha) was fourth, Chris Harris (Yamaha) fifth and Rae sixth. Newton took over at the end of the second lap and led Radcliffe by 10.4 seconds with Nelson up to third, 8.4 seconds down on Radcliffe. Leach had come off at Signpost Corner, remounted, and made it to the pits, but a long stop there dropped him down the placings. Harris was in fifth place and Dave Pither (Yamaha) was sixth. It was still a close race at half distance, Newton led Radcliffe by 15.8 seconds who in turn was 10.4 seconds ahead of Nelson. Steve Hislop (Yamaha) was now fourth, ahead of Harris and Pither. Newton increased his lead over Radcliffe to 26 seconds at the end of the fourth lap and Nelson was 19.8 seconds down on Radcliffe. Harris, Pither and Andy Graves (Yamaha) completed the top six. Radcliffe closed the gap between himself and Newton slightly on lap five, it was down to 15.4 seconds with Nelson 21 seconds down. Harris was still fourth, but Dave Pither retired at Cronk-y-Voddy, bringing Graves up to fifth and Phil Kneen (Yamaha) came on to the leaderboard in sixth place. Ian Newton won the race by 23 seconds from Radcliffe, who was runner-up in a Manx for the third time. Nelson finished third, 21 seconds down on Radcliffe. Chris Harris was fourth, Andy Graves fifth, and with the fastest lap of the race, Dave Leach finished in sixth place. There were 54 finishers and 31 riders won replicas.

Ian Newton at Sulby Bridge.

1984 Junior (6 laps / 226.38 miles)   112 entries

1. Ian Newton	Yamaha	2h. 11m. 03.0s	103.64 mph
2. Gary Radcliffe	Yamaha	2h. 11m. 26.0s	103.34 mph
3. Martyn Nelson	Yamaha	2h. 11m. 45.6s	103.08 mph
Fastest lap			
Dave Leach	Yamaha	21m. 31.2s	105.19 mph

1984 Lightweight MGP

There were 88 entries for the Lightweight, and of these, 79 lined up for the start of the race. Junior winner Ian Newton (Yamaha) was fastest in practice followed by Craig Ryding (Yamaha) and Pat McLaughlin (Yamaha). At the end of the first lap Sean Mc Stay (E.M.C.) led from Sean Collister (Yamaha) by 13.2 seconds, with Alistair Rae (Yamaha) a further 12.2 seconds down in third place. Ryding was fourth, McLaughlin fifth and Pete Bateson (Maxton) sixth. McStay increased his lead to 50.4 seconds at the end of the second lap, with Rae in second place, 21.2 seconds ahead of Collister. Bateson was fourth Dave Leach (Yamaha) fifth and McLaughlin sixth. Two of the top six went out of the race on the third lap, Collister slid off at Signpost Corner, and McLaughlin retired at Union Mills with a broken exhaust. McStay led the race from Rae by one minute 6.2 seconds, with Ryding up into third place, a further 11.4 seconds down. Bateson, Alan 'Bud' Jackson (Yamaha) and Leach completed the top six. Another two of the top six hit trouble on the final lap, third place man Ryding was reported to be touring at the Bungalow, and he eventually finished 15th, but Leach retired at the pits. McStay went on to a record breaking victory over Rae by one minute 17.0 seconds, with Bateson in third place, one minute 25.4 seconds down. Jackson finished fourth, Cliff Gobell (Yamaha) fifth and Kevin de Cruz (Yamaha) sixth. There were 47 finishers and 12 replicas were won.

1984 Lightweight (4 laps / 150.92 miles)   88 entries

1. Sean McStay	E.M.C.	1h. 26m. 46.6s	104.35 mph
			(record)
2. Alistair Rae	Yamaha	1h. 28m. 03.6s	102.83 mph
3. Pete Bateson	Maxton	1h. 29m. 29.0s	101.19 mph
Fastest lap (record)			
Sean McStay	E.M.C.	21m. 23.6s	105.81 mph

1984 Senior MGP

Graham King, Dave Pither and Ian Ogden - with silverware.

Of the total entry of 111 for the Senior, 100 lined up at the start. Buddy Yeardsley (Yamaha) was fastest in practice followed by Gary Radcliffe (Yamaha) and Graham King (Suzuki). Yeardsley led the race at the end of lap one by 2.4 seconds from Kevin Hughes (Kawasaki), who in turn was just 0.8 seconds in front of Ian Ogden (Suzuki). King, Radcliffe and Steve Dowey (Yamaha) completed the first lap leaderboard. There were just 14.6 seconds separating the top six. Buddy Yeardsley retired at Sulby with a seized engine on lap two, and Ogden took the lead from King by 7.2 seconds. Dave Pither came on to the leaderboard in third place, just 2.8 seconds down on King. Hughes was fourth, Radcliffe fifth and Martyn Nelson (Yamaha) sixth. There was yet another new leader at half distance, Pither led King by 10.4 seconds, with Radcliffe 10.2 seconds down in third place. Ogden was fourth, followed by Steve Hislop (Yamaha) and Hughes. Pither remained in control at the end of lap four, but only just, he was a mere 2.2 seconds in front of Hughes with Ogden third, a further 11.4 seconds down. The

top six was completed by King, Hislop and Steve Linsdell (Kawasaki). Pither stretched his lead at the end of lap five to 28.4 seconds from King, who was 16.8 seconds in front of Ogden who was followed by Hughes, Hislop and Linsdell. So Pither went on to complete a unique double, the Senior Manx Grand Prix and Senior Classic races. He won from Ogden by 22.8 seconds with King in third place, 13.2 seconds down on Ogden. Hughes, Hislop and Linsdell completed the leaderboard. There were 61 finishers and 23 riders won replicas.

1984 Senior MGP (6 laps / 226.38 miles)   111 entries

1. Dave Pither	Honda	2h. 08m. 38.2s	105.59 mph
2. Ian Ogden	Suzuki	2h. 09m. 01.0s	105.27 mph
3. Graham King	Suzuki	2h. 09m. 14.2s	105.10 mph
Fastest lap			
Ian Ogden	Suzuki	20m. 57.2s	108.03 mph

1985

1985 Senior Classic

The Senior Classic attracted an entry of 69, and 17 non-starters reduced the field to 52. Among the non-starters was Geoff Johnson (Norton), who was fastest in practice, but a spill at Tower Bends in Friday evening practice left him with a broken wrist. Neil Tuxworth (Matchless) was second fastest followed by Richard Cutts (Matchless). At the end of the first lap, Tuxworth led John Goodall (Matchless) by 20 seconds with Cutts in third place, a further 6.4 seconds down. The order remained the same on lap two, Tuxworth increased his lead over Goodall to 48.2 seconds, who in turn increased his advantage over Cutts to 27.4 seconds. Tuxworth, a regular TT competitor with top three placings to his credit, went on to win his first race on the TT course by one minute 10 seconds from Goodall, who beat Tony Russell (Matchless) by 32.8 seconds. Cutts finished fourth, John Knowles (Seeley) fifth and Grant Sellars (Norton) sixth. There were 30 finishers.

1985 Senior Classic (3 laps / 113.19 miles)   69 entries

1. Neil Tuxworth	Matchless	1h. 10m. 44.2s	96.01 mph
2. John Goodall	Matchless	1h. 11m. 54.2	94.45 mph
3. Tony Russell	Norton	1h. 12m. 27.0	93.73 mph
Fastest lap			
Neil Tuxworth	Matchless	23m. 20.0s	97.02 mph

1985 Junior Classic

There were 49 entries for the Junior Classic, and of these 43 faced the starter. Cliff Gobell (Aermacchi) was fastest in practice followed by John Stephens (Honda) and Chris Griffiths (Aermacchi). Stephens led Gobell at the end of the first lap by 36.8 seconds with Griffiths 13 seconds down on Gobell in third place. The order remained the same for the three laps with Stephens taking the chequered flag 56.6 seconds ahead of Gobell with Griffiths third. Phillip Woodhall (Aermacchi), David Dearden (Aermacchi) and Dave Bedlington (Aermacchi) completed the top six. There were 28 finishers.

1985 Junior Classic (2 laps / 75.46 miles)   49 entries

1. John Stephens	Honda	1h. 13m. 01.2s	93.00 mph
2. Cliff Gobell	Aermacchi	1h. 13m. 57.8	91.82 mph
3. Chris Griffiths	Aermacchi	1h. 14m. 59.4	90.56 mph
Fastest lap			
John Stephens	Honda	24m. 08.0s	93.80 mph

1985 Senior Newcomers

The entry of 25 for the Senior Newcomers was reduced by non-starters to 22. Tom Knight (Ducati) was fastest in practice followed by Robert Quinn (Yamaha) and David Lloyd (Ducati). At the end of the first lap Quinn led Knight by 7.2 seconds with John Davis (Yamaha) in third place, 31.2 seconds down on Knight. Knight closed to within 2.2 seconds of Quinn at the end of the second lap, with Davis one and a half minutes down. Quinn's race ended in a spill at the Bungalow on the third lap, so Knight had a lead of two minutes nine seconds over Davis, who in turn was one minute 23 seconds ahead of the new third place man David Lloyd. Knight won the race by two minutes 26 seconds from Davis with Michael Casey (Suzuki) in third place a further two minutes 18.6 seconds down. Adam Woodall (Kawasaki), John Weston (Yamaha) and Mick Farmer (Honda) completed the top six. David Lloyd ran out of petrol and Cronk ny Mona and pushed in to finish, last of the 15 finishers.

Man and machine in disharmony. Wayne Leatherbarrow prepares to collect his dormant Spondon Yamaha. He finished tenth in the class - despite this.

1985 Senior Newcomers (4 laps / 150.92 miles)   25 entries

1. Tom Knight	Ducati	1h. 34m. 43.2s	95.60 mph
2. John Davis	Yamaha	1h. 37m. 19.2s	93.04 mph
3. Michael Casey	Suzuki	1h. 39m. 37.8s	90.88 mph
Fastest lap			
Tom Knight	Ducati	23m. 03.0s	98.21 mph

1985 Junior Newcomers

Thirty two of the original 35 entries lined up for the Junior Newcomers. Ashley Gardner (Yamaha) was fastest in prac-

tice with Michael Dalgleish (Yamaha) next and Steve Lanyman (Yamaha) third. Gardner led John Byrne (Yamaha) at the end of the first lap by 31.4 seconds with Lanyman some 8.6 seconds down on Byrne in third place. At the end of the second lap Byrne was in front of Gardner by 9.4 seconds, with Lanyman still third, but now 60 seconds down. Gardner re-took the lead at the end of lap three by a massive four minutes 25 seconds. Byrne retired at Ballaugh and Lanyman came off at Creg-ny-Baa. The new second place man was Trevor Haywood (Yamaha) and Justin Urch (Yamaha) was third. And so they finished, Gardner won by five minutes 40 seconds from Trevor Haywood with Justin Urch third. The top six were completed by Michael Sayers (Yamaha), Henry Januszevski (Yamaha) and Jimmy Burke (Yamaha). There were 17 finishers.

1985 Junior Newcomers (4 laps / 150.92 miles) 35 entries

1. Ashley Gardner	Yamaha	1h. 31m. 58.2s	98.45 mph
2. Trevor Haywood	Yamaha	1h. 37m. 38.2s	92.74 mph
3. Justin Urch	Yamaha	1h. 38m. 15.4s	92.15 mph
Fastest lap			
Ashley Gardner	Yamaha	22m. 22.8s	101.15 mph

1985 Lightweight Newcomers

Strangely enough there were no non-starters for the Lightweight Newcomers, so 28 riders lined up on the grid. Carl Fogarty (Yamaha), son of TT competitor George, was fastest in practice followed by Gary Tate (Yamaha) and Roy Chapman (Yamaha). At the end of lap one, Fogarty led Chapman by 17.6 seconds, with Nigel Turner (Yamaha) in third place, a further 17 8 seconds down. Fogarty increased his lead over Chapman to 41 seconds at the end of the second lap and Tate was 51 seconds down on Chapman with Turner fourth. Fogarty led the race from Chapman by 40 seconds at the end of the third lap, with Tate still in third place. Roy Chapman turned the pressure on on the last lap and closed to within six seconds of the winner Fogarty. Tate finished third, 59 seconds down on Chapman and the top six were completed by Mark Linton (Yamaha), Paul Woodman (Yamaha) and Karl Fox (Yamaha). There were 19 finishers.

1985 Lightweight Newcomers (4 laps / 150.92 miles) 28 entries

1. Carl Fogarty	Yamaha	1h. 35m. 32.0s	94.78 mph
2. Roy Chapman	Yamaha	1h. 35m. 38.0s	94.68 mph
3. Gary Tate	Yamaha	1h. 36m. 37.0s	93.72 mph
Fastest lap			
Carl Fogarty	Yamaha	23m. 20.8s	97.03 mph

1985 Junior MGP

Any entry of 103 was received for the Junior, but 11 non-starters reduced this number to 92. Craig Ryding (Yamaha) was fastest in practice with Sean Collister (Yamaha) second fastest and Steve Hazlett (Yamaha) third. At the end of lap one Gary Radcliffe (Yamaha) led Ryding by 10 seconds with David Johnston (Yamaha) just two seconds down on Ryding. Decca Kelly (Yamaha) was fourth, Keith Trubshaw (Yamaha) fifth and Hazlett sixth. Ryding, with the fastest lap of the race on lap two, took the lead from Radcliffe by 2.3 seconds and Johnston was third, 18.8 seconds down on Radcliffe. Kelly was fourth, Hazlett had come up to fifth and Barrie Middleton (Yamaha) came on to the leaderboard in sixth place. Keith Trubshaw retired at Cronk-y-Voddy. Ryding still led at the end of the third lap, but by only two seconds from Radcliffe, and Hazlett was up to third, one minute behind Radcliffe, followed by Johnston, Buddy Yeardsley (Yamaha) and Kelly. Barry Middleton stopped at the Gooseneck to make adjustments, and eventually finished 17th. There was drama on lap four when it was announced that the leader Craig Ryding had retired at the Highlander, so the close race between him and Radcliffe was over. The Manx rider led at the end of lap four by 21 seconds from Johnston, Kelly was third a further 48 seconds down. Hazlett, Yeardsley and Paul Davies (Yamaha) completed the leaderboard. Radcliffe extended his lead at the end of the fifth lap over Johnston to 59 seconds, with Hazlett back up to third, 31 seconds down on Johnston, followed by Yeardsley, Kelly and Davies. So Gary Radcliffe, after finishing in second place on three occasions, finally achieved his ambition of a Manx win by 48.4 seconds from Johnston who finished 34 seconds ahead of Hazlett, Yeardsley finished fourth, Kelly fifth and Grant Goodings (Yamaha) sixth, with Paul Davies finishing seventh. There were 51 finishers and 24 replicas were won.

Gary Radcliffe at White Gates.

1985 Junior MGP (6 laps / 226.38 miles) 103 entries

1. Gary Radcliffe	Yamaha	2h. 11m. 39.6s	103.16 mph
2. David Johnston	Yamaha	2h. 12m. 28.0s	102.53 mph
3. Steve Hazlett	Yamaha	2h. 13m. 02.0s	102.10 mph
Fastest lap			
Craig Ryding	Yamaha	21m. 29.4s	105.33 mph

1985 Lightweight MGP

There were just 66 entries for the Lightweight, but luckily with just two non-starters, the field totalled 64. Craig Ryding (Yamaha) led the practice leaderboard followed by David Johnston (E.M.C.) and Alan 'Bud' Jackson (Yamaha). Johnston led Ralph Sutcliffe (Armstrong) by 17.6 seconds at the end of the first lap with Jackson a further 19.4 seconds down. Carl Fogarty (Yamaha), winner of the Lightweight Newcomers was fourth, Ryding fifth and Ashley Gardner (Waddon) winner of the Lightweight Newcomers class in sixth place. Johnston still led at the end of the second lap by 54 seconds from Fogarty with Sutcliffe now third, seven seconds down on Fogarty.

Gardner was fourth, Steve McClements (Yamaha) fifth and Mike Seward (Armstrong) sixth. Ryding was now seventh. At the end of the third lap Johnston led Sutcliffe by 52.2 seconds with Fogarty third. Gardner was fourth, Seward fifth and David Parry (Yamaha) sixth. Steve McClements retired at School House Corner, and Ryding at the Quarter Bridge. So David Johnston won by 52.4 seconds from Ralph Sutcliffe, who beat Carl Fogarty by seven seconds. Gardner took fourth place, followed by Seward and Richard Burden (Yamaha). Dave Parry finished ninth. There were 41 finishers and 13 replicas were won.

1984 Lightweight MGP (4 laps / 150.92 miles) 88 entries

1. David Johnston	E.M.C.	1h. 28m. 52.4s	101.88 mph
2. Ralph Sutcliffe	Armstrong	1h. 29m. 44.8s	100.89 mph
3. Carl Fogarty	Yamaha	1h. 29m. 51.8s	100.76 mph
Fastest lap			
Carl Fogarty	Yamaha	21m. 52.2s	103.51 mph

1985 Senior MGP

The entry of 117 for the Senior was reduced to 98 starters. Junior winner Gary Radcliffe (Yamaha) was fastest in practice followed by Robert Wright (Suzuki) and Paul Davies (Suzuki). At the end of the first lap Buddy Yeardsley (Suzuki) led Ian Ogden (Suzuki) by 11.8 seconds, with Radcliffe third 10.4 seconds down. Three Manx riders in the first three places, and another, Paul Hunt (Kawasaki) was fourth. Stuart Marshal (Suzuki) and Steve Linsdell (Yamaha) completed the top six. With the fastest lap of the race at 108.17 mph Radcliffe took over the lead by 4.2 seconds from Yeardsley at the end of the second lap, and Ogden was third 5.8 seconds down on Yeardsley. Hunt remained fourth, but Linsdell took fifth place from Marshal. Yeardsley was back in front at the end of lap three, by 5.2 seconds from Radcliffe, who led Ogden by 10.6 seconds. Linsdell and Marshal both overtook Hunt who was sixth. But the Manx battle ended on the fourth lap when Gary Radcliffe retired at the Highlander. Yeardsley led Ogden by one minute 24.2 seconds at the end of the lap, and Marshal was one minute 24 seconds down on Ogden in third place. Marshal was fourth, Hunt fifth and Robert Wright (Suzuki) sixth. Yeardsley added another seven seconds to his lead at the end of lap five and Ogden led Linsdell by one minute 19 seconds. Marshal, Hunt and Paul Davies (Suzuki) completed the top six with Wright in seventh place. So Buddy Yeardsley went on to win by one minute 59.2 seconds from Ogden who finished 41 seconds ahead of Linsdell. Stuart Marshal was fourth, Hunt fifth and Davies sixth. There were 74 finishers and 18 replicas were won.

1985 Senior MGP (6 laps / 226.38 miles) 117 entries

1. Buddy Yeardsley	Suzuki	2h. 10m. 50.6s	103.81 mph
2. Ian Ogden	Suzuki	2h. 12m. 48.8s	102.27 mph
3. Steve Linsdell	Yamaha	2h. 13m. 29.8s	101.74 mph
Fastest lap			
Gary Radcliffe	Yamaha	20m. 55.6s	108.17 mph

1986

1986 Senior Classic

The Senior Classic attracted an entry of 66, but eight non-starters reduced this figure to 58. Dave Pither (Matchless), the 1984 winner, was fastest in practice followed by John Goodall (Matchless) the 1983 winner and Bob Hirst (Matchless). At the end of the first lap Dave Roper (Matchless) winner of the 1984 Senior Classic TT led Alan Dugdale (Matchless) by just 0.8 seconds with Pither third, a further 10.4 seconds down. Roper retired near Windy Corner on the second lap, and Dugdale led Pither by 23.2 seconds, with Goodall up in to third place, 21.4 seconds down on Pither. Dugdale won the race from Dave Pither by 35.6 seconds with Goodall third, 51.8 seconds down on Pither. The top six were completed by Tony Russell (Matchless). John Knowles (Seeley) and Dave Davies (Seeley Matchless). There were 16 finishers.

1986 Senior Classic (3 laps / 113.19 miles) 66 entries

1. Alan Dugdale	Matchless	1h. 09m. 04.8s	98.31 mph
			(record)
2. Dave Pither	Matchless	1h. 09m. 40.4	97.47 mph
3. John Goodall	Matchless	1h. 10m. 32.2	96.28 mph
Fastest lap (record)			
Alan Dugdale	Matchless	22m. 54.0s	98.85 mph

1986 Junior Classic

There were 54 entries for the Junior Classic, and of these, 47 riders made it to the start line. Bill Swallow (Honda) led the practice leader-board with Dave Roper (A.J.S.), who transferred to the Senior class, second fastest and Cliff Gobell (Aermacchi) third. Swallow led the race from the start. At the end of the first lap he was 17.8 seconds ahead of Gobell, with John Kidson (Aermacchi) third, a further seven seconds down. Swallow's advantage over Gobell at the end of lap two was 42.6 seconds, with Kidson still third, 6.2 seconds down on Gobell. The race ended for Gobell on the last lap when he retired at Ballaugh. Bill Swallow won from Kidson by 53.4 seconds, with John Stephens (Honda) third, 57.4 seconds down on Kidson. Mark Linton (Aermacchi) took fourth place, James Porter (Aermacchi) was fifth and Rob Brewer (Honda) sixth. There were 37 finishers.

John Kidson crosses the tramlines at the Bungalow.

1986 Junior Classic (3 laps / 113.19 miles) 54 entries

1. Bill Swallow	Honda	1h. 11m. 51.6s	94.50 mph
			(record)
2. John Kidson	Aermacchi	1h. 12m. 45.0	93.35 mph

3. John Stephens	Honda	1h. 13m. 42.4	92.14 mph
Fastest lap (record)			
Bill Swallow	Honda	23m. 44.0s	95.38 mph

1986 Senior Newcomers

Of the 59 entries for the Senior Newcomers, 31 riders faced the starter. Nick Lynn (Honda) was fastest in practice, second fastest was Ian Mitchell (Suzuki) followed by Russ Jones (Yamaha). Jim Hunter (Suzuki) led at the end of the first lap by three seconds from Andrew Smith (Yamaha) who in turn led Mitchell by six seconds. At the end of the second lap, Hunter's lead was down to just 1.6 seconds and Mitchell was second, 19.2 seconds ahead of Dave Goodley (Kawasaki). Smith slowed and eventually finished 12th. The gap between Hunter and Mitchell was even closer at the end of lap three, just 1.4 seconds, and it was Mitchell leading! Lynn was up to third place, with Goodley fourth. Hunter set the fastest lap of the race on his final circuit, a new record at 103.05 mph, to win by 23 seconds from Mitchell, who was one minute 3.8 seconds down on Hunter. The top six were completed by Goodley, Steve Wicks (Kawasaki) and Jones. There were 22 finishers.

Jim Hunter, now a Manx 'stopover' leaves Governors Bridge.

1986 Senior Newcomers (4 laps / 150.92 miles) 39 entries

1. Jim Hunter	Suzuki	1h. 30m. 13.8s	100.35 mph
			(record)
2. Ian Mitchell	Suzuki	1h. 30m. 34.8s	99.96 mph
3. Nick Lynn	Honda	1h. 31m. 38.6s	98.80 mph
Fastest lap (record)			
Jim Hunter	Suzuki	21m. 58.0s	103.05 mph

1986 Junior Newcomers

Of the 29 entries for the Junior Newcomers, 25 made it to the starting line. Mike Swann (Yamaha) led the practice leaderboard followed by Matt Drane (Yamaha) and Geoff Baldock (Yamaha). Drane led Steve Bevington (Yamaha) at the end of lap one by 22.8 seconds, who in turn led Ian Jones (Yamaha) by 1.2 seconds. There were quite a few changes to the leaderboard at the end of lap two - Bevington came off at Cruickshanks Corner, and Drane dropped out of the top three. Jones led by 25.2 seconds from Trevor Robinson (Yamaha) with Vaughan Smith (Yamaha) third, by just 0.8 seconds. Lap three saw Drane back in front of Jones by 26.4 seconds, with Robinson 35.2 seconds down on Jones. But on the final lap, Drane came off at Cruickshanks Corner, so Jones won the race by 9.2 seconds from Robinson who finished 18.2 seconds ahead of Smith. The top six were completed by Cliff Peart (Yamaha), Phillip Matulja (Yamaha) and Roy Richardson (Yamaha). There were 15 finishers.

1986 Junior Newcomers (4 laps / 150.92 miles)

1. Ian Jones	Yamaha	1h. 34m. 05.4s	96.23 mph
2. Trevor Robinson	Yamaha	1h. 34m. 14.6s	96.08 mph
3. Vaughan Smith	Yamaha	1h. 34m. 32.8s	95.77 mph
Fastest lap			
Matt Drane	Yamaha	22m. 47.6s	99.31 mph

1986 Lightweight Newcomers

Nineteen of the original entry of 23 lined up for the start of the Lightweight Newcomers. Martin Birkinshaw (Armstrong) topped the practice leaderboard followed by Gavin Lee (Yamaha). George Higginson (Decorite) and Stewart Rae tied for the lead at the end of the first lap with a new record at 99.55 mph. They led Birkinshaw by 12.8 seconds. There were changes galore on lap two, Stewart Rae retired on the Mountain Mile and Martin Birkinshaw came off at Kerrowmoar, so Higginson led by one minute 35.2 seconds from Nigel Barton (Armstrong), who in turn was one minute 44.4 seconds ahead of Nigel Griffiths (Armstrong). The next retirement was Barton, so at the end of lap three, Higginson led Griffiths by five minutes 35.2 seconds, with Eddie Edmunds (Yamaha) third, 15.6 seconds down on Griffiths. The final lap saw the end of the race for Griffiths, so George Higginson won by the massive margin of seven minutes 09.4 seconds from Tony Tuttle (E.M.C. Rotax) with Eddie Edmunds 43.6 seconds down in third place. Tony Hutchinson (Yamaha) was fourth, Carl Marsh (Yamaha) fifth and Phillip Pennington (Suzuki) sixth. There were 12 finishers.

1986 Lightweight Newcomers (4 laps / 150.92 miles) 23 entries

1. George Higginson	Decorite	1h. 32m. 28.2s	97.92 mph
			(record)
2. Tony Tuttle	E.M.C. Rotax	1h. 39m. 37.6s	90.89 mph
3. Eddie Edmunds	Yamaha	1h. 40m. 21.2s	90.23 mph
Fastest lap (record)			
George Higginson	Decorite)		
Stewart Rae	Rotax)	22m. 44.4s	99.55 mph

1986 Junior MGP

The Junior attracted an entry of 104, reduced by non-starters to 95. Roy Chapman (Yamaha) was fastest in practice with Steve Hazlett (Yamaha) second fastest and Sean Collister (Yamaha) third. Manx rider Decca Kelly (Yamaha) led at the end of the first lap by seven seconds from fellow local Roger Sutcliffe (Yamaha) who was just 0.6 seconds ahead of Alan 'Bud' Jackson (Yamaha). Hazlett and Collister were fourth and fifth, with Norman Kneen (Yamaha) sixth. Jackson took the lead from Kelly on lap two by 2.6 seconds with Hazlett still third, 12.8 seconds down on Kelly. Collister, Sutcliffe and Kneen completed the top six leaderboard. At half distance Kelly was back in front by 16.8 seconds from Sutcliffe who lead Collister by 2.6 seconds, three Manx riders in the first three.

Jackson was fourth, Ian Standeven (Yamaha) fifth and Mike Seward (Yamaha) sixth. Hazlett had dropped to seventh and Norman Kneen retired. The lead changed again at the end of the fourth lap, Jackson led Kelly by 39.8 seconds with Sutcliffe just 1.6 seconds down in third place. Seward was fourth followed by Roy Chapman (Yamaha) and Tony Martin (Yamaha). Hazlett retired at the pits and Decca Kelly's attempt for a win ended on the fifth lap when he came off at the Gooseneck, sustaining a broken collarbone. Jackson led Sutcliffe, but by just 8.8 seconds, with Seward third, one minute 56.8 seconds down on Sutcliffe. Martin was now fourth, Justin Urch (Yamaha) fifth and Ray Evans (Yamaha) sixth. Chapman had retired at Tower Bends. The two leaders circulated on the last lap in almost identical times, 'Bud' Jackson winning from Ralph Sutcliffe by 8.2 seconds, with Seward third, two minutes 48.8 seconds down. Martin, Urch and Evans completed the top six. There were 42 finishers and 25 riders won replicas.

Alan 'Bud' Jackson at the Bungalow.

1986 Junior MGP (6 laps / 226.38 miles) 104 entries

1. Alan 'Bud' Jackson	Yamaha	2h. 10m. 55.0s	103.75 mph
2. Ralph Sutcliffe	Yamaha	2h. 11m. 03.2s	103.64 mph
3. Mike Seward	Yamaha	2h. 13m. 51.0s	101.47 mph
Fastest lap			
Alan 'Bud' Jackson	Yamaha	21m. 19.0s	106.19 mph

1986 Lightweight MGP

The entry of 94 for the Lightweight was reduced by non-starters to 72. Ralph Sutcliffe (Armstrong) was fastest in practice followed by John Davies (Yamaha) and Alan 'Bud' Jackson (Yamaha). Sutcliffe led Mick Robinson (Yamaha) at the end of the first lap by 10.2 seconds, with Sean Collister (Honda) a further 0.6 seconds down in third place. Davies was fourth, Pete Wakefield (Maxton) fifth and Stewart Rae (Rotax) sixth. Sutcliffe's lead over Robinson was cut to 0.8 seconds at the end of the second lap, with Davies up to third, 18.2 seconds behind Robinson. Wakefield, Rae and George Higginson (Decorite) completed the leaderboard, Collister was eighth. At the end of the third lap Sutcliffe had increased his advantage over Robinson to 25.2 seconds, with Davies a further 34 seconds down in third place. Collister was back up to fourth, followed by Rae and Mark Linton (Yamaha). Wakefield was seventh, and Higginson eighth. So after two second places, Ralph Sutcliffe followed father Roger's footsteps, winner of the 1970 Senior. He won by 38.4 seconds from Robinson, with Rae third, a further 28.4 seconds down. John Davies was fourth, Collister fifth and Mark Linton sixth. Pete Wakefield and George Higginson finished seventh and eighth. There were 38 finishers and 11 replicas were won.

1986 Lightweight MGP (4 laps / 150.92 miles) 94 entries

1. Ralph Sutcliffe	Armstrong	1h. 28m. 58.4s	101.77 mph
2. Mick Robinson	Yamaha	1h. 29m. 36.4s	101.05 mph
3. Stewart Rae	Rotax	1h. 30m. 04.8s	100.52 mph
Fastest lap			
Ralph Sutcliffe	Armstrong	21m. 54.2s	103.35 mph

1986 Senior MGP

Grant Goodings at Glentrammon.

The Senior entry was 116, and with 12 non-starters, 104 lined up for the start. Rich Rogers (Suzuki) topped the practice leaderboard followed by Mike Seward (Yamaha) and Grant Goodings (Suzuki). Goodings led at the end of lap one by 16 seconds from Paul Hunt (Suzuki), who in turn led Gordon Brown (Suzuki) by eight seconds. Seward, Steve Hazlett (Yamaha) and Justin Urch (Yamaha) completed the leaderboard. Goodings increased his lead to 49 seconds at the end of lap two and Seward had moved up to second, 11.8 seconds ahead of Urch. Hazlett was fourth, Rogers fifth and Ray Evans (Suzuki) sixth. Hunt had dropped to ninth and Brown to 12th. Goodings led at half distance from Seward by 55.4 seconds. with Kevin Jackson (Suzuki) third, one minute 04.8 seconds down on Seward. Hazlett was fourth, Evans fifth and Geoff Martin (Suzuki) sixth. Rogers retired at the pits and Urch on the Verandah. Seward halved Goodings lead at the end of lap four, the difference was 25 seconds, with Seward one minute 17.2 seconds ahead of Hazlett. Evans, Jackson and Gary Tate (Yamaha) completed the top six with Martin in seventh place. At the end of the fifth lap Goodings led Seward by 22.8 seconds, Jackson was back up to third, over two minutes behind Seward, Hazlett was fourth, Evans fifth and Tate sixth. So began a dramatic last lap. By Ballacraine, Seward was 18 seconds down on Goodings, by Ballaugh the difference was down to 13 seconds and at the Bungalow it was just seven seconds. Watches were poised at the finish - Goodings, No. 25 finished first - Seward - No. 50 had to finish within two minutes to win. He didn't quite

make it, losing the race by just 3.4 seconds, but he had the consolation of making Manx Grand Prix history with the first ever 110 mph lap in the Manx. Steve Hazlett took a fine third place on his 350cc Yamaha, with Kevin Jackson fourth, Gary Tate fifth and Roy Chapman sixth. Ray Evans retired at the Black Dub on the last lap. There were 68 finishers and 20 replicas were won.

1986 Senior MGP (6 laps / 226.38 miles) 116 entries

1. Grant Goodings	Suzuki	2h. 07m. 26.2s	106.58 mph (record)
2. Mike Seward	Yamaha	2h. 07m. 29.8s	106.53 mph
3. Steve Hazlett	Yamaha	2h. 11m. 17.6s	103.45 mph
Fastest lap (record)			
Mike Seward	Yamaha	20m. 26.4s	110.75 mph

1987

1987 Senior Classic

Dave Pither (Matchless) was fastest in practice with Chris Turner (Matchless) second fastest and Alan Dugdale (Matchless) third. Pither, the winner in 1984, took command of the race from the start. He became the first rider in the Classic Races to lap at 100 mph, and he did it from a standing start on the opening lap - 22m. 18.2s. 100.74 mph. He led Turner by 33.8 seconds, who in turn had an advantage of 12.6 seconds over Dugdale. Pither went even faster on the second lap with a new record at 101.31 mph and increased his lead over Turner to one minute 13.0 seconds. Dugdale, the 1986 winner, retired at Ballaugh on lap two, and Selwyn Griffiths (Matchless), winner of the 1964 Senior MGP, took third place, 41.4 seconds down on Turner. Dave Pither won the race by one minute 28.8 seconds from Chris Turner, and not only had he lapped at over 100 mph, he set a new race record at over 100 mph into the bargain. Selwyn Griffiths took third place, 29.2 seconds down on Turner, and the top six were completed by John Goodall (Matchless), Richard Cutts (Matchless) and Dave Storry (Matchless). There were 43 finishers.

1987 Senior Classic (3 laps / 113.19 miles) 72 entries

1. Dave Pither	Matchless	1h. 07m. 45.8s	100.22 mph (record)
2. Chris Turner	Matchless	1h. 08m. 14.6	98.08 mph
3. Selwyn Griffiths	Matchless	1h. 09m. 43.8	97.30 mph
Fastest lap (record)			
Dave Pither	Matchless	22m. 20.6s	101.31 mph

1987 Junior Classic

Richard Swallow (Aermacchi) had been the sensation in practice when he topped the leaderboard in 22m. 40.4s. - under two seconds away from the 100 mph lap. Second fastest was Chris Bladon (Aermacchi) and Cliff Gobell (Aermacchi) was third. Swallow led the race from start to finish, but didn't manage to get near the 100 mph lap, although he did set a new lap record on the opening lap at 96.14 mph, to lead John Kidson (Aermacchi) by one minute 2.2 seconds with Gobell in third place, 10 seconds down on Kidson. Another record by Swallow on lap two - 97.42 mph - increased his lead over Kidson to one minute 44.2 seconds with Gobell a further 42.4 seconds down. So Richard Swallow made it a rather unique double, his brother Bill having won the race in 1986. He won at a record speed by 2 minutes 28.2 seconds from John Kidson, with Gobell in third

The all-action winning style of Richard Swallow (344 Lawton Aermacchi).

place, 56.6 seconds behind Kidson. Bladon, Tony Ainslie (Ducati) and Les Trotter (Suzuki) completed the leaderboard. There were 54 finishers.

1987 Junior Classic (3 laps / 113.19 miles) 51 entries

1. Richard Swallow	Aermacchi	1h. 10m. 01.4s	96.98 mph (record)
2. John Kidson	Aermacchi	1h. 12m. 29.6	93.68 mph
3. Cliff Gobell	Aermacchi	1h. 13m. 26.2	92.47 mph
Fastest lap (record)			
Richard Swallow	Aermacchi	23m. 14.2s	97.42 mph

1987 Senior Newcomers

Colin Gable (Suzuki) led the practice leaderboard, followed by Al Dalton (Yamaha) and Steve Bushell (Yamaha). But at the end of the first lap, local rider Phil Hogg (Suzuki) led Gable by 4.4 seconds, with Dalton a further 11.2 seconds down in third place, and all three had broken the lap record from a standing start. With the fastest lap of the race, and another record at 107.33 mph, Gable took the lead at the end of the second lap by 18 seconds from Hogg, with Dalton 17.8 seconds down on Hogg. At the end of lap three, Gable increased his lead to 59.6 seconds, and Dalton took second place from Hogg by 5.4 seconds. Gable went on to win at a new record speed of 105.23 mph, and with Dalton sliding off at Governors Bridge on the last lap, Hogg took second place, 59.2 seconds down on Gable, and 19.8 seconds in front of Dalton. Dave Lawson (Suzuki) finished fourth, Steve Bushell (Yamaha) fifth and Graham Read (Suzuki), son of eight times TT winner Phil Read, finished sixth. There were 46 finishers.

1987 Senior Newcomers (4 laps / 150.92 miles)

1. Colin Gable	Suzuki	1h. 26m. 03.0s	105.23 mph (record)
2. Phil Hogg	Suzuki	1h. 27m. 02.2s	104.03 mph
3. Al Dalton	Yamaha	1h. 27m. 22.0s	103.64 mph
Fastest lap (record)			
Colin Gable	Suzuki	21m. 05.4s	107.33 mph

1987 Junior Newcomers

Billy Craine (Yamaha) was fastest in practice, Mike Bridges (Yamaha) was second fastest with Ian Dugdale (Yamaha), son of the 1986 Classic 500cc race Alan, third. Craine led the race from start to finish, at the end of the first lap he led Mike Hose (Yamaha) by 46.4 seconds, with Bridges third, 26.8 seconds down on Hose. Craine's lead over Hose at the end of the second lap was one minute 8.6 seconds, with Bridges a further 38.4 seconds down in third place. Mike Hose retired at May Hill, Ramsey with a broken chain on lap three, and Craine now led Bridges by two minutes 23.2 seconds, with Derek Young (Yamaha) up into third place, two minutes 16.8 seconds down on Bridges. But Mike Bridges ran out of luck on the final lap, retiring at Glentrammon. So Billy Craine went on to win by five minutes 06.8 seconds from Derek Young, who in turn had an advantage of one minute 10.4 seconds over Lee Finney (Yamaha). The top six were completed by Geoff Swann (Yamaha), Steve Clements (Yamaha) and Paul Ward (Yamaha). There were 11 finishers.

1987 Junior Newcomers (4 laps / 150.92 miles) 22 entries

1. Billy Craine	Yamaha	1h. 29m. 51.4s	100.77 mph
2. Derek Young	Yamaha	1h. 34m. 58.2s	95.34 mph
3. Lee Finney	Yamaha	1h. 36m. 08.6s	94.18 mph
Fastest lap			
Billy Craine	Yamaha	22m. 01.4s	102.79 mph

1987 Lightweight Newcomers

Ian Morris (Yamaha) was fastest in practice followed by Ian Simpson (Yamaha) and Dougie Black (Yamaha). Morris led at the end of the first lap by 2.6 seconds from Paul Weston (Yamaha), who in turn led Simpson by 24.6 seconds. The order remained the same on lap two, with Morris 22.6 seconds ahead of Weston, and Simpson 42.4 seconds down on Weston. The same order also on lap three with the differences increased to 27 seconds and one minute 15.4 seconds. But on the last lap Weston retired at Sulby Bridge. Ian Morris won by 2 minutes 25.2 seconds from Simpson with Kenneth Virgo (Yamaha) one minute 36.2 seconds down in third place. Nigel Jennings (Yamaha) was fourth, Steve Cook (Yamaha) fifth and Royston Edwards (Yamaha) sixth. There were 13 finishers.

1987 Lightweight Newcomers (4 laps / 150.92 miles) 23 entries

1. Ian Morris	Yamaha	1h. 33m. 31.8s	96.81 mph
2. Ian Simpson	Yamaha	1h. 35m. 57.0s	94.37 mph
3. Ken Virgo	Yamaha	1h. 37m. 33.2s	92.82 mph
Fastest lap			
Ian Morris	Yamaha	23m. 06.6s	97.95 mph

1987 Junior MGP

Craig Ryding (Kimoco) led at the end of the first lap by 25.2 seconds from Mark Linton (Yamaha), who led the third place man Steve Hazlett by 1.6 seconds. Mick Robinson (Yamaha), Stewart Rae (Yamaha) and Brown completed the top six. Ryding increased his lead at the end of the second lap to 26.8 seconds, and Hazlett was second, six seconds ahead of Linton. Robinson and Rae maintained their positions, but Gordon Brown retired at the pits with electrical trouble and Sean Collister (Yamaha) took sixth place. At half distance, Ryding led Hazlett by 30.8 seconds, and Robinson had taken third place from Linton, but he was one minute 15.2 seconds down on Hazlett. Linton was fourth, Decca Kelly (Yamaha) fifth and Ian Jones (Yamaha) sixth. Sean Collister had retired at the Hawthorn. By the time the fourth lap had been completed, Ryding led Hazlett by 31.2 seconds and Linton was back up to third place, 26.4 seconds down on Hazlett. Robinson, Kelly and Rae completed the top six with Jones in eighth place. Hazlett came back at Ryding on the fifth lap, trailing him by 24.8 seconds with Linton one minute 20 seconds down in third place. Robinson was fourth, Kelly fifth and Tony Martin (Yamaha) was up to sixth, with Jones seventh and Rae eighth. Steve Hazlett pulled back another six seconds on the final lap, but Craig Ryding beat him by 16.8 seconds, with Mark Linton in third place, one minute 52.6 seconds down on Hazlett, who scored his best placing, having been third on two previous occasions. Robinson, Kelly and Martin completed the top six. There were 46 finishers and 23 replicas were won.

1987 Junior MGP (6 laps / 226.38 miles) 103 entries

1. Craig Ryding	Kimoco	2h. 09m. 53.4s	104.57 mph
2. Steve Hazlett	Yamaha	2h. 10m. 10.2s	104.34 mph
3. Mark Linton	Yamaha	2h. 11m. 42.8s	103.12 mph
Fastest lap			
Craig Ryding	Kimoco)		
Steve Hazlett	Yamaha)	21m. 20.4s	106.08 mph

1987 Lightweight MGP

Craig Ryding (Kimoco), the Junior winner, topped the practice leaderboard followed by John Davies (Padgett Special) and Dave Moffitt (Armstrong). Ryding led the race from start to finish. At the end of lap one he was 6.5 seconds ahead of Sean Collister (Honda) who in turn led Davies by nine seconds. Mick Robinson (Yamaha) was fourth, Billy Craine (Yamaha) fifth and Peter Smethurst (Armstrong) sixth. Ryding increased his lead over Collister to one minute 03.4 seconds at the end of lap two, with Davies a further 44 seconds down in third place. Craine moved up to fourth ahead of Robinson, and Derek Glass (Yamaha) took over sixth place with Smethurst seventh. A fast pit stop by Collister closed the gap on Ryding at the end of the third lap, he was 35.2 seconds down and one minute 21.6 seconds ahead of Robinson, Craine, Davies and Glass completed the top six. Craig Ryding went on to complete only the second Junior/Lightweight double by two minutes 0.2 seconds, but Collister ran out of fuel and pushed in from Cronk-ny-Mona to finish 32nd. Mick Robinson took second place for the second year in succession, 37.2 seconds ahead of Craine. Davies, Glass and Martin Birkinshaw (Armstrong) completed the leaderboard. There were 52 finishers and 18 replicas were won.

1987 Lightweight MGP (4 laps / 150.92 miles) 89 entries

1. Craig Ryding	Kimoco	1h. 28m. 22.8s	102.45 mph
2. Mick Robinson	Yamaha	1h. 30m. 23.0s	100.18 mph
3. Billy Craine	Yamaha	1h. 31m. 00.2s	99.50 mph
Fastest lap			
Craig Ryding	Kimoco	21m. 47.2s	103.90 mph

1987 Senior MGP

Brian Raynor (Yamaha) was fastest in practice with Pete Beale (Yamaha) second and Paul Hunt (Kawasaki) third in 21m. 18.2s. At the end of the first lap Beale led by 5.4 seconds from Hunt with Steve Dowey (Yamaha) in third place 4.8 seconds down on Hunt. Raynor was fourth, Dave Sharratt (Suzuki) fifth and Kenny Harmer (Honda) sixth. Beale led by 5.6 seconds at the end of the second lap from Raynor who was 8.2 seconds up on Dowey, Harmer, Sharratt and Kevin Jackson (Suzuki) completed the leaderboard, Hunt having retired at Cronk-y-Voddy. By the end of the third lap, Raynor had taken the lead by 19.8 seconds from Beale, who had an advantage of 4.4 seconds over Dowey, followed by Harmer, Jackson and Sharratt. Raynor increased his lead over Dowey to 25.4 seconds at the end of lap four, with Beale four seconds down. Harmer remained fourth and Sharratt took fifth place from Jackson. Raynor increased his lead at the end of the fifth lap to 38.6 seconds, and strangely enough there were no further leaderboard changes to the end of the race. So Raynor won by 34.4 seconds from Dowey, with Beale third, 21.4 seconds down. Harmer was fourth, Sharratt fifth and Jackson sixth. Steve Hazlett had another fine ride to take seventh place on his 350cc Yamaha. There were 75 finishers and 26 replicas were won.

Craig Ryding leaps the Eddie Roberts built Kimoco off Sulby Bridge.

1987 Senior MGP (6 laps / 226.38 miles) 116 entries

1. Brian Raynor	Yamaha	2h. 06m. 42.0s	107.20 mph
			(record)
2. Steve Dowey	Yamaha	2h. 07m. 16.4s	106.72 mph
3. Pete Beale	Yamaha	2h. 07m. 37.8s	106.42 mph
Fastest lap			
Brian Raynor	Yamaha	20m. 38.2s	109.69 mph

1988

1988 saw major changes to the Manx programme, with the Classic 500 cc race being held on its own, and the 350 cc race incorporating a 250 cc class, so there were nine winners in all. The programme also moved to a Monday, Wednesday and Friday format.

1988 Senior Newcomers

Allan McDonald (1100 Suzuki) dominated this race from start to finish. He opened up with a lap at 107.22 mph to lead Brad Ogden (1000 Yamaha) by 21.6 seconds with Simon Beck (500 Honda) in third place a further 8.6 seconds down. Philip Gilmour (1100 Suzuki) was fourth, followed by Neil Larsen (750 Suzuki) and David Crompton. McDonald set a new lap record second time around at 109.27 mph and increased his lead over ogden to 47.6 seconds with the rest of the leaderboard unchanged. By the end of lap three McDonald's lead over Ogden was up to one minute 3.6 seconds, Beck was still third, Gilmour fourth and Crompton had overtaken Larsen. Brad Ogden lapped at 108.48 mph on the last lap, but Allan McDonald won the race by 46.2 seconds with Philip Gilmour third, ahead of Beck, Crompton and Larsen. There were 29 finishers and the first six won replicas.

1988 Senior Newcomers (4 laps / 150.92 miles) 23 entries

1. Allan McDonald	Suzuki	1h. 24m. 32.0s	107.11 mph
			(record)
2. Brad Ogden	Yamaha	1h. 25m. 18.2s	106.15 mph
3. Philip Gilmour	Suzuki	1h. 27m. 08.6s	103.91 mph
Fastest lap (record)			
Allan McDonald	Suzuki	20m. 43.0s	109.27 mph

1988 Junior Newcomers

Charles Morgan (350 Yamaha) led this class from start to finish. At the end of the first lap he led Kevin Strowger (Yamaha) by 26.6 seconds with Barry Dixon (Yamaha) in third place. The top six were completed by Francis Everard (Yamaha), Gareth Jones (Yamaha) and Martin Powell (Yamaha). On lap two Morgan increased his lead to 67 seconds and the rest of the leaderboard remained unchanged. By the time the third lap had been completed, Morgan's lead was up to one minute 25 seconds, Everard dropped off the leaderboard and Roger Jones (Yamaha) took over fourth place. Charles Morgan went on to win from Kevin Strowger by one minute 34seconds, with Barry Dixon third. Everard came back into fourth place, with Powell fifth and Gareth Jones sixth, whilst Roger Jones took eight place. There were 13 finishers and six replicas were won.

1988 Junior Newcomers (4 laps / 150.92 miles) 23 entries

1. Charles Morgan	Yamaha	1h. 32m. 22.2s	98.03 mph
2. Kevin Strowger	Yamaha	1h. 33m. 56.2s	96.39 mph
3. Barry Dixon	Yamaha	1h. 34m. 30.6s	95.81 mph
Fastest lap			
Charles Morgan	Yamaha	22m. 48.4s	99.26 mph

1988 Lightweight Newcomers

Phillip McCallen (Honda) completely re-wrote the records in the Lightweight class with another start to finish victory. From a standing start he knocked 44 seconds off the lap record at 102.41 mph and led Darren Powell (Yamaha) by one minute 19.4 seconds! Steven Elliott (Yamaha) was third and the top six were completed by Mark Langton (Yamaha), Barry Wood (Yamaha) and Richard Whiteman (Yamaha). With another lap record on the second circuit at 105 mph, McCallen increased his lead over Powell to two minutes 47 seconds - Elliott was still third followed by Langton and Whiteman. Wood had dropped off the leaderboard and Andrew Griffiths (Armstrong) came into sixth place. At the end of the third lap McCallen was almost four minutes in front of Powell, Langton had taken third place from Elliott and Whiteman and Griffiths completed the top six. With a blistering new lap record at 107.01 mph on the final lap, Phillip McCallen won from Darren Powell by five minutes 46.8 seconds at a new record speed of 103.53 mph. Langton finished third, Elliott fourth, Whiteman fifth and Paul Dave (Yamaha) took sixth place after Griffiths had retired on the last lap. There were 14 finishers, and four replicas were won.

1988 Newcomers: Richard Whiteman (Yamaha, 89) rides round Duncan Wood (Suzuki) on his way to fifth place in the Lightweight class. The picture taken at the un-named curve just above the Gooseneck.

1988 Lightweight Newcomers (4 laps / 150.92 miles) 23 entries

1. Phillip McCallen	Honda	1h. 27m. 27.4s	103.53 mph
			(record)
2. Darren Powell	Yamaha	1h. 33m. 14.2s	97.12 mph
3. Mark Langton	Yamaha	1h. 34m. 30.4s	95.81 mph
Fastest lap (record)			
Phillip McCallen	Honda	21m. 09.2s	107.01 mph

1988 Junior Classic

Richard Swallow (Aermacchi) won this race for the second year in succession and set new lap and race records. He set a new record from a standing start at 99.00 mph and led Alan

'Bud' Jackson (Aermacchi) by 12.4 seconds with John Goodall (A.J.S.) third, a further seven seconds down. The top six were completed by Mark Linton, Bill Swallow and Dave Dearden, all on Aermacchis. Richard set the first 100 mph lap in this class on lap two at 100.65 mph and led Jackson by 26.2 seconds. Linton had overtaken Goodall for third place, Bill Swallow remained fifth and John Kidson (Aermacchi) took sixth place from Dearden. With a six gallon tank fitted for a non-stop run, the leader set a new record again on the third lap at 100.80 mph and led Linton by one minute 11.4 seconds, who had taken second place from Jackson. Bill Swallow was fourth ahead now of Goodall with Dearden back in sixth place after Kidson's retirement. Richard Swallow won by almost five minutes at an average speed of 100.02 mph from Mark Linton. Bill Swallow overtook Alan 'Bud' Jackson on the last lap to finish third, with John Goodall fifth and Lawrence Parris (Aermacchi) sixth, and Dave Dearden finished seventh. There were 52 finishers and six replicas were won.

1988 Junior Classic (4 laps / 150.92 miles)

1. Richard Swallow	Aermacchi	1h. 30m. 32.0s	100.02 mph
			(record)
2. Mark Linton	Aermacchi	1h. 35m. 24.0s	94.91 mph
3. Bill Swallow	Aermacchi	1h. 35m. 57.8s	94.36 mph
Fastest lap (record)			
Richard Swallow	Aermacchi	22m. 27.4s	100.80 mph

1988 Lightweight Classic

Mike Cain (Suzuki) led this class at the end of the first lap by 56.8 seconds from David Smith (Aermacchi) with Norman Williamson (Aermacchi) third just 2.8 seconds down on Smith. Neville Watts (Honda), Eddie Crooks (Suzuki) and George Linder (Yamaha) completed the top six. Linder, who started at the back of the field, and then lost over two minutes at his pit, set a new lap record on lap two at 94.82 mph to close to just two seconds of Cain, with Williamson still third, Smith had dropped to fourth, Crooks was fifth and Watts sixth. Linder took the lead on lap three by 30 seconds from Cain with the rest of the leaderboard unchanged. George Linder won from Mike Cain by 48.6 seconds with Eddie Crooks third. Williamson retired on the last lap, and Watts took fourth place, Smith was fifth and veteran Arthur Wheeler (Guzzi) finished sixth. There were 11 finishers and five replicas were won.

1988 Lightweight Classic (4 laps / 150.92 miles)

1. George Linder	Yamaha	1h. 41m. 27.4s	89.25 mph
			(record)
2. Mike Cain	Suzuki	1h. 42m. 15.8s	88.54 mph
3. Eddie Crooks	Suzuki	1h. 45m. 42.4s	85.66 mph
Fastest lap (record)			
George Linder	Yamaha	23m. 52.4s	94.82 mph

1988 Senior Classic

Riding a specially prepared brand new 498cc Seeley, Phil Nicholls won this race after a great dice with American Dave Roper (500 Matchless). At the end of lap one Nicholls was 10 seconds ahead of Roper with Alan Dugdale (499 Cowles Matchless) third - 3.6 seconds down. The top six were completed by John Goodall (Matchless), John Knowles (Seeley) and Bill Swallow (Velocette). With the fastest lap of the race at 100.62 mph, Roper closed the gap to 1.6 seconds at the end of lap two. Third to fifth remained the same, but Dave Storry (Seeley) took sixth place from Swallow. Nicholls put in his second 100 plus lap on the third circuit and increased his lead over Roper to 20.8 seconds. Goodall took third place from Dugdale, with Knowles and Storry still fifth and sixth. Phil Nicholls went on to win from Dave Roper by 38.4 seconds with John Goodall third. Alan Dugdale, John Knowles and Dave Storry completed the top six. There were 58 finishers and six replicas were won.

Phil Nicholls at Windy Corner.

1988 Senior Classic (4 laps / 150.92 miles)

1. Phil Nicholls	Seeley	1h. 31m. 12.4s	99.28 mph
2. Dave Roper	Matchless	1h. 31m. 50.8s	98.59 mph
3. John Goodall	Matchless	1h. 32m. 29.2s	97.90 mph
Fastest lap			
Dave Roper	Matchless	22m. 29.8s	100.62 mph

1988 Junior MGP

After finishing third and second in the past two years, Steve Hazlett gained a deserved victory in the Junior race. But at the end of the first lap it was local rider Billy Craine (Yamaha) who led from fellow local Phil Hogg (Yamaha) by 6.8 seconds with Hazlett (Yamaha) third, a further 1.4 seconds down. The top six were completed by Mark Linton, Stan Rea and Nigel Barton, all Yamahas. Craine retired at Ramsey on the second lap, and Hazlett took over the lead from Hogg by 11.2 seconds with Linton third. Rea was fourth, Mick Robinson (Yamaha) was fifth and Barton and Ian Simpson (Yamaha) tied for sixth place. By the end of lap three Hazlett had a lead of one minute from Linton with Hogg third, followed by Rea, Robinson and Gordon Brown (Yamaha). There were a number of changes to the leaderboard by of the end of the fourth lap - Hazlett still led, but Rea was up to second ahead of Linton, Phillip McCallen (Yamaha) was fourth, Ian Simpson fifth and Mick Robinson sixth. Phil Hogg had dropped to ninth after a spill at Governors Bridge and an extra pit stop to check for any damage. By the time the fifth lap had been completed, Hazlett had a comfortable lead of 69 seconds over Linton, who was just a fifth of a second ahead of Rea. Robinson, Barton and Brown completed the leaderboard, with Hogg up to seventh and McCallen down to eighth. Steve Hazlett won the Junior by 71.4 seconds from Mark Linton, who just held off the challenge of Stan Rea by three fifths of a second. Mick Robinson, Nigel Barton and Phil Hogg completed the top six.

1988 Junior MGP (6 laps / 226.38 miles)

1. Steve Hazlett	Yamaha	2h. 09m. 12.0s	105.13 mph
2. Mark Linton	Yamaha	2h. 10m. 23.4s	104.17 mph
3. Stan Rea	Yamaha	2h. 10m. 24.0s	104.16 mph
Fastest lap			
Steve Hazlett	Yamaha	21m. 03.4s	107.51 mph

1988 Lightweight MGP

Phillip McCallen (Honda) once again rewrote the records with a start to finish victory. After one lap he had a lead of 51 seconds over Martin Birkinshaw (Armstrong), with Ian Dugdale (Honda) third, a further two seconds down. Mick Robinson (Yamaha) was fourth, Nick Turner (Ntraha) fifth and Derek Young (Rotax) sixth. McCallen was a minute and a half ahead of Birkinshaw at the end of lap two with a lap at over 107 mph. Third to fifth remained the same, and Ian Morris (Rotax) was sixth with Young dropping to eighth. Birkinshaw retired at the 26th milestone on lap three, and at the end of the lap McCallen led Robinson by over two minutes with Dugdale third, Young fourth, Karl Fox (Yamaha) fifth and Turner sixth. Phillip McCallen set a new lap record on his final circuit at 107.45 mph and won from Ian Dugdale by three minutes 15.2 seconds. Mick Robinson, a most consistent rider at the Manx finished third, with Derek Young, Karl Fox and Ian Morris completing the top six. 51 finished and 13 won replicas.

1988 Lightweight MGP (4 laps / 150.92 miles)

1. Phillip McCallen	Honda	1h. 25m. 41.0s	105.68 mph
			(record)
2. Ian Dugdale	Honda	1h. 26m. 56.2s	101.81 mph
3. Mick Robinson	Yamaha	1h. 29m. 03.0s	101.68 mph
Fastest lap (record)			
Phillip McCallen	Honda	21m. 04.0s	107.45 mph

1988 Senior MGP

Paul Hunt at Quarter Bridge.

From a standing start, local rider Phil Hogg (Yamaha) made Manx Grand Prix history when he became the first rider to lap in under twenty minutes - he lapped in 19m. 51.2s. - a speed of 114.02 to lead fellow Manxman Paul Hunt (Kawasaki) by 25.2 seconds, with Ian Simpson (Suzuki) third - 7.2 seconds down on Hunt. Steve Allen (Yamaha) was fourth, Steve Hazlett (Honda) fifth and Nigel Barton (Honda) sixth. Phil Hogg's race ended at Cronk ny Mona with a high speed spill on the second lap, and Hunt led Simpson by 9.6 seconds with Allen in third place. The top six were completed by Hazlett, Graham Read (Suzuki) and Al Dalton (Suzuki). By half distance Hunt led Simpson by 10.8 seconds, Allen and Hazlett maintained their positions and Dalton took fifth place from Read. Simpson retired on the fourth lap so Hunt now led Allen by 15.4 seconds with Hazlett third. The top six were completed by Read, Kevin Jackson (Yamaha) and Dalton. Hunt's lead at the of lap five over Allen was 19.6 seconds, who in turn led Hazlett by over a minute. Dalton was up to fourth, Read was fifth and Jackson sixth. So Paul Hunt went on to win the Senior by 27.4 seconds from Steve Allen with Steve Hazlett third, Al Dalton took fourth place, Graham Read fifth and Kevin Jackson sixth. There were 75 finishers and 33 replicas were won.

1988 Senior MGP (6 laps / 226.38 miles)

1. Paul Hunt	Kawasaki	2h. 02m. 42.2s	110.69 mph
			(record)
2. Steve Allen	Yamaha	2h. 03m. 09.4s	110.28 mph
3. Steve Hazlett	Honda	2h. 04m. 26.0s	109.15 mph
Fastest lap (record)			
Phil Hogg	Yamaha	19m. 51.2s	114.02 mph

1989

1989 Senior Newcomers

Chris Morris (Honda) led this race from start to finish, and indeed the top four remained the same right through the race. At the end of the first lap, Morris led Tony O'Hara (Suzuki) by fifteen seconds, with David Bowie (Suzuki) third, a further 14.2 seconds down. The top six were completed by Alan Bennallick (Yamaha), Steve Platts (Yamaha) and 'Big Mac' Chappell (Suzuki). By the end of lap two Morris had increased his lead to 27.6 seconds, Mark Stirling (Yamaha) moved up to fifth ahead of Platts, with Chappell dropping off the leaderboard to seventh place. The order remained the same on lap three, with Morris 31.8 seconds in front, and he went on to win by 41.8 seconds from O'Hara with Bowie third, and the remainder of the leaderboard unchanged. There were 34 finishers and 14 replicas were won.

1989 Senior Newcomers (4 laps / 150.92 miles)

1. Chris Morris	Honda	1h. 27m. 03.6s	104.01 mph
2. Tony O'Hara	Suzuki	1h. 27m. 45.4s	103.18 mph
3. David Bowie	Suzuki	1h. 28m. 27.6s	102.36 mph
Fastest lap			
Chris Morris	Honda	21m. 20.4s	106.08 mph

1989 Junior Newcomers

There were just eight starters for the Junior Newcomers, and at the end of the first lap David Hedison (Yamaha) led Ian Large (Yamaha) by just 3.4 seconds with Richard Mortimer (Yamaha) in third place a further 20 seconds down. Garry Bennett (Yamaha) was fourth, David Binch (Yamaha) fifth and David Meany (Yamaha) sixth. At the end of the second lap Large took the lead from Hedison by 12.2 seconds, with the rest of the leaderboard unchanged. Hedison was back in front, however, at the end of the third lap by 5.4 seconds, Bennett took third place from Mortimer, Meany was fifth and Peter Robinson (Yamaha) was sixth. Binch hit problems and his third lap took 37 minutes and he dropped to eighth. Hedison went on to win by 15.2 seconds from Large, whose machine had a slipping clutch. Bennett, Mortimer and Meany maintained their positions and Andy Coole (Yamaha) took sixth place when Robertson retired at Ballacraine on the last lap. There were seven finishers and the first four won replicas.

1989 Junior Newcomers (4 laps / 150.92 miles)

1. David Hedison	Yamaha	1h. 35m. 12.2s	95.11 mph
2. Ian Large	Yamaha	1h. 35m. 27.4s	94.86 mph
3. Garry Bennett	Yamaha	1h. 38m. 48.0s	91.65 mph
Fastest lap			
David Hedison	Yamaha	22m. 48.8s	99.23 mph

1989 Lightweight Newcomers

Hot favourite was Irishman Leslie McMaster, and at the end of the first lap his E.M.C. was some eighteen seconds ahead of Pat Sefton (Kawasaki) with Harry Corbett (Honda) a further 23 seconds down in third place. The top six were completed by Michael Jackson (Honda), Nigel Piercy (Suzuki) and Graham Morton (Kawasaki). The difference between the two leaders was down to seventeen seconds at the end of the second lap, Corbett was still third, Jackson retired at the Mountain Box and Piercy and Morton moved up one place, with John Henderson (Yamaha) coming on to the leaderboard in sixth place. On lap three McMaster had problems, the steering damper had broken and he managed to get to the pits where it was replaced, but his lap time was four minutes slower than his opening two and he dropped to eighth. Sefton took over the lead by one minute 5.4 seconds from Corbett, with Piercy third. Henderson had moved up to fourth, and with Graham Morton's retirement due to a spill at Cruickshanks Corner, Mark Pearce (Yamaha) and Steve Worth (Suzuki) came into the top six. Pat Sefton went on to win the race by 53.6 seconds from Corbett with Piercy third. McMaster really flew on the last lap at 103.57 mph and he took fourth place with Henderson fifth and Pearce sixth. There were 14 finishers and 11 replicas were won.

1989 Lightweight Newcomers (4 laps / 150.92 miles)

1. Pat Sefton	Kawasaki	1h. 33m. 27.4s	96.89 mph
2. Harry Corbett	Honda	1h. 34m. 21.8s	95.96 mph
3. Nigel Piercy	Suzuki	1h. 35m. 05.6s	95.22 mph
Fastest lap			
Leslie McMaster	E.M.C.	21m. 51.4s	103.57 mph

1989 Junior Classic

Richard Swallow became only the third rider in the history of the Manx to complete a hat trick of wins when he led the Junior Classic from start to finish on his 350cc Aermacchi. At the end of the first lap he was 18.6 seconds ahead of Ian Young (Aermacchi) with Bob Millinship (Ducati) in third place - 23.2 seconds down on Young. Mark Linton (Aermacchi), John Kidson (Aermacchi) and John Goodall (A.J.S.) completed the first lap leaderboard. The top six were unchanged at the end of the second lap, Swallow's advantage was 31.6 seconds. Surprisingly, the top five riders maintained their positions on the third lap, the exception being Goodall who retired just after Quarterbridge, bringing Alan 'Bud' Jackson (Aermacchi) into sixth place, and Swallow led by 38 seconds. He went on to win from Young by one minute and nine seconds, Linton and Kidson both overtook Millinship on the last lap and Peter Byrne (Ducati) finished sixth with Jackson dropping to eighth at the flag. There were 39 finishers and 11 riders won replicas.

1989 Junior Classic (4 laps / 150.92 miles)

1. Richard Swallow	Aermacchi	1h. 32m. 37.2s	97.76 mph
2. Ian Young	Aermacchi	1h. 33m. 46.2s	96.56 mph
3. Mark Linton	Aermacchi	1h. 35m. 33.6s	94.75 mph
Fastest lap			
Richard Swallow	Aermacchi	23m. 02.8s	98.22 mph

1989 Lightweight Classic

For the second year in succession, Mike Cain (Suzuki) led this race. At the end of the first lap he had an advantage of 21.8 seconds over David Smith (Aermacchi) with Rich Hawkins (Ducati) a further 57.6 seconds down in third place. Nev Watts (Honda), Pete Swallow (Ducati) and Richard Fitzsimmons (Suzuki) completed the top six. The order remained the same on lap two with Cain one minute ahead of Smith. But on lap three,

the Suzuki gave up the ghost at Guthrie's and Mike retired when in the lead for the second successive year. Smith took over the lead by exactly three minutes from Swallow with Watts third, ahead of Hawkins, Fitzsimmons was fifth and Geoff Hadwin (Suzuki) came into sixth place. David Smith won the race from Pete Swallow by three minutes 42 seconds, and Hawkins regained third place from Watts, with Hadwin taking fifth place from Fitzsimmons. There were fifteen finishers and ten riders, including veteran Arthur Wheeler, won replicas.

David Smith at Signpost Corner.

1989 Lightweight Classic (4 laps / 150.92 miles)

1. David Smith	Aermacchi	1h. 44m. 00.2s	87.06 mph
2. Pete Swallow	Ducati	1h. 47m. 42.2s	84.07 mph
3. Rich Hawkins	Ducati	1h. 47m. 59.2s	83.85 mph
Fastest lap			
Alan Dugdale	Aermacchi	24m. 56.2s	90.78 mph

1989 Senior Classic

American Dave Roper set a blistering pace on the opening lap on his Team Obsolete Matchless, 100.37 mph, to lead Richard Swallow (Aermacchi) by 12.8 seconds, with Phil Nicholls (Seeley) third, a further 7.4 seconds down. The top six on the opening lap were completed by Bill Swallow (Seeley), John Goodall (Matchless) and Geoff Tunstall (Seeley). On the second lap Roper broke the lap record at 102.52 mph and led Richard Swallow by 36.8 seconds, with brother Bill up to third place, thirteen seconds down. Phil Nicholls retired at the pits and John Goodall had a long stop in Ramsey and eventually finished 15th. So Tunstall was fourth, Ian Lougher (Matchless) fifth and Selwyn Griffiths (Matchless) sixth. Sensation on lap three, when Dave Roper, with a commanding lead, slid off at the Bungalow, he was uninjured but was forced to retire. The new leader at the end of the third lap was Bill Swallow, by just 0.2 of a second from brother Richard. Tunstall, Lougher and Griffiths all moved up one place and David May (Norton) took over sixth place. For part of the final lap, the brothers were together on the road, but Bill pulled out the stops and pulled away from Richard to win by 15.6 seconds. Selwyn Griffiths moved up to take third place when Geoff Tunstall slowed up to finish 10th and Ian Lougher retired at the bottom of Barregarrow. Fourth place went to May, fifth to Bill Horsman (Seeley) and the sixth finisher was Bob Hirst (Seeley). There were 49 finishers and the first 17 won replicas.

Dave Roper exhibiting his forceful style at Quarter Bridge.

1989 Senior Classic (4 laps / 150.92 miles)

1. Bill Swallow	Seeley	1h. 30m. 04.2s	100.53 mph
2. Richard Swallow	Aermacchi	1h. 30m. 19.8s	100.24 mph
3. Selwyn Griffiths	Matchless	1h. 32m. 44.4s	97.64 mph
Fastest lap (record)			
Dave Roper	Matchless	22m. 04.8s	102.62 mph

1989 Junior MGP

Dave Montgomery achieved a twelve-year-old ambition when he led the Junior from start to finish, despite having two pit stops to his rivals' one. He led at the end of the first lap on his Yamaha by three seconds from Mick Robinson (Yamaha), with Stan Rea (Yamaha) third, a further 17.6 seconds down. In fourth place was Ian Standevan (Yamaha), fifth was Andy Bassett (Yamaha) and sixth Greg Broughton (Yamaha). At the end of the second lap Montgomery increased his lead over Robinson to 27.6 seconds, with Rea still third and Standevan fourth. Nick Turner (Yamaha) came up to fifth place ahead of Bassett with Broughton down to seventh. By half distance, Montgomery led Robinson by 33.2 seconds, and Rea remained third. Ian Standevan came off at Birkins Bends and Turner moved up to fourth. Mark Linton (Yamaha) came on to the leaderboard in fifth place ahead of Bassett. There was a new second place man at the end of the fourth lap, Turner, who trailed the leader by one minute 34.4 seconds, with Robinson now third, Rea fourth followed by Linton and Bassett. By the time the fifth lap had been completed Robinson was back in second place, one minute six seconds down on Montgomery with Rea third and Linton fourth. Turner had dropped to fifth and Bassett was still sixth. On the last lap Linton had gearbox problems - losing three of the six gears and had oil on the back wheel - he stopped at the Gooseneck, was black flagged at the Bungalow and finished with a lap at 94 mph to take eighth place. Turner also had problems with a loose chain which he stopped to adjust and dropped to sixteenth. Dave Montgomery won by 42.2 seconds from Rea, Bassett moved up to third, followed by Robinson, Leslie McMaster (Yamaha) and Greg Broughton. There were 47 finishers and twenty replicas were won.

1989 Junior MGP (6 laps / 226.38 miles) 106 entries

1. Dave Montgomery	Yamaha	2h. 09m. 13.2s	105.11 mph
2. Stanley Rea	Yamaha	2h. 09m. 55.4s	104.54 mph

3. Andy Bassett	Yamaha	2h. 11m. 15.2s	103.48 mph
Fastest lap			
Dave Montgomery	Yamaha	20m. 52.2s	108.47 mph

1989 Lightweight MGP

Dave Montgomery speeds away from Ballaugh Bridge.

The four-lap Lightweight again proved to be an exciting race, with no fewer than three different leaders during the race. At the end of the first lap Karl Fox (Honda) led Derek Young (Rotax) by 4.8 seconds, with Nick Turner (Yamaha) third, eight seconds down on Young. The top six at the end of the opening lap was completed by Mark Linton (Honda), Nigel Griffiths (Yamaha) and Leslie McMaster (E.M.C.). One of the favourites, Stan Rea only got as far as Quarterbridge before sliding off. Then leader Fox retired at Ballaugh Bridge with a seized engine on lap two, and at the end of the lap Linton led Turner by 10.6 seconds with Young third, followed by McMaster, Griffiths and Mick Robinson (Yamaha). Turner had decided to go non-stop for the race, whilst Linton pitted at the end of the second lap, so by the time lap three had been completed Turner led Linton by 22.6 seconds, with Young still third, Robinson fourth, McMaster fifth and Griffiths sixth. With the fastest lap of the race on his final circuit, just 3.6 seconds outside the record, Linton closed on Turner, but finished eighteen seconds down. Robinson took third place, his 15th replica, equalling the record of Denis Parkinson, Griffiths was fourth, Young fifth, and with McMasters retirement at the Hawthorn on the last lap, Nigel Hansen (Yamaha) took sixth place. There were 51 finishers and the first 27 won replicas.

1989 Lightweight MGP (4 laps / 150.92 miles) 85 entries

1. Nick Turner	Yamaha	1h. 26m. 16.0s	104.96 mph
2. Mark Linton	Honda	1h. 26m. 34.0s	104.60 mph
3. Mick Robinson	Yamaha	1h. 27m. 45.0s	103.18 mph
Fastest lap			
Mark Linton	Honda	21m. 07.6s	107.15 mph

1989 Senior MGP

Nigel Barton amazed almost everyone on the Island by getting his RC30 Honda around three laps of the course on one tank of fuel, but he did, and established his authority on a race that surprisingly saw the first three remain the same for the full six laps. At the end of the opening lap, Barton led Allan McDonald (Honda) by 14.6 seconds with Brad Ogden (Yamaha) just two seconds down in third place. Steve Bushell (Yamaha), Nigel Nottingham (Yamaha) and Simon Beck (Honda) completed the top six. Barton's lead was 22.2 seconds at the end of the second circuit, and McDonald had increased his advantage over Ogden to 23.6 seconds. Bushell had retired at Braddan Bridge on this lap, so Nottingham moved up to fourth, Robert Quinn (Yamaha) moved on to the leaderboard in fifth place, with Norman Kneen (Yamaha) sixth and Beck seventh. With his

Nigel Barton gives the knee-slider a good workout at the Bungalow.

rivals pitting at the end of the second lap and Barton going straight through, he led at half distance by one minute 4.6 seconds. With McDonald and Ogden retaining their places on the leaderboard, the changes came in the lower half of the top six, Barrie Middleton (Honda) came up to fourth, with Quinn fifth and Kneen sixth. Nottingham had dropped to eighth. Barton's lead at the end of the fourth lap was 28 seconds, Quinn was fourth ahead of Kneen and Brian Venables (Yamaha) who had started No. 106, Middleton dropping to 10th with McDonald and Ogden stopping again at the end of the fourth lap, Barton led at the end of the fifth by one minute 22.2 seconds, and Middleton, Kneen and Venables filled fourth to sixth places with Quinn down in eighth. Nigel Barton took a precautionary fuel stop at the end of the fifth lap and went on to win from McDonald by 45.6 seconds, and Ogden completed a sub-twenty minute lap - 19m.56.8s. - on the last lap and closed to within 2.4 second of the second-place man. Middleton was fourth, Dave Castle (Yamaha) took fifth, with Kneen sixth and Brian Venables seventh. There were 74 finishers and 39 replicas were won.

1989 Senior MGP (6 laps / 226.38 miles) 116 entries

1. Nigel Barton	Honda	2h. 01m. 46.6s	111.53 mph
2. Allan McDonald	Honda	2h. 02m. 32.2s	110.84 mph
3. Brad Ogden	Yamaha	2h. 02m. 34.6s	110.81 mph
Fastest lap			
Nigel Barton	Honda	19m. 56.4s	113.53 mph

Nigel Barton made a little bit of history by being the first rider in the history of the Manx to make a scheduled rear wheel change at his pit stop.

1990

The pattern remained the same as the successful format of the previous two years, although there were changes in the capacities of some of the races. The Newcomers Senior and Senior Manx Grand Prix had a top limit of 750cc, the Junior Newcomers was for machines of 251 to 400cc two-stroke and 401cc to 600cc four-stroke, and the Lightweight Newcomers included 251 to 400cc four-strokes. The Junior Manx was for 201 to 350cc machines.

1990 Senior Newcomers

Former top moto-crosser Paul Orritt (Yamaha), in his first road race, led this class from start to finish. He opened up with a lap at 105.14 mph to lead local rider Eric Moore (Suzuki) by 24.6 seconds with Richard Harris (Yamaha) in third place, followed by Antony Woodcock (Honda), Paul Grimshaw (Honda) and Dave Hayward (Suzuki). Orritt increased his lead to over one minute by the time the second lap had been completed, and the only change to the top six was that Woodcock took third place from Harris. One minute and ten seconds was the lead Orritt had over Moore at the end of lap three, and Colin Breeze (B.S.A.) came on to the leaderboard in fifth place and Harris dropped to seventh. With the fastest lap of the race on the final circuit at 108.35 mph, Orritt won from Moore by one minute 20 seconds, Woodcock, Grimshaw, Breeze and Hayward completed the top six. There were 12 finishers and eight riders won replicas.

Big man - big bike. Paul 'Orrible' Oritt leaves Quarter Bridge

1990 Senior Newcomers (4 laps / 150.92 miles) 20 entries

1. Paul Orritt	Yamaha	1h. 25m. 27.4s	105.96 mph
2. Eric Moore	Suzuki	1h. 26m. 47.6s	104.33 mph
3. Antony Woodcock	Yamaha	1h. 29m. 03.4s	101.67 mph
Fastest lap			
Paul Orritt	Yamaha	20m. 53.6s	108.35 mph

1990 Junior Newcomers

Despite the change of capacities, it was a 350cc Yamaha that led the Junior Newcomers all the way to the flag. At the end of the first lap Lee Pullan led Andy Corbett (Yamaha) by 10.8 seconds, with Bryan Smith (Honda) in third place, 1.6 seconds down on Corbett. Mark Watts (Yamaha), Nick Wilkins (Yamaha) and Richard Hardwick (Yamaha) completed the top six. Pullan increased his lead to 14 seconds at the end of lap two, and it was Smyth in second place from Corbett by 20 seconds. Watts remained fourth, but Hardwick took fifth place from Wilkins. Smith's challenge ended in a spill at Brandywell on the third lap and Pullan led Corbett by 22.6 seconds at the end of the lap, with Watts third, Hardwick fourth, David Jackson (Yamaha) fifth and Dean Harrison (Yamaha) sixth, Wilkins was just off the leaderboard in seventh place. The only change at the end of the race was that Harrison went out on the final lap, and Wilkins moved up to sixth. Pullan won from Corbett by nine seconds. There were 17 finishers and 11 replicas were won.

1990 Junior Newcomers (4 laps / 150.92 miles) 31 entries

1. Lee Pullan	Yamaha	1h. 27m. 40.2s	103.28 mph
2. Andy Corbett	Yamaha	1h. 27m. 49.2s	103.11 mph
3. Mark Watts	Yamaha	1h. 29m. 33.2s	101.11 mph
Fastest lap			
Lee Pullan	Yamaha	21m. 30.8s	105.22 mph

1990 Lightweight Newcomers

It was another start to finish victory in the Lightweight Newcomers, Mick Lofthouse (Kawasaki) led Mark Baldwin (Kawasaki) at the end of the first lap by 42 seconds with Michael O'Connor (Suzuki) third, a further 12.2 seconds down. The top six was completed by Andy Jones (Kawasaki), Craig Mason (Kawasaki) and Lodwig Parry-Jones (Yamaha). The top

six remained unchanged at the end of the second lap and Lofthouse had increased his lead to 27.6 seconds. Third place man O'Connor retired at Quarry Bends on the third lap, so Jones, Mason and Parry-Jones moved up one place, and Pat Robinson (Kawasaki) took over sixth place. Lofthouse was leading the race by over two minutes, and went on to win by 2 minutes 38.2 seconds from Baldwin, and the rest of the top six stayed the same. There were 11 finishers and the first four won replicas.

1990 Lightweight Newcomers (4 laps / 150.92 miles) 26 entries

1. Mick Lofthouse	Kawasaki	1h. 29m. 45.0s	100.89 mph
2. Mark Baldwin	Kawasaki	1h. 32m. 23.2s	98.01 mph
3. Andy Jones	Kawasaki	1h. 34m. 03.0s	96.28 mph
Fastest lap			
Mick Lofthouse	Kawasaki	22m. 12.8s	101.91 mph

1990 Senior Classic

Alan Dugdale (Matchless) looked all set for his second Senior Classic victory when he led the race for the first three laps. At the end of the first he had a 21.2 seconds advantage over another former winner, Phil Nicholls (Seeley Matchless), who in turn led American Dave Roper (Matchless) by 13.6 seconds. The top six were completed by Bob Heath (Seeley) Richard Swallow (Aermacchi) and Dennis Gallagher (Seeley). Dugdale led at the end of the second lap by 61.4 seconds from Heath, Phil Nicholls having come off at Sulby Bridge, Roper was still third, Swallow fourth, Chris McGahan (Seeley) fifth and John Goodall (Matchless) sixth, Dennis Gallagher having dropped it at Glentrammon. The top six remained the same on the third lap, but Heath closed to within 28.2 seconds of Dugdale. On the final circuit, Alan Dugdale retired at Kerrowmoar with a broken rear sprocket, so Bob Heath won his first race on the TT course by just 3.2 seconds from the flying Roper, followed by Richard Swallow, McGahan, Goodall and Richard Cutts (Seeley Matchless). There were 51 finishers and 21 replicas were won.

1990 Senior Classic (4 laps / 150.92 miles) 119 entries

1. Bob Heath	Seeley	1h. 30m. 50.2s	99.68 mph
2. Dave Roper	Matchless	1h. 30m. 53.0s	99.63 mph
3. Richard Swallow	Aermacchi	1h. 34m. 12.2s	96.12 mph
Fastest lap			
Alan Dugdale	Matchless	22m. 13.6s	101.85 mph

1990 Junior Classic

Richard Swallow became the first rider in the history of the Manx to win the same race four years in succession when he led the Junior Classic from start to finish on his Aermacchi.

At the end of the first lap he was 41 seconds ahead of brother Bill Swallow (Aermacchi), who in turn was 23 seconds ahead of John Stephens (B.S.A.). Dave Roper (A.J.S.) was fourth, Phil Nicholls (Seeley A.J.S.) fifth and Dennis Gallagher (Seeley) sixth. Richard's lead over Bill at the end of lap two was up to 51 seconds, Roper was now third ahead of Stephens. The brothers were divided by almost three minutes at the end of the third lap - Nicholls was now up to third, Gallagher fourth, Roper fifth and John Goodall (A.J.S.) sixth.

Richard rode on to his record-breaking four in a row win from Bill by three minutes 13.6 seconds, Nicholls remained third, Gallagher fourth, but Roper retired at the pits so Goodall was fifth and Martin Orgee (Aermacchi) took sixth spot. Stephens retired at Laurel Bank on the last lap. There were 38 finishers, 11 replicas were won.

1990 Junior Classic (4 laps / 150.92 miles) 77 entries

1. Richard Swallow	Aermacchi	1h. 32m. 18.0s	98.10 mph
2. Bill Swallow	Aermacchi	1h. 35m. 31.6s	94.79 mph
3. Phil Nicholls	Seeley A.J.S.	1h. 36m. 22.0s	93.96 mph
Fastest lap			
Richard Swallow	Aermacchi	22m. 46.4s	99.40 mph

1990 Lightweight Classic

Level flight: Marek Nofer at Ballaugh Bridge.

Bob Jackson, riding a Suzuki, set the early pace in this race, run concurrently with the Junior Classic, and at the end of the first lap had a lead of just 1.2 seconds from Marek Nofer (Suzuki), who in turn led John Kidson (Aermacchi) by 14.8 seconds. Grant Goodings (Aermacchi), Mike Cain (Aermacchi) and Alan Taylor (Suzuki) completed the top six. By the time the second lap had been completed, Jackson, with a lap at 94.14 mph, led Nofer by 24 seconds. Kidson came off at Laurel Bank, Cain took third place with Taylor fourth, Barry Wood (Suzuki) fifth, Goodings dropped to sixth. Race leader Bob Jackson hit trouble on lap three, he was reported as touring at Kerrowmoar, and retired at Ramsey with an oil leak, so Nofer took over the lead from Cain by 29.6 seconds, followed by Taylor, Goodings, Wood and Norman Williamson (Aermacchi). Nofer went on to win at a record speed of 91.96 mph from Alan Taylor as second place man Mike Cain went out at Quarter Bridge. Goodings took third place, with Wood fourth, Pete Swallow (Ducati) fifth and Bob Simmons (Suzuki) sixth, Williamson having retired at Sulby Bridge. There were 21 finishers and five replicas were won.

1990 Lightweight Classic (4 laps / 150.92 miles) 43 entries

1. Marek Nofer	Suzuki	1h. 38m. 27.8s	91.96 mph
			(record)
2. Alan Taylor	Suzuki	1h. 41m. 47.0s	88.96 mph

3. Grant Goodings	Aermacchi	1h. 43m. 01.0s	87.90 mph
Fastest lap (record)			
Bob Jackson	Suzuki	24m. 02.6s	94.15 mph

1990 Junior MGP

After coming close to winning a Manx on several occasions, Belfast's Stan Rea took the honours in the Junior, reduced from six laps to four because of weather conditions.

But at the end of the first lap it was Martin Ayles (Honda) who led by 0.4 seconds from Rea (Cowles Yamaha), with Norman Kneen (Honda) in third place, a further 4.6 seconds down. The top six were completed by Gavin Lee (Yamaha), Derek Young (Yamaha) and Martin Birkinshaw (Rotax). Race leader Ayles went out at the Bungalow on lap two with a seized engine, and Lee took over the lead with Rea second, 13.4 seconds down. Kneen was third, Young fourth, Nigel Hansen (Yamaha) fifth and Derek 'Decca' Kelly (Yamaha) sixth, with Birkinshaw dropping to tenth. With the fastest lap of the race third time round at 105.30 mph, Rea took command from Lee by 54.6 seconds, with Kneen still third, Derek Young retired at Glen Helen, so Hansen was fourth, Andy Bassett (Yamaha) fifth and Mark Linton (Yamaha) sixth - Kelly dropping to seventh. Stan Rea went on to win from Gavin Lee by 47.6 seconds. Hansen put in a fast last lap to take third place from Kneen. Kelly came back up to fifth, Bassett took sixth with Linton seventh. There were 66 finishers, among them Liz Skinner, and 25 replicas were won.

1990 Junior MGP (4 laps / 150.92 miles) 115 entries

1. Stan Rea	Cowles Yamaha	1h. 28m. 50.2s	101.93 mph
2. Gavin Lee	Yamaha	1h. 29m. 37.8s	101.02 mph
3. Nigel Hansen	Yamaha	1h. 31m. 22.4s	99.10 mph
Fastest lap			
Stan Rea	Cowles Yamaha	21m. 29.8s	105.30 mph

By finishing in 15th place, Mick Robinson became the rider to have won the most replicas in the Manx, 16 in all to this point.

1990 Lightweight MGP

The four lap Lightweight was unusual, in the fact that the first four remained the same throughout the length of the race. Gavin Lee (Yamaha) led at the end of the first lap from Junior winner Stan Rea (Cowles Yamaha) by 7.8 seconds, Nigel Hansen (Yamaha) was third just two seconds down on Rea and Mark Linton (Yamaha) in fourth place, a further 5.2 seconds down. Martin Ayles (Honda) was fifth and Alan Dugdale (Yamaha) in sixth spot. With a new lap record at 109.06 mph on lap two, Lee increased his lead over Rea to 48 seconds, and the only change to the top six was that Dugdale took fifth place ahead of Derek Young (Yamaha) with Ayles dropping to seventh. With a lap of almost 109 mph third time around, Rea closed to within 4.6 seconds of Lee, and Young took fifth place from Dugdale. But on the final lap Lee set a new lap record again - 109.87 mph - to win at a new record speed from Rea, who lapped at over 109 mph himself, by 13.4 seconds, Hansen repeated his third place of the Junior with Linton fourth, followed by Young and Dugdale. There were 54 finishers and 19 replicas were won.

1990 Lightweight MGP (4 laps / 150.92 miles) 88 entries

1. Gavin Lee	Yamaha	1h. 23m. 56.2s	107.88 mph
			(record)
2. Stan Rea	Cowles Yamaha	1h. 24m. 09.6s	107.59 mph
3. Nigel Hansen	Yamaha	1h. 24m. 48.6s	106.77 mph
Fastest lap (record)			
Gavin Lee	Yamaha	20m. 36.2s	109.87 mph

1990 Senior MGP

Brian Venables takes the Martin Bullock Honda round Governors Bridge on the last lap.

It was clear from practice form that, unless they hit problems, the Senior would be a battle between Brian Venables and Simon Beck, both on 750 Hondas. They had dominated the sessions with almost every lap at over 110 mph. Beck finished top at 111.66 mph, just one second faster than Venables at 111.57 mph, and to add to the interest, Brian started at No. 1, just 10 seconds ahead of Simon at No. 4. On the first lap, Beck closed to within two seconds of Venables by Ballaugh Bridge, giving him an eight second advantage on corrected time, and he took the lead on the roads when Venables ran wide at the Verandah. Beck's opening lap was 113.30 mph, and he led his Manx rival by 10.6 seconds, with David O'Leary (Suzuki) in third place, 22.8 seconds down. The top six were completed by Nigel Nottingham (Yamaha), Tom Knight (Honda) and Roy Anderson (Yamaha). Both of the leaders were slower on lap two, but Beck had increased his lead to 21.8 seconds. With a lap at almost 113 mph, Anderson moved up to third place, and the top three

remained the same to the chequered flag. Nottingham remained fourth, Mick Noblett (Yamaha) was fifth and Martin Birkinshaw (Honda) sixth. Knight was eighth and O'Leary eleventh. At half distance, Beck led Venables by 34.2 seconds, whilst Anderson closed to within 5.4 seconds of the second place man. Noblett took fourth place from Nottingham and O'Leary came back on the leaderboard in sixth place. Birkinshaw was seventh and Knight retired at the pits. Beck was averaging over 110 mph after four laps and his lead was 37.8 seconds from Venables, who was just three seconds ahead of Anderson. Noblett was fourth, Nottingham fifth and Chris Hook (Honda) sixth. Senior Newcomers winner Paul Orritt, who had started last man at number 116, had moved through the field to ninth place. The top six remained the same at the end of the fifth lap, with Beck 31.8 seconds up on Venables, who in turn was 12.8 seconds up on Anderson. So Beck went on to win by 23.2 seconds from Venables with Anderson, who made his debut in last years Newcomers races finishing a fine third a further 23 seconds down. Noblett finished fourth, Nottingham fifth and Hook sixth. There were 69 finishers and 31 riders won replicas.

1990 Senior MGP (6 laps / 226.38 miles) 115 entries

1. Simon Beck	Honda	2h. 02m. 50.0s	110.57 mph (record)
2. Brian Venables	Honda	2h. 03m. 13.2s	110.23 mph
3. Roy Anderson	Yamaha	2h. 03m. 36.2s	109.89 mph
Fastest lap (record)			
Simon Beck	Honda	19m. 58.8s	113.30 mph

1991

The pattern for the 1991 Manx Grand Prix remained the same as the successful format of the previous two years and the capacities stayed the same as in 1990. The Senior was the only race over six lap, the Junior having been reduced to four. There were six races, two of which were divided into classes, giving a total of nine winners, and it prove to be a record breaking week.

1991 Senior Newcomers

Third fastest on the practice leaderboard Jason Griffiths, son of the 1964 Senior Manx winner Selwyn, on his first ride on a Honda, led the race from start to finish. He opened up with a new lap record at 112.06 mph to lead Chris Day (Suzuki) by 25.6 seconds with Graham Ward (Kawasaki) in third place a further 15 seconds down. Kirk Wright (Honda), Nick Morgan (Yamaha) and David Prescott (Honda) completed the top six. Griffiths upped the record to 112.57 mph second time around and led by 35.6 seconds, and the only change to the top six saw Morgan and Wright change places. Ward took over second place at the end the third lap, but was over one minute down on Griffiths, Day was third with fourth to sixth unchanged. So Griffiths went on to a record breaking victory from Graham Ward by one minute 16.2 seconds, with Day third followed by Morgan, Wright and Tim Wild (Honda), David Prescott finishing seventh. There were 19 finishers and nine replicas were won.

1991 Senior Newcomers (4 laps / 150.92 miles) 21 entries

1. Jason Griffiths	Honda	1h. 22m. 12.2s	110.15 mph (record)
2. Graham Ward	Kawasaki	1h. 23m. 28.4s	108.48 mph
3. Chris Day	Suzuki	1h. 23m. 38.2s	108.26 mph
Fastest lap (record)			
Jason Griffiths	Honda	20m. 06.6s	112.57 mph

Like father, like son, Jason Griffiths seen here at Parliament Square.

1991 Junior Newcomers

The top two on the practice leaderboard, Phil Corlett (Yamaha) and Andy Jackson (Honda) were expected to be the pacemakers in this race. Indeed, at the end of the first lap they were separated by just 0.4 seconds, with Corlett having the advantage. In third place was Rob Simm (Kawasaki) - 11.6 seconds down on Jackson, followed by Jeremy Doughty (Honda), Gary Carswell (Yamaha) and Martyn Hewlett (Honda). At the end of the second circuit, after a lap five seconds faster than Corlett, Jackson led by 4.6 seconds. Simm was still third, 25 seconds down, and the only change to the leaderboard was that Carswell took fourth place from Doughty. By the time lap three had been completed, Jackson led Corlett by 12 seconds, Simm held third, but Carswell retired at Ramsey, bringing Doughty up to fourth, Hewlett fifth and Adam Boyle (Yamaha) came onto the leaderboard in sixth place. Phil Corlett pulled out all the stops on the final lap, and with the fastest lap of the race - 107.59 mph - closed to within three seconds of Andy Jackson who set a new race record speed. Robert Simm maintained his third place, but Doughty retired at the 26th Milestone, bringing Martin Hewlett up to fourth. Ian Todhunter (Honda) came into the top six in fifth place with Adam Boyle finishing sixth. There were 14 finishers and nine replicas were won.

1991 Junior Newcomers (4 laps / 150.92 miles) 30 entries

1. Andy Jackson	Honda	1h. 26m. 00.6s	105.28 mph
			(record)
2. Phil Corlett	Yamaha	1h. 26m. 03.6s	105.21 mph
3. Rob Simm	Kawasaki	1h. 26m. 51.6s	104.25 mph
Fastest lap			
Phil Corlett	Yamaha	21m. 02.4s	107.59 mph

1991 Lightweight Newcomers

Fastest in practice, Paul Harbison (Kawasaki), led this race from start to finish. At the end of the opening lap he led Pete Turnbull (Rotax) by 15.6 seconds, with Gary Taylor (Suzuki) in third place, a further 14.2 seconds down. The top six were completed by Alan Hesselden (Kawasaki), Jim Kelly (Suzuki) and Rob Harrison (Kawasaki). Harbison increased his lead over Turnbull to 28.2 seconds after lap two, Taylor was still third, Kelly up to fourth, Hesselden fifth and Jim Stringer (Kawasaki) came up to sixth, Harrison having come off at Milntown. At the end of the third lap Harbison's lead was over one minute and the new second place man was Taylor, Hesselden was third, Stringer fourth followed by Kelly and Richard Parrott (Kawasaki), a slow lap dropped Turnbull to 11th place. There were no changes to the top six at the end of the race, and Harbison's winning margin was one minute 6.6 seconds. There were 25 finishers and 16 replicas were won

1991 Lightweight Newcomers (4 laps / 150.92 miles) 33 entries

1. Paul Harbison	Kawasaki	1h. 30m. 20.6s	100.23 mph
2. Gary Taylor	Suzuki	1h. 31m. 27.2s	99.01 mph
3. Alan Hesselden	Kawasaki	1h. 32m. 33.2s	97.83 mph
Fastest lap			
Paul Harbison	Kawasaki	22m. 14.4s	101.78 mph

1991 Junior Classic

After winning this race four years in succession, and having topped the practice leaderboard, Richard Swallow (Aermacchi) was the firm favourite again, and he led from start to finish and set a new lap record into the bargain. At the end of the opening lap, he led his brother Bill on a Aermacchi by 42.6 seconds, with Dennis Gallagher (Seeley) in third place a further 63 seconds down. They were followed by Bob Heath (Seeley), Geoff Tunstall (Seeley) and John Goodall (A.J.S.). Richard set his new lap record on lap 2 - 100.97 mph - whilst Bill had a slow lap and dropped to fifth, Gallagher was second and Heath third, with Goodall fourth and Tunstall sixth. The next rider to strike trouble was Gallagher, who retired at White Gates on the third lap, so Richard led and the new second-placed rider was Goodall, who was almost five minutes down. Heath, Tunstall, Bill Swallow and Cliff Gobell (Aermacchi) completed the top six. So Richard Swallow won this race for the fifth year in succession. equalling Dennis Parkinson's total of Manx wins, from brother Bill who set the fastest fourth lap, with Goodall third. Heath retired at Lambfell Beg, so the top six were completed by Tunstall, Gobell and Ted Edwards (Aermacchi). There were 32 finishers and 11 replicas were won.

Win number five for Richard Swallow, seen here at Creg ny Baa.

1991 Junior Classic (4 laps / 150.92 miles) 82 entries

1. Richard Swallow	Aermacchi	1h. 31m. 37.2s	98.83 mph
2. Bill Swallow	Aermacchi	1h. 36m. 30.4	93.82 mph
3. John Goodall	A.J.S.	1h. 36m. 58.2	93.38 mph
Fastest lap (record)			
Richard Swallow	Aermacchi	22m. 25.2s	100.97 mph

1991 Lightweight Classic

Alan 'Bud' Jackson won his second Manx, but after the first lap it was local rider Barry Wood (Suzuki), who led from Jackson on another Suzuki, with Bob Jackson (Suzuki) in third place, a further 4.6 seconds down. Alan Dugdale with an N.S.U. was fourth, Les Trotter (Suzuki) fifth and Ian Hogg (Suzuki) sixth. But on the second lap Jackson set the fastest lap of the race at 93.66 mph to lead Wood by 14.6 seconds. Two of the top six went out on this second lap. Alan Dugdale at the 26th Milestone and Bob Jackson at Cruickshanks, so third to sixth were now Les Trotter, Ian Hogg, Rich Hawkins (Ducati) and David Smith (Aermacchi). Jackson's lead at the end of the third lap was 27.6 seconds, but from Trotter, Wood was third, fol-

lowed by Hogg, Smith and Hawkins. 'Bud' went on to win from Wood by 54.6 seconds, Hogg was third, a slow last lap, including a push in from Governors, dropped Trotter to fourth followed by Smith and Hawkins. There were 22 finishers and eight replicas were won.

1991 Lightweight Classic (4 laps / 150.92 miles) 37 entries

1. Alan 'Bud' Jackson	Suzuki	1h. 38m. 03.2s	92.34 mph
			(record)
2. Barry Wood	Suzuki	1h. 38m. 57.8	91.50 mph
3. Ian Hogg	Suzuki	1h. 40m. 17.0	90.29 mph
Fastest lap (record)			
'Bud' Jackson	Suzuki	24m. 10.2s	93.66 mph

1991 Senior Classic

Bob Heath (Seeley) won this race for the second year in succession, and led from the drop of the flag. At the end of the opening lap he led Bill Swallow (G50 Seeley) by 31 seconds, with Alan Dugdale (Seeley) in third place, a further 2.4 seconds down. Dave Roper (Matchless) was fourth, and the top four lapped at over the ton. The top six were completed by Richard Swallow (Aermacchi) and Geoff Tunstall (Rutter Matchless). Lap two saw the end of the challenge of Dave Roper, who retired at Greeba Castle and Richard Swallow who went out at the pits. The top three remained unchanged and Heath's lead was 7.6 seconds. John Goodall (Matchless) was fourth, Tunstall fifth and Chris McGahan (G50 Seeley) sixth. With a new lap record at 103.48 mph on lap three, Heath led Swallow by 12.2 seconds, Goodall came up to third followed by Tunstall, McGahan and Andy McGladdery (Matchless). Alan Dugdale dropped to seventh and retired at Quarter Bridge on the final lap. The top six remained unchanged on the final lap, and Bob Heath won at a new record speed of 102.62 mph from Bill Swallow by 21 seconds, and both were inside the old record. There were 52 finishers and 16 replicas were won.

1991 Senior Classic (4 laps / 150.92 miles) 121 entries

1. Bob Heath	Seeley	1h. 28m. 14.4s	102.62 mph
			(record)
2. Bill Swallow	Seeley	1h. 28m. 35.4	102.21 mph
3. John Goodall	Matchless	1h. 30m. 56.8	99.56 mph
Fastest lap (record)			
Bob Heath	Seeley	21m. 52.6s	103.48 mph

1991 Junior MGP

After knocking some 39 seconds off the lap record in practice, David Milling (Yamaha) was the firm favourite for the Junior, and he set about it from the drop of the flag, leading from start to finish at a new record speed and a lap at over 112 mph into the bargain. At the end of the opening circuit he led Mick Robinson (Yamaha) by 22.8 seconds with Greg Broughton (Yamaha) a further 2.6 seconds down in third place, followed by Derek Kelly (Yamaha), Mark Baldwin (Honda) and Neil Richardson (Yamaha). With a lap at 112.31 mph, Milling led at the end of the second lap by 44.8 seconds from Broughton who had overtaken Robinson. Baldwin had passed Kelly for fourth place and Derek Wagstaff (Yamaha) came on to the leaderboard in sixth place, with Richardson seventh. The top three remained unchanged on lap three, but Nigel Hansen, who was going for a non-stop race shot up to fourth, ahead of Baldwin and Jason Griffiths (Yamaha). Kelly was eighth and Richardson had retired at the Highlander. So David Milling went on to a record breaking win by 30.8 seconds from Greg Broughton with Mick Robinson adding to his record collection of replicas in third place. Nigel Hansen's gamble of a non-stop run ended when he run out of fuel at the Bungalow, so the top six were completed by Mark Baldwin, Derek Wagstaff and John Davies (Yamaha). Jason Griffiths went out at Ramsey on the final lap when the chain jumped the sprocket. There were 40 finishers and 20 replicas were won.

1991 Junior MGP (4 laps / 150.92 miles) 96 entries

1. Dave Milling	Yamaha	1h. 22m. 33.4s	109.68 mph
			(record)
2. Greg Broughton	Yamaha	1h. 23m. 04.2s	109.00 mph
3. Mick Robinson	Yamaha	1h. 23m. 23.6s	108.58 mph
Fastest lap (record)			
David Milling	Yamaha	20m. 09.4s	112.31 mph

1991 Lightweight MGP

David Milling, double winner, at Ginger Hall

David Milling completed a double with another record breaking win in the Lightweight. On his Yamaha he led Mick Robinson (Yamaha) at the end of the opening lap by 17.2 seconds, with Mark Baldwin (Honda) in third place a further four seconds down. The top six were completed by Greg Broughton (Yamaha), Jason Griffiths (Yamaha) and Decca Kelly (Yamaha). Milling increased his lead to 26.6 seconds at the end of the second lap and it was Griffiths in second place and Broughton third, Baldwin was fourth, Robinson fifth and Neil Richardson (Yamaha) sixth, with Kelly in seventh spot. On the third lap the top five remained unchanged and Milling's lead was 26.4 seconds and Kelly took over sixth place from

Richardson who was eighth. This order remained the same to the chequered flag and Milling won by 28 seconds from Jason Griffiths. Broughton set a new lap record on the final lap, 112.05 mph, and closed to within 3.4 seconds of Griffiths. There were 50 finishers and 19 replicas were won.

1991 Lightweight MGP (4 laps / 150.92 miles) 83 entries

1. David Milling	Yamaha	1h. 22m. 12.2s	110.15 mph
			(record)
2. Jason Griffiths	Yamaha	1h. 22m. 40.2s	109.53 mph
3. Greg Broughton	Yamaha	1h. 22m. 43.6s	109.45 mph
Fastest lap (record)			
Greg Broughton	Yamaha	20m. 12.2s	112.05 mph

1991 Senior MGP

Tom Knight (Honda) had dominated the Senior practice sessions, unofficially breaking the lap record, and led the Senior from start to finish. In fact the top three remained unchanged throughout the six lap race. After lap one Knight, with a lap in 19m. 53.0s, just 1.8 seconds outside the record, led Alan Bennallick (Honda) by five seconds with Chris Hook (Honda) a further 6.2 seconds down in third place. The top six leaderboard was completed by David O'Leary (Suzuki), Nigel Nottingham (Yamaha) and Mick Noblett (Honda). Knight's lead at the end of the second lap was 20.4 seconds and he had set the new lap record at 115.67 mph. Noblett, Nottingham and Barry Dixon (Honda) completed the top six, David O'Leary had dropped to 16th, and went out at Quarter Bridge on the next lap. There were no changes to the top six at half distance, Knight led Bennallick by 33.4 seconds, and both had covered three laps in under one hour. The first five maintained station on lap four, but Chris Bray (Suzuki) took over sixth place, Dixon dropping to eighth. Knight led Bennallick by 54.6 seconds at the end of the fifth with Hook still third, Dixon came back on to the leaderboard in fourth place, Nottingham was fifth and Mark Livingston (Yamaha) came on to the leaderboard in sixth place, Chris Bray having retired at Ballaugh Bridge. So Tom Knight won the fastest Manx in history by 55 seconds at a speed of 113.54 mph and the only change to the top six was that Livingston took fifth place from Nottingham whose Honda slowed on the final laps of the race. There were 64 finishers and the top 35 finishers averaged over 100 mph, with the first 26 winning replicas.

1991 Senior MGP (6 laps / 226.38 miles) 105 entries

1. Tom Knight	Honda	1h. 59m. 37.6s	113.54 mph
			(record)
2. Alan Bennallick	Honda	2h. 00m. 32.6s	112.67 mph
3. Chris Hook	Honda	2h. 01m. 56.6s	111.38 mph
Fastest lap			
Tom Knight	Honda	19m. 34.2s	115.67 mph

1992

The pattern for the 1992 Manx Grand Prix remained the same as the successful format of the previous two years, and the capacities stayed the same as in 1991. The Senior was reduced to four laps because of weather conditions so with the Junior having been reduced to four, there were no six lap races. There were six races, two of which were divided into classes, giving a total of nine winners, and it was again to prove to be a record breaking week.

1992 Senior Newcomers

Tim Leech (Kawasaki) topped the practice leaderboard at 111.12 mph, followed by Brian Gardiner (Honda) at 107.37 mph and Steve Gordon (Suzuki) at 106.40 mph, and that's the order they finished the race! At the end of the opening lap Leech led Gardiner by 33.6 seconds with Gordon a further 5.8 seconds down in third place. The top six were completed by Ian Smith (Honda), Andrew Powell (Honda) and Mick Edwards (Yamaha). At half distance Leech had increased his lead over Gardener to 53 seconds and the top six remained the same. With a faster lap than the leader on the third circuit, Gardiner closed the gap to 46 seconds, and the only change to the leaderboard was that Mark Turner (Suzuki) took sixth place, with Edwards dropping to equal seventh. So Tim Leech won by 42.6 seconds from Brian Gardiner who set the fastest lap of the race on his last lap with Steve Gordon in third place. Ian Smith held on to fourth, Mark Turner was fifth, and Bob Farrington (Suzuki) took sixth place. Edwards was seventh and Powell, with a 33 minute last lap, 11th. There were 13 finishers and four replicas were won.

1992 Senior Newcomers (4 laps / 150.92 miles) 19 entries

1. Tim Leech	Kawasaki	1h. 23m. 01.6s	109.06 mph
2. Brian Gardiner	Honda	1h. 23m. 44.0s	108.41 mph
3. Steve Gordon	Suzuki	1h. 24m. 43.2s	106.88 mph
Fastest ap			
Brian Gardiner	Honda	20m. 30.2s	110.41 mph

1992 Junior Newcomers

Ian King (Pirelli Honda) had dominated the practice sessions in this class, and topped the leaderboard in 21m. 00.0s. - 107.80 mph, followed by Ashley Law (Honda) at 105.93 mph and Rob I'anson (Honda) at 104.34 mph. It was a start to finish victory for King, who also broke the longest standing lap record on the TT course, beating the late Norman Brown's 1983 time. At the end of the opening lap, he led I'anson by 22.8 seconds, with Graham Webster (Honda) third 29.2 seconds down. They were followed by Jon Wright (Yamaha), Simon Smith (Honda) and Gary Rowe (Honda). King had over a minute advantage at the end of lap two, with the rest of the top six unchanged. The first two retained their positions at the end of the third lap, but Wright was third, Smith fourth, Webster fifth and Rowe remained sixth. And that's the order they finished with King having a one minute 7.2 seconds advantage over I'anson. There were 10 finishers and seven of them won replicas.

1992 Junior Newcomers (4 laps / 150.92 miles) 17 entries

1. Ian King	Honda	1h. 24m. 35.4s	107.04 mph
			(record)
2. Rob I'anson	Honda	1h. 26m. 42.2s	104.43 mph
3. Jon Wright	Yamaha	1h. 28m. 35.4s	102.21 mph
Fastest lap (record)			
Ian King	Honda	20m. 50.6s	108.61 mph

1992 Lightweight Newcomers

New Irish star James Courtney (Yamaha) also dominated this class during practice and indeed was some seven miles an hour faster than the second place man on the leaderboard David Collister (Yamaha) with Brad Evans (Yamaha) in third place. As expected Courtney leapt into the lead from the drop of the flag and led Phil Reid (Yamaha) by 34.8 seconds at the end of the first lap, with Evans in third place, 19.8 seconds down. Craig Hunt (Kawasaki), Anthony Roberts (Yamaha) and Mick Fallon (Kawasaki) completed the top six. The top four remained unchanged on the second lap, and Courtney increased his lead to one minute 10 seconds. David Chambers (Yamaha) moved up to fifth, Roberts was sixth and Fallon seventh. No change to the top five after lap three, with Fallon in sixth place ahead of seventh place Roberts. So James Courtney completed his expected victory at a new record speed, with Reid in second place. Third place man throughout Evans had the misfortune to retire at Cronk-ny-Mona on the last lap, letting Hunt on to the top three leaderboard, and he was followed by Chambers, Fallon and Roberts. There were 14 finishers and eight replicas were won.

1992 Lightweight Newcomers (4 laps / 150.92 miles) 31 entries

Now a TT star; James Courtney at Quarter Bridge.

1. James Courtney	Yamaha	1h. 26m. 40.0s	104.48 mph (record)
2. Phil Reid	Yamaha	1h. 28m. 37.6s	102.17 mph
3. Craig Hunt	Kawasaki	1h. 31m. 09.0s	99.34 mph
Fastest lap			
James Courtney	Yamaha	21m. 23.0s	105.86 mph

1992 Junior Classic

The Classic Junior/Lightweight races were delayed by bad weather and eventually got under way some four hours late at 2 p.m., and even then conditions were far from ideal. Bill Swallow (Aermacchi) had been fastest in practice at 98.09 mph, followed by Bob Heath (A.J.S.) and Geoff Tunstall (Aermacchi). At the end of the opening lap Swallow led Tunstall by 30.6 seconds with Dave Storry (Seeley) in third place followed by Heath, Kenny Shepherd (Aermacchi) and Grant Sellers (Aermacchi). With a lap some 37 seconds faster than Tunstall, and indeed the fastest of the Race, Swallow increased his lead to one minute 17.6 seconds at the end of the second circuit, and Heath took third place from Storry, Bill Horsman (Seeley) took fifth place, with Sellars sixth and Shepherd seventh. With the weather conditions worsening, the Clerk of the Course announced that the race would be stopped after three laps, so Bill Swallow won by over two minutes from Tunstall with Heath third, followed by Storry, Horsman and Shepherd with Sellars in seventh place. There were 34 finishers and 12 riders won replicas.

1992 Junior Classic (3 laps / 113.19 miles) 68 entries

1. Bill Swallow	Aermacchi	1h. 14m. 04.8s	91.67 mph
2. Geoff Tunstall	Aermacchi	1h. 16m. 16.4s	89.04 mph
3. Bob Heath	A.J.S.	1h. 16m. 57.0s	88.25 mph
Fastest lap			
Bill Swallow	Aermacchi	24m. 21.2s	92.95 mph

1992 Lightweight Classic

The three Suzuki riders, Bob Jackson, 'Bud' Jackson and Barry Wood topped the practice leaderboard and at the end of the first lap it was Bob who led Barry by 45 seconds with Bud in third place, 13.8 seconds down. They were followed by Mike Cain (Aermacchi), Derek Whalley (Ducati) and Ken Stewart (Ducati). At the end of the second lap, Bob led by one minute 45.6 seconds, with Bud still third, Cain fourth, Whalley fifth, but Martin Crooks (Crooks Suzuki) took sixth place from Stewart who was seventh. So after many years of trying, Bob Jackson won a race on the TT course, his winning margin being over two and a half minutes from Barry Wood who finished runner-up for the second year in succession, 1991 winner Bud Jackson was third and the rest of the top six remained unchanged. There were 26 finishers, including the only lady competitor Phillipa Wheeler, and five replicas were won.

1992 Lightweight Classic (3 laps / 113.19 miles) 44 entries

1. Bob Jackson	Suzuki	1h. 15m. 55.4s	89.45 mph
2. Barry Wood	Suzuki	1h. 18m. 29.8s	86.51 mph
3. Alan 'Bud' Jackson	Suzuki	1h. 19m. 07.6s	85.82 mph
Fastest lap (record)			
Bob Jackson	Suzuki	24m. 42.0s	91.65 mph

1992 Senior Classic

The Senior Classic produced the closest ever finish to a Manx race, and indeed equalled the closest ever finish on the TT course, and to make it even more exciting, the two riders Bob Heath (Seeley) and Bill Swallow (Seeley Matchless) started together at No's 1 & 2, and were never more than half a second apart for the entire 150 miles. Bob led by 0.6 seconds at the end of the opening lap at 101.34 mph, with Steve Linsdell (Norton) third, Dave Roper (Matchless) fourth, Geoff Tunstall (Matchless) fifth and Jack Gow (Norton) sixth. At the end of the second lap Swallow led Heath by 0.6 seconds, and the rest of the leader board remained the same. Still riding only yards apart, Swallow still held the advantage at the end of lap three, but by just 0.2 seconds, and the only change to the leaderboard was that Gow overtook Tunstall for fifth place. And so to the final lap - both riders appeared out of the dip at Governors almost side by side and it was a flat out dash to the flag - Bob Heath took victory by 0.2 seconds from Bill Swallow - just about half a machines length in a truly tremendous race. Linsdell held third throughout, Gow took fourth place at the finish, followed by

Tunstall and Dave Storry. It was Bob Heath's third win in a row. There were 55 finishers and the first 20 won replicas.

1992 Senior Classic (4 laps / 150.92 miles) 113 entries

1. Bob Heath	Seeley	1h. 28m. 02.6s	102.84 mph (record)
2. Bill Swallow	Seeley Matchless	1h. 28m. 02.8s	102.84 mph
3. Steve Linsdell	Norton	1h. 29m. 41.2s	100.96 mph
Fastest lap (record)			
Bob Heath	Seeley	21m. 48.2s	103.82 mph

1992 Junior MGP

The Junior was postponed from the Wednesday to Thursday due to weather conditions, and the decision was absolutely correct as we saw a record breaking race. In practice the top five - Andy Jones (Yamaha), Richard Smith (Honda) Mark Baldwin (Yamaha), Craig Mason (Yamaha) and Mick Robinson (Yamaha) were separated by just 3.6 seconds. At the end of the first lap, Smith led Mark Watts (Yamaha) by 0.2 seconds, with Baldwin third, followed by Robinson, Decca Kelly (Yamaha) and James Courtney (Yamaha). Watts was the leader at the end of the second lap by 2.2 seconds from Baldwin with Smith third, Kelly fourth, Robinson fifth and David O'Leary (Yamaha) sixth with Courtney seventh. There was a new leader again at the end of the third lap - Baldwin by 10 seconds from O'Leary, Robinson was third, Kelly fourth, Watts fifth and Jones in sixth place - Smith was seventh, and Courtney, who had gone past the end of the pits instead of coming in at the end of the second lap, had to be pushed back up pit lane by Davy Wood, had dropped to 11th place. And so to the final circuit, and with the fastest lap of the race - 112.06 mph, David O'Leary snatched a dramatic win from Mark Baldwin by just 4.6 seconds, with Robinson winning his 19th replica in third place. They were followed by Decca Kelly, Mark Watts and Andy Jones, with James Courtney finishing in 10th place. There were 69 finishers and 38 replicas were won.

1992 Junior MGP (4 laps / 150.92 miles) 115 entries

1. David O'Leary	Yamaha	1h. 22m. 16.6s	110.05 mph (record)
2. Mark Baldwin	Yamaha	1h. 22m. 21.2s	109.95 mph
3. Mick Robinson	Yamaha	1h. 22m. 46.2s	109.40 mph
Fastest lap			
David O'Leary	Yamaha	20m. 12.0s	112.06 mph

1992 Lightweight MGP

After so nearly winning the Junior, Mark Baldwin (Yamaha), starting at No. 1, made no mistake in the Lightweight, he just cleared off from the line and led from start to finish. At the end of the opening lap he led Mark Watts (Yamaha) by 25.8 seconds with Nigel Hansen (Yamaha) in third place a further 9.6 seconds down. Mick Robinson (Yamaha), Decca Kelly (Yamaha) and James Courtney (Yamaha) completed the top six leaderboard. Baldwin increased his lead to almost a minute at the end of the second lap, but from Hansen, Robinson was third, Watts fourth, Courtney fifth and Kelly sixth. More changes at the completion of lap three, Baldwin led from Courtney, who had a superb pit stop this time, by one minute 15 seconds, Robinson was third, Hansen fourth, Kelly fifth and Nigel Jennings (Yamaha) sixth - Mark Watts having retired at Quarter

And they finished closer than this! It's finishing order as Bob Heath and Bill Swallow attack the mountain climb from the Gooseneck.

bridge. So Mark Baldwin won from Robinson, with Courtney third, Nigel Hansen was fourth, Decca Kelly fifth and Sean Collister (Yamaha) sixth, Jennings taking seventh place. There were 45 finishers and 13 replicas were won.

1992 Lightweight MGP (4 laps / 150.92 miles) 95 entries

1. Mark Baldwin	Yamaha	1h. 28m. 22.8s	102.45 mph
2. Mick Robinson	Yamaha	1h. 30m. 04.2s	100.53 mph
3. James Courtney	Yamaha	1h. 30m. 29.8s	100.06 mph
Fastest lap (record)			
Mark Baldwin	Yamaha	21m. 40.4s	104.45 mph

Mick Robinson thought that 1992 would mark the last 'proper' Manx, having reached the age of 40, and with two more replicas, he took his record number to 20 - will that total ever be beaten? No one expected the age limit rule to be changed.

1992 Senior MGP

Allan Bennallick keeps it low at Ballaugh Bridge.

The weather conditions for the Lightweight had not been ideal, and the decision was reached that the Senior Manx should be reduced from six laps to four. In practice, Alan Bennallick (Honda) had been the only rider to break 20 minutes - 19m. 50.4s. - 114.10 mph, Nigel Davies, Brian Venables and Bob Quinn, all Hondas had been next fastest. With the weather as it was however, there would be no records in this race. At the end of the opening lap it was Chris Day (750 Kawasaki) who led Bennallick by five seconds, Wattie Brown (Honda) was third a further 11.6 seconds down and followed by Billy Craine (Kawasaki), Quinn and Mark Livingston (Honda). Day still led at the end of lap two, by 37.6 seconds, but from Craine, with Bennallick in third place, Brown was fourth, David O'Leary (Honda) fifth and Quinn sixth, Livingston having retired at Ballaugh Bridge on this lap. As the riders completed their third lap and set off on the final circuit, Bennallick was the leader but only by 11.4 seconds from Craine, Day had slipped off at Quarter Bridge and continued, was now third, followed by Brown, Quinn and Phil Corlett (Yamaha) with O'Leary in seventh place. And so to the final lap, Craine had the bit between his teeth and really went for it and cut the lead to six seconds, but on the Mountain the Kawasaki motor cried enough, and he had to push in from Cronk-ny-Mona to finish to a standing ovation in 56th place. So Alan Bennallick became the first Cornishman to win a Manx, he took the flag some 26.6 seconds ahead of Chris Day, with Wattie Brown in third place. With the fastest lap of the race on his final circuit, O'Leary took fourth place with Quinn and Corlett completing the top six leaderboard. There were 69 finishers and the first 19 won replicas.

1992 Senior MGP (4 laps / 150.92 miles) 105 entries

1. Alan Bennallick	Honda	1h. 24m. 00.8s	107.78 mph
2. Chris Day	Kawasaki	1h. 24m. 27.4s	107.21 mph
3. Wattie Brown	Honda	1h. 25m. 02.0s	106.49 mph
Fastest lap			
David O'Leary	Honda	20m. 26.4s	110.75 mph

1993

For 1993, the Senior was reduced to four laps, so there were no six-lap races, it was to prove to be a record breaking week, with not a little controversy!

1993 Senior Newcomers

Michael Brown (Kawasaki) had topped the practice leaderboard at 110.27 mph - 30.8 seconds ahead of Mark Campion (Kawasaki), but at the end of the opening lap it was Campion in the lead from Brown by 6.6 seconds, with Nick Cook (Kawasaki) third, a further 1m 22s down. The top six was completed by Anthony Williams (Honda), Ivor Uren (Suzuki) and Terry Young (Honda). The top six remained unchanged on lap two, but the difference between first and second was down to 6.4 seconds. It was a race out front between the top two with the rest of the field way off the pace of the two leaders. The end of lap three and Campion led by 10 seconds, but with the fastest lap of the race on the final lap at 112.05 mph, Brown took the honours from Campion by 22.4 seconds with the remaining four places unchanged. There were nine finishers and four replicas were won.

1993 Senior Newcomers (4 laps / 150.92 miles) 12 entries

1. Michael Brown	Kawasaki	1h. 22m. 58.0s	109.14 mph
2. Mark Campion	Kawasaki	1h. 23m. 20.4s	108.65 mph
3. Nick Cook	Kawasaki	1h. 29m. 44.4s	100.90 mph
Fastest lap			
Michael Brown	Kawasaki	20m. 06.8s	112.55 mph

There were only nine starters from twelve entries, but no retirements at all in the Senior Newcomers race.

1993 Junior Newcomers

Chris Richardson had dominated the practice leaderboard on his Honda, 12 seconds faster than Marc Flynn (Honda). But the day before the race, engine problems with the Honda forced him to change back to his original Yamaha.

At the end of the first lap Richardson led Flynn by 26.6 seconds with a new lap record at 111.53 mph. Simon Trezise was third, a further 28.6 seconds with Richard Stockdale, Eddie Sinton and Sandra Barnett, all on Hondas, completing the top six. At half distance Richardson had extended his lead over

Flynn to 35.4 seconds, Stockdale took third place from Trezise with Sinton and Sandra Barnett holding their fifth and sixth places. There was no change to the top six at the end of lap three, but Richardson's lead had been reduced to 25.8 seconds. On the final lap Richardson hit mechanical problems and he retired at Handleys Corner, so Flynn went on to an unexpected win by 1m. 41.2s. from Stockdale with Trezise third, the top six was completed by Sinton, Barnett and Stuart Edwards (Honda). There were 15 finishers and 10 replicas were won.

Sandra Barnett became the fastest ever lady solo rider on the course with a lap at 106.21. It was a speed she was to beat in the Senior.

1993 Junior Newcomers (4 laps / 150.92 miles) 24 entries

1. Marc Flynn	Honda	1h. 23m. 03.2s	109.02 mph (record)
2. Richard Stockdale	Honda	1h. 24m. 44.4s	106.85 mph
3. Simon Trezise	Honda	1h. 25m. 28.8s	105.93 mph
Fastest lap (record)			
Chris Richardson	Honda	20m. 17.8s	111.53 mph

1993 Lightweight Newcomers

The race had a really dramatic ending - at the end of the first lap the leader was Peter Bell (Honda) by 10 seconds from Ian McVeighty (Yamaha) with Shaun Brown (Honda) in third place a further 19.6 seconds down, followed by Andy Thompson (Kawasaki), Phil Thornton (Kawasaki) and Barry Green (Kawasaki). McVeighty surprised everyone by going straight through at the end of the second lap, whereas all the other riders stopped for fuel. He led the race from Bell by 4.4 seconds with the fastest lap of the race at 103.46 mph, Brown, Thompson and Thornton retained their places and Garry Greenway (Kawasaki) took sixth place from Green. Lap three completed and McVeighty led Bell by one minute 31 seconds, and the only change to the top six was that Green jumped to fifth place ahead of Greenway with Thornton down to seventh. Both the leaders were indicated at Signpost Corner on the last lap, but it was Peter Bell who crossed the line to win by one minute 35.8 seconds from Brown with Greenway third, Green took fourth, Thornton fifth and poor McVeighty, who had run out of petrol at Governors on the last lap, pushed in to finish in sixth place. There were 14 finishers and 10 replicas were won.

1993 Lightweight Newcomers (4 laps / 150.92 miles) 27 entries

1. Peter Bell	Yamaha	1h. 29m. 32.6s	101.12 mph
2. Shaun Brown	Honda	1h. 31m. 08.4s	99.35 mph
3. Garry Greenway	Kawasaki	1h. 32m. 46.8s	97.59 mph
Fastest lap			
Ian McVeighty	Yamaha	21m. 52.8s	103.46 mph

1993 Junior Classic

The Classic Junior was expected to be a battle between the Seeley of Bob Heath and the Aermacchi of Bill Swallow, with 1992 Lightweight Manx winner Mark Baldwin on the Aermacchi featuring well in practice and Dave Roper on the exotic ex-works Benelli four also likely to be on the pace. It was Swallow who led at the end of the first lap by 15.8 seconds from Bob Heath with Geoff Tunstall (FCL Aermacchi) in third place, a further 32.8 seconds down, followed by Jack Gow (A.J.S.), John Loder (Greeves) and Mark Baldwin. Dave Roper dropped the sweet-sounding Benelli on the opening lap. Heath lapped at over 100 mph on the second lap to reduce the deficit on Swallow to 7.8 seconds, Baldwin, with a lap at 99.05 mph took third place ahead of Tunstall, Gow and Loder. At the end of the third lap, Bob Heath, with a lap at 100.65 mph led from Mark Baldwin by two minutes 5.6 seconds with Jack Gow third, John Goodall (A.J.S.) fourth, Danny Shimmin (A.J.S.) fifth and Bill Horsman (A.J.S.) sixth. Swallow toured in in eighth place and retired, Geoff Tunstall retired at Signpost and Loder dropped to 11th place. Bob Heath went on to win his fourth Classic race and his first Junior by two minutes 17.4 seconds from Baldwin with Gow third, the only change to the top six was that Shimmin took fourth place from Goodall. There were 38 finishers and 17 replicas were won.

1993 Junior Classic (4 laps / 150.92 miles) 70 entries

1. Bob Heath	Seeley	1h. 31m. 03.0s	99.45 mph
2. Mark Baldwin	Aermacchi	1h. 33m. 20.4s	97.01 mph
3. Jack Gow	A.J.S.	1h. 34m. 39.6s	95.66 mph
Fastest lap			
Bob Heath	Seeley	22m. 29.4s	100.65 mph

1993 Lightweight Classic

After lapping at over 98 mph in practice on his 250 Suzuki, Bob Jackson was firm favourite to repeat his 1992 victory - and he led the race from start to finish with Wattie Brown (Suzuki) in second place throughout. At the end of the first lap Steve Richardson (Yamaha) held third place, followed by Nick Turner (Yamaha), Ewan Hamilton (Suzuki) and Joey Dunlop (Aermacchi), making his Manx GP debut. On lap two Bob Jackson lapped at 99.05 mph - a new record - but Joey retired at the bottom of Bray Hill, so 'Bud' Jackson came on to the leaderboard in sixth place. Nick Turner retired on the Mountain Mile on the third lap and Steve Richardson dropped to seventh, so Hamilton was third, 'Bud' Jackson fourth with Alan Beck (Suzuki) and David Smith (Aermacchi) coming into the top six. The only change to the top six at the flag was that Richardson took sixth place from Smith. There were 26 finishers and, with record speeds, just seven replicas were won.

1993 Lightweight Classic (4 laps / 150.92 miles) 48 entries

1. Bob Jackson	Suzuki	1h. 33m. 12.2s	97.15 mph

2. Wattie Brown	Suzuki	1h. 36m. 04.8s	94.24 mph
3. Ewan Hamilton	Suzuki	1h. 38m. 35.2s	91.85 mph (record)
Fastest lap (record)			
Bob Jackson	Suzuki	22m. 51.2s	99.05 mph

1993 Senior Classic

Another Heath v Swallow race on their Seeley's was expected, and at the end of the opening lap Bob led Bill by 17.2 seconds with Bob Jackson (Seeley) in third place, followed by Bill Horsman (Matchless), Dave Storry (Seeley) and Danny Shimmin (Matchless). On his second lap, Bob Heath broke his own lap record at 104.38 mph and led Bill Swallow by 28.6 seconds, Horsman took third place from Jackson and Shimmin moved ahead of Storry. Bob Heath's race ended at Ginger Hall on the third lap, leaving Bill Swallow leading Horsman by 23.4 seconds, Jackson was third, Shimmin fourth and Chris McGahan (Seeley) and John Goodall (Matchless) came on the leaderboard. Dave Storry had clutch problems, came into the pits in seventh place and was in for almost ten minutes before getting away. Bill Swallow went on to win by 20.8 seconds and the top six remained the same. There were 65 finishers and 24 replicas were won.

Bill Horsman came from Australia to claim second place on his Seeley. He went one better in 1997.

1993 Senior Classic (4 laps / 150.92 miles) 118 entries

1. Bill Swallow	Seeley	1h. 28m. 08.0s	102.74 mph
2. Bill Horsman	Matchless	1h. 28m. 28.8s	102.34 mph
3. Bob Jackson	G50 Seeley	1h. 29m. 24.0s	101.28 mph
Fastest lap (record)			
Bob Heath	Seeley	21m. 41.2s	104.38 mph

1993 Junior MGP

There was a dramatic ending to the four-lap Junior Manx - but more of that later. The battle for honours was expected to be between Nigel Davies on the 600 Honda and James Courtney on the 250 Honda - both had lapped at over 111 mph in practice. At the end of the first lap Davies led Courtney by just 1.2 seconds with Brian Venables (Honda) in third place 16.4 seconds down. The top six was completed by Nigel Hansen (Yamaha), Greg Broughton (Yamaha) and Neil Richardson (Yamaha). Davies increased his lead to 8.2 seconds at half distance with Venables still third, Broughton moved ahead of Hansen and Nigel Jennings (Yamaha) took sixth with Richardson dropping to seventh. At the end of the third lap the difference between the two leaders was 23.8 seconds, they were followed by Venables, Broughton, Hansen and Richardson. So Davies crossed the line some 48.8 seconds ahead of Courtney, with Venables, Broughton, Richardson and Hansen completing the top six. But after the post-race examinations, three riders were excluded for having oversize engines, including the winner Davies, third place man Venables and 12th finisher Marc Flynn. So James Courtney was declared the winner, with Broughton second and Richardson third, Hansen took over fourth place, Alan Marshal (Honda) fifth and Jennings sixth. There were 67 finishers and 33 replicas were won.

1993 Junior MGP (4 laps / 150.92 miles) 112 entries

1. James Courtney	Honda	1h. 21m. 54.6s	110.55 mph (record)
2. Greg Broughton	Yamaha	1h. 22m. 55.6s	109.19 mph
3. Neil Richardson	Yamaha	1h. 23m. 31.4s	108.41 mph
Fastest lap			
James Courtney	Honda	20m. 10.4s	112.21 mph

1993 Lightweight MGP

James Courtney (Honda) was firm favourite to take the honours in the Lightweight with a host of Yamahas likely to challenge. He led at the end of the opening lap by 8.2 seconds from Nigel Hansen with Neil Richardson third, a further 6.4 seconds down, followed by Chris Cannell, Greg Broughton and Andy Jackson, all on Yamahas. With the fastest lap of the race second time around, Courtney increased his lead over Hansen to 14.4 seconds, Richardson still third, Broughton up to fourth, Wilkins (Honda) was fifth with Jackson sixth and Cannell seventh. Courtney completed the Junior/Lightweight double by 22.2 seconds from Nigel Hansen with Broughton in third place, Richardson was fourth, Jackson fifth and Cannell sixth. Nick Wilkins came off at Ginger Hall on the last lap. There were 50 finishers and 28 replicas were won.

1993 Lightweight MGP (4 laps / 150.92 miles) 81 entries

1. James Courtney	Honda	1h. 22m. 33.0s	109.69 mph
2. Nigel Hansen	Yamaha	1h. 22m. 53.2s	109.24 mph
3. Greg Broughton	Yamaha	1h. 22m. 59.4s	109.11 mph
Fastest lap			
Greg Broughton	Yamaha	20m. 19.8s	111.35 mph

Decca Kelly, who should have started at No. 2, had to fit a replacement radiator on the start line. Starting last on the road, he came through the field for a fine seventh place.

1993 Senior MGP

This was to prove to be the fastest race in the history of the Manx at the time, and Nigel Davies (Honda) made up for his disappointment of the Junior. He smashed the outright lap record on his opening lap at a speed of 116.53 mph, and led Brian Venables (Honda), who was also inside the old record, by 6.4 seconds. David Black (Kawasaki) was third followed by Tim Leech (Kawasaki), Nick Morgan (Ducati) and Wattie

Brown (Honda). Davies knocked another second of the record on the second lap to lead Venables by 27.2 seconds, Black and Leech retained their positions, but Brown took fifth place from Morgan. The difference between Davies and Venables at the end of lap three was 38.2 seconds, Brown had moved up to third, Morgan fourth, Leech fifth and Black was down to sixth.

So Nigel Davies went on to win at a new record speed from Brian Venables by one minute 4.8 seconds. Wattie Brown retained his third place as he did in 1992. The top six was completed by Morgan, Leech and Chris Hook (Honda), David Black having retired at the bottom of Barregarrow on the final lap. There were 53 finishers and 19 replicas were won.

Nigel Davies leaves Parliament Square.

1993 Senior MGP (4 laps / 150.92 miles) 94 entries

1. Nigel Davies	Honda	1h. 18m. 45.6s	114.97 mph (record)
2. Brian Venables	Honda	1h. 19m. 50.4s	113.41 mph
3. Wattie Brown	Honda	1h. 21m. 00.4s	111.78 mph
Fastest lap (record)			
Nigel Davies	Honda	19m. 24.4s	116.65 mph

Sandra Barnett (Honda) became the fastest lady rider on the TT course when she took fifteenth place and lapped at 108.21 mph.

1994

The pattern for the 1994 Manx Grand Prix races remained the same as the previous year, all the races were over four laps - 150.92 miles. There were six races, two of which were divided into classes, giving a total of nine winners, and two riders were destined to score doubles.

1994 Senior Newcomers

At the end of the first lap, Duncan Muir (Honda), who had gradually increased his speed during the practice week, after a spill on the first practice lap, led the race by 20 seconds from Mark Diffey (Kawasaki) with Dean Nelson (Yamaha) in third place, a further 18.9 seconds down. Alistair Howarth (Suzuki), Graham Kerr (Yamaha) and Keith Nicholls (Yamaha) completed the top six. The top five remained the same at the end of lap two, and Muir increased his lead to 38.2 seconds. Nicholls dropped to ninth place and David Black (Yamaha) took over sixth. No change in the top six at the end of the third lap, and Muir led Diffey by 42.8 seconds. On the final lap Diffey set the fastest lap of the race at 109.56 mph to cut into Muir's lead, but the local rider held on to win by 18.2 seconds, Nelson was third, Howarth fourth, Black took fifth place and Kerr completed the top six. There were nine finishers and four replicas were won.

Duncan Muir; a Gooseneck shot.

1994 Senior Newcomers (4 laps / 150.92 miles) 15 entries

1. Duncan Muir	Honda	1h. 24m. 43.7s	106.87 mph
2. Mark Diffey	Kawasaki	1h. 25m. 01.9s	106.49 mph
3. Dean Nelson	Yamaha	1h. 26m. 22.6s	104.83 mph
Fastest lap			
Mark Diffey	Kawasaki	20m. 39.7s	109.56 mph

1994 Junior Newcomers

Paul Kirkby (Honda), who had topped the practice leaderboard, led at the end of the first lap by 6.3 seconds from Phil Stewart with Tony Cross (Honda) 21.1 seconds down in third place. The top six was completed by Tim Camp (Honda), Andy Tuck (Yamaha) and Jonathan Dunne (Honda). The gap between the first and second was down to 15.9 seconds at half distance, Camp, Tuck and Dunne moved up one place as Cross dropped to sixth. Stewart was increasing the pressure on Kirkby and at the end of the third lap was just 5.9 seconds down - Camp remained third, Dunne moved up to fourth, Tuck was fifth and Chris Jones (Yamaha) took over sixth place with Cross dropping to ninth. On the final lap Phil Stewart set the fastest lap of the race - 108.96 mph, to take victory from Kirkby by 7.3 seconds with the rest of the top six unchanged.

There were nine finishers and seven replicas were won.

1994 Junior Newcomers (4 laps / 150.92 miles) 16 entries

1. Phil Stewart	Honda	1h. 25m. 46.3s	105.57 mph
2. Paul Kirby	Honda	1h. 25m. 54.0s	105.41 mph
3. Tim Camp	Honda	1h. 27m. 27.5s	102.94 mph
Fastest lap			
Phil Stewart	Honda	20m. 46.3s	108.98 mph

1994 Lightweight Newcomers

Emlyn Hughes (Yamaha) led this race from start to finish, with Gary Walker (Yamaha) in second place throughout.

Hughes led at the end of the first lap by 9.6 seconds and Garry

Linham (Honda) was just 0.4 seconds down on Walker. Tommy Diver (Yamaha), Joss Armer (Honda) and John Ashford (Honda) completed the top six. These six riders maintained their places on laps two and three, Hughes led Walker by 23.1 seconds and by 44.1 seconds after lap three. Emlyn Hughes went on to win by 32 seconds from Gary Walker, and with the fastest lap of the race on the final circuit at 106.04 mph, Tommy Diver took third place from Linham with Armer and Ashford completing the leaderboard. There were 16 finishers and eight replicas were won.

1994 Lightweight Newcomers (4 laps / 150.92 miles) 21 entries

1. Emlyn Hughes	Yamaha	1h. 27m. 15.8s	103.76 mph
2. Gary Walker	Yamaha	1h. 27m. 47.8s	103.13 mph
3. Tommy Diver	Yamaha	1h. 27m. 49.8s	103.09 mph
Fastest lap			
Tommy Diver	Yamaha	21m. 20.9s	106.04 mph

1994 Senior Classic

With Bill Swallow (Seeley) and Bob Heath (Seeley) starting at numbers 1 and 2, a tremendous race appeared to be in prospect. But at the end of the first lap Heath led Swallow by 28.4 seconds with Wattie Brown (Seeley) in third place, a further eight seconds down. Glen English (Matchless), Bob Jackson (Matchless) and Mick Robinson (Seeley) completed the top six. The difference between Bob and Bill after lap two was 48 seconds and Jackson had moved up to third, English was fourth, Brown fifth and John Goodall (Matchless) sixth, with Robinson dropping to eighth. Three of the leaders retired on lap three - Wattie Brown at the pits, Mick Robinson at Quarter Bridge and Glen English at Kirk Michael - so the top six were Bob Heath, by over a minute from Bill Swallow, Bob Jackson still third, Jack Gow (Norton) fourth, John Goodall fifth and Mark Baldwin (Petty Manx) sixth. Bob went on to win at a new race record by one minute 21.5 seconds from Bill and the only change to the top six was that Mark Baldwin took fifth place from John Goodall. There were 56 finishers and 20 replicas were won.

1994 Senior Classic (4 laps / 150.92 miles) 121 entries

1. Bob Heath	Seeley	1h. 27m. 33.6s	103.41 mph
			(record)
2. Bill Swallow	Matchless	1h. 28m. 55.1s	101.83 mph
3. Bob Jackson	Matchless	1h. 29m. 11.5s	101.52 mph
Fastest lap			
Bob Heath	Seeley	21m. 48.4s	103.81 mph

1994 Junior Classic

In this race Bob Heath (Seeley) started No. 1 with Bill Swallow (Aermacchi) at No. 2. But at the end of the first lap it was Mark Baldwin (Aermacchi) who led Bob Heath by 10.7 seconds with Bill Swallow 0.3 seconds down on Bob in third place. Joey Dunlop (Aermacchi), Geoff Tunstall (Aermacchi) and John Goodall (A.J.S.) completed the first lap top six. Baldwin set the fastest lap of the race on lap two, and led Heath by 25.5 seconds and Swallow was 0.3 seconds down on Heath - they were virtually riding side by side. Dunlop and Tunstall held their places, but Jack Gow (Seeley) took sixth place from Goodall. Drama on lap three as news came that the leader Mark Baldwin had retired at the Verandah, so as they crossed the line at the start of the final lap Bill led Bob by 0.2 seconds, and memories of their titanic battle in the 1992 Classic 500 were rekindled. Joey Dunlop was now up to third followed by Goodall, Tunstall and Gow. But a close finish was not to be, Bill Swallow retired at Lezayre on the final lap, so Bob Heath won by 1m.32.3s., and became the first rider to complete a Classic double and notch up his sixth Manx win from Joey Dunlop who picked up his first Manx replica, with John Goodall third, Geoff Tunstall fourth, Danny Shimmin (A.J.S.) and Dave Montgomery (Aermacchi) completing the leaderboard, Gow having retired on the Mountain Mile on the final lap. There were 46 finishers and eight replicas were won.

Joey Dunlop at Governors Bridge. Unlike his brothers Jim and Robert, Joey never campaigned the Manx until his rides in the Classic.

1994 Junior Classic (4 laps / 150.92 miles) 82 entries

1. Bob Heath	Seeley	1h. 31m. 18.9s	99.16 mph
2. Joey Dunlop	Aermacchi	1h. 32m. 52.2s	97.50 mph
3. John Goodall	A.J.S.	1h. 34m. 29.2s	95.83 mph
Fastest lap			
Mark Baldwin	Aermacchi	22m. 33.1s	100.38 mph

1994 Lightweight Classic

The top three remained unchanged throughout this four lap race. Bob Jackson (PB Suzuki) led brother 'Bud' (Jackson Suzuki) by almost a minute at the end of the first lap, with Wattie Brown (Crooks Suzuki) third, 33.1 seconds further down. The top six was completed by Bill Robertson (Suzuki), Les Trotter (Crooks Suzuki) and David Nobbs (Jackson Suzuki). The time gap between the first three extended as the race progressed - changes to the leaderboard on lap two - Les Trotter retired at Appledene so Peter Robertson (Suzuki) came up to sixth place. At the end of the third lap, the order was Bob Jackson, 'Bud' Jackson, Brown, Robertson, Nobbs and Peter Robertson, and they all retained these positions at the chequered flag. Elder brother Tom Jackson finished 23rd so the Jackson brothers won the team prize. There were 15 finishers and six replicas were won.

1994 Lightweight Classic (4 laps / 150.92 miles) 41 entries

1. Bob Jackson	Suzuki	1h. 34m. 26.1s	95.88 mph
2. 'Bud' Jackson	Suzuki	1h. 38m. 18.5s	92.11 mph
3. Wattie Brown	Suzuki	1h. 40m. 57.1s	89.69 mph
Fastest lap			
Bob Jackson	Suzuki	23m. 08.3s	97.83 mph

1994 Junior MGP

So near a winner in the Manx, Brian Venables (Honda) made no mistake in the Junior with a start to finish victory. He led at the end of the first lap by 4.2 seconds from Roy Richardson (Honda), with Derek Kelly (Yamaha) in third place, a further 6.5 seconds down. Tony Duncan (Yamaha), Eddie Sinton (Honda) and Greg Broughton (Yamaha) completed the first lap leaderboard. On lap two Richardson retired at Bishopscourt, so Venables led Duncan by 18 seconds, with Kelly third and Broughton fourth - all local riders - fifth was Phil Reid (Honda) and Sinton was sixth. The top four remained the same at the end of lap three and Venables' lead was 20.5 seconds. Ian Kirk (Yamaha) took fifth place with Sinton still sixth - Reid had dropped to eighth. Brian Venables won his first Manx by 12.7 seconds from Tony Duncan with Derek 'Decca' Kelly third, Graham Morton (Honda) was fourth, Chris Cannell (Yamaha) fifth and Phil Reid sixth with Ian Kirk finishing ninth. Broughton dropped to 16th place. There were 73 finishers and an amazing 52 replicas were won.

1994 Junior MGP (4 laps / 150.92 miles) 113 entries

1. Brian Venables	Honda	1h. 22m. 31.8s	109.72 mph
2. Tony Duncan	Yamaha	1h. 22m. 44.5s	109.43 mph
3. Derek 'Decca' Kelly	Yamaha	1h. 22m. 49.5s	109.32 mph
Fastest lap			
Brian Venables	Honda	20m. 15.4s	111.75 mph

1994 Lightweight MGP

After competing in the Manx since 1976, and being so near a winner a number of times, Derek 'Decca' Kelly (Yamaha) led the Lightweight from start to finish, with fellow Manxman Tony Duncan (Yamaha) second throughout. At the end of the first lap, they were separated by ten seconds, with Nigel Jennings (Yamaha) in third place, 4.6 seconds down on Duncan. Chris Cannell (Yamaha), Phil Reid (Honda) and Greg Broughton (Yamaha) completed the top six. Kelly's lead over Duncan was 16.9 seconds at the end of the second lap, Reid moved up to third, Jennings was fourth, Ian Kirk (Yamaha) fifth and Cannell sixth - Broughton was in eighth place. Kelly added 10 seconds to his lead after the third lap had been completed, and Reid was just 1.4 seconds down on Duncan. Broughton was up to fourth followed by Jennings and Cannell. The top six leaderboard men all retained their positions on the final lap - Derek Kelly achieved his life-long ambition with a win by 24.4 seconds from Duncan and Reid was just 1.8 seconds down in third place. There were 48 finishers and 22 replicas were won.

1994 Lightweight MGP (4 laps / 150.92 miles) 75 entries

1. Derek 'Decca' Kelly	Yamaha	1h. 22m. 33.2s	109.68 mph
2. Tony Duncan	Yamaha	1h. 22m. 57.6s	109.15 mph
3. Phil Reid	Honda	1h. 22m. 59.4s	109.11 mph
Fastest lap			
Derek 'Decca' Kelly	Yamaha	20m. 25.1s	110.87 mph

1994 Senior MGP

After finishing second in the Senior twice before, Brian Venables (Honda) added the Senior to his Junior win with another start to finish victory. At the end of the first lap he led Nigel Nottingham (Yamaha) by 23.7 seconds with Chris Hook (Honda) in third place, just 1.6 seconds down on Nottingham.

Out on his own - Decca Kelly at Guthrie's

Michael Brown (Kawasaki), Mike Casey (Honda) and Nick Morgan (Kawasaki) completed the leaderboard. Venables lead at the half-way stage was 30.3 seconds from Hook, who was just 0.2 seconds ahead of Nottingham, but Nigel stalled his engine in the stop box and that probably cost him the chance to challenge for second place. Brown and Casey remained fourth and fifth, but with Morgan's retirement at Crosby Crossroads, Roy Richardson brought his Honda into sixth place. The final two laps of the Senior saw no change to the top six, so Venables won by 32.6 seconds from Hook, who had an advantage of 12.8 seconds over Nottingham at the finish. There were 55 finishers and 25 replicas were won.

1994 Senior MGP (4 laps / 150.92 miles) 98 entries

1. Brian Venables	Honda	1h. 20m. 31.5s	112.45 mph
2. Chris Hook	Honda	1h. 21m. 14.1s	111.69 mph
3. Nigel Nottingham	Yamaha	1h. 21m. 16.9s	111.40 mph
Fastest lap			
Brian Venables	Honda	19m. 41.4s	114.97 mph

1995

The pattern for the 1995 Manx Grand Prix races remained the same as the previous year, and all races were over four laps of the course - 150.92 miles. There were six races, two of which were divided into classes, giving a total of nine winners, and 11 lap and race records were to be broken.

1995 Senior Newcomers

At the end of the first lap, Peter Barnett (Honda), husband of Sandra Barnett, the fastest lady ever round the TT course, led from Jason Harte (Suzuki) by 10.7 seconds with Robbie Watterson (Kawasaki) in third place a further 12.4 seconds down. Mike Brown (Honda), Ian Thompson (Yamaha) and John Quail (Honda) completed the top six. There were no changes to the top six leaderboard at half distance, and the lead for Barnett over Harte increased to 25.5. seconds, and Watterson had closed the gap on the second place man to 8.7 seconds. By the time the riders had completed lap three Jason Harte had closed to within 2.5 seconds of the leader, and the only change was that Quail took over fifth place from Thompson. Barnett got the message and set the fastest lap of the race on the final lap at 108.88mph - but his pursuer Jason Harte slid off at the Creg. So Peter Barnett won by just over a minute from Watterson with Brown third. The top six was completed by Quail, Thompson and Andrew Kirk (Honda). There were 11 finishers and seven replicas were won.

1995 Senior Newcomers (4 laps / 150.92 miles) 17 entries

1. Peter Barnett	Honda	1h. 24m. 13.4s	107.52 mph
2. Robbie Watterson	Kawasaki	1h. 25m. 15.9s	106.20 mph
3. Mike Brown	Honda	1h. 25m. 40.3s	105.69 mph
Fastest lap			
Peter Barnett	Honda	20m. 47.5s	108.88 mph

1995 Junior Newcomers

Ricky Mitchell (Yamaha) led this race from start to finish, but for the first two laps he was challenged hard by Paul Dedman (Kawasaki). At the end of the opening lap Mitchell had a lead of 8.9 seconds over Dedman with Adrian McFarland (Honda) in third place a further 6.9 seconds down. Barry Hall (Honda), Adrian Archibald (Honda) and Chris Heath (Yamaha) completed the top six. As the leaders came in for their pit stops at half distance the gap between first and second was 10.2 seconds, and both had lapped at over 111mph. McFarland was still third, but Heath had moved up to fourth, followed by Hall and Archibald. Paul Dedman's race ended on the third lap, so Mitchell led from McFarland by 39 seconds. Heath was third,

Two more successful candidates from the 'Davy Wood School of Road Racing'; Adrian McFarland (33) and Ricky Mitchell (30), plus their crews, with 'their maun' Davy Wood.

Hall fourth, Archibald fifth and Carl Rennie (Yamaha) took over sixth place. The order remained the same at the finish, but Adrian McFarland set a new lap record at 112.07 mph in his pursuit of Mitchell. There were 34 finishers and 23 replicas were won.

1995 Junior Newcomers (4 laps / 150.92 miles) 45 entries

1. Ricky Mitchell	Yamaha	1h. 21m. 54.0s	110.56 mph
2. Adrian McFarland	Honda	1h. 22m. 20.7s	109.96 mph
3. Chris Heath	Yamaha	1h. 24m. 19.7s	107.38 mph
Fastest lap (record)			
Adrian McFarland	Honda	20m. 11.9s	112.07 mph

1995 Lightweight Newcomers

Norman Gordon (Yamaha) led this race from start to finish and won at record breaking speed. At the end of the opening lap he led Russell Waring (Yamaha) by 8.8 seconds with Sean Jackson (Yamaha) in third place, just half a second down. Colm Fitzgerald (Yamaha), Richard Foxon (Yamaha) and Mick Presland (Yamaha) completed the top six. Gordon's lead was 10.9 seconds at the end of the second lap, but from Jackson who led Waring by 3.9 seconds, with the rest of the top six unchanged. By the time they had completed the third lap, Gordon led by 11.7 seconds, with the leaderboard unchanged. Gordon went on to win at a record speed of 106.25mph from Jackson and Waring, Fitzgerald took fourth place and Foxon fifth, but Mick Presland retired at Kirk Michael on the last lap, so Jonathan Cutts (Yamaha) took over sixth place. There were 15 finishers and six replicas were won.

1995 Lightweight Newcomers (4 laps / 150.92 miles) 20 entries

1. Norman Gordon	Yamaha	1h. 25m. 13.5s	106.25 mph
			(record)
2. Sean Jackson	Yamaha	1h. 25m. 30.9s	105.89 mph
3. Russell Waring	Yamaha	1h. 26m. 05.2s	105.18 mph
Fastest lap (record)			
Sean Jackson	Yamaha	20m. 47.7s	108.86 mph

1995 Lightweight Classic

With the firm favourite for a fourth successive win in this race, Bob Jackson, retiring at Sarah's Cottage on the first lap - the title was really up for grabs. Wattie Brown (Crooks Suzuki) led first time round by 3.4 seconds from Alan 'Bud' Jackson (Jackson Suzuki) with Les Trotter (Crooks Suzuki) a further 39 seconds down in third place. The top six was completed by Stephen Smith (Suzuki), Alan Beck (Suzuki) and David Smith (Yamaha). Wattie Brown retired at Ballacraine on lap two, so Jackson led Trotter by 37 seconds with Stephen Smith third, Beck fourth, David Smith fifth and David Nobbs (Suzuki) came on to the leaderboard in sixth place. After the early retirements things settled down and the only change to the leaderboard for the final two laps was that Alan Beck took over third place, so 'Bud' won his third Manx from Les by just under one minute. There were 18 finishers and eight replicas were won.

1995 Lightweight Classic (4 laps / 150.92 miles) 35 entries

1. Alan 'Bud' Jackson	Jackson Suzuki	1h. 36m. 55.4s	93.42 mph
2. Les Trotter	Crooks Suzuki	1h. 37m. 54.1s	92.49 mph
3. Alan Beck	Suzuki	1h. 38m. 42.3s	91.74 mph
Fastest lap			
Wattie Brown	Crooks Suzuki	23m. 39.6s	95.68 mph

1995 Senior Classic

Bob Heath (Seeley) who had topped the practice leaderboard at 106.22mph, led at the end of the first lap by 29.2 seconds from Glen English (Matchless) with Bill Swallow (Seeley) a further 1.4 seconds down in third place. The top six was completed by Robert Holden (Petty Norton), Steve Linsdell (Norton) and Wattie Brown (Seeley G50). With a lap at 105.96 on the second circuit, Heath increased his lead to 24.1 seconds, but from Swallow who was 9.6 seconds ahead of Holden. English dropped to fourth, Linsdell was fifth and John Goodall (Matchless) took sixth place - Wattie Brown having retired after a spill at Quarter Bridge. The top four remained the same as they started their last lap - Goodall moved up to fifth and Mervyn Elwood (Arter Matchless) took sixth place - Steve Linsdell retired at Sulby Bridge. Just as Bob Heath appeared to be strolling on to another victory, gearbox trouble hit at the Gooseneck on the final lap - so Bill Swallow notched up win number five with Holden second and Heath third. John Goodall retired, so Bill Horsman (Seeley) took fourth place ahead of Elwood with Steve Ruth (Seeley) taking sixth place. There were 52 finishers and 15 replicas were won.

"Wattie Brown having retired after a spill at Quarter Bridge." So reads the text; this is the photographic proof of Wattie Brown about to relinquish sixth place in the Senior Classic.

1995 Senior Classic (4 laps / 150.92 miles) 118 entries

1. Bill Swallow	Seeley	1h. 27m. 33.6s	103.41 mph
2. Robert Holden	Petty Norton	1h. 28m. 06.1s	102.78 mph
3. Bob Heath	Seeley	1h. 28m. 17.7s	102.55 mph
Fastest lap (record)			
Bob Heath	Seeley	21m. 21.5s	105.99 mph

1995 Junior Classic

In this race Bob Heath (Seeley) made up for his disappointment in the Senior Classic with a record breaking win. He led Glen English (Aermacchi) by 9.7 seconds at the end of the first lap with John Goodall (A.J.S.) in third place, 41.2 seconds down. Dave Montgomery (Aermacchi), Danny Shimmin (RM 7R) and Grahame Rhodes (Aermacchi) completed the leader-

board. Bill Swallow had retired at the Creg. The top three retained their places at half distance, but Shimmin took fourth place followed by Rhodes and John Loder (Aermacchi), Dave Montgomery was seventh. Two of the top six went out on lap three - English at Quarter Bridge and Montgomery at Hillberry - so Heath led Goodall by just under three minutes, Shimmin moved up to third with Rhodes fourth, Bob Newby (Mularney Norton) fifth and Tim Johnson (Norton) sixth. At the flag the top five remained the same, but Johnson retired at Sulby Crossroads and Grant Sellars (Aermacchi) took sixth place. There were 42 finishers and nine replicas were won.

1995 Junior Classic (4 laps / 150.92 miles) 85 entries

1. Bob Heath	Seeley	1h. 30m. 14.6s	100.34 mph
2. John Goodall	A.J.S.	1h. 34m. 24.8s	95.91 mph
3. Danny Shimmin	RM 7R	1h. 34m. 47.3s	95.53 mph
Fastest lap			
Bob Heath	Seeley	22m. 28.0s	100.76 mph

1995 Junior MGP

Another local victory seemed to be on the cards as Mike Casey (Honda) and Tony Duncan (Yamaha) were first and second on the practice leaderboard. It was Duncan who led at the end of the first lap, but only by 0.3 seconds from Ian Kirk (Yamaha) with Keith Townsend (Honda) in third place, a further 1.2 seconds down. Casey was fourth followed by Ricky Mitchell (Yamaha) and Rob Bardwell (Honda). Ian Kirk came off at Bedstead on lap two, Tony Duncan set a new lap record at 112.76mph and led Townsend by 10.2 seconds. Casey, Mitchell and Bardwell all moved up one place and Chris Cannell (Yamaha) took over sixth place. Starting the final lap, Tony Duncan had a lead of 18.3 seconds - but from Ricky Mitchell, Mike Casey was still third, Keith Townsend had dropped to fourth followed by Rob Bardwell and Chris Cannell. Tony Duncan went on to win by 12.1 seconds from Ricky Mitchell, Keith Townsend fought back to take third place with Mike Casey in fourth. Rob Bardwell came off at Greeba Castle on the final lap so Chris Cannell took fifth place and Adam Woodhall (Honda) came on to the top six leaderboard. There were 83 finishers and 46 replicas were won.

1995 Junior MGP (4 laps / 150.92 miles) 121 entries

1. Tony Duncan	MSR Yamaha	1h. 21m. 20.0s	111.33 mph
2. Ricky Mitchell	Yamaha	1h. 21m. 32.1s	111.05 mph
3. Keith Townsend	Butler Honda	1h. 21m. 38.5s	110.91 mph
Fastest lap (record)			
Tony Duncan	MSR Yamaha	20m. 04.5s	112.76 mph

1995 Lightweight MGP

Tony Duncan wheeled his Yamaha out again for the Lightweight and set off for another start to finish record breaking win. At the end of the opening lap he led Russell Henley (Yamaha) by 10.9 seconds, who in turn led Chris Cannell (Yamaha) by 1.5 seconds. The top six was completed by Greg Broughton (Yamaha), Alan Marshal (Yamaha) and Sean Jackson (Yamaha). At half distance Duncan's lead, with the help of a record lap at 112.49mph, was up to 30.3 seconds, but from Cannell, who was just 1.1 seconds ahead of Henley.

Marshal, Jackson and Derek Wagstaff (Yamaha) completed the top six, Broughton had pushed in from Governor's Bridge to retire. The top three remained the same at the end of lap three, but Jackson had moved up to fourth with Wagstaff fifth and Marshal sixth. There were no changes to the top six at the end of the race, Duncan completed his double by 1m. 9.5s. There were 53 finishers and 25 replicas were won.

Tony Duncan heels into Ballacraine, adding two more race wins to sponsor Ray Cowles Manx GP winning collection.

1995 Lightweight MGP (4 laps / 150.92 miles) 84 entries

1. Tony Duncan	MSR Yamaha	1h. 21m. 30.2s	111.10 mph
			(record)
2. Chris Cannell	Pergola Yamaha	1h. 22m. 39.7s	109.54 mph
3. Russell Henley	Mannin Yamaha	1h. 23m. 00.3s	109.09 mph
Fastest lap (record)			
Tony Duncan	MSR Yamaha	20m. 07.4s	112.49 mph

1995 Senior MGP

Nigel Nottingham (Yamaha) had topped the practice leaderboard, but at the end of the opening lap it was Chris Hook (Honda) who led the race by 3.6 seconds from Mike Casey (Honda) with Roy Richardson (Honda) in third place, just 1.8 seconds down on Casey. Keith Townsend (Honda), Nick Morgan (Kawasaki) and Graham Morton (Honda) completed the top six, with Nottingham in seventh place. Hook still led at half distance by 6.8 seconds from Casey with Richardson still third. Morton had taken over fourth place with Townsend fifth, and Paul Dedman (Kawasaki), who had start number 103, had flown through the field to take sixth place. There was real drama in the pits, however, Nick Morgan toured in to retire, and the machines of Chris Hook and Nigel Nottingham would just not start after their stops and both retired. At the completion of lap three Mike Casey led the race from Keith Townsend by 15.2 seconds, with Richardson third, Morton fourth, Dedman fifth and Adrian McFarland (Honda) in sixth place. So Mike Casey went on to win by 10.6 seconds, but from Roy Richardson with Keith Townsend in third place. Morton, Dedman and McFarland held their positions to the flag. There were 69 finishers and 36 replicas were won.

1995 Senior MGP (4 laps / 150.92 miles) 109 entries

1. Mike Casey	Bullock Honda	1h. 20m. 59.2s	111.81 mph
2. Roy Richardson	Honda	1h. 21m. 09.8s	111.56 mph
3. Keith Townsend	Butler Honda	1h. 21m. 16.3s	111.41 mph

My Winning Ride - Mike Casey, 1995 Senior Manx

My Winning Ride
Mike Casey, 1995 Senior Manx

The story of my winning ride in the 1995 Senior Manx Grand Prix actually began immediately after the 1994 Senior Manx. We were having a drink in the beer tent when I was approached by local sponsor Martin Bullock, who offered me a ride on the RC30 Honda that had just been ridden to victory by Brian Venables.

A year later I was on the start line waiting to set off in the first practice. I have always prepared my own machines, but now all the work was being done by ex-TT racer Richard Rose, which meant all I had to do was turn up and concentrate on the riding.

I completed two laps on the RC30 and was pleased to find that it was virtually perfect straight away. I was also riding a 600 Honda for the team and completed one lap on it at the end of practice. When the times came out I was fastest in both classes, which was a perfect start to the week.

Practice week went extremely well, Richard and myself were very happy with the setup of the bikes, although I couldn't help thinking about the well-known racers proverb "good practice, bad race".

The Junior race was on the Wednesday and I thought I had a really good chance of a top three position, however, things didn't go as planned and I ended up finishing fourth.

On Senior race day, we decided to take it easy off the start and try to relax and ride smoothly.

All went well until I was going into Ballacraine on the first lap when I noticed one of the front brake discs had warped, causing the bike to judder, but as long as I braked carefully it wouldn't be too much of a problem.

I got my first signal from sponsor Alan Kelly at the 13th Milestone and was astonished to see that I was leading, as I was not really trying at this point. By the time I reached Ramsey, Chris Hook was leading by one second.

Chris and I traded first and second places until the end of the second lap, but as I was riding down to Brandish, the bike cut out in top gear. Luckily it cleared itself on the way down to Hillberry and I entered the pits in second place, seven seconds behind.

The pit stop went well but as I exited pit lane I was amazed to see Chris Hook's bike stopped at the side of the road, I learnt later that his gearbox had locked up. This was confirmed at Ballacraine where I got a signal 'first plus seventeen seconds'. I was now leading on the road, and second place was now held by Roy Richardson (Honda), who had started in front of me. All I had to do was stay ahead of Roy and I would win.

The last lap was a fantastic experience. People were waving all the way around the course and I managed to recognise quite a few of them, but I didn't wave back very much as I didn't want anything to go wrong.

I rode out of Governor's Bridge onto the Glencrutchery Road and saw the chequered flag. This was it, after ten years of trying, I was going to win the Manx. I finished the race scarcely able to believe it had happened; it was only when I came back down to earth I realised with sadness that by winning I could not return and had ridden in my last Manx.

This article was written by Mike in May, shortly before his fatal accident in practice for the 1998 TT races.

Top: Mike at Windy Corner. Bottom: Mike gives Manx Radio's Geoff Cannell a first-hand account of his winning ride. Behind Mike stands Richard Rose, main spanner-man for the Martin Bullock team.

Fastest lap				
Chris Hook	Honda		19m. 55.5s	113.61 mph

1996

1996 Senior Newcomers

Paul Duckett (Kawasaki), who had topped the practice leaderboard at 104.44 mph, led this race from start to finish. At the end of the opening lap he led Stephen Nugent (Marshal Yamaha) by 10.3 seconds, with David Hodgkinson (Honda) in third place, a further 4.9 seconds down. Ian Shaw (Kawasaki) held fourth place, followed by Justin Noone (Sally Long Honda) and Paul Humble (Honda). It was an unusual race, in the fact that the top six remained unchanged for the entire 150.92 miles. Second time round Duckett was 10 seconds ahead of Nugent with Hodgkinson just half a second down. By the time lap three had been completed the difference between the first two was just 2.7 seconds, but with the fastest lap of the race on lap four, Duckett won by 20.7 seconds from Nugent, who finished 4.1 seconds in front of Hodgkinson. There were 14 finishers and 11 replicas were won.

1996 Senior Newcomers (4 laps / 150.92 miles) 16 entries

1. Paul Duckett	Kawasaki	1h. 28m. 52.3s	101.89 mph
2. Stephen Nugent	Marshal Yamaha	1h. 29m. 14.0s	101.47 mph
3. David Hodgkinson	Honda	1h. 29m. 18.1s	101.40 mph
Fastest lap			
Paul Duckett	Kawasaki	21m. 43.3s	104.21 mph

1996 Junior Newcomers

Gordon Blackley (Honda) topped the practice leaderboard in this class, and led the four-lap race from start to finish. At the end of the opening lap he was 5.7 seconds ahead of Darren Soothill, who in turn led Olaf Jones by 29.6 seconds. The top six was completed by Brodie Branch, Bill Hutcheson and John Leigh-Pemberton - all on Hondas. As in the Newcomers Senior race the top six stayed the same for the entire race. It was a close battle between the first two, however, at the end of lap two the difference was exactly the same as at the end of lap one - 5.7 seconds. It was 4.2 seconds at the end of lap three and Blackley went on to win by 8.4 seconds. There were 20 finishers and seven replicas were won.

1996 Junior Newcomers (4 laps / 150.92 miles) 21 entries

1. Gordon Blackley	Honda	1h. 24m. 35.4s	107.04 mph
2. Darren Soothill	Honda	1h. 24m. 43.8s	106.87 mph
3. Olaf Jones	Honda	1h. 26m. 14.2s	105.00 mph
Fastest lap			
Gordon Blackley	Honda	20m. 41.7s	109.38 mph

1996 Lightweight Newcomers

This race was expected to be a battle between Derek Cohen and Chris Moore on their Yamahas, as they had dominated the practice leaderboard. It turned out to be that way, but only for half a lap. Cohen led Moore at Glen Helen and Ramsey Hairpin but retired at Tower Bends, so Moore had a comfortable lead of just over a minute at the end of the first lap from David Taylor (Kawasaki) who led Andrew Yarnold (Kawasaki) by 11.2 seconds. Paul White (Honda), Toby Marshal (Yamaha) and Tim Darvell (400 Yamaha) completed the top six. Marshal retired at the pits so Pamela Cannell (Honda) moved into sixth place. Chris Moore continued to increase his lead at the front, but Darvell's race ended in a spill at the Waterworks and Andrew Yarnold retired at Gardeners Lane, Ramsey. Monica Floding (Honda) moved up to fourth place ahead of Cannell. Chris Moore went on to win by 3m 33.4 seconds from David Taylor,

Bob Jackson (Matchless, 5) is about ten seconds up on Bill Horsman (Seeley) at Sulby Bridge. They finished the race with exactly that number of seconds between them in second and third places.

with Paul White in third place - with the two local lady newcomers in fourth and fifth places. There were just five finishers and two replicas were won.

1996 Lightweight Newcomers (4 laps / 150.92 miles) 10 entries

1. Chris Moore	Yamaha	1h. 35m. 07.2s	95.19 mph
2. David Taylor	Kawasaki	1h. 38m. 40.6s	91.76 mph
3. Paul White	Honda	1h. 45m. 56.3s	85.47 mph
Fastest lap			
Chris Moore	Yamaha	23m. 15.6s	97.32 mph

1996 Senior Classic

Bob Heath (Seeley) who had topped the practice leaderboard at over 105 mph, was again firm favourite to take the honours. At the end of the opening lap he led Bob Jackson (Matchless) by 37.5 seconds with Glen English (Beale Matchless) a further 2.6 seconds down in third place. Bill Horsman (Seeley), Wattie Brown (Seeley G50) and John Goodall (Matchless) completed the top six - and just 27 seconds covered second to sixth place. The top two retained their places at half distance and Bob Heath had increased his advantage to 63 seconds. Glen English retired at the pits, so Bill Horsman took over third place with Wattie Brown fourth. Mervyn Elwood (Matchless G50) came into fifth place ahead of John Goodall. Heath added another 11 seconds to his lead over Jackson after the completion of the third lap with Horsman still third. Brown's race ended on this lap with retirement at Snugborough. Elwood and Goodall were fourth and fifth with Steve Ruth (Seeley) taking over sixth spot. Bob Jackson was slightly quicker than Heath on the final circuit, but the Walsall rider took his fifth Senior Classic, and his eighth win overall, by 68.9 seconds and the rest of the leaderboard was unchanged. Steve Ruth won a M.G.P.R.A. medal for his first 100 mph classic lap. There were 64 finishers and 24 replicas were won.

1996 Senior Classic (4 laps / 150.92 miles) 114 entries

1. Bob Heath	Seeley	1h. 27m. 21.5s	103.65 mph
			(record)
2. Bob Jackson	Matchless	1h. 28m. 30.6s	102.30 mph
3. Bill Horsman	Seeley	1h. 28m. 40.6s	102.11 mph
Fastest lap			
Bob Heath	Seeley	21m. 40.2s	104.46 mph

1996 Junior Classic

Bob Heath (Seeley) also topped the Junior Classic leaderboard, and with Bill Swallow starting at No. 1 and Bob Heath at 2, memories of their titanic battle of a few years ago were to the fore in many peoples minds. Bill Swallow (Aermacchi) had other ideas however and at the end of the first lap he led Bob Heath by 26 seconds with Bill Horsman (Aermacchi) in third place - 0.4 seconds down on Heath. The top six was completed by Glen English (Aermacchi), Bob Newby (Mularney Manx Norton) and Steve Ruth (Aermacchi). Swallow's advantage at half distance was 33.6 seconds - but from Horsman with Heath in third place, 33.7 seconds down. The rest of the top six remained the same. At the end of the third lap the top three were the same - Steve Ruth retired at Governors Bridge and English dropped to eighth. Bob Newby was fourth, John Loder (Greeves) was fifth and John Goodall (A.J.S.) was sixth. Bill Swallow went on to win his third Junior Classic and sixth win overall by 35.2 seconds from Horsman and Heath took third. Newby took fourth, John Goodall fifth and Glen English came back on to the leaderboard in sixth place. John Loder had a problem on the last lap, stopping at the Highlander for adjustments, and finished 15th. There were 39 finishers and 11 replicas were won.

1996 Junior Classic (4 laps / 150.92 miles) 82 entries

1. Bill Swallow	Aermacchi	1h. 29m. 00.4s	101.73 mph
			(record)
2. Bill Horsman	Aermacchi	1h. 29m. 35.6s	101.07 mph
3. Bob Heath	Seeley	1h. 31m. 43.1s	98.72 mph
Fastest lap (record)			
Bill Swallow	Aermacchi	22m. 08.6s	102.23 mph

Bill Swallow thought the handling of his race-winning machine was not as precise as should be. A post race inspection revealed broken spokes and a cracked rear hub!

1996 Lightweight Classic

The only lap record in the Manx at under 100 mph was the Classic Lightweight, but with Bob Jackson (PB Suzuki) lapping at 100.26 mph in practice, hopes were high that he could repeat that feat in the race. But at the end of the opening lap it was Gary Long (Suzuki), with a lap at 99.67 mph, who led the race by 14.4 seconds from Bob Jackson with brother 'Bud' (Jackson Suzuki) in third place, some 35.4 seconds adrift. Ewan Hamilton (Suzuki), Les Trotter (Crooks Suzuki) and Barry Wood (Suzuki) completed the top six. History was made on the second lap when Bob Jackson lapped in 22m 33.4seconds - 100.34 mph, but he was still 8.1 seconds down on Long. 'Bud' Jackson was still third but Ewan Hamilton retired at Ramsey. This brought Les Trotter up to fourth followed by Barry Wood and Steve Smith (Suzuki). Long's challenge ended on lap three when he retired at Hillberry so Bob had a lead of over two minutes from his brother with Les Trotter third. Wood and Smith both moved up one place with Phillip Shaw (Suzuki) coming into the top six. Bob set another lap record on his final lap - 100.90 mph - and won from 'Bud' by 3m. 18.1seconds. Les Trotter went out on this final lap at Westwood, so Barry Wood took third place. Smith was fourth, Shaw fifth and Dave Thurlow (Suzuki) took sixth place. There were 13 finishers and four replicas were won.

1996 Lightweight Classic (4 laps / 150.92 miles) 36 entries

1. Bob Jackson	PB Suzuki	1h. 30m. 50.1s	99.68 mph
			(record)
2. Alan 'Bud' Jackson	Suzuki	1h. 34m. 08.1s	96.19 mph
3. Barry Wood	Suzuki	1h. 37m. 01.2s	93.33 mph
Fastest lap (record)			
Bob Jackson	PB Suzuki	22m. 26.1s	100.90 mph

1996 Junior MGP

Firm favourite for Junior honours was Ricky Mitchell (GS Honda) who had knocked some ten seconds off the lap record in practice. What an explosive start he made - on the

opening lap he set a new absolute lap record in 19m. 20.4s. - speed of 117.05 mph, and led Roy Richardson (Honda) by 32.7 seconds, with Keith Townsend (Butler Honda) in third place some 10.2 seconds down. Adrian Archibald (Honda), Adam Woodhall (Honda) and Alistair Howarth (Kawasaki) completed the top six. With a lap at over 116 mph second time around, Mitchell increased his lead to 66.5 seconds from Archibald with Townsend in third. Richardson retired at the pits and Chris Hook (Honda) shot up to fourth place ahead of Woodhall and Adrian McFarland came onto the leaderboard in sixth place with Howarth in seventh place. Lap three saw Ricky Mitchell increase his lead over Adrian Archibald and Chris Hook moved up to third. McFarland was fourth, Townsend fifth and Woodhall sixth. The top five remained the same on the final lap and Ricky Mitchell won comfortably at a record 114.58 mph, and the battle for sixth place went to Alistair Howarth with Woodhall taking seventh place. There were an amazing 96 finishers and 42 replicas were won.

1996 Junior MGP (4 laps / 150.92 miles) 119 entries

1. Ricky Mitchell	Honda	1h. 19m. 01.6s	114.58 mph (record)
2. Adrian Archibald	Honda	1h. 20m. 21.6s	112.68 mph
3. Chris Hook	Honda	1h. 21m. 15.5s	111.43 mph
Fastest lap (record)			
Ricky Mitchell	Honda	19m. 20.4s	117.05 mph

1996 Lightweight MGP

Russell Henley (Yamaha) had been the fastest in practice and he confirmed this form with a start to finish victory. He started at No. 2 alongside Mick Robinson (Honda) and they crossed the line at the end of the first lap side by side, almost touching, and couldn't be separated on the watches. They led Barry Wood (Honda) by thirteen seconds with Chris Cannell (Yamaha) fourth, Alex Marshal (Yamaha) fifth and Richard Quayle (Yamaha) sixth. At half distance Russell led Mick by 9.7 seconds. Locals Barry Wood and Chris Cannell were still third and fourth, but Alan Marshal slid off at Ginger Hall so Richard Quayle moved up to fifth and Dave Vale (Yamaha) came in to sixth place. There were changes at the end of the third lap - the top four remained the same but Derek Wagstaff (Yamaha) and Gary Linham (Yamaha) came into the top six with Quayle and Vale seventh and eighth. Russell Henley won by 4.8 seconds, but from Barry Wood who passed Mick Robinson on the last lap. Cannell, Wagstaff and Linham held on to their top six places. There were 47 finishers and 31 replicas were won.

1996 Lightweight MGP (4 laps / 150.92 miles) 66 entries

1. Russell Henley	Yamaha	1h. 22m. 53.3s	109.24 mph
2. Barry Wood	Honda	1h. 22m. 58.1s	109.14 mph
3. Mick Robinson	Honda	1h. 23m. 10.0s	108.88 mph
Fastest lap			
Derek Wagstaff	Yamaha	20m. 20.2s	111.15 mph

1996 Senior MGP

Adrian Archibald (Honda), Ricky Mitchell (Honda) and Keith Townsend (Honda) had all lapped at over 113 mph in practice, so another record-breaking race looked on the cards. Ricky Mitchell opened with a blistering lap at 116.90 mph and led Roy Richardson (Honda) by 17.7 seconds with Adrian Archibald and Keith Townsend third and fourth. The top six were completed by Gary Carswell and Paul Dedman - both on Kawasakis. The leaderboard was unchanged at half distance and Ricky's lead was extended to 24.4 seconds. At the end of the third lap Mitchell had a new pursuer - Archibald had taken second place from Richardson and was 32.1 seconds down on the leader with the other top six places unchanged. Adrian Archibald literally flew around the 37.73 miles on his final lap and set a new absolute Manx Grand Prix course record in 19m. 19.1s. - 117.18 mph - but couldn't prevent Mitchell completing

Mick Robinson, adding to his record-breaking tally of Manx replicas; a Gooseneck shot.

his double, and his third Manx win in two years. The rest of the leaderboard remained the same at the flag. There were 90 finishers and 33 replicas were won.

1996 Senior MGP (4 laps / 150.92 miles) 117 entries

1. Ricky Mitchell	Honda	1h. 18m. 33.1s	115.27 mph (record)
2. Adrian Archibald	Honda	1h. 18m. 44.0s	115.01 mph
3. Roy Richardson	Honda	1h. 19m. 01.6s	114.58 mph
Fastest lap (record)			
Adrian Archibald	Honda	19m. 19.1s	117.18 mph

1997

1997 Senior Newcomers

John Bradshaw (620 Honda) had topped the practice leaderboard, but a spill in practice had damaged his machine so he was a non-starter. Darren Lindsay (600 Suzuki), second fastest in practice, led at the end of the opening lap by 14.3 seconds from Gary Sansom (750 Honda) who in turn led Derek Heron (600 Yamaha) by 33.4 seconds. Paul Mercer (850 Yamaha), Matty Bruce (600 Honda) and Steven Hayhurst (640 Honda) completed the top six. The leaderboard remained unchanged at half distance, and Lindsay had a 53.7 second advantage over Sansom. At the end of lap three the difference between the first two was almost two minutes and the only change in the top six was that Matty Bruce took over fourth place from Paul Mercer. Darren Lindsay went on to win by almost three minutes and the top six remained unchanged. There were 10 finishers and six replicas were won.

1997 Senior Newcomers (4 laps / 150.92 miles) 14 entries

1. Darren Lindsay	Suzuki	1h. 26m. 05.6s	105.17 mph
2. Gary Sansom	Honda	1h. 29m. 16.5s	101.43 mph
3. Derek Heron	Yamaha	1h. 31m. 00.7s	99.49 mph
Fastest lap			
Darren Lindsay	Suzuki	21m. 12.4s	106.74 mph

1997 Junior Newcomers

Richard Britton, Junior Newcomers winner, pictured at the Bungalow.

Steve Ellis on his 600 Cowles Honda had topped the practice leaderboard with a lap at 109.41 mph, with Paul Kellett (600 Honda) second. Sure enough Steve led at the end of the first lap at 111.97 mph - just 6.4 seconds outside Jason Griffiths seven year old record. He led Richard Britton (600 Schimmel Honda) by 31 seconds with Paul Kellett in third place a further 26.1 seconds down. Geoff Downey (600 Honda), Leslie Williams (600 Honda) and Martin McCloy (600 Honda) completed the top six. Sadly, Steve Ellis retired with ignition trouble on Bray Hill on lap two, so the leader at half distance was Richard Britton by 24.4 seconds from Paul Kellett, Downey, Williams and McCloy all moved up one place and Uel Duncan (600 Honda) came into sixth place. The top three maintained station on lap three but McCloy took over fourth place followed by Duncan and Williams. Richard Britton went on to win by 33.2 seconds from Kellett, Downey held third place, Leslie Williams took back fourth place with McCloy and Duncan completing the leaderboard. There were 15 finishers and eight replicas were won.

1997 Junior Newcomers (4 laps / 150.92 miles) 25 entries

1. Richard Britton	Schimmel Honda	1h. 23m. 21.7s	108.62 mph
2. Paul Kellett	Honda	1h. 23m. 54.9s	107.90 mph
3. Geoff Downey	Honda	1h. 25m. 59.0s	105.31 mph
Fastest lap			
Steve Ellis	Cowles Honda	20m. 13.0s	111.97 mph

1997 Lightweight Newcomers

Local rider Nigel Beattie (250 MB Yamaha) had been the only rider in practice to lap at over the 100 - 101.59 mph, but at the end of the opening lap it was Dave Jones (250 Yamaha) who led from Lawrence Palmer (250 Yamaha) by 25.8 seconds with Beattie in third place a further 18.6 seconds down. The top six was completed by Jim Halligan (249 Honda), Mark Marshal (250 Yamaha) and Tony Cawte (249 Yamaha). Jones increased his lead to 40.1 seconds at half distance and the only change to the leaderboard was that Cawte took fifth place from Marshal. As they crossed the line to start their final lap Dave Moore had a lead of over one minute, but from Nigel Beattie with Lawrence Palmer in third spot and the remaining leaderboard men maintained their places. Dave Jones won at 102.61 mph, and the only change at the finish to the top six was that James Croft (250 Suzuki) took sixth place after Mark Marshal came off at Keppel Gate - he was uninjured. There were eight finishers and four replicas were won

1997 Lightweight Newcomers (4 laps / 150.92 miles) 15 entries

1. Dave Jones	Yamaha	1h. 28m. 14.8s	102.61 mph
2. Nigel Beattie	MB Yamaha	1h. 29m. 17.5s	101.41 mph
3. Lawrence Palmer	Yamaha	1h. 29m. 29.9s	101.17 mph
Fastest lap			
Dave Jones	Yamaha	21m. 46.9s	103.93 mph

1997 Senior Classic

Firm favourite Bob Heath (499 Seeley) who had lapped at 105.98 mph in practice, just one tenth of a second outside his own lap record, was second at the end of the first lap by 1.5 seconds to Bob Jackson (500 Norton), with Bill Swallow (499 Petty Norton) in third place a further 24.2 seconds down, followed by Tony Myers (492 Seeley), Bill Horsman (499 Molnar Norton) and Wattie Brown (499 Petty Manx). On lap two Bob Heath set the first ever Classic 106 plus lap to take the lead from

Bob Jackson by 3.6 seconds and the rest of the top five remained the same, but Wattie Brown retired at Quarry Bends and Frenchman Bruno Leroy (496 Seeley G50) took over sixth place. With the fastest lap of the race on lap 3 - 106.74 mph - Heath extended his lead over Jackson to 16.7 seconds, Swallow remained third, Horsman took fifth place from Myers and Leroy remained sixth. Bob Heath notched up another 106 plus on the final lap to win from Bob Jackson by 34.4 seconds with the top six remaining the same. There were 57 finishers and 14 replicas were won.

1997 Senior Classic (4 laps / 150.92 miles)   111 entries

1. Bob Heath	Seeley G50	1h. 25m. 19.2s	106.13 mph
			(record)
2. Bob Jackson	Norton	1h. 25m. 53.6s	105.42 mph
3. Bill Swallow	Petty Norton	1h. 27m. 00.7s	104.06 mph
Fastest lap (record)			
Bob Heath	Seeley G50	21m. 12.5s	106.74 mph

1997 Junior Classic

Bob Heath (349 Seeley) again topped the practice leaderboard and was all out for his 10th Manx victory in a race reduced to three laps because of a delayed start due to the weather. He led Bill Horsman (349 Aermacchi) on the end of the opening lap by 36.9 seconds with Graham Wilson (344 Aermacchi) in third place nearly a minute down. Mick Robinson (348 Aermacchi), John Goodall (349 A.J.S.) and John Loder (350 Greeves) made up the first lap leaderboard. The difference between the first two at the end of the second lap was 42.3 seconds. Wilson was still third, but Goodall and Loder both overtook Robinson. Drama on the final lap - as Bob Heath rounded Glen Helen his chain came off and he cruised to a halt at Sarah's Cottage - he replaced the chain and continued, was then black flagged at the Bungalow, stopped for seven seconds and proceeded. Whilst all this was going on, Bill Horsman was writing a bit of Manx history, by becoming the first Australian to win a Manx. He won by 47.4 seconds, Bob Heath finished second over two minutes up on Graham Wilson. John Goodall and John Loder held their positions but Grahame Rhodes (344 Aermacchi) took sixth place from Mick Robinson. There were 44 finishers and 10 replicas were won.

1997 Junior Classic (3 laps / 113.19 miles)   77 entries

1. Bill Horsman	Aermacchi	1h. 08m. 27.3s	99.20 mph
2. Bob Heath	Seeley 7R	1h. 09m. 15.1s	98.06 mph
3. Graham Wilson	Aermacchi	1h. 11m. 21.4s	95.17 mph
Fastest lap			
Bob Heath	Seeley 7R	22m. 30.5s	100.57 mph

1997 Lightweight Classic

This race, run concurrently with the Junior Classic was also reduced to three laps, and the firm favourite was Bob Jackson (250 PB Suzuki), he had come to within three-tenths of a second of his own lap record in practice and led Gary Long (249 Suzuki) by 11.9 seconds at the end of the first circuit with Bill Swallow (249 Aermacchi), completing in his first 250cc Classic Race in third place, 10.7 seconds down. Suzuki mounted Wattie Brown, Barry Wood and Bud Jackson made up the top six. The top two remained the same after lap two had been completed and the difference was 63.1 seconds. But Bill Swallow went out at the Verandah, Wattie Brown at Governors Bridge and Barry Wood at Ballacraine. Bud Jackson shot up to third place. Ewan Hamilton, Phillip Shaw and Dave Thurlow, all on Suzukis, came into the top six. Bob Jackson went on to a comfortable victory and the only change to the top six at the flag was that Stephen Smith (247 Suzuki) took sixth spot from Dave Thurlow. There were 23 finishers and five replicas were won.

1997 Lightweight Classic (3 laps / 113.19 miles)   42 entries

1. Bob Jackson	PB Suzuki	1h. 09m. 50.3s	97.24 mph
2. Gary Long	Suzuki	1h. 10m. 07.6s	96.84 mph
3. Alan 'Bud' Jackson	Suzuki	1h. 13m. 50.0s	91.98 mph
Fastest lap			
Bob Jackson	PB Suzuki	22m. 44.7s	99.52 mph

1997 Junior MGP

David Black (600 Honda) had topped the practice leaderboard at 110.65 mph - eight other riders had also topped the 110 mark and were separated by just 5.9 seconds - a close race looked on the cards. At the end of the opening lap it was Keith Townsend (599 DC Butler Honda) who led at 113.67 mph - 1.5 seconds ahead of Roy Richardson (600 BDC Europe Suzuki) with Adam Woodhall (600 Bullock Honda) in third place a further 16.2 seconds down. Chris Hook, Gordon Blackley and Darren Soothill, all on Hondas made up the top six, and remarkably 105 riders completed the first lap. Keith Townsend's race ended at Sulby Bridge on lap two, so Richardson took over the lead by 36.4 seconds from Chris Hook with Woodhall in third place - they were followed by Soothill, Gary Carswell (Kawasaki) and Carl Rennie (600 Honda). Gordon Blackley had run out of fuel and pushed in to eighth place. Richardson had an advantage of 45.4 seconds over Hook as they started their last lap - Soothill had taken third spot from Woodhall, Carswell was still fifth, but Blackley had grabbed sixth place from Rennie. The top five remained the same to the flag, but Gordon Blackley again had a long push in, the smaller tank on his Honda had dried up again - he finished 37th but had the consolation of winning a replica. Bill Hutcheson (600 Honda) took sixth place. There were 97 finishers and 47 replicas were won.

1997 Junior MGP (4 laps / 150.92 miles)   122 entries

1. Roy Richardson	BDC Suzuki	1h. 20m. 11.3s	112.92 mph
2. Chris Hook	Honda	1h. 21m. 04.2s	111.69 mph
3. Darren Soothill	Whitwell Honda	1h. 21m. 23.1s	111.26 mph
Fastest lap			
Roy Richardson	BDC Suzuki	19m. 46.7s	114.45 mph

1997 Lightweight MGP

Garry Linham (250 Honda) showed his practice form to be true when he opened with a lap at 109.48 mph to lead Barry Wood (250 Manton Honda) by 8.5 seconds, with Chris Cannell (250 MB Pergola Yamaha) 10.9 seconds further down. Then came Norman Gordon (250 Yamaha), Brian Kneale (250 DTR Yamaha) and Adam Nowell (250 Clark Yamaha). The top two maintained station at half distance, but Brian Kneale moved up to third, Chris Cannell was fourth, Norman Gordon dropped to

fifth and Brian Spooner (250 Honda) took sixth place - Adam Nowell having been black-flagged for a loose exhaust pipe - he repaired it in the pits but dropped down to eventually finish 42nd. Another shake-up at the end of lap three - Garry Linham still led by 25.2 seconds but from Brian Kneale and Norman Gordon, Chris Cannell was fourth, Barry Wood fifth and Brian Spooner sixth. The top five held their places on the final circuit, but Mick Robinson (250 Honda) won his 26th replica for taking sixth place from Brian Spooner. There were 51 finishers and 28 replicas were won.

1997 Lightweight MGP (4 laps / 150.92 miles) 71 entries

1. Gary Linham	Honda	1h. 23m. 01.9s	109.05 mph
2. Brian Kneale	DTR Yamaha	1h. 23m. 15.3s	108.76 mph
3. Norman Gordon	Yamaha	1h. 23m. 31.8s	108.40 mph
Fastest lap			
Barry Wood	Manton Honda)	20m. 21.9s	111.16 mph
Norman Gordon	Yamaha)	20m .21.9s	111.16 mph

1997 Senior MGP

Roy Richardson (750 JSB Bullock Honda) was all fired up for the Junior/Senior double, and led at the end of the first lap by 6.2 seconds from Gary Carswell (750 W&C Kawasaki) who in turn had a 10.6 seconds advantage over third place-man Keith Townsend (750 DC Butler Honda). Three 600 Hondas filled the next three places - Chris Hook, Gordon Blackley and Adam Woodhall. In this race 104 riders completed the first lap. The top four remained the same at half distance - Steve Ellis (600 Cowles Honda) slotted unto fifth place ahead of Blackley with Woodhall slipping to seventh. Roy Richardson's dream of a double ended however with a retirement and Gordon Blackley also went out at the pits with tyre troubles. So the third lap leaderboard read - Carswell by 30.2 seconds from Townsend followed by Hook, Ellis, Woodhall and Alistair Howarth (600 Honda). The top five finished the race in the same order - and Darren Soothill (600 Honda) snatched sixth place from Howarth by just 2.4 seconds. There were 93 finishers and 47 replicas were won.

1997 Senior MGP (4 laps / 150.92 miles) 116 entries

1. Gary Carswell	W&C Kawasaki	1h. 19m. 29.3s	113.91 mph
2. Keith Townsend	DC Butler Honda	1h. 19m. 55.9s	113.28 mph
3. Chris Hook	Honda	1h. 20m. 35.4s	112.36 mph
Fastest lap			
Roy Richardson	Honda	19m. 25.9s	116.50 mph

Gary Carswell, the latest in a long line of local Manx GP winners, pictured at Tower Bends.

Lap and Race records

Lightweight
Lap	Tony Duncan	249 Yamaha	20.07.4	112.49	1995
Race	Tony Duncan	249 Yamaha	1.21.30.2	111.10	1995

Junior
Lap	Ricky Mitchell	600 Honda	19.20.4	117.05	1996
Race	Ricky Mitchell	600 Honda	1.19.01.6	114.58	1996

Senior
Lap	Adrian Archibald	600 Honda	19.19.1	117.18	1996
Race	Ricky Mitchell	600 Honda	1.18.33.1	115.27	1996

Newcomers Races

Lightweight
Lap	Sean Jackson	250 Yamaha	20.47.7	108.86	1995
Race	Norman Gordon	250 Yamaha	1.25.13.5	106.25	1995

Junior
Lap	Adrian McFarland	600 Honda	20.11.9	112.07	1995
Race	Ricky Mitchell	600 Yamaha	1.21.54.0	110.56	1995

Senior
Lap	Jason Griffiths	750 Honda	20.06.6	112.57	1991
Race	Jason Griffiths	750 Honda	1.22.12.2	110.15	1991

Classic races

500 c.c
Lap	Bob Heath	499 Seeley	21.12.5	106.74	1997
Race	Bob Heath	499 Seeley	1.25.19.2	106.13	1997

350 c.c.
Lap	Bill Swallow	349 Aermacchi	22.08.6	102.23	1996
Race	Bill Swallow	349 Aermacchi	1.29.00.4	101.73	1996

250 c.c.
Lap	Bob Jackson	250 Suzuki	22.26.1	100.90	1996
Race	Bob Jackson	250 Suzuki	1.30.50.1	99.68	1996

Adrian Archibald (600 Vent Axia Honda), current outright Manx Grand Prix lap record holder.

The Travelling Marshals

Left: Albert Moule checks the problem on A. Henthorn's early Gold Star at Parliament Square. As he was posted as a retirement, it must be assumed that the problem was terminal.

Below: A Manx Norton may not be the ideal tool for a travelling marshal, but Geoff Duke used one in 1956. Geoff is seen here at Braddan Bridge.

Left: Dennis Margan hustles his Gold Flash through Cronk ny Mona in 1953. Dennis was invited to be a marshal, but was required to provide his own transport!

Below: 'Kipper' Killip takes a BSA Lightning round the Gooseneck. 1998 sees the end of Kipper's travelling marshal duties, which started in 1960.

INDEX OF RIDERS 1983 - 1997
Key to Abbreviations

S. Senior Manx Grand Prix; S(N). Senior Newcomers; S(Sn.). Senior Snaefell; J. Junior Manx Grand Prix; J(N). Junior Newcomers; J(Sn.). Junior Snaefell; L. Lightweight; Cl. Classic

R. Retired; D. Disqualified; Ex. Excluded; N.F. Non-finisher; F. Finisher *The figures equal the position at end of race.*

Adams, Mark
1987 S/N. 34 Suzuki
Adams, Sean
1990 L/N.R. Suzuki
Adams, Stewart
1994 S/Cl.45 Rickman Weslake
1994 J/Cl.26 Norton
Adams, Richard
1989 S/Cl.R. Velocette
1990 S/Cl.34 Velocette
1991 S/Cl.R. Norton
1993 S/Cl.23 Norton
1996 S/Cl.28 Norton
1996 J/Cl.16 Norton
Aiken, Alex G.
1983 J.R. Yamaha
1983 S.R. Moto Guzzi
1988 S.53 Suzuki
1989 S.28 Yamaha
1990 S.52 Suzuki
1992 S.52 Suzuki
1993 S.24 Yamaha
1995 S.R. Yamaha
1996 J.58 Yamaha
1996 S.29 Yamaha
1997 J.48 Yamaha
1997 S.R. Yamaha
Ainley, Tony M.
1997 S/Cl.53 Velocette
Ainslie, Anthony
1983 L/Cl. 3 Ducati
1983 S.60 Triumph
1985 J/Cl.10 Ducati
1986 J/Cl.7 Ducati
1987 J/Cl.5 Ducati
1988 J/Cl.9 Ducati
Aitkin, Eddie I.
1997 J/N.8 Honda
Akerman, Derek
1984 S.R. Yamaha
1986 S.65 Yamaha
Alexander, Andy J. P.
1987 S/Cl.20 Triumph
1988 S/Cl.R. Triumph
Alexander, Brian
1991 S/Cl.40 Seeley
1992 S/Cl.30 Seeley
Alexander, Ian C.
1983 L/N.R. Yamaha
1983 L.65 Yamaha
1984 S.58 Suzuki
Alexander, Ian C.
1985 S/Cl.R. Vincent
1987 S/Cl.R. Vincent
Allan, Derek J.
1983 J.10 Yamaha
1983 L.33 Yamaha
1984 J.R. Yamaha
1984 S.23 Dawson Yamaha
1987 J.10 Yamaha
1991 S.R. B.S.A.
1995 J/Cl.R. Aermacchi
Allan, Robbie C.
1984 J/Cl.23 Ducati
1985 S/Cl.R. B.S.A./Ducati
1986 S/Cl.19 B.S.A./Ducati
1987 J/Cl.16 B.S.A./Ducati
1988 S/Cl.R. Ducati
1988 S/Cl.R. Ducati/B.S.A.
1989 S/Cl.40 Seeley
1989 J/Cl.R. Ducati
1990 J/Cl.R. Greeves
1990 S/Cl.14 Seeley Weslake
1992 S/Cl.R. Seeley Weslake
1992 S/Cl.25 Weslake
1992 J/Cl.20 Ducati

1993 S/Cl.R. Rickman Weslake
1993 J/Cl.18 Ducati
1995 S/Cl.R. Norton Weslake
1995 J/Cl.R. Ducati
1996 S/Cl.10 Norton Weslake
1996 J/Cl.R. Manx Norton
1997 S/Cl.R. Nourish Weslake
Allan, Vic
1991 J/Cl.R. Ducati
1992 S/Cl.R. Seeley Weslake
1993 S/Cl.R. Seeley
1993 J/Cl.37 Greeves
Allen, Mike R. M.
1984 J/N.3 Kawasaki
1987 S.16 Suzuki
Allen, Steve
1987 S/N.8 Suzuki
1988 S.2 Yamaha
Alexander, Brian
1993 S/Cl.34 Seeley
Allison, Mark
1993 J/N.9 Honda
1993 J.36 Honda
Alton, Rob
1997 J/N.R. Honda
Anderson, Eric
1985 J/Cl.18 Ducati
1986 J/Cl.26 Ducati
1988 J/Cl.36 Ducati
Anderson, Hugh R.
1985 S/Cl.R. Matchless
Anderson, Roy
1989 S/N.R. Suzuki
1990 S.3 Yamaha
Anderson, Tony
1986 J/N.10 Yamaha
1987 J.R. Yamaha
1988 L.7 Yamaha
1989 L.R. Yamaha
Anderton, Terry R.
1988 S/Cl.54 Velocette
Andrews, Richard J.
1983 J.R. Yamaha
Angold, Chris
1987 J/N.8 Yamaha
1990 J.48 Kawasaki
1990 L.36 Kawasaki
Antill, Tim
1995 S/Cl.R. Metisse
1995 J/Cl.30 Seeley
1996 S/Cl.R. NRE Weslake
1997 J/Cl.R. Petty Manx
1997 J/Cl.R. Seeley 7R
Antoni, Charlie
1985 L/N.R. Yamaha
1985 L.25 Yamaha
Appleton, Brian
1983 S.R. Suzuki
1984 S.16 Suzuki
1985 S.23 Suzuki
1986 S.14 Suzuki
1987 S.11 Suzuki
1988 S.39 Suzuki
1989 S.R. Suzuki
1990 S.30 Suzuki
1991 S.30 Suzuki
1992 S.23 Harris Kawasaki
1993 S.R. Suzuki
1994 S.28 Yamaha
1996 S.52 Yamaha
1997 S.63 Yamaha
Archibald, Adrian
1995 J/N.5 Honda
1995 S.10 Honda
1996 J.2 Vent Axia Honda
1996 L.2 Vent Axia Honda

Armer, Joss
1994 L/N.5 Honda
1994 L.R. Honda
1994 J.35 Honda
1995 J.36 Honda
1995 L.16 Honda
Armes, Phil W.
1984 L/N.1 Yamaha
1984 L.12 Yamaha
Armstrong, George
1983 J/Cl.R. Ducati
1983 S.R. Sparton
Armstrong, Graham J.
1983 J.28 Yamaha
1984 J.R. Yamaha
1984 L.R. Yamaha
1985 J.22 Yamaha
1985 L.R. Armstrong
1986 J.R. Yamaha
1986 S.R. Yamaha
1987 S.R. Suzuki
Armstrong, Ian
1995 J/N.8 Honda
1995 S.15 Honda
Armstrong, John S.
1985 S/Cl.11 Norton
1986 S.59 Triumph
1987 S.61 Triumph
1988 S/Cl.21 Triumph
Armstrong, Mark
1990 J/N.R. Yamaha
Ashby, Roger
1989 J/Cl.39 A.J.S.
1992 S/Cl.52 Matchless
1992 J/Cl.22 A.J.S.
1993 J/Cl.R. A.J.S.
1994 J/Cl.25 A.J.S.
1994 S/Cl.R. Matchless
1995 S/Cl.37 Norton
1995 J/Cl.27 A.J.S.
1996 S/Cl.R. Norton
1996 J/Cl.18 A.J.S.
1997 S/Cl.R. Norton
1997 J/Cl.R. A.J.S.
Ashford, John
1994 L/N.6 Padgett Honda
1994 L.R. Padgett Honda
Atkins, Alan
1983 J.4 Yamaha
1983 S.R. Yamaha
Atkinson, Chris
1983 J.43 Yamaha
Auckland, David
1987 S/Cl.29 Norton
1988 S/Cl.12 Norton
Ayles, Martin R.
1988 L/N.12 E.M.C.
1988 L.31 E.M.C.
1989 J.R. Yamaha
1989 L.11 Honda
1990 L.R. Honda
1990 L.12 Honda

Babb, Gerry
1988 J/Cl.R. Honda
1989 L/Cl.R. Honda
Bacon, Andy N.
1988 S/N.R. Yamaha
1996 L/Cl.11 Suzuki
1996 L.43 Yamaha
1997 L/Cl.18 Suzuki
Bacon, Chris J.
1983 L/Cl.8 Fahron

1984 J.53 Fahron
1984 L.35 Fahron
1987 S.R. Kawasaki
Baddeley, Ian
1995 J/N.30 Honda
1995 J.71 Honda
1997 S.70 Honda
Baird, John
1983 L.41 Yamaha
1988 S/N.24 Suzuki
Bairstow, Richard
1991 L/N.15 Suzuki
1991 L.49 Suzuki
1993 S/Cl.42 Matchless
1995 L.41 Yamaha
1997 L/Cl.21 Suzuki
1997 L.35 Yamaha
Baker, Ian
1996 J/N.13 Honda
Baker, John R.
1983 L.46 Yamaha
1984 L.54 Yamaha
1985 J.R. Yamaha
1987 J.R. Yamaha
1987 L.37 Yamaha
1989 J.30 Yamaha
1989 L.38 Yamaha
Baldock, Geoff E.
1986 J/N.R. Yamaha
1986 L.R. Yamaha
1988 S.7 Yamaha
1989 S.9 Yamaha
Baldwin, Mark
1990 L/N.2 Kawasaki
1990 L.19 Kawasaki
1991 J.4 Honda
1991 L.4 Honda
1992 J.2 Yamaha
1992 L.1 Yamaha
1993 S/Cl.12 Aermacchi
1993 J/Cl.2 Aermacchi
1994 J/Cl.R. Aermacchi
1994 S/Cl.5 Petty Manx
Balmain, Paul
1997 L/N.8 Honda
Bandeen, Chad
1985 S/Cl.29 Norton
Bannister, Simon
1987 S/N.43 Suzuki
Barber, Mark
1992 L/N.7 Kawasaki
1992 L.38 Kawasaki
Bardwell, Bob J.
1987 L/N.R. Suzuki
1987 L.40 Suzuki
1988 J.36 Suzuki
1988 L.17 Suzuki
1989 S.23 Suzuki
1990 S.22 Crooks Suzuki
1991 S.8 Crooks Suzuki
1992 S.11 Crooks Suzuki
1993 S.9 Crooks Suzuki
1994 S.7 Crooks Suzuki
1995 J.R. Honda
Barker, Nigel
1987 S/N.30 Suzuki
1991 S. Kawasaki
1992 S.65 Kawasaki
1996 L.46 Yamaha
Barnett, Peter
1995 S/N.1 Honda
1996 J.22 Honda
1996 S.19 Honda
Barnett, Sandra
1993 J/N.5 Honda
1993 S.15 Honda
1995 J/C.R. Greeves

Barrett, David
1994 J/Cl.35 Ducati
Barrett, Paul
1989 S/Cl.R. Norton
1992 S/Cl.R. Aermacchi
Barron, Gerald
1983 L/N.10 Yamaha
1983 L.41 Yamaha
1984 J.R. Yamaha
1984 L.13 Rotax
1985 J.35 Yamaha
1985 L.31 Rotax
1986 L.18 Rotax
Bartling, Simon
1983 S/N.R. Yamaha
1983 L.56 Yamaha
Barton, Chris J.
1986 J/N.R. Yamaha
1988 J.R. Armstrong
Barton, John A.
1988 J/Cl.21 Aermacchi
1989 J/Cl.12 Metisse
1989 L.19 Rotax
Barton, Nigel
1989 J.R. Yamaha
1989 S.1 Honda
Bas, Ray
1995 J/N.24 Honda
1995 S.51 Honda
1996 J.33 Honda
1996 S.38 Honda
Bassett, Andy
1983 L.7 Yamaha
1985 J.19 Yamaha
1985 S.27 Kawasaki
1986 J.13 Harris Yamaha
1986 L.12 Harris Yamaha
1987 J.13 Yamaha
1987 L.9 Yamaha
1988 J.R. Yamaha
1988 L.11 Yamaha
1989 J.3 Yamaha
1989 L.8 Yamaha
1990 J.6 Yamaha
1990 L.16 Yamaha
Batchelor, Steve
1989 S/N.17 Suzuki
Bates, David
1986 S/Cl.R. Triumph
1987 S/Cl.34 Triumph
Bateson, Andrew
1986 S/N.R. Suzuki
Bateson, Peter
1983 L.43 Maxton
1984 L.3 Maxton
Batty, John
1991 S.58 Yamaha
Batty, Neil
1991 J/N.9 Yamaha
Baxter, Michael W.
1983 J.R. Yamaha
1984 L.49 Yamaha
1984 J.49 Yamaha
1984 L.R. Yamaha
1985 J.40 Yamaha
1985 L.R. Yamaha
1986 J.R. Yamaha
1989 L.39 Kawasaki
1990 L.46 Kawasaki
1993 J/Cl.R. Ducati
Beale, Peter
1983 L.43 Yamaha
1985 J.38 Yamaha
1985 S.28 Yamaha
1986 J.R. Yamaha
1986 S.R. Yamaha

1987 J.21	Yamaha	**Bell, Peter**		**Binch, David**		1997 S.R.	Honda	**Borthwick, Neil J.**		
1987 S.3	Yamaha	1993 L/N.1	Yamaha	1989 J/N.7	Yamaha	**Blacklock, Alan**		1987 L/N.R.	Armstrong	
1988 S.22	Yamaha	1993 L.R.	Yamaha	1990 J.38	Yamaha	1989 S/Cl.R.	Norton	1987 L.49	Armstrong	
1989 S.R.	Honda	**Bellerby, Mike J.**		1990 L.24	Yamaha	1991 S/Cl.48	Norton	1988 S.R.	Suzuki	
1990 S.16	Yamaha	1988 S/Cl.53	B.S.A.	1991 J.R.	Yamaha	1991 J/Cl.26	Ducati	**Bowden, Robert**		
1992 J.R.	Yamaha	1991 S/Cl.50	Norton	1991 L.20	Yamaha	**Blackstock, Peter J.**		1990 L/N.7	Gower Power	
1992 S.R.	Yamaha	1992 S/Cl.R.	Norton	1992 J.R.	Yamaha	1988 S/Cl.R.	Norton	1994 J.66	Honda	
1993 J.25	Honda	1992 J/Cl.30	Norton	1992 L.28	Yamaha	**Blackwell, Dean**		1994 L.32	Honda	
1993 S.R.	Yamaha	1993 S/Cl.54	Norton	1993 J.22	Yamaha	1987 L/N.10	Yamaha	**Bowers, Ned**		
1994 J.R.	Yamaha	1994 S/Cl.38	Norton	1993 L.R.	Yamaha	1988 L.35	Yamaha	1983 S.37	Ducati	
1994 S.23	Yamaha	1994 J/Cl.27	Norton	1994 J.20	Yamaha	1989 J.36	Yamaha	1984 S.39	Ducati	
1995 J.9	Kawasaki	**Bennallick, Alan**		1994 L.12	Yamaha	1989 L.48	Yamaha	1985 S.35	Suzuki	
1995 S.19	Beale Yamaha	1989 S/N.4	Yamaha	1997 J.43	Yamaha	1990 J.61	Honda	1987 S.33	Yamaha	
Beattie, Garry E. R.		1990 S.17	Yamaha	1997 L.9	Yamaha	1991 J.R.	Honda	1988 S.61	Yamaha	
1983 L/N.R.	Yamaha	1991 S/Cl.R.	Triumph	**Bingley, Tony**		1991 L.R.	Honda	1989 S.36	Suzuki	
1983 L.20	Yamaha	1991 S.2	Honda	1992 S/Cl.40	Seeley	1992 J.32	Yamaha	**Bowers, Ricky**		
1984 J.R.	Yamaha	1992 S.1	Honda	1993 S/Cl.51	Seeley	1992 S/Cl.27	Yamaha	1990 S/Cl.44	Triumph	
1984 L.R.	Yamaha	**Bennett, Garry**		1995 S/Cl.35	Seeley	1993 J.23	Yamaha	1990 S.67	Triumph	
1985 L.11	Gregory Yamaha	1989 J/N.3	Yamaha	1995 S/Cl.44	Seeley G50	1993 L.17	Yamaha	1991 S/Cl.45	Triumph	
1986 J.18	Yamaha	1990 J.50	Kawasaki	1996 S/Cl.52	Seeley G50	1994 J.31	Yamaha	1991 S.52	Triumph	
1986 L.R.	Greg Yamaha	1992 J.41	Honda	1997 S/Cl.R.	Seeley G50	1994 L.13	Yamaha	1992 S/Cl.44	Triumph	
1987 J.R.	Yamaha	1992 S.44	Honda	**Birkinshaw, Martin**		1995 J.31	Yamaha	1992 S.R.	Triumph	
Beattie, Nigel G.		**Bennett, Steven A.**		1986 L/N.R.	Armstrong	1995 L.15	Yamaha	1993 S/Cl.48	Triumph	
1997 L/N.2	Yamaha	1985 L/N.17	Ducati	1986 L.R.	Armstrong	**Blackwell, Ian R.**		1993 S.43	Triumph	
1997 L.R.	MB Mannin Yamaha	**Bennett, Vincent**		1987 L.6	Armstrong	1987 L/N.12	Yamaha	1994 S/Cl.R.	Dresda Triumph	
Beattie, Stephen		1989 S/N.12	Yamaha	1987 J.R.	Yamaha	**Bladon, Chris**		1994 S.R.	RN Trident	
1995 S/N.R.	Yamaha	1990 S.34	Yamaha	1988 L.R.	Armstrong	1983 J/Cl.7	Aermacchi	1995 S/Cl.46	Dresda Triumph	
Beck, Alan		1991 S.17	Yamaha	1988 J.R.	Armstrong	1984 J/Cl.4	Aermacchi	1995 S.66	RN Trident	
1992 L/Cl.R.	Suzuki	**Bennie, Alan**		1989 J.R.	Armstrong	1985 J/Cl.R.	Aermacchi	1996 S/Cl.R.	RN Trident	
1993 L/Cl.5	Suzuki	1995 J/N.19	Honda	1989 L.R.	Armstrong	1985 J.R.	Yamaha	1997 S.86	RN Trident	
1994 L/Cl.R.	Suzuki	1995 S.34	Honda	1990 J.11	Rotax	1986 J/Cl.14	Aermacchi	**Bowie, David**		
1995 L/Cl.3	Suzuki	1996 J.20	Honda	1990 S.7	Honda	1986 J.36	Yamaha	1989 S/N.3	Suzuki	
Beck, Robin		1996 S.22	Honda	**Birks, Charles**		1987 J/Cl.4	Aermacchi	1989 L.18	Kawasaki	
1986 S/N.R.	Honda	1997 J.16	Honda	1984 L/N.R.	Yamaha	1987 J.R.	Yamaha	1990 J.12=	Kawasaki	
1987 S.R.	Honda	1997 S.34	Honda	**Birtles, D.**		1987 J/Cl.13	Aermacchi	1990 S.10	Honda	
1988 S.R.	Honda	**Bentley, Bob**		1987 S/N.9	Suzuki	1988 J.32	Yamaha	**Bowler, Roger D.**		
Beck, Simon A.		1985 L/N.R.	Yamaha	**Birtwistle, Alan**		1989 J/Cl.9	Aermacchi	1988 S/Cl.R.	Metisse	
1988 S/N.4	Honda	**Bernier, Robert L.**		1994 J.52	Yamaha	**Blair, Alistair**		1990 S/Cl.28	Matchless	
1989 S.13	Honda	1983 J.R.	Yamaha	1994 L.22	Yamaha	1983 S/N.R.	Honda	1991 S/Cl.47	Matchless	
1990 S.1	Honda	1985 J.R.	Yamaha	1996 J.R.	Honda	1985 S.44	Honda	1993 S/Cl.39	Matchless	
Bedlington, J. David		**Bevan, Colin**		1996 S.61	Honda	**Blake, Mike R.**		1994 S/Cl.R.	Matchless	
1983 J/Cl.10	Aermacchi	1991 S/Cl.R.	Honda	1997 S.88	Honda	1987 J/N.7	Yamaha	1995 S/Cl.R.	Matchless	
1985 J/Cl.8	Aermacchi	1991 J/Cl.R.	Honda	1997 S.75	Honda	1987 L.39	Yamaha	**Bowran, Kevin A.**		
Begg, George N.		**Bevington, Steven J.**		**Black, Bruce**		1988 L.26	Yamaha	1986 L/N.7	Yamaha	
1985 S/Cl.R.	Norton	1986 J/N.R.	Yamaha	1995 J/N.11	Kawasaki	1988 J.43	Yamaha	1987 L.R.	Yamaha	
1988 S/Cl.38	Norton	1987 J.31	Yamaha	1995 S.25	Kawasaki	1989 J.18	Yamaha	**Boyd, Ian**		
Beharrell, Trevor		1988 J.R.	Yamaha	**Black, David**		1989 L.9	Yamaha	1988 J/Cl.40	Aermacchi	
1983 J/Cl.15	A.J.S.	1990 J.9	Yamaha	1988 S/N.9	Suzuki	1992 J.38	Yamaha	1989 J/Cl.18	Aermacchi	
1984 J/Cl.R.	A.J.S.	1991 J.R.	Yamaha	1989 S.17	Suzuki	1992 L.R.	Yamaha	**Boyd, Sammy N.**		
1986 J/Cl.11	A.J.S.	1991 L.R.	Yamaha	1990 J.20	Suzuki	1993 J.43	Yamaha	1989 J/Cl.R.	Aermacchi	
1987 J/Cl.8	A.J.S.	**Bezzant, Alan**		1990 S.31	Suzuki	1993 L.27	Yamaha	**Boyes, Stephen**		
1988 J/Cl.18	A.J.S.	1984 L/N.8	Yamaha	1991 S.25	Honda	1997 L.38	Yamaha	1983 J.R.	Yamaha	
1988 S/Cl.R.	Matchless	1984 L.48	Yamaha	1992 J.21	Yamaha	**Blease, Tim S.**		1983 S.7	Padgett Yamaha	
1989 J/Cl.38	A.J.S.	1985 L.40	Yamaha	1992 S.12	Honda	1983 J/Cl.27	Aermacchi	1996 L/Cl.R.	Suzuki	
1989 S/Cl.13	Matchless	1986 J.R.	Yamaha	1993 J.17	Honda	**Boast, Peter**		**Boyle, Adam**		
1990 S/Cl.R.	Matchless	1986 L.37	Yamaha	1994 S/N.5	Yamaha	1983 J.R.	Yamaha	1991 J/N.6	Yamaha	
1991 S/Cl.14	Matchless	1987 J.R.	Yamaha	1994 J.13	W&C Yamaha	1983 S.28	Yamaha	**Boyle, Tony**		
1991 S/Cl.R.	A.J.S.	1988 J.R.	Yamaha	1994 S.44	Yamaha	**Boland, Robert**		1995 L/N.9	Yamaha	
1992 S/Cl.18	Matchless	1988 S.R.	Yamaha	1994 S.R.	Kawasaki	1984 J/N.7	Yamaha	1995 L.43	Yamaha	
1992 J/Cl.18	A.J.S.	1989 L.R.	Yamaha	1996 S/Cl.40	Norton	**Bone, Dave**		1996 S.63	Honda	
1993 S/Cl.R.	Matchless	1990 J.R.	Yamaha	1996 J.13	Honda	1995 J/N.32	Honda	**Bradley, Pat**		
1993 J/Cl.17	A.J.S.	1990 S.68	Yamaha	1996 S.23	Honda	1995 S.62	Honda	1991 L/N.R.	Kawasaki	
Bell, Derek		1991 J.44	Yamaha	1997 S/Cl.14	Norton	1996 J.82	Honda	1994 J.64	Yamaha	
1983 L.28	Yamaha	1992 J.65	Yamaha	1997 J.9	Honda	1996 S.80	Honda	1994 L.29	Yamaha	
Bell, Graeme		1993 J.47	Kawasaki	1997 S.14	Honda	1997 J.R.	Yamaha	1995 J.46	Yamaha	
1987 S/N.35	Suzuki	1993 S.R.	Kawasaki	**Blackburn, Neil**		**Bool, Rich**		1995 L.29	Kawasaki	
1988 S.65	Yamaha	1994 J.57	Yamaha	1983 S/Cl.21	Triumph	1984 J/Cl.32	Ducati	**Bradley, Ray R.**		
1989 S.64	Suzuki	1994 S.43	Yamaha	1983 L.66	Yamaha	1985 J/Cl.25	Ducati	1985 J/Cl.14	Ducati	
Bell, Karl		1995 J.59=	Kawasaki	1984 S/Cl.19	Triumph	1986 J/Cl.R.	Ducati	1986 J/Cl.R.	Aermacchi	
1990 J/N.R.	Yamaha	1995 S.41	Kawasaki	1984 L.45	Yamaha	1987 J/Cl.30	Ducati	1987 J/Cl.7	Aermacchi	
1991 J.41	Spondon	1996 J.R.	Kawasaki	1985 S/Cl.22	Seeley Triumph	1988 J/Cl.45	Ducati	1989 J/Cl.7	Aermacchi	
1991 L.50	Kawasaki	1996 S.45	Kawasaki	1985 L.R.	Yamaha	1989 L/Cl.15	Ducati	**Bradshaw, Peter I.**		
1992 J.59	Spondon Yamaha	1997 J.64	Kawasaki	1986 S/Cl.27	Triumph	1990 L/Cl.18	Ducati	1988 S/N.20	Honda	
1992 L.31	Yamaha	1997 S.65	Kawasaki	1986 L.38	Yamaha	1991 L/Cl.22	Ducati	1989 S.40	Honda	
1993 J.45	Spondon Yamaha	**Biddulph, Bob**		1987 S/Cl.32	Triumph	1994 J/Cl.32	Ducati	1990 S.15	Honda	
1993 L.32	Spondon Yamaha	1984 S/Cl.32	Velocette	1987 L.42	Yamaha	1995 J/Cl.40	Ducati	1992 S.41	Honda	
1994 J.43	Spondon Yamaha	1985 J/Cl.R.	A.J.S.	1990 S/Cl.R.	Seeley Triumph	1996 J/Cl.R.	Ducati	**Brammon, Patrick**		
1994 L.16	Spondon Yamaha	1986 J/Cl.30	A.J.S.	1991 S/Cl.46	Seeley Triumph	**Boothby, Graham C.**		1989 S/N.10	Suzuki	
1995 J.27	Spondon Yamaha	1987 J/Cl.34	A.J.S.	1993 S/Cl.61	Seeley Triumph	1986 S/Cl.23	Norton	**Branch, Brodie**		
1995 L.13	Spondon Yamaha	1988 S/Cl.32	A.J.S.	1994 S/Cl.49	Seeley Triumph	1987 S/Cl.28	Norton	1996 J/N.4	Honda	
1996 J.50	Spondon Yamaha	1988 S/Cl.27	Matchless	1994 L.48	Yamaha	**Borland, Colin**		**Brandon, Geoff H.**		
1996 L.R.	Spondon Yamaha	1989 J/Cl.35	A.J.S.	**Blackley, Gordon**		1994 S/N.R.	Harris KTM	1988 S/Cl.R.	Norton	
1997 J.83	Spondon Yamaha	1989 J/Cl.49	Seeley	1996 J/N.1	Honda	1996 J.89	Yamaha	**Brasier, David**		
1997 L.R.	Spondon Yamaha	1990 J/Cl.R.	A.J.S.	1997 J.37	Honda	1996 S.85	Yamaha	1996 L/Cl.R.	Aermacchi	

1997 L/Cl.23	Ducati	1997 J.94	Ducati
Bray, Chris		1997 S.59	Ducati
1984 S/N.4	Yamaha	**Brown, Craig**	
1985 S.50	Kawasaki	1996 S/N.8	Honda
1986 S.22	Yamaha	1996 S.R.	Honda
1987 S.22	Yamaha	**Brown, David**	
1990 S.18	Yamaha	1995 S.35	Honda
1991 S.R.	Suzuki	1996 S.40	Honda
1996 S.12	CAM Kawasaki	**Brown, David E**	
1997 S.16		1983 J.R.	Yamaha
Breeze, Colin S.		1983 L.19	Yamaha
1990 S/N.5	B.S.A.	1984 J.11	Yamaha
1997 J/Cl.R.	Aermacchi	1984 S.31	Ducati
1997 S.10	Kawasaki	1985 J.R.	Yamaha
Brew, Allan		1985 S.36	Ducati
1994 S/Cl.R.	B.S.A. Gold Star	1987 S.R.	Yamaha
1995 S/Cl.31	Seeley G50	**Brown, David**	
1996 S/Cl.23	Seeley G50	1995 J.54	Honda
1997 S/Cl.23	Seeley G50	1996 J.48	Honda
Brew, Andrew P.		**Brown, Gordon**	
1983 S/N.8	Suzuki	1986 J.R.	Yamaha
1983 L.35	Yamaha	1986 S.R.	Yamaha
1984 J.31	Yamaha	1987 J.R.	Yamaha
1984 L.R.	Yamaha	1988 J.R.	Yamaha
1985 J.36	Brew Yamaha	1988 L.R.	Rotax
1985 L.R.	Brew Yamaha	**Brown, Michael**	
1986 J.16	Brew Yamaha	1993 S/N.1	Kawasaki
1986 L.32	Brew Yamaha	1993 S.10	Kawasaki
1987 J.37	Brew Yamaha	1994 J.28	Yamaha
1987 L.16	Padgett Yamaha	1994 S.4	Kawasaki
1992 S.46	Honda	**Brown, Michael D.**	
1994 S/Cl.R.	B.S.A.	1995 S/N.3	Honda
1994 L.44	Honda	1995 S.R.	Honda
Brewer, Robert		**Brown, Pete**	
1986 J/Cl.6	Honda	1989 J/Cl.32	A.J.S.
Bridges, Michael J.		1989 S/Cl.34	Norton
1987 J/N.R.	Yamaha	**Brown, Ron**	
Brind, Martin D.		1983 L.R.	Maxton Yamaha
1987 S/N.37	Suzuki	1984 L.29	Maxton Yamaha
Britton, Richard		1985 L.29	Maxton Yamaha
1997 J/N.1	Honda	1985 L.29	Maxton Yamaha
1997 J.R.	Schimmel Honda	1986 S.66	Honda
1997 S.8	Schimmel Honda	1987 J/Cl.24	Ducati
Brooker, A. Bill		1988 J/Cl.49	Ducati
1987 S/Cl.19	Matchless	1990 J/Cl.29	Ducati
1990 S/Cl.R.	Matchless	1991 S/Cl.31	Norton
1991 S/Cl.27	G50 Matchless	**Brown, Shaun**	
1992 S/Cl.R.	Matchless	1993 L/N.2	Honda
1994 S/Cl.25	Matchless	1993 L.R.	Honda
1996 S/Cl.R.	G50 Matchless	1993 L.R.	Honda
1997 S/Cl.R.	Matchless	1994 J.25	Yamaha
Brophy, James		1994 L.R.	Yamaha
1991 S/N.8	Honda	**Brown, Steve**	
Brough, Dave		1991 L/N.22	Yamaha
1994 J/N.R.	Maxton Yamaha	1991 L.42	Yamaha
Brough, David G.		**Brown, Wattie**	
1985 S/N.R.	Seeley Suzuki	1983 J.R.	Yamaha
Broughton, Greg		1988 S/Cl.R.	Velocette
1986 J/N.R.	Yamaha	1989 S/Cl.17	Velocette
1986 L.23	Yamaha	1990 S/Cl.19	Velocette
1987 J.R.	Yamaha	1990 S.14	Suzuki
1987 L.20	Yamaha	1991 S/Cl.R.	B.S.A.
1988 J.R.	Yamaha	1991 J/Cl.R.	B.S.A.
1988 S.14	Yamaha	1991 S.R.	Suzuki
1989 J.6	Yamaha	1992 S.3	Honda
1989 S.16	Yamaha	1993 L/Cl.2	Suzuki
1990 J.10	Yamaha	1993 S.3	Honda
1991 J.2	Yamaha	1994 L/Cl.3	Crooks Suzuki
1991 L.3	Yamaha	1994 S/Cl.R.	Seeley G50
1992 J.R.	Yamaha	1995 S/Cl.R.	Seeley G50
1992 L.R.	Yamaha	1995 L/Cl.R.	Crooks Suzuki
1993 J.2	Yamaha	1996 S/Cl.R.	Seeley G50
1993 L.3	Yamaha	1997 S/Cl.R.	Petty Manx
1994 J.16	Yamaha	1997 L/Cl.R.	Suzuki
1994 L.4	Yamaha	**Brownrigg, Brian**	
1995 J.R.	DTR Yamaha	1983 J.37	Yamaha
1995 L.R.	DTR Yamaha	1983 S.44	Honda
1996 L.11	DTR Yamaha	1984 L.38	Honda
Brown, Andrew		1986 S.57	Honda
1993 S/N.8	Ducati	1987 L.38	Special
1994 S.R.	Ducati	**Bruce, I. Matty**	
1995 J/Cl.39	Ducati	1997 S/N.4	Ducati
1995 S.57	Ducati	1997 S.69	Honda
1996 S.50	Ducati	**Bryant, Ian J.**	

1983 J/Cl.25	Aermacchi	1997 S/Cl.20	Seeley G50
Buckley, Richard J.		1997 J/Cl.21	Norton
1986 S/N.19	Ducati	**Byrne, Peter J. W.**	
1987 S.R.	Ducati	1985 L/N.18	Ducati
1990 J.60	Kawasaki	1986 J/Cl.13	Ducati
1990 L.49	Kawasaki	1987 J/Cl.7	Ducati
Bullock, James S.		1988 J/Cl.17	Ducati
1988 S/N.R.	Suzuki	1989 J/Cl.6	Ducati
1988 L.49	Yamaha	1990 J/Cl.R.	Ducati
Burbridge, John K.		**Byrne, Trevor**	
1988 S/N.14	Suzuki	1986 S/N.R.	Kawasaki
1989 S.R.	Suzuki	1987 S.28	Honda
Burden, Richard		1988 S.61	Suzuki
1984 L/N.R.	Harris Rotax		
1984 L.20	Harris Rotax	**Cadger, William F.**	
1985 L.6	Honda	1983 J/Cl.R.	B.S.A.
Burden, Trevor		1985 J/Cl.R.	B.S.A.
1988 S/N.R.	Suzuki	1986 S/Cl.25	B.S.A.
1989 S.30	Suzuki	1987 S/Cl.R.	Seeley
1990 S.35	Honda	**Cain, Anthony M.**	
1993 S.R.	Honda	1997 J/N.R.	Yamaha
1994 S.37	Honda	**Cain, Michael A.**	
1995 J.53	Honda	1987 J/Cl.10	Suzuki
1995 S.37	Honda	1988 L/Cl.2	Suzuki
1996 S.42	Honda	1989 L/Cl.R.	Suzuki
1997 J.60	Honda	1990 L/Cl.R.	Aermacchi
1997 S.50	Honda	1991 L/Cl.R.	Aermacchi
Burgess, Peter		1992 L/Cl.4	Aermacchi
1991 L/N.14	Suzuki	**Cain, Mike**	
1991 L.43	Suzuki	1995 J/N.26	Kawasaki
1992 J.54	Suzuki	1995 S.R.	Kawasaki
1992 L.R.	Suzuki	**Cale, Andrew C.**	
1993 J.49	Yamaha	1985 S/N.8	Kerby Honda
1993 S.40	Yamaha	1986 S.R.	Yamaha
1994 J.R.	Yamaha	1988 S.R.	Honda
1994 L.R.	Yamaha	**Callon, Kevin**	
1995 J.R.	Yamaha	1992 J/N.7	Yamaha
1995 L.23	Yamaha	1992 S.39	Yamaha
1996 L.56	Yamaha	**Callow, Stephen**	
1996 L.23	Yamaha	1983 S.55	Suzuki
1997 J.53	Honda	1986 S.64	Honda
1997 S.66	Honda	1992 L.45	Yamaha
Burke, James M.		**Calvin, Geoffrey**	
1985 J/N.6	Yamaha	1993 L/N.R.	Yamaha
Burman, Alan P.		**Calwell, Andy**	
1983 L.27	Yamaha	1997 J/N.R.	Honda
1984 J.R.	Yamaha	**Calwell, David**	
1984 L.16	Yamaha	1995 J/N.31	Honda
1985 S.54	Kawasaki	1996 J.R.	Honda
1986 S.42	Kawasaki	**Camp, Tim**	
1987 S.36	Honda	1994 J/N.3	Honda
1990 S.65	Kawasaki	1994 J.36	Honda
1991 L/Cl.R.	Ducati	**Campbell, Des**	
1993 J.R.	Honda	1992 J/N.R.	Suzuki
Burton, Paul		1993 J.R.	Honda
1995 L/Cl.R.	Yamaha	1993 S.R.	Honda
1996 J.95	Yamaha	**Campion, Mark**	
1996 L.44	Yamaha	1993 S/N.2	Kawasaki
1997 L.44	Yamaha	1993 S.11	Kawasaki
Bushell, Steve W.		**Campion, Sean**	
1987 S/N.5	Yamaha	1988 J/N.13	Yamaha
1988 S.17	Yamaha	**Cannell, Chris**	
1989 S.R.	Yamaha	1990 J/N.8	Yamaha
Butcher, Andy		1990 L.58	Yamaha
1995 J/N.22	Honda	1991 L.14	Yamaha
1995 S.49	Honda	1992 J.R.	Yamaha
Buxton, Anita		1992 L.29	Yamaha
1996 J/N.14	Yamaha	1993 J.18	Yamaha
Byers, Eddie		1993 L.6	Yamaha
1984 S/N.1	Suzuki	1994 J.5	Yamaha
1984 S.21	Suzuki	1995 J.5	Pergola Yamaha
1985 S.12	Suzuki	1995 L.2	Pergola Yamaha
1986 S.R.	Suzuki	1996 J.18	Pergola Yamaha
1987 S.R.	Suzuki	1996 L.4	Pergola Yamaha
1988 S.R.	Suzuki	1997 J.R.	Pergola Yamaha
1989 S.R.	Kawasaki	1997 L.4	MB Pergola Honda
1991 S/Cl.33	Matchless	**Cannell, Chris**	
1992 S/Cl.R.	G50 Seeley	1991 J.20	Yamaha
1993 S/Cl.27	Seeley	1994 L.6	Yamaha
1994 S/Cl.19	Seeley	**Cannell, Pamela**	
1995 S/Cl.17	Seeley G50	1996 L/N.5	Honda
1995 J/Cl.24	Norton	**Cannon, Rick**	
1996 S/Cl.46	G50 Seeley	1983 J.R.	Yamaha
1996 J/Cl.26	Norton	1983 L.23	Yamaha

Capes, Derek E. E.			
1983 J/Cl.13	Aermacchi		
Carey, Colin			
1989 S/N.26	Ducati		
1990 J.R.	Kawasaki		
Carr, Stephen			
1997 J/N.14	Honda		
Carswell, Gary			
1991 J/N.R.	Yamaha		
1991 S.R.	Yamaha		
1994 J.46	Yamaha		
1994 S.36	Yamaha		
1995 J.37	Yamaha		
1995 S.16	Kawasaki		
1995 L.R.	Yamaha		
1996 J.21	Yamaha		
1996 S.5	Kawasaki		
1997 J.5	Kawasaki		
1997 S.1	W&C Kawasaki		
Carter, Larry			
1989 S/N.18	Honda		
Carthy, Stephen			
1983 S/N.1	Suzuki		
Cartright, Robert A.			
1985 L/N.14	Yamaha		
1985 L.33	Yamaha		
1986 S.R.	Honda		
Casey, Mike			
1985 S/N.3	Suzuki		
1986 J.R.	Yamaha		
1986 S.41	Suzuki		
1987 J.R.	Yamaha		
1988 J.R.	Yamaha		
1988 L.R.	Yamaha		
1991 S.R.	Yamaha		
1992 J.R.	Yamaha		
1992 S.R.	Honda		
1993 S.8	Honda		
1994 S.5	Honda		
1995 J.4	Bullock Honda		
1995 S.1	Bullock Honda		
Castle, David E.			
1987 S/N.24	Suzuki		
1988 J.39	Yamaha		
1988 S.26	Suzuki		
1989 S.5	Yamaha		
1990 S.8	Honda		
Cathcart, Alan			
1985 S/Cl.8	Paton		
Catterall, Paul			
1986 S/N.R.	Kawasaki		
1993 J.60	Honda		
1993 S.53	Honda		
1994 J.68	Honda		
1994 S.46	Kawasaki		
1995 J.62	Honda		
1995 S.R.	Honda		
1997 J.96	Honda		
1997 S.92	Honda		
Cavenby, Gerald A.			
1988 S/N.17=	Yamaha		
Cawte, Tony M.			
1997 L/N.5	Yamaha		
Chadwick, Ricky			
1997 J/N.11	Honda		
Chalkley, Gary			
1996 J/N.15	Yamaha		
1997 S.81	Honda		
Chalmers, Ian			
1989 L/N.13	Kawasaki		
Chambers, David			
1992 L/N.4	Yamaha		
1992 L.20	Yamaha		
1993 L.R.	Yamaha		
Chambers, Tom			
1989 J/Cl.R.	Ducati		
1989 S.R.	Kawasaki		
Chamley, Alan			
1995 L/N.12	Honda		
1996 L.35	Honda		
1997 L.33	Honda		
Chapman, Frank, J.			
1984 S/N.11	Laverda		
Chapman, Roy			

1985 L/N.2 Symbol Yamaha	1983 S.54 Spondon	1995 S/Cl.18 Norton	**Coogan, Brian**	**Courtney, James, P. J.**	
1985 L.R. Symbol Yamaha	1984 J.R. Spondon Yamaha	1996 S/Cl.R. Norton	1995 J/N.12 Kawasaki	1984 J/N.R. Yamaha	
1986 J.R. Yamaha	1984 S.R. Spondon Yamaha	1996 S/Cl.R. Norton	1995 S.32 Kawasaki	1985 J.R. Yamaha	
1986 S.6 Honda	1985 J.50 Spondon	1997 S/Cl.R. Norton	**Cook, Peter**	1986 L.R. Yamaha	
Chappell, Mac	1985 S.69 Spondon	**Collard, William J.**	1983 J.19 Yamaha	1987 L.51 Yamaha	
1989 S/N.7 Suzuki	1986 J.41 Spondon	1983 S/Cl.R. Norton	1983 L.R. Armstrong	1988 J.R. Yamaha	
Charlesworth, Keith R.	1986 L.33 Yamaha	1983 J.R. Yamaha	1984 J.R. Yamaha	1988 L.47 Yamaha	
1983 J.R. Yamaha	1987 J.R. Spondon	1984 J.R. Norton	**Cooke, Steve J.**	1989 J.R. Yamaha	
1984 J.R. Yamaha	1987 J.50 Spondon	1984 J/Cl.R. Norton	1987 L/N.5 Yamaha	**Cowan, Gary**	
1984 L.30 Yamaha	1988 J.R. Spondon	1986 S/Cl.12 Norton	1987 L.33 Yamaha	1984 J/N.1 Yamaha	
Cheers, Eric	1989 J.47 Spondon	1987 S/Cl.14 Norton	1988 S.31 Suzuki	**Cowin, Peter D.**	
1988 J/Cl.41 Aermacchi	1989 L.50 Spondon	1988 J/Cl.26 Norton	1989 J.33 Suzuki	1985 J/N.R. Yamaha	
1988 S/Cl.28 Aermacchi	1991 J/Cl.32 Ducati	1988 S/Cl.14 Norton	1989 L.24 Suzuki	1986 J.R. Yamaha	
1989 J/Cl.26 Aermacchi	1992 J/Cl.R. Ducati	1989 S/Cl.R. Norton	1990 J.R. Yamaha	**Cox, Peter M.**	
1990 J/Cl.18 Aermacchi	1993 J/Cl.R. Ducati	1990 S/Cl.R. Norton	1990 L.41 Yamaha	1983 J.33 Yamaha	
1991 S/Cl.44 Aermacchi	1994 J/Cl.R. Ducati	1991 S/Cl.22 Seeley	1991 J.17 Suzuki	1983 S.40 Yamaha	
1991 L/Cl.13 Suzuki	1995 J/Cl.42 Ducati	1992 S/Cl.21 Seeley	1991 S.22 Suzuki	1984 J.42 Yamaha	
1992 S/Cl.50 Aermacchi	1997 J/Cl.44 Ducati	1993 S/Cl.30 Seeley	1992 J.R. Honda	1984 S.44 Yamaha	
1992 L/Cl.17 Suzuki	**Clay, Stuart**	1994 S/Cl.R. Seeley	1993 J.R. Honda	1986 J.34 Yamaha	
1993 S/Cl.53 Aermacchi	1987 S/N.31 Yamaha	1996 S/Cl.33 Seeley G50	1993 L.14 Honda	1986 S.54 Yamaha	
1993 L/Cl.R. Suzuki	**Clegg, Nigel J.**	**Collingswood, Steve**	**Coole, Andy**	1987 J.36 Yamaha	
Chorley, Neil	1987 L/N.11 Maxton	1996 J/N.15 Kawasaki	1989 J/N.6 Yamaha	**Craine, Billy A.**	
1983 J/N.18 Yamaha	1987 L.R. Maxton Yamaha	1996 S.R. Kawasaki	1989 J.45 Yamaha	1987 J/N.1 Yamaha	
1983 L.55 Yamaha	**Clements, Alan**	**Collister, David**	1989 L.R. Yamaha	1987 L.3 Yamaha	
1984 J.43 Yamaha	1991 L/N.12 Suzuki	1992 L/N.R. Yamaha	1990 J.R. Yamaha	1988 J.R. Yamaha	
1984 L.26 Yamaha	1991 J.36 Mowlem Suzuki	1992 L.14 Yamaha	1990 L.17 Yamaha	1988 S.R. Yamaha	
1985 J.26 Yamaha	1991 L.R. Mowlem Suzuki	**Collister, Sean**	1991 J.R. Yamaha	1991 J.R. Yamaha	
1985 L.R. Yamaha	**Clements, Steve J.**	1983 J.5 Yamaha	1991 L.R. Yamaha	1992 J.R. Kawasaki	
1986 J.R. Yamaha	1987 J/N.5 Yamaha	1983 L.3 Yamaha	1993 J.R. Padgett Honda	1992 S.56 Kawasaki	
1986 S.R. Yamaha	1988 J.25 Yamaha	1984 J.R. Yamaha	**Coonie, David**	1993 S.R. Kawasaki	
1987 J.33 Yamaha	1989 J.29 Yamaha	1984 L.R. Yamaha	1994 L/N.R. Yamaha	**Crane, Terry J.**	
1987 S.R. Yamaha	1989 L.42 Yamaha	1985 J.R. Yamaha	1994 L.45 Yamaha	1988 S/N.16 Suzuki	
1988 J.21 Yamaha	1990 J.28 Yamaha	1985 L.R. Yamaha	**Cooper, David**	**Craven, Mark**	
1988 L.36 Yamaha	1990 L.27 Yamaha	1986 J.R. Yamaha	1984 J.R. Yamaha	1989 S/N.24 Suzuki	
1989 J.26 Yamaha	1991 J.46 Yamaha	1986 L.5 Yamaha	1985 J.32 Yamaha	1989 J.R. Yamaha	
1990 S.39 Suzuki	1991 L.R. Yamaha	Cowin Padgett Yamaha	1986 J.24 Yamaha	1990 S/Cl.R. Triumph	
Christian, Dennis	1992 J.42 Yamaha	1987 J.R. Yamaha	1986 S.R. Yamaha	**Crawford, Jeremy**	
1986 S/Cl.17 Norton	1992 L.13 Yamaha	1987 L.32 Honda	1987 J.16 Yamaha	1983 J/N.6 Maxton Yamaha	
1989 J/Cl.27 Ducati	1993 J.R. Yamaha	1988 J.7 Yamaha	1987 S.37 Yamaha	1984 S.R. Yamaha	
1989 S/Cl.R. Norton	1997 J.76 Yamaha	1989 J.R. Yamaha	1989 J.28 Yamaha	**Crawford, Steve**	
1990 S/Cl.R. Norton	1997 L.22 Yamaha	1990 L.21 Yamaha	1990 J.22 Yamaha	1986 J/Cl.17 Honda	
1993 S/Cl.R. Velocette	**Clowes, Simon**	1990 J.21 Yamaha	1991 J.R. Yamaha	1987 S.39 Suzuki	
1993 J/Cl.R. Ducati	1990 L/N.R. Yamaha	1990 L.7 Yamaha	1991 L.37 Yamaha	1988 S.R. Suzuki	
Christie, Sandy	**Clutterbuck, Len**	1991 J.14 DTR Yamaha	1992 J.39 Yamaha	**Crellin, John**	
1989 S/N.9 Yamaha	1994 S/Cl.46 Seeley	1991 L.17 DTR Yamaha	**Copland, Martin L.**	1983 J.13 Yamaha	
1991 S.R. Yamaha	1995 S/Cl.34 Seeley G50	1992 J.16 DTR Yamaha	1983 L/N.17 Yamaha	1983 S.8 Suzuki	
Clark, Colin	1995 J/Cl.31 Seeley 7R	1992 L.6 DTR Yamaha	1983 L.61 Yamaha	**Cretney, David**	
1991 S.53 Suzuki	1996 S/Cl.42 Seeley G50	1993 J.13 Yamaha	**Corbett, Andy**	1983 S/Cl.13 Honda	
1992 S.R. Suzuki	1996 J/Cl.30 Seeley 7R	1993 L.9 Yamaha	1990 J/N.2 Yamaha	1983 S.62 Honda	
1993 S.R. Suzuki	1997 S/Cl.27 Seeley 7R	1994 J.15 MB Yamaha	**Corbett, Harry**	1993 J.R. Honda	
1994 S.R. Suzuki	1997 S/Cl.R. Seeley 7R	1994 L.10 MB Yamaha	1989 L/N.2 Honda	**Croft, James**	
1995 S.65 Suzuki	**Coates, Ivan**	1995 J.25 DTR MB Yamaha	**Corlett, Phil**	1997 L/N.6 Suzuki	
1996 S.R. Suzuki	1996 J/Cl.31 Ducati	1995 L.11 Mannin Honda	1991 J/N.2 Yamaha	**Cronshaw, John**	
Clark, Gloria	1997 S/Cl.R. Petty Manx	1996 J.38 DTR MB Yamaha	1991 S.18 Yamaha	1983 S/Cl.R. B.S.A.	
1989 S/N.31 Ducati	1997 J/Cl.R. Honda	1996 L.9 DTR MB Yamaha	1992 J.9 Yamaha	1984 S/Cl.4 Unity B.S.A.	
1991 S.55 Yamaha	**Coates, Richard**	1997 J.46 DTR MB Yamaha	1992 S.6 Yamaha	1985 S/Cl.R. Unity B.S.A.	
1992 J.64 Yamaha	1983 J.R. Yamaha	1997 L.13 DTR Yamaha	**Costello, Maria**	1986 S/Cl.R. Unity B.S.A.	
Clark, Gordon	1983 L.2 Cotton	**Colville, Stephen D.**	1996 S/N.10 Honda	1987 S/Cl.R. Unity B.S.A.	
1990 S/N.R. Suzuki	**Cohen, Derek**	1983 S/N.R. Yamaha	1996 S.73 Honda	**Crooks, Eddie**	
Clarke, Colin A.	1996 J/N.R. Yamaha	**Colvin, Rob E.**	1997 J.77 Honda	1983 L/Cl.R. Suzuki	
1984 S/N.R. Suzuki	1996 L.17 Yamaha	1984 L/N.R. Yamaha	1997 S.57 Honda	1984 J/Cl.6 Crooks Suzuki	
1986 S.61 Suzuki	1997 J.55 Yamaha	1986 J.37 Yamaha	**Cotgrave, Geoffrey**	1985 J/Cl.R. Crooks Suzuki	
1987 S.R. Suzuki	1997 L.12 Yamaha	1986 S.R. Yamaha	1983 S.R. Yamaha	1986 J/Cl.R. Crooks Suzuki	
1988 S.70 Suzuki	**Coleman, John**	1987 J.41 Yamaha	1984 L.31 Yamaha	1987 J/Cl.9 Crooks Suzuki	
Clarke, Martin	1984 J.R. Yamaha	1994 J.71 Yamaha	1985 L.14 Yamaha	1988 L/Cl.3 Crooks Suzuki	
1994 J/N.9 Honda	1984 S.R. Yamaha	1994 L.33 Yamaha	1986 J.29 Yamaha	**Crooks, Martin B.**	
1994 J.R. Honda	1986 J.R. Yamaha	1995 L.34 Yamaha	1986 L.19 Yamaha	1984 L/N.R. Crooks Suzuki	
1996 L.42 Honda	1986 S.56 Yamaha	1996 J.77 Yamaha	1987 J.R. Yamaha	1985 J.44 Crooks Suzuki	
Clarke, Nigel	1987 J.46 Yamaha	1996 L.R. Yamaha	1987 L.23 Yamaha	1985 L.23 Crooks Suzuki	
1988 L/N.8 Rotax	1988 J.R. Yamaha	1997 J.75 Honda	**Coulter, Alex**	1986 J.35 Crooks Suzuki	
1988 L.21 Rotax	1989 J.R. Yamaha	1997 L.28 Yamaha	1986 L/N.R. Waddon Rotax	1986 L.27 Crooks Suzuki	
1989 J.R. Armstrong	1990 J.44 Yamaha	**Connor, Michael**	1986 L.R. Waddon Rotax	1987 S.56 Suzuki	
1989 L.R. Rotax	1991 J.R. Yamaha	1995 S/N.10 Kawasaki	1987 L.45 Rotax Waddon	1988 J.40 Suzuki	
1990 J.26 Spondon	1992 J.R. Yamaha	1995 S.61 Kawasaki	1988 L.R. Rotax	1988 L.23 Suzuki	
1990 L.20 Armstrong	1993 J.R. Yamaha	1996 J.72 Yamaha	1991 S.62 Suzuki	1989 L.26 Suzuki	
Clarke, Paul	**Colin, Mike**	1996 S.R. Yamaha	1992 S.R. Suzuki	1990 L/Cl.9 Crooks Suzuki	
1989 S/Cl.46 Ducati	1987 S/Cl.24 Norton	1997 J.56 Yamaha	1993 S.50 Suzuki	1992 L/Cl.6 Crooks Suzuki	
Clay, Arthur	1988 S/Cl.R. Norton	1997 S.71 Norton	1994 S.R. Suzuki	1993 L/Cl.9 Crooks Suzuki	
1989 J.R. Yamaha	1989 S/Cl.R. Norton	**Conway, Tony**	1995 S.68 Suzuki	**Cross, Tony**	
1989 L.41 Suzuki	1990 S/Cl.17 Norton	1984 J.R. Yamaha	**Courtney, James**	1994 J/N.8 Honda	
1990 J.R. Yamaha	1991 S/Cl.R. Norton	1985 J.R. Yamaha	1992 L/N.1 Yamaha	1994 S.25 Honda	
1990 L.43 Kawasaki	1992 S/Cl.28 Norton	1985 L.R. Yamaha	1992 J.10 Yamaha	**Crossan, Adrian**	
Clay, Barry	1993 S/Cl.R. Norton	1986 J.40 Yamaha	1992 L.3 Yamaha	1994 L/N.14 Kawasaki	
1983 J.45 Yamaha	1994 S/Cl.22 Norton	1987 L.46 Yamaha	1993 J.1 Honda	1994 L.39 Kawasaki	
		1996 J.92 Yamaha	1993 L.1 Honda		

172 The History of the Manx Grand Prix 1923-1998

1995 J.65	Kawasaki	1995 J.32	Honda	1988 S.69	Yamaha	1995 J/N.9	Honda	1989 L/Cl.11	Honda
1995 L.35	Kawasaki	1996 J.45	Honda	1991 S.51	Suzuki	1996 J.9	FC Moore Honda	1989 S.65	Honda
1996 J.44	Honda	**Cutts, John**		**Davis, John**		1996 S.21	FC Moore Honda	1990 L/Cl.7	Honda
1996 S.39	Honda	1995 L/N.6	Yamaha	1985 S/N.2	Yamaha	1997 J.14	Honda	1992 J/Cl.R.	Honda
1997 J.34	Honda	1995 L.36	Yamaha	1986 J.R.	Yamaha	1997 S.21	Honda	1995 L/Cl.R.	Suzuki
1997 S.41	Honda	1996 J.71	Yamaha	1986 S.R.	Suzuki	**Dickenson, John**		1997 L/Cl.R.	Suzuki
Crossland, Philip		1996 L.25	Yamaha	1987 S.26	Suzuki	1983 J.R.	Yamaha	**Donovan, Jeff**	
1986 S/Cl.22	Matchless	1997 J.R.	Yamaha	**Davis, Ken**		1983 L.R.	Maxton yamaha	1987 S/N.26	Yamaha
Crowe, Robert		1997 L.17	Yamaha	1995 J/N.18	Chaintec Honda	1984 J.40	Yamaha	**Doughty, Jeremy**	
1990 L/N.R.	Suzuki	**Cutts, Richard H.**		1995 S.38	Chaintec Honda	1984 L.R.	Yamaha	1996 J/N.R.	Honda
1991 J.29	Suzuki	1983 S/Cl.5	Seeley	1996 J.53	Chaintec Honda	1985 S.41	Suzuki	**Douglas, Alan**	
1991 L.R.	Suzuki	1983 S.15	Kawasaki	1996 S.R.	Chaintec Honda	**Diffey, Mark**		1983 J.R.	Yamaha
1992 J.47	Yamaha	1984 S/Cl.R.	Matchless	1997 J.17	Chaintec Honda	1994 S/N.2	Kawasaki	1983 S.23	Yamaha
1992 L.R.	Yamaha	1985 S/Cl.4	Matchless	1997 S.24	Honda	1994 S.R.	Kawasaki	1984 S.47	Moto Guzzi
Crowson, William		1986 S/Cl.10	Matchless	**Davy, Graham R.**		**Diver, Tommy**		1985 S.R.	Kawasaki
1988 S/Cl.40	Seeley	1987 S/Cl.5	Matchless	1983 S/N.7	Suzuki	1994 L/N.3	Yamaha	1986 J.10	Yamaha
Cruddas, Stirling		1988 J/Cl.15	Aermacchi	**Dawson, Robin**		1994 L.17	Yamaha	1986 S.13	Yamaha
1996 S/N.9	Honda	1988 S/Cl.7	Seeley	1991 S/N.18	Suzuki	**Dixon, Barry**		**Dowey, Steve**	
1996 S.55	Honda	1989 S/Cl.R.	Seeley	1991 S.61	Suzuki	1988 J/N.3	Yamaha	1983 S.4	Yamaha
1997 J.78	Honda	1990 S/Cl.6	Seeley Matchless	**Dawson, Wally**		1989 J.R.	Yamaha	1984 S.R.	Yamaha
1997 S.64	Honda	1991 S/Cl.7	Seeley Matchless	1987 S/Cl.R.	Norton	1990 S.19	Honda	1986 S.R.	Honda
Cudworth, Neil		1992 S/Cl.R.	Matchless	1988 S/Cl.R.	Norton	1991 S.5	Honda	1987 S.2	Yamaha
1983 J.12	Yamaha			1989 S/Cl.R.	Norton	1992 J.27	Honda	**Downes, Christopher J.**	
1983 S.22	Yamaha	**Dalgleish, Michael N.**		1990 S/Cl.16	Norton	1992 S.R.	Honda	1987 S/N.19	Suzuki
1984 J.10	Yamaha	1985 J/N.R.	Yamaha	1991 S/Cl.13	Norton	**Dixon, Keith**		1988 S.R.	Suzuki
1984 S.18	Yamaha	**Dalton, J. Al**		1992 S/Cl.9	Norton	1993 S/Cl.45	Seeley	1990 S.24	Yamaha
1985 J.R.	Yamaha	1987 S/N.3	Yamaha	1993 S/Cl.11	Norton	1994 S/Cl.24	Seeley G50	1991 S.10	Honda
1985 S.18	Yamaha	1988 S.4	Suzuki	1994 S/Cl.56	Norton	1994 J/Cl.R.	Seeley 7R	1992 J.28	Honda
1986 J.R.	Yamaha	**Daly, John Jnr**		1995 S/Cl.R.	Norton	1995 S/Cl.21	Seeley	1992 S.9	Honda
1987 J.14	Yamaha	1983 S/Cl.R.	B.S.A.	1996 S/Cl.17	Norton	1995 J/Cl.21	Seeley	**Downey, Geoff**	
1987 S.40	Yamaha	1985 S/Cl.R.	B.S.A.	1997 S/Cl.R.	Norton	1996 S/Cl.30	Seeley G50	1997 J/N.3	Honda
1988 J.16	Yamaha	**Darby, Anthony**		**Day, Paul**		1996 J/Cl.20	Seeley 7R	1997 J.44	Honda
1988 L.22	Yamaha	1989 S/N.R.	Yamaha	1988 L/N.6	Yamaha	1997 S/Cl.52	Seeley	**Dowty, Bob K.**	
1989 J.14	Yamaha	1990 S.66	Kawasaki	**Day, Chris**		1997 J/Cl.16	Seeley	1994 J/N.R.	Yamaha
1989 L.28	Yamaha	**Darvell, Tim**		1990 S/N.3	Suzuki	**Dobson, Charlie E.**		1994 J.72	Yamaha
1990 J.19	Yamaha	1996 L/N.R.	Yamaha	1991 S.R.	Suzuki	1986 S/Cl.17	Matchless	1995 L/Cl.12	Dowty Suzuki
1990 L.22	Yamaha	1996 L.47	Yamaha	1992 J.7	Yamaha	1988 J/Cl.24	A.J.S.	1995 L.50	Yamaha
1991 J.7	Yamaha	**Darwood, Brian D.**		1992 S.2	Kawasaki	1988 S/Cl.19	Matchless	1996 L/Cl.R.	Suzuki
1991 L.9	Yamaha	1987 S/N.28	Honda	**Day, William H.**		1989 J/Cl.R.	A.J.S.	1996 L.39	Yamaha
1993 J.34	Yamaha	1988 S.56	Honda	1983 L/Cl.9	Greeves	1989 S/Cl.R.	Seeley	1997 L/Cl.16	Suzuki
1993 L.22	Yamaha	**Davies, Andy**		**Daynes, Mark J.**		1990 J/Cl.R.	A.J.S.	1997 L.47	Yamaha
1994 J/Cl.R.	Aermacchi	1987 S.64	Yamaha	1986 S/N.R.	Kawasaki	1990 S/Cl.36	Matchless	**Drage, Al**	
1995 J.47	Yamaha	**Davies, David C. E.**		1987 S.54	Yamaha	1992 S/Cl.27	Seeley G50	1984 S/N.14	Yamaha
1995 L.19	Yamaha	1986 S/Cl.6	Matchless	1989 S.63	Yamaha	1993 S/Cl.R.	Matchless	**Drane, Matt**	
1996 J.57	Yamaha	**Davies, John D.**		1991 S.R.	Suzuki	1993 J/Cl.26	A.J.S.	1986 J/N.R.	Yamaha
1996 L.19	Yamaha	1983 J.R.	RDV	1993 J.66	Rotax	1994 J/Cl.R.	A.J.S.	**Duckett, Paul**	
1997 J.52	Yamaha	1983 S.R.	Suzuki	**Dearden, David J.**		1994 S/Cl.R.	Matchless	1996 S/N. 1	Kawasaki
1997 L.16	Yamaha	1984 J.R.	Yamaha	1983 L/N.3	Yamaha	1995 S/Cl.29	Matchless	1996 S.R.	Kawasaki
Cummins, Billy L.		1984 S.R.	Suzuki	1983 L.15	Yamaha	1995 J/Cl.28	A.J.S.	1997 S.23	Kawasaki
1984 J/N.12	Yamaha	1985 J.13	Yamaha	1984 S/Cl.10	B.S.A.	**Dock, Dave**		**Duckett, Vin F.**	
1984 L.R.	Suzuki	1985 S.10	Suzuki	1984 J.R.	Armstrong	1983 L/Cl.7	Ducati	1990 S/Cl.R.	Seeley Matchless
1985 J.45	B & G Yamaha	1986 J.26	Yamaha	1984 L.8	Armstrong	1983 J.48	Aermacchi	1991 S/Cl.18	Seeley Matchless
1985 S.R.	B & G Yamaha	1986 L.4	Yamaha	1985 J/Cl.5	Aermacchi	1983 L.R.	Ducati	1991 J/Cl.R.	Aermacchi
1986 J.R.	Yamaha	1987 J.R.	Yamaha	1986 J/Cl.R.	Aermacchi	1984 J/Cl.25	Aermacchi	1992 S/Cl.R.	Matchless
1986 S.35	Yamaha	1987 L.4	Padgett SPC	1987 S/Cl.7	Seeley	1984 L.43	Ducati	1992 J/Cl.R.	Aermacchi
1987 J.R.	Yamaha	1988 J.R.	Yamaha	1988 J/Cl.7	Aermacchi	1985 J/Cl.28	Aermacchi	1993 S/Cl.25	Matchless
1987 L.R.	Yamaha	1988 L.8	Padgett Spl	1988 S/Cl.43	Seeley	1985 S.74	Vincent	1993 J/Cl.10	Aermacchi
1988 J.R.	Yamaha	1989 J.R.	Yamaha	**De Kruz, Kevin**		1986 J/Cl.24	Aermacchi	1994 S/Cl.14	Seeley Matchless
1989 J.R.	Yamaha	1989 L.10	Padgett	1983 L/N.4	Yamaha	1987 J/Cl.R.	Aermacchi	1994 J/Cl.37	Drixton Aermacchi
1989 S.45	Yamaha	1990 J.16	Honda	1983 L.9	Yamaha	1988 L/Cl.7	Ducati	1995 S/Cl.15	Seeley Matchless
1990 J.37	Yamaha	1990 L.8	Honda	1984 L.6	Yamaha	1989 L/Cl.7	Ducati	1995 J/Cl.11	Drixton Aermacchi
1990 L.26	Rotax	1991 J.6	Padgett Honda	**Dedman, Paul**		1990 L/Cl.13	Ducati	1996 S/Cl.16	Seeley Matchless
1992 L/Cl.15	Suzuki	1991 L.30	Padgett Honda	1995 S.5	Kawasaki	1990 S/Cl.49	Aermacchi	1996 J/Cl.R.	Seeley 7R
1993 L/Cl.R.	Suzuki	1992 L/Cl.R.	Padgett Yamaha	1996 J.R.	Kawasaki	1991 S/Cl.R.	G50 Matchless	1997 J/Cl.24	Seeley Matchless
1993 S.35	Yamaha	1993 L/Cl.R.	Yamaha	1996 S.6	Kawasaki	1991 L/Cl.15	Ducati	1997 J/Cl.13	Seeley 7R
1994 L/Cl.R.	Suzuki	1995 J.22	Padgett Honda	**De Groome, Ken A.**		1992 S/Cl.35	G50 Matchless	**Duffy, Frank**	
1996 S.81	Yamaha	1995 S.R.	Padgett Honda	1986 S/Cl.32	Matchless	1992 L/Cl.16	Ducati	1988 L/N.10	Yamaha
1997 L.27	Yamaha	1996 J.41	Padgett Honda	1987 S/Cl.R.	Matchless	1993 S/Cl.35	G50	1988 L.24	Yamaha
Cunliffe, Carl N.		1996 S.10	Padgett Yamaha	1988 S/Cl.49	Velocette	1993 L/Cl.15	Ducati	1989 L.29	Honda
1984 J/N.R.		1997 S.15	Padgett Yamaha	1989 S/Cl.39	Matchless	1994 J/Cl.13	Aermacchi	**Dugdale, Alan**	
1985 J.41	Yamaha	**Davies, Nigel**		1991 S/Cl.R.	Matchless	1994 S/Cl.29	G50	1986 S/Cl.1	Cowles Matchless
1985 S.R.	Yamaha	1991 J.25	Suzuki	1992 S/Cl.R.	Matchless	1995 S/Cl.36	Rickman Metisse	1987 S/Cl.R.	Cowles Matchless
Curry, Fred		1991 S.15	Suzuki	1993 S/Cl.59	Matchless	1995 J/Cl.19	Aermacchi	1988 S/Cl.4	Cowles Matchless
1983 J/Cl.16	Aermacchi	1993 J.D.	Honda	1995 S/Cl.R.	Matchless Spl	1996 S/Cl.56	Rickman G50	1989 L/Cl.R.	Aermacchi
1983 J.39	Yamaha	1993 S.1	Norton	1997 S/Cl.R.	Matchless	1996 J/Cl.21	Aermacchi	1989 S/Cl.R.	Matchless
1983 S.26	Kawasaki	**Davies, Paul A.**		**Denison, Mike**		1997 S/Cl.24	Rickman G50	1990 S/Cl.R.	Yamaha
1984 J/Cl.14	Aermacchi	1983 J.R.	Yamaha	1992 S/N.R.	Trident	1997 J/Cl.39	Ducati	1990 S/Cl.R.	Matchless
1984 J.47	Yamaha	1983 S.R.	Yamaha	**Dettloff, Kerry B.**		**Donan, John**		1991 S/Cl.R.	Seeley
1984 S.60	Kawasaki	1984 J.R.	Cowles Yamaha	1985 J/N.R.	Yamaha	1988 S/N.25	Kawasaki	1991 L/Cl.R.	N.S.U.
1985 J/Cl.R.	Yamaha	1985 J.7	Yamaha	1986 S.31	Yamaha	**Donovan, Brian P.**		**Dugdale, Ian**	
1985 J.31	Yamaha	1985 S.6	Suzuki	1988 S.35	Yamaha	1986 J/Cl.31	Honda	1987 J/N.R.	Maxton
1985 S.24	Suzuki	**Davis, Andy**		1989 S.41	Yamaha	1987 S.75	Honda	1987 L.7	Honda
Cutler, Lee		1986 J/N.14	Honda	1991 S.23	Yamaha	1988 L/Cl.8	Honda	1988 J.11	Maxton
1995 J/N.13	Honda	1987 S.64	Yamaha	**Dey, Steve**		1988 L.50	Rotax	1988 L.2	Honda

1990 J.R.	Maxton Yamaha	1997 S/Cl.33	Norton	**Emberton, Ian**		1995 J/Cl.14	Aermacchi	1987 J/Cl.16	Suzuki
1990 L.6	Maxton Yamaha	1997 J/Cl.R.	Norton	1989 S/N.30	Honda	1996 S/Cl.R.	Aermacchi	1988 L/Cl.R.	Suzuki
1992 J.R.	Yamaha	**Edmonds, Rick G.**		**English, Glen**		1996 J/Cl.17	Aermacchi	1989 L/Cl.6	Suzuki
1992 S.48	Suzuki	1986 L/N.3	Eddison Yamaha	1991 J/Cl.R.	Ducati	1997 S/Cl.46	Aermacchi	1990 L/Cl.15	Suzuki
1993 S.41	Suzuki	1986 L.20	Eddison Yamaha	1993 J/Cl.R.	Ducati	1997 J/Cl.R.	Aermacchi	1991 L/Cl.12	Suzuki
Duncan, Tony		**Edwards, Allan J.**		1994 S/Cl.R.	Matchless	**Faragher, Robert W.**		1992 L/Cl.24	Suzuki
1989 L/N.9	Yamaha	1988 J/Cl.19	Ducati	1995 S/Cl.R.	Beale Matchless	1988 J.R.	Yamaha	**Fleming, Peter**	
1989 J.R.	Yamaha	**Edwards, Keith R.**		1995 S/Cl.R.	Aermacchi	**Fargher, Chris**		1988 J/Cl.37	Aermacchi
1989 L.31	Yamaha	1983 J.26	Yamaha	1996 S/Cl.R.	Beale Matchless	1983 J.1	Yamaha	1988 S/Cl.R.	Aermacchi
1990 J.56	Yamaha	1984 J.32	Yamaha	1996 J/Cl.6	Aermacchi	1983 L.1	Rotax	1990 J/Cl.20	Aermacchi
1990 L.32	Kawasaki	1986 J.R.	Yamaha	**English, Paul W.**		**Farmer, Mark**		1991 J/Cl.R.	Ducati
1991 J.R.	Yamaha	1987 J.24	Yamaha	1984 L/N.3	Yamaha	1985 S/N.6	Honda	**Fletcher, David P.**	
1991 L.27	Kawasaki	1988 J.49	Yamaha	1984 S.63	Yamaha	**Farrimond, Mark D.**		1983 L/Cl.R.	Ossa
1992 J.12	Yamaha	1990 S/Cl.R.	Velocette	**Eorton, Garry**		1983 J/N.R.	Yamaha	**Flockhart, Charles A.**	
1992 L.R.	Yamaha	1992 S/Cl.R.	Velocette	1994 J.53	Yamaha	1983 L.47	Yamaha	1984 S/N.10	Ducati
1993 J.R.	Yamaha	**Edwards, Laurence G**		**Evans, Brad**		**Farrington, Bob**		1985 S/Cl.23	Velocette
1994 J.2	Yamaha	1983 J/N.15	Yamaha	1992 L/N.R.	Yamaha	1992 S/N.6	Suzuki	1985 S.68	Triumph
1994 J.2	Yamaha	1984 J/Cl.13	Ducati	**Evans, John G**		1993 S.R.	Suzuki	1986 S/Cl.R.	Velocette
1995 J.1	MSR Yamaha	1984 J.26	Yamaha	1983 L.59	Yamaha	1996 S.67	Honda	1986 S.67	Triumph
1995 L.1	MSR Yamaha	1987 S.48	Yamaha	**Evans, Paul W.**		1997 J.87	Honda	1987 S/Cl.23	Velocette
Duncan, Uel K.		1989 L.16	Suzuki	1986 S/N.10	Ducati	1997 S.73	Honda	1987 S.R.	Triumph
1997 J/N.6	Honda	1996 L.26	Spondon Yamaha	**Evans, Ray**		**Faulkner, Chris**		1988 J/Cl.48	B.S.A.
1997 J.38	Honda	**Edwards, Mark**		1983 J.32	Maxton	1983 J.R.	Yamaha	1988 S/Cl.R.	Velocette
Dunlop, Joey		1993 L/N.R.	Yamaha	1983 L.29	Yamaha	1983 S.3	Yamaha	1989 J/Cl.33	Velocette
1993 L/Cl.R.	Aermacchi	1993 J.30	Yamaha	1984 J.24	Maxton	**Faulkner, John H.**		1989 S/Cl.20	Velocette
1994 J/Cl.2	Aermacchi	**Edwards, Mick**		1984 S.R.	Suzuki	1986 S/N.R.	Metisse Norton	1990 J/Cl.33	Velocette
Dunlop, Malcolm P.		1992 S/N.7	Yamaha	1985 J.16	Greenhall Yamaha	1987 S/Cl.17	Norton	1990 S/Cl.24	Velocette
1983 S.52	Suzuki	**Edwards, Robert**		1985 S.14	Greenhall Suzuki	1988 S/Cl.16	Norton	1991 S/Cl.R.	Velocette
Dunlop, Robert		1983 J/Cl.R.	Aermacchi	1986 J.6	Yamaha	1989 S/Cl.47	Norton	1991 L/Cl.18	Velocette
1983 J/N.1	Yamaha	**Edwards, Roy J.**		1986 S.R.	Suzuki	1990 S/Cl.18	Norton Metisse	1992 S/Cl.37	Velocette
Dunn, Mike		1987 L/N.6	Yamaha	1987 J.15	Maxton	1991 S/Cl.R.	Norton Metisse	1993 J/Cl.55	Velocette
1992 J/Cl.R.	Greeves	**Edwards, Stuart**		1987 S.34	Suzuki	1992 S/Cl.19	Norton	1993 J/Cl.35	Velocette
1993 L/Cl.R.	Suzuki	1993 J/N.6	Honda	1988 J.15	Yamaha	1994 S/Cl.R.	Rickman Metisse	**Floding, Monica**	
1996 J/Cl.R.	Greeves	1993 S.22	Honda	1988 S.R.	Yamaha	**Fegan, Adrian**		1996 L/N.4	Honda
1997 J/Cl.41	Greeves	1994 J.26	Honda	1989 J.R.	Yamaha	1993 L/N.10	Honda	1997 L.50	Yamaha
Dunne, Jonathan		1994 S.R.	Honda	1989 S.32	Yamaha	1993 L.48	Honda	**Flynn, Marc**	
1994 J/N.4	Honda	1995 J.7	Honda	**Evans, Richard V.**		**Ferguson, Euan B.**		1993 J/N.1	Honda
Durvan, Kelvin		1995 S.8	Honda	1988 L/N.14	Yamaha	1983 S/Cl.20	Norton	1993 J.D.	Honda
1983 J/N.20	Yamaha	1996 J.12	Honda	1988 L.R.	Yamaha	1985 S/Cl.R.	Norton	**Fogarty, Carl G.**	
Dutton, Trevor G.		1996 S.R.	Honda	**Evans, Russell**		1986 S/Cl.R.	Norton	1985 L/N.1	Yamaha
1985 S/N.13	Yamaha	1997 J.25	Honda	1983 S.R.	Yamaha	1990 S/Cl.40	Aermacchi	1985 L.3	Yamaha
1986 J.R.	Maxton	1997 S.19	Honda	1984 S.R.	Yamaha	1991 S/Cl.R.	Norton	**Forth, Barry J.**	
1986 S.R.	Maxton	**Edwards, Ted**		1985 S.R.	Maxton Yamaha	1991 J/Cl.R.	Aermacchi	1987 J.R.	Yamaha
Duxbury, Dave		1989 J/Cl.11	Ducati	1986 S.32	Suzuki	1992 S/Cl.R.	Norton	**Foster, Alan**	
1993 S/Cl.33	Norton	1990 J/Cl.9	Ducati	1987 S.R.	Yamaha	1992 J/Cl.32	Aermacchi	1994 S/Cl.R.	Norton Dominator
1994 S/Cl.16	Norton	1991 J/Cl.6	Aermacchi	1988 S.36	Yamaha	1993 S/Cl.R.	Norton	**Foster, Peter**	
Dyer, Lee		1993 L/Cl.16	Greeves	**Everard, Francis**		1993 J/Cl.R.	Aermacchi	1985 L/N.9	Yamaha
1991 S/N.15	Kawasaki	1994 L/Cl.7	Greeves	1988 J/N.4	Yamaha	1994 J/Cl.R.	Aermacchi	1986 S.R.	Suzuki
		1995 L/Cl.R.	Greeves	1988 J.R.	Yamaha	1994 J/Cl.53	Norton	1987 S.46	Kawasaki
East, Chris		1996 S/Cl.31	B.S.A.	**Ewles, John**		1995 S/Cl.R.	Norton	1990 J.55	Kawasaki
1987 S/Cl.12	Matchless	1997 S/Cl.R.	B.S.A.	1992 L/N.R.	Suzuki	1995 J/Cl.R.	Aermacchi	1991 J.31	Kawasaki
1988 S/Cl.12	Matchless	1997 L/Cl.10	Greeves	1992 L.35	Suzuki	1997 S/Cl.54	Seeley G50	1991 S.26	Honda
1989 S/Cl.7	Matchless	**Edwards, William L.**		1993 L.R.	Suzuki	1997 J/Cl.42	Aermacchi	1992 J.43	Honda
1990 S/Cl.10	Matchless	1983 L/N.7	Yamaha	**Eyes, Graham N.**		**Fiford, Jerry**		1992 S.27	Honda
1991 S/Cl.11	Matchless	1983 L.30	Yamaha	1997 J/N.13	Honda	1988 J/Cl.31	Ducati	1993 J.54	Yamaha
1992 S/Cl.18	Matchless	**Elder, Kidge**		1997 S.84	Honda	**Finch, Frank**		1993 S.17	Honda
1993 S/Cl.16	Matchless	1984 J/N.20	Yamaha	**Eyre, Robert**		1985 S/N.7	Suzuki	**Fowler, Neil**	
1995 S/Cl.9	Matchless	1987 S.71	B.M.W.	1987 S.R.	Suzuki	1985 S.21	Suzuki	1983 J.R.	Yamaha
1996 S/Cl.27	Matchless	**Elliott, Martin R.**				**Finney, Lee S.**		1983 S.R.	Yamaha
1996 J/Cl.R.	Seeley	1984 J/N.8	Yamaha	**Fairhurst, Damion**		1987 J/N.3	Yamaha	1984 S.R.	Yamaha
1997 S/Cl.12	Matchless	**Elliott, Steven**		1983 J.R.	Maxton	**Fisher, Mark**		**Fox, Karl G.**	
1997 J/Cl.14	Seeley	1988 L.N.4	Yamaha	1983 S.16	Maxton	1997 J/Cl.R.	Ducati	1985 L/N.6	Yamaha
East, Dave		1988 L.13	Yamaha	**Fallon, Mick**		**Fisher, Trevor**		1985 L.19	Yamaha
1988 S/Cl.R.	Velocette	1991 L.28	Mowlem Kawasaki	1992 L/N.5	Kawasaki	1995 S/N.11	Honda	1986 L.15	Yamaha
Easton, Adam B.		**Ellis, Don J.**		1992 L.40	Kawasaki	1996 J.94	Yamaha	1987 J.27	Yamaha
1983 J/Cl.28	Norton	1983 S/Cl.R.	B.S.A.	**Fallowfield, Len**		1996 S.90	Yamaha	1987 L.18	Yamaha
1985 S/Cl.24	Manx Norton	1984 J/Cl.20	B.S.A.	1984 J/Cl.15	Aermacchi	**Fitzgerald, Colm**		1988 J.R.	Yamaha
1986 J/Cl.35	Manx Norton	1985 J/Cl.25	B.S.A.	1985 J/Cl.12	Aermacchi	1995 L/N.4	Yamaha	1988 L.5	Honda
1987 J/Cl.23	Norton	1986 S/Cl.R.	B.S.A.	1986 J/Cl.15	Aermacchi	**Fitzgerald, John T**		1989 L.R.	Honda
1988 J/Cl.R.	Norton	1988 S/Cl.57	B.S.A.	1987 J/Cl.11	Aermacchi	1983 J/Cl.18	Aermacchi	1990 J.17	Honda
1988 S/Cl.R.	Norton	1993 S/Cl.R.	B.S.A.	1988 S/Cl.R.	Aermacchi	1983 S.R.	Spondon	1990 L.13	Honda
1989 J/Cl.R.	Norton	**Ellis, Steve**		1989 S/Cl.23	Aermacchi	1984 J/Cl.10	Aermacchi	1991 J.R.	Honda
1990 J/Cl.27	Norton	1997 J/N.R.	Cowles Honda	1989 J/Cl.R.	Aermacchi	1984 S.R.	Spondon Ducati	1992 J.26	Honda
1990 S/Cl.41	Norton	1997 S.4	Cowles Honda	1990 J/Cl.24	Aermacchi	1985 J/Cl.13	Aermacchi	1992 S.50	Honda
1991 S/Cl.R.	Norton	**Ellison, Karl**		1990 S/Cl.R.	Aermacchi	1986 S.34	Yamaha	1993 J.16	Honda
1991 J/Cl.R.	Norton	1987 S/N.10	Yamaha	1991 J/Cl.9	Aermacchi	1987 S.32	Suzuki	1993 S.18	Honda
1993 S/Cl.43	Norton	**Elwood, Mervyn**		1992 S/Cl.29	Aermacchi	1988 S.38	Suzuki	1995 L/Cl.13	N.S.U.
1993 J/Cl.R.	Norton	1992 S/Cl.15	Matchless	1992 J/Cl.17	Aermacchi	**Fitzsimmons, Richard A.**		1996 L/Cl.R.	Suzuki
1994 S/Cl.55	Norton	1994 J/Cl.15	A.J.S.	1993 J/Cl.39	Aermacchi	1983 L/Cl.1	Suzuki	1997 L/Cl.R.	Suzuki
1994 J/Cl.39	Norton	1994 S/Cl.R.	Matchless	1993 J/Cl.15	Aermacchi	1983 L.52	Suzuki	**Foxon, Richard**	
1995 S/Cl.30	Norton	1995 J/Cl.5	Arter Matchless	1994 J/Cl.9	Aermacchi	1984 J/Cl.11	Suzuki	1995 L/N.5	Yamaha
1995 S/Cl.23	Norton	1995 J/Cl.R.	Seeley 7R	1994 S/Cl.R.	Aermacchi	1984 L.32	Suzuki	1995 L.20	Yamaha
1996 S/Cl.37	Norton	1996 J/Cl.4	Seeley G50	1995 S/Cl.33	Aermacchi	1985 L.30	RAF Suzuki	**Franklin, Byron G.**	
1996 J/Cl.R.	Norton	1996 J/Cl.9	Seeley 7R			1986 J/Cl.19	Suzuki	1983 S/N.R.	Honda

Franklin, Colin
1984 J/N.R. Yamaha
Fraser, Calum
1993 J/N.8 Honda
1993 S.R. Honda
Fraser, Willie
1989 S/N.11 Honda
Freak, Richard J.
1983 J.43 Yamaha
1983 L.58 Yamaha
1984 S/Cl.21 Velocette
French, Ian F.
1984 L/N.7 Rotax
1984 L.R. Yamaha
1985 J.R. Yamaha
1985 L.27 Yamaha
1986 J.32 Yamaha
1986 L.R. Yamaha
1987 J.R. Yamaha
1987 L.36 Yamaha
1988 J.R. Yamaha
1989 J.R. Yamaha
Frost, Martin
1991 J/N.R. Yamaha
1991 J.R. Yamaha
Frost, Rob
1992 L/N.R. Suzuki
Fryer, Frank
1989 S.69 Suzuki
Gabbott, Bob
1989 J/Cl.R. Excelsior
1990 J/Cl.31 E.M.B.
1991 J/Cl.21 Excelsior
1994 J/Cl.30 E.M.B. Manxman
Gable, Colin C.
1987 S/N.1 Suzuki
Gaites, Brett
1983 L/Cl.4 Greeves
Gallagher, Denis
1984 J/Cl.9 Cowles A.J.S.
1989 S/Cl.R. Seeley
1990 J/Cl.4 Seeley
1990 S/Cl.R. Seeley
1991 S/Cl.R Seeley
1991 J/Cl.R. Seeley
1992 S/Cl.R. Seeley
1992 J/Cl.8 Aermacchi
1996 S/Cl.7 Seeley Weslake
1997 S/Cl.R. Seeley Weslake
1997 J/C.R. Aermacchi
Gant, Mark P.
1988 J/N.12 Honda
1989 J/Cl.31 Ducati
1989 S/Cl.43 Ducati
1990 J/Cl.R. Ducati
1990 S/Cl.48 Rickman
1991 S/Cl.34 Matchless
1991 J/Cl.22 Ducati
1993 S/Cl.65 Matchless
1993 S/Cl.34 Ducati
1995 S/Cl.R. Metisse
1996 S/Cl.60 Matchless
1997 S/Cl.45 Matchless
Gardiner, Brian
1992 S/N.2 Honda
1992 S.22 Honda
Gardner, Ashley A.
1985 J/N.1 Yamaha
1985 L.4 Waddon
Garrett, James
1984 J.R. Craig Yamaha
1984 S.20 Craig Yamaha
Garside, Mark
1996 S/N.11 Honda
Gavin, Richie
1989 S/N.15 Yamaha
1990 J.32 Suzuki
George, Alex J. S.
1992 S/Cl.11 Manx Norton
George, Owen
1987 S/N.25 Yamaha
1988 S.50 Yamaha
1989 S.42 Yamaha

1990 J.59 Kawasaki
1990 S.56 Suzuki
1991 S.R. Suzuki
Gibbon, Alan
1988 S/N.R. Suzuki
Gibson, Alex
1991 J/N.R. Honda
1992 S.55 Suzuki
Gibson, James
1983 S.R. Kawasaki
1985 S.R. Kawasaki
1987 S.R. Yamaha
Gilbert, Steve
1993 S/N.7 Honda
1994 J.50 Honda
1994 S.30 Kawasaki
1996 J.34 Honda
1996 S.30 Honda
1997 J.26 Honda
1997 S.30 Honda
Gilbody, Martin J. F.
1985 J/N.12 Yamaha
1986 J.R. Yamaha
Gillard, Roy
1995 S/Cl.50 Ducati
1996 S/Cl.51 Ducati
1996 J.R. Ducati
1997 S/Cl.50 Matchless
1997 J/Cl.R. Ducati
Gilmour, Phil
1988 S/N.3 Suzuki
1989 S.31 Spondon Yamaha
1990 S.9 Honda
1991 S.12 Honda
1992 S.19 Yamaha
Gilroy, Paul R.
1995 L/N.14 Yamaha
1995 L.53 Yamaha
1997 L/Cl.46 Yamaha
Gimpsey, Gordon
1991 S/N.R. Suzuki
Gladwin, Brent E.
1983 S/N.2 Yamaha
Glass, Derek P.
1987 J.11 Yamaha
1987 L.5 Yamaha
Glauser, Franz
1994 S/Cl.34 Seeley
1994 J/Cl.18 Aermacchi
1995 S/Cl.19 Seeley
1995 S/Cl.16 Aermacchi
1996 S/Cl.14 Seeley
1996 J/Cl.14 Aermacchi
1997 S/Cl.10 Seeley
1997 J/Cl.11 Aermacchi
Glazier, Keith
1991 S/N.16 Yamaha
1995 S.67 Yamaha
Gobell, Cliff
1983 L.R. Nice Yamaha
1984 L.5 Yamaha
1985 J/Cl.2 Aermacchi
1986 J/Cl.R. Aermacchi
1987 J/Cl.3 Aermacchi
1988 J/Cl.11 Aermacchi
1989 J/Cl.13 Aermacchi
1990 J/Cl.R. Aermacchi
1991 J/Cl.5 Aermacchi
1992 S/Cl.R. Weslake
1992 S/Cl.15 Ducati
1993 S/Cl.20 Weslake
Goddard, Glynn
1995 J/N.29 Honda
1995 J.73 Honda
Goddard, Paul A. J.
1986 S/N.13 Honda
1987 S.R. Yamaha
Godward, Graham
1985 J/Cl.7 Aermacchi
1986 J/Cl.12 Aermacchi
1987 J/Cl.R. Aermacchi
1989 J/Cl.R. Aermacchi
1991 J/Cl.R. Aermacchi
1992 S/Cl.R. Matchless

1993 S/Cl.R. Matchless
Goodall, John H.
1983 S/Cl.1 Matchless
1984 S/Cl.7 Matchless
1985 S/Cl.2 Matchless
1986 S/Cl.3 Matchless
1987 S/Cl.4 Matchless
1988 J/Cl.5 A.J.S.
1988 S/Cl.3 Matchless
1989 S/Cl.15 Matchless
1989 J/Cl.R. A.J.S.
1990 J/Cl.5 A.J.S.
1990 S/Cl.5 Matchless
1991 S/Cl.3 Matchless
1991 J/Cl.3 A.J.S.
1992 S/Cl.8 Matchless
1992 J/Cl.R. A.J.S.
1993 S/Cl.6 Matchless
1993 J/Cl.5 A.J.S.
1994 S/Cl.6 Matchless
1994 J/Cl.3 A.J.S.
1995 S/Cl.R. Matchless
1995 J/Cl.2 A.J.S.
1996 S/Cl.5 Matchless
1996 J/Cl.5 A.J.S.
1997 S/Cl.22 Matchless
1997 J/Cl.4 A.J.S.
Goodings, Grant
1984 J.8 Yamaha
1984 S.15 Yamaha
1985 J.6 Yamaha
1985 S.R. Yamaha
1986 S.1 Suzuki
1990 L/Cl.3 Aermacchi
1990 S/Cl.R. Seeley Matchless
Goodley, David R. C.
1986 S/N.4 Kawasaki
Goodwin, Anthony
1984 J/N.10 Yamaha
1984 S.R. Yamaha
Goodwin, Richard P.
1986 L/N.R. Yamaha
1986 L.28 Yamaha
1987 J.R. Yamaha
1987 L.R. Yamaha
1988 J.9 Yamaha
1988 L.R. Yamaha
1989 J.R. Yamaha
1989 L.R. Yamaha
1990 J.24 Yamaha
1990 L.15 Yamaha
Gordon, Norman
1995 L/N.1 Yamaha
1995 L.7 Yamaha
1997 J.10 Honda
1997 L.3 Yamaha
Gordon, Fraser
1989 S/N.22 Honda
Gordon, Steve
1992 S.N.3 Suzuki
1992 S.20 Suzuki
1993 S.R. Yamaha
Gow, Jack
1983 J/Cl.6 Aermacchi
1990 S/Cl.R. Triumph Weslake
1991 S/Cl.18 Manx Norton
1992 S/Cl.4 Norton
1992 J/Cl.9 A.J.S.
1993 S/Cl.R. Norton
1993 J/Cl.3 A.J.S.
1994 J/Cl.R. Richards Seeley
1994 S/Cl.4 Wardrope Norton
1995 S.R. Weslake Seeley
Graham, Heath
1992 S/Cl.R. Seeley
1994 S/Cl.34 Seeley
1994 S/Cl.R. Seeley
1995 S/Cl.22 Seeley
1995 J/Cl.R. Seeley
1995 J.72 Yamaha
1997 S/Cl.30 Seeley
1997 S/Cl.27 Seeley 7R
1997 J.R. Harris Yamaha
Graham, Jim

1993 S/Cl.R. Matchless
1994 J/Cl.11 Aermacchi
1995 J/Cl.12 Aermacchi
Graham, M. Ross
1997 S/Cl.49 Matchless
Graham-Troll, Matthew
1994 L/N.11 Kawasaki
Grainger, Stephenson
1995 S/Cl.48 Seeley
Granados, Wyatt
1987 L/N.R. Yamaha
1987 L.29 Yamaha
1990 J.34 Yamaha
1993 J.55 Yamaha
1993 L.R. Yamaha
Grant, Donald McG.
1984 S/Cl.R. Norton
Grant, Lindsay, A.
1985 L/N.15 Ducati
1986 J/Cl.21 Ducati
1988 J/Cl.20 Ducati
Grant, Mark
1994 S/Cl.31 Matchless
Graves, Andrew M
1983 S.17 Yamaha
1984 J.5 Yamaha
Gray, Carl
1985 S/Cl.R. Triumph
1986 S/Cl.21 Triumph
1988 S/Cl.24 Triumph
Gray, Ian E.
1984 L/N.5 Yamaha
1984 L.34 Yamaha
1985 S/Cl.R. Norton
1985 S.59 Honda
1987 S/Cl.37 Norton
1988 S/Cl.R. Norton
1989 S/Cl.37 Norton
1990 S/Cl.R. Norton Metisse
1991 S/Cl.R. Norton Metisse
1992 S/Cl.R. Metisse
1993 S/Cl.R. Weslake
1994 S/Cl.37 Weslake Metisse
1995 S/Cl.R. Weslake Metisse
1996 S/Cl.54 Weslake Metisse
1997 S/Cl.R. Weslake Metisse
Green, Barry
1993 L/N.4 Kawasaki
1993 L.33 Kawasaki
Green, Simon
1992 L/N.12 Kawasaki
Greenham, David
1984 J.R. Yamaha
Greenham, Geoffrey J.
1983 J/Cl.20 Ducati
1983 S.38 Yamaha
1984 J.R. Yamaha
1985 J.R. Yamaha
1985 L.R. Yamaha
Greenway, Garry
1993 L/N.3 Kawasaki
1993 L.36 Kawasaki
1994 L.20 Kawasaki
1995 L.22 Kawasaki
Greenwood, Roger
1983 S/Cl.16 Norton
Grew, John J.
1988 L/Cl.R. B.S.A.
1988 S/Cl.25 Triumph
1989 L/Cl.13 B.S.A.
1989 S/Cl.19 Velocette
Grey, Mick
1992 L/N.10 Kawasaki
Grey, Tony
1984 J/N.R. Yamaha
1986 J.31 Yamaha
1986 S.20 Kawasaki
1987 J.32 Yamaha
1987 S.R. Kawasaki
1988 S.30 Suzuki
1990 J.40 Yamaha
1990 S.26 Yamaha
Griffin, David
1984 S/N.R. Suzuki
1985 S.R. Suzuki

Griffiths, Andrew D.
1988 L/N.R. Armstrong
1988 L.20 Armstrong
1989 L.26 Armstrong
Griffiths, Ann
1993 L/N.R. Kawasaki
1993 J.67 Kawasaki
1995 J.R. Yamaha
Griffiths, D. Chris M.
1983 J/Cl.3 Aermacchi
1984 J/Cl.R. Aermacchi
1985 J/Cl.3 Aermacchi
Griffiths, David K.
1987 J/N.10 Yamaha
Griffiths, Jason
1991 S/N.1 Honda
1991 J.R. Yamaha
1991 L.2 Yamaha
Griffiths, Kevin
1989 J.40 Yamaha
Griffiths, Michael
1983 S.45 Laverda
1984 S.54 Laverda
Griffiths, Nigel M.
1986 L/N.R. Armstrong
1986 L.R. Armstrong
1987 J.43 Yamaha
1987 L.R. Armstrong
1988 L.9 Yamaha
1989 J.R. Yamaha
1989 L.4 Yamaha
1991 J.R. Yamaha
1991 L.10 Yamaha
Griffiths, Peter J.
1983 S/N.R. Honda
1984 S/Cl.25 Triumph
1985 S/Cl.38 Triumph
1987 S/Cl.31 Triumph
1988 S/Cl.34 Triumph
Griffiths, Selwyn G.
1987 S/Cl.3 Matchless
1988 J/Cl.R. A.J.S.
1988 S/Cl.R. Matchless
1989 S/Cl.3 Matchless
1989 J/Cl.R. A.J.S.
1990 J/Cl.7 Cowles A.J.S.
1990 S/Cl.R. Cowles Matchless
1991 S/Cl.R. Matchless
Griffiths, Terence
1983 L.32 Yamaha
1984 J.R. Yamaha
1985 L.R. Yamaha
Grigson, David M.
1984 L/N.2 Yamaha
1984 L.14 Yamaha
1985 J/Cl.R. Bultaco
1985 L.7 Yamaha
1986 J.15 Yamaha
1986 L.9 Yamaha
1987 J.R. Yamaha
Grimshaw, Paul
1990 S/N.4 Honda
1991 S.24 Kawasaki
Grindey, Philip A.
1991 L/N.9 Kawasaki
1991 J.32 Kawasaki
Grindley, Phil
1992 J.29= Yamaha
1994 J.29 Yamaha
Grindrod, Martin P.
1987 J/N.11 Yamaha
Grundison, Dave
1992 J/N.R. Rotax
Gunson, Mark
1987 S/N.36 Honda
1988 S/Cl.32 Seeley
1989 S/Cl.14 Seeley
1991 S/Cl.R. Seeley
1991 J/Cl.R. Seeley
Guslov, Peter
1991 J/N.11 Honda
1992 J.R. Rotax
1992 S.58 Kawasaki
1993 J.29 Honda

1993 S.33		Honda
1994 J.48		Honda
1997 J.69		Honda

Guymer, Malcolm F
1986 S/N.		Suzuki
1987 S.18		Yamaha
1988 S.20		Yamaha

Gwatkin, John
1990 L/Cl.R.		Ducati
1994 L/Cl.15	Jackson	Suzuki
1995 L/Cl.17		Suzuki
1997 L/Cl.R.		Suzuki

Hackshall, David
| 1995 J/N.R. | | Yamaha |
| 1995 J.79 | | Yamaha |

Haddock, Roger F.
| 1983 J/Cl.5 | | A.J.S. |

Haddon, Nigel
| 1995 J/N.10 | | Honda |
| 1995 S.14 | | Honda |

Hadwin, Chris
1983 S.R.		Yamaha
1984 J.R.		Yamaha
1984 S.52		Yamaha

Hadwin, Geoff
1983 J.44		Yamaha
1983 L.51		Yamaha
1984 J/Cl.26	Crooks	Suzuki
1984 L.33		Yamaha
1985 L.R.		Yamaha
1989 L/Cl.5		Suzuki
1990 L/Cl.8		Suzuki
1993 L/Cl.13		Suzuki

Hadwin, Keith
| 1989 S/N.33 | | Honda |
| 1990 L.53 | | Kawasaki |

Halford, Chris G.
1986 S/N.R.		Kawasaki
1987 S.53		Kawasaki
1988 S.R.		Suzuki
1989 S.R.		Suzuki

Hall, Barry
| 1995 J/N.4 | | Honda |
| 1995 S.9 | | Honda |

Halligan, Jim
| 1997 L/N.4 | | Honda |
| 1997 L.29 | | Honda |

Halliwell, Paul
| 1984 S/N.R. | | Yamaha |

Hamilton, Ewan W.
1987 L/N.7		Yamaha
1987 L.R.		Yamaha
1988 L.16		Yamaha
1989 J.R.		Yamaha
1989 L.46		Yamaha
1990 J.23	Spondon	Yamaha
1991 J.12		Yamaha
1991 L.R.		Yamaha
1992 L/Cl.R.		Suzuki
1992 L.12		Yamaha
1993 L/Cl.3		Suzuki
1994 L/Cl.R.		Suzuki
1995 S/Cl.R.	NRE	Weslake
1995 L/Cl.R.		Suzuki
1996 S/Cl.25	Seeley	Weslake
1996 L/Cl.R.		Suzuki
1997 L/Cl.4		Suzuki

Hammond, Colin
1983 L/Cl.2		Bultaco
1983 L.34	Spondon	Rotax
1984 J/Cl.R.		Bultaco
1984 L.R.	Spondon	Rotax
1985 L.16	Spondon	Rotax
1986 L.14	Spondon	Rotax
1987 J.39		Rotax Spl
1987 L.25	Spondon	Rotax

Hammond, John E.
1985 J/Cl.9		Aermacchi
1987 J/Cl.R.		Aermacchi
1990 J/Cl.R.		Aermacchi
1992 J/Cl.R.		Aermacchi
1993 J/Cl.23		Aermacchi
1994 J/Cl.R.		Aermacchi

| 1995 J/Cl.R. | | Aermacchi |

Hammond, Stephen G.
1983 J/N.19		Yamaha
1984 J.29		Yamaha
1985 J.R.	Motrac	Yamaha

Hanna, Ray S.
| 1984 L.R. | | Yamaha |

Hansen, Nigel L.
1988 L/N.R.		Yamaha
1988 L.42		Yamaha
1989 J.13		Yamaha
1989 L.6		Yamaha
1990 J.3		Yamaha
1990 L.3		Yamaha
1991 J.R.		Yamaha
1991 L.R.		Yamaha
1992 L.4		Yamaha
1993 J.4		Yamaha
1993 L.2		Yamaha
1994 J.7		Yamaha
1994 L.8		Yamaha

Harbison, Paul
| 1991 L/N.1 | | Kawasaki |
| 1991 L.15 | | Kawasaki |

Harding, Mark J.
| 1983 L/N.R. | | Rotax |
| 1983 L.R. | | Rotax |

Harding, Steve
| 1992 J/N.8 | | Yamaha |

Hardisty, Ian
1995 L/N.7	Cowles	Honda
1995 L/Cl.11	Cowles	Ducati
1996 J.42	Cowles	Honda
1996 L.16	Cowles	Honda

Hardman, Colin
1985 J/Cl.R.		Suzuki
1985 J.R.		Yamaha
1986 J/Cl.20		Suzuki
1986 L.R.		Rotax
1987 L.R.		Rotax
1988 L.R.		Rotax
1992 J/Cl.R.		Ducati
1993 J/Cl.R.		Ducati

Hardwick, John
| 1990 L/N.11 | | Honda |
| 1991 S.64 | | Suzuki |

Hardwick, Richard
| 1990 J/N.5 | | Yamaha |

Hargreaves, John
1983 S/Cl.23		Norton
1984 S/Cl.26		Norton
1985 S/Cl.31		Norton
1986 S/Cl.31		Norton
1987 S/Cl.38		Norton
1988 S/Cl.52		Triton
1989 S/Cl.44		Norton
1990 S/Cl.R.		Norton

Harley, Colin
| 1991 L/N.25 | | Kawasaki |

Harley, Dave
| 1992 J.68 | | Yamaha |

Harling, Alan
1988 S/N.27		Trident
1990 S/Cl.R.		Norton
1991 S/Cl.R.		Norton
1992 S/Cl.32		Norton
1993 S/Cl.36		Norton
1994 S/Cl.16		Norton
1994 S/Cl.R.		Norton
1995 S/Cl.R.		Norton
1995 S/Cl.R.		Norton
1996 S/Cl.R.		Norton
1996 S/Cl.22		Norton
1997 S/Cl.R.		Seeley
1997 S/Cl.R.		Norton

Harmer, Kenny
1983 S.R.		Triumph
1984 S/Cl.R.		Triumph
1984 S.37		Triumph
1985 S/Cl.R.		Triumph
1985 S.R.		Triumph
1986 S.R.		Suzuki
1987 S.4		Honda

Harper, Colin

1985 S/N.12	Peacock	Honda
1986 J.39		Yamaha
1986 S.R.		Honda
1988 S.52		Honda
1989 S.67		Honda

Harris, Anthony
| 1988 S/N.13 | | Kawasaki |

Harris, Chris A.
1983 J.7		Yamaha
1984 S.R.		Yamaha
1985 J.18		Yamaha
1985 S.22		Yamaha
1986 J.7		Yamaha
1986 S.12	Cowles	Suzuki
1987 J.R.		Yamaha
1987 L.R.		Armstrong
1988 J.18		Yamaha
1988 S.58		Kawasaki
1989 J.R.		Yamaha
1989 S.R.		Kawasaki
1990 J.35		Yamaha
1990 L.38		Kawasaki
1991 J.43		Yamaha
1991 S.33		Honda
1992 J.34		Yamaha
1992 L.R.		Yamaha
1993 J.21		Yamaha
1993 L.13		Yamaha

Harris, Lawrence
| 1992 S/Cl.46 | | Norton |

Harris, Nigel
| 1990 S/N.12 | | B.S.A. |

Harris, Richard
1990 S/N.7		Yamaha
1990 J.51		Yamaha
1991 S.16		Yamaha

Harris, Stuart
| 1993 L/N.13 | | Suzuki |

Harris, Tony
| 1991 S/Cl.R. | | B.S.A. |
| 1991 S.46 | | Suzuki |

Harrison, A. Clive
1988 L/N.13		Yamaha
1988 L.43		Yamaha
1990 L.52		Yamaha

Harrison, Dean
1990 J/N.R.		Yamaha
1990 J.R.		Suzuki
1991 J.11		Honda
1992 J.24		Honda
1992 L.9		Honda
1993 J.R.		Honda
1993 S.42		Yamaha

Harrison, John
1987 J/N.28		Aermacchi
1988 J/Cl.35		Aermacchi
1989 J/Cl.19		Aermacchi
1990 J/Cl.17		Aermacchi
1991 J/Cl.7		Aermacchi

Harrison, John R.
| 1997 L/N.R. | | Kawasaki |

Harrison, Mike A.
1984 S.28		Honda
1985 S.39		Suzuki
1990 J/Cl.25		Ducati
1991 J/Cl.24		Ducati

Harrison, Rob
1991 L/N.R.		Kawasaki
1992 J.60		Kawasaki
1992 L.R.		Kawasaki

Hart, Johannes R.
| 1989 L/Cl.R. | | Ducati |
| 1990 L/Cl.R. | | Yamaha |

Harte, Jason
1995 S/N.R.		Suzuki
1995 S.22		Suzuki
1996 J.14		Honda
1996 S.11		Honda

Harvey, Terence
| 1985 J/N.R. | | Yamaha |

Haskell, G. Vic
1988 S/Cl.R.		Seeley
1991 J/Cl.19		B.S.A.
1992 S/Cl.43		Seeley

1992 J/Cl.R.		B.S.A.
1993 S/Cl.R.		Seeley
1993 J/Cl.30		B.S.A.
1994 J/Cl.22		B.S.A.
1994 S/Cl.R.		Seeley
1995 S/Cl.R.		Seeley
1995 J/Cl.R.		Seeley
1996 S/Cl.R.	Seeley	Weslake
1996 J/Cl.R.	Rickman	Goldstar
1997 S/Cl.36	Seeley	Weslake
1997 J/Cl.28	Rickman	Goldstar

Haslam, Neil
1988 S/N.12		Suzuki
1989 S.R.		Suzuki
1990 S.36		Yamaha

Hattersley, John
| 1989 S/Cl.33 | | Seeley |

Hawkins, Rich
1989 L/Cl.3		Ducati
1990 L/Cl.16		Ducati
1991 L/Cl.6		Ducati
1992 L/Cl.R.		Ducati
1994 J/Cl.7		Ducati
1996 J.67	Tigcraft	Rotax
1996 S.62	Tigcraft	Rotax

Hayden, Chris
1986 J/N.9		Yamaha
1987 J.26		Yamaha
1988 J.31		Yamaha
1988 S.71		Vincent
1989 J.42		Yamaha
1990 S.47		Kawasaki

Hayhurst, Phil R.
1995 J/Cl.R.		Seeley
1996 J/Cl.R.		Seeley
1997 L.49		Suzuki

Hayhurst, Steven W.
| 1997 S/N.6 | | Honda |

Haynes, Geoff
1992 J/N.R.		Yamaha
1992 J.R.		Yamaha
1993 J.65		Yamaha
1993 L.47		Yamaha
1994 J.R.	DTR	Yamaha
1995 J.69	DTR	Yamaha
1995 L.R.	DTR	Yamaha
1996 J.81	DTR	Yamaha
1996 L.R.	DTR	Yamaha
1997 J.R.	DTR	Yamaha
1997 L.R.		Yamaha

Haynes, Ray
1983 J.25		Yamaha
1983 L.36		Yamaha
1984 J.21		Yamaha
1984 S.61		Yamaha
1985 J.21		Yamaha
1985 S.20		Yamaha
1986 J.R.		Yamaha
1986 L.11		Yamaha
1987 J.25		Yamaha
1987 L.26		Yamaha
1988 J.34		Yamaha
1988 L.32		Yamaha
1989 J.31		Yamaha
1989 L.35		Yamaha
1990 J.R.		Yamaha
1997 L/Cl.15		Suzuki

Hayward, Alan
1992 L/N.14		Suzuki
1992 L.R.		Suzuki
1994 J.R.		Yamaha
1994 L.35		Yamaha
1995 J.R.		Yamaha
1995 L.46		Yamaha

Hayward, Dave
| 1990 S/N.6 | | Suzuki |
| 1990 S.37 | | Suzuki |

Haywood, Trevor A.
| 1985 J/N.2 | | Yamaha |
| 1986 J.R. | | Yamaha |

Hazlett, Stephen J.
1984 J/N.3		Yamaha
1985 J.3		Yamaha
1985 S.R.		Yamaha

1986 J.R.		Yamaha
1986 S.3		Yamaha
1987 J.2		Yamaha
1987 S.7		Yamaha
1988 J.1		Yamaha
1988 S.3		Honda

Heath, Bob
1989 S/Cl.R.		Seeley
1990 S/Cl.1		Seeley
1991 S/Cl.1		Seeley
1991 S/Cl.R.		Seeley
1992 S/Cl.1		Seeley
1992 S/Cl.3		A.J.S.
1993 S/Cl.R.		Seeley
1993 J/Cl.1		Seeley
1994 J/Cl.1		Seeley
1994 J/Cl.1		Seeley
1995 S/Cl.3		Seeley
1995 J/Cl.1		Seeley
1996 S/Cl.1		Seeley
1996 J/Cl.3		Seeley
1997 S/Cl.1		Seeley
1997 J/Cl.2		Seeley

Heath, Chris
| 1995 J/N.3 | | Yamaha |

Hedison, David
| 1989 J/N.1 | | Yamaha |
| 1996 J.93 | Spondon | Yamaha |

Heenan, David
| 1983 J.31 | | Yamaha |
| 1984 S.R. | | Suzuki |

Hemmings, Mick
1991 S/Cl.25		Matchless
1992 S/Cl.R.		G50 Matchless
1993 S/Cl.17		McIntyre
1994 J/Cl.R.		McIntyre
1994 S/Cl.13		McIntyre
1996 S/Cl.11		McIntyre
1996 J/Cl.R.		McIntyre

Henderson, John
1989 L/N.5		Yamaha
1989 L.22		Yamaha
1991 J/Cl.R.		Aermacchi
1992 J/Cl.11		Aermacchi
1993 J/Cl.R.		Aermacchi
1994 J/Cl.R.		Aermacchi

Hennessey, Eugene
| 1988 S/N.17 | | Suzuki |
| 1989 S.54 | | Honda |

Henley, Russell
1993 L/N.R.		Yamaha
1993 L.16		Yamaha
1994 J.11		Yamaha
1994 L.R.		Yamaha
1995 J.R.	Mannin	Yamaha
1995 L.3	Mannin	Yamaha
1996 J.R.	MB Mannin	Yamaha
1996 L.1	MB Mannin	Yamaha

Henthorn, Jeff
1994 J/N.7		Honda
1994 S.39		Honda
1995 J.55		Honda
1995 S.36		Honda

Heppenstall, Peter
1987 S/N.33		Honda
1991 S.63		Honda
1992 J.58		Honda
1992 S.66		Honda
1993 S.46		Honda

Herbertson, Mark
| 1994 S/Cl.30 | Seeley | Matchless |
| 1996 S/Cl.45 | | B.S.A. |

Heron, Derek
| 1997 S/N.3 | | Yamaha |
| 1997 J.73 | | Yamaha |

Hersevoort, John J.
1985 S/N.R.		Honda
1986 S.68		Honda
1987 S.R.		Honda

Hesselden, Alan
1991 L/N.3		Kawasaki
1994 J.41		Honda
1995 J.23		Honda
1995 S.31		Honda

176 The History of the Manx Grand Prix 1923-1998

1996	J.32	Honda	**Hines, Ben**		1988	S.74	Norton	1994	J.39	Honda	1985 S/Cl.14 Norton
1996	S.28	Honda	1991	S/N.19	Suzuki	1989	S/Cl.21	Norton	1994	S.18	Honda	1985 J.R. Maxton
1997	J.32	Honda	1991	S.R.	Suzuki	1990	L/Cl.12	Ducati	1996	S.14	Suzuki	1986 S/Cl.29 Norton
1997	S.29	Honda	**Hirst, Bob**		1991	S/Cl.32	Norton	1997	S.22	Suzuki	1986 S.R. Cagiva
Hewlett, Martin			1983	S/Cl.2	Seeley	1991	L/Cl.19	Ducati	**Howard, Wayne**			1988 S/Cl.38 Seeley
1991	J/N.4	Honda	1984	S/Cl.5	Seeley	1991	S/Cl.31	Norton	1995	S/N.R.	Harris Suzuki	1988 S/Cl.51 Norton
Hibbert, David M.			1987	S/Cl.R.	Matchless	1992	S/Cl.R.	Norton	**Howarth, Alastair**			1989 J/N.30 Seeley
1983	L/N.R.	Armstrong	1988	S/Cl.20	Seeley	1992	J/Cl.R.	Ducati	1994	S/N.4	Suzuki	1989 S/Cl.22 Norton
1983	L.R.	Armstrong	1989	S/Cl.6	Seeley	1993	S/Cl.R.	Norton	1994	S.19	Suzuki	1990 J/Cl.R. Seeley
Hickey, Ian			1990	S/Cl.9	Seeley	1994	J/Cl.R.	Ducati	1995	J.12	Honda	1991 S/Cl.31 Arter Matchless
1990	S/N.8	Kawasaki	1992	S/Cl.13	Seeley	1994	S/Cl.28	Norton	1995	S.24	Kawasaki	**Hutcheson, Bill**
1991	S.44	Kawasaki	1993	S/Cl.10	Seeley	1995	S/Cl.24	Norton	1996	J.6	Kawasaki	1996 J/N.5 Honda
1992	J.48	Yamaha	1994	S/Cl.R.	Seeley	1995	J/Cl.32	Ducati	1996	S.7	Kawasaki	1997 J.6 Honda
1992	S.62	Yamaha	1995	S/Cl.8	Seeley	1996	S/Cl.R.	Norton	1997	J.11	Kawasaki	1997 S.9 Honda
1993	J.R.	Yamaha	1995	J/Cl.8	A.J.S.	1996	J/Cl.R.	Ducati	1997	S.7	Honda	**Hutchinson, Anthony R.**
1993	S.40	Yamaha	1996	J/Cl.R.	A.J.S.	1997	S/Cl.40	Norton	**Howarth, Ian M.**			1986 L/N.4 Yamaha
1994	J.55	Honda	1997	S/Cl.15	Seeley	1997	J/Cl.33	Norton	1987	L/N.R.	Waddon	1986 L.21 Yamaha
1994	S.R.	Honda	1997	J/Cl.R.	A.J.S.	**Holmes, David J.**			1987	L.R.	Waddon	**Huws, Huw**
1995	J.49	Honda	**Hislop, Steve R.**			1987	S/N.46	Yamaha	**Howe, Graham D.**			1992 J/N.10 Yamaha
1995	S.30	Honda	1983	J/N.2	Yamaha	**Hook, Chris J.**			1983	J.15	Yamaha	1993 S.51 Norton
1996	J.37	Honda	1983	L.11	Yamaha	1988	S/N.7	Yamaha	1983	L.13	Yamaha	1994 S.54 Norton
1996	S.R.	Honda	1984	J.R.	Yamaha	1989	J.R.	Yamaha	**Howe, Robert K.**			1995 S.60 Norton
1997	J.29	Honda	1984	S.5	Yamaha	1989	S.20	Suzuki	1983	J.17	Yamaha	1996 S.79 Norton
1997	S.37	Honda	**Hodges, Maurice S.**			1990	S.6	Honda	1983	S.R.	Yamaha	1997 S.85 Pierce Norton
Hickey, Phil			1983	S/Cl.7	Seeley Unity	1991	J.27	Suzuki	1984	J.R.	Yamaha	
1992	S/N.8	Suzuki	**Hogg, Brian P.**			1991	S.3	Honda	1984	S.R.	Yamaha	**Ianson, Rob**
1992	S.68	Suzuki	1987	S/N.32	Kawasaki	1993	J.11	Honda	**Hudson, Martin**			1992 J/N.2 Honda
1993	S.34	Suzuki	1988	J.45	Yamaha	1993	S.6	Honda	1992	S/N.9	Yamaha	1992 S.42 Honda
1994	J.R.	Yamaha	1988	L.38	Yamaha	1994	J.33	Yamaha	1995	S.R.	Tigcraft BMW	**Ingleby, Hans**
1994	S.40	Suzuki	1989	J.R.	Kawasaki	1994	S.2	Honda	**Hudspeth, Andrew S.**			1987 S/N.44 Suzuki
1995	J.R.	Yamaha	1989	L.R.	Kawasaki	1995	J.8	Honda	1987	J/N.R.	Yamaha	**Innocent, Bill W.**
1995	L.38	Yamaha	1990	J.R.	Kawasaki	1995	S.R.	Honda	**Hudziack, Anthony**			1984 S/Cl.R. Triumph
1996	J.86	Yamaha	1990	L.33	Kawasaki	1996	J.3	Honda	1985	J/N.R.	Yamaha	**Inwood, Ken F. H.**
1996	L.R.	Yamaha	1991	J.26	Kawasaki	1997	J.2	Honda	**Hughes, Chris A.**			1983 S/Cl.4 Norton
1997	S.76	Honda	1991	L.31	Kawasaki	1997	S.3	Honda	1987	S/N.16	Suzuki	1984 S/Cl.9 Norton
Hicks, Howard J.			1992	J.R.	Yamaha	**Horgan, John**			1988	S.R.	Suzuki	1985 S/Cl.7 Norton
1983	J/N.7	Yamaha	1992	L.18	Yamaha	1991	J/N.14	Kawasaki	**Hughes, Emlyn**			1986 S/Cl.8 Norton
1985	S.R.	Kawasaki	1993	J.20	Yamaha	**Hornby, Robert**			1994	L/N.1	Yamaha	**Irwin, Richard N.**
Hierons, Tony			1993	L.19	Yamaha	1988	S/N.22	Honda	1994	L.R.	Yamaha	1983 S/N.R. Honda
1996	S/Cl.61	Aermacchi Metisse	1993	J.34	Yamaha	**Horsman, Bill**			**Hughes, Ian**			1984 J/Cl.3 Aermacchi
Higginson, Frank			1994	L.R.	Yamaha	1989	S/Cl.5	Seeley	1994	L/N.13	Kawasaki	1985 J/Cl.R. Aermacchi
1983	J.R.	Yamaha	**Hogg, David**			1990	J/Cl.34	McIntyre	1995	J.63	Honda	**Ivory, Carlton P.**
1984	S/Cl.28	Triumph	1990	J/N.R.	Yamaha	1990	S/Cl.R.	Matchless	1995	S.R.	Honda	1984 S/N.16 Kawasaki
1985	S/Cl.R.	Triumph	1991	J.R.	Yamaha	1992	J/Cl.R.	Seeley	1997	J.68	Honda	1985 J.51 Yamaha
1986	S/Cl.R.	Triumph	1992	J.50	Yamaha	1992	J/Cl.5	Seeley	1997	S.80	Honda	1985 S.72 Kawasaki
1987	S/Cl.43	Triumph	1993	J.26	Yamaha	1993	S/Cl.R.	Matchless	**Hughes, J. A.**			1986 J.42 Yamaha
1988	S/Cl.46	Triumph	1993	L.18	Yamaha	1993	J/Cl.6	A.J.S.	1993	S/Cl.R.	Norton	1986 S.R. Yamaha
1989	S/Cl.R.	Triumph	1994	J.44	Yamaha	1995	S/Cl.4	Seeley	1995	S/Cl.51	Seeley Norton	1987 J.45 Yamaha
1990	S/Cl.R.	Triumph	1994	L.15	Yamaha	1996	S/Cl.3	Seeley	**Hughes, Kevin**			1988 J.47 Yamaha
1991	S/Cl.41	Triumph	1995	J.26	Yamaha	1996	J/Cl.2	Aermacchi	1983	S/N.R.	Laverda	1989 J.35 Yamaha
1993	S/Cl.R.	Triumph	1995	L.R.	Yamaha	1997	S/Cl.4	Molnar Norton	1984	S.4	Kawasaki	1989 L.44 Yamaha
1993	J/Cl.32	Triumph	1996	J.R.	Yamaha	1997	J/Cl.1	Aermacchi	**Hughes, Tony L.**			1990 J.R. Yamaha
1994	S/Cl.R.	Triumph	1996	L.14	Yamaha	**Hose, Michael**			1985	J/N.13	Yamaha	1990 L.54 Yamaha
1995	S/Cl.R.	Triumph	**Hogg, Ian**			1987	J/N.R.	Yamaha	1985	L.34	Yamaha	1991 J.33 Yamaha
1996	S/Cl.R.	Triumph	1991	L/Cl.3	Suzuki	**Hosie, Bruce R.**			1995	S/Cl.R.	Norton	1991 L.R. Suzuki
1996	J/Cl.32	Ducati	**Hogg, John S.**			1985	S/Cl.27	Norton	**Humble, Paul**			1992 J.56 Yamaha
1997	S/Cl.51	Triumph	1983	L/N.R.	Yamaha	1987	S/Cl.22	Weslake	1996	S/N.6	Honda	1992 L.R. Yamaha
1997	J/Cl.35	Ducati	1983	L.R.	Yamaha	1988	S/Cl.R.	Weslake	1996	S.58	Honda	1993 J.57 Yamaha
Higginson, George			1984	J.50	Yamaha	1989	S/Cl.R.	Metisse	1997	J.R.	Honda	1993 L.35 Yamaha
1986	L/N.1	Decorite	1986	S.R.	Kawasaki	1990	J/Cl.R.	Seeley	1997	S.51	Honda	1994 J.62 Yamaha
1986	L.8	Decorite	**Hogg, Phil J.**			1990	S/Cl.R.	Weslake Metisse	**Humphreys, Daniel**			1994 L.30 Yamaha
Hildige, Carl			1987	S/N.2	Suzuki	1991	S/Cl.R.	Seeley	1994	L/N.9	Yamaha	1995 J.61 Yamaha
1996	S/N.13	Honda	1988	J.6	Yamaha	1991	J/Cl.R.	Seeley	1994	L.25	Yamaha	1995 L.31 Yamaha
1996	S.84	Honda	1988	S.R.	Yamaha	1992	S/Cl.R.	Seeley	1995	L.14	Yamaha	1995 L.R. Yamaha
1997	S.89	Honda	**Hold, John**			1992	J/Cl.31	B.S.A.	**Humphries, Colin**			1996 L.24 Yamaha
Hildige, Shawn			1989	S/N.R.	Yamaha	1993	S/Cl.R.	Seeley	1995	S/Cl.41	Seeley	1997 J.R. Yamaha
1992	S/N.R.	Kawasaki	1990	S.61	Yamaha	1994	J/Cl.40	Seeley	**Hunt, Craig**			1997 L.39 Yamaha
1994	J.R.	Yamaha	1991	S.49	Yamaha	1994	S/Cl.R.	Seeley	1992	L/N.3	Kawasaki	
1994	S.55	Yamaha	1992	S.43	Yamaha	1995	S/Cl.R.	Seeley	1992	L.26	Kawasaki	**Jackson, Alan 'Bud'**
Hill, Brian			1993	J.33	Honda	1995	J/Cl.26	Seeley	1993	J.25	Yamaha	1983 J.R. Yamaha
1989	S/N.14	Honda	1993	S.R.	Honda	1996	J/Cl.39	Seeley	**Hunt, Derek**			1983 L.5 Armstrong
Hill, Jeff			**Holden, Robert**			1996	J/Cl.24	Seeley	1983	L/Cl.R.	Greeves	1984 J.13 Yamaha
1991	L/N.R.	Honda	1995	S/Cl.2	Petty Norton	1997	S/Cl.35	Seeley	**Hunt, Kieron**			1984 L.4 Fowler Yamaha
1991	L.24	Honda	**Holland, Graham M.**			1997	J/Cl.26	Seeley	1983	J.R.	Yamaha	1985 L.R. Yamaha
1992	J.31	Yamaha	1988	L/N.12	Yamaha	**Hosie, Duncan T.**			1983	S.11	Yamaha	1986 J.1 Fowler Yamaha
1992	L.R.	Yamaha	1988	L.R.	Yamaha	1984	S/Cl.R.	Norton	**Hunter, Jim D.**			1986 L.R. Fowler Yamaha
Hill, Robert C.			**Holliland, Derrick**			1985	S/Cl.R.	Norton	1986	S/N.1	Suzuki	1987 J/Cl.33 Aermacchi
1983	J/Cl.19	Aermacchi	1983	S.58	Norton	1987	S/Cl.36	Norton	1993	J/Cl.R.	Aermacchi	1988 J/Cl.4 Aermacchi
1985	J/Cl.R.	Aermacchi	1984	S/Cl.18	Norton	1989	J/Cl.R.	A.J.S.	**Hurlstone, John R.**			1989 J/Cl.8 Aermacchi
1986	J/Cl.R.	Aermacchi	1985	S/Cl.R.	Norton	**Hounsell, Peter A.**			1984	S/Cl.R.	Metisse	1989 S/Cl.R. Aermacchi
1987	J/Cl.12	Aermacchi	1985	S.71	Norton	1983	J/N.R.	Yamaha	1985	J/Cl.15	Honda	1991 L/Cl.1 Suzuki
1988	J/Cl.23	Aermacchi	1986	S/Cl.24	Norton	1984	J.R.	Yamaha	1986	S/Cl.R.	Triumph	1992 L/Cl.3 Suzuki
Hill, Steven J.			1987	S.70	Norton	1985	J.R.	Yamaha	**Hurst, Graham R.**			1993 L/Cl.4 Suzuki
1986	J/N.11	Yamaha	1988	S/Cl.58	Norton	1985	S.R.	Yamaha	1984	S/Cl.30	Domiracer	1994 L/Cl.2 Jackson Suzuki

The History of the Manx Grand Prix 1923-1998 177

1995 L/Cl.1	Jackson Suzuki	1997 S/Cl.R.	B.S.A.	Jones, Chris		1988 L.R.	Yamaha	1997 S.61	Kawasaki
1996 L/Cl.2	Jackson Suzuki	**Jefferies, Nick**		1984 J/N.R.	Yamaha	1989 J.R.	Yamaha	**Kershaw, Kevin**	
1997 S/Cl.17	Seeley Weslake	1983 J.R.	Yamaha	1984 L.42	Yamaha	1989 L.R.	Rotax	1983 S/Cl.R.	Velocette
1997 L/Cl.3	Clucas Suzuki	1983 S.1	Suzuki	1985 J.R.	Yamaha	1990 J.63	Yamaha	1983 S.R.	Yamaha
Jackson, Andy		**Jefferson, Tim**		1985 S.56	Yamaha	1990 L.51	Yamaha	1984 S/Cl.22	Velocette
1991 J/N.1	Honda	1988 J/Cl.R.	Brancato Ducati	**Jones, Chris**		1991 J.R.	Yamaha	1984 J.R.	Maxton Yamaha
1991 S.R.	Honda	1988 L.40	Yamaha	1994 J/N.6	Yamaha	1991 L.47	Yamaha	1985 S/Cl.R.	Velocette
1992 J.15	Honda	**Jeffs, Christopher**		1995 J.51	Yamaha	1992 J.61	Yamaha	1985 J.R.	Yamaha
1992 L.30	Kawasaki	1983 L/Cl.R.	Bultaco	**Jones, C. Roland**		1992 L.39	Yamaha	**Kiddie, John**	
1993 J.12	Yamaha	1983 S.R.	Spondon Yamaha	1989 L/N.10	Suzuki	1993 J.48	Yamaha	1983 J/Cl.17	Honda
1993 L.5	Yamaha	1984 S.55	Spondon Yamaha	1989 L.R.	Suzuki	1993 L.31	Yamaha	**Kidson, John**	
Jackson, Bob		1985 S.58	Spondon Yamaha	1990 J.62	Suzuki	1994 J.R.	Yamaha	1986 J/Cl.2	Aermacchi
1987 J/Cl.R.	Greeves	1987 S.R.	Yamaha	1990 L.44	Suzuki	1994 L.27	Yamaha	1987 J/Cl.2	Aermacchi
1989 L/Cl.R.	Suzuki	**Jenkins, Gerry**		**Jones, Dave M.**		1995 J.59=	Yamaha	1988 J/Cl.R.	Aermacchi
1990 L/Cl.R.	Suzuki	1989 J/Cl.R.	Greeves	1997 L/N.1	Yamaha	1995 L.27	Yamaha	1989 J/Cl.4	Aermacchi
1991 L/Cl.R.	Suzuki	1990 J/Cl.R.	Greeves	1997 L.24	Yamaha	1995 J.88	Yamaha	1990 L/Cl.R.	Aermacchi
1992 L/Cl.1	Suzuki	**Jennings, Martin**		**Jones, Doug**		1996 L.33	Yamaha	**Killworth, Robert J.**	
1993 S/Cl.R.	G50 Seeley	1984 J/N.R.	Yamaha	1996 S/Cl.R.	Norton	1997 J.91	Yamaha	1987 S/N.41	Yamaha
1993 L/Cl.1	Suzuki	1984 S.43	Yamaha	1996 J/Cl.R.	Norton	1997 L.34	Yamaha	1988 S/Cl.45	Triumph
1994 S/Cl.3	Matchless	1985 J.R.	Yamaha	**Jones, Gareth J.**		**Kelly, Derek A. 'Decca'**		**Kimberley, Ian S.**	
1994 L/Cl.1	PB Suzuki	1985 S.R.	Yamaha	1988 J/N.6	Yamaha	1983 J.18	Yamaha	1988 S/N.10	Yamaha
1995 L/Cl.R.	Seeley	1986 J.R.	Yamaha	1989 S.44	Yamaha	1983 S.R.	Yamaha	1989 S.62	Yamaha
1995 L/Cl.R.	Suzuki	1986 S.R.	Yamaha	**Jones, Ian**		1984 J.16	Yamaha	**King, Graham W.**	
1996 S/Cl.2	Matchless	1987 J.R.	Yamaha	1986 J/N.1	Yamaha	1984 S.R.	Yamaha	1983 J.R.	Yamaha
1996 L/Cl.1	PB Suzuki	**Jennings, Nigel A.**		1986 L.R.	Yamaha	1985 J.5	Yamaha	1983 S.13	Yamaha
1997 S/Cl.2	Norton	1987 L/N.4	Yamaha	1987 J.9	Yamaha	1985 S.R.	Yamaha	1984 S.3	Suzuki
1997 L/Cl.1	PB Suzuki	1987 L.27	Yamaha	1987 L.R.	Yamaha	1986 J.R.	Yamaha	**King, Ian**	
Jackson, David A.		1990 J.R.	Yamaha	**Jones, Kevin**		1987 J.5	Yamaha	1992 J/N.1	Pirelli Honda
1990 J/N.4	Yamaha	1990 L.23	Yamaha	1989 S.33	Yamaha	1987 L.R.	Yamaha	1992 S.7	Pirelli Honda
1990 S.63	Yamaha	1991 J.8	Yamaha	1990 S.25	Yamaha	1988 J.R.	Yamaha	**King, Ray M. J.**	
Jackson, Kevin		1991 L.8	Yamaha	**Jones, Martin**		1988 L.R.	Yamaha	1988 J/Cl.R.	Aermacchi
1983 S.14	PM Suzuki	1992 J.17	Yamaha	1985 S/N.14	Honda	1989 J.R.	Yamaha	1989 J/Cl.R.	Aermacchi
1984 S.12	Suzuki	1992 L.7	Yamaha	1986 J/Cl.34	Aermacchi	1989 L.R.	Yamaha	1990 J/Cl.19	Aermacchi
1985 S.13	Crooks Suzuki	1993 J.6	Yamaha	1987 J/Cl.19	Aermacchi	1990 J.5	Yamaha	1991 S/Cl.37	Seeley Matchless
1986 S.4	Suzuki	1993 L.8	Yamaha	**Jones, Neil**		1991 J.R.	Yamaha	1991 J/Cl.23	Aermacchi
1987 S.6	Suzuki	1994 J.12	Yamaha	1995 L/N.8	Yamaha	1991 L.6	Yamaha	1994 J/Cl.R.	Aermacchi Metisse
1988 S.6	Yamaha	1994 L.5	Yamaha	1995 L.40	Yamaha	1992 J.4	Yamaha	1994 S/Cl.47	Norton
Jackson, Mark A.		**Jeremiah, Jeff**		1996 S.41	Honda	1992 L.5	Yamaha	1995 S/Cl.R.	Aermacchi Metisse
1987 S/N.13	Honda	1983 J/N.10	Yamaha	1997 J.31	Honda	1993 J.10	Yamaha	1995 J/Cl.25	Aermacchi Metisse
1988 S.40	Honda	**Jessop, Andrew C. E.**		1997 S.R.	Honda	1993 L.7	Yamaha	1996 S/Cl.53	Aermacchi
1989 S.43	Suzuki	1984 S/N.17	Laverda	**Jones, Olaf**		1994 J.3	Yamaha	1996 J/Cl.25	Aermacchi
1991 S.R.	Honda	**Johnson, Neil F.**		1996 J/N.3	Honda	1993 L.R.	Yamaha	**Kinloch, Peter**	
Jackson, Michael		1983 J/N.17	Yamaha	**Jones, Roger**		1994 L.1	Yamaha	1990 S/N.R.	Suzuki
1989 L/N.R.	Seabank Honda	1984 J.39	Spondon Yamaha	1988 J/N.8	Yamaha	1996 S/Cl.48	Ducati	**Kirk, Andy**	
1989 L.R.	Seabank Honda	1984 S.R.	Spondon Yamaha	1989 J.R.	Yamaha	1996 L/Cl.12	Ducati	1995 S/N.6	Honda
Jackson, Sean		**Johnson, Tim**		1990 J.R.	Yamaha	1997 S/Cl.R.	Ducati	1995 S.50	Honda
1995 L/N.2	Yamaha	1989 S/N.32	B.S.A.	**Jones, Russ**		1997 L/Cl.R.	Ducati	1996 J.51	Honda
1995 L.4	Yamaha	1990 S/Cl.R.	Velocette	1986 S/N.6	Yamaha	**Kelly, Glenn T.**		1996 S.R.	Honda
Jackson, Tom		1991 S/Cl.30	Velocette	1987 S.63	Yamaha	1983 L/N.15	Yamaha	1996 J.51	Honda
1994 L/Cl.13	Jackson Suzuki	1992 S/Cl.42	Velocette	1994 J.R.	Yamaha	1983 L.R.	Yamaha	1997 S.R.	Honda
1995 L/Cl.10	Jackson Suzuki	1992 J/Cl.R.	Norton	**Jones, Stuart J.**		1984 L.44	Yamaha	**Kirk, Eric J.**	
1997 S/Cl.R.	Dawson Jawa	1993 S/Cl.21	Velocette	1986 S.22	Yamaha	**Kelly, Jim**		1983 J/Cl.24	A.J.S.
1997 L/Cl.12	Jackson Suzuki	1993 J/Cl.12	Norton	1988 S.19	Yamaha	1991 L/N.5	Suzuki	1985 J/Cl.R.	N.S.U.
Jacques, Bernard		1994 S/Cl.R.	Velocette	1993 S/Cl.14	Matchless	1993 J.R.	Yamaha	1990 L/Cl.R.	N.S.U.
1983 S.59	Laverda	1995 S/Cl.16	Velocette	1994 S/Cl.9	Seeley Matchless	1993 L.24	Yamaha	1991 J/Cl.R.	A.J.S.
1984 S.53	Laverda	1995 J/Cl.R.	Norton	1995 S/Cl.R.	Seeley Matchless	**Kendall, Simon**		1992 J/Cl.13	A.J.S.
1994 J.70	Yamaha	1996 S/Cl.R.	Norton	**Jones, Tony G.**		1989 S/N.19		1993 J/Cl.16	A.J.S.
1994 S.47	Yamaha	1996 J/Cl.R.	Norton	1983 J/Cl.21	Aermacchi	1990 S.57	Honda	1994 J/Cl.R.	A.J.S.
Jaermann, Peter		1997 S/Cl.28	Velocette	1984 J/Cl.17	Aermacchi	1991 S.47	Honda	1994 S/Cl.R.	Matchless
1991 S/N.14	Honda	1997 J/Cl.9	Norton	**Jowett, Keith**		**Kent, Neil A.**		**Kirk, Ian**	
James, Lewis G.		1997 S.R.	B.S.A.	1987 S/N.18	Suzuki	1986 J/N.15	Yamaha	1992 L/N.R.	Suzuki
1983 J/N.R.	Yamaha	**Johnston, David A.**		1988 J.R.	Yamaha	1987 J.42	Yamaha	1992 L.33	Suzuki
1983 L.R.	Yamaha	1984 L/N.R.	Waddon	1988 S.42	Honda	1987 L.R.	Yamaha	1993 J.19	Yamaha
Jameson, Gary J.		1984 L.7	Waddon	**Judkins, Les**		1988 J.R.	Yamaha	1993 J.12	Yamaha
1988 L/N.R.	Yamaha	1985 J.2	Yamaha	1990 J/Cl.R.	Ducati	1988 L.39	Yamaha	1994 J.9	Yamaha
Jamison, Gary		1985 L.1	E.M.C.	1991 J/Cl.R.	Ducati	1989 J.R.	Maxton	1994 L.R.	Yamaha
1986 J/N.13	Yamaha	**Johnstone, Archie**		1992 J/Cl.R.	Ducati	1990 J.R.	Yamaha	1995 J.R.	Yamaha
1986 L.17	Yamaha	1983 S/N.13	Suzuki	**Katuszonek, Peter**		1990 L.39	Honda	**Kirk, Mark**	
1989 S.R.	Suzuki	**Jones, Andy**		1992 L/N.8	Suzuki	1991 J.R.	Honda	1994 J/N.R.	Yamaha
Januszewski, Henry A.		1990 L/N.3	Kawasaki	**Kellett, Paul J.**		1991 L.33	Padgett Honda	1994 L.R.	Yamaha
1985 J/N.5	Yamaha	1991 J.13	Yamaha	1997 J/N.2	Honda	1994 J.56	Padgett Honda	1995 J.78	MBK Yamaha
1985 L.R.	Yamaha	1991 L.R.	Yamaha	**Kelly, David A.**		1994 L.R.	Honda	1995 L.R.	Yamaha
1986 J.8	Yamaha	1992 J.6	Yamaha	1983 J.30	Yamaha	1995 J.R.	Honda	1996 L.41	Yamaha
1986 L.R.	Yamaha	1992 L.R.	Yamaha	1983 S.35	Yamaha	1995 L.30	Yamaha	**Kirkby, Paul**	
1987 J.R.	Yamaha	**Jones, Arthur**		1984 J.44	Yamaha	1996 J.59	Padgett Honda	1994 J/N.2	Honda
1987 S.R.	Yamaha	1994 S/Cl.52	Seeley Matchless	1984 S.R.	Yamaha	1996 L.15	Padgett Honda	1994 J.19	Honda
Jarman, Alan		1995 S/Cl.45	Seeley Matchless	1985 J.R.	Yamaha	1997 J.90	Padgett Honda	**Kirwan, Dave S.**	
1983 J/N.22	Yamaha	1996 S/Cl.50	Seeley Matchless	1985 S.49	Yamaha	1997 L.21	Padgett Honda	1993 J/Cl.36	Aermacchi
1984 S.R.	Norton	1997 S/Cl.R.	Seeley G50	1986 J.R.	Yamaha	**Kerr, Graham**		1994 S/Cl.R.	Seeley Weslake
Jarmann, Peter		**Jones, Brian**		1986 S.44	Yamaha	1994 S/N.6	Yamaha	1995 S/Cl.R.	Seeley Weslake
1992 S/Cl.45	B.S.A.	1991 L/N.23	Kawasaki	1987 J.R.	Yamaha	1994 S.R.	Yamaha	1995 J/Cl.22	Aermacchi
1992 L.34	Kawasaki	1993 J/Cl.49	Seeley	1988 J.46	Yamaha	1995 J.41	Honda	1996 S/Cl.44	Weslake
1995 S/Cl.23	B.S.A.	1994 J/Cl.R.	Ducati			1995 S.43	Honda	1996 J/Cl.23	Aermacchi
1996 S/Cl.38	B.S.A.	1994 S/Cl.36	Seeley			1997 J.70	Kawasaki	**Kirwan, Mal L.**	

178 The History of the Manx Grand Prix 1923-1998

Year/Race	Make	Year/Race	Make	Year/Race	Make	Year/Race	Make	Year/Race	Make
1983 J/Cl.8	Aermacchi	1996 J.49	Honda	1992 S.18	Honda	1996 J.16	Yamaha	1991 L.40	Yamaha
1988 J/Cl.R.	Aermacchi	1996 S.47	Honda	**Lawless, Neil**		1996 S.25	Yamaha	1991 J.37	Yamaha
1989 S/Cl.R.	Norvel	**Knight, Ray L.**		1996 S/N.12	Honda	**Lewis, Philip S.**		1992 S.R.	Honda
1990 J/Cl.16	Aermacchi	1984 S/Cl.R.	RSM-Triumph	1996 S.86	Honda	1985 L/N.R.	Yamaha	**Lloyd, Kevin**	
1990 L.R.	Norvel	1985 S/Cl.10	RSM-Triumph	**Lawson, David**		1985 L.26	Yamaha	1983 L/N.14	Yamaha
1991 J/Cl.13	Aermacchi	1986 S/Cl.14	RSM-Triumph	1987 S/N.4	Suzuki	**Lewis, Richard**		1985 J.33	Yamaha
1992 S/Cl.33	Seeley	1987 S/Cl.15	RSM-Triumph	**Lawson, Graeme**		1996 J/N.10	Honda	1985 S.62	Yamaha
1993 J/Cl.13	Aermacchi	1988 S/Cl.R.	Triumph	1987 S/N.R.	Kawasaki	1997 J.59	Honda	**Lockwood, Peter**	
1995 J/Cl.13	Aermacchi	**Knight, Tom B.**		1988 S.13	Yamaha	1997 S.62	Honda	1992 S/Cl.53	Matchless
1995 J/Cl.11	Aermacchi	1985 S/N.1	Ducati	**Lawson, Mike**		**Liddle, Kevin**		1992 J/Cl.33	A.J.S.
Kneale, Brian P.		1986 S.9	Ducati	1990 J/N.7	Kawasaki	1987 L/N.8	Yamaha	1993 S/Cl.56	Matchless
1988 L/N.R.	Yamaha	1987 S.R.	Ducati	1991 S.38	Kawasaki	1989 S.R.	Yamaha	1994 S/Cl.R.	Matchless
1988 L.37	Yamaha	1988 S.12	Yamaha	1995 J.21	Honda	**Lilley, John**		1994 J/Cl.31	A.J.S.
1990 J.54	Yamaha	1989 S.19	Ducati	**Lawson, Paul**		1995 J/N.33	Yamaha	1995 S/Cl.47	Matchless
1990 L.31	Yamaha	1991 S.1	Honda	1996 J/N.12	Honda	1995 L.49	Yamaha	1995 J/Cl.37	A.J.S.
1991 S.31	Yamaha	**Knowles, Andy**		1997 J.62	Honda	**Linder, George**		1996 S/Cl.63	Matchless
1993 J.R.	Yamaha	1985 S/N.11	Yamaha	**Lawton, Alan T.**		1988 L/Cl.1	Yamaha	1996 J/Cl.38	A.J.S.
1993 S.30	Honda	1985 S.60	Kawasaki	1983 S/Cl.R.	Norton	1990 L/Cl.R.	Yamaha	**Loder, John**	
1995 J.30	Honda	1986 S.58	Norton	1984 S/Cl.3	Norton	1992 L/Cl.R.	Yamaha	1983 S.34	Fahron
1995 L.12	Honda	1987 S.R.	Seeley	1985 S/Cl.R.	Norton	**Lindsay, Darran R.**		1984 S/Cl.12	B.S.A.
1996 J.31	Cowles Yamaha	1988 S.18	Yamaha	1986 S/Cl.R.	Norton	1997 S/N.1	Suzuki	1984 J.R.	Yamaha
1996 L.10	Cowles Yamaha	1989 S.14	Yamaha	1990 S/Cl.R.	Norton	1997 S.31	Suzuki	1984 S.R.	Fahron
1997 J.22	DTR Yamaha	1991 S.13	Yamaha	**Lawton, Ken D.**		**Lindsay, Ken**		1985 S/Cl.R.	B.S.A.
1997 L.2	DTR Yamaha	**Knowles, John**		1985 S/Cl.R.	B.S.A.	1990 L/Cl.17	Ducati	1985 J.25	Jewel Yamaha
Kneen, Chris		1983 S/Cl.11	Seeley	1986 S/Cl.16	B.S.A.	**Linham, Garry**		1986 S/Cl.18	B.S.A.
1983 J.R.	Yamaha	1983 J.8	Yamaha	1987 S/Cl.R.	B.S.A.	1994 L/N.4	Honda	1987 S/Cl.R.	Gold Star
1983 L.R.	Yamaha	1983 S.19	Yamaha	1988 S/Cl.R.	B.S.A.	1994 L.14	Honda	1988 J/Cl.R.	B.S.A.
1984 J.34	Yamaha	1984 S/Cl.8	Seeley G50	**Leach, Dave**		1996 J.10	Yamaha	1988 S/Cl.26	B.S.A.
1984 S.R.	Yamaha	1985 J.R.	Seeley	1983 J.R.	Yamaha	1996 L.6	Yamaha	1989 J/Cl.R.	Greeves
1985 J.42	Yamaha	1985 S/Cl.5	Seeley	1983 L.4	Yamaha	1997 J.20	Honda	1989 S/Cl.R.	B.S.A.
1985 S.29	Yamaha	1986 S/Cl.5	Seeley	1984 J.6	Yamaha	1997 L.1	Honda	1990 J/Cl.R.	Greeves
1986 J.R.	Yamaha	1986 S.37	Honda	1984 L.R.	Yamaha	**Linsdell, Steve**		1990 S/Cl.R.	B.S.A.
1987 J.23	Yamaha	1987 S/Cl.8	Seeley	1991 S/Cl.R.	Matchless	1983 S/Cl.R.	Seeley	1991 J/Cl.11	Greeves
1987 L.22	Yamaha	1988 S/Cl.6	Seeley	1997 S/Cl.9	Weslake	1983 S.R.	Moriwaki	1992 S/Cl.R.	B.S.A.
1988 S.R.	Kawasaki	1990 S/Cl.12	Seeley	**Leatherbarrow, Wayne E.**		1984 S/Cl.R.	Enfield Seeley	1992 J/Cl.R.	Greeves
1989 S.R.	Suzuki	1991 S/Cl.10	Seeley	1985 S/N.10	Spondon Yamaha	1984 S.6	Moriwaki	1993 S/Cl.7	Seeley
1990 S.64	Suzuki	1992 S/Cl.R.	Seeley	1987 S.31	Yamaha	1985 S/Cl.R.	Seeley Enfield	1993 J/Cl.8	Greeves
1991 S.50	Suzuki	**Knox, James A.**		**Leddy, Ricky**		1985 S.3	Flitwick Yamaha	1994 J/Cl.R.	Greeves
1992 S.63	Suzuki	1984 J/N.R.	Yamaha	1995 S/N.8	Honda	1992 S/Cl.3	Norton	1994 S/Cl.R.	KSS Seeley
1993 S.44	Suzuki	**Kormendy, Nick**		1995 S.R.	Honda	1993 S/Cl.R.	Norton	1995 J/Cl.R.	Greeves
1994 S.42	Suzuki	1990 L/N.R.	Kawasaki	1996 L.37	Yamaha	1994 J/Cl.R.	Lawton Aermacchi	1996 S/Cl.R.	KSS Seeley
1995 J.74	Yamaha	1990 L.33	Kawasaki	**Lee, David C.**		1994 S/Cl.R.	Norton	1996 J/Cl.15	Greeves
1995 S.42	Honda			1984 S/N.R.	Honda	1995 S/Cl.R.	Flitwick Norton	1997 S/Cl.R.	Seeley G50
1996 J.83	Yamaha	**Langton, Mark**		**Lee, Gavin B.**		**Linton, Dick**		1997 J/Cl.5	Greeves
1996 S.75	Yamaha	1988 L/N.3	Yamaha	1986 L/N.R.	Yamaha	1983 S/Cl.R.	Linto	**Lofthouse, Mick**	
1997 S.88	Windsor Kawasaki	**Lanyman, Steve**		1987 J.22	Yamaha	1984 S/Cl.20	Linto	1990 L/N.1	Kawasaki
Kneen, Mark		1985 J/N.R.	Yamaha	1987 L.15	Yamaha	**Linton, Mark**		**Logan, Doug**	
1993 L/N.11	Yamaha	1986 J.R.	Yamaha	1988 J.26	Yamaha	1985 L/N.4	Yamaha	1993 J/N.11	Yamaha
1993 L.49	Yamaha	**Large, Ian**		1988 L.R.	Yamaha	1985 L.12	Yamaha	1993 J.63	Yamaha
1994 J.R.	Yamaha	1989 J/N.2	Yamaha	1989 L.7	Yamaha	1986 J/Cl.4	Aermacchi	1994 J.R.	Honda
1994 L.R.	Yamaha	1989 J.20	Yamaha	1990 J.2	Yamaha	1986 L.6	Yamaha	1995 J.R.	Honda
1995 L.32	Yamaha	**Larsen, Neil**		1990 L.1	Yamaha	1987 J.3	Yamaha	1995 S.53	Honda
Kneen, Norman		1988 S/N.6	Suzuki	**Lee, Martin J.**		1987 L.R.	Yamaha	1996 J.47	Honda
1989 S.6	Yamaha	1989 S/Cl.35	Velocette	1983 J.23	Yamaha	1988 J/Cl.2	Aermacchi	1996 S.32	Honda
1990 J.4	Honda	1989 S.24	Yamaha	1984 J.R.	Yamaha	1988 J.2	Yamaha	1997 J.47	Honda
1990 L.9	Honda	1990 S/Cl.45	Velocette	**Leech, Tim**		1988 L.R.	Yamaha	1997 S.49	Honda
1991 J.R.	Yamaha	1991 S/Cl.R.	Velocette	1992 S/N.1	Maxton Kawasaki	1989 J/Cl.3	Aermacchi	**Long, Gary**	
1992 J.R.	Yamaha	1991 J/Cl.27	Velocette	1992 S.14	Maxton Kawasaki	1989 J.8	Yamaha	1996 J/Cl.R.	Suzuki
1992 S.R.	Yamaha	1991 S.27	Suzuki	1993 S.14	Honda	1989 L.2	Honda	1997 L/Cl.2	Suzuki
1993 J.R.	Yamaha	1992 S/Cl.31	Velocette	1993 S.5	Maxton Kawasaki	1990 J.7	Yamaha	**Long, Gordon B.**	
1995 J.15	Kawasaki	1992 J/Cl.21	A.J.S.	**Leeson, Don**		1990 L.4	Yamaha	1983 L/N.16	Yamaha
1995 S.18	Kawasaki	1992 S.17	Suzuki	1995 L/Cl.16	Suzuki	**Livingston, Ken**		1983 L.68	Yamaha
1996 J.11	Kneenja Kawasaki	1993 S/Cl.18	Seeley	1997 L/Cl.17	Suzuki	1991 S/N.13	Cagiva	**Long, Harry**	
1996 S.15	Kneenja Kawasaki	1993 S.19		**Leigh Pemberton, John**		**Livingston, Mark D.**		1984 S/Cl.29	B.S.A.
1997 J.12	Kneenja Kawasaki	1994 J/Cl.19	Drixton Aermacchi	1996 J/N.6	Honda	1983 S/N.R.	Honda	1985 S/Cl.30	B.S.A.
1997 S.45	Kneenja Kawasaki	1994 S.13	Yamaha	**Leonard, Sean**		1987 S.41	Suzuki	1986 S/Cl.28	B.S.A.
Kneen, Phil		1996 S/Cl.R.	Seeley Weslake	1986 J/N.R.	Maxton	1988 L/N.9	Honda	1987 S.Cl.37	B.S.A.
1989 S.34	Yamaha	1996 S.16	Yamaha	1986 L.R.	Maxton	1988 S.46	Suzuki	1988 S/Cl.R.	B.S.A.
1990 J.R.	Yamaha	1997 S/Cl.13	Seeley Weslake	**Leroux, Patrick**		1989 S.18	Suzuki	**Longstaff, Ian D.**	
Kneen, Richard		1997 S.25	Yamaha	1997 S/Cl.57	Velocette	1990 J/Cl.R.	Honda	1984 S/N.R.	Honda
1990 L.28	RGC Suzuki	**Lavery, Brian P.**		**Leroy, Bruno**		1990 S.12	Suzuki	**Longstreeth, Dave**	
1991 L.R.	Yamaha	1987 S/N.38	Yamaha	1996 S/Cl.24	Norton	1991 S.6	Suzuki	1995 S/Cl.R.	Velocette
1992 L.R.	Honda	1988 S.72	Yamaha	1997 S/Cl.6	G50 Seeley	1992 J.18	Honda	**Lord, Steve**	
Knight, Nick		1991 J.R.	Yamaha	**Leslie, Graham**		1992 S.R.	Honda	1991 J/N.7	Yamaha
1990 J/N.14	Honda	1991 S.57	Yamaha	1983 L.24	Yamaha	**Lloyd, David J.**		1991 S.54	Yamaha
1991 S.37	Honda	1992 J.62	Yamaha	1984 J.28	Yamaha	1985 S/N.15	Ducati	1992 J.R.	Yamaha
1992 S.60	Honda	1992 S.60	Yamaha	1986 S.R.	Ducati	1992 L.17	Yamaha		
1992 S.28	Kawasaki	1993 S.38	Yamaha	**Lewis, Greg**		1987 S.55	Ducati	1993 L.28	Yamaha
1993 J.40	Honda	1993 J.R.	Yamaha	1993 L/N.7	Honda	1989 S.70	Ducati	1994 J.R.	RG Honda
1993 S.26	Honda	**Law, Adrian E.**		1993 L.R.	Honda	1992 J.33	Ducati	1994 S.32	RG Honda
1994 J.54	Honda	1983 J.R.	Yamaha	1994 J.38	Yamaha	1992 S.R.	Ducati	**Lougher, Ian**	
1994 S.26	Honda	1983 L.57	Yamaha	1994 S.16	Yamaha	1993 J.R.	Harris Ducati	1983 J/N.3	Yamaha
1995 J.34	Honda	**Law, Ashley**		1995 J.18	Yamaha	**Lloyd, Derek**		1984 J.R.	Yamaha
1995 S.29	Honda	1992 J/N.R.	Honda	1995 S.13	Yamaha	1990 L/N.R.	Yamaha		

1989 S/Cl.R. Matchless
Lovett, Andy
1997 J/N.7 Honda
1997 J.62 Honda
Low, Doug A.
1987 J/Cl.29 Royal Enfield
1988 S.37 Suzuki
1989 S.56 Suzuki
1991 S.11 Suzuki
1991 J/Cl.R. Greeves
Lowdon, Derek R.
1985 L.23 Crooks Suzuki
1988 L.28 Yamaha
Lowson, Ian
1983 J/N.R. Yamaha
Ludlow, Neil
1995 J/N.23 Knotts Honda
Lumley, Brian
1988 J/Cl.47 Norton
Lund, Brian
1983 J.R. Yamaha
Lunney, Phil A.
1984 S/N.R. Yamaha
1986 S.49 Yamaha
1987 S.49 Yamaha
1988 S.49 Yamaha
Lynch, Declan P.
1985 J/N.R. Yamaha
Lynch, Pat
1989 S/N.8 Suzuki
Lynn, Nick J.
1986 S/N.3 Honda

McAleer, Liam
1992 L/N.R. Kawasaki
1993 J.64 Kawasaki
1993 L.45 Kawasaki
1994 J.67 Crossan
1994 S.48 Crossan Honda
1995 J.R. Honda
1995 S.R. Honda
1996 S.82 Crossan Honda
1997 J.89 Crossan Honda
1997 S.68 Crossan Honda
McBride, Brian
1993 S/N.9 Honda
McBride, John
1983 J.29 Yamaha
1983 S.31 Yamaha
1984 J.37 Yamaha
1984 S.32 Yamaha
1985 J.R. Yamaha
1985 S.16 Yamaha
1986 S.16 Suzuki
1987 S.10 Suzuki
1988 S.R. Suzuki
1989 S.48 Suzuki
1992 J.44 Honda
1992 S.37 Honda
1993 J.41 Honda
1993 S.31 Honda
1995 J.58 Honda
1995 S.39 Honda
1996 J.64 Honda
1996 S.51 Honda
Macbride, Tony J.
1997 L/N.7 Kawasaki
1997 S/Cl.56 Norton
McCabe, Decland R.
1984 L/N.R. Yamaha
1984 10 Yamaha
McCallen, J. Phillip
1988 L/N.1 Honda
1988 L.1 Honda
McCallister, Ronnie
1992 L.25 Suzuki
1993 J.R. Yamaha
McCallum, I. Bruce
1983 S/Cl.10 Matchless
1984 S.36 Harris Suzuki
1985 S.R. Ducati
1986 S.36 Ducati
1988 S/Cl.9 Seeley
1989 S/Cl.R. Seeley
1990 S/Cl.15 Seeley
McCartney, Andrew
1991 L/Cl.17 Suzuki
McClements, Stephen
1983 J.R. Yamaha
1983 L.6 Yamaha
1984 L.R. Yamaha
1985 L.R. Yamaha
1986 J.12 Yamaha
1986 L.R. Yamaha
McCloy, Andy
1989 S/N.16 Suzuki
1992 S.21 Honda
1993 S.R. Honda
1994 J.21 Honda
1994 S.20 Honda
1995 J.17 Honda
1996 J.40 Honda
1996 S.27 Honda
1997 J.36 Honda
1997 S.38 Honda
McCloy, Martin
1997 J/N.5 Honda
1997 J.R. Team Fab Honda
McCormack, William H.
1983 S/N.5 Kawasaki
McCormick, John D.
1984 S.R. Kawasaki
1985 S.4 Peckett Kawasaki
1986 S.52 McNab Kawasaki
1987 S.42 Suzuki
McDiarmid, Stewart N.
1983 S/N.9 Yamaha
1983 L.R. Yamaha
1986 S.R. Ducati
McDonald, Allan
1988 S/N.1 Suzuki
1989 J.11 Yamaha
1989 S.2 Honda
McDonald, Marc R.
1995 J/N.15 Honda
1995 J.39 Honda
1996 J.17 Honda
1996 L.12 Yamaha
1996 S.18 Honda
1997 J.85 Yamaha
1997 L.8 Yamaha
1997 S.18 Suzuki
McDonnell, Eugene P.
1983 J/N.5 Yamaha
McDonnell, Angus
1994 L/N.15 Kawasaki
1994 L.R. Kawasaki
McDowell, Robert
1983 L/N.R. Yamaha
McFarland, Adrian
1995 J/N.2 Schimmel Honda
1995 S.6 Schimmel Honda
1996 J.4 Schimmel Honda
1996 S.8 Schimmel Honda
McGahan, Chris J.
1986 S/Cl.13 Seeley
1988 S/Cl.10 Matchless
1989 S/Cl.8 Seeley
1990 S/Cl.4 Seeley
1991 S/Cl.5 G50 Seeley
1992 S/Cl.7 Seeley
1992 J/Cl.R. Aermacchi
1993 S/Cl.5 Seeley
1994 S/Cl.12 Trekdean Seeley
1995 S/Cl.R. Trekdean Seeley
1997 S/Cl.7 Trekdean Seeley
1997 J/Cl.R. Oldfield Aermacchi
McGarrity, Michael
1983 J/N.R. Yamaha
1993 L/Cl.R. N.S.U.
1994 L/Cl.R. N.S.U.
McGee, Peter
1993 L/N.R. Yamaha
1994 L.40 Yamaha
McGinty, Terry
1996 S/Cl.R. Matchless G50
1997 S/Cl.19 Seeley G50
1997 J/Cl.17 Seeley 7R
McGladdery, Andy
1991 S/Cl.6 Matchless
McGovern, Chris D.
1988 S/N.R. Yamaha
1989 S.73 Kawasaki
1995 J.77 Kawasaki
1995 L.45 Kawasaki
1996 J.78 Honda
1996 L.30 Honda
1997 J.86 Honda
1997 L.31 Honda
McHenry, Herbie P.
1988 J/N.R. Yamaha
McIlroy, Brian F.
1985 J/N.R. Yamaha
McKinstry, David
1983 L.R. Yamaha
McLachlan, Victor J.
1985 S/Cl.R. Triumph
1986 S/Cl.36 Triumph
McLaughlin, Patrick
1983 L.R. Yamaha
1984 J.R. Yamaha
1984 L.R. Yamaha
McLean, Nigel
1991 L/N.17 Suzuki
1993 J.39 Yamaha
McLoy, Andy
1995 S.11 Honda
McManus, Bridget
1996 S/N.7 Honda
1996 S.60 Honda
1997 J.57 Honda
1997 S.60 Honda
McManus, James
1983 S/N.11 Suzuki
1984 J.R. Yamaha
1984 S.R. Yamaha
1985 J.30 Yamaha
1985 S.15 Yamaha
1986 J.R. Yamaha
1986 S.R. Yamaha
1987 J.R. Yamaha
1987 S.44 Yamaha
McManus, John
1983 S.R. Suzuki
1984 S.38 Kawasaki
1985 S.25 Kawasaki
1986 S.33 Kawasaki
1987 S.R. Yamaha
1988 S.47 Yamaha
McMaster, Leslie
1989 L/N.4 E.M.C.
1989 J.5 Yamaha
1989 L.R. E.M.C.
McMillan, Ian
1987 L/N.R. Yamaha
1987 L.31 Yamaha
McNulty, Vince
1985 J/N.14 Yamaha
McStay, Sean
1984 J/N.R. Yamaha
1984 L.1 E.M.C.
McVeighty, Ian
1993 L/N.6 Yamaha
1993 L.20 Yamaha
1994 J.27 Yamaha
1994 L.R. Yamaha
McVey, John
1993 L/N.14 Yamaha
1993 L.50 Yamaha
McVittie, Colin
1987 S/N.22 Yamaha
1988 S.57 Yamaha
Maddocks, John F.
1988 S/Cl.56 Norton
Maddocks, Peter W.
1988 J/Cl.R. Honda
Madsen-Mygdal, David
1983 J.R. Yamaha
1983 L.60 Yamaha
1984 J.R. Yamaha
1984 S.R. Kawasaki
Maher, Philip D.
1983 J/N.R. Yamaha
Mainwaring, Stephen
1983 S.R. Suzuki
1988 S.29 Suzuki
Mannion, Leo
1985 J/N.R. Yamaha
Margrain, Beth
1991 L/N.18 Kawasaki
1992 J.R. Yamaha
1992 L.21 Yamaha
Marks, Paul R.
1987 S/N.21 Kawasaki
1988 S.45 Kawasaki
1989 S.R. Suzuki
1990 S.50 Suzuki
1991 S.32 Suzuki
1992 J.55 Suzuki
1992 S.36 Suzuki
1993 J.R. PRM Suzuki
1993 S.52 PRM Suzuki
1994 J.59 Honda
1994 S.R. Honda
1995 S.R. Honda
1996 S.69 Honda
1997 S.48 Honda
Marsh, Carl
1986 L/N.5 Yamaha
1986 L.30 Yamaha
Marshal, Alan
1983 J.23 Yamaha
1983 L.18 Yamaha
1984 J.R. Yamaha
1984 S.26 Yamaha
1986 S.55 Honda
1987 S.R. Honda
1988 S.60 Honda
1989 S.22 Honda
1991 S.20 Honda
1992 J.13 Honda
1992 S.16 Honda
1993 J.5 Honda
1993 S.12 Honda
1994 J.R. Honda
1995 J.10 Yamaha
1995 L.6 Yamaha
1996 L.R. Yamaha
Marshal, Gary
1986 S/N.17 Honda
1987 S.66 Honda
1988 S/Cl.R. Norton
1988 S.R. Yamaha
1990 S.62 Yamaha
Marshal, Mark G.
1997 L/N.R. Yamaha
1997 L.41 Yamaha
Marshal, Stuart C
1984 S/N.2 Honda
1985 S.4 Suzuki
1987 S.8 Honda
1990 J.R. Honda
Marshal, Toby
1996 L/N.R. Yamaha
1996 L.38 Yamaha
1997 J.84 Yamaha
1997 L.26 Yamaha
Marston, Donald A.
1983 L/N.6 Rotax
1983 L.21 Rotax
Martin, Dean C.
1983 S.R. Honda
1995 J.56 Honda
1995 L.28 Honda
1996 J.54 Padgett Honda
1996 L.18 Padgett Honda
1997 J.56 Padgett Honda
1997 L.15 Padgett Honda
Martin, Gary P.
1983 J/Cl.14 A.J.S.
1983 J.R. Yamaha
1984 S/Cl.R. Norton
1984 J.R. Yamaha
1985 J.R. Yamaha
Martin, Geoffrey D.
1983 J.R. Yamaha
1983 S.39 Suzuki
1984 S.29 Suzuki
1985 J/Cl.23 Honda
1985 S.17 Suzuki
1986 J/Cl.28 Honda
1986 S.7 Suzuki
1987 S.9 Suzuki
1988 S.23 Suzuki
1989 S.25 Yamaha
1990 S.49 Suzuki
Martin, Paddy R.
1983 J.R. Yamaha
1983 S.42 Honda
1984 S.57 Kawasaki
1985 S.R. S & S Kawasaki
1986 S.R. Suzuki
1987 S.R. Suzuki
1989 S.55 Yamaha
1997 L.30 Honda
Martin, Paul W.
1983 J.R. Shepherd
1983 S.29 Suzuki
Martin, Tony
1983 S/Cl.R. B.S.A.
1983 J.20 Yamaha
1984 J.18 Yamaha
1984 L.R. Yamaha
1985 J.12 Yamaha
1985 L.15 Yamaha
1986 J.4 Yamaha
1986 L.13 Yamaha
1987 J.6 Yamaha
1987 L.13 Yamaha
Mason, Craig
1990 L/N.4 Kawasaki
1991 J.16 Kawasaki
1991 L.18 Kawasaki
Mason, Tony
1989 L/Cl.R. Ariel
1990 J.R. E.M.C.
1990 L.45 E.M.C.
1991 L/Cl.11 N.S.U.
1992 L/Cl.9 N.S.U.
1994 S/Cl.R. Norton
1994 L/Cl.9 Crooks Suzuki
1995 S/Cl.R. Norton
1995 L/Cl.R. Crooks Suzuki
1996 L/Cl.R. Crooks Suzuki
Mateer, Brian
1992 L/N.13 Suzuki
1992 L.41 Suzuki
1993 J.56 Suzuki
1993 L.38 Suzuki
1994 J.49 Yamaha
1994 L.18 Yamaha
1995 J.42 Yamaha
1995 L.R. Yamaha
1996 J.62 Yamaha
1996 L.20 Yamaha
1997 J.42 Yamaha
1997 L.14 Yamaha
Matthews, Stuart J.
1984 J/N.15 Yamaha
Matulja, Philip
1986 J/N.5 Yamaha
1986 L.22 Yamaha
1988 J.22 Yamaha
1988 L.19 Yamaha
Mawdsley, Kevin M.
1984 J/N.6 Yamaha
1985 J.8 Yamaha
Maxwell, Joe
1991 L/Cl.20 Ducati
May, David J.
1987 S/Cl.42 Norton
1988 J/Cl.28 Norton
1988 S/Cl.17 Norton
1989 S/Cl.4 Norton
1989 J/Cl.R. Norton
1991 S/Cl.9 Norton
1991 J/Cl.10 Norton
Mead, David
1993 J/N.R. Honda
1995 J/Cl.41 Petty Norton

1995 S.69	Kawasaki	1988 L.30	Yamaha	1986 L.R.	Maxton	Moss, Richard J.		1993 J/Cl.R.	A.J.S.
Meaney, Dave		1989 S/Cl.27	Seeley	1987 S.35	Suzuki	1984 L.R.	Yamaha	1994 S/Cl.R.	Matchless
1989 J/N.5	Yamaha	1989 S.66	Yamaha	1990 S.42	Suzuki	1985 L.32	Honda	1995 S/Cl.7	Seeley G50
Meli, Sergio		**Mitchell, Dennis J.**		1991 S.36	Suzuki	**Mould, John A.**		1995 S/Cl.R.	A.J.S.
1992 S/Cl.R.	Seeley Weslake	1985 J/N.15	Yamaha	1995 J.67	Yamaha	1983 J.9	Yamaha	1996 S/Cl.32	Seeley
1993 S/Cl.	Seeley Weslake	1985 L.37	Yamaha	1995 L.R.	Yamaha	1983 L.R.	Yamaha	1996 J/Cl.R.	Aermacchi
1993 J/Cl.R.	Greeves	**Mitchell, Ian**		**Moore, Robert A.**		1984 J.R.	Yamaha	1997 S/Cl.5	Seeley
1995 S/Cl.40	Seeley Weslake	1986 S/N.2	Suzuki	1983 L/Cl.R.	Crooks Suzuki	1984 L.13	Maxton Yamaha	1997 S/Cl.R.	A.J.S.
1995 J/Cl.R.	Ducati	1987 S.12	Suzuki	1983 J.47	Yamaha	1985 J.9	Maxton Yamaha	**Mylchreest, Cliff**	
Mellish, Anthony M.		**Mitchell, John**		1984 L.40	Spondon Yamaha	1985 S.R.	Maxton Yamaha	1989 J.R.	Yamaha
1984 J/N.R.	Spondon Yamaha	1994 S/Cl.54	Norton	1985 L.36	Yamaha	**Muir, Duncan**		**Neate, John P.**	
1984 S.R.	Spondon Yamaha	1995 S/Cl.R.	Norton	1986 L.35	Yamaha	1994 S/N.1	Honda	1983 J/N.11	Yamaha
Mellor, Philip, G.		1996 S/Cl.R.	Norton	1987 L.41	Yamaha	1994 S.12	Kawasaki	**Neilson, Neil**	
1983 L.R.	Rotax	1997 S/Cl.48	Norton	1988 L.R.	Yamaha	**Mullaney, Mark**		1985 J/Cl.R.	Aermacchi
1984 S.56	Honda	**Mitchell, Ricky**		**Moore, Seamus P.**		1994 S/N.2	Yamaha	**Nelson, Dean**	
1985 J.27	Yamaha	1995 J/N.1	Yamaha	1987 S/N.12	Harris F2	**Munro, Neil**		1994 S/N.3	Yamaha
1985 S.38	Yamaha	1995 J.2	Yamaha	**Morgan, Charlie**		1987 S/N.7	Suzuki	1994 S.14	Yamaha
Mercer, Paul F.		1996 J.1	GS Honda	1989 J.15	Yamaha	1989 S.60	Yamaha	1996 S.26	Yamaha
1997 S/N.5	Yamaha	1996 L.1	GS Honda	1989 L.45	Rotax	**Munro, Rob**		1997 S.12	Yamaha
Middleton, Barrie J.		**Moffatt, Malcolm A. C.**		**Morgan, Nick**		1991 J/N.12	Honda	**Nelson, A. Martyn**	
1983 L/N.1	Yamaha	1985 S/Cl.R.	B.S.A.	1991 S/N.4	Yamaha	**Munsey, Roger**		1983 J.R.	Yamaha
1983 L.10	Yamaha	1986 S/Cl.R.	B.S.A.	1992 J.R.	Yamaha	1992 J/Cl.19	A.J.S.	1983 S.R.	Yamaha
1984 L.9	Yamaha	**Moffitt, Chris**		1992 S.13	Kawasaki	1994 J/Cl.8	A.J.S.	1984 J.3	Yamaha
1985 J.23	Yamaha	1994 L/N.R.		1993 J.R.	Yamaha	1995 S/Cl.14	MB Seeley	1984 S.9	Yamaha
1989 S.4	Honda		Gower Power Honda	1993 S.4	Ducati	1996 S/Cl.35	MB Seeley	**Neumair, Reinhard**	
Milbourn, Nicholas		1994 J.60	Gower Power Honda	1994 J.24	Honda	1997 S/Cl.34	MB Seeley	1992 S/Cl.R.	B.S.A.
1985 L/N.R.	Rotax	1994 L.19	Gower Power Honda	1994 S.R.	Honda	**Murden, Phil**		1993 S/Cl.63	B.S.A.
Milburn, Gary		**Moffitt, David J.**		**Morris, Chris**		1992 L/N.R.	Yamaha	1994 S/Cl.43	B.S.A.
1997 J/N.9	Honda	1986 L/N.R.	Yamaha	1989 S/N.1	Honda	1992 L.36	Yamaha	1995 S/Cl.35	B.S.A.
1997 J.80	Honda	1986 L.R.	Yamaha	1991 J.42	Kawasaki	1993 J.38	Yamaha	1995 J/Cl.R.	Aermacchi
Miley, Andy		1987 J.R.	Yamaha	1991 S.19	Honda	1993 S.25	Yamaha	1996 S/Cl.64	Norton
1993 S.R.	Kawasaki	1987 L.R.	Armstrong Rotax	**Morris, Clin**		1994 J.45	Yamaha	1996 J/Cl.33	Aermacchi
1994 S.45	Kawasaki	1988 J.R.	Yamaha	1996 L/Cl.R.	Suzuki	1994 S.29	Yamaha	1997 S/Cl.38	Norton
Millar, Jimmy		1988 L.48	E.M.C.	**Morris, Ian G.**		1995 J.11	Honda	1997 J/Cl.30	Aermacchi
1983 J/Cl.4	Aermacchi	**Molnar, Andy**		1987 L/N.1	Yamaha	1995 S.20	Honda	**Neumuller, Philip**	
Miley, Andy		1986 S/Cl.35	Norton	1988 J.8	Yamaha	1996 J.R.	Honda	1984 J/Cl.29	B.S.A.
1992 L/N.R.	Rotax	1989 S/Cl.38	Norton	1988 L.6	Rotax	1997 J.27	Honda	1985 J/Cl.R.	Greeves
1992 L.R.	Rotax	1995 S/Cl.R.	Norton	1989 J.R.	Maxton	1997 S.36	AJM Honda	**Neve, Andy**	
1996 J.63	Honda	1996 S/Cl.59	Norton	1989 L.R.	Kimoco	**Murden, Rupert C. H.**		1995 J/N.28	Honda
1996 S.56	Honda	1996 J/Cl.36	Norton	**Morris, Simon**		1983 L/Cl.R.	Aermacchi	1996 J.66	Honda
1997 J.71	Honda	**Monk, Kevin E. J.**		1983 J/Cl.29	Ducati	1983 S.57	Bonneville	1996 S.54	Honda
1997 S.52	Honda	1988 S/Cl.R.	Triumph	1984 J/Cl.18	Ducati	1984 J/Cl.8	Aermacchi	**Neville, Gary P.**	
Miller, David		**Montgomery, David R.**		1987 S.69	Ducati	1985 J/Cl.21	Aermacchi	1985 L/N.11	Yamaha
1990 S/N.11	Yamaha	1983 J.R.	Yamaha	**Morris, Stephen John**		1985 S.63	Harris Kawasaki	1985 L.21	Yamaha
1992 S.61	Kawasaki	1983 S.R.	Suzuki	1987 J/Cl.15	Aermacchi	1986 L.26	Yamaha
1993 S.49	Kawasaki	1984 J.14	Yamaha	1989 S/N.29	Yamaha	1987 S.R.	Ducati	1987 J.30	Yamaha
1994 S.49	Kawasaki	1984 S.22	Suzuki	1990 S.46	Honda	1989 L/Cl.R.	Aermacchi	1987 L.30	Yamaha
1995 S.46	Kawasaki	1985 J.11	Yamaha	1992 J.66	Kawasaki	1990 L/Cl.R.	Aermacchi	1989 J.25	Yamaha
1996 S.43	CAM Kawasaki	1985 S.11	Suzuki	1992 S.67	Honda	1993 S/Cl.37	Norton	1989 S.74	Suzuki
1997 S.77	CAM Kawasaki	1986 J.14	Yamaha	1993 S.39	Honda	**Murphy, Kevin P.**		1990 J.45	Yamaha
Miller, George		1986 S.10	Yamaha	1994 S.51	Honda	1984 S/N.13	Honda	1990 S.53	Suzuki
1988 J/Cl.46	Aermacchi	1987 J.7	Yamaha	**Morrissey, Paul**		1994 L.43	Honda	1991 J.R.	Yamaha
1989 J/Cl.22	Aermacchi	1987 S.R.	Yamaha	1994 L/N.12	Honda	1995 L.39	Suzuki	1991 L.R.	Yamaha
Miller, Jazz		1988 J.12=	Yamaha	1994 L.42	Honda	1996 L.31	Honda	1992 J.R.	Yamaha
1996 J/N.17	Yamaha	1988 S.11	Suzuki	1995 L.48	Kawasaki	**Murray, Ken G.**		1992 L.16	Yamaha
1996 S.87	Yamaha	1989 J.1	Yamaha	**Morss, Gordon**		1985 J/N.R.	Yamaha	**New, Roy**	
Miller, Keith		1989 S.15	Suzuki	1983 L/Cl.R.	Greeves	1986 J.R.	Yamaha	1992 S/N.R.	Suzuki
1985 S/N.R.	Kawasaki	1993 J/Cl.7	Aermacchi	1983 J.R.	Yamaha	1986 S.30	Suzuki	1992 S.R.	Suzuki
Milling, Dave S.		1994 S/Cl.27		1983 S.61	Triumph	1987 S.25	Suzuki	**Newbery, Kevin R.**	
1989 S/N.R.	Suzuki		Meadows Aermacchi	**Mortimer, Richard**		1988 J.14	Yamaha	1984 L/N.6	Maxton
1990 J.8	Yamaha	1994 J/Cl.6		1989 J/N.4	Yamaha	1988 S.27	Yamaha	1984 L.37	Maxton
1991 J.1	Yamaha		Meadows Aermacchi	**Morton, Graham**		1989 J.10	Yamaha	1985 L.R.	Rotax
1991 L.1	Yamaha	1995 S/Cl.26		1989 L/N.R.	Kawasaki	1989 S.26	Yamaha	1986 L.R.	Maxton
Millinship, Bob J.			Meadows Aermacchi	1991 J.R.	Suzuki	**Murray, Steve**		1987 J.44	Yamaha
1985 L/N.13	Ducati	1995 J/Cl.R.		1992 J.29=	Honda	1992 S/Cl.16	Seeley	1987 L.34	Maxton
1986 J/Cl.8	Ducati		Meadows Aermacchi	1993 J.15	Yamaha	1993 S/Cl.13	Seeley	1988 J.42	Yamaha
1987 J/Cl.R.	Ducati	1996 S/Cl.29	Seeley Matchless	1993 L.11	Yamaha	**Murtagh, David**		1988 L.43	Rotax
1988 J/Cl.10	Ducati	1996 J/Cl.10		1994 J.4	Padgett Honda	1995 J/N.20	Yamaha	**Newby, Bob**	
1989 J/Cl.5	Ducati		Meadows Aermacchi	1994 L.9	Padgett Honda	1996 J.52	Yamaha	1994 S/Cl.R.	Manx Norton
1990 S.54	Honda	1997 S/Cl.29	Seeley Matchless	1995 S.4	Christie Honda	1996 S.48	Yamaha	1994 J/Cl.R.	Manx Norton
1990 S/Cl.R.	Ducati	1997 J/Cl.12		1996 S.9	Honda	**Myatt, Neil**		1995 J/Cl.5	Mularney Manx
1992 J/Cl.10	Ducati		Meadows Aermacchi	1997 S/Cl.R.	Christie Seeley	1990 J/N.8	Yamaha	1996 J/Cl.4	Mularney Manx
1992 S.29	Harris Suzuki	**Moore, Chris**		1997 J.8	A&D Christie Honda	1991 S.45	Yamaha	**Newman, Dave A.**	
1995 S/Cl.R.	Ducati	1996 L/N.1	Yamaha	1997 S.R.	Honda	1994 J.63	Yamaha	1986 S/N.18	Honda
1995 J/Cl.9	Ducati	1996 L.29	Yamaha	**Moss, Philip J.**		1994 S.53	Yamaha	1987 S.52	Suzuki
1996 S/Cl.R.	Ducati	**Moore, David**		1985 J/Cl.R.	Norton	**Myers, Tony**		**Newton, David A.**	
1997 S/Cl.R.	Ducati	1988 L/N.9	Yamaha	1986 J/Cl.33	Norton	1986 S/Cl.R.	Ducati	1984 S/Cl.16	Tricati
1997 J/Cl.10	Ducati	1989 S.R.	Honda	1988 J/Cl.50	Norton	1987 S/Cl.30	Norton	1985 S/Cl.12	Tricati
Milnes, Paul		**Moore, Eric**		1988 S/Cl.44	Norton	1988 S/Cl.R.	Norton	1986 S/Cl.R.	Triumph
1985 J/N.R.	Spondon Yamaha	1990 S/N.2	Suzuki	1989 J/Cl.R.	Norton	1990 J/Cl.30	Myers	1987 S/Cl.18	Tricati
1986 S.63	Suzuki	1990 S.23	Suzuki	1990 J/Cl.27	Seeley	1990 S/Cl.43	Norton	1988 S/Cl.R.	Tricati
1987 L.43	Armstrong	**Moore, Peter J**		1991 J/Cl.R.	Aermacchi	1991 J/Cl.R.	A.J.S.	1988 S/Cl.R.	Ducati
Minchell, John		1984 J/N.R.	Harris	1991 J/Cl.R.	Aermacchi	1992 S/Cl.R.	Ducati	1988 S/Cl.R.	Tricati
1984 J/Cl.27	B.S.A.	1986 J.R.	Harris	1992 S/Cl.R.	Seeley	1992 J/Cl.14	A.J.S.	1989 J/Cl.37	Ducati

The History of the Manx Grand Prix 1923-1998 181

1989 S/Cl.32	Tricati	1994 S/Cl.R.	RSM-Triumph	1992 S.4	Honda	1983 J.36	Yamaha	1992 S/Cl.36	Ducati
Newton, Ian		1994 J/Cl.R.	RSM-Triumph	**Ollerton, Paul**		1983 S.25	Kawasaki	1992 J/Cl.16	Ducati
1983 J/N.R.	Yamaha	1995 S/Cl.43	RSM-Triumph	1989 S/N.23	Yamaha	1984 S/Cl.24	B.S.A.	1993 S/Cl.R.	Ducati
1984 J.1	Yamaha	**Noone, Justin**		**O'Neill, Charlie**		1984 J.R.	Yamaha	1993 S/Cl.25	Ducati
1984 L.R.	Armstrong	1996 S/N.5	Sally Long Honda	1985 J/N.R.	Yamaha	1985 S/Cl.R.	B.S.A.	1994 J/Cl.12	Ducati
Newton, Joe		**Norris A. J. Bill**		1986 J.R.	Yamaha	1993 S/Cl.R.	B.S.A.	1994 S/Cl.40	Ducati
1987 S/N.45	Suzuki	1986 L/N.10	Rotax	1986 S.R.	Yamaha	**Parker, Graeme**		**Partington, Tim H.**	
Nicholls, Keith P.		1986 L.R.	Rotax	**Ono, Katsugi**		1989 S/N.13	Yamaha	1983 S/N.12	Yamaha
1983 J/N.4	Yamaha	1987 S.R.	Suzuki	1988 S/Cl.R.	Matchless	1992 J.R.	Yamaha	1984 L.47	Yamaha
1994 S/N.7	Yamaha	**Notley, Paul**		**Orford, Neil**		1991 S.41	Yamaha	**Parvin, Michael I.**	
1994 S.35	Yamaha	1989 S/N.34	Honda	1997 J/N.R.	Honda	1992 S.30	Honda	1985 J/N.11	Yamaha
Nicholls, Phil		**Nottingham, Nigel**		1997 J.92	Honda	1994 J.61	Yamaha	**Paterson, George**	
1988 S/Cl.1	Seeley	1988 S/N.8	Suzuki	**Orgee, Martin J.**		1994 L.26	Yamaha	1988 S/Cl.36	Norton
1989 S/Cl.R.	Seeley	1989 J.22	Yamaha	1986 S/Cl.R.	Aermacchi	**Parker, Steve**		1989 S/Cl.R.	Norton
1990 J/Cl.3	Seeley A.J.S.	1989 S.12	Yamaha	1987 J/Cl.R.	Aermacchi	1983 L/N.R.	Yamaha	1990 J/Cl.R.	Norton
1990 S/Cl.R.	Matchless	1990 J.30	Suzuki	1988 J/Cl.27	Aermacchi	1983 L.R.	Yamaha	1990 S/Cl.R.	Norton
1993 S/Cl.15	Seeley	1990 S.5	Yamaha	1988 S/Cl.31	Norton	**Parker, Tate**		1992 L/Cl.20	Suzuki
Niven, Ron F.		1991 J.R.	Kawasaki	1989 J/Cl.10	Aermacchi	1994 S/Cl.41	Norton	1993 L/Cl.10	Suzuki
1983 J/Cl.R.	Aermacchi	1991 S.7	Yamaha	1989 S/Cl.R.	Norton	1994 J/Cl.38	B.S.A. Goldstar	1996 S/Cl.R.	Suzuki
1984 J/Cl.33	Aermacchi	1992 S.10	Yamaha	1990 J/Cl.6	Aermacchi	1996 S/Cl.R.	Rickman B.S.A.	1997 L/Cl.13	Suzuki
1985 J/Cl.16		1993 S.13	Yamaha	1991 J/Cl.R.	Aermacchi	1996 J/Cl.R.	B.S.A. Goldstar	**Paterson, Ian M.**	
	Lawton Aermacchi	1994 J.18	Yamaha	**Ormerod, Paul S.**		**Parkhill, William C.**		1984 J/N.R.	Yamaha
1986 J/Cl.15	Aermacchi	1994 S.3	Yamaha	1986 S/N.22	Suzuki	1987 J/Cl.R.	Triumph	1985 J.R.	Yamaha
1987 J/Cl.17	Aermacchi	1995 J.38	Honda	1986 L.34	Yamaha	1988 S/Cl.50	B.S.A.	1986 S.R.	Suzuki
1988 J/Cl.R.	Aermacchi	1995 S.R.	Yamaha	1988 S.66	Suzuki	**Parkinson, Kate**		1987 S.14	Yamaha
1988 S/Cl.R.	Aermacchi	1995 S.R.	Honda	**Ornsby, Dave**		1991 L/N.11	Kawasaki	**Patt, Derwent**	
1990 S/Cl.R.	Matchless	1996 J.43	Yamaha	1990 J/N.11	Honda	1991 L.R.	Kawasaki	1983 S.36	Yamaha
Nobbs, David		1996 S.17	Mistral Yamaha	**Orritt, Paul**		1992 J.49	Kawasaki	1984 L.27	Yamaha
1983 L/Cl.R.	Bultaco	**Nowell, Adam**		1990 S/N.1	Yamaha	1992 L.19	Honda	**Pattinson, Ian**	
1984 J/Cl.R.	Yamaha	1995 J/N.16	Honda	1990 S.11	Yamaha	**Parris, Lawrence**		1995 J/N.21	Yamaha
1992 L/Cl.25	Honda	1996 J.26	Honda	**O'Shaughnessy Noel**		1983 J/Cl.2	Aermacchi	1996 J.29	Kawasaki
1993 L/Cl.12	Suzuki	1996 S.R.	Honda	1988 J/N.10	Yamaha	1984 J/Cl.1	Aermacchi	1996 S.31	Kawasaki
1994 L/Cl.5	Jackson Suzuki	1997 J.R.	Clark Yamaha	1988 J.R.	Yamaha	1985 J/Cl.6	Aermacchi	1997 J.13	Kawasaki
1995 L/Cl.6	Suzuki	1997 L.42	Clark Yamaha	1989 J.41	Yamaha	1986 J/Cl.R.	Aermacchi	1997 S.20	Kawasaki
1996 L/Cl.R.	Suzuki	**Nugent, Stephen**		**Outhwaite, John**		1987 J/Cl.R.	Aermacchi	**Payton, Nick M.**	
Noble, Ben		1996 S/N.2	Marshal Yamaha	1988 L/N.R.	Yamaha	1988 J/Cl.6	Aermacchi	1983 S/Cl.12	Velocette
1983 J/Cl.26	Norton	1996 S.35	Marshal Yamaha	**Oversby, Alan**		1989 S/Cl.R.	Norton	1984 S/Cl.13	Velocette
1984 J/Cl.19	Norton	1997 J.33	Marshal Honda	1988 S/Cl.18	Triumph	1990 S/Cl.R.	Norton	1986 S/Cl.15	Velocette
1985 J/Cl.19	Norton	1997 S.13	Young Honda	1989 S/Cl.R.	Triumph	**Parrish, Basil C.**		**Peabody, Robert J.**	
1986 J/Cl.27	Norton	**Nutland, Geoff**		1992 S/Cl.R.	Triumph	1983 J/N.21	Yamaha	1983 L/Cl.R.	Bultaco
1987 J/Cl.25	Norton	1991 S/N.10	Kawasaki	**Owen, Dai**		1984 J.46	Yamaha	1983 L.R.	Yamaha
1988 J/Cl.44	Ducati	1991 S.42	Kawasaki	1990 L/N.8	Yamaha	1985 J.37	Yamaha	**Pearce, Keith**	
1989 J/Cl.29	Norton	1992 S.31	Kawasaki	1990 L.48	Yamaha	1986 J.R.	Yamaha	1984 S/N.9	Laverda
1990 J/Cl.23	Norton	1993 J.R.	Yamaha	1991 L.38	Kawasaki	1986 S.38	Yamaha	1984 S.51	Laverda
1991 J/Cl.R.	Norton	1993 S.R.	Kawasaki	**Owen, David W.**		1987 J.37	Yamaha	1987 S.68	Laverda
1992 J/Cl.29	Norton			1988 J/N.11	Yamaha	1988 J.30	Yamaha	**Pearce, Mark**	
1993 J/Cl.31	Norton	**O'Brien, Kevin**		1988 J.48	Yamaha	1989 J.R.	Yamaha	1989 L/N.6	Yamaha
1994 J/Cl.33	Norton	1986 J/N.R.	Yamaha	1989 J.46	Yamaha	1990 J.49	Yamaha	1989 L.32	Yamaha
1995 J/Cl.35	Norton	1986 L.R.	Yamaha	1989 L.37	Yamaha	**Parrott, Philip J.**		**Pearson, Gav**	
1996 J/Cl.35	Norton	1988 J.R.	Yamaha	**Owen, Gareth**		1983 L.37	Yamaha	1989 L/Cl.12	Ducati
Noblett, Mick D.		**O'Brien, Steve**		1983 S/Cl.22	Norton	1984 L.22	Yamaha	1991 J/Cl.25	Ducati
1983 J.R.	Yamaha	1991 S/N.R.	Suzuki	1985 S/Cl.R.	Velocette	1985 L.R.	Yamaha	1993 S/Cl.R.	Ducati
1983 S.10	Honda	1991 S.56	Suzuki	1986 S/Cl.R.	Velocette	**Parrott, Richard**		1994 S/Cl.48	Ducati
1984 J.R.	Yamaha	1992 S.54	Suzuki	**Owen, Meredydd**		1991 L/N.6	Kawasaki	**Pearson, John P.**	
1984 S.R.	Suzuki	1994 J.R.	Yamaha	1995 S/Cl.R.	Seeley	1992 L.10	Kawasaki	1983 J.R.	Yamaha
1989 S.10	Suzuki	1994 L.46	Honda	1996 S/Cl.34	Seeley G50	**Parry, David**		1983 L.48	Yamaha
1990 S.4	Honda	1996 L.45	Cowles Yamaha	1997 S/Cl.21	Seeley G50	1984 L.R.	Yamaha	1984 J.R.	Yamaha
1991 S.4	Honda	**O'Callaghan, Fred**		1997 J/Cl.20	Seeley	1985 L.9	Yamaha	1984 S.R.	Yamaha
1991 J.R.	Yamaha	1983 J/Cl.9	Aermacchi	**Padgett, Don**		1986 L.R.	Yamaha	1986 S.R.	Honda
1992 S/Cl.12	Matchless	1984 J/Cl.5	Aermacchi	1983 J/Cl.R.	Aermacchi	1988 L.R.	Yamaha	**Pearson, Kevin M.**	
Nofer, Marek		**O'Connor, Michael**		1984 J/Cl.12	Aermacchi	**Parry-Jones, Beth**		1983 S.27	Yamaha
1983 S.R.	Yamaha	1990 L/N.R.	Suzuki	**Padgett, Gary**		1995 J.68	Honda	1984 J.19	Yamaha
1984 J.23	Yamaha	**O'Hara, Tony**		1980 L/N.1	Padgett Yamaha	1995 S.56	Honda	1984 S.14	Yamaha
1984 S.19	Yamaha	1989 S/N.2	Suzuki	1980 L.19	Padgett Yamaha	**Parry-Jones, Lodwig**		1985 J.R.	Yamaha
1986 J.R.	Yamaha	**Ogden, Brad P.**		**Page, Martin E. G.**		1990 L/N.5	Yamaha	1985 S.40	Yamaha
1986 S.R.	Yamaha	1988 S/N.2	Yamaha	1987 S/Cl.35	Norton	1991 L/Cl.10	Ducati	1986 S.24	Honda
1987 J.12	Yamaha	1989 S.3	Yamaha	1988 J.R.	Norton	1992 L/Cl.R.	Ducati	**Peart, Cliff**	
1988 J.R.	Yamaha	1993 J.R.	Honda	1989 J/Cl.25	A.J.S.	1993 L/Cl.14	Ducati	1986 J/N.4	Yamaha
1988 S.15	Suzuki	**Ogden, Ian**		1989 S/Cl.36	Matchless	1995 L/Cl.9	Ducati	1986 L.R.	Yamaha
1990 L/Cl.1	Suzuki	1984 J.R.	SGB Yamaha	1990 J/Cl.14	Seeley	1997 S/Cl.29	Ducati	1987 J.R.	Yamaha
Nolan, Emmet		1984 S.2	SGB Suzuki	1990 S/Cl.R.	Seeley	**Parshley, Robert S.**		1987 S.17	Honda
1986 S/N.14	Honda	1985 S.2	Suzuki	1991 S/Cl.R.	Seeley	1983 S/N.R.	Ducati	**Peile, John R.**	
1991 S.R.	Yamaha	**Older, Derek G.**		1991 J/Cl.12	Seeley	1983 S.R.	Ducati	1983 J/N.16	Yamaha
1992 S.45	Yamaha	1983 J/Cl.8	Norton	1992 S/Cl.23	G50 Matchless	**Parsons, Laurie D. S.**		**Pellow, Mike C.**	
Noon, Stuart L.		**O'Leary, David**		**Pain, Stephen D.**		1985 J/Cl.17	Ducati	1983 S.R.	Suzuki
1987 S/Cl.R.	RSM-Triumph	1988 J.R.	Yamaha	1983 J.21	Yamaha	1986 J/Cl.23	Ducati	1984 S.35	Suzuki
1990 J/Cl.R.	RSM-Triumph	1988 S.R.	Honda	1983 S.21	Yamaha	1987 J/Cl.R.	Ducati	1987 S.23	Suzuki
1990 S/Cl.R.	RSM-Triumph	1989 J.7	Yamaha	**Palmer, Lawrence**		1988 J/Cl.R.	Ducati	**Penfold, Brian E.**	
1991 S/Cl.28	RSM-Triumph	1989 S.11	Suzuki	1997 L/N.3	Yamaha	1988 S/Cl.R.	Ducati	1986 S/Cl.11	Norton
1991 J/Cl.14	RSM-Triumph	1990 J.R.	Yamaha	1997 L.23	Yamaha	1989 J/Cl.24	Ducati	1987 S/Cl.11	Norton
1992 S/Cl.24	RSM-Triumph	1991 J.R.	Yamaha	**Panter, Paul**		1990 L/Cl.13	Ducati	1988 S/Cl.R.	Norton
1992 J/Cl.19	RSM-Triumph	1991 S.R.	Suzuki	1990 S/N.R.	Honda	1990 S/Cl.29	Ducati	1989 S/Cl.18	Norton
1993 J/Cl.31	RSM-Triumph	1992 J.1	Yamaha	**Parker, Colin T.**		1991 S/Cl.R.	Ducati	1990 S/Cl.R.	Norton
1993 J/Cl.R.	RSM-Triumph							1991 S/Cl.17	Norton

1992 S/Cl.R.	Norton	1995 J.35	Yamaha	1995 L/Cl.14	Suzuki	**Price, Robert A.**		1989 J.R.	Yamaha
1992 J/Cl.25	Norton	1995 L.R.	Yamaha	**Potter, Stephen**		1983 S/N.3	Yamaha	1989 S.53	Honda
1993 S/Cl.26	Norton	**Pink, Richard D.**		1996 J/N.R.	Yamaha	1984 S/Cl.31	B.S.A. Metisse	1990 S.29	Honda
1993 J/Cl.R.	Norton	1997 S/N.10	Yamaha	**Potts, Andy**		1984 S.17	Yamaha	**Raynor, Brian**	
1994 S/Cl.R.	Norton	**Pither, Dave**		1996 J/N.11	Spondon	1985 S/Cl.13	B.S.A.	1983 S.R.	Honda
1995 S/Cl.21	Norton	1984 S/Cl.1	G50 Matchless	**Poulter, Bob**		1986 S/Cl.26	B.S.A.	1984 S.R.	Honda
1997 S/Cl.37	Norton	1984 J.R.	Inwood Yamaha	1993 S/Cl.47	Seeley	1987 S/Cl.13	B.S.A.	1986 S.48	Honda
Pennington, J. Grenville		1984 S.1	Honda	1994 S/Cl.23	Seeley	1988 S/Cl.29	B.S.A.	1987 S.1	Yamaha
1989 L/N.R.	B.S.A.	1986 S/Cl.2	Matchless	1996 S/Cl.36	Seeley G50	1989 S/Cl.9	B.S.A.	**Raynor, John B.**	
Pennington, Philip		1987 S/Cl.1	Matchless	**Powell, Andrew**		1990 S/Cl.Ex		1983 J/Cl.23	Aermacchi
1986 L/N.6	Suzuki	**Platts, Steve**		1992 S/N.11	Honda	1991 S/Cl.36	B.S.A.	1984 J/Cl.R.	Aermacchi
1987 L.11	Yamaha	1989 S/N.6	Yamaha	1992 S.35	Honda	1992 S/Cl.22	B.S.A.	1985 J/Cl.R.	Aermacchi
1989 L.30	Yamaha	1991 S.R.	Honda	1993 J.24	Yamaha	1993 S/Cl.28	B.S.A.	1986 J/Cl.32	Honda
Pereira, Chris A.		**Plummer, Neil**		1993 S.20	Yamaha	1994 S/Cl.R.	B.S.A.	1987 J/Cl.R.	Aermacchi
1984 J/Cl.31	Ducati	1991 L/N.16	Kawasaki	1993 J.R.	Yamaha	1995 S/Cl.R.	B.S.A.	1988 J/Cl.25	Aermacchi
Perrin, Chris		1991 J.39	Kawasaki	**Powell, Darren W.**		**Price, Robert J.**		1988 S/Cl.R.	Aermacchi
1990 S/N.R.	Kawasaki	1992 J.53	Kawasaki	1988 L/N.2	Yamaha	1983 L/Cl.6	Greeves	1989 S/Cl.31	Aermacchi
1991 S.29	Yamaha	1992 L.R.	Kawasaki	1988 L.R.	Yamaha	1986 J/Cl.36	Greeves	1990 J/Cl.26	Honda
Perrin, Peter		1993 J.51	Yamaha	**Powell, Martin**		1986 J.30	Yamaha	1990 S/Cl.R.	Honda
1995 J/Cl.R.	Yamaha	1993 L.29	Yamaha	1988 J/N.5	Yamaha	1990 J.33	Kawasaki	**Rea, Stanley W**	
1997 S.67	Kawasaki	1994 J.R.	Yamaha	1988 L.27	Yamaha	1990 L.30	Kawasaki	1984 J/N.4	Yamaha
Peters, Colin B.		1995 J.52	Yamaha	1989 J.19	Yamaha	1991 J.24	Kawasaki	1986 J.R.	Yamaha
1988 S/Cl.47	Norton	1995 L.25	Yamaha	1989 S.47	Suzuki	1991 L.25	Kawasaki	1986 S.19	Yamaha
1989 S.68	Kawasaki	1997 S.79	Honda	1990 J.39	Yamaha	**Priestley Mark A.**		1987 J.R.	Yamaha
Peters, David		**Plunkett, Aidan**		1990 S.44	Suzuki	1988 S/N.29	Kawasaki	1987 S.51	Yamaha
1983 J/N.R.	Yamaha	1991 J/N.10	Honda	1991 J/Cl.R.	Aermacchi	1989 J.R.	Yamaha	1988 J.3	Yamaha
Petty, Chris R.		1993 J.53	Honda	**Powell, Richard**		1989 S.57	Suzuki	1988 L.R.	Yamaha
1986 S/N.8	Kawasaki	1993 S.45	Honda	1996 J/Cl.R.		1990 J.41	Kawasaki	1989 J.2	Yamaha
Phillips, Alan J.		1996 J.76	Honda		Saxon Walker Ducati	1990 S.55	Yamaha	1989 L.R.	Yamaha
1983 S.43	Norton	**Pollard, Martin**		**Powell, Robert J.**		**Probett, Damion**		1990 J.1	Cowles Yamaha
1984 S.49	Norton	1985 J/N.16	Yamaha	1983 S.R.	Kawasaki	1990 J/N.15	Tigcraft Yamaha	1990 L.2	Cowles Yamaha
1985 S.52	Norton	1985 L.39	Yamaha	**Power, Jon**		**Protheroe, Brian**		**Read, Graham P.**	
1986 S.53	Norton	**Pollock, John**		1989 S/N.R.	Yamaha	1983 S.63	Seeley Suzuki	1987 S/N.6	Suzuki
1987 S.71	Norton	1983 S/N.4	Suzuki	1992 S.15	Yamaha	**Pullan, Lee**		1988 S.5	Suzuki
1988 S.68	Kawasaki	1984 S.R.	Suzuki	**Power, Virginia**		1990 J/N.1	Spondon	**Redfearn, Nick**	
1989 S.59	Yamaha	1985 S.46	Suzuki	1994 L/N.16	Kawasaki	**Pullen, Danny R.**		1996 J/N.8	Yamaha
1990 S/Cl.38	RSM-Triumph	1987 S.38	Suzuki	1994 L.47	Kawasaki	1997 L/N.R.	Honda	1996 S.57	Yamaha
1991 S/Cl.38	RSM-Triumph	1988 S.64	Suzuki	1995 J.76	Yamaha	1997 L.R.	Honda	**Reed, Nigel**	
1991 J/Cl.15	RSM-Triumph	1991 J.40	Suzuki	1995 S.63	Yamaha	**Purves, David**		1995 L/Cl.R.	Suzuki
1992 S/Cl.49	RSM-Triumph	1991 L.41	Suzuki	1996 J.84	Yamaha	1993 L/N.8	Suzuki	1995 L.R.	Suzuki
1992 J/Cl.26	RSM-Triumph	**Ponting, Adrian**		1996 S.77=	Yamaha	1993 L.46	Suzuki	1997 L.37	Yamaha
1993 S/Cl.44	RSM-Triumph	1995 L/N.11	Suzuki	1997 J.95	Kawasaki	1994 J.40	Honda	**Regan, Tony**	
1993 J/Cl.28	RSM-Triumph	1995 L.44	Suzuki	1997 S.91	Kawasaki	1994 S.34	Honda	1987 S/Cl.25	Triumph
1994 J/Cl.R.	RSM-Triumph	**Poole, Edward**		**Powis, Clive H.**		**Quail, John**		1989 S/Cl.41	Triumph
1994 S/Cl.32	RSM-Triumph	1994 S/Cl.42	Norton	1983 J.11	Maxton Yamaha	1995 S/N.4	Kirwans Honda	**Reid, Phil**	
1995 S/Cl.27	RSM-Triumph	1995 S/Cl.32	Norton	1983 L.22	Maxton Yamaha	1995 S.26	Honda	1993 L/N.2	Yamaha
1996 S/Cl.R.	RSM-Triumph	1997 S/Cl.47	Norton	1984 J.R.	Maxton Yamaha	1996 J.61	Honda	1993 J.9	Yamaha
1997 S/Cl.R.	RSM-Triumph	1997 J/Cl.34	Norton	1984 L.R.	Maxton Yamaha	1996 S.R.	Honda	1992 S.24	Yamaha
Phillips, Joe		**Porter, Dennis W.**		**Pratt, Ian R.**		**Quaye, Tom**		1993 L.R.	Honda
1983 L/N.R.	Yamaha	1985 S/Cl.R.	Honda	1983 J/N.8	Yamaha	1991 S.48	Laverda	1994 J.6	Honda
1984 S.R.	Yamaha	1990 S/Cl.47	Norton	**Prescott, Dave W.**		1995 J/Cl.20	Honda	1994 L.3	Padgett Honda
1986 J.25	Yamaha	**Porter, James W.**		1991 S/N.7	Honda	1995 S.40	Ducati	1996 J.27	Honda
1987 J.R.	Yamaha	1985 J/Cl.R.	Ducati	1991 S.R.	Honda	1996 J/Cl.12	Honda	1996 L.R.	Honda
1987 S.65	Yamaha	1986 J/Cl.5	Aermacchi	1992 S.38	Honda			**Reid, Sean**	
1988 J.20	Yamaha	1987 J/Cl.13	Aermacchi	1994 S.21	Honda	**Quayle, Richard**		1988 S/N.19	Yamaha
1988 L.R.	Yamaha	1989 J/Cl.15	Aermacchi	1997 J.82	Honda	1996 J.19	Yamaha	1989 L.34	Kawasaki
1990 J.R.	E.M.C.	1990 J/Cl.10	Aermacchi	1997 S.46	Ducati	1996 L.7	Yamaha	**Rennie, Carl**	
1991 J.R.	E.M.C.	**Potter, Alan**		**Presland, Mick**		**Quinn, Dennis W.**		1995 J/N.6	Yamaha
1991 L.R.	E.M.C.	1983 J.41	Yamaha	1995 L/Cl.R.	Yamaha	1983 L/N.5	Yamaha	1995 S.21	Yamaha
1992 J.R.	Yamaha	1983 L.R.	Yamaha	1995 L.45	Yamaha	1983 L.25	Yamaha	1996 J.8	Yamaha
1992 L.R.	Yamaha	1984 J.R.	Yamaha	1996 J.69	Yamaha	1989 S.8	Yamaha	1996 S.13	Honda
Phillips, John D.		1984 S.50	PEM Suzuki	1996 L.32	Yamaha	**Quinn, Robert**		1997 J.7	Honda
1983 J.49	Yamaha	1985 J.43	Yamaha	1997 J.81	Yamaha	1991 J.21	Kawasaki	1997 S.11	Honda
1985 S.73	Cliffe Suzuki	1985 S.R.	Suzuki	1997 L.20	Yamaha	1992 S.5	Honda	**Rennie, Paul**	
1987 J.R.	Cliffe Yamaha	1986 L.R.	Armstrong	**Press, Martin J.**				1996 J/N.20	Honda
1988 L.44	Yamaha	1987 J.R.	Yamaha	1984 L/N.4	Armstrong	**Radcliffe, Gary**		1997 L.51	Honda
Phillips, Patrick H.		1987 L.R.	Armstrong	1984 L.R.	Armstrong	1983 J.3	Yamaha	**Reynolds, Andy**	
1988 S/N.15	Honda	1988 J.R.	Yamaha	1985 L.R.	Armstrong	1983 S.9	Yamaha	1985 S/Cl.20	Velocette
1990 S.45	Yamaha	1988 L.46	Yamaha	**Prewer, Stephen P.**		1984 J.2	Yamaha	1990 S/Cl.35	Seeley Matchless
1994 S.33	Kawasaki	1989 S/Cl.48	Ducati	1987 S/N.R.	Triumph	1984 S.R.	Yamaha	1991 S/Cl.29	G50 Seeley
Phillips, Tim		1989 L.49	Armstrong	1988 S.R.	Triumph	1985 J.1	Fowler Yamaha	1992 S/Cl.26	G50 Matchless
1996 J/N.19	Honda	1990 J/Cl.22	Aermacchi	1989 S/Cl.R.	Norton	1985 S.R.	Fowler Yamaha	1992 J/Cl.23	Seeley
Piercy, Nigel		1990 J.R.	Yamaha	1990 S/Cl.R.	Weslake	**Rae, Alastair J.**		1993 S/Cl.32	Matchless
1989 L/N.3	Suzuki	1991 J/Cl.R.	Ducati	1991 S/Cl.21	Weslake	1984 J.R.	Yamaha	1993 J/Cl.22	A.J.S.
1991 S.21	Yamaha	1992 J/Cl.R.	Aermacchi	1992 S/Cl.R.	Manx Weslake	1984 L.2		1994 S/Cl.21	Seeley Matchless
1992 J.23	Yamaha	**Potter, Brian**		1993 S/Cl.R.	Manx Weslake	**Ray, David**		1994 J/Cl.14	Seeley A.J.S.
1993 J.8	Honda	1990 L/Cl.20	Suzuki	1995 S/Cl.R.	Manx Weslake	1988 S/N.R.	Yamaha	1995 S/Cl.10	Seeley G50
1993 L.15	Yamaha	1991 L/Cl.18	Suzuki	1996 S/Cl.R.	Manx Weslake	**Raybould, Stuart**		1995 J/Cl.R.	Seeley 7R
Pike, Andy		1992 L/Cl.22	Suzuki	1997 S/Cl.R.	Manx Weslake	1985 J/N.R.	Yamaha	1996 S/Cl.13	Seeley G50
1996 J/Cl.R.	Aermacchi	1993 L/Cl.21	Suzuki	**Price, Dexter G.**		1985 L.R.	Yamaha	1996 J/Cl.13	Seeley 7R
1997 J/Cl.22	Aermacchi	1994 L/Cl.R.	Suzuki	1986 S/N.20	Kawasaki	1986 J.17	Yamaha	1997 S/Cl.R.	Seeley G50
Pinches, Dave		**Potter, Mick P.**		1990 S.41	Kawasaki	1986 L.R.	Yamaha	1997 J/Cl.18	Seeley 7R
1994 L/N.7	Yamaha	1987 J/N.R.	Yamaha	1994 J/Cl.R.	Greeves	1987 J.R.	Yamaha	**Reynolds, Peter H.**	
1994 L.24	Yamaha	1988 L/Cl.R.	Suzuki	1994 L.37	Kawasaki	1987 S.47	Suzuki	1984 S/Cl.27	Matchless

The History of the Manx Grand Prix 1923-1998 183

1985 S/Cl.26	Matchless
1987 S/Cl.41	Matchless
1990 J/Cl.32	Ducati
1991 J/Cl.R.	Ducati
1993 J/Cl.38	Ducati

Rhodes, Graham C.
1985 J/Cl.22	Velocette
1987 J/Cl.20	Velocette
1988 J/Cl.29	Velocette
1988 S/Cl.R.	Matchless
1990 S.43	Suzuki
1993 J/Cl.11	Aermacchi
1994 J/Cl.21	Aermacchi
1995 J/Cl.4	Aermacchi
1996 J/Cl.9	Seeley
1996 J/Cl.R.	Aermacchi
1997 S/Cl.R.	Seeley
1997 J/Cl.6	Aermacchi

Rice, Bill
1983 J.R.	Zeger
1983 S.R.	Zeger
1984 J.51	Yamaha
1984 S.R.	Yamaha
1985 J.R.	Shields Egli
1985 S.43	Zeger
1986 J.R.	Yamaha
1986 S.R.	Suzuki
1987 J.R.	Egli Yamaha
1988 S.R.	Suzuki
1990 S.60	Yamaha
1995 S.59	Anderton Honda
1996 S.83	Anderton Honda
1997 S.90	Anderton Honda

Rice, Seamus J.
1984 S/N.5	Yamaha

Richards, Brian
1983 S/Cl.17	Seeley G50
1985 S/Cl.15	Seeley
1986 S/Cl.9	Seeley
1987 S/Cl.9	Seeley
1988 J/Cl.R.	Seeley
1988 S/Cl.8	Seeley
1989 J/Cl.R.	Seeley
1989 S/Cl.R.	Seeley
1990 J/Cl.12	Seeley
1990 S/Cl.22	Seeley
1991 S/Cl.20	Seeley
1991 J/Cl.8	Seeley

Richards, John
1993 L/N.9	Yamaha
1993 L.37	Yamaha
1994 L.28	Chatenay Honda
1995 S/Cl.R.	Matchless
1995 J.40	Yamaha
1995 L.17	Yamaha
1996 S/Cl.R.	Seeley
1996 L.27	Walker Yamaha
1997 S/Cl.16	Seeley G50
1997 S.39	Honda

Richardson, Chris
1993 J/N.R.	Honda
1993 S.7	A.W. Honda

Richardson, Ken M.
1983 S.R.	Suzuki
1984 S.25	Suzuki
1985 S.31	Suzuki
1986 S.40	Suzuki
1987 S30	Suzuki
1988 S.R.	Suzuki

Richardson, Neil
1989 L/N.8	Yamaha
1989 L.R.	Yamaha
1990 J.27	Yamaha
1991 J.R.	Yamaha
1991 L.7	Yamaha
1992 J.R.	Yamaha
1992 L.R.	Yamaha
1993 J.3	Yamaha
1993 L.4	Yamaha

Richardson, Peter F.
1997 J/Cl.20	Bullock Ducati

Richardson, Roy
1986 J/N.6	Yamaha
1989 S.61	Honda

1990 L.29	Kawasaki
1991 L.26	Honda
1992 L.24	Honda
1993 J.R.	Honda
1994 J.R.	Honda
1994 S.6	Honda
1995 S.2	Honda
1995 J.R.	Honda
1996 J.R.	Honda
1996 S.3	JSB Bullock Honda
1997 J.1	BDC Europe Suzuki
1997 S.R.	JSB Bullock Honda

Richardson, Scott
1993 J/N.R.	Yamaha
1993 J.37	Yamaha
1994 J.37	Rotax
1994 S.22	Rotax
1995 J.19	Honda
1995 S.12	Honda
1996 J.28	FC Moore Honda
1996 S.24	FC Moore Honda
1997 J.23	FC Moore Honda
1997 S.27	FC Moore Honda

Richardson, Stephen
1983 J.R.	Yamaha
1983 S.6	Suzuki
1984 J.27	Yamaha
1984 S.11	Suzuki

Richardson, Steve
1992 L/Cl.R.	Yamaha
1993 L/Cl.6	Yamaha

Ridgeway, Gareth M.
1987 L/N.9	Yamaha

Rimmer, John
1994 S/Cl.R.	Seeley
1995 S/Cl.38	Seeley
1995 J/Cl.R.	Seeley
1996 S/Cl.R.	Seeley
1997 S/Cl.43	G50 Seeley

Ritchie, Alex
1983 J/N.9	Yamaha

Rivers, Gary
1985 L/N.12	Yamaha
1986 J.R.	Yamaha

Roberts, Anthony
1992 L/N.6	Yamaha
1992 L.R.	Yamaha

Roberts, David, J.
1983 L.39	Yamaha
1984 S.R.	Yamaha
1988 S.54	Honda
1989 S.51	Yamaha
1990 L.42	Kawasaki

Roberts, Victor G.
1983 S/Cl.14	Seeley G50

Robertson, Bill
1989 L/Cl.R.	Villiers
1990 S/Cl.R.	Seeley
1992 S/Cl.R.	Suzuki
1993 L/Cl.8	Suzuki
1994 L/Cl.4	Suzuki
1995 L/Cl.D	Suzuki
1996 L/Cl.R.	Suzuki
1997 L/Cl.R.	Suzuki

Robertson, Drew M.
1985 J/Cl.27	Aermacchi
1986 S/Cl.R.	Norton
1987 S/Cl.R.	Aermacchi
1988 S/Cl.R.	Aermacchi
1989 J/Cl.34	Aermacchi
1990 J/Cl.R.	Aermacchi
1991 S/Cl.42	Seeley
1991 S/Cl.R.	Aermacchi

Robertson, Peter
1989 J/N.R.	Yamaha
1989 J.43	Yamaha
1990 J.43	Yamaha
1990 L.50	Yamaha
1991 J.28	Yamaha
1991 L.46	Yamaha
1992 L/Cl.13	Suzuki
1993 L/Cl.11	Suzuki

1994 L/Cl.6	Suzuki
1995 L/Cl.R.	Suzuki
1996 L/Cl.7	Suzuki
1997 L/Cl.9	Suzuki

Robinson, Allan
1984 S/Cl.R.	Norton/Triumph
1985 S/Cl.28	Triumph/Norton
1986 S/Cl.30	Norton
1987 S/Cl.39	Triumph
1988 S/Cl.42	Matchless
1989 S/Cl.42	Triumph

Robinson, Brian
1985 S/Cl.21	Triton
1986 S/Cl.R.	Triumph
1987 S/Cl.R.	Triumph
1988 S/Cl.R.	Triumph
1989 J/Cl.36	Norton
1989 S/Cl.R.	Weslake
1990 S/Cl.23	Weslake
1991 S/Cl.R.	Weslake
1991 L/Cl.R.	Honda

Robinson, David J.
1983 J/N.12	Yamaha
1984 J.41	Yamaha
1984 S.41	Yamaha

Robinson, Herb
1995 S/Cl.R.	Seeley
1996 S/Cl.R.	Seeley
1996 J/Cl.27	Seeley 7R
1997 S/Cl.R.	Seeley G50
1997 S/Cl.31	Seeley 7R

Robinson, Mark
1993 J/N.14	Yamaha
1993 J.R.	Yamaha
1994 J.R.	Yamaha

Robinson, Mick, S.
1983 J.14	Yamaha
1983 L.8	Yamaha
1984 J.17	Yamaha
1984 L.R.	Yamaha
1985 J.14	Yamaha
1985 L.10	Yamaha
1986 J.11	Yamaha
1986 J.2	Yamaha
1987 J.4	Yamaha
1987 L.2	Yamaha
1988 J.4	Yamaha
1988 L.3	Yamaha
1989 J.4	Yamaha
1989 L.3	Yamaha
1990 J.15	Yamaha
1991 J.3	Abinger Yamaha
1991 L.5	Abinger Yamaha
1992 J.3	Abinger Yamaha
1992 L.2	Abinger Yamaha
1993 S/Cl.8	Seeley
1994 S/Cl.R.	Seeley
1995 S/Cl.R.	Seeley
1996 J.24	Honda
1996 L.3	Honda
1997 S/Cl.8	Seeley G50
1997 J/Cl.7	Aermacchi
1997 L.6	Honda

Robinson, Neil
1991 L/N.R.	Kawasaki
1991 L.23	Kawasaki
1993 J.32	Yamaha
1993 J.39	Yamaha

Robinson, Pat
1990 L/N.6	Kawasaki
1991 L.36	Kawasaki
1992 J.52	Kawasaki
1992 L.37	Kawasaki
1994 S.31	Honda

Robinson, Philip J.
1988 S/Cl.39	B.S.A.
1989 S/Cl.26	Seeley B.S.A.
1990 J/Cl.R.	Seeley B.S.A.
1990 S/Cl.R.	Seeley Matchless
1991 S/Cl.43	Seeley Matchless

Robinson, Rob
1991 J/N.R.	Yamaha
1992 L/Cl.R.	Honda
1992 S.R.	Yamaha

1993 L/Cl.25	Honda
1994 J/Cl.R.	Honda

Robinson, Steve
1985 L.41	Yamaha
1986 L.42	Yamaha
1987 L.48	Yamaha

Robinson, Steve
1992 S/Cl.R.	Norton
1993 S/Cl.62	Norton

Robinson, Steve
1995 J/N.17	Robinson Honda
1995 J.45	Honda

Robinson, Stuart G. E.
1987 S/Cl.40	B.S.A.
1988 S/Cl.48	B.S.A.
1990 S/Cl.50	B.S.A.
1992 S/Cl.51	B.S.A.
1993 S/Cl.58	B.S.A.
1994 S/Cl.39	B.S.A.
1995 S/Cl.55	B.S.A.
1996 J/Cl.34	Seeley Goldstar
1997 J/Cl.40	Seeley Goldstar

Robinson, Trevor
1986 J/N.2	Yamaha

Robson, Barry R.
1983 S/Cl.18	Ducati
1984 S/Cl.14	Ducati
1985 S/Cl.16	Ducati
1986 S/Cl.20	Ducati
1989 S/Cl.R.	Ducati
1990 S/Cl.37	Ducati

Robson, Peter
1990 S/Cl.R.	Weslake
1991 S/Cl.R.	Norton
1992 S/Cl.34	Norton
1993 S/Cl.41	Norton
1993 J/Cl.21	Manx Norton
1994 J/Cl.R.	Manx Norton
1994 S/Cl.17	Petty Manx
1995 S/Cl.11	Petty Manx
1995 J/Cl.18	Manx Norton

Rodger, Ian
1991 S/N.11	Yamaha

Roe, Dan H.
1997 J/N.10	Honda
1997 S.82	Honda

Roebuck, Ted
1983 L/N.13	Maxton
1983 L.53	Maxton
1988 J.33	Yamaha
1988 L.R.	Yamaha
1989 J.R.	Yamaha
1989 L.27	Yamaha
1990 J.25	Yamaha
1990 L.11	Yamaha

Roebury, Ron C.
1983 J/Cl.11	Honda

Rogers, Richard O.
1983 J.R.	Yamaha
1983 S.24	Yamaha
1984 J.22	Yamaha
1984 S.24	Suzuki
1985 J.10	Suzuki
1985 S.34	Suzuki
1986 J.8	Yamaha
1986 S.R.	Suzuki
1987 J.R.	Yamaha
1987 S.15	Suzuki
1988 J.R.	Yamaha
1988 S.16	Suzuki
1989 J.12	Yamaha
1989 S.21	Yamaha
1990 J.47	Yamaha
1991 J.22	Yamaha
1991 S.R.	Suzuki
1994 S/Cl.R.	Matchless
1995 J.57	Yamaha
1995 S.45	Yamaha

Rollston, Mark
1996 J/N.9	Honda
1996 S.88	Honda
1997 S.58	Honda
1997 S.53	Honda

Rome, Paul G.

1985 L/N.R.	Armstrong
1985 L.R.	Armstrong
1986 J.R.	Yamaha
1986 L.R.	Armstrong
1987 J.R.	Yamaha
1987 S.R.	Suzuki
1988 J.R.	Yamaha
1988 S.R.	Yamaha
1990 J.R.	Yamaha

Rondelli, Gino
1983 J.R.	Yamaha
1985 S.R.	P&M Suzuki
1987 S.13	Yamaha
1988 S.10	Suzuki
1989 J.R.	Yamaha
1989 S.R.	Suzuki
1990 J.R.	Yamaha

Rooney, T. Kenneth
1987 S/N.40	Suzuki
1988 S.R.	Suzuki

Rope, David
1984 L.R.	Yamaha
1986 S.29	Harris
1988 S.63	Harris

Roper, David
1983 S/Cl.9	Matchless
1986 S/Cl.R.	Matchless
1988 S/Cl.2	Matchless
1989 S/Cl.R.	Matchless
1990 J/Cl.R.	A.J.S.
1990 S/Cl.2	Matchless
1991 S/Cl.R.	Matchless
1991 S/Cl.16	A.J.S.
1992 S/Cl.38	Matchless
1993 J/Cl.R.	Benelli

Rose, Graham C.
1985 J/Cl.26	Ducati
1986 J/Cl.R.	Ducati
1987 J/Cl.31	Ducati
1988 J/Cl.51	Ducati

Rose, Keith
1991 L/N.21	Kawasaki
1991 L.45	Kawasaki

Rose, Richard W.
1983 S.33	Fahron
1984 S.34	Honda

Rose, Stephen R.
1983 L.67	Yamaha

Ross, Gordon
1989 S/N.25	Honda

Rothwell, Cyril
1996 S/Cl.R.	Seeley Triumph
1997 S/Cl.R.	Seeley Triumph

Rowe, Gary
1992 J/N.6	Honda
1993 J.R.	Honda
1993 S.R.	Honda
1994 J.R.	Spondon Gilera
1994 S.R.	Spondon Gilera
1995 S.55	Suzuki
1996 S.74	Suzuki
1997 L.36	Yamaha
1997 S.78	Suzuki

Rowles, Derek G.
1984 S/Cl.23	Triumph

Rowntree, Gordon F.
1984 J/N.5	Yamaha

Russell, Alan
1991 J/N.R.	Yamaha
1995 J.64	Honda
1996 J.65	Honda
1997 J.97	Honda
1997 S.55	Honda

Russell, Andy
1993 J/Cl.27	Honda
1994 J/Cl.27	Honda
1995 S/Cl.R.	Norton
1996 S/Cl.15	Norton
1997 S/Cl.R.	Norton

Russell, Tony R.
1983 J.R.	Yamaha
1983 L.31	Yamaha
1985 S/Cl.3	Seeley Matchless
1985 J.R.	Yamaha

Year	Class	Machine
1986	S/Cl.4	Matchless
1987	S/Cl.R.	Matchless
1988	S/Cl.39	Oulton
1988	S/Cl.R.	Seeley
1989	S/Cl.16	Seeley
1991	S/Cl.52	Triton
1992	S/Cl.R.	Triumph
1993	S/Cl.R.	Triumph
1994	S/Cl.R.	Seeley Triumph
1995	S/Cl.R.	Triumph
1996	S/Cl.49	Triumph

Ruth, John G.
1986	J/Cl.25	A.J.S.
1987	S/Cl.26	Norton
1988	S/Cl.15	Matchless
1989	J/Cl.20	A.J.S.
1989	S/Cl.12	Seeley

Ruth, Steve
1995	S/Cl.6	Seeley
1996	J/Cl.R.	Aermacchi
1996	S/Cl.6	Seeley

Rutter, Frank
1991	S/Cl.R.	Seeley
1992	S/Cl.R.	Seeley
1996	S/Cl.20	Seeley
1996	J/Cl.R.	Seeley
1997	S/Cl.25	Seeley

Rutzen, David W.
1983	J.R.	Yamaha
1983	S.12	Suzuki
1984	J.9	Yamaha
1984	S.7	Suzuki

Ryder, Andrew
1993	S/Cl.50	B.S.A.
1995	S/Cl.R.	B.S.A.
1996	S/Cl.R.	B.S.A.

Ryding, Craig
1983	J.R.	Yamaha
1984	J.R.	Yamaha
1984	L.15	Yamaha
1985	J.R.	Yamaha
1985	L.R.	Cotton
1987	J.1	Kimoco
1987	L.1	Kimoco

Salter, Colin
1989	L/N.14	Yamaha
1991	L.R.	Yamaha
1992	J.R.	Yamaha
1992	L.43	Yamaha
1993	J.61	Yamaha
1993	L.44	Yamaha
1994	L.38	Yamaha
1994	J.R.	Yamaha
1995	L.47	Yamaha
1996	J.90	Yamaha
1996	L.40	Yamaha
1997	L.45	Yamaha

Salter, Graham
| 1988 | S/N.23 | Rotax |

Samuel, John G.
1984	S/N.6	Honda
1985	J.R.	Padgett Yamaha
1985	S.45	Padgett Yamaha
1986	S.50	Honda

Sanby, Charlie
1990	S/Cl.7	Seeley G50
1992	S/Cl.R.	Seeley
1992	J/Cl.12	Norton

Sanders, Gary
| 1985 | J/N.7 | Beckett Yamaha |

Sanpher, Ian
| 1988 | L/N.R. | Yamaha |

Sansom, Gary L.
| 1997 | S/N.2 | Honda |
| 1997 | S.R. | Honda |

Saville, Dave
| 1992 | S/Cl.R. | Norton |
| 1993 | S/Cl.R. | Norton |

Saville, Richard
| 1984 | J/N.19 | Yamaha |

Sawyer, Geoff B.
| 1987 | J/N.9 | Yamaha |

1988	S/Cl.33	Matchless
1988	L.45	Rotax
1989	S/Cl.30	Matchless
1989	S.R.	Ducati
1990	S/Cl.R.	Matchless
1991	S/Cl.23	Matchless
1991	J/Cl.28	Aermacchi
1992	S/Cl.R.	Matchless
1992	J/Cl.R.	Aermacchi
1993	S/Cl.22	Matchless
1993	J/Cl.R.	Aermacchi
1994	J/Cl.R.	Aermacchi
1994	S/Cl.18	Matchless
1995	S/Cl.13	DTR Matchless
1995	J/Cl.7	DTR Aermacchi
1996	J/Cl.R.	Matchless
1996	J/Cl.R.	Aermacchi Metisse
1997	S/Cl.41	Matchless

Sayers, Mick
1985	J/N.4	Yamaha
1985	S.19	Yamaha
1989	J.R.	Yamaha
1989	L.33	Yamaha

Schneider, Gerd
| 1997 | L/Cl.R. | Jawa |

Schoenemann, John A.
| 1984 | S/N.R. | Suzuki |

Schyma, John
1983	S/N.14	Ducati
1984	S.R.	Suzuki
1985	J.47	Yamaha
1985	S.55	Suzuki
1986	J.R.	Yamaha
1986	S.R.	Yamaha
1987	J.R.	Yamaha
1988	S.48	Suzuki
1989	S.R.	Suzuki
1993	S.48	Honda
1994	S.41	Honda
1995	S.47	Honda
1996	S.59	Honda
1997	J.67	Suzuki
1997	S.58	Suzuki

Scott, Dominic
1991	L/N.19	Kawasaki
1991	L.48	Kawasaki
1992	J.69	Suzuki
1992	L.R.	Suzuki
1995	J.66	Yamaha
1995	L.26	Yamaha
1996	J.73	Yamaha
1996	L.28	Yamaha

Scott, Stephen
1992	L/N.9	Yamaha
1992	L.R.	Yamaha
1993	J.46	Honda

Searle, Pete
1987	S/N.15	Honda
1988	S.R.	Yamaha
1989	S.46	Ducati

Seawright, Wallace
1995	J/N.27	Yamaha
1995	S/Cl.28	Seeley
1996	S/Cl.R.	Seeley G50
1997	S/Cl.19	Seeley

Sefton, Pat
1989	L/N.1	Kawasaki
1989	L.R.	Yamaha
1992	S.40	MV Agusta

Sellars, Adrian R.
1987	S/Cl.R.	Norton
1988	S/Cl.37	Norton
1989	S/Cl.29	Norton
1989	S/Cl.R.	Norton
1990	S/Cl.R.	Norton
1990	S/Cl.33	Norton

Sellars, Grant W.
1983	S/Cl.6	Norton
1983	S.46	Norton
1984	S/Cl.11	Norton
1984	S.48	Norton
1985	S/Cl.6	Norton
1986	S/Cl.R.	Norton
1987	S/Cl.27	Norton

1988	J/Cl.16	Norton
1988	S/Cl.12	Norton
1989	S/Cl.14	Norton
1989	S/Cl.R.	Norton
1990	J/Cl.11	Norton
1990	S/Cl.13	Norton
1991	S/Cl.16	Norton
1991	J/Cl.R.	Aermacchi
1992	S/Cl.20	Manx Norton
1992	J/Cl.7	Aermacchi
1993	J/Cl.19	Norton
1993	J/Cl.9	Aermacchi
1994	J/Cl.R.	Petty Manx
1994	S/Cl.15	Norton
1995	S/Cl.12	Norton
1995	J/Cl.6	Aermacchi
1996	J/Cl.19	Norton
1996	J/Cl.8	Aermacchi
1997	S/Cl.R.	Norton
1997	J/Cl.R.	Aermacchi

Sells, Dave
1985	S.R.	Triumph
1986	S/Cl.34	Triton
1988	S/Cl.R.	Norton
1989	S/Cl.R.	Triton
1990	S/Cl.46	Triton
1991	S/Cl.R.	B.S.A.
1991	J/Cl.29	B.S.A.
1992	S/Cl.41	B.S.A.
1993	S/Cl.R.	B.S.A.
1993	L.42	Honda
1994	J.R.	Yamaha
1995	J.R.	Yamaha
1995	L.37	Honda
1996	J.R.	Yamaha
1996	S.70	Yamaha
1997	S/Cl.R.	B.S.A.
1997	S.87	Yamaha

Senior, Dennis M.
1986	J/N.7	Yamaha
1987	J.40	Yamaha
1988	S/Cl.22	Ducati
1988	J.17	Yamaha
1990	S.51	Honda

Senior, Des
| 1996 | S.49 | Honda |

Seward, Michael P.
1984	J/N.2	Yamaha
1984	L.11	Yamaha
1985	J.R.	Yamaha
1985	L.5	Armstrong
1986	J.3	Yamaha
1986	S.2	Yamaha

Sewart, Geoff E.
| 1984 | L.23 | Yamaha |
| 1985 | J.R. | Yamaha |

Shacklady, Ian T.
| 1985 | S/N.R. | Suzuki |

Shackleford, Brian
1995	J/Cl.R.	B.S.A.
1997	J/Cl.R.	B.S.A.
1997	J/Cl.R.	B.S.A.

Shannon, Keith
1990	J/N.12	Yamaha
1990	J.R.	Yamaha
1991	J.15	Yamaha
1991	L.13	Yamaha

Sharratt, Andrew
1990	S/N.10	Suzuki
1990	S.59	Suzuki
1991	J.R.	Suzuki
1991	L.R.	Suzuki

Sharratt, Dave J.
1983	J.22	Yamaha
1983	S.32	Yamaha
1986	S.12	Suzuki
1987	S.5	Suzuki
1988	S.8	Suzuki

Shaw, Alan C.
| 1984 | S/N.R. | Yamaha |

Shaw, Godfery
1992	J/Cl.34	Honda
1994	J/Cl.R.	Meta Honda
1994	S.50	Honda

1995	J.70	Meta Honda
1995	S.58	Meta Honda
1996	J.85	Meta Honda
1996	S.77=	Meta Honda

Shaw, Ian
| 1996 | S/N.4 | Kawasaki |
| 1996 | S.33 | Kawasaki |

Shaw, Malcolm
| 1988 | S/N.21 | Suzuki |
| 1989 | S.R. | Suzuki |

Shaw, G. Philip
1994	L/Cl.1	Suzuki
1995	L/Cl.8	Suzuki
1997	L/Cl.5	Suzuki

Sheehan, Tony
| 1987 | S/N.42 | Suzuki |

Shepherd, Kenneth
1989	J/Cl.R.	Aermacchi
1990	S/Cl.R.	Manx Goldie
1992	J/Cl.6	Aermacchi

Shepherd, Peter J.
| 1985 | J/N.17 | Yamaha |
| 1986 | L.R. | Yamaha |

Shields, David R.
| 1988 | S/N.R. | Yamaha |

Shillings, Peter
1983	J.R.	Yamaha
1983	L.16	Yamaha
1984	J.12	Yamaha
1984	L.R.	Yamaha
1985	J.R.	Yamaha
1985	S.R.	Yamaha
1987	S.55	Suzuki
1992	J.R.	Yamaha
1992	J.44	Yamaha

Shimmin, Danny
1987	J/Cl.21	Norton
1988	J/Cl.42	Norton
1992	S/Cl.17	G50 Matchless
1993	S/Cl.4	Matchless
1993	J/Cl.4	A.J.S.
1994	S/Cl.7	RM G50
1994	J/Cl.5	RM 7R
1995	S/Cl.R.	RM G50
1995	J/Cl.3	RM 7R
1996	S/Cl.12	G50 Matchless
1996	J/Cl.7	A.J.S.

Shone, David
| 1983 | J/N.23 | Yamaha |

Shorter, Cliff J.
1986	J/Cl.37	Ducati
1987	J/Cl.27	Ducati
1988	J/Cl.30	Ducati
1989	J/Cl.28	Ducati
1990	J/Cl.R.	Ducati
1991	J/Cl.20	Ducati
1992	J/Cl.24	Ducati
1994	J/Cl.23	Ducati
1995	J/Cl.29	Ducati
1996	J/Cl.R.	Ducati
1997	J/Cl.36	Ducati

Shortland, Anthony R.
1983	L/N.12	Yamaha
1983	L.R.	Yamaha
1984	L.18	Yamaha
1985	J.39	Yamaha
1985	L.R.	Yamaha
1988	L.12	Yamaha

Shortland, Vince
1989	J.17	Yamaha
1989	L.14	Yamaha
1991	J.23	Yamaha
1991	L.34	Yamaha
1992	J.35	Yamaha
1992	L.22	Yamaha

Simm, Rob
| 1991 | J/N.3 | Kawasaki |

Simmonds W. Graham
1989	J.44	Yamaha
1989	L.51	Yamaha
1990	J.R.	Yamaha

Simmons, Bob M.
| 1983 | L/Cl.R. | Suzuki |
| 1983 | J.40 | Yamaha |

1983	S.51	Yamaha
1984	J/Cl.30	Suzuki Spl.
1984	J.R.	Yamaha
1984	L.R.	Suzuki
1985	J/Cl.20	Suzuki
1986	J/Cl.29	Suzuki
1987	J/Cl.22	Suzuki
1988	L/Cl.R.	Suzuki
1989	L/Cl.R.	Suzuki
1990	L/Cl.6	Suzuki
1991	L/Cl.R.	Suzuki
1992	L/Cl.14	Suzuki
1993	L/Cl.17	Suzuki
1994	L/Cl.10	Suzuki
1995	L/Cl.R.	Suzuki
1996	L/Cl.8	Suzuki
1997	L/Cl.R.	Suzuki

Simmons, William G.
1983	J/N.R.	Yamaha
1984	J.R.	Yamaha
1984	L.36	Yamaha
1985	J.R.	Yamaha
1985	S.35	Yamaha
1987	J.R.	Yamaha
1987	L.R.	Yamaha
1988	J.R.	Yamaha
1988	L.R.	Yamaha

Simms, John
| 1990 | S/N.R. | Triumph |

Simpson, Ian T.
1987	L/N.2	Yamaha
1987	L.12	Yamaha
1988	J.R.	Yamaha
1988	S.R.	Suzuki

Sinclair, David
| 1983 | L/Cl.R. | Ducati |
| 1983 | S.56 | Honda |

Sinclair, Jon C. M.
1988	J/N.7	Yamaha
1989	J/Cl.17	Aermacchi
1989	S/Cl.28	Seeley
1990	J/Cl.R.	Aermacchi
1990	S/Cl.25	Matchless
1997	L.R.	Yamaha

Sinclair, Simon A.
| 1997 | J/N.12 | Honda |

Sinton, Eddie
1993	J/N.4	Moore Honda
1993	S.R.	Moore Honda
1994	J.8	Moore Honda
1994	S.11	Kawasaki

Skidmore, Michael D.
1983	L/N.8	Yamaha
1983	L.R.	Yamaha
1984	J.33	Yamaha
1984	L.R.	Yamaha
1985	J.15	Yamaha
1985	S.66	Yamaha
1986	J.22	Yamaha
1986	S.18	Yamaha

Skinner, David J.
1985	J/N.R.	Yamaha
1986	S.R.	Kawasaki
1987	J.R.	Yamaha
1987	L.47	Yamaha
1988	J.R.	Yamaha

Skinner, Liz
1989	L.43	Yamaha
1990	L.64	Kawasaki
1990	L.47	Kawasaki

Skripek, Christopher
1990	L/N.10	Yamaha
1990	J.66	Yamaha
1990	L.52	Yamaha

Slater, Colin
| 1995 | L.75 | Yamaha |

Smallbone, Nigel W.
| 1985 | S/Cl.R. | Triumph |
| 1995 | S/Cl.52 | Triumph |

Smallman, Tom
1993	L/N.12	Honda
1993	J.62	Honda
1994	J.73	Honda
1994	L.R.	Yamaha

1995 J.83 Yamaha
1995 L.R. Yamaha
1996 L.R. Yamaha
1997 L.48 Yamaha
Smethurst, Peter A.
1985 L/N.8 Armstrong
1987 L.52 Armstrong
1988 L.R. Armstrong
1989 J.R. C.W.H.
1989 L.R. Armstrong
1993 L.R. Armstrong
Smith, Andrew G. C.
1986 S/N.12 Yamaha
Smith, Alan F.
1983 S/Cl.R. Matchless
1983 S.R Kawasaki
1984 S/Cl.R. Matchless
1985 S/Cl.R. Matchless
1986 S/Cl.R. Matchless
Smith, Bill
1983 L/N.11 Yamaha
1983 L.R. Yamaha
1984 L.24 Yamaha
1987 J.R. Yamaha
Smith, Chris J.
1986 S/N.21 B.S.A.
1988 S/Cl.23 B.S.A.
1989 S/Cl.R. B.S.A.
Smith, David
1989 L/Cl.1 Aermacchi
1989 S/Cl.R. Matchless
1990 L/Cl.R. Aermacchi
1994 L/Cl.R. Aermacchi
1995 L/Cl.5 Yamaha
1996 L/Cl.R. Yamaha
Smith, David
1983 L/Cl.R. Aermacchi
1987 J/Cl.14 Aermacchi
1988 L/Cl.5 Aermacchi
1991 S/Cl.R. Aermacchi
1991 L/Cl.5 Aermacchi
1992 S/Cl.R. Aermacchi
1992 L/Cl.R. Aermacchi
1993 L/Cl.7 Aermacchi
1995 L.51 Yamaha
1997 L/Cl.8 Yamaha
Smith, David, C. P.
1983 J/Cl.32 Honda
1983 S.47 Ducati
1985 J/Cl.24 Honda
Smith, Ian
1992 S/N.4 Honda
1992 S.25 Honda
1993 J.52 Kawasaki
1993 S.14 Honda
1994 J.22 Yamaha
1994 S.8 Honda
1995 S.R. Honda
1996 J.36 Kawasaki
1996 S.20 Honda
1997 J.21 Honda
1997 L.19 Yamaha
1997 S.17 Honda
Smith, John, N.
1983 S.48 Honda
1984 S.R. Honda
1985 S.R. Honda
1986 J.36 Yamaha
1986 S.R. Honda
1987 L.R. Rotax
1989 S/Cl.R. Matchless
1990 L/Cl.19 Ducati
1991 S/Cl.R. Matchless
1992 S/Cl.R. Triumph
1993 S/Cl.R. Triumph
1995 J/Cl.R. Ducati
1997 S/Cl.42 Rickman G50
Smith, Martin J
1987 S/N.27 Yamaha
1988 S.44 Yamaha
1989 J.34 Yamaha
1989 S.37 Yamaha
1990 S/Cl.R. Triton
1990 S.40 Suzuki
1991 S/Cl.R. Triton
1991 S.28 Honda
1992 S/Cl.55 Triton
1992 S.34 Honda
1993 J.59 Suzuki
1993 S.23 Honda
1994 J.32 Honda
1994 L.31 Suzuki
1995 J.24 Honda
1995 S.27 Honda
1996 J.25 Honda
1996 S.36 Honda
1997 J.19 Honda
1997 S.33 Honda
Smith, Neil E.
1983 S/Cl.15 Norton G.S.
1984 S/Cl.R. Norton JAP
1985 L.R. Yamaha
Smith, Richard A.
1987 S/N.17 Suzuki
1988 S.R. Suzuki
1989 S.50 Honda
1991 S.R. Suzuki
1992 J.11 Honda
1992 S.8 Honda
Smith, Richmond
1987 S/N.39 HQ Hagon
Smith, Sean
1983 J/N.R. Yamaha
1985 J.R. Yamaha
1985 S.37 Yamaha
1986 J.26 Yamaha
1986 S.27 Suzuki
1988 S.59 Yamaha
Smith, Simon
1992 J/N.4 Honda
1992 S.32 Honda
Smith, Steve V.
1986 J/N.3 Yamaha
1986 L.R. Yamaha
1987 J.19 Yamaha
1987 L.10 Yamaha
1988 J.12= Yamaha
1988 L.10 Yamaha
1989 J.38 Yamaha
1989 L.17 Yamaha
1990 J.12= Yamaha
1990 L.18 Yamaha
1991 J.9 Yamaha
1991 L.11 Yamaha
1994 L/Cl.R. PB Suzuki
1995 L/Cl.4 Suzuki
1996 L/Cl.4 Suzuki
1997 L/Cl.6 Suzuki
1997 L.18 Yamaha
Smith, Stewart
1985 S/N.R. Maxton Yamaha
1986 J.38 Maxton
1986 L.31 Yamaha
1987 J.R. Yamaha
1987 L.R. Yamaha
1988 J.27 Yamaha
1988 L.15 Yamaha
1989 J.23 Yamaha
1989 L.40 Yamaha
1990 J.14 Yamaha
1990 L.10 Yamaha
1991 J.10 Yamaha
1991 L.R. Yamaha
Smith, Tony
1993 S/Cl.58 Matchless
1994 S/Cl.44 Matchless
Smith, Trevor
1989 S/N.27 Yamaha
Smyth, Brian
1990 J/N.R. Honda
1991 S.35 Honda
Smyth, G. John
1984 J/N.14 Yamaha
1985 J.16 Yamaha
1988 S.21 Suzuki
1989 S.R. Suzuki
Smyth, John
1985 L.R. Yamaha
Smyth, Laurence
1997 S/N.9 Yamaha
1997 S.93 Yamaha
Snaith, Jim
1993 J/N.15 Yamaha
Snee, Thomas M.
1985 S/Cl.R. Triumph
1985 J.R. Yamaha
1986 J.R. Yamaha
1986 L.39 Yamaha
Snow, Doug
1995 J/Cl.36 Ducati
1996 J/Cl.R. Ducati
1997 J/Cl.25 Ducati
Snow, John
1995 J/Cl.38 Drixton Aermacchi
1997 S/Cl.55 Drixton Aermacchi
1997 J/Cl.43 Drixton Aermacchi
Soothill, Darren
1996 J/N.2 Honda
1997 J.3 Whitwell Honda
1997 S.6 Whitwell Honda
Spain, E. Paul
1987 S/N.29 Suzuki
Speak, Andrew
1985 S/N.R. Suzuki
Spence, Cyril D. H.
1983 J/N.30 Yamaha
1984 J.25 Yamaha
Spence, Ian
1983 L.64 Yamaha
1984 J.52 Yamaha
1984 L.46 Yamaha
Spenceley, Adrian
1991 J/N.13 Yamaha
Spencer, Andy
1992 S/N.12 Norton
1994 S/Cl.R. Norton
1995 J.R. Ducati
1996 S/Cl.R. Norton
1996 J.96 Ducati
1997 S/Cl.R. Norton
Spencer, Steve
1991 S/Cl.R. Norton
Spencer, Steve
1995 S/N.9 Yamaha
1995 S.64 Yamaha
Spencer, Stewart
1988 J/N.9 Honda
Spong, John
1993 J/Cl.20 Ducati
1995 S/Cl.R. Norton
1995 J/Cl.15 Ducati
1996 J/Cl.R. Ducati
1997 J/Cl.R. Ducati
Spooner, Brian
1994 L/N.8 Honda
1994 L.21 Honda
1995 J.50 Honda
1995 L.18 Honda
1996 J.46 Honda
1996 L.13 Honda
1997 J.45 Honda
1997 L.7 Honda
Sproston, Andrew
1985 L/N.7 Suzuki
1985 L.22 Yamaha
1986 L.R. Yamaha
1987 J.R. Yamaha
1987 L.R. Yamaha
Stables, Adrian
1987 J/N.R. Yamaha
1988 J.R. Yamaha
1988 L.41 Yamaha
1991 J.35 Yamaha
1991 L.R. Yamaha
Stafford, Neil
1988 S.51 Yamaha
Stafford, Sid
1991 L/N.20 Kawasaki
Staley, V. John
1983 J.38 Yamaha
1985 J.49 Yamaha
Stallard, Rowland
1994 S/Cl.50 Norton
1994 J/Cl.36 Ducati
1995 S/Cl.43 Norton
1995 J/Cl.R. Ducati
1996 S/Cl.R. Manx Norton
Standevan, Ian
1983 J.R. Yamaha
1984 J.20 Yamaha
1984 S.R. Yamaha
1985 J.R. Yamaha
1986 J.R. Yamaha
1987 J.R. BVM Yamaha
1988 J.R. Yamaha
1989 J.R. Yamaha
Steed, Mark A.
1986 J/N.12 Yamaha
1987 J.38 Yamaha
1988 J.37 Yamaha
1988 L.34 Yamaha
Steele, Frank J.
1994 L/Cl/14 Ducati
1996 L/Cl/10 Suzuki
Steele, Roger
1984 J/N.18 Yamaha
1985 J.34 Yamaha
1985 S.R. Yamaha
1986 S.21 Suzuki
1987 S.24 Suzuki
1988 S.24 Suzuki
1989 S.29 Suzuki
1990 S.33 Suzuki
1992 J.R. Honda
1995 S/Cl.49 Matchless
1996 S/Cl.41 G50 Matchless
1997 S/Cl.32 Rickman G50
Stenton, Dave
1996 S/N.R. Yamaha
1996 S.89 Yamaha
Stephens, John
1983 S/Cl.12 Norton
1984 J/Cl.2 Honda
1985 J/Cl.1 Honda
1986 J/Cl.3 Honda
1987 J/Cl.R. B.S.A.
1990 J/Cl.R. B.S.A.
Stephens, Robert T.
1985 L/N.10 Rotax
1985 L.28 Rotax
Stevens, Nigel
1991 L/N.13 Kawasaki
1992 J.63 Yamaha
Stewart, Douglas G.
1983 S.49 Honda
Stewart, Ken J. C.
1989 L/Cl.R. Ducati
1991 L/Cl.14 Ducati
1992 L/Cl.7 Ducati
1992 J.57 Yamaha
1994 J/Cl.R. Aermacchi
1995 J/Cl.R. Aermacchi
Stewart, Phil
1994 J/N.1 Honda
1994 J.R. Honda
1994 S.17 Honda
1996 J.R. Yamaha
1996 S.R. Yamaha
1997 J.15 Honda
1997 S.26 Honda
Stewart, Raymond J.
1983 J/N.R. Yamaha
1983 S.R. Yamaha
Stimson, Chris J.
1984 S/Cl.R. Norton
Stirling, Mark
1989 S/N.5 Yamaha
1989 J.R. Yamaha
1990 S.21 Yamaha
Stockdale, Colin
1984 S.R. Honda
1985 S.61 Honda
Stockdale, Richard
1993 J/N.2 Honda
Stoddart, John
1984 J/N.13 Armstrong
1984 L.25 Armstrong
Storry, David M.
1983 S/Cl.R. Seeley
1984 S/Cl.R. B.S.A.
1985 S/Cl.R. Weslake
1986 S/Cl.R. Seeley
1987 S/Cl.6 Matchless
1988 J/Cl.14 Seeley
1988 S/Cl.5 Seeley
1989 J/Cl.R. Seeley
1989 S/Cl.R. Seeley
1990 J/Cl.8 A.J.S.
1990 S/Cl.8 Matchless
1991 S/Cl.8 Seeley
1991 J/Cl.R. Seeley
1992 S/Cl.6 Seeley
1992 J/Cl.4 Seeley
1993 S/Cl.40 Seeley
Stothert, Neil T.
1983 J/N.R. Maxton
1983 L.R. Maxton Yamaha
1984 J.36 Maxton Yamaha
1984 L.19 Yamaha
1985 J.R. Maxton Yamaha
1985 S.30 Maxton Yamaha
Stott, Arthur
1983 L/N.18 Yamaha
Stott, Richard
1983 J.35 Yamaha
1984 S.40 Norton
1985 J.R. Yamaha
Stratford, Mervyn
1992 L/Cl.23 Greeves
1993 L/Cl.R. Greeves
1994 L/Cl.R. Greeves
1995 L/Cl.R. Greeves
1996 L/Cl.R. Greeves
1997 L/Cl.14 Greeves
Stratford Parsons, Martin
1987 L/N.13 Ducati
1988 L/Cl.R. Ducati
1988 S/Cl.R. Ducati
1989 L/Cl.8 Ducati
1990 L/Cl.R. Ducati
1990 S/Cl.42 Ducati
Stringer, Jim
1991 L/N.4 Kawasaki
1991 L.29 Kawasaki
1992 J.R. Yamaha
1993 J.R. Yamaha
1993 L.21 Yamaha
Strowger, Kevin A.
1988 J/N.2 Yamaha
1988 J.24 Yamaha
1990 J.18 Honda
1990 L.14 Honda
Stuart, Forbes
1988 S/N.26 Yamaha
Sunderland, Eric R.
1983 J.R. Yamaha
1983 L.17 Yamaha
1984 L.21 Pharaoh Yamaha
1991 S.26 Seeley
1992 S/Cl.R. G50 Seeley
1993 S/Cl.R. Seeley
1994 J/Cl.R. Manx Norton
1994 S/Cl.20 Seeley
1996 S/Cl.R. Seeley
1996 J/Cl.R. Seeley
Sutcliffe, Ralph
1983 J.R. Yamaha
1983 S.30 Suzuki
1984 J.R. Raglan Yamaha
1984 S.R. Kelly Suzuki
1985 J.20 Raglan Yamaha
1985 L.2 Cowles Armstrong
1986 J.2 Yamaha
1986 L.1 Cowles Armstrong
Sutcliffe, Roger
1987 S/Cl.10 Cowles Matchless
Sutton, Michael A.
1990 L/N.9 Yamaha
1992 L.R. Yamaha
1993 L.23 Yamaha

1994 J.R.	Yamaha
1994 L.R.	Yamaha
1995 J.33	Yamaha
1995 L.R.	Yamaha
1996 S/Cl.R.	Seeley
1996 L.21	Honda
1997 J.50	Honda
1997 L.40	Honda

Sutton, Rob
| 1990 J/N.17 | Kawasaki |
| 1990 J.65 | Kawasaki |

Swainson, Jon
| 1995 L/N.15 | Yamaha |

Swallow, Alec
| 1986 S/Cl.R. | Velocette |
| 1987 S.59 | Suzuki |

Swallow, Bill
1983 S/Cl.R.	Velocette
1984 S/Cl.6	Velocette
1985 S/Cl.R.	Velocette
1986 J/Cl.1	Honda
1988 J/Cl.3	Aermacchi
1988 S/Cl.30	Velocette
1989 S/Cl.1	Seeley
1989 J/Cl.R.	Aermacchi
1990 J/Cl.2	Aermacchi
1990 S/Cl.R.	Seeley
1991 S/Cl.2	G50 Seeley
1991 J/CR.	Aermacchi
1992 S/Cl.2	Seeley Matchless
1992 J/Cl.1	Aermacchi
1993 S/Cl.1	Seeley
1993 J/Cl.R	FCL Aermacchi
1994 J/Cl.R	Aermacchi
1994 S/Cl.2	Seeley
1995 S/Cl.1	Seeley
1995 J/Cl.R.	Aermacchi
1996 S/Cl.R.	Seeley
1996 J/Cl.1	Aermacchi
1997 S/Cl.3	Petty Norton
1997 L/Cl.R.	Aermacchi

Swallow, Peter
1983 S.R.	Ducati
1984 S/Cl.R.	Norton
1984 S.R.	Norton
1985 S/Cl.9	Metisse Norton
1985 S.53	Metisse Norton
1986 S/Cl.R.	Norton
1988 S/Cl.11	Norton
1988 S.75	Honda
1989 J/Cl.2	Ducati
1989 S/Cl.11	Norton
1990 L/Cl.5	Ducati
1990 S/Cl.26	Norton
1991 S/Cl.12	Petty
1991 L/Cl.7	Ducati
1992 S/Cl.14	Norton
1992 L/Cl.18	Ducati
1993 S/Cl.R.	Manx Norton
1994 J/Cl.10	Petty Manx
1994 S/Cl.R.	Petty Manx
1995 S/Cl.20	Petty Manx
1995 J/Cl.10	Petty Manx
1996 J/Cl.R.	Petty Manx
1997 J/Cl.19	Petty Manx

Swallow, Richard
1987 J/Cl.1	Lawton Aermacchi
1988 J/Cl.1	Lawton Aermacchi
1988 S/Cl.R.	Lawton Aermacchi
1989 J/Cl.1	Aermacchi
1989 S/Cl.2	Aermacchi
1990 J/Cl.1	Aermacchi
1990 S/Cl.3	Aermacchi
1991 J/Cl.1	Aermacchi

Swann, Geoff
1987 J/N.4	Yamaha
1987 L.R.	Yamaha
1988 J.R.	Yamaha
1988 S.67	Suzuki

Swann, Michael
| 1986 J/N.R. | Yamaha |
| 1986 L.R. | Kimoco Rotax |

Swiers, Keith
| 1992 J/Cl.R. | A.J.S. |

Swindell, Jane
1994 L/N.10	Yamaha
1994 L.41	Yamaha
1995 L.R.	Yamaha
1996 L.36	East Yamaha

Sykes, Simon J.
| 1985 S/N.R. | Kawasaki |
| 1986 S.R. | Yamaha |

Tabiner, Cliff
| 1983 S/N.R. | Suzuki |

Tagg, Andy
| 1992 L/N.R. | Kawasaki |
| 1993 L/Cl.24 | Ducati |

Tams, Raymond G.
1988 L/Cl.10	Ducati
1989 L/Cl.14	Ducati
1990 L/Cl.14	Ducati

Tannock, Steve
| 1994 S/N.R. | Spondon Yamaha |
| 1994 S.52 | Yamaha |

Tansley, Jeff
| 1995 J/N.7 | Yamaha |
| 1995 J.13 | Yamaha |

Tate, Gary E.
1985 L/N.3	Yamaha
1985 L.8	Yamaha
1986 S.5	Yamaha

Taylor, Alan
1990 L/Cl.2	Suzuki
1990 S/Cl.R.	B.S.A.
1992 L/Cl.R.	Suzuki

Taylor, Bob
1991 J/Cl.R.	Ducati
1992 J/Cl.R.	Yamaha
1994 L/Cl.R.	Yamaha
1995 L/Cl.R.	Yamaha
1996 J/Cl.R.	Yamaha

Taylor, David
1992 S/N.R.	Honda
1992 S.53	Honda
1993 S.37	Honda

Taylor, David
1996 L/N.2	Kawasaki
1996 L.34	Kawasaki
1997 J.54	Kawasaki
1997 L.25	Kawasaki

Taylor, Francis
1995 J/Cl.17	Ducati
1996 S/Cl.22	Ducati
1996 J/Cl.29	Ducati
1997 S/Cl.18	Ducati
1997 J/Cl.8	Ducati

Taylor, Gary
| 1991 L/N.2 | Suzuki |

Taylor, Gordon
1994 S/N.9	Yamaha
1995 L.33	Yamaha
1995 S.54	Yamaha
1996 J.68	Yamaha
1996 S.71	Yamaha
1997 J.61	Kawasaki
1997 S.56	Kawasaki

Taylor, Keith
1996 J/N.7	Honda
1997 J.30	MB Mannin Honda
1997 S.40	Honda

Taylor, Lee
| 1989 S/N.20 | Yamaha |
| 1990 S.58 | Yamaha |

Taylor, Martin
| 1996 L/Cl.R. | Suzuki |
| 1997 L/Cl.19 | Suzuki |

Taylor, Mike
1983 J/N.14	Shepherd
1984 S.45	Honda
1985 J.29	Yamaha
1986 J.R.	Yamaha
1986 S.R.	Yamaha
1987 S.27	Suzuki
1988 S.41	Suzuki
1989 S.49	Suzuki
1991 S.40	Suzuki

| 1992 S.26 | Suzuki |

Taylor, Peter D.
| 1983 L.R. | Yamaha |

Taylor, Robert R.
1983 J.R.	Yamaha
1983 S.41	Yamaha
1984 J.R.	Yamaha
1984 S.46	Yamaha
1985 J.R.	Yamaha
1985 S.47	Yamaha
1986 J.23	Yamaha
1986 S.26	Yamaha
1987 J.20	Maxton
1987 S.R.	Maxton
1988 J.35	Yamaha
1990 J/Cl.R.	Ducati

Taylor, Robin
| 1983 L/N.19 | Honda |

Taylor, Wayne
1995 J/N.R.	Honda
1996 J.39	Honda
1996 S.R.	Honda
1997 J.28	Quiver Honda
1997 S.32	Quiver Honda

Teague, Gary
| 1991 L/N.7 | Suzuki |
| 1993 J.35 | Honda |

Teague, Jon
1990 J/N.10	Honda
1991 S.43	Honda
1991 J.45	Kawasaki
1992 J.51	Honda
1992 S.57	Honda
1993 S.27	Honda

Teale, Nick
| 1995 J/N.14 | Kawasaki |
| 1995 S.R. | Kawasaki |

Teare, Jeff
1992 S/N.13	Norton
1995 S/Cl.R.	Norton
1997 S/Cl.R.	Norton

Temple, Dennis
1995 J/N.R.	Maxton Yamaha
1995 J.80	Maxton Yamaha
1996 J.80	Honda
1996 S.R.	Honda
1997 J.93	Honda

Ten Cate, Grieko
| 1995 S/N.R. | Triumph |

Thain, Glen
| 1985 L/N.R. | Decorite |

Thomas, Stan
1986 S/N.16	Norton
1987 S.58	Norton
1988 S.34	Norton
1989 S.39	Suzuki
1990 S.27	Honda
1992 S.R.	Norton
1993 J.27	Yamaha
1993 S.R.	Norton
1994 J.42	Yamaha
1994 S.38	Norton
1995 J.R.	Yamaha
1995 S.52	Norton
1996 S.55	Yamaha
1996 S.43	Yamaha
1997 J.35	Yamaha
1997 S.47	Yamaha

Thompson, Andy
| 1993 L/N.R. | Kawasaki |
| 1993 L.30 | Kawasaki |

Thompson, Ian
1995 S/N.5	Yamaha
1995 S.33	Yamaha
1996 S.46	Yamaha
1997 J.55	Yamaha
1997 S.R.	Yamaha

Thompson, James M. G.
| 1984 S/N.R. | B.S.A. |
| 1986 J/Cl.18 | Ducati |

Thompson, Mick D.
1986 L/N.9	Honda
1987 J.29	Yamaha
1987 L.24	Yamaha

1988 S.R.	Suzuki
1992 L.23	Honda
1994 J.R.	Yamaha
1994 S.24	Honda
1996 S.65	Suzuki

Thompson, Sam D.
| 1988 J/Cl.34 | Aermacchi |
| 1989 J/Cl.R. | Aermacchi |

Thomson, A. Charles
1987 J.18	Yamaha
1988 L.R.	Yamaha
1989 S.37	Yamaha
1990 J.R.	Yamaha

Thornton, Peter
1992 L/Cl.21	Ducati
1993 J/Cl.29	Ducati
1994 J/Cl.28	Ducati
1995 J.82	Ducati
1995 J.87	Honda
1996 S.76	Honda
1997 J.79	Honda
1997 S.74	Honda

Thornton, Phil
1993 L/N.5	Kawasaki
1993 L.41	Kawasaki
1994 J.69	Kawasaki
1994 L.R.	Kawasaki

Thrush, Jez P.
1985 J/N.9	Maxton
1986 S.R.	Suzuki
1987 S.19	Suzuki
1988 J.19	Yamaha
1988 S.33	Suzuki

Thurlow, Dave
1991 L/Cl.R.	Yamaha
1992 L/Cl.10	Yamaha
1993 L/Cl.18	Yamaha
1994 L/Cl.3	Yamaha
1995 L/Cl.7	Suzuki
1996 L/Cl.6	Suzuki
1997 L/Cl.7	Suzuki

Todd, Paul A.
1983 J.6	Yamaha
1983 L.R.	Yamaha
1984 J.R.	Yamaha
1984 L.R.	Yamaha

Todhunter, Ian
| 1991 J/N.5 | Honda |

Tomlinson, Neil M.
1983 J/N.R.	Yamaha
1983 L.40	Yamaha
1986 J.R.	Yamaha
1986 L.R.	Yamaha
1987 J.R.	Yamaha
1987 L.21	Yamaha
1989 J.R.	Yamaha

Toner, Joe B.
1986 S/N.9	Suzuki
1987 S.R.	Suzuki
1989 S.35	Yamaha
1990 S.20	Yamaha
1991 S.9	Honda
1993 S.42	Yamaha
1993 S.21	Honda
1994 J.51	Honda
1994 S.R.	Honda
1995 S.17	Honda

Tonkin, Steve
| 1993 S/Cl.R. | Matchless |
| 1994 S/Cl.8 | Beale Matchless |

Torpey, Martin
1992 L/N.R.	Kawasaki
1993 J.58	Honda
1993 L.R.	Kawasaki
1994 L.36	Kawasaki

Townsend, Keith
1993 J/N.7	Honda
1993 J.31	Honda
1995 J.10	Honda
1994 S.10	Honda
1995 J.3	DC Butler Honda
1995 S.3	DC Butler Honda
1996 J.5	DC Butler Honda

1996 S.4	DC Butler Honda
1997 J.R.	DC Butler Honda
1997 S.2	DC Butler Honda

Townsend, Neil
| 1996 J/Cl.37 | A.J.S. Seeley |
| 1997 J/Cl.38 | A.J.S. Seeley |

Tree, Richard C. E.
1983 L/N.14	Ducati
1984 J/Cl.16	Aermacchi
1984 L.41	Ducati
1985 J/Cl.11	Aermacchi
1985 J.46	Aermacchi
1986 J/Cl.10	Aermacchi
1987 J/Cl.R.	Aermacchi
1987 S.57	Norton
1988 J/Cl.8	Aermacchi
1990 J/Cl.R.	Aermacchi
1990 S/Cl.11	Matchless
1992 S/Cl.47	Norton
1992 J/Cl.28	Aermacchi
1993 S/Cl.29	Seeley
1993 J/Cl.14	Aermacchi
1995 S/Cl.25	Seeley
1995 J/Cl.R.	Aermacchi
1997 S/Cl.R.	Seeley G50
1997 J/Cl.R.	Aermacchi

Trezise, Simon
| 1993 J/N.3 | Honda |

Trimble, Barry J.
| 1986 S/N.11 | Yamaha |
| 1987 S.20 | Yamaha |

Trollope, Dennis C.
1983 S/Cl.19	Norton
1984 S/Cl.15	Norton
1985 S/Cl.R.	Norton
1987 S/Cl.21	Matchless
1988 J/Cl.R.	Aermacchi
1988 S/Cl.22	G50
1989 J/Cl.21	Aermacchi
1989 S/Cl.25	Matchless
1990 J/Cl.R.	Aermacchi
1990 S/Cl.32	G50 Matchless
1991 S/Cl.35	G50 Matchless
1991 J/Cl.R.	Aermacchi
1992 S/Cl.54	Petty G50
1992 J/Cl.R.	Aermacchi
1993 J/Cl.R.	Matchless
1993 J/Cl.R.	Aermacchi
1994 J/Cl.R.	Aermacchi
1994 S/Cl.26	Petty G50
1997 S/Cl.31	Seeley Matchless
1997 J/Cl.23	Aermacchi

Trotter, Les
1983 S/Cl.R.	Ridgeon
1986 J/Cl.9	Suzuki
1987 J/Cl.6	Suzuki
1988 L/Cl.R.	Suzuki
1990 L/Cl.R.	Suzuki
1991 L/Cl.4	Suzuki
1992 L/Cl.8	Suzuki
1993 L/Cl.R.	Suzuki
1994 L/Cl.R.	Crooks Suzuki
1995 L/Cl.2	Crooks Suzuki
1996 L/Cl.R.	Kirk Seeley G50
1996 L/Cl.R.	Suzuki
1997 L/Cl.R.	Crooks Suzuki

Trout, Bernard H.
1988 L/Cl.R.	Ducati
1989 L/Cl.R.	Ducati
1990 L/Cl.R.	Ducati

Trubshaw, Keith
1983 J.2	Yamaha
1983 S.5	Yamaha
1984 J.R.	Yamaha
1984 S.8	Yamaha
1985 J.R.	Yamaha
1985 S.9	Yamaha

Tuck, Andy
1994 J/N.5	Honda
1995 J.43	Yamaha
1996 J/Cl.19	A.J.S.
1996 S.34	Yamaha
1997 J.41	Yamaha

1997 S.42	Yamaha	1989 J.R.	Yamaha	**Vernall, Tim N.**		1996 S/N.14	Honda	1996 J.60	Honda
Tuley, David		1989 L.R.	Rotax	1983 S/N.R.	Honda	**Wallis, David**		1996 S.64	Honda
1993 J/N.13	Yamaha	1995 J.44	Yamaha	1984 S.59	Honda	1987 S/N.11	Suzuki	1997 J.49	Honda
1995 J.81	Yamaha	1995 L.24	Yamaha	1985 S.51	Kerby Honda	**Walls, Stephen D.**		1997 S.44	Honda
1996 J.91	Yamaha			1986 S.51	Kerby Honda	1984 S/N.8	B.S.A.	**Watmough, Peter**	
1997 L.43	Yamaha	**Unsworth, Vernon**		1987 S.60	Honda	1985 S/Cl.R.	B.S.A.	1991 L/N.24	Honda
Tunstall, Geoff D.		1983 L/N.9	Shepherd Yamaha	1988 S.60	Honda	**Walmsley, Alfie**		1991 L/Cl.16	Yamaha
1989 S/Cl.10	Seeley	1984 J.R.	Shepherd Yamaha	1989 S/Cl.R.	B.S.A.	1991 J.30	Yamaha	1992 L/Cl.R.	Yamaha
1989 J/Cl.R.	Seeley	1984 L.R.	Shepherd Yamaha	1990 S/Cl.R.	B.S.A.	1991 S.34	Suzuki	1993 L/Cl.23	Yamaha
1991 S/Cl.4	Rutter Matchless	**Upton, Nick**		1992 J/Cl.R.	Aermacchi	1992 J.19	Yamaha	1995 L/Cl.R.	Yamaha
1991 J/Cl.4	A.J.S.	1992 J/N.9	Yamaha	1993 J/Cl.33	Aermacchi	1992 L.R.	Yamaha	**Watson, Duncan**	
1992 S/Cl.5	Matchless	1993 S.69	Yamaha	1994 J/Cl.20	Aermacchi Metisse	**Walmsley, Andrew**		1989 S/N.28	Honda
1992 J/Cl.2	Aermacchi	1993 S.29	Kawasaki	1995 J/Cl.R.	Aermacchi Metisse	1990 J/N.13	Yamaha	1989 S/Cl.45	Velocette
1993 S/Cl.38	Matchless	**Urch, Justin M.**		1997 J/Cl.R.	Aermacchi Metisse	1990 J.57	Yamaha	1990 S/Cl.30	Rickman Weslake
1993 J/Cl.R.	FCL Aermacchi	1985 J/N.3	Yamaha	**Vernon, Gary**		**Walter, Kevin B.**		1991 S/Cl.R.	Rickman Weslake
1994 S/Cl.11	Matchless	1986 J.5	Yamaha	1983 L.63	Yamaha	1985 L/N.16	Rotax	1992 S.59	BMW
1994 J/Cl.4	FCL Aermacchi	1986 S.R.	Suzuki	**Vincent, Jon**		1985 L.R.	Rotax	1993 S.32	Broon Suzuki
Tunstall, Ian E.		1987 J.R.	Yamaha	1993 L/N.R.	Yamaha	1986 J.R.	Yamaha	1994 S/Cl.R.	Matchless
1983 L.45	Yamaha	1987 S.R.	Yamaha	1993 L.34	Yamaha	1986 S.46	Suzuki	1995 J.R.	Bentley Yamaha
1984 L.R.	Yamaha	1988 J.R.	Yamaha	**Vine, Nigel A.**		**Walton, Chris J.**		**Watson, Russell**	
1985 J.R.	Yamaha	1988 S.R.	Yamaha	1987 J/Cl.26	Aermacchi	1985 J/Cl.R.	Aermacchi	1992 L/Cl.19	Ducati
1985 L.18	Yamaha	1989 J.21	Yamaha	1989 J/Cl.23	Aermacchi	1986 J/Cl.22	Aermacchi	**Watt, James G.**	
1986 J.R.	Yamaha	1989 S.27	Yamaha	**Vine, Rob**		1987 J/Cl.18	Aermacchi	1983 S.64	Laverda
1986 S.25	Yamaha	1990 J.R.	Yamaha	1984 S/Cl.2	Matchless	1988 J/Cl.33	Aermacchi	**Watt, Ian**	
1987 J.35	Yamaha	1990 S.13	Yamaha	**Vines, John E.**		1989 J/Cl.16	Aermacchi	1991 S/N.12	Honda
1987 L.28	Yamaha	1997 S.28	Honda	1983 S/Cl.R.	Norton	1989 S/Cl.R.	Triumph Seeley	1992 S.49	Honda
1988 J.R.	Yamaha	**Uren, Ivor**		**Virgo, Kenneth J.**		1990 J/Cl.R.	Aermacchi	**Watterson, Robbie**	
1988 L.R.	Yamaha	1993 S/N.5	Suzuki	1987 L/N.3	Yamaha	1990 S/Cl.R.	Aermacchi	1995 S/N.2	Kawasaki
Turnbull, Pete		1993 S.R.	Suzuki	1987 L.19	Yamaha	1991 S/Cl.51	Triumph	1995 S.23	Kawasaki
1991 L/N.10	Rotax	1994 S.R.	Honda	1988 J.29	Yamaha	1991 J/Cl.17	Aermacchi	**Watts, Mark**	
1991 J.R.	Rotax	1996 J.79	Honda	1988 L.44	Armstrong	1992 J/Cl.27	Aermacchi	1990 J/N.3	Yamaha
1991 L.19	Rotax	1996 S.68	Honda	1989 J.R.	Yamaha	1993 J/Cl.27	Aermacchi	1991 S.14	Yamaha
1992 J.22	Yamaha	1997 J.72	Honda	1989 L.R.	Armstrong	1994 J/Cl.24	Aermacchi	1992 J.5	Yamaha
1992 L.R.	Yamaha	1997 S.72	Honda	1990 J.R.	Yamaha	1995 J/Cl.33	Aermacchi	1992 L.R.	Yamaha
1995 J.14	Yamaha	**Uttley, Gabriel H.**		1990 L.37	Yamaha	1996 J/Cl.R.	Aermacchi	**Watts, Mark**	
1995 L.10	Yamaha	1984 S/N.12	Honda	1991 J.R.	Yamaha	1997 J/Cl.R.	Aermacchi	1995 J/N.34	MWR Rotax
1997 J.18	Yamaha	1985 S.33	Honda	1991 L.32	Armstrong	**Ward, Brian W.**		**Watts, R. Nev**	
1997 L.R.	Yamaha			1992 L.8	Yamaha	1984 S/N.15	Suzuki	1988 L/Cl.4	Honda
Turner, Chris J.		**Vale, David J.**		1993 J.R.	Yamaha	1985 J.R.	Yamaha	1989 L/Cl.4	Honda
1983 S/N.R.	Honda	1988 L/N.11	Yamaha	**Vollans, Gary**		1985 S.70	Suzuki	1990 L/Cl.11	Honda
1984 S.10	Honda	1988 L.29	Yamaha	1995 J/N.25	Honda	1986 L.41	Yamaha	1991 L/Cl.9	Honda
1987 S/Cl.2	Matchless	1990 J.36	Honda			1987 L.R.	Yamaha	1992 L/Cl.12	Honda
Turner, David		1991 J.19	Honda	**Wagstaff, Derek G.**		**Ward, Brian**		1993 L/Cl.19	Honda
1988 S/Cl.55	Triumph	1991 L.16	Honda	1986 J/N.8	Yamaha	1986 L/N.12	Yamaha	**Webb, Tom**	
1990 S/Cl.39	Triumph	1992 J.25	Yamaha	1987 J.R.	Yamaha	**Ward, Graham**		1987 S/N.14	Suzuki
1991 S/Cl.39	Triumph Daytona	1992 L.R.	Yamaha	1987 L.R.	Yamaha	1991 S/N.2	Kawasaki	**Webb, Tony J.**	
1991 S.R.	Triumph	1995 L.16	Padgett Honda	1988 J.38	Yamaha	**Ward, Mark R.**		1987 S/Cl.R.	Triumph
1992 S/Cl.R.	R. Weslake	1995 L.9	Padgett Honda	1988 L.18	Yamaha	1983 J/Cl.R.	Aermacchi	1988 S/Cl.41	Triumph
1994 S/Cl.R.	Rickman Weslake	1996 J.15	Padgett Honda	1989 J.24	Suzuki	1984 S.R.	Ducati	1989 S/Cl.24	Triumph
1994 S.R.	Triumph Trident	1996 L.8	Padgett Honda	1989 L.12	Suzuki	**Ward, Mick**		1990 S/Cl.R.	Triumph
1996 S/Cl.	Rickman Weslake	1997 J.40	Honda	1990 J.31	Suzuki	1983 S/Cl.17	Aermacchi	1991 S/Cl.24	Triumph
Turner, Glyn		1997 L.11	Honda	1990 L.21	Suzuki	1984 J/Cl.24	Aermacchi	1993 L/Cl.22	Honda
1983 L.26	Yamaha	**Vanderplank, Simon P.**		1991 J.5	Yamaha	1985 J/Cl.R.	Greeves	**Webster, Bernard P.**	
1984 L.17	Yamaha	1995 L/N.13	Kawasaki	1991 L.12	Yamaha	**Ward, Paul A.**		1986 L/N.11	Yamaha
Turner, Mark		1995 L.52	Kawasaki	1992 J.14	Yamaha	1987 J/N.6	Yamaha	1986 L.25	Yamaha
1992 S/N.5	Suzuki	1996 J.75	Honda	1993 J.R.	Yamaha	1989 L.13	Rotax	1987 J.R.	Yamaha
1994 S/N.8	Kawasaki	1996 S.66	Honda	1992 L.R.	Yamaha	1991 L.44	Rotax	1987 L.14	Yamaha
1994 S.R.	Kawasaki	1997 J.R.	Honda	1993 L.10	Yamaha	**Waring, David**		1989 J.32	Yamaha
1995 J.R.	Yamaha	1997 S.83	Honda	1994 J.23	Yamaha	1984 S/N.7	Kawasaki	1989 L.25	Rotax
1995 S.44	Yamaha	**Vanderplank, Simon**		1994 L.11	Yamaha	1985 S.42	Yamaha	1990 J.29	Yamaha
Turner, Nick J.		1988 S/N.5	Yamaha	1995 J.20	Yamaha	**Waring, Russell**		1990 L.25	Rotax
1985 L/N.R.	Trtax	**Varney, David J.**		1995 L.5	Yamaha	1995 L/N.3	Yamaha	**Webster, Geoff**	
1985 L.13	Trtax	1984 J/Cl.21	Aermacchi	1996 J.23	Yamaha	1995 L.8	Yamaha	1993 J.R.	Honda
1986 J.R.	Ntrax	**Venables, Brian**		1996 L.5	Yamaha	**Warren, Brian R.**		1993 S.47	Honda
1986 L.10	Ntrax	1984 J/N.9	Yamaha	1997 J.24	Yamaha	1984 J/Cl.28	A.J.S.	1994 J.47	Honda
1988 J.R.	Yamaha	1985 J.R.	Yamaha	1997 L.10	Yamaha	**Waterfield, Al J.**		1994 S.R.	Honda
1988 L.R.	Yamaha	1985 S.R.	Yamaha	**Wakefield, Peter**		1989 S/N.21	Suzuki	1995 J.28	Honda
1989 J.16	Yamaha	1986 S.28	Suzuki	1983 S/N.10	Suzuki	1990 S.32	Suzuki	1995 S.28	Honda
1989 L.1	Yamaha	1987 S.29	Suzuki	1984 J.35	Yamaha	1991 S.R.	Suzuki	1996 J.35	GLSM Honda
1993 L/Cl.R.	Yamaha	1988 L.R.	Armstrong	1984 S.27	Suzuki	1992 S.33	Suzuki	1996 S.37	GLSM Honda
1996 S/Cl.26	Seeley G50	1989 S.7	Yamaha	1985 S.26	Suzuki	1993 S.16	Honda	1997 J.39	GLJ Honda
1996 L/Cl.R.		1990 S.2	Honda	1986 J.27	Yamaha	1994 S.27	Spondon Suzuki	1997 S.35	GLJ Honda
Tuttle, Anthony A.		1991 S.R.	Honda	1986 L.7	Maxton	1995 S.R.	Spondon Suzuki	**Webster, Graham**	
1986 L/N.2	E.M.C. Rotax	1992 J.8	Honda	**Walker, David**		1996 S.72	Spondon Suzuki	1992 J/N.5	Honda
1986 L.16	E.M.C. Rotax	1992 S.R.	Honda	1992 S/N.10	Tigcraft Suzuki	1997 S.43	Spondon Suzuki	1992 S.47	Honda
Tuxworth, Neil		1993 J.D.	Honda	**Walker, Gary**		**Wateridge, Mark**		**Weeks, Jim**	
1983 S/Cl.3	Matchless	1993 S.2	Honda	1994 L/N.2	Yamaha	1990 J/N.16	Kawasaki	1995 S/N.7	Honda
1984 S/Cl.R.	Matchless	1994 J.1	Bullock RG Honda	1994 L.R.	Yamaha	1991 S.60	Kawasaki	1995 S.48	Honda
1985 S/Cl.1	Cowles Matchless	1994 S.1	Bullock Honda	**Walker, John**		1992 J.67	Yamaha	1996 L/Cl.R.	Suzuki T20
Tyrell, Mark J.		**Verity, Nigel**		1991 J/Cl.31	Norton	1992 S.51	Yamaha	**Welburn, Alan L.**	
1987 S/N.R.	Yamaha	1984 J/N.16	Yamaha	1992 S/Cl.48	B.S.A.	1993 J.28	Yamaha	1986 S/N.R.	Suzuki
1987 L.R.	Yamaha	1985 S.32	Suzuki	1993 S/Cl.52	Norton	1993 S.28	Triumph	1987 J.R.	Spondon
1988 J.10	Yamaha	1986 S.23	Suzuki	1994 S/Cl.R.	Norton B.S.A.	1994 J.30	Honda	1988 J.28	Yamaha
1988 L.R.	Yamaha	1987 S.21	Yamaha	**Walker, Keith**		1994 S.R.	Triumph	1989 J.27	Yamaha

1989 S.58	Suzuki	**Wild, Tim**		1988 S.25	Suzuki	1993 J.50	Honda	1985 S.57	Yamaha
Wells, John		1991 S/N.6	Honda	1989 S.R.	Honda	1994 S/Cl.10	Matchless	1986 J.R.	Yamaha
1985 J/N.10	Yamaha	**Wildman, Les**		**Wilson, Graham**		**Wood, Nat**		1986 S.45	Yamaha
1990 S.48	Kawasaki	1990 J/N.9	Yamaha	1993 S/Cl.R.	B.S.A.	1983 S/N.6	Honda	1989 J.37	Yamaha
Weston, John		1991 J.28	Kawasaki	1994 S/Cl.33	Seeley	**Wood, Neil**		**Wright, Bernie**	
1985 S/N.5	Yamaha	1991 S.R.	Yamaha	1995 S/Cl.R.	G50	1994 L/Cl.R.	Greeves	1983 L.R.	Yamaha
Weston, Paul		1992 J.R.	Kawasaki	1996 S/Cl.8	Craven G50	**Wood, Sid**		1984 J.R.	Yamaha
1987 L/N.R.	Yamaha	1992 L.32	Kawasaki	1997 S/Cl.R.	Craven G50	1987 S.73	Kawasaki	1984 L.R.	Yamaha
1987 L.17	Yamaha	**Wilkerson, Roger**		1997 J/Cl.3	Aermacchi	**Wood, Steven J.**		1986 S/Cl.R.	Triumph
Whalley, Derek		1997 S/N.8	Ducati	**Wilson, Jeff**		1986 S/N.R.	Kawasaki	1986 J.R.	Triumph
1993 S/Cl.24	Seeley	**Wilkins, Nick**		1995 L/N.10	Yamaha	1987 S.73	Kawasaki	1988 S/Cl.R.	Triumph
1993 J/Cl.R.	Ducati	1990 J/N.6	Cowles Yamaha	1996 J.74	Honda	**Woodhall, Adam J.**		1989 S/Cl.R.	Triumph
1994 S/Cl.R.	Seeley	1990 J.R.	Cowles Yamaha	1996 S.44	Suzuki	1985 S/N.4	Kawasaki	1990 S/Cl.21	Weslake
1995 S/Cl.R.	Seeley	1991 L.21=	Rotax	**Wilson, Laurence A. U.**		1986 J.R.	Yamaha	1991 S/Cl.19	NRE Weslake
1995 L/Cl.R.	Bultaco	1992 L.11	Cowles Honda	1988 S/N.11	Honda	1986 S.60	Honda	1992 S/Cl.R.	Metisse
1996 S/Cl.R.	G50	1993 J.7	Cowles Honda	1989 S.52	Yamaha	1987 S.R.	Suzuki	1994 S/Cl.R.	NRE Weslake
1996 L/Cl.R.	Bultaco	1993 L.R.	Cowles Honda	**Wilson, Peter J.**		1991 S/Cl.R.	Norton	1995 S/Cl.R.	NRE Weslake
1997 S/Cl.11	Seeley G50	**Wilkinson, Dale**		1988 L/Cl.11	Honda	1994 J.14	Yamaha	1996 S/Cl.R.	NRE Weslake
1997 J/Cl.15	Ducati	1986 S/Cl.33	Gold Star	1989 L/Cl.9	Honda	1994 S.9	Yamaha	1996 J/Cl.39	Aermacchi
Wheeler, Arthur F.		1988 J/Cl.43	B.S.A.	1990 L/Cl.10	Honda	1995 J.6	Honda	1997 S/Cl.R.	NRE Seeley
1983 L/Cl.5	Moto Guzzi	**Williams, Anthony**		1991 L/Cl.8	Honda	1995 S.7	Honda	1997 J/Cl.R.	Aermacchi
1984 J/Cl.22	Moto Guzzi	1993 S/N.4	Honda	1992 L/Cl.11	Honda	1996 J.7	MB Mannin Honda	**Wright, Bob**	
1985 J/Cl.R.	Moto Guzzi	1994 S.R.	Honda	1993 S/Cl.60	Triumph	1996 S.R.	Honda	1987 S.45	Suzuki
1986 J/Cl.R.	Moto Guzzi	**Williams, David A.**		1993 L/Cl.20	Honda	1997 J.4	Bullock Honda	**Wright, Charles C.**	
1987 J/Cl.32	Moto Guzzi	1983 S.R.	Honda	1994 L/Cl.12	Honda	1997 S.5	Bullock Honda	1983 S/N.R.	Yamaha
1988 L/Cl.6	Moto Guzzi	**Williams, Derek L.**		1995 L/Cl.15	Honda	**Woodall, Philip**		**Wright, Jon**	
1988 S/Cl.35	Moto Guzzi	1983 J.R.	Yamaha	1997 J/Cl.32	Honda	1983 J/Cl.31	A.J.S.	1992 J/N.3	Yamaha
1989 L/Cl.10	Moto Guzzi	1984 J.R.	Yamaha	**Wilson, Stephen D.**		1984 J/Cl.7	Aermacchi	**Wright, Kirk**	
1989 S/Cl.R.	Moto Guzzi	1986 J.R.	Yamaha	1987 S/N.23	Rickman	1985 J/Cl.4	Aermacchi	1991 S/N.5	Honda
Wheeler, Chris		1987 J.R.	Yamaha	1989 S.72	Rickman	1986 S/Cl.7	Seeley	1991 S.R.	Honda
1984 J/N.17	Yamaha	1988 J.41	Yamaha	1990 S.38	Yamaha	1986 S.43	Ducati	**Wright, Martyn**	
Wheeler, Philippa		1988 L.R.	Yamaha	1991 S.59	Yamaha	**Woodcock, Antony**		1988 J/N.R.	Yamaha
1991 L/Cl.21	Ducati	1989 J.R.	Yamaha	1992 J.36	Yamaha	1990 S/N.3	Honda	**Wright, Robert A.**	
1992 L/Cl.26	Ducati	1989 L.R.	Yamaha	1992 S.R.	Yamaha	**Woodcock, Chris D.**		1983 S.53	Kawasaki
1993 L/Cl.26	Ducati	1990 J.42	Yamaha	**Wilson, Stephen J.**		1990 S/Cl.20	Seeley	1984 S.33	Kawasaki
1995 J/Cl.R.	Ducati	1990 L.35	Yamaha	1985 L/N.R.	Yamaha	1991 J.18	Yamaha	1985 S.8	Suzuki
Whitby, Keith		1991 J.R.	Yamaha	**Wingrave, Rob**		1992 J.20	Yamaha	1986 S.11	Suzuki
1989 S/Cl.R.	Seeley	1991 L.R.	Yamaha	1994 S/Cl.51	Norton	1992 L.R.	Yamaha	1987 S.45	Suzuki
1991 S/Cl.R.	Seeley	**Williams, Derek**		1994 J/Cl.29	Norton	**Woodman, Paul M.**		1988 S.R.	Yamaha
1993 L.43	Honda	1994 L/Cl.R.	Suzuki	1995 S/Cl.42	Norton	1985 L/N.5	Yamaha	**Wynne, Pat**	
White, Martin		1996 L/Cl.R.	Suzuki	1995 J/Cl.34	Norton	1985 L.17	Yamaha	1983 L.62	Yamaha
1991 L/N.8	Suzuki	1997 L/Cl.R.	Suzuki	1996 S/Cl.57	Norton	1986 J.28	Yamaha	1984 L.39	Yamaha
1992 J.40	Yamaha	**Williams, Keith**		1996 J/Cl.28	Norton	1986 S.39	Suzuki	1985 L.38	Yamaha
1992 L.42	Yamaha	1991 S/N.9	Yamaha	1997 S/Cl.39	Norton	1989 L.23	Honda	1986 L.26	Yamaha
White, Paul		1994 J.58	Yamaha	1997 J/Cl.24	Norton	**Woods, Dave**		1987 L.35	Yamaha
1996 L/N.3	Honda	1994 S.15	Yamaha	**Winn, Stephen R.**		1997 J/N.15	Honda	1988 L.51	Armstrong
White, Roger E. V.		1995 J.29	Honda	1983 L.R.	Yamaha	**Woolams, Dave**		1990 L/Cl.21	Ducati
1983 J.R.	Maxton Yamaha	1995 S.R.	Yamaha	**Winyard, Mark**		1985 S.48	Kawasaki	1993 L/Cl.R.	Ducati
1983 S.20	Maxton Yamaha	1996 J.30	Honda	1983 S/N.R.	Yamaha	**Worth, Andy**		1995 L/Cl.18	Ducati
1984 J.R.	Yamaha	1996 S.R.	Honda	**Withers, Mick R.**		1990 L/N.R.	Kawasaki	1996 L/Cl.13	Ducati
1984 S.R.	Yamaha	**Williams, Les**		1984 J.38	Yamaha	1991 J.38	Suzuki	1997 L/Cl.22	Ducati
Whitehead, Ian		1997 J/N.4	Honda	1985 J.28	Yamaha	1991 L.39	Suzuki	**Wyse, James F.**	
1989 L/N.R.	Yamaha	1997 S.54	Honda	1987 J.17	Yamaha	1993 L.R.	Yamaha	1986 S/N.15	Kawasaki
1991 S/Cl.49	Velocette	**Williams, Michael P.**		1987 S.62	Yamaha	1994 J.65	Kawasaki	1987 S.67	Kawasaki
1993 S/Cl.64	Velocette	1983 J.R.	Yamaha	**Wood, Barry**		1994 L.34	Kawasaki	1988 S.R.	Kawasaki
Whitehouse, David		1983 L.14	Yamaha	1988 L/N.7	Yamaha	**Worth, Steve**			
1996 L/Cl.9	Yamaha	**Williams, Paul John**		1988 L.25	Yamaha	1989 L/N.7	Suzuki	**Yarnold, Andrew**	
1997 L/Cl.11	Yamaha	1983 L/N.2	Yamaha	1989 L.15	Yamaha	**Worthington, Nigel**		1996 L/N.R.	Kawasaki
Whiteley, Peter		1983 L.54	Yamaha	1990 L/Cl.4	Suzuki	1992 L/N.11	Suzuki	1996 L.R.	Kawasaki
1990 S/N.R.	Suzuki	1984 L.R.	Yamaha	1990 S.28	Yamaha	**Worton, Garry**		**Yeardsley, C. Buddy**	
Whiteman, Richard		**Williams, Wilf**		1991 L/Cl.2	Suzuki	1989 L/N.12	Yamaha	1983 J.R.	Yamaha
1988 L/N.5	Yamaha	1992 S.64	Yamaha	1991 L.21=	Spondon Rotax	1989 L.47	Yamaha	1983 S.2	Suzuki
1988 L.14	Yamaha	**Williamson, Glenn**		1992 L/Cl.2	Suzuki	1990 J.53	Yamaha	1984 J.R.	Martland Yamaha
1989 J.39	Suzuki	1989 L/N.11	Kawasaki	1992 L.R.	Rotax	1990 L.40	Yamaha	1984 S.R.	Suzuki
1989 L.20	Suzuki	**Williamson, Norman**		1994 J.17	Yamaha	1991 J.R.	Yamaha	1985 J.4	Martland Yamaha
Whitham, James M.		1983 J.16	Yamaha	1994 L.7	Yamaha	1991 L.35	Yamaha	1985 S.1	Wilson Suzuki
1985 L/N.R.	Suzuki	1983 S.18	Yamaha	1996 L/Cl.3	Suzuki	1992 J.46	Yamaha	**Yeats, John**	
Whittaker, Graham J.		1984 J.15	Maxton Yamaha	1996 L.2	Padgett Yamaha	1992 L.15	Yamaha	1995 S/Cl.R.	Metisse
1983 L.R.	Yamaha	1984 S.R.	Maxton Yamaha	1997 L/Cl.R.	Honda	1993 J.44	Yamaha	1996 S/Cl.58	Metisse
1984 L.28	Yamaha	1986 J.20	Maxton Yamaha	1997 L.5	Manton Honda	1993 L.26	Yamaha	1997 S/Cl.R.	Metisse
1985 L.20	Yamaha	1986 S.62	Maxton	**Wood, Duncan**		1994 L.23	Yamaha	**Young, Derek A.**	
1986 J.R.	Yamaha	1988 L/Cl.R.	Aermacchi	1988 S/N.28	Suzuki	1995 J.48	Yamaha	1987 J/N.2	Yamaha
1986 L.26	Yamaha	1989 L/Cl.R.	Aermacchi	**Wood, Jackie J.**		1995 L.21	Yamaha	1987 L.8	Rotax
Wicks, Steven		1989 J.R.	Yamaha	1985 J/Cl.R.	Aermacchi	1996 J.70	Yamaha	1988 J.44	Yamaha
1986 S/N.5	Kawasaki	1989 S.71	Honda	**Wood, Matt J.**		1996 J.22	Yamaha	1988 L.4	Rotax
1987 S.R.	Suzuki	1990 L/Cl.R.	Aermacchi	1983 L/N.R.	Cotton Rotax	1997 J.74	Honda	1989 J.9	Yamaha
Wield, Chas		1990 J.46	Yamaha	1983 L.R.	Cotton Rotax	1997 L.32	Yamaha	1989 L.5	Rotax
1995 S/Cl.39	Seeley Velocette	**Willis, Anthony G.**		1985 S.65	Honda	**Wragg, Jules**		1990 J.R.	Robson Yamaha
1996 S/Cl.62	Seeley Velocette	1984 J/N.11	Yamaha	1987 S.50	Honda	1993 J/N.10	Honda	1990 L.5	Robson Yamaha
1996 J/Cl.R.	Metisse Velocette	**Wilson, Andy**		1988 S.43	Suzuki	1993 S.36	Honda	**Young, Ian**	
1997 S/Cl.26	Seeley G50	1996 J/N.18	Honda	1991 S.39	Honda	**Wren, Edwin**		1989 J/Cl.2	Aermacchi
1997 J/Cl.37	Metisse Viper	**Wilson, Colin**		1992 J.45	Harris	1983 L.50	Yamaha	**Young, Terry**	
Wilcox, John		1984 S/N.R.	Suzuki	1992 S.R.	Harris	1984 J.45	Yamaha	1993 S/N.6	Honda
1983 J.50	Yamaha	1987 S.43	Honda	1993 S/Cl.9	G50	1985 J.R.	Yamaha		

The History of the Manx Grand Prix 1923-1998 189

The Manx Grand Prix Riders Association

The Manx Grand Prix Riders Association

The M.G.P.R.A. was formed in 1973 after several riders and former riders had made suggestions that it would be nice to have an organisation which would be exclusively for themselves. The new TT Clerk of the Course Jack Wood approached Bob Dowty Senior to see if he would help get the Association off the ground. Sixty-one members attended an inaugural meeting where draft objects and rules were laid down at the first meeting which was held on Sunday 1st September 1974 at the Woodbourne Hotel, Douglas. In a very short time 104 members were recruited.

There are many founder members who are still very active and keep a keen interest on how the Association runs, they include Jack Wood, Bob Dowty Snr, George Costain, Roger Sutcliffe, Alan Shepherd and Eddie Crooks, plus many more who cannot make the Manx race week but who look forward to receiving 'Out of the Mist', the Associations newsletter which keeps everyone up to date.

In the early days, the membership was £2; today it is £5 minimum for life membership, a bargain! Membership now stands at over 700.

As the Association was gaining more and more members who were over for the races, it was not easy to meet each other. In the late 80s it was decided by the Committee that it would be a good idea to have a regular meeting place (the TT Riders Association were faced with the same problem).

In 1989, the M.G.P.R.A., together with the T.T.R.A. decided to jointly purchase a Portacabin so that all members had a meeting place when they came to the races. This is solely for members and their guests. (To be a member of either Association one has to have ridden in either the TT or the MGP).

'The 38th Milestone'

The M.G.P.R.A. hold their Annual General Meeting at 11 am on the Sunday between practice and race week, in the Mike Hailwood Centre, followed by a well-organised buffet arranged and supplied by the wives of the Committee members, "Thank you girls".

During race week the '38th' is alive as riders past and present meet and greet each other, possibly for the first time since they raced together many years ago. It is manned and run by ex-rider Tom Thorp and his wife Frances, who have made the Island their home. They both put a lot of unseen time and effort into running the '38th' for both organisations, it is such a comfortable and relaxing venue for members and guests to meet and enjoy a cuppa and refreshments.

Both associations rely on donations, however small, which enables them to provide assistance to any member who may find themselves in difficulty.

For those wishing to find the '38th Milestone, it is situated at the rear of the Grandstand, opposite the Press Office. It proudly flies the banner of both organisations during race periods, and is open from Thursday afternoon of practice week onwards. Frances and Tom will be delighted to make the acquaintance of any ex-riders, and sign them up for either of the organisations.

For those who are unable to get to the Island, they can send their subscription or write for details to Mrs Francis Thorp, MGPRA, Mountain View, Glen Maye, Isle of Man, IM5 3BJ.

'Mine hosts' of the 38th Milestone, Francis and Tom Thorp with Joey Dunlop, a rider who is eligible for membership of the MGPRA, but is better known for his TT exploits.

Club Team Awards

Senior Manx Grand Prix Team Prize
The G J A Brown Trophy

Year	Club	Riders
1928	Southport & District M.C.C.	P. Hunt; W. L. Birch; G. L. Emery
1929	not awarded	
1930	Crewe M.C.C.	A. Ashley; A. Brewin; D. Kenyon
1931	Crewe M.C.C.	Herbert & Harold Hartley; R. G. Williamson
1932	Grantham & District M.C.C.	F. L. Frith; S. C.Vince; J. F. Clay
1933	Kirkcaldy M.C.C.	J. K. Swanston; J. H. Blyth; J. Mc.L. Leslie
1934	B.M.C.R. C.	D. J. Pirie; R. Harris; L. R. Courtney
1935	Grimsby & District M.C.C.	F. L. Frith; A. Munks; M. Cann
1936	Perth & District M.C.C.	J. H. Blyth; K. Bills; T. McEwan
1937	Peveril (I.O.M.) M.C.& L.C.C.	W. A. Rowell; H. M. Rowell; J. Cannell
1938	Derby & District M.C.C.	J. Lockett; P. M. Aitchison; R. Lee
1946	Bradford & District M.C.C.	E. E. Briggs; A. E. Moule; K. Bills
1947	Pathfinder & Derby M.C.C.	C. F. Salt; W. McVeigh; C. H. Francis
1948	Peveril (I.O.M.) M.C.& L.C.C.	D.G.Crossley; T. P. Crebbin; J. W. Moore
1949	B.M.C.R.C.	G. E. Duke; F. Norris; H. J. D. Boynton
1950	Mont Christie M.C.C.	R. H. Sherry; P. Simister; D. E. R. Morgan
1951	King's Norton M. C. C.	D. E. Bennett; G. E. Read; F. Norris
1952	B.M.C.R. C.	D. K. Farrant; H. A.Pearce; K. R. Campbell
1953	Louth & District M.C.C.	J. Duncan; J. Hartle; A.Jervis
1954	Southern (I.O.M.) M.C.C	G. R. Costain; W. S. Mizen; E. B.Crooks
1955	Ringwood M.C.C.	G. B.Tanner; R. B.Cortvriend; F. A.Rutherford
1956	Southern (I.O.M.) M.C.C.	W. A. Holmes; E. B. Crooks; R. Dowty
1957	Southern (I.O.M.) M.C.C.	W. A. Holmes; E. B. Crooks; R. Dowty
1958	Southern (I.O.M.) M.C.C.	E. B. Crooks; R. Dowty; M. S. Kelly
1959	Ramsey & District M.C.C.	E. B. Crooks; M. S. Kelly; F. Fisher
1960	B.M.C.R. C. 'A'	E. Minihan; P. W. Read; R. S. Mayhew
1961	Barnet & District M.C.	E. Minihan; R. P. Dawson; P. J. Darvill
1962	Barnet & District M.C.	P. J. Darvill; R. P. Dawson; N. J. Price
1963	Dundee & Angus M.C.C.	R. H. M. Lister; P. N. Elmore; D. Reid
1964	not awarded	
1965	West Bromwich M.C.& C.C.	M. Uphill; S. Spencer; D. Brown
1966	not awarded	
1967	not awarded	
1968	Wirall '100' M.C.C.	M. D. J. Taylor; E. Bilsborrow; C.Wilkinson
1969	Carmarthen M.C.	R. Davies; G. C. Pantall; D. Grant
1970	Andreas Racing Association	D. Shimmin; T. N. Kelly; G. M. Short
1971	not awarded	
1972	Southern 67 R. C.C.	T. C. Parker; K. F. H. Inwood; A. Ayers
1973	R.A.F. M.S.A.	J. H. Goodall; P. H. Reid; D. Arnold
1974	Cheshire M.C.R.C.C. 'C'	F. Higginson; B. Peters; J. Knowles
1975	Newmarket M.C.C. 'C'	D. Featherstone; R. Barber; G. Barstard
1976	not awarded	
1977	Market Drayton M.C.	R. Monnery; E. Cornes; G. Wylie
1978	Bon Accord	G. Linder; G. Paterson; S. Bradley
1979	Darley Moor M.C.R.C. 'A'	J. McEntee; D. Ashton; A. Cooper
1980	Andreas Racing Association 'A'	G. Radcliffe; R. Luckman; M. Kneen
1981	Aintree 'B'	S. Anderson; R. Evans; D. Smith
1982	Farnham Royal M.C.& L.C.	G. Farmer; R. Cutts; R. Rogers
1983	Aintree 'A'	M. Noblett; R. White; C. Faulkner
1984	Andreas Racing Association 'E'	A. Phillips; B. Appleton; B. Jacques
1985	Aintree 'A'	K. Trubshaw; R. Evans; S. Marshal
1986	R.A.F. M.S.A. 'A'	G. Goodings; I. Tunstall; G. Tate
1987	Market Drayton	D. Sharratt; G. Martin; R. Steele
1988	Newmarket	S. Bushell; J. Dalton; P. Beale
1989	North Glos. M.C.C.	C. Hook; B. Middleton; N. Larsen
1990	R.A.F. M.S.A. 'A'	S. Beck; M. Livingston; J. Urch
1991	North Gloucester M.C.C.	C. Hook; N. Larsen; S. Cook
1992	Pegasus M.C. & L.C.C.	R. Smith; C. Downes; D. O'Leary
1993	North Gloucester M.C.C.	C. Hook; N. Larsen; N. Hansen
1994	Andreas Racing Association 'B'	B. Appleton; C. Kneen; D. Muir
1995	Andreas Racing Association 'B'	M. Casey; N. Kneen; G. Carswell
1996	M.C.R.R.C. of Ireland	A. McFarland; R. Mitchell; A. Archibald
1997	North Gloucester M.C.C.	K. Townsend; C. Hook; N. Larsen

Junior Manx Grand Prix Team Prize
The J W Davie Trophy

Year	Club	Riders
1931	Crewe M.C.C.	R. Harris; E. N. Lea; D. J. P. Whittingham
1932	Derby & District M.C.C.	R. Fidgeon; H. L. Daniell; J. F. Clay
1933	Kirkcaldy M.C.C.	J. K. Swanston; J. H. Blyth; J. Mc.L. Leslie
1934	Cambridge University M.C.C	J. H. White; J. H. Fell; S. B. Darbishire
1935	Kirkcaldy M.C.C.	J. K. Swanston; J. H. Blyth; T. McEwan
1936	not awarded	
1937	Wakefield & District M.C.C.	D. Parkinson; M. Cann; A. E. Moule
1938	Wakefield & District M.C.C.	D. Parkinson; T. McEwan; J. F. R. Martin
1946	Dublin & District M.C.C.	E. Lyons; P. D. Gill; H. Tyson
1947	Bradford & District M.C.C.	E. E. Briggs; A. E. Moule; J. M. Crow
1948	B.M.C.R.C.	A. F. Wheeler; R. H. Dale; D. G. Crossley
1949	B.M.C.R.C.	G. E. Duke; F. Norris; R. Pratt
1950	Peveril (I.O.M.) M.C.& L.C.C.	D. G. Crossley; D. Christian; R. Hunt
1951	Mont Christie M.C.C.	R. H. Sherry; G. Clark; D. E. R. Morgan
1952	Peveril (I.O.M.) M.C. & L.C.C.	D. Ennett; D. Christian; J. J. Wood
1953	Peveril (I.O.M.) M.C. & L.C.C.	D. Christian; J. J. Wood; E. B.Crooks
1954	Ringwood M.C.C.	G. B.Tanner; D. Powell; P. Tait
1955	Southern (I.O.M.) M.C.C.	W. A. Holmes; E. B. Crooks; E. Dow
1956	Windsford & District M.C.C.	E. F. H. Boyce; G. D. Alcock; J. R. Hurlstone
1957	Southern (I.O.M.) M.C.C.	C. Broughton; W. S. Mizen; W. R. Anderson
1958	Peveril (I.O.M.) M.C.& L.C.C.	E. B. Crooks; R. Dowty; M. S. Kelly
1959	Horsforth & D. M.C.C. 'B'	G. Bell; P. J. Darvill; A. Craven
1960	Scottish A.C.U. 'A'	I. P. Wallace; W. Milne; J. Adam
1961	Border M.R. C. 'B'	D. Pratt; F. Reynolds; P. Huby
1962	B.M.C.R.C. 'B'	D. E. Watson; S. G. Griffiths; P. B. James
1963	Barnet Club	P. J. Darvill; J. T. Griffiths; S. G. Griffiths
1964	not awarded	
1965	Whitley & District M.C.C.	B. J. Davies; W. Scott; D. P. May
1966	East Grinstead M.C.C.	R. W. Baylie; A.C.Peck; R. L. Knight
1967	Solway M.C.C.	C. E. Dobson; R. A. Graham; J. B. Lishman
1968	Cheshire M.C.R.R.C.	C. D. Wild; J. Duffy; P. Welfare
1969	Cheshire M.C.R.R.C.	P. Welfare; C. D. Wild; J. Duffy
1970	Andreas Racing Association	J. K. Cowley; R. W. Bryant; R. B. Sutcliffe
1971	Cheshire M.C.R.R.C. 'C'	J. B. Hall; E. W. Ramsey; D. A. Naylor
1972	Southern 67 R. C.C.	K. G. Hampton; T. C. Parker; M. J. Trimby
1973	Racing 50 Club 'C'	D. Lunn; E. Roberts; C.Crosby
1974	Racing 50 Club 'A'	M. Kirwan; D. Richardson; M. Harrison
1975	Pontypool & D. M.C.C.	D. Williams; C. Bond; J. Davis
1976	Racing 50 Club 'A'	K. Riley; J. Knowles; E. Martin
1977	Cheltenham M.C.	T. Russell; J. Goodall; J. Bishop
1978	Cheltenham M.C.	G. Ridgeon; J. Stone; T. Russell
1979	Waterloo & D. M.C.	K. Trubshaw; P. Daniels; C. Mylchreest
1980	Waterloo & D. M.C.	P. Daniels; K. Trubshaw; C. Mylchreest
1981	Andreas Racing Association 'B'	R. Coates; C. Grose; K. Wilson
1982	Farnham Royal M.C.& L.C.	G. Farmer; K. Edwards; R. Williams
1983	British Formula R.C.	A. Marshal; D. Sharratt; T. Martin
1984	not awarded	
1985	Dundrod & District M.C.C.	D. Johnson; S. Hazlett; G. Barron
1986	not awarded	
1987	Scottish A.C.U.	S. Rae; D. Allan; D. Glass
1988	North Glos. M.C.C.	S. Clements; T. Roebuck; K. Virgo
1989	M.C.R. R. C.Ireland	S. Rea; D. Young; L. McMaster
1990	Andreas Racing Association 'A'	N. Kneen; G. Broughton; A. Bassett
1991	Auto 66	Stephen Smith; D. Wagstaff; Stewart Smith
1992	R.A.F.M.S.A.	Andy Jones; R. Smith; M. Livingston
1993	Scottish A.C.U.	N. Hansen; G. Morton; B. Hogg
1994	Andreas Racing Association 'A'	G. Broughton; D. Kelly; T. Duncan
1995	Andreas Racing Association 'A'	C. Cannell; M. Casey; S. Collister
1996	M.C.R.R.C. of Ireland	A. McFarland; R. Mitchell; A. Archibald
1997	Andreas Racing Association	N. Kneen; G. Carswell; D. Black

Lightweight Manx Grand Prix Team Prize
The Bills/Harding Trophy

Year	Club	Riders
1969	Coleraine & D. M.C.C.	E. T. P. McCready; A. Mayrs W. M. Galbraith
1970	Coleraine & D. M.C.C.	A. Mayrs; E. T. P. McCready; W. M. Galbraith
1971	Racing 50 Club 'A'	L. Trotter; D. Lunn; R. J. E. Cope
1972	Newmarket & D. M.C.& L.C.	D. Arnold; P. H. Reid; E. R. Piner
1973	Newmarket & D. M.C.& L.C.	C. Revett; P. H. Reid; D. Arnold
1974	Batley M.C.& L. C.	D. Padgett; S. Ward; B. Robson
1975	Midland M.C.R. C. 'A'	J. Stone; J. Baker; G. Pinch
1976	Midland M.C.R. C.	J. Stone; S. Davies; B. Jackson
1977	Andreas Racing Association 'A'	D. Padgett; D. Cassidy; K. Harrison
1978	Midland M.R. C.	J. Stone; A. Atkins; E. Sunderland
1979	Mid-Antrim M.C.	M. Barr; C. Law; R. Campbell
1980	Louth	G. Tunstall; S. Williams; G. Padgett
1981	Andreas Racing Association 'A'	C. Grose; C. Cannell; C. Fargher
1982	M.C.R.R.C.of Ireland 'A'	G. Adams; S. McClements; D. Bell
1983	Andreas Racing Association 'A'	R. Coates; S. Collister; C. Fargher
1984	Aintree 'D'	N. Chorley; G. Sewart; N. Stothert
1985	North Glos. M.C.C.	B. Moore; P. Lewis; R. Burden
1986	Darley Moor	J. Davies; R. Haynes; P. Wakefield
1987	North Gloucestershire	B. Moore; N. Jennings; K. Virgo
1988	Loughshinny M.C.C.	D. Young; F. Duffy; P. McCallen
1989	Pegasus (Grantham)	M. Robinson; R. Whiteman; P. Ward
1990	Auto 66	Stephen Smith; D. Wagstaff; Stewart Smith
1991	Pegasus M.C.& L.C.C.	M. Robinson; P. Ward; D. Cooper
1992	North Gloucestershire 'A'	N. Jennings; S. Clements; K. Virgo
1993	Scottish A.C.U.	G. Morton; B. Hogg; J. Teague
1994	Andreas Racing Association 'A'	G. Broughton; D. Kelly; T. Duncan
1995	Auto 66	R. Henley; P. Turnbull; K. Bell
1996	Southern 100	B. Wood; S. Collister; D. Kelly
1997	Southern 100	B. Wood; S. Collister; B. Kneale

Newcomers Team Prize
The Padgett Trophy

Year	Club	Riders
1986	B.M.C.R.C.	N. Lynn; P. Goddard; P. Evans
1987	Clubman's Racing.	S. Bushell; C. Gable; G. Read
1988	Wirral 100	L. Wilson; B. Dixon; D. Moore
1990	North Glos M.C.C.	T. Quaye; L. Pullan; P. Orritt
1991	Waterloo & District M.C.C.	D. Prescott; C. Day; K. Parkinson
1992	M.C.R.R.C.Ireland	B. Gardiner; I. King; J. Courtney
1993	North Yorks R.R.S.C.	S. Edwards; Mark Allison; S. Brown
1994	A team with a tricky	T. Camp; G. Linham; J. Swindell
1995	M.C.R.R.C.Ireland	R. Mitchell; A. Archibald; A. McFarland
1996	R.A.F. M.S.A.	G. Blackley; D. Soothill; B. Brunch
1997	M.C.R.R.C. Ireland 'A'	R. Britton; M. McCloy; G. Downey

Classic Team Prize

Year	Club	Riders
1986	North West Kent C.R.M.C.	R. Tree; J. Porter; J. Ruth
1987	Scottish Classic Racing	R. Allan; B. Richards; D. Storry

Senior Classic Team Prize
The Gwen Crellin Trophy

Year	Club	Rider
1988	Darley Moor R.R.C.	A. Dugdale; D. Roper; P. Barrett
1989	North West Kent C.R.M.C.	B. Penfold; C. McGahan; J. Ruth
1990	Worcester Auto	J. Goodall; R. Hirst; C.East
1991	Classic Racing M.C.C.	J. Gow; D. Storry; B. Richards
1992	Worcester Auto	J. Goodall; B. Hirst; C. East
1993	Worcester Auto	J. Goodall; B. Hirst; C. East
1996	S.C.R.M.C. 'B'	R. Allan; D. Gallagher; E. Hamilton
1997	Southern 100 'A'	B. Heath; B. Jackson; D. Whalley

Junior/Lightweight Classic Team Prize
The Manx Telecom Trophy

Year	Club	Rider
1988	Classic M.C.R.C. 'A'	A. Ainslie; L. Grant; A. Edwards
1989	Classic M.C.R.C. 'A'	R. Millinship; P. Byrne; E. Edwards
1990	Scottish C.M.C.C. 'A'	D. Gallagher; B. Richards; A. Taylor
1991	Classic Racing M.C.C.	G. Tunstall; D. Roper; D. May
1992	Scottish C.R.M.C.A.	D. Storry; J. Gow; B. Horsman
1993	Fleetwood & District M.C.C.	D. Montgomery; V. Duckett; M. Baldwin
1994	The Jackson Brothers	Bob Jackson; Bud Jackson; T. Jackson
1995	S.C.R.M.C. 'B'	T. Myers; G. Sellars; P. Jarmann
1996	Southern 100 'A'	B. Heath; G. English; D. Shimmin
1997	Southern 100 'A'	B. Heath; J. Loder; D. Whalley

Special Awards

The Lord Wakefield Cup

To the driver making the best overall performance in the opinion of the Club Committee in the Junior and/or Senior Manx Grand Prix who is not a winner of any race

1973	David Williams	1980	Nick Jefferies	1987	Steve Hazlett		
1974	Wayne Dinham	1981	Kenny Shepherd	1988	Nigel Barton	1994	Nigel Nottingham
1975	Ken Inwood	1982	Gary Radcliffe	1989	Allan McDonald	1995	Keith Townsend
1976	Rob Buxton	1983	Keith Trubshaw	1990	Martin Birkinshaw	1996	Adrian Archibald
1977	John Robinson	1984	Martyn Nelson	1991	Chris Hook	1997	Chris Hook
1978	Clive Watts	1985	Paul Davies	1992	Chris Day		
1979	John Robinson	1986	Michael Seward	1993	Chris Hook		

The Lady Hill Rose Bowl

To the driver who is a local resident making the most meritorious performance during the Senior Manx Grand Prix in the opinion of the Club Committee

1934	Bertie Rowell	1955	Eddie Crooks	1969	Roger Sutcliffe	1984	Ian Ogden
1935	Bertie Rowell	1956	Eddie Crooks	1970	Roger Sutcliffe	1986	Paul Hunt
1936	Bertie Rowell	1957	Alan Holmes	1971	Neil Kelly	1987	John McBride
1937	Bertie Rowell	1958	Bob Dowty	1972	Danny Shimmin	1988	Paul Hunt
1938	J.K. Kermode	1959	Mike Kelly	1973	Neil Kelly	1989	Norman Kneen
1946	Harold Rowell	1960	Mike Kelly	1974	Danny Shimmin	1990	Brian Venables
1947	Don Crossley	1961	Mike Kelly	1975	Danny Shimmin	1991	Philip Gilmour
1948	Don Crossley	1962	Mike Kelly	1978	Rob Brew	1992	Phil Corlett
1949	Dennis Christian	1963	Dennis Craine	1979	Rob Brew	1993	Brian Venables
1950	Don Crossley	1964	Mike Kelly	1980	Mike Kneen	1994	Brian Venables
1951	Don Crossley	1966	Randall Cowell	1981	Richard Coates	1995	Mike Casey
1953	Jack Wood	1967	Nigel Warren	1982	Gary Radcliffe	1996	Gary Carswell
1954	George Costain	1968	George Short	1983	Clifford Yeardsley	1997	Gary Carswell

The York Trophy

To the driver who is a local resident making the most meritorious performance during the Junior Manx Grand Prix in the opinion of the Club Committee

Year	Driver	Year	Driver	Year	Driver	Year	Driver
1953	Bill Harding	1980	Mike Kneen	1986	Ralph Sutcliffe	1992	Derek Kelly
1954	Pete Kissack	1981	Dave Broadhead	1987	Decca Kelly	1993	Greg Broughton
1956	Dennis Craine	1982	Gary Radcliffe	1988	Phil Hogg	1994	Brian Venables
1957	Dennis Christian	1983	Chris Fargher	1989	Andy Bassett	1995	Tony Duncan
1958	Bob Dowty	1984	Gary Radcliffe	1990	Norman Kneen	1996	Norman Kneen
1971	Ken Huggett	1985	Gary Radcliffe	1991	Greg Broughton	1997	Gary Carswell

The Wallace Cup

To the driver who is a local resident making the most meritorious performance during the Newcomers race in the opinion of the Club Committee

Year	Driver	Year	Driver	Year	Driver	Year	Driver
1978	Rob Brew	1985	Ashley Gardner	1990	Eric Moore		
1981	Clifford Yeardsley	1986	Barry Trimble	1991	Philip Corlett	1995	Robbie Watterson
1982	Brian Lund	1987	Billy Craine	1992	David Chambers	1996	Paul Duckett
1983	Andrew Brew	1988	Philip Gilmour	1993	Ian McVeighty	1997	Nigel Beattie
1984	Brian Venables	1989	Ian Large	1994	Duncan Muir		

The Ray Cowles Trophy

To the competitor in any Manx Grand Prix (but excluding the Newcomers Race) who in the opinion of the Club Committee makes the best performance on a four-stroke machine of British manufacture

Year	Driver	Year	Driver	Year	Driver	Year	Driver
1978	Malc Wheeler	1983	Grant Sellars	1988	Phil Nichols	1993	Bill Swallow
1979	Dave Ashton	1984	Kenny Shepherd	1989	Bill Swallow	1994	Bob Heath
1980	Dave Ashton	1985	Alan Phillips	1990	Bob Heath	1995	Bill Swallow
1981	Jim Anderson	1986	Alan Phillips	1991	Bob Heath	1996	Bob Heath
1982	Brian Garratt	1987	Richard Tree	1992	Bob Heath	1997	Bob Heath

The Cromie McCandless Trophy

To the driver who is an Irish resident making the most meritorious performance during the Manx Grand Prix in the opinion of the Club Committee

Year	Driver	Year	Driver	Year	Driver
1992	James Courtney	1994	Emlyn Hughes	1996	Ricky Mitchell
1993	James Courtney	1995	Ricky Mitchell	1997	Richard Britton

The Naylor Trophy

To the driver who has the fastest race time on a British four stroke twin cylinder in the Classic Senior race.

Year	Driver	Year	Driver	Year	Driver	Year	Driver
1984	Neil Blackburn	1988	John Faulkner	1992	John Faulkner		
1985	Ray Knight	1989	Bob Price	1993	Cliff Gobell	1996	Denis Gallagher
1986	Ray Knight	1990	Robbie Allan	1994	Alan Phillips	1997	Tony Myers
1987	Bob Price	1991	Bernie Wright	1995	Alan Phillips		

The Dick Linton Trophy

To the driver who is a newcomer making the most meritorious performance during a Classic race in the opinion of the Club Committee

Year	Driver	Year	Driver	Year	Driver	Year	Driver
1987	Bill Brooker	1990	Alan Taylor	1993	Roger Munsey	1996	Bruno Leroy
1988	Alan Oversby	1991	Mick Hemmings	1994	Jim Graham	1997	Ross Graham
1989	Rich Hawkins	1992	Mervyn Elwood	1995	Ian Hardisty		

The Seymour Trophy

To the driver who is a National of a European country outside the British isles making the most meritorious performance in the opinion of the Club Committee

Year	Driver	Year	Driver
1994	Franz Glauser	1996	Franz Glauser
1995	Franz Glauser	1997	Bruno Leroy

The Lesley Anne Trophy

To the lady driver making the most meritorious performance in the opinion of the Club Committee

Year	Driver	Year	Driver	Year	Driver
1992	Kate Parkinson	1994	Jane Swindell	1996	Bridget McManus
1993	Sandra Barnett	1995	Beth Parry-Jones	1997	Bridget McManus

Riders with most wins

Rider	Wins	Breakdown
Bob Heath	9	6 Senior Classic - 3 Junior Classic
Bill Swallow	6	3 Senior Classic - 3 Junior Classic
Dennis Parkinson	5	3 Lightweight - 1 Junior - 1 Senior
Richard Swallow	5	5 Junior Classic
Bob Jackson	5	5 Lightweight Classic
Austin Munks	4	2 Junior - 1 Senior - 1 Lightweight
Ken Bills	3	2 Junior - 1 Senior
James Courtney	3	1 Junior - 1 Lightweight - 1 Newcomers
Alan 'Bud' Jackson	3	1 Junior - 2 Lightweight Classic
Ricky Mitchell	3	1 Junior N/c - 1 Junior - 1 Senior
Doug Pirie	3	2 Junior - 1 Senior
Dave Pither	3	1 Senior - 2 Senior Classic
Eric Briggs	2	1 Senior - 1 Junior
Jimmy Buchan	2	1 Senior - 1 Junior
Maurice Cann	2	1 Senior - 1 Junior
Don Crossley	2	1 Senior - 1 Junior
Tony Duncan	2	1 Junior - 1 Lightweight
Chris Fargher	2	1 Junior - 1 Lightweight
John Findlay	2	1 Senior - 1 Junior
Alan Holmes	2	1 Senior - 1 Junior
Tim Hunt	2	1 Senior - 1 Junior
Tom Knight	2	1 Newcomers - 1 Senior
Eric Lea	2	1 Senior - 1 Junior
George Linder	2	1 Senior - 1 Lightweight Classic
Phillip McCallen	2	1 Lightweight - 1 Newcomers
Dave Milling	2	1 Junior - 1 Lightweight
Bernard Murray	2	1 Senior - 1 Junior
Len Randles	2	2 Amateur
Craig Ryding	2	1 Junior - 1 Lightweight
Geoff Tanner	2	1 Senior - 1 Junior
Malcolm Uphill	2	1 Senior - 1 Junior
Brian Venables	2	1 Senior - 1 Junior
Clive Watts	2	1 Senior - 1 Junior
Buddy Yeardsley	2	1 Senior - 1 Newcomers

Bob Jackson - 5 Lightweight Classic wins

Fastest laps - Riders over 108 mph

	Rider	Machine	Race	Time	Speed
1.	Adrian Archibald	600 Honda	96 S	19.19.1	117.18
2.	Ricky Mitchell	600 Honda	96 J	19.20.4	117.05
3.	Nigel Davies	750 Honda	93 S	19.24.4	116.65
4.	Roy Richardson	750 Honda	97 S	19.25.9	116.50
5.	Brian Venables	750 Honda	93 S	19.32.0	115.89
6.	Gary Carswell	750 Kawasaki	97 S	19.32.1	115.88
7.	Tom Knight	750 Honda	91 S	19.34.2	115.67
8.	Keith Townsend	750 Honda	96 S	19.38.6	115.24
9.	Allan Bennallick	750 Honda	91 S	19.49.6	114.17
10.	Phil Hogg	989 Yamaha	88 S	19.51.2	114.02
11.	Steve Ellis	600 Honda	97 S	19.52.4	113.99
12.	Chris Hook	600 Honda	71 S	19.52.4	113.91
13.	Bill Hutcheson	600 Honda	97 S	19.54.6	113.70
14.	Darren Soothill	600 Honda	97 S	19.58.4	113.62
15.	Nigel Barton	748 Honda	89 S	19.56.4	113.53
16.	Brad Ogden	1000 Yamaha	89 S	19.56.8	113.49
17.	Paul Dedman	750 Kawasaki	96 S	19.58.4	113.34
18.	Wattie Brown	750 Honda	93 S	19.58.6	113.32
	Nick Morgan	888 Ducati	93 S	19.58.6	113.32
20.	Mike Casey	749 Honda	95 S	19.58.7	113.31
21.	Simon Beck	748 Honda	90 S	19.58.8	113.30
22.	Alastair Howarth	600 Kawasaki	96 S	20.00.4	113.19
23.	David Black	750 Kawasaki	93 S	20.00.2	113.17
24.	Allan McDonald	750 Honda	89 S	20.01.4	113.05
25.	Nigel Nottingham	750 Yamaha	94 S	20.01.9	113.01
	Adam Woodhall	600 Honda	97 S	20.01.9	113.01
27.	Mick Noblett	750 Honda	91 S	20.02.0	113.00
28.	Roy Anderson	750 Yamaha	90 S	20.03.6	112.85
29.	Tim Leech	750 Kawasaki	93 S	20.04.0	112.81
30.	Tony Duncan	249 Yamaha	95 J	20.04.5	112.76
31.	Graham Morton	750 Honda	95 S	20.04.7	112.74
32.	Adrian McFarland	600 Honda	96 S	20.05.2	112.70
33.	Adam Woodhall	600 Honda	96 J	20.05.8	112.64
34.	Carl Rennie	600 Honda	97 S	20.06.4	112.58
35.	Jason Griffiths	750 Honda	91 S N/c	20.06.6	112.57
36.	Michael Brown	750 Kawasaki	93 S N/c	20.06.8	112.55
	Gordon Blackley	600 Honda	97 S	20.06.8	112.55
38.	Richard Britton	600 Honda	97 S	20.07.3	112.50
39.	Paul Hunt	997 Kawasaki	88 S	20.07.4	112.49
40.	Chris Richardson	600 Honda	93 S	20.08.2	112.42
41.	Colin Breeze	750 Kawasaki	97 S	20.09.0	112.34
42.	David Milling	249 Yamaha	91 J	20.09.4	112.31
43.	Ian Simpson	1052 Suzuki	88 S	20.09.8	112.27
44.	James Courtney	250 Honda	93 J	20.10.4	112.21
45.	Ian Kirk	250 Yamaha	95 J	20.11.2	112.14
46.	Steve Allen	998 Yamaha	88 S	20.11.6	112.10
47.	David O'Leary	250 Yamaha	92 J	20.12.0	112.06
48.	Greg Broughton	250 Yamaha	91 L	20.12.2	112.05
49.	Neil Larsen	750 Yamaha	96 S	20.13.6	111.92
50.	Dean Nelson	750 Yamaha	97 S	20.15.8	111.71
51.	Steve Gordon	749 Yamaha	93 S	20.17.2	111.59
52.	Chris Bray	749 Kawasaki	96 S	20.18.3	111.49
53.	Norman Kneen	599 Yamaha	96 S	20.18.4	111.48

Fastest laps - Classic races

	Rider	Machine	Race	Time	Speed
1.	Bob Heath	499 Seeley	97 Senior	21.12.5	106.74
2.	Bob Jackson	500 Norton	97 Senior	21.24.0	105.78
3.	Bill Swallow	499 Petty Norton	97 Senior	21.39.1	104.55
4.	Bill Horsman	499 Norton	97 Senior	21.47.2	103.90
5.	Tony Myers	499 Seeley	97 Senior	21.50.7	103.63
6.	Robert Holden	498 Petty Manx	95 Senior	21.55.5	103.25
7.	Glen English	500 Matchless	95 Senior	22.02.1	102.73
8.	Dave Roper	500 Matchless	89 Senior	22.04.8	102.52
9.	Steve Linsdell	500 Norton	95 Senior	22.05.7	102.45
10.	Mervyn Elwood	496 Seeley	96 Senior	22.10.0	102.12
11.	Jack Gow	492 Norton	94 Senior	22.13.4	101.86
12.	Alan Dugdale	496 Matchless	90 Senior	22.13.6	101.85
13.	John Goodall	496 Matchless	96 Senior	22.14.4	101.78
14.	Wattie Brown	499 Norton	97 Senior	22.15.7	101.69
15.	Bruno Leroy	496 Seeley	97 Senior	22.18.4	101.48
16.	Dave Pither	500 Matchless	87 Senior	22.20.6	101.31
	Steve Ruth	496 Seeley	96 Senior	22.20.7	101.31
18.	Mark Baldwin	500 Petty Manx	94 Senior	22.22.2	101.19
19.	Danny Shimmin	498 Matchless	93 Senior	22.25.2	100.97
	Richard Swallow	349 Aermacchi	91 Junior	22.25.2	100.97
21.	Bob Jackson	250 PB Suzuki	96 Lightweight	22.26.1	100.90
22.	Dave Storry	498 Seeley	93 Senior	22.30.2	100.59
22.	Chris McGahan	496 Seeley	93 Senior	22.32.8	100.40
23.	Mick Robinson	496 Seeley	94 Senior	22.34.6	100.27
24.	Phil Nicholls	499 Seeley	90 Senior	22.34.8	100.25

100mph Classic Laps

The Manx Grand Prix Riders Association awards a gold medal to the driver who achieves a 100 mph lap in the Classic races

	Rider	Total		Rider	Total
1.	Bill Swallow	31	13.	Robert Holden	4
2.	Bob Heath	31		Danny Shimmin	4
3.	Bill Horsman	19		Wattie Brown	4
4.	Bob Jackson	18	16.	Mark Baldwin	3
5.	John Goodall	10		Alan Dugdale	3
6.	Steve Linsdell	8		Bruno Leroy	3
7.	Jack Gow	7		Tony Myers	3
	Dave Roper	7		Phil Nicholls	3
	Richard Swallow	7	21.	Mick Robinson	2
10.	Wattie Brown	6		Chris McGahan	2
11.	Glen English	5		Dave Pither	2
	Mervyn Elwood	5		Steve Ruth	2
			25.	Dave Storry	1

Doubles

Doubles, winning two races in one week, are far more difficult to attain in the Manx Grand Prix Races than in the T.T., as the rules of the Manx debar a winner of any race, other than the Newcomers and Classic Races, from competing again. Nevertheless a total of 22 riders have achieved the feat, but it must be said that the earlier doubles were achieved before the ruling of winners not entering again was introduced.

The first double in 1929 was unusual, in that the winners of both of the races were disqualified, and the runner-up in both races, Eric Lea, was declared the winner. The first 'winning' double was achieved in 1936 by Austin Munks.

Year	Rider	Races
1929	Eric Lea	Senior and Junior
1936	Austin Munks	Senior and Junior
1937	Maurice Cann	Senior and Junior
1938	Ken Bills	Senior and Junior
1947	Eric Briggs	Senior and Junior
1955	Geoff Tanner	Senior and Junior
1956	Jimmy Buchan	Senior and Junior
1957	Alan Holmes	Senior and Junior
1965	Malcolm Uphill	Senior and Junior
1968	John Findlay	Senior and Junior
1974	Bernard Murray	Senior and Junior
1979	Clive Watts	Senior and Junior
1983	Chris Fargher	Junior and Lightweight
1984	Dave Pither	Senior and Classic 500cc
1987	Craig Ryding	Junior and Lightweight
1988	Phillip McCallen	Newcomers 250 and Lightweight
1991	David Milling	Junior and Lightweight
1993	James Courtney	Junior and Lightweight
1994	Brian Venables	Senior and Junior
1994	Bob Heath	Classic 500 and Classic 350
1995	Tony Duncan	Junior and Lightweight
1996	Ricky Mitchell	Senior and Junior

In 1994 Bob Heath became the first rider to win two Classic Races in a week, and took his total of wins to six, and in 1995 with victory in the Junior Classic notched up his seventh win, the most successful rider in the history of the Manx. In 1991 Richard Swallow made history when he won the Classic Junior Race for the fifth year in a row, and equalled the record of Denis Parkinson with five wins. Four other riders have won three races in succession, Denis Parkinson won the 1936, 1937 and 1938 Lightweight Races, Ken Bills won the 1938 Senior and Junior Races and the 1946 Junior and almost made it four in a row when he finished second in the 1946 Senior, Bob Heath won the Senior Classic Race in 1990, 1991 and 1992, and Bob Jackson won the Lightweight Classic Race in 1992, 1993 and 1994.

Fastest laps - Ladies

	Rider	Machine	Race	Time	Speed
1.	Sandra Barnett	750 Honda	1993	20.55.2	108.21
7	Bridget McManus	600 Honda	1997	21.24.4	105.75
3.	Maria Costello	600 Honda	1997	21.55.0	103.29
4.	Beth Parry-Jones	599 Honda	1995	22.27.8	100.77
5.	Jane Swindell	250 Yamaha	1995	22.42.3	99.70
6.	Virginia Power	600 Yamaha	1996	22.44.1	99.57
7.	Kate Parkinson	250 Kawasaki	1992	22.49.0	99.21

Close finishes

A total of 29 Manx Grand Prix Races have been won by a margin of 10 seconds or less. The closest ever finish came in the 1992 Senior Classic when **Bob Heath** beat **Bill Swallow** by 0.2 seconds, the closest ever finish to a race on the T.T. Course including massed start T.T. Races.

1.	1992	Cl.S	Bob Heath	beat	Bill Swallow	by 0.2s.
2.	1983	L.	Chris Fargher	beat	Dick Coates	by 0.6s.
3.	1976	S.	Les Trotter	beat	Danny Shimmin	by 1.4s.
4.	1980	L.	Steve Williams	beat	Bob Jackson	by 2.8s.
	1979	N/c. J	Roger Luckman	beat	Rob McElnea	by 2.8s.
	1990	N/c. J	Lee Pullan	beat	Andy Corbett	by 2.8s.
7.	1956	S.	Jimmy Buchan	beat	Bob Anderson	by 3.2s.
8.	1986	S.	Grant Goodings	beat	Mike Seward	by 3.6s.
	1974	S.	Bernard Murray	beat	Norman Tricoglus	by 3.6s.
	1991	N/c. J	Andy Jackson	beat	Philip Corlett	by 3.6s.
11.	1977	L.	Dave Hickman	beat	Richard Swallow	by 3.8s.
12.	1992	J.	David O'Leary	beat	Mark Baldwin	by 4.6s.
13.	1970	S.	Roger Sutcliffe	beat	Ken Huggett	by 4.8s.
	1996	L.	Russell Henley	beat	Barry Wood	by 4.8s.
15.	1983	J.	Chris Fargher	beat	Keith Trubshaw	by 5.6s.
16.	1965	J.	Malcolm Uphill	beat	Nigel Warren	by 6.0s.
	1985	N/c. L	Carl Fogarty	beat	Roy Chapman	by 6.0s.
18.	1971	S.	Nigel Rollason	beat	Ken Huggett	by 6.2s.
19.	1936	J.	Austin Munks	beat	Jack Blyth	by 7.0s.
	1969	S.	Gordon Daniels	beat	Gordon Pantall	by 7.0s.
21.	1983	Cl.S	John Goodall	beat	Bob Hirst	by 7.2s.
22.	1994	N/c. J	Phil Stewart	beat	Paul Kirkby	by 7.7s.
23.	1958	Sn. S	Peter Richardson	beat	David Williams	by 8.2s.
	1986	J.	Alan 'Bud' Jackson	beat	Ralph Sutcliffe	by 8.2s.
25.	1996	N/c. J	Gordon Blackley	beat	Darren Soothill	by 8.4s.
26.	1978	S.	George Linder	beat	Steve Ward	by 8.8s.
27.	1990	Cl.S	Bob Heath	beat	Dave Roper	by 9.0s.
28.	1986	N/c. J	Ian Jones	beat	Trevor Robinson	by 9.2s.
29.	1936	S.	Austin Munks	beat	Jack Blyth	by 10s.

In complete contrast, the biggest winning margin in the Manx came in the 1926 Race when **Rex Adams** beat **M. I. Dawson** by 12m. 08s.!

All photographs for The History of the Manx Grand Prix have been sourced by

FoTTofinders

FoTTofinders Bikesport Photo Archives is a photograph cataloguing service, combining commercial collections and private picture galleries within a single database.

We have access to over half a million images of TT racing; from 1907 when the first TT races were held on the 15.8 mile St. John's-Kirk Michael-Peel circuit, through to this year's wet, but exciting TT '98.

In addition, we have pictures from most years of the Manx Grand Prix (1923 to date), the Southern 100 (1955 to date), as well as hundreds of images from the Ulster Grand Prix between the years 1950 to 1959.

UK short-circuit meetings: The collections within FoTTofinders include pictures from UK short-circuit race meetings from 1950 to 1956.

FoTTofinders is an on-going service; no catalogues will be published, but we will try and find photographs of any riders. There are, currently, over 180,000 images fully catalogued by year; rider; machine; location; riding number. (Please note: We try our best to answer every query as quickly as we possibly can, but, with the size and scope of the unaccessioned collections, we cannot always be as successful or as quick as some people would like.

The database is being added to daily, and we are touch with other Bikesport photographers, who also have their collections on databases.

For further details, please contact Bill Snelling or Pat Burgess at

FoTTofinders
Lossan y Twoaie, Glen Road, Laxey, Isle of Man, British Isles, IM4 7AN
Tel: (01624) 862238 • Fax: (01624) 862298 • Email: amulree@mcb.net

Howard Davis (350 A.J.S.) winner of the 1921 Senior TT, and second in the Junior race on the same machine

Travelling marshal Robin Sherry at Braddan Bridge, 1980. Robin was winner of the 1951 Junior Manx.

When did Joey Dunlop first ride at the Manx Grand Prix? It wasn't in the 1993 Lightweight Classic on an Aermacchi. Joey is shown here at Sulby Bridge in practice, 1983, during filming for Duke Marketing's video V-4 Victory. (Note we asked when at - not when in!)